CAPITAL
MARKETS
IN INDIA

CAPITAL MARKETS IN INDIA

ICAI-CMA - JAICO Finance & Accounting Series

JAICO PUBLISHING HOUSE

Ahmedabad Bangalore Bhopal Bhubaneswar Chennai
Delhi Hyderabad Kolkata Lucknow Mumbai

Published by Jaico Publishing House
A-2 Jash Chambers, 7-A Sir Phirozshah Mehta Road
Fort, Mumbai - 400 001
jaicopub@jaicobooks.com
www.jaicobooks.com

CAPITAL MARKETS IN INDIA
ISBN 978-81-8495-232-2

First Jaico Impression: 2013

Printed by
Kadambari Printers (P) Ltd.
114, Patparganj Industrial Area, Delhi-110092

Foreword

It gives me immense pleasure to write the foreword to this book. This initiative is quite remarkable and new in the history of **The Institute of Cost Accountants of India,** particularly in the field of research publications, being a collaborative effort with a reputed publishing house like **JAICO.** I believe this research publication will find wide exposure and circulation through this collaborative initiative.

There have been enormous changes in the way the market functions and trading is carried out. Since the use of the latest technology to widening the markets and market activities, a host of eventful changes have taken place. A series of new investment avenues and market entities, starting from Mutual Funds to Venture Capital Funds have come to the fore, broadening the markets in a big way.

We can easily perceive sea changes in the way primary markets are regulated. Amid all this growth and widening of the markets, safeguarding the investors' interest has remained paramount and significant changes have been made on that front as well.

This publication gives a comprehensive assessment of the Capital Markets in India. The book is rich in details and analysis of various dimensions which have a bearing on an evolving capital market in India. The authors, Mr. Amal Krishna Dey and Dr. Pankaj Kr. Roy have done a commendable job in blending theory with sound practical experience.

I must congratulate the CMA, Manas Kumar Thakur, Chairman, Research and Innovation Committee and his expert research team members of the Institute for this noble initiative, as well as for putting in continuous effort to enhance research activities for the greater interest of society.

I am confident that this volume will be a rich contribution and be of huge interest to policy planners, investors, researchers and students of capital market.

CMA Rakesh Singh
President
The Institute of Cost Accountants of India

THE INSTITUTE OF COST ACCOUNTANTS OF INDIA

The Institute of Cost Accountants of India is a statutory body set up under an Act of Parliament in the year 1959. The Institute as a part of its obligation regulates the profession of Cost and Management Accountancy, enrolls students for its courses, provides coaching facilities to the students, organizes professional development programs for its members and undertakes research programs in the field of Cost and Management Accountancy. The Institute also pursues the vision of cost competitiveness, cost management, efficient use of resources and a structured approach to cost accounting as the key drivers of the profession.

After an amendment to the Act passed by the Parliament of India, the Institute has now been renamed as "The Institute of Cost Accountants of India," instead of "The Institute of Cost and Works Accountants of India". This step is aimed towards synergizing with global management accounting bodies, sharing the best practices and it will be useful for a large number of trans-national Indian companies operating from India and abroad to remain competitive. The Institute has its headquarters in Kolkata and also has an office in Delhi. It operates through its four regional councils situated in Kolkata, Delhi, Mumbai and Chennai and 95 Chapters situated in other important cities in the country as well as from eight overseas centres. It is under the administrative control of the Ministry of Corporate Affairs, Government of India. At present the Institute has more than 50,000 members and 5 lakh students across the globe.

The Institute apart from being a member of the International Federation of Accountants (IFAC), South Asian Federation of Accountants (SAFA), Confederation of Asian & Pacific Accountants (CAPA), National Advisory Committee on Accounting Standards (NACAS), and National Foundation for Corporate Governance (NFCG) is also a member of the Government Accounting Standards Advisory Board (GASAB). In addition it is also a member of chambers of commerce of different industries, viz. CII, FICCI, ASSOCHAM, Bharat Chamber of Commerce, Indian Chamber of Commerce etc.

Vision Statement

"The Institute of Cost Accountants of India would be the preferred source of resources and professionals for the financial leadership of enterprises globally."

Mission Statement

"The CMA professionals would ethically drive enterprises globally by creating value to stakeholders in the socio-economic context through competencies drawn from the integration of strategy, management and accounting."

About the Authors

Amal Krishna Dey has a background in research, teaching and the newspaper and finance industry. In the early 1970s he worked as researcher in agricultural economics and taught econometrics at the Visva-Bharati University, Santiniketan, West Bengal, India. During the 1980s, 1990s and early 2000 he worked as chief research writer on corporate and stock market performance in *Commerce Weekly*, Bombay and *Business Standard* and *Ananda Bazaar Patrika*, Calcutta and published numerous research articles on capital markets, and agricultural, industrial, corporate and development economics in *Economic and Political Weekly*, *Desh* and other reputed periodicals and dailies. He has also authored books on the share market and development economics. At present he is a freelance consultant for an in-house publication of the Exim Bank of India, Kolkata, and is also associated with two reputed financial services organisations of Kolkata as a flexi time chief adviser, freelance journalist and is a life member of the Press Club, Kolkata.

Dr. Pankaj Kumar Roy obtained a PhD from the Department of Business Management, University of Calcutta with specialisation in industrial sickness. Dr. Roy is a life member of the Indian Accounting Association. Now he is the Head of the Department of Commerce and an associate professor, New Alipore College, Kolkata. He also acts as technical advisor of the ICFAI, Calcutta Chapter and is also a flexi time faculty member of the IISWBM and BSE Ltd joint programme. He has published a number of research articles in reputed journals and dailies and has also authored a book on the share market.

Acknowledgements

We would like to express our gratitude to Dr. Debaprosanna Nandy, the Director, (Research and Journals), The Institute of Cost Accountants of India (ICAI). Our special thanks go to Dr. Sumita Chakraborty, Joint Director, (Research) and, ICAI; she toiled endlessly by taking on the herculean task of editing. We would specially like to thank Mr. Manas Kumar Thakur, Chairman, Research and Innovation Committee, ICAI, for his sincere efforts in making our dream a reality. We are highly indebted to Professor Asish Bhattacharyya, Advisor (Advanced Studies), ICAI for his valuable suggestions. We are also very grateful to Mr. Soumen Mukherjee of Jaico Publishing House, who has played a pivotal role in the publication of this research work.

Thanks are also due to Dr. Gautam Mitra, Associate Professor, Burdwan University for making chapter 8 so interesting and rich. We are also grateful to different columnists of reputed business journals like the *Business Standard* and *Economic Times* including *Economic Times Wealth*, *National Stock Exchange*, *Bombay Stock Exchange* and *The Ananda Bazaar Patrika*, for their valuable inputs from time to time, the advice of experts like Mr. Ambarish Dutta, MD and CEO, BSE Ltd., Mr. Pradeep Gooptu, Former Editor, *The Business Standard*, Calcutta and *The Business Line*, Calcutta to name a few.

We have tried our level best to acknowledge every one as far as possible. In spite of our best and honest efforts if anyone or any organization is left unacknowledged, we tender our profuse apologies.

Preface

The emergence of the Indian capital market as an attractive avenue for international investors has been an important financial story of recent times. The entry of world players has revolutionized Indian capital markets, largely for the better. But problems of understanding the management systems and behaviour of the capital market scientifically are vastly ignored by general investors and unless they look at things more scientifically, the good times for investors, big and small, might not last long. Further, understanding the management system of the capital market is a must for students of economics, commerce, cost and management accountancy & chartered accountancy, different management systems, and business journalism as it will obviously help them in their studies and professional life.

The Indian capital market is significant in terms of its degree of development in volume of trading and the use of technology. Behaviour of the Indian capital market, especially, the stock market is always interesting, challenging and rewarding, provided one understands it in its truest sense.

During our work as business research journalists and teachers of economics & commerce, we have tried to explain the different investment theories and scientific planning of investment and how different laws of the land can influence investment planning. Until recently, the Indian capital market behaved according to the rules of speculators and brokers, and we sometimes doubted how far scientific investment planning is valid in the Indian context.

However, more recently we have noticed, across classrooms as well as in press conferences, seminars, and general investing communities that people are increasingly becoming more interested in the scientific parameters which affect the capital market in general and the stock market in particular. Especially after liberalization of the Indian economy in the early nineties, general investors find that the Indian capital market is behaving in a rational way which was entirely beyond their imagination and understanding. So, they are now eager to know how one can achieve maximum gain from the Indian stock or capital market, with minimum risk. Thus the investing community is now increasingly becoming aware of scientific analysis of the capital market to reap the best from their investments. A large number of investors now apply scientific reasoning to the movements of prices of share scrips, bonds or mutual funds rather than listening to rumours.

Scientific reasoning of the movements of the capital market mostly depends on the different scientific parameters and changed laws and regulations implemented by the regulatory authorities from time to time. Besides these, other fundamental and technical reasons also influence the Indian capital market, more precisely the Indian stock market.

Keeping all the above mentioned aspects and the basic subject matter of capital market in mind, we have divided this book into ten chapters.

In the first chapter we have described the different capital markets of the world with a brief history, definitions of the capital and money market and the differences between them. In the second chapter, different instruments of the capital market, including company shares, have been taken care of in detail. In the third chapter, different aspects of investments in the capital market are discussed in depth. In the fourth chapter, scientific discussions of the movement of prices of company shares, debentures, mutual funds etc., have been clarified with the help of fundamental and technical analysis. In the fifth chapter, the role of different financial institutions, including banks and foreign financial institutions, in the capital market has been described. The sixth chapter involves a discussion on different laws and regulations affecting the Indian capital market. How tax laws can affect the investments in the capital market and how these can be taken care of by the investing community has been elaborated in chapter seven. In the eighth chapter, the role of derivatives, options and futures in the capital market is discussed. Computer screen based trading of securities, demat (dematerialised) trading through demat accounts in banks and trading through the internet has been detailed in chapter nine and in chapter ten, the security of investors has been discussed.

We hope that this book provides a comprehensive idea about the role and functioning of the capital market in India and will be a great help to students of business management, economics and business journalism, commerce, cost and management accountants and also lay people in understanding the scientific parameters of the capital market mechanism in India.

Contents

Capital Markets and Stock Exchanges and their History

It may sound strange but it is a fact that only two per cent of the Indian population pays income tax. But what is stranger as well as amazing in our country is that around three per cent of the population invests their money in the share market. At the end of March, 2010, in India, around 3 crore investors invested their investable surplus in different stock exchanges, and as a result the market capitalization of the Bombay Stock Exchange alone stood at Rs. 61.64 lakh crore during that period.

Share markets or stock exchanges are the only legal markets trading in companies' shares and government bonds or securities. The behavior of the Indian capital market, especially the stock market, is always interesting and challenging, and if one understands it, it becomes pleasantly rewarding. Trading in company shares is also done outside the stock exchanges, which is known as 'kerb' trading. Though this type of trading is not legal, at times trends in share price movements are also influenced by 'kerb' trading.

In general, the financial market consists of four markets: Forex market, capital market, money market and credit market. All the four markets play a crucial role in the economy, in creating a financial system. To understand a country's financial market, it is necessary to understand each market separately.

FOREX MARKET

The Forex market ensures exchange in foreign currencies (short term and long term currency finance) by main players, like Exim Bank, Forex dealers, banks and other Financial Institutes (FIs).

CAPITAL MARKET

The capital market is the financial market where industry and government raises capital. The capital market consists of two markets – the equity market and the debt or bond market. The equity market, more commonly known as the stock or share market, is where equity shares are traded. Equity shares represent a certain share of ownership and therefore, every equity shareholder is considered an owner of the company issuing the shares. The basic purpose of an equity market is to provide a facility whereby corporates or companies can raise scarce capital by selling fresh shares to the public, these are known as Initial Public Offers (IPOs) or more commonly as primary issues. The market pertaining to primary issues is called the primary market. But, the general public is unlikely to subscribe to primary issues if there is not enough liquidity in the market. To overcome such a situation, the market facilitates transfer of ownership or simple trading of equity shares in the market known as the secondary market. Thus, the market provides much sought after liquidity through an active secondary market. When the general public is confident about liquidity, they can freely participate in the fund or capital raising activity. Lack of liquidity may result in share prices falling lower than their actual intrinsic value. Thus, the equity market provides a primary market backed by a liquid secondary market. All these aspects of market mechanisms or instruments will be discussed in detail in the following chapters.

MONEY MARKET

The money market can be defined as a short-term debt market. In the money market, corporates, banks and other financial institutions borrow money for a short period, ranging from one day to one year. The different instruments in the money market include government issued treasury bills, commercial papers issued by the corporate sector, and a certificate of deposit issued by banks. The banks that lend and borrow money on a short-term basis in the market from the inter-bank form the money market. The rate of lending and borrowing – the

Table 1.1 Difference between Capital Market and Money Market

Points of Difference	Money Market	Capital Market
1. Terms of funds	It provides funds for short term investments.	It provides funds for long- term investments.
2. Objective	Lending and borrowing to facilitate adjustment of liquidity position are the main objectives of the money market.	Mobilization and effective utilization of resources lending are the main objectives of this market.
3. Purpose of utilization	The funds provided by this market are generally utilized for working capital.	The funds provided by this market are utilized for both fixed and working capital.
4. Underwriting	Underwriting is a secondary function.	Underwriting is a primary function.
5. Middleman or link	It works as middleman between the depositor and the borrower.	It works as middleman between the investor and the entrepreneur.
6. Opportunities	It provides opportunities to commercial banks, business corporates, non-banking financial concerns etc., to invest their short-term surplus funds.	It provides opportunities to investment institutions, to raise capital from the public and invest in securities so as to earn and give the highest possible return with the lowest risk.
7. Physical location	It does not have any physical location.	It may have a physical location, like the stock exchange.
8. Form of funds	It provides short-term funds in the form of treasury bills, CDs, MMMFs etc.	It provides short-term funds in the form of debt and equity.

interest rate – depends on the demand and supply of money in the market. When money is scarce in the market, obviously the rate moves up and vice versa. The supply of money also tells on the yields of other instruments.

The difference between the capital market and the money market is explained in Table 1.1.

CREDIT MARKET OR DEBT MARKET

The credit market or debt market is the market where bonds and debentures of companies are traded. Like the equity market, the credit or debt market is used to raise debt capital from common investors. The market, where the corporate sector or the government directly borrows from the investing public by issuing debentures or bonds is called the primary market and the market where these instruments are traded is called the secondary debt market.

In India, the secondary debt market is not as vibrant as the secondary equity market. The secondary debt or bond market goes up when interest rates go down. Because of the lower rate of interest, the required rate of return goes down and investors are willing to buy the bonds at higher prices such that the yield matches the prevailing interest rate. In a vibrant secondary debt market, as in a developed economy, the speculators take positions in the long-term bonds based on the expected interest rate trend in the future. This does not prevail in the present capital market in India. The credit market usually provides short term, medium term and long term loans to corporate and individuals by banks, FIs and Non-Banking Financial Companies (NBFCs).

Table 1.2 Types of Markets, Objectives, Players and Regulators

Type of Market	Objectives	Players	Regulators
Forex market	Short and long term foreign currency finance	Exim Bank, banks, corporate and Forex	Reserve Bank of India (RBI)
Capital market	Long-term finance	Banks, individuals, corporate and FIIs, FDIs, MFs etc.	Securities Exchange Board of India (SEBI)
Money market	Short-term finance	Banks, individuals, corporate and FIIs, FDIs, MFs etc. dealers	Reserve Bank of India (RBI)
Credit market	Short-term finance	Banks, individuals, corporate and FIIs, FDIs, MFs etc.	Reserve Bank of India (RBI)

The central bank, apart from Open Market Operations (OMOs), regulates money supply by using tools like the Cash Reserve Ratio (CRR), bank rate and Statutory Liquidity Ratio (SLR). The amount of cash that a country's banks is required to maintain with the central bank (RBI) is determined by the CRR, while the SLR determines the liquid funds the banks are required to maintain with the central bank, either in the form of cash or government securities. The bank rate is the interest rate at which the central bank lends funds to other banks. While OMOs are used to manage the transitory liquidity in the system, the regulating tools are used to steer the long-term trend of money supply in the economy. When the CRR is increased, money flows from the system to the central bank (RBI), thus arresting the money supply within the system. Changes in the SLR result in a similar effect. The rate sends a signal of the interest rate to the economy.

When the bank rate is lowered, it means that banks can borrow from the central bank at a lower rate, thus enabling them to lend at a lower rate.

One may wonder why markets and money move together. Most people attribute the link between the amount of money in the economy and the movements in the stock markets to the amount of liquidity in the system. This is not entirely correct. About 70 years ago, John Maynard Keynes[1], the father of market economics, discovered the link between money and stock markets. Being an aggressive investor in the stock markets, Keynes realized that the factor connecting money and stocks was the interest rates. Thus, it can be easily understood that an increase in interest rates would tend to suck money out of shares into bonds or deposits. A fall in the interest rates would have the opposite effect. This argument has been established both by statistical tests and more precisely by econometric tests and practical experience. Hence, any announcement of a bank rate cut brings some sort of relief for the stock markets.

In short it can be said that while the capital market provides long term capital for an enterprise, the money market provides for short term financial needs. The RBI, commercial banks and other financial institutions control the money market of a country, while with the financial institutions, FIIs, Foreign Direct Investments (FDIs), Mutual Funds (MFs), corporate, individuals, merchant banks, etc. control capital markets. Share markets or stock exchanges of a country take an active part in transferring the domestic savings into development of capital in the economy. In one of his books, John Kenneth Galbraith, the famous market economist opined that, *"The stock market is but a mirror which provides an image of the underlying or fundamental economic situation."* The Indian capital market is going through a quantitative as well as qualitative change. The liberalization of the Indian economy and the entry of world players in the Indian capital market revolutionized the Indian capital market, largely for the better. More and more people from India and other countries are attracted by the Indian capital market, especially stock markets.

At present in India, more than 7,000 share brokers (discussed later) and around half a million sub-brokers are working on behalf of the investing people of the country. A discussion on the stock broking business is given later in this chapter. In 1946, there were only 7 stock exchanges in India. At present, the number has grown to 24 exchanges. According to a conservative estimate, there are more than 10,000 listed companies in these 24 stock exchanges. According to the number of listed companies, India ranked second after USA. India is one of the most divergent markets in the world in terms of types of companies that have gone public. The current market capitalization is in the region of US$ 200 billion (2011). Around 25 to 30 per cent of this is held by mutual funds and other financial institutions, and the balance as floating stock by the public. In other words, market capitalization in terms of

---

[1]J.M. Keynes: *The General Theory of Employment, Interest and Money*, Macmillan, for Royal Economic Society, 3rd ed., New York, USA, 1973

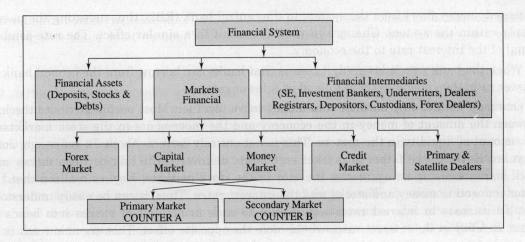

```
                        ┌─────────────────┐
                        │ Financial System │
                        └─────────────────┘
```

Financial Assets (Deposits, Stocks & Debts)

Markets Financial

Financial Intermediaries (SE, Investment Bankers, Underwriters, Dealers Registrars, Depositors, Custodians, Forex Dealers)

Forex Market | Capital Market | Money Market | Credit Market | Primary & Satellite Dealers

Primary Market COUNTER A | Secondary Market COUNTER B

Chart 1.1   Flow Chart of Financial System

available floating stock is around US$ 50 billion. Against this, the stocks of a number of public sector companies, which only have large notional market capitalization, are not yet traded actively. Hence, the actual float is around US$ 45 billion.

The stock market provides a market place for the purchase and sale of securities evidencing the ownership of business property or of a public or business debt. The origin of the stock market therefore goes back to the time when securities representing this property or promises to pay were first issued and made transferable from one person to another. By the 1830s, there was a perceptible increase in the volume of business, not only in loans but also in corporate stocks and shares. In Bombay (now Mumbai), business passed to the share of banks like 'The Commercial bank, The Chartered Mercantile Bank, The Chartered Bank, The Oriental Bank and last, but not least, to The Old Bank of Bombay,' and among the prominent shareholders were the cotton presses. During the American Civil War in the 1860s, the cotton mills of England, which earlier imported only 20 per cent of their cotton from India, had no choice but to substantially increase their imports of cotton from India. The cotton prices soared and Indian business received a big boost[2].

In 1836, in Calcutta (now Kolkata), the news paper *'The Englishman'* reported quotations of 4 per cent, 5 per cent, 6 per cent loans of the East India Company as well as shares of the Bank of Bengal for which there were buyers at a premium of Rs. 5,000 and sellers at a premium of Rs. 7,500.

The trading list was boarded in 1839 and Calcutta newspapers then gave a quotation of banks like the Union Bank and Agra Bank and of business ventures like Bengal Bonded Warehouse, the Docking Company and the Steam Tug Company. Brokers then were not a numerous community and in Bombay between 1840 and 1850 there were only half a dozen

---

[2]Paras Dagli, 'Circa, Capital Market', Smart Investor, *Business Standard*, 8 January, 2001

brokers recognized by banks and merchants. In 1956, the Companies Act introducing limited liability was enacted and with it commenced the era of modern joint stock enterprise in India.

The rise of stock brokers in the stock markets of India is quite interesting. It is known that a stock exchange is a market for dealing in equities and other securities. However, the investing public is not permitted to enter the trading floor of a stock exchange to do business. The investor must employ the services of a registered member of a recognized stock exchange who is commonly known as a stock broker or share broker (both the brokers and sub-brokers must be registered with Securities Exchange Board of India (SEBI). Their registration with SEBI was made mandatory during the late 1990s and this mandatory rule is discussed in Chapter 2 and Chapter 3). These stock brokers buy and sell the shares in a stock market on behalf of an investor, who is known to them as a client, but cannot trade in shares in their own name. In Chapter 3, we have repeated this definition for smooth and comparable reading.

From the year 1850 to 1865, the history of brokers and their rise to power in Bombay is given in the book by Premchand Roychand. The 1850s witnessed a rapid development of commercial enterprises. The extension of railways, the introduction of telegraphs and a gradual improvement in the system of communications promoted internal trade and commerce, and at the same time, the demand for European manufactures increased in the country and was accompanied by the growth of a corresponding demand in Europe for our exports. Stock brokers shared in this general progress. During that period, 'hundis' and bills of exchange were common practice amongst the trading community and both the businesses were very prosperous as was that of brokerage.

The brokerage business attracted many men into the field and by 1860 the number of brokers increased to 60. Their legendary leader was Premchand Roychand who had entered the trade in 1850. He was the first broker who could read and write English. Within six or seven years, he almost monopolized the broking business in shares, stocks, bullion and other bonds and held all the strings in his hands.

During the American Civil War and the consequent surge of cotton prices in India, Premchand Roychand established himself as one of the biggest cotton brokers and was known as cotton bull. He also founded the Bank of Bombay, the Asiatic Bank and a host of other institutions and also started huge speculative trading activity. Actually, all his life, although he remained a broker, Premchand Roychand directed his financial genius to other pursuits and manifold activities, land and sea reclamations and trading. He captured the imagination of Indians and Europeans alike and all the enterprises were either promoted by him or promoted through his goodwill or help. So, not only shares but also all the best gilt-edged securities of those days gave him a splendid opportunity to display his brilliant financial strategy for which he was crowned the 'Napoleon' of finance.

According to the analyst, Paras Dagli[3], Roychand was the first market speculator in the history of Indian broking. He utilized a loophole in the law, which allowed banks to give an advance on government securities and other public companies. Roychand promised the banks

---

[3]Reserve Bank of India Bulletin, June 1960, p. 801

quick and better returns on their loans. Banks started lending funds to buy stocks that were assumed to have sound fundamental values (backgrounds), without checking their credentials. Roychand used this money to increase the prices of certain favored stocks. One such stock, The Backbay Reclamation Company, traded at Rs. 50,000 even in 1860. Premchand Roychand was a famous model millionaire at that time. He donated a lot of money for social causes. He launched a scholarship named after him for the students of Calcutta University and the Rajabai Tower at Bombay is named after his mother. Roychand's speculative bull runs continued for some time and finally collapsed in 1865 when the American Civil War ended and a number of companies went bankrupt and their stock prices became zero. Interestingly, almost a hundred and twenty five years later another big bull, Harshad Mehta used the same *modus operandi* to artificially boost share prices to an unsustainable level. This story of share speculation is discussed in Chapter 5.

A craze for the demand of shares was observed during 1860 to 1865, that is, during the time of the famous Premchand Roychand. We have already mentioned earlier that demand for Indian cotton increased significantly during the middle of the nineteenth century. The supply of cotton from the USA to Europe stopped due to the American Civil War in 1860-61, so, the demand for Indian cotton increased manifold. During that period the largest amount of cotton stock was available in the Bombay Presidency, alone. As the Civil War progressed, the price and demand of cotton kept rising. The large exports of cotton were paid for in bullion which poured into Bombay from Liverpool in the form of silver and gold. Between 1861-62 and 1864-65, a total amount of Rs. 85 crore of bullion came into the country. Out of this Bombay alone absorbed Rs. 52 crore, giving an average of Rs. 13 crore per annum (see Table 1.3).

Table 1.3 Imports of Gold and Silver

Year	India (Rs. crore)	Bombay (Rs. crore)
1861-62	17.73	9.48
1862-63	19.63	13.98
1863-64	18.97	16.13
1864-65	28.49	12.19
Total	84.82	51.78

Source: The Stock Exchange Official Directories, Bombay.

In addition to the wealth of the city, the import of this entire bullion served as fresh capital for a number of new ventures. As observed by the Bank of Bombay Commission in its report:

"The great sudden wealth produced by the prices of cotton shortly after the commencement of the American Civil War, coupled with the want of legitimate means of investment, was at this time producing its natural result in the development of excessive speculation........ From the period everyone in Bombay appears to have become wild with the spirit of speculation. Companies were started for every

imaginable purpose – banks and financial associations, land reclamation, trading, cotton cleaning, pressing and spinning, hotel companies, shipping and steamer companies and companies for bricks and tiles."

The capital drawn into these new ventures, during 1863 to 1865, was about Rs. 30 crores and the premia they faced in the market amounted to nearly Rs. 38 crores. More than 125 concerns were involved and in not a few cases the premia exceeded the paid up capital (see Table 1.4).

Table 1.4 Flotation of New Companies: 1863 to 1865

Nature of Companies	Number of Companies	Paid up Capital (Rs. crore)	Market Premium (Rs. crore)
Banks	25	13.64	10.94
Financial associations	69	6.22	4.42
Land reclamation companies	7	8.34	17.56
Miscellaneous companies	30	1.56	5.00
Total	131	29.76	37.92

Source: The Stock Exchange Official Directories, Bombay.

The first vital spark of the speculation which eventually burst into a huge conflagration was kindled by the Asiatic Banking Corporation. Originally named the Bombay Joint Stock Bank, it was established in 1863 with a capital of Rs. 50 lakhs, which doubled within a year of the charter being obtained. Its share was rigged up to a premium of 65 per cent in a few short months and it was the forerunner of 94 other monetary institutions which came into existence on its heels.

It was also in 1863 that the charter of the old Bank of Bombay was amended and its capital doubled from Rs. 52 lakhs to Rs. 104 lakhs. At the same time, the ban on the bank prohibiting it from making advances on personal security was removed and permission to advance on government securities was enlarged to cover securities of other public companies in India. This new freedom was fully exploited. Premchand Roychand dominated the bank and under his influences the bank advanced on variety of supposed substantial securities with highly fictitious values. The reckless lending policy of the Bank of Bombay was in a large measure imitated by others and it was in a considerable degree responsible for the speculation that followed.

During the period from 1861 to early 1865, there was nothing, however wild that was floated, whose shares did not command a premium. We have already mentioned earlier that The Back Bay Reclamation share of Rs. 5,000 paid up was at a Rs. 50,000 premium. The Port Canning share with Rs. 1,000 paid up was at Rs. 11,000 premium, while the Mazgaon Land share was at a Rs. 9,000 premium and the Elphinstone Land share at more than 500 per cent premium. Some of the banks and financial associations' shares reached a premium of 50 per cent to 100 per cent without being tested by returns. The Asiatic Bank share of

Rs. 200 was quoted at Rs. 460 in August 1864 and the Bank of Bombay share with Rs. 500 paid up reached a maximum price of Rs. 2,850.

It appeared during that period, that men and women, master and servant, employer and employee, banker and merchant, trader and artisan, rich and poor of all races and creeds, officials in high positions included, were deeply involved in commuting bits of paper, variously called *allotments, scrips* and *shares* into gold and silver.

The madness which seized the population at large was indescribable. The people only woke up when the American Civil War ended. Then, they all rushed to sell their securities but there were no buyers and the entire wealth received during the American Civil War was represented by a huge mass of un-saleable papers.

On the 1st July, 1865, the fatal day arrived, when hundreds of time bargains matured which no one was in a position to fulfill. A disastrous slump followed and so completely overwhelmed the commercial city of Bombay that the shares of the Bank of Bombay, which had previously touched Rs. 2,850 could only fetch Rs. 87 and the Back Bay Reclamation shares not more than Rs. 1,750 against its peak price of Rs. 50,000, while a share of the solid Elphinstone Company could only be sold at Rs. 450, that of Colaba at Rs. 975, Mazgaon at Rs. 515 and Frere Land at Rs. 115.

Like the South Sea bubble and tulip mania of the eighteenth century in Europe, the craze for shares from 1861 to 1865 caused widespread despair and Premchand Roychand and his broker friends were 'anathematized'. A large number of companies failed and there were few left solvent in Bombay. A special legislation, Act XXVIII of 1865, had to be enacted to deal with the mass failures swiftly and expeditiously. The liquidation went on till 1872.

The depression was long and severe; the share craze had certain lasting effects. The expansion of liquid capital and the establishment of a regular market in securities were its direct results and they helped to make Bombay what it is today even after it changed its name to Mumbai, – the chief centre of the money and capital market and the financial capital of India.

To understand the present role of share brokers, their speculation procedures and *modus operandi*, the past history of the Indian capital market and the activities of the most famous broker of that time have been discussed in the above paragraphs.

The births of share markets or stock exchanges in different parts of the world are quite interesting. There are different opinions regarding the origin of stock exchanges. Some think that the origin of the stock market relates back to the year 1494, when the Amsterdam Stock Exchange was set up. Others believe that in 1531, in Antwerp, Belgium, traders regularly gathered together at a market square in the heart of the city to speculate in shares and commodities, and this gave birth to the concept of the stock exchange [3]. The term stock is derived from the French word *souche* (stump of a tree) and refers to tally of credits and debits. A number of researchers think that world's first organized stock exchange was set up in Amsterdam (Netherlands) in 1602. At the end of the eighteenth century (1790-92), came the New York Stock Exchange (NYSE) one of the most powerful stock exchanges in the world today.

To understand the Indian capital market, it is essential to learn the history of Indian stock markets and those around the world.

THE BIRTH OF THE BOMBAY (NOW MUMBAI) STOCK EXCHANGE

During the share craze of 1861 to 1865, the number of brokers greatly increased and they gained great influence, authority and wealth. Between 1840 and 1850, only half a dozen brokers had sufficed for the limited business that then existed and their meeting place was under the wide spreading *Banyan* trees in front of the town hall at Cotton Green where Elphinstone or Horniman Circle is now situated. Brokers continued to meet there till 1855 and by that time their number had increased to between 30 and 40. After 1855, brokers again made their market place under the shade of some *Banyan* trees, between the Old Fort Walls and the old Mercantile Bank, on the open site now facing the Central Bank of India head office building at the junction of Meadows Street and Mahatma Gandhi Road.

By 1860, the number of brokers was 60 and during the exciting period of the American Civil War their number increased to about 200 to 250. Brokers were then a privileged class, they created as much noise as they pleased and obstructed the streets, the shops and the lower premises of banks. Bank managers went to their rooms through a serried rank of brokers, bowing to them right and left, and police had only *salams* for them.

The end of the American Civil War brought disillusionment and many failures and the brokers decreased in number and prosperity. Bank managers all of a sudden discovered that they were a nuisance to their customers and made arrangements to clear their steps, and police drove them from place to place, and wherever they went, through sheer habit they overflowed into the streets, till in 1874, in a street that is now appropriately called Dalal Street after them, they found a place where they could conveniently assemble; and on the place where they assembled once stood the office of The Advocate of India.

It was in those turbulent times between 1868 and 1875 that brokers organized themselves into an informal association, and finally, as recited in the Indenture constituting the Articles of Association of the Exchange, on or about 9th July, 1875 a few native brokers doing brokerage business in shares and stocks resolved upon forming in Bombay an association for protecting the charter, status, and interest of native share and stock brokers and providing a hall or building for the use of the members of such an association. This association, which took shape in 1875 was called the Native Share and Stock Brokers' Association, can be considered as the first stock exchange of Asia. The stock exchange of Tokyo was established in 1878.

On the 5th February, 1887, at a meeting held in Brokers' Hall it was resolved to execute a formal Deed of Association, constitute the first managing committee and appoint the first trustees. Accordingly, an indenture was executed on 3rd December, 1887, constituting the Articles of Association of the Exchange and Stock Exchange was formally established in Bombay (Mumbai). Along with the Native Share and Stock Brokers' Association, the association is now alternatively also known as 'The Stock Exchange'. The word 'Native' in the original title which still survives marked no distinction from a parallel foreign association, for none existed. It was a sign of exclusiveness and pride, and Article II of the Articles of Association specially declared "that on the other person except natives of the said Association". The Articles of Association so adopted by the exchange form, with modifications and amendments, the basis of its government to this day.

In 1899, the Brokers' Hall was formally inaugurated by James M. McLean, M.P. previously an editor of the *Bombay Gazette*. In 1928, the present premises were acquired and a new building was constructed and occupied in 1930. It is said that while digging the land it was found that the land was home to a *naag devta* (serpent) and his wife. Prayers were offered through a Hindu Brahmin and the *naag devta* couple was requested to shift elsewhere, which they did and as tribute, the entrance of the current building is in the shape of the hood of a cobra. The present 28 storied, two phased building called Phiroze Jeejeeboy Towers is named after the late Phiroze Jamshedji Jeejeeboy who was the chairman of the Stock Exchange from 1973 to 1983 and was occupied in phases from 1980-81.

However, when the exchange was constituted in 1875, the entrance fee for new members was Re. 1 and there were 318 members on the list. The number of members increased to 333 in 1896, 362 in 1916 and 478 in 1920 and the entrance fee was raised to Rs. 5 in 1877, Rs. 1,000 in 1896, Rs. 2,500 in 1916 and Rs. 48,000 in 1920. In 1994, the membership fee was Rs. 4 crore but during the depressed investment climate in 1998 it came down to Rs. 90 lakh. It was observed in the history of the movement of the entrance fee, that whenever the investment climate improved the entrance fee for brokers increased and it decreased during the time of market depression.

In 2010-11, the exchange had more than 6000 listed companies and around 650 broking members with right of nomination, that is, they are entitled to transfer their right of membership with the approval of the governing board. The value of the right of nomination – called a 'Seat' on the London and New York stock exchanges and known as 'Card' on Bombay Stock Exchange – has fluctuated according to the ebb and flow of market activity. The price of a 'Card' was Rs. 1,800 in 1910 before the First World War, Rs. 48,111 in 1920 during the post First World War boom, Rs. 6,700 in 1932 during the great world depression, Rs. 64,000 in 1946 during the post Second World War boom and Rs. 14,000 in 1954 during the slump that followed the World War II boom, while ten years later the value was in the neighborhood of Rs. 32,000.

CONSOLIDATION OF THE BOMBAY STOCK EXCHANGE

The organization of the stock exchange in Bombay (Mumbai) coincided with the recovery from the seven-year depression following the share craze from 1862 to 1865. The enterprise was promoted by first generation brokers, although they ruined the general shareholders of that time, they had grand conceptions of genius before their time, the fulfillment of which we only see today. After 1872, the capitalists steadily promoted only those enterprises which were useful and remunerative, such as mills, presses, mining companies etc. With the firm establishment of the cotton industry, credit was restored and prosperity came back to Bombay. At the same time, a new departure in commerce and industry was taken by building new sea-docks and the extension of railway facilities for transport of goods.

In these new developments, the stock exchange played an important role. The object of forming an association was to facilitate the negotiation of the sale and purchase of joint stock securities promoted throughout the Presidency of Bombay, which was fulfilled. Outside it, no securities could be negotiated, purchased or sold. In those days, it was very difficult to float a public company and secure large amounts of capital subscribed. It must be mentioned, to the credit of the brokers, that they always tried their best to popularize the new issues to enable the companies to secure the necessary capital. The stock exchange thus channeled the flow of investment into stocks, shares and gilt-edged securities and materially helped government, trade and industry.

As the exchange grew in size, so did its accommodation. The premises, as we have already indicated earlier, were taken in 1874 in Dalal Street on a rent of Rs. 130 per month. They were given up when the building now known as the stock exchange old building was acquired on the same street for Rs. 97,000 in 1895. In the central court-yard of these premises, in what is now the Brokers' Hall, flourished two sturdy *Peepal* trees, which still survive. As we mentioned earlier, on the 18th January, 1899, the Brokers' Hall was inaugurated by James M. McLean, M.P. In the course of his inaugural address he declared:

> "*A Bombay native broker is a very useful member of the society, whose virtues are not sufficiently recognized, although his faults are emblazoned forth. With rare exceptions, he is honest to the backbone and pays up his own misfortunes or the defaults of his customers to the last pie............................ Without doubt this is largest a rupee paper market in India, whether as regards the volume of business or extent of the fluctuations. The Bombay Port Trust and the Bombay Municipality are under a debt of gratitude to them for raising their credit to enable them to borrow at the lowest rates obtaining in India, next to government paper. India being the original home of options, a native broker would give few points to the brokers of the other nations in the manipulations of puts and calls............... A native has borne a considerable share in the building of the present Bombay.................. A portion of the prosperity of Bombay is owing to the mill industry and its every stride forwarded the brokers have a considerable share.*"[4]

The Bombay Stock Exchange was at last comfortably housed, though for a time, a throng of dealers in government securities preferred to remain outside. After the First World War, the adjoining old building which changed hands for Rs. 73,000 in 1913 was bought in 1920 at Rs. 10,30,000 to enlarge the trading hall for transacting the increasing volume of business. In 1928, the premises were further extended by acquiring the adjoining plot of land abutting Apollo Street and flanked by Dalal Street and Hamam Street, from the Bombay Municipal Corporation for Rs. 5 lakhs. A new building was constructed on the site at a cost of another Rs. 5 lakhs and it was thrown open for public use on 1st December, 1930. The process of extension, adoption and renovation is a continuous process even today. Lately, the surrounding property has been absorbed and it is proposed to rebuild all the stock exchange properties to handle the constant growth of the institution.

---

[4]ibid

The Bombay Stock Exchange is not only the oldest stock exchange but also the oldest association in the country. Among the twenty-four stock exchanges recognized by the Government of India under the Securities Contracts (Regulation) Act, 1956, it was the first one to be recognized and it is the only one that has been granted the privilege of permanent recognition. Likewise, it is acknowledged to be the best organized and the largest – be it as a market for gilt-edged securities or for new issues of capital; or in regard to paid up capital and market value of listed securities or average size of listed companies; or from the point of view of turnover, price continuity, liquidity and negotiability, in all of which it enjoys outstanding pre-eminence. Out of the total share trading in India, more than 60 per cent trading is done through the clearing house of the Bombay Stock Exchange. The primacy of this stock exchange places it at the heart of the capital market. The exchange thus helps to make Bombay "the chief centre of money and capital markets"[5] and contributes in no small measure to the importance of the city as "the financial capital of India."[6]

Normally, companies having an issued capital of Rs. 3 crore (Rs. 30 million) to Rs. 10 crore (Rs. 100 million) listed on any recognized stock exchange can seek listing at the Bombay Stock Exchange (BSE) based on the following criteria:

The company should have made profits for at least three years.

Its minimum market capitalization (the term capitalization is discussed later) should be Rs. 20 crores, based on the average price of the previous six months.

The share should have traded, during the previous six completed months, for a minimum of half of the total trading days on any stock exchange.

The minimum average daily traded volume during the past three completed months should be 500 shares with a minimum of five trades per day.

Public holdings (including corporate) should be a minimum of 25 per cent and there should be a minimum of 15 shareholders per 1 lakh of capital in the public category.

At present, trading in shares is done through an online computer system which is commonly known as Bombay Stock Exchange Online Trading (BOLT). Trading through the 'internet' has also started here. All these operating systems in trading shares have been discussed in the relevant chapter.

The Bombay Stock Exchange (BSE) has developed software to monitor capital adequacy of its members. Even as the capital adequacy and members' security deposit is a part of the Carry Forward System (CAFS) functionally, the surveillance thereof is a function under the Capital Adequacy Monitoring System (CAMS).

The members' capital is defined as the sum of their cash deposit with the exchange, long term fixed deposit with a bank on which the exchange has lien, approved securities lodged with

---

[5]ibid
[6]Larissa Fernand: 'OTCEI: Online and ahead', *Business Standard*, 26 April, 1995.

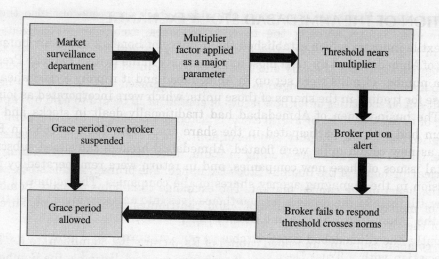

Chart 1.2   The Capital Adequacy Watch

the exchange with margin cover. Besides, a member is required to maintain a base minimum capital at any point of time.

In the new formula which came into force from the first day of December, 1995, a capital adequacy of 3 per cent would imply that a member's gross open position should not exceed 33.33 times his/her capital. Gross open position comprises gross sales, gross purchases and gross inter-client business. Broadly, monitoring would involve:

Interacting with members for deposit of cash and securities with banks.

Valuation of securities deposited by members at daily closing rates.

Calculation of the required capital and shortfall if any, for members.

Informing members about shortfall in capital or its imminence.

Cautioning members about the suspension of trading in case of shortfall in capital for a predetermined period of time.

CAFS would recalculate the capital adequacy on a daily basis on the basis of the day's transaction data downloaded from BOLT. The latest capital adequacy status would then be uploaded to the BOLT, to track shortfalls on the subsequent day.

One of the major parameters for monitoring capital adequacy is the multiplier factor (in the new formula it is 33.33). Alert signals will be sent to the members at the threshold nearing the multiplier factor. The exchange would allow a certain grace period before suspension of trading in case of capital inadequacy.

The members would also be required to deposit with the bourse, a minimum security deposit either in cash or approved securities or a combination thereof.

FOUNDATION OF THE AHMEDABAD STOCK EXCHANGE

The cotton textile industry which established the primacy of Bombay also contributed to the development of Ahmedabad as the next most important city in the British Bombay Presidency. After 1880, a number of mills were set up in Ahmedabad and it rapidly forged ahead. Soon the need arose for trading in the shares of those units, which were incorporated as joint stock companies. The businessmen of Ahmedabad had traditionally dealt in stocks and shares. Many of them had actively participated in the share craze from 1861 to 1865 in Bombay. Accordingly, as new cotton mills were floated, Ahmedabad brokers canvassed subscriptions for the capital issues of those new companies, and in return were remunerated by the way of a commission in the managing agency shares of the companies. The volume of business steadily grew, till in 1894 the brokers formed themselves into an association under the name and style of the "Ahmedabad Shares and Stock Brokers' Association."

Subsequently, the Ahmedabad Stock Exchange was organized as a voluntary non-profit making association with a Trust Deed and a Deed of Association on the same lines as the Bombay Stock Exchange. It followed the Bombay rules and practices and not a few of the members and their relatives were also members of the Bombay Stock Exchange. This close correspondence has been maintained ever since. The Ahmedabad market concentrated its business in shares of local textile mills and of the managing Agency Houses controlling those companies. After the First World War substantial business was witnessed in its trading in the Manekchowk area where members used to congregate and trade under the open sky. Business continued to expand and the exchange thereupon purchased a nearby property and constructed its own building in the 1920s at a cost of Rs. 3,60,000. In 1950, it acquired another adjoining property for Rs. 70,000.

FORMATION OF THE CALCUTTA STOCK EXCHANGE ASSOCIATION

From a get together under a *Neem* tree way back in the 1830s, the Calcutta stock broking fraternity has come a long way. Though the once famous shelter for Calcutta stock brokers no longer exists, the roots laid in the 19th Century have dug themselves deep into the city and the region. The north-eastern region today plays a crucial role in the country's capital market, while the Calcutta Stock Exchange has emerged as the second largest 'bourse' in India. The investors from the eastern zone are also at the forefront today.

The stock exchanges at Bombay and Ahmedabad were well set up as properly organized associations in the beginning of the 20th Century. Though stock broking was practiced in Calcutta as early as 1836, the members of the broking profession had neither any code of conduct for their guidance nor any permanent place for congregation. The centre of their activity was under a *Neem* tree, where at present, stands the office of the Chartered Bank (now known as Standard Chartered Bank) on Netaji Subhash Road. In 1905, the Chartered Bank began to construct its own building, which led brokers to shift the arena of their operations to the neighborhood of the present Allahabad Bank.

The brokers had no shelter and business was carried in an open area. The inconvenience of such trading, promoted brokers to organize themselves, and in May 1908, an association was formed under the name of the Calcutta Stock Exchange Association at 2, China Bazar Street.

On 7th June, 1923, the association was registered as a limited liability concern, with an authorized capital of Rs. 3 lakhs divided into 300 shares of Rs. 1,000 each. The shares were subdivided into four shares of Rs. 250 each in 1959. The golden jubilee of the association was celebrated in 1958, the diamond jubilee in 1968 and the platinum jubilee in 1983.

The present stock exchange building at 7, Lyons Range which was constructed in 1928 with an amount of Rs. 3,77,000 and which has been the office of the stock exchange for the last 84 years, has become too small to accommodate the enormous increase, not only in the number of members of the exchange but also the phenomenal growth in the volume of business being handled by the members of the exchange. The authorities of the stock exchange have already initiated measures for obtaining larger premises, so the hardship faced by members due to acute shortage of space is mitigated.

At the time of incorporation in 1908, the stock exchange had 150 members as compared to 50 native and 5 European brokers who traded towards the close of the 19th Century. Today the total membership has risen to more than 800, which includes several corporate and institutional members.

The number of companies listed on the exchange is about 4000. The trading business of the exchange is around Rs. 3 lakh crore. The Calcutta Stock Exchange has been granted permanent recognition by the Indian Government with effect from 14th April, 1980 under relevant provisions of the Securities Contracts (Regulation) Act, 1956, with a view to render useful service to investors.

This exchange was a pioneer in forming an Investor Service Cell in 1986. At present the cell handles, on an average, more than five thousand complaint letters from investors, per year. The stock exchange also runs a free training program for prospective entrants, to the broking profession.

Like BOLT of the Bombay Stock Exchange, the Calcutta Stock Exchange too started an online trading system called C-Star. It has very limited success in making members of the National Stock Exchange (NSE) or Bombay Stock Exchange accept the C-Star screen. But 10 of the 24 odd stock exchanges in the country have now suddenly made a bee-line for membership of the Calcutta Stock Exchange for obvious reasons. Almost all of them have been gasping for breath over the last few years with business all but nil.

FORMATION OF THE MADRAS STOCK EXCHANGE

Some business in stocks and shares was apparently transacted in Madras by a broker or two after the First World War and a stock exchange was formed in 1920 only to go out of existence in 1923. In 1927, there were two brokerage firms, one European and the other Indian; a Bombay firm opened a branch in Madras in that year. Very few transactions were done by these brokers and reported in the press. In the next four years, a few more brokers joined the trade, and though there was no organized exchange, they helped to float many electricity companies, textile mills and planting and industrial concerns.

The stock and share business was almost entirely in the hands of two or three European firms and two Indian firms up to 1933-34; their daily business was mostly confined to gilt-edged securities and south Indian plantations, the principal interest being the London shares. With the establishment of trunk telephone facilities in 1933, business gradually broadened as south Indian investors became interested in stock and shares quoted on the Bombay Stock Exchange and Bombay and Calcutta investors developed an interest in Madras scrips. A few more Indian firms were started in 1935 by former assistance or constituents of English firms and business continued to develop.

The boom during the 1930s, the First World War and post-war was followed by a world depression. The improvement in business conditions and stock market activity in 1935 was marked by a growing public interest in stocks, shares and securities. In south India, there was a rapid increase in the number of textile mills and many new plantation companies were floated. To cater to this expanding trade in plantation and mill shares, a stock exchange was organized in Madras (now Chennai) on the 4th September, 1937, under the name of "Madras Stock Exchange Association (Private) Ltd."

The Madras stock exchange had 5 members and 84 companies on its list at the time of its birth in 1937. Since then, with the rapid industrialization of Madras and neighboring states, the exchange expanded in its membership and the scope of its activities. It was reorganized as a new company limited by guarantee under the name of the Madras Stock Exchange Ltd., on the 29th April, 1957, and in May 1961 it acquired a building of its own at the cost of Rs. 2,10,000. Its activities are steadily expanding and companies covering all types of industries, including banks and insurance companies, are on its trading list.

FORMATION OF SOME RIVAL STOCK EXCHANGES

Apart from the Madras Stock Exchange, rival stock exchanges were set up in Bombay (now Mumbai) and Calcutta (now Kolkata) in 1937 and 1938 respectively. The stock boom in 1937 stimulated considerable interest in Calcutta, and as prices soared and the volume of business increased, a number of new entrants invaded the field with a view to exploiting the favorable opportunities and making a future for themselves. Accordingly, another stock exchange under the name of the Bengal Share and Stock Exchange Ltd., was organized in Calcutta in 1937 with the object of doing forward business in stocks and shares on a monthly settlement basis.

For much the same reason, and for the second time in the history of Bombay, a new stock exchange limited by guarantee was started in February 1938 under the name of the Indian Stock Exchange Ltd. It had an influential Board of Directors consisting of well known business personalities and industrialists like Sir Choonolal B. Meheta, Sir Behram Karajia and others. Most of them were ineligible for membership of the existing stock exchange because its rules, sanctioned by the government, prohibited members from engaging themselves as principals or employees in any business other than that of stocks and shares. The object of the promoters of the new exchange therefore was to force themselves into the stock exchange trade through the back-door by forming a new association. Apart from these industrialists and dealers, the membership of the Indian Stock Exchange Ltd., was drawn at different stages from the speculative elements which had been driven out from the bullion, cotton, seeds and other forward markets after they came under government control.

The Indian Stock Exchange Ltd., functioned sporadically, and whenever it did, its interest was restricted to two or three highly speculative scrips. The exchange failed to win public support and its repeated applications for recognition in Bombay under the Securities Contracts Control Act was refused by the State Government of Bombay. The Government of India also rejected its application for recognition when the Securities Contracts (regulation) Act came into force in 1957; but in view of the principle of unitary control, 25 of its members were then admitted to the membership of the Bombay Exchange on concession terms. Since then, the Indian Stock Exchange Limited has ceased to function and is now in morbid condition.

INFLUENCE OF THE INDIAN FREEDOM FIGHTING *(SWADESHI)* MOVEMENT ON THE FORMATION OF INDIAN STOCK EXCHANGES

In the beginning of the 20th Century, the industrial revolution was on the way in India. Its first outpost had already been planted in the middle of the 19th Century. There was then a revolution in transport and means of communications with an increase in the network of railways, roads and telegraphs. A new form of industry was established through the plantations operated by tea, coffee and indigo estates. These followed by two of the most important industries in India – the cotton mill industry in Bombay financed by Indian capital and enterprise and the jute industry in Bengal were dominated by the Europeans. The industrial revolution thereafter spread to the mining and other miscellaneous industries such as coal, manganese, gold and mica, rice mills, oil mills etc.

The early years of the 20th Century saw the birth of the Indian *Swadeshi* movement. The institution of the Indian Industrial Conference in 1905 in association with the Indian National Congress was the first definite sign of an alliance between economic and political discontent. The *Swadeshi* movement let loose a great wave of industrial enthusiasm in the country and an important stage in industrial advance under Indian enterprise was reached with the inauguration of the Tata Iron & Steel Co. Ltd. in 1907. These developments were portents of the industrial progress to come and of the part to be played by the stock exchanges.

Apparently, the *Swadeshi* movement, though it had a direct influence on the formation of stock exchanges, indirectly had a definite role in the formation of stock exchanges even in the pre-independence era.

IMPACT OF THE FIRST WORLD WAR ON THE INDIAN CAPITAL MARKET

On the eve of the First World War, the stock market in India consisted of three stock exchanges at Bombay, Calcutta and Ahmedabad. As hostilities progressed, Europe ceased to produce any manufactured articles except those required for the war.

The imports of manufactured goods into India stopped almost completely and a boom ensued in all industrial enterprises. Mills, factories and workshops worked round the clock, fabulous profits were earned and large dividends were declared. Cotton and jute textiles, steel, sugar, paper, flour mills and all companies generally enjoyed phenomenal prosperity. Wealth accumulated, the volume of money increased and the stock exchanges soon became the centre of attraction for all.

During the war and the post-war boom, the roaring trade in stocks and shares led to the formation of rival stock exchanges in Bombay and Ahmedabad. A few limited companies were formed and incorporated in Bombay under the name and style of the Bombay Stock Exchange Ltd., in December 1917 and an unincorporated body called the Gujarat Share and Stock Exchange was established in Ahmedabad in 1920.

The Bombay Stock Exchange Ltd., had on its managing committee a number of well-known industrialists and businessmen like Sir Purshottamdas Thakurdas, Sir Chunilal V. Meheta, Sir Ibrahim Rahamtoolla, Shri Rameswardas Birla and others – men of high reputation but who were not conversant with the working of stock exchanges. They claimed they would introduce reforms in matters in which, it was said, the existing stock exchange in Bombay was deficient, but they found the same impracticable and were unable to move an inch further and they had to close their doors within three years. As Shri Bulabhai Desai commented in his Minority Report of the Stock Exchange Enquiry Committee of 1923, *"For some time past no business is being transacted on the new exchange and it is now practically a dead institution. The figures relating to the business of the Association point to the same conclusion."* An attempt was made to revive the Bombay Stock Exchange Ltd. in 1922 but it failed. After the passing of the Bombay Securities Contracts Control Act in 1925, it made a last ditch effort to obtain official recognition under the Act, but the government refused. Thereafter it went into liquidation and wound up its affairs. The fact was that, in spite of highly influential persons, the new exchange did not command the confidence of the public which continued to support the existing association which is commonly known as 'The Stock Exchange, Bombay (BSE). Now it has been renamed as 'The Stock Exchange, Mumbai (BSE).

Apart from Bombay and Ahmedabad, a new stock exchange was also organized in Madras (now Chennai) under the name of the Madras Stock Exchange on 6th of April, 1920, and in northern India also the Late Harikishan and others attempted to establish a registered stock exchange in the 1920s but did not succeed. The Madras Stock Exchange had 100 members on its rolls when it started and dealt mainly in mills' shares. However, when the boom faded, followed by company failures and a sharp fall in prices in 1921-22, the Madras Stock Exchange became moribund for want of business. By 1923, the number of its members reduced from 100 to only 3 and so it went out of existence at that time.

Over and above the two new exchanges in Calcutta and Bombay, the Lahore Stock Exchange was formed in 1934. It had a brief career and merged with the Punjab Stock Exchange Ltd., which was incorporated in 1936. There were thus eight stock exchanges in India. Two each in Bombay, Calcutta and Ahmedabad and one each in Madras and Lahore, when the Second World War broke out in 1939.

RESULTANT BOOM OF THE SECOND WORLD WAR AND FORMATION OF OTHER STOCK EXCHANGES

The Second World War touched off a brief boom which was followed by a slump. The situation changed radically in 1943 when India was fully mobilized as a supply base. Mills, factories and workshops were running day and night. Prosperity was rapidly increasing, inflationary finance expanded, money became cheaper and paper wealth multiplied. This war time boom brought unprecedented property to the stock exchanges. On account of restrictive controls on cotton, jute, bullion, seeds and other commodities, those dealing in them found the stock market the only outlet for their activities. They were anxious to join the trade and their number swelled due to numerous others who saw in the expanding volume of business and swiftly rising prices an opportunity for accumulating large fortunes overnight. Many new associations were constituted for the purpose and organization of stock exchanges in all parts of the country assumed the proportion of a craze.

In Ahmedabad where the Ahmedabad Share and Stock Broker Association recognized by the government and the Gujarat Share and Stock Exchange already existed, as many as four new stock exchanges were set up one after another. Two of them disappeared with equal speed, but the Indian Share and Stock Brokers' Association established in 1943 managed to survive till 1957-58. In that year, some of its members as well as those of the Gujarat Share and Stock Exchange were absorbed on concessional terms by the Ahmedabad Shares and Stock Brokers' Association which was the only stock exchange in Ahmedabad recognized by the Government of India under the Securities Contracts (Regulation) Act, 1956.

In Calcutta over and above the Calcutta Stock Exchange Association Ltd., the Bengal Share and Stock Association Ltd., was organized.

In Delhi, two new stock exchanges, the Delhi Stock and Share Brokers' Association Ltd., and the Share Stock and Share Exchange Ltd., were floated and later, in June, 1947, amalgamated into the Delhi Stock Exchange Association Ltd.

Two other stock exchanges were also formed. The U.P. Stock Exchange Ltd., was incorporated in Kanpur in 1940 and the Nagpur Stock Exchange Ltd., was incorporated in Nagpur. In the Indian States (former Princely States), the Hyderabad Stock Exchange Ltd., was incorporated in 1944 as a company limited by guarantee and recognized under the Hyderabad Securities Contracts Control Act which was enacted in that year on the lines of the Bombay Securities Contracts Control Act of 1925. A small stock exchange also sprang up in Bangalore city of Mysore State.

This mushrooming growth of stock exchanges fed on the war time boom and suffered almost a total eclipse in the aftermath of the depression. The stock exchanges in Lahore closed down during the holocaust which followed the partition of India in 1947 and later one of them migrated to Delhi where it was merged with the Delhi Stock Exchange. Most of the other stock exchanges withered away or languished till 1957 when they applied to the Indian Government for recognition under the Securities Contracts (Regulation) Act that came into force in 1957. Only the established stock exchanges in Bombay, Calcutta, Madras, Ahmedabad,

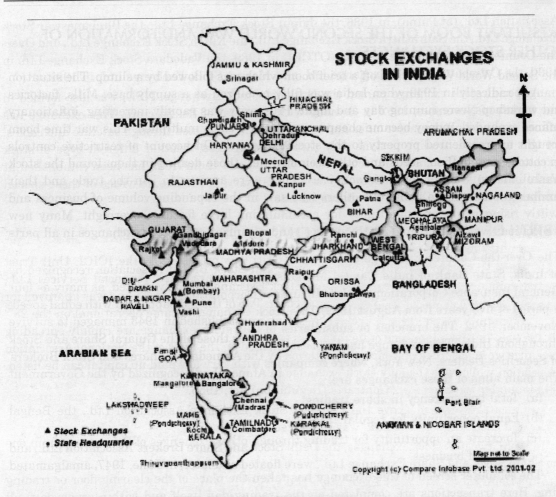

STOCK EXCHANGES IN INDIA

Copyright (c) Compare Infobase Pvt. Ltd. 2001-02

Note: We gratefully acknowledge Infobase Pvt. Ltd. for use of the map.

Delhi, Hyderabad and Indore were recognized under the Act. Some members of the other associations were required to be admitted by the recognized stock exchanges on a concession basis, but acting on the principle of unitary control, all these pseudo stock exchanges were refused recognition by the Government of India and they thereupon ceased to function or exist.

The Bangalore Stock Exchange Ltd. was subsequently registered in 1957 and recognized in 1963. Fourteen more stock exchanges were recognized under the Securities Contracts (Regulation) Act, 1956. These are the Cochin Stock Exchange Ltd., in 1980, the Uttar Pradesh Stock Exchange Association Ltd., (at Kanpur) and Pune Stock Exchange Ltd., in 1982, the Ludhiana Stock Exchange Association Ltd., in 1983, the Gauhati Stock Exchange Ltd., in 1984, the Kanara Stock Exchange Ltd., (at Mangalore), in 1985, the Magadha Stock Exchange

Association Ltd., (at Patna), in 1986, the Jaipur Stock Exchange Ltd., the Bhubaneswar Stock Exchange Ltd., the Saurashtra Stock Exchange Ltd., the Kutch Stock Exchange Ltd., and Over-the-Counter Stock Exchange of India (OTCEI) in 1989, the Vadodara Stock Exchange Ltd. in 1990, the Coimbatore Stock Exchange Ltd. and Meerut Stock Exchange Ltd. in 1991.

A special stock exchange named the National Stock Exchange (NSE) was also formed in the month of November, 1992 in Bombay with a capital of Rs. 25 crore. This exchange has offices in almost all the major cities and towns of India connected through satellite and cables. In this exchange, trading is done only through computers. Another different type of stock exchange named the Inter-connected Stock Exchange of India (ISE) has been established at Vashi in Navi Mumbai (New Bombay) on 22nd January, 1998. The activities of these special exchanges, including OTCEI, are discussed later.

BIRTH OF OVER THE COUNTER EXCHANGE OF INDIA (OTCEI)

The Over-the-Counter Exchange of India (OTCEI) was promoted by the ICICI, Unit Trust of India, State Bank of India Capital Markets Ltd., Canara Bank Financial Services Ltd., General Insurance Corporation and Life Insurance Corporation of India and was approved for a period of five years from August 1989. This stock exchange became operational on the 28th November, 1992. The branches or subsidiaries of this stock exchange are rapidly spreading throughout India. This exchange has been established on the lines of the National Association of Securities Dealers, New York, where companies with very low paid up capital can be listed. The main aims of those exchanges are:

(a) Total transparency in share trading.

(b) Equal opportunity for regular trading.

(c) To create an opportunity for trading through other exchanges of the country from one centre of business.

The computer screen of this exchange has taken the place of the clearing floor or trading ring. Here transactions are completed on the trading day itself and within seven days all dealings are made to completion. So, the exchange is gradually becoming a favorite trading place for the small investors of the country.

The four main conditions for membership of the OTCEI are:

(a) The paid up capital of the company should be between Rs. 30 lakh and Rs. 25 crore

(b) Debentures of those companies, which are not listed on any other exchange can be listed here.

(c) To increase the awareness of general investors, the companies that are already listed with other exchanges in the country can also be listed here.

(d) In spite of being listed on the other stock exchanges, only those debentures can be listed on the exchange which are certified debentures of the OTCEI.

The number of listing companies in the exchange is increasing very rapidly which means that popularity of this exchange is fast increasing.

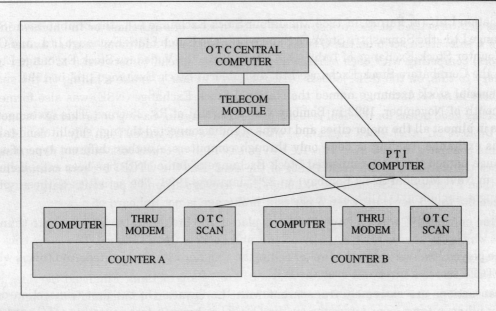

Chart 1.3 The Work System of the OTCEI Market

In fact the Over-the-Counter Exchange of India (OTCEI) operates in more than 25 cities of India. This ring-less, electronic screen based, nationwide stock exchange links small investors across the country giving them the prime benefits of transparency and quick settlement.

According to an article of Larissa Fernand[7], while the OTCEI is more than a giant step away from being able to compete with the Bombay Stock Exchange (BSE) on an equal level in terms of companies and volume, it is proving to be a viable option for investors. It is more beneficial for those who trade in small amounts, are not interested in speculative activities and are afraid of being cheated by brokers or sub-brokers.

There are two inherent advantages in the state of the art technological set up of the OTCEI, namely, it makes for extremely convenient trading and gives investors the best possible deal, cost wise. Buy and sell quotes for every scrip listed on the exchange are stored in the central computer at the OTCEI. All the members, dealers and representatives' offices are linked to the central computer via computer modems. An investor specifies the scrip he wishes to buy or sell and this order is keyed in at the local counter and transmitted to the central computer (see Chart 1.3).

After that, the order is processed and matched with the prevailing rates. The investor and dealer can then view the rates on a television monitor that has a decoder to access the OTCEI rates on the tele-text. If the investor prefers to view the rates in the comfort of his home, he simply attaches a decoder at a cost of around Rs. 10,000 (at 1999-2000 prices) to his television set.

---

[7]ibid

The deal is settled at the lowest quoted price in case of a purchase or the highest in the case of a sale. Each scrip on the OTCEI has compulsory and additional market makers (the sponsors) competing with each other, which brings the spread to between 3 to 3.5 per cent. Contrary to this, on the BSE, jobbers (discussed in Chapter 3) make a killing on the spread and there is no set limit.

Getting good prices for the deal is just a part of the bargain. Saving on brokerage is another plus. Brokers on other stock exchanges often fix a fee that varies from day to day, deal to deal and customer to customer. This fee can go sky high or touch rock-bottom, depending on volumes transacted and the profitability of the deal. But the OTCEI brokers cannot charge more than 2 per cent. BSE brokers, although they average around 2 per cent, charge anything between 0.5 to 3.5 per cent. Even 5 per cent brokerage is not unheard of.

Often on the BSE when a buying order is placed, the broker states a higher rate than the one at which the shares were actually bought and pockets the difference. The same trick can also be played inversely with the broker selling at a higher rate than stated. And this is where the OTCEI scores a direct hit over the BSE.

Transactions are extremely transparent with the former. On the first transaction or by simply filling a form, every investor on the OTCEI is given a free investing OTC card that carries a permanent code. This code is used for all the transactions and application slip (PCS) once the deal is through. This receipt, replaced later with a permanent counter receipt, mentions the time of trading, brokerage fee, and the prices at which the deal was executed.

At the time of sale, the investor gets a Sale Confirmation Slip (SCS) from the counter in which he deals. This effectively clips the wings of the broker. But a BSE broker will never show the investors the transaction sheet which carries the exact rate at which the deal is struck.

While payments from a BSE broker can take a month, 45 days or even 90 days after settlement, the OTCEI boasts of state of the art delivery and settlement. When trading with a listed instrument, OTCEI gives, through the T+3 settlements, where T stands for day of transaction, (done on a daily basis), payment within 7 days. In the permitted section, the T+7 settlements (done on a weekly basis), will settle the trade within 10 days.

Investors, if disappointed about the number companies, should be happy about the comparatively minimized risks on the OTCEI. Here, the guidelines demand that each issue gets a sponsor who buys the shares from the company at a mutually agreed price. The sponsor then sells the issue in the market at a premium. An example can be cited of the deal between the Times Guaranty Financials and Melstar Information Technologies. In the later part of 1995, Times Guaranty Financials bought out a deal of Rs. 4.86 crore of Melstar Information Technologies.

The shares had been bought at Rs. 75 premium by the sponsor who offloaded them at Rs. 125. The sponsor was required to give two way quotes for the scrip for 18 months. Considering that they have to be compulsory market makers, merchant bankers are careful to keep away from bogus issues.

Secondly, there is little tendency of overpricing or overselling as the sponsor may be the eventual loser. This reduces investor risk to an extent. So what is sacrificed in terms of volumes is made up in reliability. The trade-off between reliability volumes need not indicate one between reliability and profitability opined Fernand.

It is true that, an overly technology dependent exchange may put off some investors fearful of a breakdown in communications since it is on line via modems, connected through telephone lines. But on the plus side, the number of companies listed and volumes traded may not pose a problem for long as the OTCEI plans a major expansion. OTCEI officials plan to increase the number of its members in almost all cities and towns of the country. Soon investors in any part of the country will be linked electronically.

Table 1.5 List of Stock Exchanges in India (Situation up to 2010)		
Sr. No.	*Name of the Stock Exchanges*	*Locations*
1.	Ahmedabad Stock Exchange Limited	Ahmedabad
2.	Bangalore Stock Exchange Limited	Bangalore
3.	Bhubaneshwar Stock Exchange Limited	Bhubaneshwar
4.	Bombay Stock Exchange Limited	Mumbai
5.	Calcutta Stock Exchange Association Limited	Kolkata
6.	Cochin Stock Exchange Limited	Cochin
7.	Coimbatore Stock Exchange	Coimbatore
8.	Delhi Stock Exchange Limited	New Delhi
9.	Gauhati Stock Exchange Limited	Gauhati
10.	Interconnected Stock Exchange of India Limited	Navi Mumbai
11.	Jaipur Stock Exchange Limited	Jaipur
12.	Ludhiana Stock Exchange Limited	Ludhiana
13.	Madhya Pradesh Stock Exchange Limited	Indore
14.	Madras Stock Exchange Limited	Chennai
15.	MCX Stock Exchange Limited	Mumbai
16.	National Stock Exchange of India Limited (NSE)	Mumbai
17.	OTC Exchange of India	Mumbai
18.	Pune Stock Exchange Limited	Pune
19.	United Stock Exchange of India Limited (USE)	Mumbai
20.	Uttar Pradesh Stock Exchange Association Limited	Kanpur
21.	Vadodara Stock Exchange Limited	Vadodara

Source: Securities Exchange Board of India (SEBI)

Note: Hyderabad Stock Exchange, Magadh Stock Exchange, Saurashtra Kutch Stock Exchange and Mangalore Stock Exchange have been de-recognized by SEBI.

Listing norms in the NSE are as follows:

(a) The paid up capital of the applicant should be at least Rs. 10 crore and market capitalization should be at least Rs. 20 crore.

Or

(b) The market capitalization should be at least Rs. 40 crore.

(c) For computing paid up equity capital, the existing capital and capital raised for the proposed issue for listing will be taken into account. Also, for computing market capitalization, average weekly high and low prices for the previous six months will be considered. Necessary adjustments will be made for rights/bonus issues and the share should have traded on at least half of the trading days during the previous six months.

Also, either the company seeking listing or the promoting company should have a three year track record. An audited balance sheet should be submitted for the three previous financial years. The company should have been referred to the Board for Industrial Financial Reconstruction (BIFR), its net worth should have been wiped out by accumulated losses and it should not receive a winding up petition from a court.

(d) Unless the applicant is listed on an another recognized stock exchange for at least three years, the project/activity plan must have been appraised by a financial corporation, or a scheduled commercial bank with a paid up capital exceeding Rs. 50 crore, or a category I Merchant Banker with a net worth of at least of Rs. 10 crore.

(e) The applicant should have paid dividend in at least 2 out of 3 financial years preceding the year in which listing application has been made or the net worth of the company should be at least Rs. 50 crore.

A NEW STOCK EXCHANGE WITH A DIFFERENCE: INTER-CONNECTED STOCK EXCHANGE OF INDIA (ISE)

In an article, published on the Internet, S.D. Irani[8] stated that, there are very few countries which have more than one stock exchange, India is one of them. Actually, Mumbai city (Bombay) alone has three stock exchanges, namely the Bombay Stock Exchange (BSE), the National Stock Exchange (NSE) and the Over the Counter Exchange of India (OTCEI). Hence one would have thought that there is no room for more exchanges – at least not in Mumbai. However, recently, a new stock exchange was granted recognition by the Securities and Exchange Board of India (SEBI) as a 'regional stock exchange' for Navi Mumbai. This new stock exchange is the Inter-connected Stock Exchange of India (ISE).

The ISE is a stock exchange like any other exchange, but at the same time it is quite different and unique in certain respects. It was on 22nd January, 1998, that the ISE was incorporated as a company limited by a guarantee. Within a short span of time, the ISE has already become an institution.

Of course, the reasons for such a rapid development are not far to seek. Unlike other exchanges, the ISE has been promoted by 15 regional stock exchanges, so as to provide trading

---

[8]S.D. Irani: An article on internet (e-mail:sdirani@use.net), Tata McGraw-Hill Publishing Company Limited, New Delhi, 1993.

linkage/connectivity to all the participating exchanges and thereby enable them to widen their own market. As a result, the ISE is a national-level exchange with a presence in several cities across the country. The ISE provides trading, clearing, settlement, risk management and surveillance support to the Inter-Connected Market System (ICMS).

A unique feature of the ISE is that it addresses the needs of small companies and retail investors. This it intends to achieve with the guiding principle of optimizing the infrastructure and harnessing the potential of regional markets and thereby transforming them into liquid and vibrant markets. Obviously, technology and networking will play a very important role in achieving the ISE's goals Irani opined. Irani also observed that the core objectives of the ISC are as follows[9]:

To create a single integrated national-level solution with access to multiple markets for providing high-quality, low-cost services to millions of investors across the country.

To create a liquid and vibrant national-level market for all listed companies in general and small companies in particular.

To provide trading, clearing and settlement facilities to traders and dealers across the country at their doorstep with a decentralized support system.

Dealership Network

According to the ISE, there are in all about 4,500 traders in its participating exchanges of which about 500 have shown an interest in trading on the ISE. In order to leverage its infrastructure and expand its nationwide reach, the ISE has also appointed 500 additional dealers across 70 cities other than the participating exchange centers. These dealers are supported by strategically located regional offices at Delhi, Calcutta, Chennai and Nagpur.

Membership of ISE

Another unique feature of the ISE is that it has also floated a wholly-owned subsidiary, namely, ISE Securities & Services Limited (ISS), to acquire membership of the NSE and other premier exchanges, so that traders and dealers of the ISE can access other markets in addition to the local market and the ISE. This will provide investors in smaller cities a one-stop solution for cost-effective and efficient trading in securities.

The ISE has already obtained membership of NSE and, in the coming months, it plans to obtain membership of some of the other important exchanges in the country. In other words, unlike other exchanges, membership on the ISE opens up vistas for dealers/traders not only on one exchange, but simultaneously on several exchanges located in different parts of the country.

---

[9]ibid

Listing of Securities

The ISE recently commenced listing of securities and it already has several companies listed on it. In addition to the International InfoTech Park, Vashi, the ISE is the regional exchange for three other technology parks in the vicinity. This makes the ISE a unique exchange as it can have technology companies for listing.

With the SEBI code for corporate governance being made a part of the listing agreement, there is an increase in responsibility on the part of companies and exchanges for better investor protection. With a focus on this, the ISE has decided to facilitate better governance and regulatory compliance through greater pro-activeness, decentralization and better use of technology. Towards that goal, the ISE has regional offices headed by a senior officer in all metros. This will result in convenience and low-cost regulatory compliance of the companies listed on the ISE. At present, other stock exchanges are all centralized as far as compliances are concerned.

The IPO Distribution System

Another feature of the ISE is that it intends to play an active role in the marketing of primary issues as well. The Initial Public Offering Distribution Chain (IPO DC) represents a system whereby issue of securities in the primary market is made through the stock exchange mechanism by utilizing the existing infrastructure network of the stock exchange. This could be in addition to the present non-computerized public offering system. IPO DC's main aim is to reduce the time taken for allotment of securities and bring down discrepancies/errors inherent in any manual system.

According to the ISE, under the proposed system, allotment of securities is expected to take not more than 15 days from the date of closure of the issue. The investor parts with his funds only when he has been provisionally allocated the securities. There will, therefore, be no question of refund of application money. Either all or some of the empanelled members of the stock exchange, as may be the rule of the concerned stock exchange, shall be appointed by the issuer company for the purpose of accepting applications from investors, placing of orders and for compulsory underwriting of the issue.

These members will not levy any service charge on their clients for rendering this additional service. The concerned members will act as collection centers/agents when the issue is open to the public for subscription. Interested investors could approach their preferred member(s) and place suitable orders for subscribing to the issue. The placement of the orders would be done through the stock exchange's trading network.

After finalizing the basis of allotment, the registrar to the issue will send the information regarding the allotment to the stock exchange, which, in turn, will inform the concerned members. It will be the responsibility of the members (brokers) to inform their clients. Additionally, the details of allotment would also be posted on the stock exchange's web site, which can be accessed directly by investors.

Successful applicants can then fill up the application forms electronically through the Internet wherever access to the Internet is available. Wherever Internet access is unavailable, the applicants will fill up the application forms as is being done at present.

Payment for the shares allotted will also be made electronically through the payment gateway system or through physical instruments. The IPO DC system will have sufficient checks and controls to ensure that information is properly fed into the electronic system and that correct payments are made. The concerned members may also be provided with a software module to take care of the capture and uploading of details from the manual application forms.

After receiving the data and the full money, the registrar to the issue will allot the securities and also issue dematerialized shares. Based on the information received from investors about their DPs, investors' accounts with the DPs would be credited for the shares finally allotted. Throughout the entire subscription and allotment, SEBI will have the right to carry out inspection of the records maintained by investors, members, registrars to the issue and bankers to the issue.

According to the ISE, as it is a technology-driven stock exchange with a potential membership base of around 5000 members (4500 members from the participating exchanges and 500 dealers), the IPO DC system can be an excellent proposition for issuer companies to market their IPOs. These members, spread over more than 75 cities across the country, are all linked through leased lines or VSATs with the ISE, Vashi. Further, their existing relationship with the clearing banks of ISE (HDFC Bank, Vysya Bank, Stanchart, Grindlays Bank, etc.) could be used for the payment system. Besides this, the ISE has professionally qualified and well-trained manpower at its registered office at Vashi, the participating exchanges and major metros in India.

There is no doubt that, in the coming years, the capital market will have to play a greater role in resource mobilization. Apart from institutional investors, it is very important that retail investors are treated with extra care. The ISE seems to hold that promise and the fact that it is managed by a group of committed professionals and has a countrywide presence, will enable it to reach out to small investors in remote parts of the country through its members located there. Hopefully, small investors, particularly in the interior towns of the country, should be able to take advantage of the ISE. This should also be the case with companies with a small capital base.

We have stated earlier that the Stock Exchange of Mumbai (BSE) and the National Stock Exchange (NSE) are the country's two leading exchanges. The country's regional exchanges are connected via the Inter-connected Stock Exchange (ISE). The BSE and NSE allow nationwide trading via their Very Small Aperture Terminus (VSATs) systems.

Their workstations are connected to a stock exchange's central computer via satellite using VSATs. The orders placed by brokers reach the exchange's central computer and are matched electronically.

CAPITAL MARKETS OF THE WORLD

To understand the capital market of India, some idea about the world capital market is necessary, as since the late 1990s India has been interacting with the world capital market in a greater way than before.

In the history of the organized world capital market, the New York Stock Exchange of the United States of America can be considered a pioneer. It was established on 'Wall Street' in New York City in 1792. Hence the exchange is popularly known as 'Wall Street' or 'Big Board'. Share trading in New York, like Calcutta, also started under the shade of a tree. In the late Eighteenth Century, trading in shares, bonds and securities began under the shade of a sycamore tree at 23, Wall Street in New York City.

The first merchant exchange was started in a coffee house named *Tuntin* at the crossing of Wall Street and Water Street. Its board room shifted to Hanover Street in 1827. The office building of the merchant exchange was destroyed by a fire in 1835. So, trading continued in a nearby warehouse of straw and hay. During that time a rival merchant exchange named *Brosh* was also trading in shares and bonds.

The share market of New York was formally founded as the New York Stock Exchange in 1863 and constructed its own four storied building in 1865. At that time, the membership fee was US\$ 3,000. Though the number of members was small at the beginning, it crossed the 1000 mark within a short period. At present the number of members is more than 1400. Most of the members of the exchange are representatives of large financial institutes. In this exchange, stocks and shares of more than 1600 business houses are traded. There are two other exchanges named the American Stock Exchange and the Commodity Exchange of New York. But more than 60 per cent trading is done through the New York Stock Exchange.

The New York Stock Exchange is the largest stock exchange in the United States by dollar volume and total market capitalization of companies listed. The biggest stock exchange by share volume is the NASDAQ, a fully electronic exchange, and a comparatively newer one (the history of NASDAQ is discussed later).

The oldest and the largest well organized stock exchange in the world is the London Stock Exchange. This exchange was established during the early eighteenth century but it was recognized as a full fledged stock exchange in 1885. At present it has its own office building which is situated on Labert Street. The number of members of the exchange is around 4,000. The functioning of the exchange is directed by a committee known as The Council of London Stock Exchange. The exchange is popularly known as Harlay Street. To the business community of the world, the London Stock Exchange is known as an ideal exchange for trading. Brokers and jobbers (the role of brokers and jobbers is discussed in Chapter 3) deal in special bonds and shares, the brokers finish the transaction with jobbers on behalf of their investing clients.

There is a definite influence of the London Stock Exchange on the society of Britain. So, the German philosopher and politician, Bismarck, correctly opined that actual understanding of the British nation can be obtained in the London Stock Exchange not in the 'House of

Commons'. The world famous economist, Keynes, was a very regular player in the London Stock Exchange while he was the Manager of Cambridge University; he invested money of the university in the stock market and improved the fund position of the university.

The share market of Paris is famous as the *Bourse de Paris*. The Government of France controls this share market. Here trading is also done in commodities in addition to shares and bonds. Both brokers and jobbers have to deposit a certain amount of money with the government as security for which they are entitled to interest.

The Paris Stock Exchange was established in 1808. Gradually trading in this exchange moved from floor trading to computer controlled trading which is known as the *Ralit* system. Earlier, shifting capital from other businesses to the share market was banned but later this restriction was lifted.

Though internationally not recognized, the share market of Germany can be considered as one of the oldest share markets of the world. The Frankfurt Stock Exchange was established as *Frankfurter Wertpapaier Bourse* in 1585. Later, the exchange was renamed as 'Frankfurt of Main.' The Berlin Stock Exchange was established in 1685, the Hanover Stock Exchange in 1787, the Stuttgart Stock Exchange in 1861 and the Düsseldorf Stock Exchange in 1935. Later, stock exchanges were also established in Hamburg, Munich etc.

It is quite well known that the share market is a product of capitalist economy. But after opening up their economy, the socialist and former communist countries also started well defined stock exchanges. The former Soviet Union, presently known as the Confederation of Independent States (CIS) opened a stock exchange in Moscow on the 12th November, 1990. This stock exchange is known as the Moscow International Stock Exchange. Later, the Siberia Stock Exchange was established in 1991.

In China, after the introduction of market economy, a 'Stock Exchange Executive Council' was formed in 1989. Its membership was restricted to banks and other financial institutions. The Shanghai Stock Exchange was established in 1990. This exchange had 171 members and the number of listed companies was 38.

The stock market became so popular in China that very recently a large number of people formed a serpentine queue to collect share application forms of a certain company. Since many of them were not able to get the application forms, a riot broke out in that area and the news was prominently published in all the major newspapers of the world.

The socialist countries gradually accepted that capital is the life-blood of a country's businesses and industries and that capital can be created through the stock markets of a country. In the government sponsored daily of China *'Legal Daily'* it was reported that Karl Marx invested £ 200 in a company's shares in 1864 and later when the market boomed he sold his shares for £ 400, thus making a profit of £ 200 per share within a short span of time.

It is true that in a share market one cannot expect to profit all the time. At times, one has to face a crash as well. On Monday, the 27th October, 1997 a big crash was observed across all the share markets of the world. Just ten years before, a similar crash was also observed on a Monday of 1987. In the world of share markets that Monday was branded as 'Black Monday'.

Analysts felt that the stock market crash of the world during the late eighties was mainly due to the handing over of Hong Kong to China. But analysts in Hong Kong felt that a fall on the New York Stock Exchange led to a worldwide crash. Other experts felt that uncertainty in the money markets of Asia prevented the investors from investing in shares in a big way even before the handing over of Hong Kong.

It was quite evident that after the handing over of Hong Kong, all the money markets of South-East Asia faced total non-confidence from the investing public. Hence the share markets witnessed a crash. The effects of this crash were also felt in the share markets of Bombay and Calcutta along with Hong Kong, Tokyo, New York, Frankfurt and Paris. The stock markets across the globe again faced a market crash during early 2009, which was mainly due to an economic meltdown in the developed countries, more particularly in the USA. In the USA most of the big financial institutions incurred a heavy loss due to their bad credit policy and a resultant failure in recovery of disbursed loans.

These financial institutions were the main sources of the money market and the capital market; they failed to supply much needed capital for businesses and industries and hence the overall economic growth faced an unprecedented setback. This economic meltdown led to a crash in the stock markets of the USA, which ultimately affected the stock markets across the globe including the markets of India.

Table 1.6 Some Important Stock Markets of the World

Name of the Country	Establishment of First Stock Exchange	Number of Listed Companies*
United States of America	1790	7,607
England	1801	1,646
Canada	1852	1,124
Australia	1884	1,070
South Africa	1887	647
Israel	1953	558
France	1808	472
Germany	1585	426
Spain	1831	376
Denmark	1861	285
Holland	1876	245
Switzerland	1873	215
Italy	1821	210
Nigeria	1960	174
Belgium	-	165
Turkey	1866	152
Greece	1876	143

Note:
1. *According to available data.
2. To get a more comprehensive picture of share markets of the world, see Appendix.
Sources: Different stock exchange publications of the respective countries.

In any country where a capitalist economy prevails, formation of private capital is one of the main criteria for the development of trade and industry. In the creation of private capital, share markets of a country play a major role. Hence, the share market and trading in shares are expanding beyond the boundaries of countries.

Opening up the economy in different countries influenced their share markets positively. Investors of one country built up an international relationship with the investors of other countries. The countries of South-East Asia specially, Japan, Hong Kong, Singapore, China, Malaysia, Indonesia and Thailand developed a mutual relationship among their investors. The share trading system which had begun in the USA and the United Kingdom more than two hundred years ago and in India more than a hundred years ago, began to influence the countries of South-East Asia in the last two and half decades. So, it can be said that the share markets of India are the oldest ones in South-East Asia.

Table 1.7 Some Important Stock Markets of Asia and Latin America

Name of the Country	Establishment of First Stock Exchange	Number of Listed Companies*
India	1875	7,811
Brazil	1843	2,906
Japan	1878	2,155
Pakistan	1947	653
Hong Kong	-	450
South Korea	-	693
Malaysia	1973	410
Thailand	1975	347
Chile	1893	263
Peru	1860	233
Philippines	1927	182
Argentina	-	180
Singapore	-	178
Mexico	1946	183
Indonesia	-	205
Sri Lanka	1960	200
Bangladesh	1960	153

Note:
1. * According to available data.
2. To get a more comprehensive picture of share markets of the world, see Appendix.
Sources: Different stock exchange publications of the respective countries.

It is well known that investment means the use of money to earn a considerable profit by way of interest, dividend or capital appreciation. It is obvious that well planned investments alone can ascertain a regular income, capital appreciation and can be used to meet the financial requirements of the investors.

The financial and economic meanings of investment are related to each other, because investment is part of the savings of individuals, which flow to the capital market either directly or through institutions divided into new and secondary financing. The capital market is considered as a meeting place of suppliers (investors) and users (business organizations) of long term funds.

Different scholars have defined investment in their own way. According to F. Amleng, investment may be defined as the purchase by an individual or institutional investor of a financial or real estate asset that produces a return proportional to the risk assumed over a future investment period. Fisher and Jordan said that investment can be defined as commitment of funds made in the expectation of some rate of return. If the investment is properly undertaken, the return will be commensurate with the risk (discussed in Chapter 2) the investor assumes.

In short, investment means the use of funds for a profitable productive purpose. There are various avenues of investment in India, which are presented in Chart 1.4.

It is obvious from our discussion on investment and trading of securities that trading in shares and participation in capital market in India is not new to the Indian investors. But to understand the movements of the share market scientifically is very new to Indian investors. After the entry of foreign financial institutions in the Indian arena, scientific understanding of the movements of stock and share prices, that is, the overall behavior of the stock market

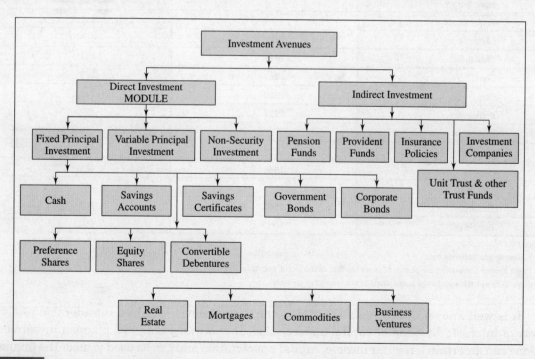

Chart 1.4   Different Avenues for Investment

is the need of the day. But before that it is essential to understand the total mechanism of the Indian stock market. In the next chapter we discuss the market mechanism or different instruments of the Indian capital market.

FOR FURTHER READING

1. Chowdhury, Utpal K., *The Market Gridlock, Smart Investor*, Business Standard, 23 April, 2001.

2. *All About Money Supply*, Economic Times, Calcutta, 2001.

3. ET in the Class Room, *The Economic Times*, 9 January, 2001.

4. Parekh, H.T., *The Bombay Money Market*, Book Publication.

Different Instruments of the Indian Capital Market

2

Before undertaking the tasks of stock market analysis it is necessary to understand clearly the different instruments or mechanisms of the Indian capital market in general, and the Indian stock market in particular. So, here we will try to explain most of the instruments of the Indian capital market.

DEFINITION AND EXPLANATION OF COMPANY SHARES

Generally, share means equity shares or ordinary shares of a company. The terms shares and stocks refer to more or less the same thing. While in India the term, share is more common, the term stock is more common in western markets. In fact, stock means representation of ownership in a company. Stock, share, security, equity and scrip mean the same thing.

A share certificate is a document that certifies a person's ownership of the interest in the share-holding of the company. Holding an equity share is evidence of a certain proportional ownership in a company. When in need of capital to run a company, the principal owner of the company issues or sells paper certificates in which the principal owner promises to consider the holders of those certificates as part owner of the company. In other words, they have a certain share in the ownership of the company. Hence the physical evidence of this ownership is a document called the share certificate.

The ownership rights are proportionate to the shares one owns. If a shareholder purchases 100 shares of a company which issued 10,000 shares, then that holder would own one per cent of the company. That means that the shareholder would own one per cent of its land, factory, equipment, patents, bank balances, and all its other assets. Hence by purchasing the shares of the company the investor is actually purchasing a fractional ownership of the company.

Each company issues shares of a certain fixed denomination called face value or par value of that share. This is clearly indicated on the share certificate. Though there are other denominations of face values, most of the shares have a face value of either Rs. 1 or Rs. 10 or Rs. 100. The face value is the value of the share when it was first issued by the company. The first issue of shares of a company is known as the Initial Public Offering (IPO). The company continues to retain its face value of the share, as far as the company is concerned, irrespective of the price at which it may later be bought or sold in the stock markets.

By selling shares, the company collects a total amount of money which is known as share capital or paid up capital of that company. If the company makes significant profits, the shareholders of the company receive a dividend as a certain percentage of its profit, determined on the basis of the face value of its share by the Board of Directors of the company in its Annual General Meeting (AGM). In short, dividend is the amount of money or stock that a company distributes to its shareholders, in the ratio in which they hold shares in the company. If the company incurs losses, the shareholders also have to take a certain responsibility, though it remains limited according to the amount of paid up capital. Shareholders have the right to vote in annual general meetings of the company. They can appoint a proxy to vote on their behalf, elect directors and appoint auditors.

In case a company issues new shares in any financial year, then these shares are eligible only for pro rata dividend in respect of the financial year in which they are issued. The old and the new shares thus carry disproportionate rights as to dividend, although their market price remains the same. To compensate the buyer to whom these new shares are delivered for loss of pro rata dividend, the seller of new shares has to pay the buyer, the dividend declared in respect of old shares. This old-new compensatory value is called the new share dividend. The exchange publishes a list of the scrips that are eligible to receive the pro rata dividend per settlement.

According to Section 82 of the Companies Act, 1956, the company share is the transferable property of its holder. So, it can be transferred. According to Section 83 of this Act, every share should have a distinctive number, price and value of that certificate which should be mentioned on it. Shares of a company can be inherited but there are certain formalities in transferring the share certificates.

AUTHORIZED CAPITAL

The amount of capital (in form of equity shares) that a company can issue as per provisions of its Memorandum of Association (MoA) which is signed at the time of the formation of the company, is known as authorized capital.

ISSUED CAPITAL

This is the amount of capital (in form of equity shares) actually offered by the company to the investing public, promoters and others for subscription. It is a part of the authorized capital. A part of the authorized capital may be withheld by the company for subsequent issue or issues.

SUBSCRIBED CAPITAL

This is the part of the issued capital that has actually been taken or subscribed to by the investors, the actual amount paid by the investing public is called paid up capital. Generally, the terms subscribed capital and paid up capital are used to denote the same thing. For example, the authorized capital of company 'A' is 100 crore shares of Rs. 10 each as on 31st March, 2009, whereas the issued subscribed and paid up capital stood at 47.38 crore shares of Rs. 10 each as on that date.

ISSUE PRICE

For the new issues or IPOs, the price at which the equity share is offered to the investors for subscription, is known as par value or face value of that share. In case of most of the new issues, it can be Rs. 10, Rs. 50, or Rs. 100 per share. However, an existing company with established profitable business, healthy reserve (discussed latter) position and proven earning power may issue shares at a price higher than the face value or par value. The difference between the issue price and the par value in such a case is known as securities premium. For example, if a company's public issue is priced at Rs. 100 per share of Rs. 10, then it effectively means that the premium per share of that company is Rs. 90. A company, however, is legally not permitted to issue shares at a discount to face value or par value.

Sometimes a few companies divide the existing face value into two or more parts. This system is known as split. Actually a split is a book entry wherein the face value of the share is altered to create a greater number of shares outstanding without calling for fresh capital or altering the share capital account. For example, if a company announces a two-way split, it means that a share having a face value of Rs. 10 is split into two shares of face value of Rs. 5 each and a person holding one share now holds two shares.

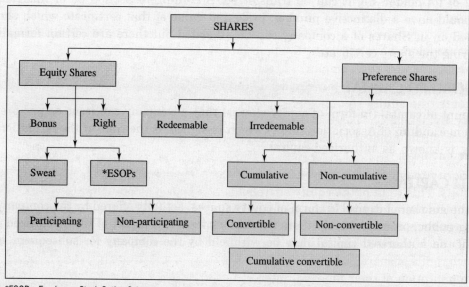

*ESOP = Employees Stock Option Scheme

Chart 2.1   Different Characteristics of Shares

The company shares are mainly divided into two parts. Chart 2.1 explains the divisions of shares more clearly.

EQUITY SHARES

An equity share signifies proportionate ownership of a company. If a company has issued 1,00,000 shares of Rs. 10 each, and if an investor or shareholder buys 1,000 shares of this company, then 1/100th part of the company belongs to that shareholder, including its plants & machinery, earnings, dividend, loans and losses. The total value of issued equity shares is the equity capital of the company. In other words it can be said that the capital of a company can be divided into several parts with definite value and each of the parts is called as share. A company issues shares to raise money or capital to build new plants, and to increase production. Thereby, the company hopes to increase its profit. Part of this profit is paid to shareholders as dividend and the balance ploughed back into business. To meet the expansion needs, most of the listed companies issue equity shares. This process of raising money by issuing equity shares is known as equity financing.

Equity capital of a company helps the company as a permanent source of working capital, but does become a liability. It also helps the company in getting loans from banks and financial institutions. According to Section 83 of the Companies' Act 1956, every equity share certificate is inscribed with the name of the investors, distinctive number of shares, price or value of shares and the number of shares the shareholder owns. The Companies Act, 1956 has limited the types of shares only to preference shares and equity shares.

RIGHTS AND LIMITATIONS OF EQUITY SHAREHOLDERS

1. Right to get dividends if the company makes residual profits. Though the equity shareholders have the right to claim on profits, if the profits are insufficient to pay the dividends, the company directors may skip the dividend payment to equity shareholders and only pay dividends to preference shareholders. In case of sufficient profits, the equity shareholders cannot legally force the directors of the company to pay dividends. The board of directors of the company has the legal right to decide how much of the profit is to be distributed as dividend and how much is to be retained in the business.

2. Priority to get shares of the company if the company plans to market a new issue of equity. This right of the equity shareholders is known as pre-emptive right. This right protects their interest in the company. As per Section 81 of the Companies Act, 1956, whenever a company proposes to increase its capital by issuing further shares, it must offer such shares to the existing shareholders. Such shares are called right shares and such rights of shareholders are known as pre-emptive rights. They protect shareholders from dilution of their financial interest in the company.[1]

---

[1]Alok Goyal et al., *Financial Market Operations*, V. K. Publications, New Delhi, India

3. Right to vote in the determination of the amount of dividend, appointment of new directors, and restructuring of business strategy. Hence, it can be said that the equity shareholders have full rights in the company as owners of the company and exercise indirect control over the working of the company.

4. Right to sell their shares in the share market through brokers at any time preferred by the shareholders. The liability of the equity shareholders is limited to the number of shares they have purchased. In case of liquidation, they are liable to pay if the shares are only partly paid up.[2]

5. If the company ceases to function, the shareholders have a right to get an appropriate share of its assets. The claim of the equity shareholders on the assets of the company is also residual. In case of liquidation, the preference shareholders will be repaid first after paying the debts and the equity shareholders are paid last. It may happen that they do not get anything in case of liquidation.

In short, when one buys a company's equity; one is in effect financing it, and being compensated with a stake in the business. He/She becomes part-owner of the company and is entitled to dividends and other benefits that the company may announce, but without any guarantee of a return on his investments

The ups and downs of the prices of equity shares in the stock markets make investment in shares free from income tax. Profits from equity shares and units of the Unit Trust of India are free from income tax. Equity shareholders are also benefited when the company issues rights or bonus shares.

BONUS SHARES

Companies do not generally distribute their entire profits to the shareholders as dividend. A fairly large part of the profit is retained and added to what is commonly called 'reserves' of the company. As the name indicates 'reserves' are back up funds which the company keeps to meet unforeseen increases in expenditure, and for financing future expansion-cum-diversification programs. Over the years, most profit making companies build up large reserves. There is also a sizeable increase in their assets, sales and the volume in business. When such growth takes place, companies often find that their equity capital is too small compared to the expansion of their business operation. It is not advantageous for companies to operate a continuously expanding business on a narrow capital base. Therefore, in order to expand their equity capital, they capitalize a part of their reserves by issuing bonus shares to their existing shareholders.

Bonus shares as their name implies, are issued free to their shareholders proportionately to the number of shares held by them. It is essentially a book transfer by which some amount of money equal to the value of bonus shares is transferred from the head 'reserves' to the head 'equity capital' in the company's book of accounts. With the issues of bonus shares, a shareholder can expand the size of his shareholding without diluting his proportional ownership of the company.

---

[2]Ibid.

Any talk of bonus shares invariably leads to a fall in the market price of shares. This does not, however, affect the shareholders adversely because this fall in the market price is more than offset by an increase in the size of his shareholding. To illustrate how this happens, let us assume that an investor owns 100 shares of a company, when the company issues bonus shares in the ratio of 1:1 (that is one bonus share for every share held by the investor). Let us also assume the market price to be Rs. 50 per share prior to the bonus issue. With the issue of bonus shares the investor's shareholding doubles to 200 shares. At the same time, the market price of the shares should probably fall from Rs. 50 to Rs. 25 per share. Even though the price has fallen, the investor does not lose because the value of his shareholding remains Rs. 5,000. The fall in price from Rs. 50 to Rs. 25 per share is fully compensated by the increase in the investor's holding from 100 shares to 200 shares. Actually, share prices generally do not fall to the same extent as the proportion in which bonus shares are issued. Ex-bonus price of the company shares is often a little higher than what it should be. In this case, the ex-bonus price of the company shares would probably fall to around Rs. 27 per share.

Companies usually continue to pay the same rate of dividend after the issue of bonus shares as they were paying prior to the bonus issue. This benefits the shareholders because they get the same rate of dividend on a large holding. A company will not normally issue bonus shares unless it is confident that its future growth prospects justify an expansion of equity capital. Therefore, the expectation of a bonus issue by any company normally creates a climate of optimism and cheer in the stock markets. This usually results in a rise in the price of a company's share just before the announcement by it of a bonus issue. By issue of bonus shares, reserve is converted into share capital and it is called capitalization of reserve. The value of bonus shares is not taxable to the shareholders. If shareholders sell the original shares after getting the bonus shares, they are likely to get some tax benefits as well.

In this connection, it will be relevant to mention some of the important guidelines issued by the Securities & Exchange Board (SEBI) in 2000 regarding bonus issue. These are:

1. No bonus issue will be made within 12 months of any public issue or right issue.
2. Bonus issue will be made out of free reserves built out of genuine profits.
3. Reserves created by revaluation of fixed assets, are not to be capitalized.
4. Residual reserves after proposed capitalization will be required to be equal to at least 40 per cent of the increased paid-up capital.
5. Bonus issue will not be made until and unless partly paid shares are converted into fully paid shares.
6. Declaration of the bonus issue instead of dividend is not to be made.
7. A company must implement the proposal of bonus issue within 6 months after taking the approval of the Board of Directors.

There must be a provision in the Articles of Association of the company for capitalization of reserve i.e. bonus issue and if there is no provision regarding the matter, the company shall pass a resolution at its general body meeting by making a provision in the Articles of Association for capitalization.

RIGHTS SHARES

Companies often require additional funds for their working capital or for their expansion and diversification plans. They sometimes raise these funds by sale of additional equity shares on rights basis to their existing shareholders. These are known as rights shares because shareholders by virtue of their existing share-holdings have a prior-right to buy these shares.

According to Section 81 of the Companies Act, 1956, if a company wants to issue new equity shares, the company has to offer these new equities to the existing shareholders as they have the first rights to those shares. The right shares offer is open exclusively to existing shareholders of the issuing company for 15 days. After that time period, the offer is open to all.

The number of right shares offered to each existing shareholder is directly proportional to the number of equity shares he owns. Right shares are offered either at par or at premium. When such shares are offered at their face value, they are said to be offered 'at par', and when the sale price is higher than the face value, they are said to be offered at 'premium'. Here, premium is the difference between the issue prices of the right shares and its face value. In order to make the right issue attractive, the price of the right shares is invariably fixed at a level far below the prevailing market price of the company's share. The issue of right shares increases the equity capital of the issuing company but does not dilute the shareholders proportionate ownership in it.

After the issue of right shares, the shares of a company which become low-priced ones in the stock market are called deferred shares. These shares are also called founder shares. These shares are issued to the promoters and founders of the company. These shares are issued in small dominations. As these shares carry voting rights, the management of the company remains in the hands of promoters. Payment of dividend on these shares is made last. The Companies Act, 1956 has put restrictions on the issue of such types of shares by a public limited company.

The relevant important SEBI guidelines issued regarding rights issue are:

1. Period of rights issue shall not be kept open for more than 60 days.
2. The quantum of right issue shall not exceed the amount specified in the letter of order. Retention of over-subscription is not permissible under any circumstances.
3. The gap between the closure of rights issue and public issue must not exceed 30 days.
4. Minimum subscription clause is applicable for both right issue and public issue.
5. Letter of offer for right issue containing disclosures will be vested by SEBI from time to time.

EX-DIVIDEND, CUM-DIVIDEND, EX-BONUS, CUM-BONUS, EX-RIGHTS AND CUM-RIGHTS

Ex-dividend quote is the price of a share which does not contain dividend declared by the company or the share price after the payment of dividend; hence the new buyer will not be entitled to the dividend amount. The shares become cum-dividend immediately after the company declares dividend containing basis, till the book closure (book closure is the period during which company does not entertain share transfer). Definitions are more or less the same for bonus and rights.

Let us say that the present market price of a company's share is Rs. 400/- per share. If the company announces a bonus issue at ratio 1:1, that is one bonus share for every share (equity held), then the price of the ex-bonus share will be Rs. 400/2 = Rs. 200 per share. After the bonus issue, the total number of shares of the company will be doubled. So, the market will automatically adjust the ex-bonus price of its share.

Apart from equity shares, preference shares, bonus shares and rights shares, there are two other equity issues called sweat equity issue and equity issue under Employees Stock Option Schemes (ESOPs). Both the issues are meant for employees of the company only and not for the general public.

SWEAT EQUITY SHARES

As per Section 79A of the Companies (Amendment) Act, 1999, a company, including a public limited one, can issue sweat equity shares. Sweat equity shares are equity shares issued by the company to an employee or directors at a discount or under any other condition except cash for providing know-how or making available rights in the nature of Intellectual Property Rights (IPR) or for value addition. A company may issue sweat equity shares after fulfilling the following conditions:

1. The issue of sweat equity shares is authorized by a special resolution passed by the company in the annual general meeting.

2. The said resolution must specify the number of shares, their values and for which class of employees or directors such equity shares are to be issued. The company can issue such shares only after completing one year from the date of commencement of business and equity shares of the company must be listed on a recognized stock exchange and must follow the regulations made by the Securities and Exchange Board of India (SEBI).

3. Sweat equity shares may be issued by unlisted companies in accordance with the guidelines made by the SEBI for this purpose. All the limitations, restrictions and provisions relating to equity shares are applicable to sweat equity shares also.

It is believed that the issue of sweat equity will encourage an employee or a director to work at his best as he will have a 'sense of belonging'. It is one way of rewarding the employee or director. These shares are called sweat equity shares because they have been earned by hard work (sweat) and in another sense, the employees feel happy with the issue of such shares and so the company expects more loyalty and more participation of the employees.

ISSUE OF EQUITY SHARES UNDER EMPLOYEES STOCK OPTION SCHEME (ESOP)

Employees Stock Option Scheme (ESOP) is a form of compensation extended to the employees by issuing stocks i.e. equities at a discounted price as compared to the market price. The SEBI prohibits the outstanding stock options in case of IPO (discussed later) for employees whether vested or not. If employee stock options are outstanding at the time of IPOs by an unlisted company, the promoters' contributions should be calculated on the basis of enlarged capital if all vested options are being exercised.

The issue of ESOPs, is assured to be made to the approval of the shareholders in a special resolution. If ESOPs are more than 1 per cent of the total shares, special approval is necessary in the Annual General Meeting (AGM). The operation of ESOPs is made under the supervision and direction of a Compensation Committee formed by the Board of Directors, where the majority are independent directors.

The ESOP scheme is designed as a voluntary scheme to boost employees' participation in the company. Goyal[3] opined that this scheme is particularly beneficial for companies that depend on the talent of the employees for the main activities of the company, such as software companies. The following are the guidelines regarding the ESOP scheme in India:

Every listed company may offer its securities to its employees through an ESOP scheme, but subject to some specified conditions. These conditions are:

1. The size of the issue of ESOP should not exceed 5 per cent of the paid-up capital of the company in a year.
2. The promoters and part-time directors of the company are not entitled to the securities of the company, even if they are employees of the company.
3. In devising the ESOP including terms of payment, the company has full liberty
4. The issue of shares under ESOP on a preferential basis can be made under two conditions. First, the issue price should not be less than the higher of the weekly average of high and low of the closing prices of the related shares quoted on a stock exchange during the previous six months and second, the issue price should not be less than the higher of the weekly average of high and low of the closing prices of the related shares quoted on a stock exchange during two weeks preceding the relevant date.

On the basis of the report submitted by the J.R. Verma Panel, in June, 2002, the SEBI put a lock-in period of 3 years on sweat equity shares to employees and directors on the 4th October, 2002. SEBI also announced a new pricing formula on the line of preferential allotments during the same period.

---

[3]Ibid.

PREFERENCE SHARES

Preference shares are not like ordinary equity shares, they are one kind of bond or debt-instrument. So, they have a pre-determined interest rate. In the case of squaring any liability, the preference shareholders get priority. That is, at the time of liquidation, they get preference in getting back their invested money. Preference shareholders can attend Annual General Meetings (AGMs) of the company, but they do have any voting rights.

Preference shares give a fixed rate of dividend which is normally less than 20 per cent per annum. They give preferential right over equity shares as regards of payment of dividends. Preference shareholders do not have the rights to get dividend like equity shareholders. It is up to the board of directors of the company whether the preference shareholders are entitled to the dividend or not in a particular year. If the board decides to pay dividend, the preference shareholders get dividends along with equity shareholders and at the time of payment of dividend, tax is not deducted at source. There is another kind of share or stock which also gives a fixed rate of dividend, this stock is known as common stock. This is stock with a fixed dividend that is paid before preferred stock dividends. Generally, the preferred dividend is higher than the common stock dividend. In the USA, to differentiate equity shares from preference shares, equity shares are referred to as common stock.

The preference shares are divided into nine classes as follows:

REDEEMABLE PREFERENCE SHARES

Usually, the share capital of a company is not refunded to the shareholders so long as the company is in existence. However, an exception is usually made in the case of preference shareholders. In such cases the preference shares are called redeemable preference shares as their share capital can be refunded or redeemed from the company after a certain fixed period of time.

IRREDEEMABLE PREFERENCE SHARES

The holders of this type of shares can get a certain percentage of the dividend every year but cannot redeem their invested money before the company winds up.

CUMULATIVE PREFERENCE SHARES

Companies which make losses are sometimes not in a position to pay any dividend to their preference shareholders. To provide for such an eventuality, companies issue what are called cumulative preference shares. Unpaid dividends on these shares do not lapse, but are allowed to accumulate till the company is in a position to clear all the arrears of accumulated dividends to its equity shareholders until such arrears of accumulated preference dividends have been paid. This gives added security to preference shareholders by assuring them of their fixed dividend, irrespective of the losses which company may incur.

NON-CUMULATIVE PREFERENCE SHARES

If a company is not able to pay dividend to its preference shareholders in a year, this dividend cannot be accumulated in the next year for this type of preference shareholders and hence these shares are called non-cumulative preference shares.

PARTICIPATING PREFERENCE SHARES

The holders of this type of shares get an additional share of profits over and above the specified dividend. Additional profits are given according to the company's law. At the time of winding up the company, participating preference shareholders enjoy a proportionate part of the surplus assets of the company.

NON-PARTICIPATING PREFERENCE SHARES

The holders of this type of shares can get dividend every year at a certain rate, but do not get any additional share of the profit. Neither are they entitled to get a proportionate share of assets if and when the company winds up.

CONVERTIBLE PREFERENCE SHARES

After a certain period of time, the preference shares which are eligible for conversion into equity shares are known as convertible preference shares.

NON-CONVERTIBLE PREFERENCE SHARES

Shareholders of this type of shares are entitled to get interest every year at a certain pre-determined rate, but these shares are never converted into equity shares. Hence this type of shares are called non-convertible preference shares.

CUMULATIVE CONVERTIBLE PREFERENCE SHARES

This financial instrument has been introduced in India since 1985. The rate of dividend for this type of shares is fixed at 10 per cent per annum. Within three to five years, this type of preference shares are converted into equity shares on a priority basis.

UNLISTED COMPANIES/SECURITIES

When a listed company does not obey the rules and regulations of stock exchanges or the company winds up its business, the stock exchanges strike the company's name off its registers so its shares are not traded. This process is known as delisting of a company.

In India, there is no organized market for unlisted securities. Hence, it is difficult to sell the shares of an unlisted company as is done in the case of companies that are listed on stock exchanges. Therefore, the Over the Counter Exchange of India (OTCEI) has come forward with a plan to provide a segment which will permit trading in such securities.

The objective of launching trading in the unlisted securities segment is to provide an exit route for investments made by venture capital and private equity funds. Further, it is expected to broad base the existing informal market to make it more liquid and to promote organized trading in unlisted securities. It is also expected to act as a preparatory ground for an IPO that may be planned for some time in the future.

By definition, only qualified participants can trade in this segment. Corporates including selected banks, venture capital funds, private equity funds or mutual funds, Unit Trust of India (UTI), state level institutions and companies wishing to make strategic investments and high net worth individuals can participate in this segment. All qualified participants need to have a minimum stipulated net worth of Rs. 2.5 crores.

The unlisted securities market can act as an ideal launch pad to complement the country's IPO market. This is because it helps companies not having a track record to still access the stock market platform with limited trading facility to raise funds. This also provides an ideal exit route for private equity and venture capital funds, thereby attracting fresh capital through such investment vehicles and at the same time preventing flight of capital.

Any entrepreneur who needs funds for a project has three options. He can either approach a venture capital fund or go to a bank or financial institute or raise money through the IPO route. Banks and financial institutions normally doubt the ability of inexperienced entrepreneurs and hesitate in financing their projects.

In the absence of a healthy track record, listing norms of large stock exchanges prohibit entrepreneurs from raising money through the IPO route. The listing norms of large exchanges require that any company, planning to raise money through an IPO route, needs to have a three-year profitability record.

This is where the new listing norms of the OTCEI are useful. The exchange has done away with the three-year track record requirement for companies planning an IPO. This means that even inexperienced entrepreneurs can raise money using the IPO route, by approaching OTCEI.

While the OTCEI has done away with the three-year track record criteria for companies planning an IPO, it has laid down stringent norms to ensure that only genuine entrepreneurs raise money from the market. The exchange will set up a high powered panel of chartered accountants, which will do the diligence of such companies and their projects. Also market making will be mandatory for a period of 18 months at these counters. Such companies without any track record have to be introduced through a sponsor.

According to the SEBI norms regarding securities, all companies which have a paid up capital of less than Rs. 3 crores (excluding premium), have to be listed with the OTCEI. During the late 1990s and early 2000s, when there was a boom in information technology (InfoTech) business, it was found that InfoTech companies preferred to approach the OTCEI to raise funds as they did not require a huge capital to start their enterprise.

DEFENSIVE STOCKS

It is generally known that in a bullish market, that is when an increasing trend prevails in the stock markets, the share prices increase rapidly and when the share prices decrease, that is at the time of a bearish market, the share prices decline rapidly. But the shares of some companies increase or decrease slowly compared to other shares, these shares are called defensive stocks. Actually, these shares are more or less unaffected by swings in the market. Typically, these are shares of traditional companies engaged in stable and mature industries. Their earnings do not fluctuate very widely from year to year. Over the years, they developed standard dividend payment practices and followed them scrupulously. The dividend yield, i.e. dividend expressed as a percentage of the market price usually works out higher than that of super stock and emerging blue chips.

SUPER STOCKS

The share of established companies whose assets, sales turnover and profits continue to grow rapidly are, appropriately called super stock or super share. Rapid growth can be achieved by following an aggressive policy of expanding profitable manufacturing facilities and widening the marketing net work, or else through diversification into profitable new lines of activity. Such companies are usually led by a very high growth-oriented entrepreneurial type of management. They enjoy full advantage of tax incentives available for growth through expansion, modernization, diversification, mergers and acquisitions.

The classic example of a super stock in India is the stock of Hero-Honda which has achived remarkable success by concentrating all its energies on the two wheeler market and by refusing to diversify into unrelated activities. On the other hand, Reliance Industries which has successfully diversified into multifarious and unrelated activities like textiles, petrochemicals, refineries, finance, infrastructures etc. is doing remarkably well even after the division of the total business between two brothers, Mukesh and Anil Ambani. The ultimate test of super stock is the quality of its management as evidenced by a strong and growing financial ratio like Earning Per Share (EPS), which can be derived by dividing the net profit of the company by the total number of shares issued by the company; and a relatively high market price.

BLUE CHIP STOCK OR SHARES

Shares of well-established and financially strong corporations, with little investment risk and a history of earnings and dividend payments are known as blue-chip shares. These stocks usually form the base of a portfolio and allow for higher gain (and higher risk) speculation in other stocks. Investment in such stocks is more for capital appreciation than for return on investment since most blue chips trade at high market prices. Indian companies like Tata Steel Company, Indian Tobacco Company etc. are known as blue-chip companies. It is always advisable to allocate a portion of the intending investors' annual income for the purchase of investment stocks over the long term.

Some stocks bank on their past glory. Once this fact is widely recognized, the market down grades such stocks and their prices tumble. These shares are termed as low-quality, high-priced, yesterday's blue-chips. Such scrips should be sold fast. One should not think about such shares again until they return to the growth track.

EMERGING BLUE CHIPS

Shares of relatively newer companies which are performing in an outstanding manner are known as emerging blue-chips. Such companies are usually headed by ambitious, first generation entrepreneurs. Their success is based on technology, marketing, pricing and/or some other unique quality.

The success if the IT company, Infosys Technologies is largely attributed to a highly professional approach of its promoter, Mr. Narayan Murthy and his excellent pioneering efforts.

The detergent company, Nirma's success is attributed to cost-effective technology and an effective marketing approach.

The success of the pharmaceutical company, Dr. Reddy's Laboratories, is largely attributed to low-cost bulk drugs manufactured by high technology.

Emerging blue-chips eventually grow into established super stocks. With time, they mature, gain stature, gather financial muscle and marketing clout and become trend setters in the stock markets.

Some of the companies' shares are popular and command a high price in the stock markets. As long as their glamour lasts, such shares perform well in the market. These shares are termed as high-quality, high-priced, emerging blue-chips. Such scrips should be sold fast. One should not think about such shares again until they return to the growth track.

ONE DECISION STOCK

If investors take a decision to hold shares of companies, which have the potential to record an increase in price in the stock markets, then these shares are termed as one decision stock.

PORTFOLIO

A collection of stocks, mutual funds or other securities that is owned by an investor is known as the portfolio of the investor. If the shares have the power to earn in risky market conditions, it is called an efficient portfolio.

There is a proverb in the market that all investors are savers but all savers cannot be good investors. After liberalization and globalization of the Indian economy, the investment process has turned out to be a science as well as an art. It is a science because good and profitable investment requires a lot of systematic thinking and analysis, and it is an art because a lot of steps need to be considered to make the investment safe.

Generally, every investor is primarily concerned about the safety of his investment. Adequate protection should exist against the risk of loss of capital. It is not guaranteed that a highly safe investment will generate relatively high returns. However, it is always advisable that the general investor should look for a safe investment. Apart from safety, an investor must also take care of sound liquidity coupled with marketability of the investments. So, a calculative risk can always be taken in selecting well diversified securities in the construction of a portfolio, as it is quite well known in the market that a safe portfolio generates low returns whereas a portfolio with some risky securities may sometimes generate surprisingly high returns. It is true that fixed income securities provide safety but their rate of return is very low. Alternatively, construction of a portfolio by properly selecting different securities is likely to achieve the objective of both safety and satisfactory yield as the risk is spread out due to diversification among different types of securities. Chart 2.2 will help one to understand the selection of a healthy portfolio.

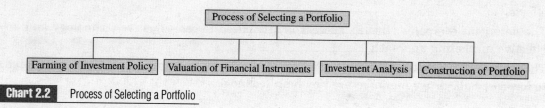

Chart 2.2   Process of Selecting a Portfolio

1. Farming of investment policy consists of:
   (a) Determination of investment amount
   (b) Determination of portfolio objectives
   (c) Identification of potential investment assets
   (d) Allocation of wealth to assert categories.
2. Valuation of financial investment consists of:
   (a) Valuation of stocks
   (b) Valuation of debentures
   (c) Valuation of bonds
   (d) Valuation of others assets
3. Investment analysis should consist of the steps shown in Chart 2.3.

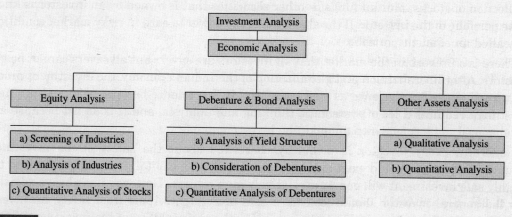

Chart 2.3   Investment Analysis

4. Portfolio construction may consist of the steps shown in Chart 2.4.

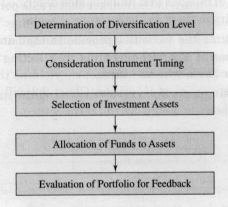

Determination of Diversification Level

Consideration Instrument Timing

Selection of Investment Assets

Allocation of Funds to Assets

Evaluation of Portfolio for Feedback

Chart 2.4   Portfolio Construction

PORTFOLIO CONSULTANTS

We have already mentioned that a combination of securities such as stocks, bonds, and money market instruments is called as portfolio. Harry Markowitz, the famous international economist, is considered the father of modern portfolio theory. As early as in 1952, he brought in the concept of portfolio. Portfolio consultants are persons or financial firms or companies who advise, direct or undertake the management of funds on behalf of their clients. Portfolio managers deal with the process of selecting securities from a number of opportunities available with different expected returns and carrying different levels of risks. The selection of securities is made with a view to provide the maximum yield to the investors with minimum risk.

Peter L. Bernstein and Aswath Damodaran[4] described the job of the portfolio managers as shown in Chart 2.5.

In their book, Bernstein and Damodaran opined that most of the stock market savvy investors mainly exercise their intuition in selecting securities from the open market for the construction of their portfolios. Yet an understanding of the investment process is critical for every investor, and the functions of the process should be communicated by advisers. The investment process, outlined by the authors is as follows:

1. The steps in creating a portfolio and emphasis on the sequence of actions involved, from understanding the investor's risk performances to selecting and allocating assets and then evaluating their performance. By emphasizing the sequence, the process provides an orderly way in which an investor can create a personal portfolio or portfolio for some one else.

---

[4]Peter L. Bernstein and Aswath Damodaran: *Investment Management*, John Wiley and Sons Inc., Third Avenue, USA

2. The investment process provides a structure that allows investors to see sources of the different investment strategies and philosophies described in the press and investment newsletters, and to trace them to their common roots.

3. The process emphasizes the various components that are needed for an investment strategy to be successful, thereby revealing why some strategies that look good on paper never work for those who use them.

The exercise of constructing a portfolio revolves around the intention of profitable return. Now let us discuss what exactly is meant by the term return.

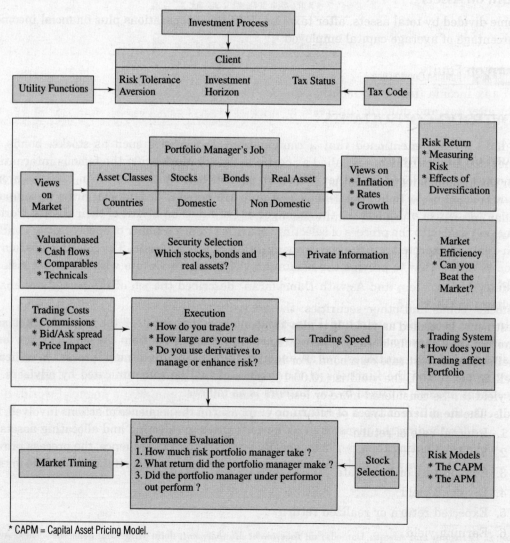

* CAPM = Capital Asset Pricing Model.

Chart 2.5   Job of Portfolio Managers

RETURN

It can be understood from the word itself that the application of some effort in getting something back can be termed as return. In the financial world return refers to some profits or loss against some investments. Expectation of a positive return is the motivation of every investment. A positive return or rate of return is always associated with some kind of risk. It is generally accepted that the higher the risk, the greater is the return expected by an investor. There are different types of returns against different financial items.

Return on Assets

Income divided by total assets, after taxation. Profit from operations plus financial income as a percentage of average capital employed.

Return on Equity

After tax income (latest 12 months) divided by shareholders equity (from balance sheet). Profit after tax and minority interests as a percentage of average equity excluding minority interests.

Return on Investments

After tax income (latest 12 months) divided by total of shareholders equity plus long term debt, plus other long term liabilities. In fact, there are two components in return on investments, regular income in the form of interest or dividend and capital appreciation. This can be calculated as

$$R_1 = \text{Income } (+/-) \text{ Price appreciation (depreciation)}$$

Yield

In stocks, bonds and other securities, the amount of money returned to investors on their investments is termed as yield. It is also known as rate of return. Interest and dividends paid to mutual fund shareholders as a percentage of the share price Net Asset Value (NAV) is also the effective interest rate on a bond. For instance, if a bond pays 10.00 interest annually, and is selling for 100.00, the yield is (10.00/100.00) = 10 per cent. But in the true sense, return and yield can be considered more or less the same in the arena of the financial world. Below we discuss the different types of return or yield which are as follows:

1. Internal rate of return
2. Yield to maturity
3. Coupon rate or bond rate
4. Dividend yield
5. Expected return or realized return
6. Earning yield
7. Holding period return

8. Real and nominal return
9. Basic yield
10. Gross and net yield
11. Current yield
12. Required rate of return

The detailed discussion on the above mentioned types of returns are given below.

Internal Rate of Return (IRR)

It is the rate at which the sum of discounted cash inflows equals the sum of discounted cash outflows and is also the rate which discounts the cash flow to zero. IRR is also known as yield rate.

Coupon Rate/Bond Rate

The interest rate received on the face value or par value of the bond is known as coupon rate or bond rate. If a company or government issues a 10 year bond with Rs. 100 as face value and 14 per cent annual rate of interest, it would be described as a 14 per cent bond or debenture and may be said have a coupon rate of 14 per cent.

Expected/Realized Return

Most of the investors know that return is not assured. At best, it can be speculated and it may be realized later on. So, the expected return is an anticipated or predicted or desired return by the investor which is subject to uncertainty. Realized return refers to what is actually earned and received.

Holding Period Yield (HPY)

It measures the total return from an investment during a given or designated time period in which the asset is held by an investor. It should be noted that HPY does not mean that a security is actually sold and gain or loss is actually realized by the investor. The concept of HPY is applicable whether one is measuring the realized return or estimating the future or expected return. HPY can be calculated as:

$$HPY = (C_{PR} + P_{Ct})/Ps$$

Where

C_{PR} = Any cash payment received

P_{Ct} = Price change over holding period

Ps = Price at which asset or security is purchased

Basic Yield

It is the lowest yield actually attained in the market. Basic yield is associated with high grade bonds. It can be understood by noting the concept of pure rate of interest, which is unique and absolutely without risk; it implies absolute safety and certainty of principal income and also freedom from losses through changes in commodity prices, interest rates and taxes. The basic yield, however, does not imply either risk less or uniqueness.

Current Yield

It is the ratio of interest per year to the current market price of the bond or security. It does not consider the return earned by the investor due to appreciation in the value of the bond. Bonds are offered to the public with coupon rate. Current yield is also known as market yield or running yield.

Yield to Maturity (YTM)

It is the assured or promised rate of return an investor receives from a bond purchased at the current market price and held till maturity. It is also known as redemption yield. It may be expressed as:

$$YTM = I_t \, (+/-) \, A_{a/d} \, /Vrf$$

Where,

I_t = Annual interest rate of the asset

$A_{a/d}$ = Appreciation or depreciation of the asset

Vrf = Redemption value of face value

Dividend Yield

It is the ratio per share of the expected dividend, gross of tax to the current market price of the share.

Earnings Yield

Earning yield is the ratio of expected earning per share (discussed later) of the firm to the current market price of the share. There is no difference between dividend yield and earnings yield if a firm's payout ratio (discussed later) is 100 per cent.

Nominal Rate of Return

It is the return in nominal rupees; the real return is equal to nominal return adjusted for inflation.

Gross and Net Yield

Gross yield is realized by the investor before paying any tax and net yield is gross yield less income tax paid. It can be expressed as:

Net yield = Gross yield – Applicable taxes thereon

Required Rate of Return (RRR)

It is defined as the minimum expected rate of return needed by an investor to purchase the security, given its risk. The RRR has two components namely, the risk free rate of return or time value of money and the risk premium. It is the return that an investor must get for facing the risk by investing his money in all those generating investments. RRR is an important factor to be considered for buying securities. It may be expressed as:

$$\text{RRR} = \text{Time value of money} + \text{Inflation premium} + \text{Risk premium}$$

Or

$$\text{RRR} = \text{Risk free rate of return} + \text{Risk premium}$$

RISKS

During the discussion on returns and yields, the term risk has been mentioned several times. Below we discuss the meaning of risk in the financial world.

It may be said that all kinds of financial investments involve some kind of risk. So, the objective of any investor who intends to invest in the capital market is to minimize the risk and maximize return. The value of any financial asset depends on its risk and return. Risk can be defined as the probability of future loss that can be foreseen. Some market analysts[5] define risk as the chance factor in trading in which expected or perspective advantage, gain, profit or return may be measurable.

One may be confused about the actual meaning of risk. According to John J. Hampton,[6] risk can be defined as the chance of a future that can be foreseen. Actually, risk means estimating the degree of the loss happening. We have mentioned in the previous paragraph that risk is a measurable element. Risk and return are inseparable. Return is an expected income from the investment. Agreeing with Hampton, it can be said that risk can be quantified by using precise statistical techniques. The investment process must be considered in terms of both aspects of risks and return. The rate of return required by an investor from his investments to a great extent depends upon the risk involved in his investment. It is an accepted fact that the higher the risk, the greater is the return expected by the investor.

A number of market analysts and researchers have classified risk into three groups which are shown in Chart 2.6.

Now, Total Risk = Systematic risk + Unsystematic risk + Other risks.

A number of market economists[7] and market analysts tried to analyze the risk elements of a security in different ways but they more or less agreed that the measures of risks involve price movements of securities in the market. This was denoted by β (Beta).

Gangadharan and Babu, in their book, defined β as the measure of relative risk of a security or its sensitivity to the movements in the market. It is a measure of volatility or the systematic risk faced by an asset or portfolio or project. Statistically it can be calculated as:

$$\text{Beta } (\beta) = \text{Cov } (R_A, R_{MP})/\sigma_{RMP}^2$$

[5]V. Gangadharan and Ramesh G. Babu: *Investment Management*, Anmol Publication, New Delhi, India

[6]John J. Hampton, *Financial Decision Making*, John Wiley and Sons, Inc., Third Avenue, USA

[7]National Stock Exchange: 'Surveillance in Stock Exchanges Models', Work Book, NSE, Mumbai

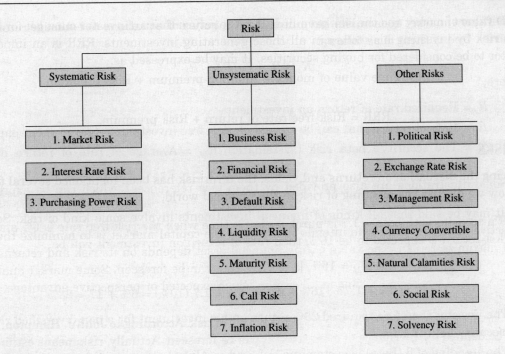

Chart 2.6   Classification of Risk

Where, Cov (R_A, R_{MP}) = the covariance between return of assets (R_A) and returns of market portfolio (R_{MP}) and σ^2_{RMP} = the variance of returns on the market portfolio.

Beta (β) shows how the price of a security responds to the market factors. The more responsive the price of a security to the changes in the market, the higher will be its β. β can also be derived by relating the return on security with returns for the market. Market return is measured by the average return of a large sample of stocks.

The β for the overall market is considered to be equal to 1.00 and other b*s are viewed in relation to this value. The value of β can be positive or negative. Financial consultants, large broker firms and investment companies provide data on β for a large number of stocks. It can also be derived as:

$$R_s = \alpha + \beta_{RM} + e_{its}$$

Where,

R_s = Estimated return on stock; α = The intercept of the line of linear regression between R_s and R_M;

β = The slope of the line of linear regression between R_s and R_M; R_M = Return on market index;

e_{it} = Error term.

Different market economists have deduced a number of equations to estimate return on security. One of them is as follows:

$$R_s = R_f + \beta_s \, (R_M - R_f)$$

Where,

R_s = Required rate of return on investment

R_f = Rate of return that can be earned on risk free investments (government papers)

β_s = The security's beta risk (systematic); R_M = Average of rate of return on all securities

Some illustrations are also provided by them (see references), which can be expressed as:

If a security with beta = 1.7 is purchased at a time when the risk free rate is 6% and the market return is expected to be 16%, then rate of return on investment will be

$$R_f = 6\%, \, R_M = 16\%, \, \beta_s = 1.7$$

$$R_s = 6\% + 1.7\% \, (16\% - 6\%) = 6\% + 1.7 \, (10\%) = 6\% + 17 = 23\%$$

The investor therefore required 23% return on his investment for a non-diversified risk of the security beta of 1.7%.

The standing of β (Beta) is systematic risk and α (Alpha) measures the unsystematic risk of the company. The difference between expected return and actual earned return is termed as α. Hence, when α = 0, the actual return is equal to the expected return of a security.

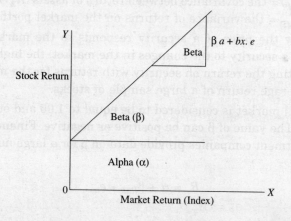

| **Chart 2.7** | Relationship between Index and Stock Return - I |

A number of eminent economists have suggested that only one regression model cannot be considered optimum or can explain all the factors that influence the growth of any economic phenomenon including portfolio of securities growth.

With the help of a formula we may reach a conclusion that in a situation when correlation (r) of return is positive, it is the effect on risk when two securities are combined. Their deductions are as follows:

Let there be N number of securities in the portfolio, now the general formula is

$$\sigma_p^2 = W_x^2\,\sigma_x^2 + 2W_xW_y\,C_{xy} + W_y^2\,\sigma_y^2$$

where,

σ_p^2 = The variance of return for the portfolio

W_x = The portion of the fund invested in security x

W_y = The portion of the fund invested in security y

C_{xy} = the covariance between return on security x and return on security y

$C_{xy} = r_{xy}\,\sigma_x\,\sigma_y$

If there is perfect positive correlation between the securities x and y, so that, $r_{xy} = +1$ and $C_{xy} = \sigma_x\,\sigma_y$, then by substituting these values in the general formula;

$$\sigma_p^2 = W_x^2\sigma_x^2 + 2W_xW_y\,\sigma_x\sigma_y + W_y^2\,\sigma_y^2$$

Or,
$$\sigma_P^2 = (W_x\,\sigma_x + W_y\,\sigma_y)^2$$

Hence,
$$\sigma_P = W_x\,\sigma_x + W_y\,\sigma_y \text{ if } r_{xy} = +1$$

Gangadhar and Babu mentioned that this is an important result. If two securities' returns are perfectly positive the risk combination can be measured through the calculation of standard deviation of return on securities. Diversification does not provide risk reduction but only risk averaging.

They argued that sometimes the diversification process can help to eliminate the risk of a portfolio. It can eliminate the risk in case of perfectly negative correlated returns therefore, if $r_{xy} = -1$, then the general formula turns out to be as follows;

$$\sigma_p^2 = W_x^2\,\sigma_x^2 - 2W_xW_y\,\sigma_x\sigma_y + W_y^2\,\sigma_y^2$$

Or,
$$\sigma_P^2 = (W_x\,\sigma_x - W_y\,\sigma_y)^2 \text{ If } r_{xy} = -1 \text{ and } \sigma_P = 0$$

This may be represented as,

$$W_x = \frac{W_y\sigma_y}{\sigma_x}$$

Or,

$$\sigma_P = (W_x\,\sigma_x - W_y\,\sigma_y)^2 \text{ If } r_{xy} = -1 \text{ and } \sigma_P = 0, \text{ as, } (W_x + W_y) = 1 \text{ and } W_y = 1 - W_x$$

Or,

$$0 = W_x \, \sigma_x - W_y \, \sigma_y, \text{ or}$$

$$0 = W_x\sigma_x - (1 - W_x) \, \sigma_y, \text{ or, } 0 = W_x \, \sigma_x - \sigma_y + W_x \, \sigma_y, \text{ or, } 0 = W_x \, (\sigma_x + \sigma_y) - \sigma_y$$

Or,

$$\sigma_y = W_x \, (\sigma_x + \sigma_y)$$

Or,

$$W_x = \frac{\sigma_y}{\sigma_x + \sigma_y}$$

Similarly,

$$W_y = \frac{\sigma_x}{\sigma_x + \sigma_y}$$

If the two securities are perfectly negatively correlated, it is possible to combine them in a manner that will eliminate all risks. Some risk can be reduced by pooling all the securities. Selection of better securities for a portfolio is the important task of a portfolio manager.

In case of un-correlated returns, the general formula turns out to be;

$$\sigma_p^2 = W_x^2 \, \sigma_x^2 + 2W_x W_y r_{xy} \, \sigma_x \, \sigma_y + W_y^2 \, \sigma_y^2$$

Or,

$$\sigma_P^2 = W_x^2 \, \sigma_x^2 + W_y^2 \, \sigma_y^2 \text{ if } r_{xy} = 0$$

If the diversification process helps the portfolio to reduce the risk either of a single security or a component of securities, it will remain the same irrespective of the number of securities in the portfolio. If all the returns are uncorrelated the formula becomes (when the portfolio consists of 4 securities)

$$\sigma_P^2 = W_1^2 \, \sigma_1^2 + W_2^2 \, \sigma_2^2 + W_3^3 \, \sigma_3^3 + W_4^4 \, \sigma_4^4 + 2W_1 W_2 \, r_{12} \, \sigma_1 \, \sigma_2 + 2 \, W_1 W_3 \, r_{13} \, \sigma_1 \sigma_3$$

$$+ 2W_1 W_4 \, r_{14} \, \sigma_1 \, \sigma_4 + 2 \, W_2 W_3 \, r_{23} \, \sigma_2 \, \sigma_3 + 2 \, W_2 W_4 \, r_{24} \, \sigma_2 \, \sigma_4 + 2 \, W_3 W_4 \, r_{34} \, \sigma_3 \, \sigma_4$$

When,

$$\sigma_1 = \sigma_2 = \sigma_3 = \sigma_4 \text{ (S.Ds are equal)}$$

and

$$\sigma_{12} = \sigma_{13} = \sigma_{14} = \sigma_4 = \sigma_{23} = \sigma_{24} = \sigma_{34} \text{ (Covariance of each pair of securities are equal);}$$

and $W_1 = W_2 = W_3 = W_4$ (Portfolio containing securities are equal);

Then,

$$\sigma_P^2 = W_1^2 \, \sigma_1^2 + W_1^2 \, \sigma_1^2 + W_1^2 \, \sigma_1^2 + W_1^2 \, \sigma_1^2 + 2W_1^2 \, \sigma_{12} + 2W_2^1 \, \sigma_{12}$$

$$+ 2W_1^2 \, \sigma_{12} + 2 \, W_1^2 \, \sigma_{12} + 2W_1^2 \, \sigma_{12} + 2W_1^2 \, \sigma_{12}$$

Or,

$$\sigma_P^2 = 4W_1^2 \, \sigma_1^2 + 12 \, W_1^2 \, \sigma_{12}$$

σ_P = Standard deviation of return on portfolio

W_1 = The proportion of funds invested in security 1 of a portfolio

W_2 = The proportion of funds invested in security 2 of a portfolio

σ_1 = Standard deviation of return for security 1

σ_2 = Standard deviation of return for security 2

W_3 = The proportion of funds invested in security 3 of a portfolio

W_4 = The proportion of funds invested in security 4 of a portfolio

σ_3 = Standard deviation of return for security 3

σ_4 = Standard deviation of return for security 4

Diversification can lead to substantial risk when the components of a portfolio are uncorrelated. An investor can reduce the overall risk of the portfolio by including a sufficient number of securities in his portfolio. The process of including enough securities in a portfolio to minimize the incidence of risk is known as portfolio insurance.

The ideal portfolio is a combination of risk less and risky securities. If return from security A is certain, and that from security B is uncertain, then $\sigma_A = 0$ and the combination is deduced by Gangadhar and Babu as follows:

$$\sigma_P = W^2 A_0 + 2W_A W_{B0} + W^2 B_s^2 B$$

Hence,

$$\sigma_P = W_B \sigma_B \text{ if } \sigma_A = 0$$

Usually the borrowed fund is a costly investment and it enhances the leverage. If borrowed capital is invested in a risk alternative, then the leverage increases the expected return on investment. Sometimes the expected return may decline with an unfavorable outcome. Borrowing increases risk and expenses. Leverage increases risk and return. The individual investors can borrow from a number of sources. The borrower has to meet the cost of the fund. The interest rate will depend upon a number of factors, i.e. the length of time involved, the amount of money borrowed, the purpose of the loan, the lender, the collateral etc. There is a chance that the loan amount will not be repaid in full in time, the rate charged of course is higher and the loan will be risk less. We also advocate trying an alternative method of ideal combination of portfolio or coefficient of determination r^2.

Let us consider, X is the market return (Index) and Y is the stock return of an individual security in a portfolio. Since the distribution of Y is not specified,

We note that:

$$\sigma_{XY}^2 = \frac{1}{n-2} \Sigma (Y - Y_c)^2 \tag{1}$$

Where, σ_{XY}^2 = Standard deviation of regression or standard risk estimate with degrees of freedom considered to be $n - k$ (here $k > 2$).

Equation (1) consists of deviations $e = Y - Y_c$. Let us investigate this aspect of σ_{XY}^2 using a diagram. From Chart 2.8, we may establish the relationship

$$Y - \overline{Y} = (Y - Y_c) + (Y_c - \overline{Y}) \tag{2}$$

Where,

$Y - \overline{Y}$ = *Total risk* in the portfolio

$(Y - Y_c)$ = *Unexplained risk* components (securities) in the portfolio

$(Y_c - \overline{Y})$ = *Explained risk* component or risk less components (securities) in the portfolio.

$(Y - \overline{Y})$ shows the *total risk* (or total deviation) and may be considered as the risk between an individual security Y and the arithmetic mean $\overline{Y}$ which is an estimate of Y when no regression line is used.

$(Y_c - \overline{Y})$ is called the *explained risk*, and it may be thought of as the amount of risk removed when the regression line is fitted to points.

$e = Y - Y_c$ is the deviation we defined earlier but will also be called the *unexplained risk* in harmony with the other two terms. It is the risk that still remains after the regression line has been fitted.

Each point can be decomposed in the manner explained above.

As is seen, the estimated residual variance or standard risk σ^2_{XY} is an average of the sum of squared unexplained risks. We note that when $e = Y - Y_c$ becomes zero in Chart 2.8, point Y coincides with Y_c and falls on the regression line, AB, and

$$\sigma^2_{XY} = \frac{\Sigma(Y - Y_c)^2}{n - 2} = \frac{\Sigma e^2}{n - 2} = 0$$

That is, the residual variance is zero and we have a perfect fit. On the other hand, when $(Y_c - Y)$ becomes equal to zero, that is, there is no improvement in selection of the portfolio due to regression, then Y_c coincides with $\overline{Y}$ and

$$\sigma^2_{XY} = \frac{\Sigma(Y - Y_c)^2}{n - 2}\ \frac{\Sigma(Y - \overline{Y})^2}{n - 2}$$

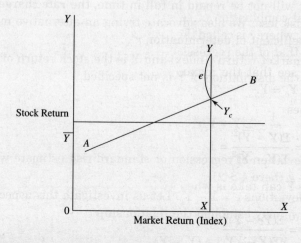

Chart 2.8   Relationship between Index and Stock Return - II

As is seen the smallest value $Y - Y_c$ can take is

$$e = Y - Y_c = 0$$

and the largest value $Y - Y_c$ can take is

$$e = Y - Y_c = Y - \overline{Y}$$

Hence, it seems reasonable to evaluate $Y - Y_c$ with respect to $Y - \overline{Y}$.

It turns out that we may perform this evaluation by utilizing the following relationship:

$$\Sigma(Y - \overline{Y})^2 = \Sigma(Y - Y_c)^2 + \Sigma(Y_c - \overline{Y})^2 \qquad (3)$$

Where, the sum is taken over the sample portfolio. This is the basic relation in regression analysis. $\Sigma(Y - \overline{Y})^2$ is called the *total sum of square of risks* and Equation (3) shows how it can be split (partitioned) into two parts: $\Sigma(Y - Y_c)^2 = e^2$ which is called the *unexplained risks*; and $\Sigma(Y_c - \overline{Y})^2$ which is called the *explained risks*.

We are interested in the relation between $\Sigma(Y_c - \overline{Y})^2$ and $\Sigma(Y - \overline{Y})^2$

So let us divide both sides of Equation (3) by $\Sigma(Y - \overline{Y})^2$

$$1 = \frac{\Sigma(Y - Y_c)^2}{\Sigma(Y - \overline{Y})^2} + \frac{\Sigma(Y_c - \overline{Y})^2}{\Sigma(Y - \overline{Y})^2} \qquad (4)$$

And r can be defined as

$$r^2 = \frac{\Sigma(Y_c - \overline{Y})^2}{\Sigma(Y - \overline{Y})^2} \qquad (5)$$

$$= \frac{\text{Explained risks}}{\text{Total risks}}$$

Determination of an ideal combination of securities in a portfolio is represented by the *coefficient of determination* r^2; where r is called the *correlation coefficient of the sample portfolio*. The sign of r is the same as that of the regression coefficient b.

From Chart 2.8, we can see that the maximum value $Y_c - \overline{Y}$ can take occurs when Y_c coincides with Y and we get $Y_c = Y$.

Then Equation (5) becomes

$$r^2 = \frac{\Sigma(Y - \overline{Y})^2}{\Sigma(Y - \overline{Y})^2} = 1$$

The minimum value $Y_c - \overline{Y}$ can take is when Y_c coincides with $\overline{Y}$ and we get,

$$r^2 = \frac{\Sigma(Yc - \overline{Y})^2}{\Sigma(Y - \overline{Y})^2}$$

$$r^2 = \frac{\Sigma(\overline{Y} - \overline{Y})^2}{\Sigma(Y - \overline{Y})^2} = 0$$

Hence $1 \le r^2 \le 0$

And the *correlation coefficient of the sample portfolio is* $1 \le r \le -1$

The sign of r is the same as that of b or the coefficient β.

r^2 as measure of improvement

The basic relation is, schematically,

$$\underset{\substack{Total \\ risk}}{\Sigma(Y - \overline{Y})^2} = \underset{\substack{Unexplained \\ risk}}{\Sigma(Y - Y_c)^2} + \underset{\substack{Explained \\ risk}}{\Sigma(Y_c - \overline{Y})^2}$$

And

$$r^2 = \frac{Explained\ risks}{Total\ risks}$$

When the unexplained risk = 0, then total risk is equal to the explained risk. Hence

$$r^2 = \frac{Explained\ risks}{Total\ risks}$$

$$= \frac{Total\ risks}{Total\ risks} = 1$$

When the explained risk = 0, then

$$r^2 = \frac{Explained\ risks}{Total\ risks}$$

$$r^2 = \frac{0}{Total\ risks} = 0$$

Thus r^2 shows the relative reduction in the total risks when the regression line is fitted. For example, when $r^2 = 0.7$, it means that there has been a 70 per cent reduction in total risk. $r^2 = 1.0$ shows there has been 100 per cent reduction in total risks and the portfolio which represents this phenomenon, is considered the ideal portfolio. But this phenomenon very rarely occurs. Even a portfolio which represents a maximum reduction in total risks is certainly considered the most ideal portfolio. Hence it can be said that r^2 shows that amount of improvement in construction of a portfolio which is brought about by fitting the regression line.

We have also found that calculation of the correlation coefficient between the dependent variable (stock return) and explanatory variables (different securities) and further between two explanatory variables and the formation of a correlation coefficient matrix sometimes help to identify the individual and total effect of selected securities on stock return and subsequently lead to the construction of an ideal portfolio.

The standard formula, which is also known as the Karl Pearson's formula, for the correlation coefficient is given by:

$$r = \frac{\Sigma xy}{\sqrt{(\Sigma x^2)\,(\Sigma y^2)}} = \frac{\text{cov}\,(x, y)}{\sigma_x \sigma_y}$$

Where, r represents the co-efficient of correlation, x (security) is the explanatory variable and y is the dependent variable (stock return).

In the above paragraphs, we have discussed details of portfolio construction and related returns, yields and risks. Now let us consider other instruments of the capital market.

NON-VOTING SHARES

It is well known that equity shareholders of a company have the power to vote in taking decisions in a company's affairs. It is a common phenomenon throughout the world including India. In other countries, the companies issue shares along with equity shares which have no voting power in the decision making of a company's affairs. But the holders of these shares get dividends at a higher rate than the equity shareholders. These shares are known as non-voting shares. Earlier, these shares were in circulation in our country. In 1966, the then finance minister of India, P. Chidambaram, in his budget speech announced the re-introduction of non-voting shares. But later, he withdrew his proposal.

CYCLICAL SHARES

These are shares of companies engaged in businesses, which are susceptible to fluctuations caused by trade cycles. They do extremely well during boom periods but hit the bottom during recessions. Due to this cyclical nature of the fortunes of these industries, the share prices go up and down in a cyclical manner. Examples of cyclical shares would be those of companies in aluminum, automobiles, housing, plantation, sugar industries etc.

FLOATING STOCKS AND SHARES

Floating stock and floating shares are somewhat different. The portion of the subscribed equity capital of a company that takes part in daily trading in the stock markets, is called floating stock. On the other hand, shares which are purchased in view of quick short term gains are called floating shares. Investors generally do not take delivery of these shares, but keep them with the broker and after taking advantage of the bull phase (upward price trend of shares) and bear phase (downward price trend of shares) of the market, sell those shares for quick profit.

VOLATILE SHARES

The prices of the shares of a company which move up and down in short intervals are known as volatile shares. These shares can be determined according to following manner:

$$\text{Volatile Shares} = \frac{\text{Highest price} - \text{Lowest price}}{\text{Highest price}}$$

The prices of shares of a well managed company with a small equity base move in a linear way. Shares of such companies are cornered or sold very easily in the stock market. These shares are price sensitive. There are other types of shares which are interest sensitive. The prices of the shares of some companies change with a change in the government's policy of bank interest rates. Shares of such companies are called interest sensitive shares.

The shares of the companies which have low P/E ratios (discussed later), but yield good dividend and follow a policy of high dividend payout are termed as income shares. More clearly it can be said that such shares have consistently paid high dividends. Contrary to what one might think, after some time on the stock exchange, there really are such stocks. When an investor finds one he should grab it and cherish it 'till death or inflation do one part'. If one has a good base of income shares, one can afford to speculate in higher risk stocks. But one should keep an eye on the fundamentals of the company. Consistent does not mean forever.

TURNAROUND SHARES

A turnaround share is one whose market price is currently lower than its intrinsic value because the company has gone through a bad patch. When such a company begins to turn the corner, or is taken over by another more successful company, shrewd bargain-hunters pick up its shares at a relatively lower price and reap a fortune when the anticipated favorable turn of events takes place. Shares of some blue-chip companies of today were once similarly available at steep discounts.

Shares of the shoe company Bata and music products company Gramophone Company, for instance, were discount shares in the late 1980s and early 1990s until the companies were restructured. Tata Tea was a sick discount share in 1979-80 before the tea industry showed a relatively better performance.

GROWTH SHARES

These shares have a strong position in a growth market. They enjoy an above-average rate of growth of profitability, tend to be highly volatile on the stock exchange and in general offer low current and high capital gains yield to investors.

GILT-EDGED SECURITIES

These are debt-instruments issued by the Central, State and quasi-government authorities. They typically have a redemption period of 10 years to 20 years and carry interest at very low rates. Banks and other financial companies are required to hold a specific number of these securities.

The shares or securities that generate steady earnings for their investors, and are likely to continue steady earnings in the future, are known as gilt stock. Investments in these shares are safe and secure.

ACTIVE SHARES, INACTIVE SHARES AND INACTIVELY TRADED SHARES

Trading of established profit making companies' shares are done frequently in the stock markets. Shares of these companies are traded at least three times a week. The prices of these shares react or fluctuate according to political and economic fluctuations in a country. These types of company shares are known as active shares.

The shares of some of the companies are traded very rarely and investors seldom show any interest in them. Such shares are called inactive shares.

Some listed shares are not traded in the stock markets for weeks or months and are only traded once or twice in a year. These shares are known as inactively traded shares.

MANIPULATED SHARES, WIDOW AND ORPHAN STOCK, AND YO-YO STOCK

Before issuing rights shares or equity shares, some companies try to corner the shares of their own companies by their own appointed people in the disguise of investors. This way they try to artificially push up the prices of their shares in the stock markets. The shares of these companies are called manipulated shares.

The share prices of some companies show a steady trend and rarely show any declining trend in the stock markets. Such shares are known as widow or orphan stock.

The share prices of some companies move up and down like a yo-yo. These types of shares are called yo-yo stocks.

BAROMETER STOCK, BETA SHARES, CATS AND DOGS, AND LONG DATED STOCK

At times the movement of share prices in stock exchanges is influenced by a particular share, which actually determines the direction of the trend of prices in the stock market. That trend setter stock of a particular company is called a barometer stock.

Share prices of some listed companies remain at a very low level and are traded very rarely. Internal capital of these companies also erodes very quickly. The shares of such companies are called beta shares.

Shares of some new, financially week companies are seldom traded in the stock markets. Though in a bullish market these shares record some earnings, in a bearish market trading in these shares very rarely takes place. These shares are called cats and dogs.

Securities of the British government, which mature after 15 years or more, are called long dated stock.

PSU STOCKS

Companies which are mainly owned by the government of India are called Public Sector Undertaking or PSUs. The shares of these companies are known as PSU shares. The government has initiated steps to disinvest its holdings in several PSUs.

MNC STOCKS

There are several reputed Multi National Companies (MNCs) operating successfully in India. Prior to the dismantling of the respective provision of the Foreign Exchange Regulation Act (FERA), these were generally known as FERA companies. With FERA practically redundant, it will be more appropriate to refer to them as MNCs. Investors have a great fancy for these MNC stocks due to their strong financial performance over the years.

BENAMI-SHARES

People with unlimited black money buy a large number of shares from the stock markets in fictitious names. These shares are called unnamed or benami shares. These people not only buy shares in fictitious name, but also sell in due time and make profits. Any investor who buys these types of shares is likely to be cheated.

TAINTED SHARES

During the share-scam by Harshad Mehta in 1992 and later by others, a large number of shares were in the hands of convicted brokers or traded by them. The share market regulatory authority, SEBI announced that these shares as tainted ones and declared trading in these shares illegal.

VALUATION OF EQUITY SHARES

Most of the general investors face some sort of dilemma in making a decision to buy, hold or sell. To make such a decision, scientific valuation of equity shares is necessary. A number of economists have suggested ways of determining the valuation of equity shares.

The authors opined that a security analyst should evaluate the past performance of a particular company's scrip when a person is faced with the problem of making a decision to buy, hold or sell. With the result of the evaluation and his personal experience, any knowledgeable analyst can predict the future performance of the observed equity share and its relative market position. The detailed data available to the analyst for this task far exceeds his human capabilities of assimilation. The prediction of the analyst will normally be based on several basic attributes of the security and he will modify these results in the light of his intuitive beliefs.

It is quite obvious that the valuation of equity shares will be quite difficult and different because the return on equity shares is uncertain and is likely to change from time to time. The amount of return and degree of variability of return together will determine the value

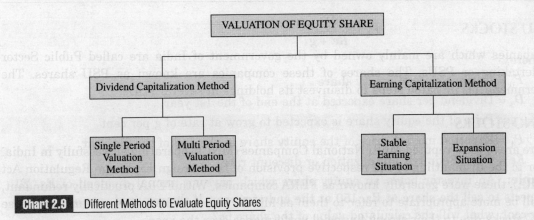

Chart 2.9 Different Methods to Evaluate Equity Shares

of a share. The authors suggest that if the value of a share is lower than the intrinsic value, then the share is undervalued and is a good buy because the same can be sold when it is overvalued in the market. To evaluate equity shares, different methods can be adopted as shown in Chart 2.9.

Dividend Capitalization Approach (Method)

Conceptually this can be considered a very sound approach. According to this approach, the valuation of an equity share is equivalent to the present value of its future dividends plus the present value of the price expected to be realized on its sale.

This approach is based on the following assumptions:

1. Dividends are paid annually.
2. The dividend is received a year after the purchase of an equity share.

   This approach is divided into two types:

   (a) Single period valuation method
   (b) Multiple period valuation method

Single period valuation method: In this approach, it is assumed that the investor expects to hold the equity share for a year. In this situation, the value of the equity share can be calculated as follows:

$$P_0 = \frac{D_1}{1 + Ke} + \frac{P_0(1 + g)}{1 + Ke}$$

Or,
$$P_0 = \frac{D_1 + P_0(1 + g)}{1 + Ke}$$

Or,
$$P_0(1 + Ke) = D_1 + P_0(1 + g)$$

Or,
$$P_0(1 + Ke - 1 - g) = D_1; \text{ or, } P_0(Ke - g) = D_1$$

So,
$$P_0 = \frac{D_1}{Ke + g}$$

Where,

P_0 = Current price of equity share

D_1 = Dividend per share expected at the end of the 1st year

g = Price of the equity share is expected to grow at rate of g per cent

P_1 = Expected market price of the equity share at the end of the 1st year

Ke = Cost of equity/Capitalization or discount rate

Example: An investor holds an equity share which pays an annual dividend of Rs. 20. He expects to sell the share at Rs. 150 at the end of a year. If the required rate of return is 20 per cent, what will the calculated value of the share be?

As
$$D_1 = 20, P_1 = 150, Ke = 20\%$$

$$P_0 = \frac{D_1}{1 + Ke} + \frac{P_1}{1 + Ke}$$

$$= \frac{20}{1 + 0.20} + \frac{150}{1 + 0.20} = 150 \text{ (approximately)}$$

Multiple period valuation method: Until the company goes into liquidation, the equity shares of the company are perpetual. They do not have a maturity period. The investor or holder of equity shares in general expects cash inflows in the form of dividends year after year. Then the value of an equity share is equivalent to the present value of its future stream of dividends. In a situation where the dividend per share remains constant, the value of an equity share can also be determined on the basis of valuation methods applied to value the debentures or bonds.

$$P_0 = \frac{D_1}{(1 + Ke)} + \frac{D_2}{(1 + Ke)^2} + ... + \frac{D_n}{(1 + Ke)^n} + \frac{P_n}{(1 + Ke)^n}$$

$$= \sum_{t=1}^{n} \{Dt/(1 + Ke)^t\} + \{Pn/(1 + Ke)^n\}$$

The investor plans to hold the security for n years and sell it thereafter at a price P_n.

Zero Growth Model

$$P_0 = \frac{Di}{Ke}$$

Where

P_0 = Current value of equity share

Di = Expected annual dividend per equity share

Ke = Rate of capitalization

Following the method advocated by Gangadhar and Babu, the current value of an equity share can be estimated by the formula given below:

$$Ecv = \frac{Di}{Ke}$$

Where

Ecv = Current value of equity share

Di = Expected annual dividend per equity share

Ke = Rate of capitalization

Example: The Company X currently pays an annual dividend of Rs. 75 per equity share, it is expected that the company will continue this rate of paying dividends in the future as well. The present capitalization rate of the company is 25 per cent. What will be the estimated value of equity share of the company?

As

$$Ecv = \frac{Di}{Ke} = \frac{75}{25} \times 100 = \text{Rs. } 300$$

From the Constant Growth Model (proposed by Myron J. Gordon):

$$P_0 = \frac{D_1}{(1 + Ke)} + \frac{D_2}{(1 + Ke)^2} + \dots + \frac{D_{n+1}}{(1 + Ke)^{n+1}}$$

Or,

$$P_0 = \frac{D_1}{(1 + Ke)} + \frac{D_1(1 + g)}{(1 + Ke)^2} + \dots + \frac{D_1(1 + g)^n}{(1 + Ke)^{n+1}}$$

With the help of a geometrical progression the aforesaid expression can be written as:

$$P_0 = \frac{D_1}{Ke - g}$$

Growth of Dividend

On the basis of their earning and retention policies, most of the profit making companies increase their rate of paying out dividends every year. So, if the company does not make any new issue of shares or does not increase its paid up capital, the company would have an increased earning per share per annum. The growth rate of a dividend can be calculated by a simple formula:

$$G_d = \frac{D_2 - D_1}{D_1} \times 100$$

Where

G_d = The growth in dividends

D_1 = The dividend at the end of the 1st year

D_2 = The dividend at the end of the 2nd year

Now with the conventional formula, the market price per share can be calculated as:

$$Pc = \frac{D_1}{Ke - G_d}$$

Where

Pc = Current market price of an equity share

D_1 = Dividend at the end of the 1st year

G_d = Growth rate of dividend

Ke = Rate of capitalization

Example: The Company X earns 20 per cent of its capital employed; it has a share capital of Rs. 20,00,000. The policy of the company is to retain 80 per cent of its earnings.

	The Company X	
	1st Year	2nd Year
	Rs.	Rs.
Total Earnings (20% of 20,00,000)	4,00,000	4,64,000
Retained Earnings (–)	3,20,000	3,71,000
Dividend Distributed	80,000	92,000

Now, growth of dividend,

$$G_d = \frac{D_2 - D_1}{D_1} \times 100$$

$$= \frac{92,000 - 80,000}{80,000} \times 100$$

$$= 16\%$$

Now let us determine the valuation of the equity share of the company with a growth rate of dividend with the conventional formula of market price per share, which we have already mentioned above, i.e.

$$Pc = \frac{D_1}{Ke - G_d}$$

Example: The Company ABC Ltd. is expected to pay a dividend of Rs. 25 per share. Dividends are expected to grow at the rate of 15 per cent and capitalization rate is 20 per cent, then the market value of the share of the company will be:

$$Pc = \frac{D_1}{Ke - G_d} = \frac{25}{(0.20 - 0.15)} = \frac{25}{0.05} = 500$$

Earnings Capitalization Method (Approach)

This approach is classified into two categories:

1. Valuation of an equity share when the earnings of the company are stable
2. Valuation of an equity share when the earnings of the company are increasing and can be estimated by:

$$Pc = \frac{E_1}{Ke}$$

Where

Pc = The current value of an equity share

E_1 = The expected earnings for the share at the end of the 1st year

Ke = The capitalization rate

Example: The Earning Per Share (EPS)* of a company is 25, rate of capitalization is 30 per cent and retained earnings is 0, then the price of the equity share of the company will be

$$Pc = \frac{E_1}{Ke} \times 100 = \frac{25}{30} \times 100 = 83.33$$

Broadly EPS is defined by $\dfrac{\text{Profit after tax of the company}}{\text{Total number of equity shares}}$

The value of the equity share of a company which is sinking can also be determined by

$$Ve = \frac{Dc}{Ke - g}$$

Where

Ve = Value of the equity share

Dc = Current dividend

Ke = Capitalization rate

g = Rate of growth/decline of the company

Example: If a company is sinking (declining) at the rate of 5 per cent per annum, the capitalization rate of the company is 15 per cent and current dividend is Rs. 2 per share, the value of the company's share will be:

$$Ve = \frac{2(1 - 0.05)}{0.15 - (-0.05)} = \frac{2(0.95)}{0.15 + 0.05} = \frac{1.90}{0.20} = \text{Rs. } 950$$

In the discussion and deduction of mathematical formulae regarding the valuation of equity shares, we have followed the mainly the mathematical logic of Gangadhar and Babu[8] and other authors.

---

*The EPS will be discussed later.

[8]V. Gangadhar and Ramesh G. Babu: *Investment Management,* Anmol Publication, New Delhi, India

Now let us turn to other instruments of capital market investment.

DEBENTURES

When expanding the business, making structural changes, diversifying and modernization, companies require funds. At times, companies take short term loan from banks for these purposes. Companies also raise funds by issuing debentures to the general public. Debentures are sometimes also referred to as bonds. There is, in fact, no material difference between the two – the latter is of common American usage. A debenture is actually a loan. When an investor buys a debenture, he becomes a creditor of the company. A debenture holder lends his money to the company for a specified period of time and at a fixed rate of interest which is generally higher than bank deposits. So, generally investors are attracted by the debentures. The debenture certificate that investors receive from the company is an acknowledgement of the debt that the company owes the investors.

While equity shares are considered as ownership securities, debentures are considered as creditorship securities. Therefore, a debenture holder does not have any voting rights. But equity shareholders have voting rights in the functioning of the company's affairs. The debenture holder gets a fixed rate of interest whereas the equity shareholder gets varying returns in the form of dividends. Unlike preference shares, barring some exceptions, there is no provision for accumulation of interest in the case of debentures; holders have to be paid their interest even if the company has to borrow money or sell its assets to do so.

Companies follow the same rules in the case of public issues of debentures, as in the case of equity shares. Therefore, one can buy debentures by applying for them in the same way as one would for equity shares.

DIFFERENT TYPES OF DEBENTURES

Debentures can be issued as either secured or unsecured, and redeemable or irredeemable. At present, companies generally issue only secured and redeemable debentures, unsecured and irredeemable debentures are rarely issued.

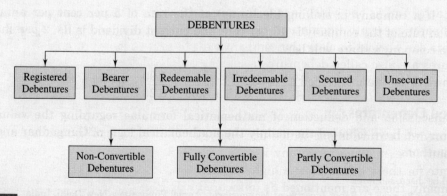

Chart 2.10 Different Types of Debentures

There are different types of debentures that are circulated in our country, which are classified in Chart 2.10.

REGISTERED DEBENTURES

The name and address of the debenture holders are registered in the debentures holder-register. According to Sections 108 and 111 of the Companies Act, these debentures can be transferred through transfer certificates. Interest or coupon of interest is given for these types of debentures.

Bearer Debentures

In bearer debentures, the names of the debenture holders are not registered and as in the case of promissory notes, anyone can encash these debentures on maturity. The company does not keep any register for these types of debenture holders. Interest coupons are generally attached with these debentures and so, at regular intervals, interest can be withdrawn through these coupons. Otherwise, the value of the debentures is paid on maturity.

Redeemable Debentures

A redeemable debenture is one which is issued for a certain fixed period of time. On the expiry of this period, the money invested by the debenture holders is returned to them. In other words, debenture holders can redeem their money on expiry of the date fixed for redemption of the debentures.

Irredeemable Debentures

An irredeemable debenture is one which is issued for a certain fixed period, but unlike redeemable debentures, the money invested by the debenture holders is not returned to them. Only interest is paid at regular intervals. However, if the company ceases to function, the investors' money is returned to them before that of the equity holders.

Secured Debentures

A secured debenture is one which is made secure through a mortgage of the company's assets. If the company goes into liquidation, or fails to pay due interest on its debentures, then these assets can be sold to clear the company's debts to its debenture holders. These types of debentures are also called debentures issued as co-lateral security. In the balance sheet of the company these are mentioned as secured loan.

Unsecured Debentures

An unsecured debenture is one which does not carry any security like secured debentures. The company does not mortgage any assets against these debentures. But sometimes the interest rate for these debentures is higher than for other debentures. In the balance sheet of the company, these are mentioned as unsecured loans.

Non-Convertible Debentures

Those debentures which do not contain any provision for conversion into equity shares are called non-convertible debentures. Non-convertible debentures normally have face value of Rs. 100/- and earn a fixed interest of 14 per cent to 16 per cent per annum. These are usually redeemable after a period of five to seven years.

The interest on non-convertible debentures does not qualify for exemption under Section 80L of the Income Tax Act. Under this section, dividends, interest on bank deposits, etc., are exempt from income tax up to a ceiling Rs. 10,00,000 per annum. This means that investors in high tax brackets, or those who have not fully availed of the tax exemptions under Section 80L, will not find non-convertible debentures an attractive investment avenue, particularly when they are bought from the open market at a good discount.

Non-Convertible Debenture (NCD) with detachable equity warrants: These debenture holders have an option to buy a specific number of equity shares at a fixed rate on the expiry of a certain period. This is the lock-in period for NCDs after which the debenture holder has to exercise his option for equity shares. If such an option is not exercised within the stipulated period, the company will be at liberty to dispose of the unapplied portion of shares in the market. The warrants (discussed below) attached to the NCDs can be converted into shares only if they are fully paid.

Convertible Debentures

Convertible debentures are those which, under specific terms and conditions, are made convertible into to equity shares of the same company. Actually convertible debentures can be converted either fully or in part, into equity shares of the same company under specified terms and conditions which vary from company to company. So, it is essential to study carefully the implication of the various terms and conditions for conversion into equity shares, before buying a convertible debenture of any company.

Convertible debentures are an ideal investment for conservative investors in many ways. They give high yield, carry low risk as debentures are secured and an annual interest is assured. Further, they have a fairly good scope for capital appreciation (which is represented by the difference between the conversion price and market price of the shares so converted). They are essentially a compromise between equity shares and non-convertible debentures – they combine the capital appreciation of the former with the stability of income, and safety of capital, of the latter. Convertible debentures have a better market than non-convertible debentures. They are not only readily saleable but usually command a high premium too. Their market value is linked to the market price of the equity share in to which they are to be converted.

Convertible debentures redeemable at premium: These debentures are issued at par but with an option to the investor to sell debentures later on to the issuer at a premium. They are basically similar to convertible debentures but carry less risk.

Debt equity swap: These are a type of convertible debentures and are the offers to exchange debentures for equity. This type of instrument is quite risky for the investor because the anticipated capital appreciation may not materialize.

Zero-coupon convertible notes: These types of debentures have a right to be converted into shares. But on the date of conversion, the accrued or unpaid interest has to be sacrificed. These types of convertible notes are quite sensitive to change in the interest rates.

Secured Premium Notes (SPN) with detachable warrants: These notes are repayable after a lock-in period. The detachable warrants are to be converted into shares within a specified period. No interest is payable during the lock-in period. No interest will be payable on SPNs if the holder sells them back to the company after the lock-in period. However, the investor will be entitled to additional interest in installments if the redemption is made after expiry of the SPN.

The attached warrant assures the right to the holder to apply and get equity shares allotted. This right is available only if the SPN if fully paid up for. The conversion of detachable warrants into equity shares will have to be done within the time limit allowed by the company.

Warrants: A warrant is another type of convertible debenture which entitles the holders to purchase a specific number of shares at a specific rate before a specific period. These warrants may be issued with debentures or equity shares. They are also called sweeteners. The number of shares the investor is entitled to, the expiration date, along with the stated/exercise price etc. are clearly specified in the warrants.

The warrants have a secondary market. They are generally issued by new/growing firms and venture capital firms. They do not contain any floatation cost when they are exercised; the firm receives additional funds at a price lower than the current market rate, yet higher than that prevailing at the time of issue. But since 1993, very few companies have issued warrants.

According to Gangadhar and Babu[9], a warrant is a company or corporate created option to purchase a stated number of common shares at a specified price within a specified time. Generally, warrants are attached to bonds, debentures and equity issues, and have long term maturities; they help companies in raising fresh capital. Warrants can be detached from the securities and traded separately. The range of maturity of warrants can be 3 to 10 years; perpetual warrants are available in a board. Warrants can be traded on a stock exchange or the Over The Counter Stock Exchange (OTCEI). With some differences, warrants are similar to call options. Options are standardized but warrants are not. Normally, warrants are issued on a long term basis, but options expire in nine months

Warrants are issued in the ratio determined by the issuing company, such as, one warrant per share. A warrant holder has no equity right in the company so the investor is not entitled to dividends or the right to vote in company affairs. In the market warrants sometimes fetch a premium. That is, in the market, they are also sold at higher prices then the original minimum price of the warrant. The value of a warrant depends upon stock potential for the

---

[9]Ibid

rising price. High dividend payout may also have an adverse effect on the price of a warrant. A considerable number of investors purchase warrants for speculative purposes. The issue of warrants provides benefits both to companies and investors.

Benefits for investors are:

1. Low requirement for investment
2. Better liquidity
3. Good opportunity for capital gains

Benefits for companies are:

1. Warrants facilitate raising funds for companies i.e., the corporate sector
2. There is no obligation to pay interest and repayment of principal
3. Issue of warrants does not have flotation costs

The authors also provided a formula to value the warrant, which is given below:

$$Pw = \int (Po, Tn, Pc, Ri, Fc)$$

Where

Pw = Market price of the warrant

Po = Option price of the equity share

Tn = Duration of the issue

Ri = The ratio between shares outstanding and warrants

Fc = The equity share price

$$V = (Pc - Po)N$$

Where

V = Value of the warrant

Pc = Current price of the equity share

Po = Option price of the equity share

N = Number of shares that may be purchased with one warrant

Fully Convertible Debentures

When convertible debentures issued by a company, are entirely convertible into equity shares of the same company after a specified time period and with a specified conversion ratio, then the convertible debentures are called as fully convertible debentures. Holders of fully convertible debenture are benefited during conversion into equity as it is always much less than the prevailing market price of the equity during the time of conversion.

Fully Convertible Debentures (FCDs) with zero-interest: These debentures are automatically and compulsorily converted into shares after a specific time period. These types of debentures generally have no interest. No interest will be paid during the lock-in period. FCDs may be converted into shares if they are fully paid. If the company goes for rights issue meanwhile, it shall only do so after the FCD holders are offered securities.

Fully Convertible Debentures (FCDs) with interest: These debentures do not yield any interest for a short period. After this short period, the debenture holders have the option to apply for equity shares issued at a premium without paying the premium. Such an option should be indicated in the application form itself. A specified rate of interest is payable on FCDs between the two conversion dates in lieu of which shares are issued.

Partly Convertible Debentures

Some convertible debentures are partly converted into equity shares, according to the terms and conditions of the issue, after a specified time period. The unconverted part of these debentures is virtually treated as non-convertible debentures. In the terminology of the share market, this unconvertible part is also known as khoka or koka. Sometimes, the conversion of debentures into equity are left to the wishes of the debenture holders according to the terms and conditions. So, it is only the convertible portion that imparts investment value to a convertible debenture, and not the non-convertible portion.

Secured zero interest bearing partly convertible debentures with detachable separately tradable warrants: This type of debenture gives zero interest but is secured in nature. Such debentures have two parts: Part A and Part B. According to the usual terms of a partly convertible debenture, Part A is convertible into shares at a fixed rate on a date of allotment. Part B is non-convertible and is redeemable at par on expiry of the specified period. It also contains a separately tradable warrant which can be converted into equity shares.

Besides the types of debentures described above, there are other types of debentures called: (i) Zero rated debentures. Investors, generally buy these debentures for capital gains not for interest rates. (ii) Debentures which have the option to exit either by the company or debenture holders from the term of issue and the coupon rate is specified at the time of issue are known as convertible debentures with option. (iii) Third party convertible debentures are the debts with a warrant which entitle the holders to subscribe to the equity of another firm at a preferential price instead of the market price. The interest rate offered is generally lower in comparison to simple debentures due to conversion option.

According to market analysts, S.S. Grewal and Novjot Grewal, convertible debentures are ideal investments in the following situations:

1. When a company's expansion project has a long gestation period, it is better to go in for its convertible debentures rather than equity shares. In this way one can get the twin benefits of a high and stable income during the gestation period, and conversion to equity shares at a relatively low price once the company goes into commercial production.

2. Convertible debentures are normally safer investments than equity shares during the tail end of a boom. This is because they are not likely to be affected to the same extent as equity shares when the boom gives way to a depression. During the ensuing depression, when the company's profits slump and dividends are cut, the holder of convertible debentures will continue to get 12 per cent to 15 per cent per annum interest as the case may be.

3. Convertible debentures are ideal investments when the future of the company is uncertain and difficult to predict. They allow one to adopt a wait-and-watch policy, without any of the risks involved in equity investments at such a time.

PUBLIC SECTOR BONDS

Public Sector Undertakings (PSUs) are permitted to raise capital from the general public through the issue of bonds. These bonds are fixed interest-rate securities which carry a certain per cent of fixed interest determined by the Board of Directors of the PSU along with government advisers. Some PSUs are permitted by the government to issue tax-free bonds carrying a lower interest rate per annum than the bonds with taxable interest income. These bonds are normally targeted at investors in the higher tax brackets. For an investor in the highest income tax bracket these bonds are most beneficial to minimize the incidence of his tax liability.

The future outlook for investments in debentures and bonds is now brightening with full and effective functioning of the National Stock Exchange (NSE). The main purpose of the NSE is to provide a vibrant secondary market (discussed in the next chapter) for corporate debentures, PSU bonds and other government bonds and securities. With the liberalization and gradual globalization of the Indian economy, interest rates in India, that is, banks' lending rate to industry and interest paid by banks to their depositors, will perforce have to fall in line with international interest rates. The fall in interest rates in bank deposits will make debentures and bonds, which carry higher interest rates, more attractive to investors as a whole. In the situation when banks' interest rates are expected to fall, debentures and bonds are likely to provide excellent investment opportunities to risk-averse investors who seek twin benefits of higher annual income combined with a decent capital appreciation.

Besides public sector undertakings, financial institutions in India have also used innovative securities. These are listed below:

Floating Rate Bonds (FRBs):   The interest rates on these bonds is linked to some other rates, such as, bank rate, maximum interest on term deposits, prime lending rate, yield on treasury bills etc. The floating rate is fixed in terms of a margin above/below the benchmark rate. It ensures that neither the borrower nor the lender suffer from changes in interest rates. For example, during a certain period of time, the State Bank of India's floating rate bond issue was linked to maximum interest on term of deposit which was 10 per cent per annum at that time. The floor rate was 12 per cent per annum in this case.

Zero-coupon bonds/Deep discount bonds: No interest is payable on these bonds. These bonds are sold to customers at a discount rate. They have a long maturity period, generally 20 to 25 years. The return to the investor is the difference between the acquisition value and the redemption value. An example is the deep discount bonds of the Sardar Sarovar Nigam Limited (the project was aimed at developing an irrigation system and generation of hydro-electricity in India) which were issued at a price of Rs. 3,600 per bond and have a redemption value of Rs. 1,11,000 after 21 years.

Easy exit bonds with a floating interest rate: The rate of interest on these bonds is flexible. It means it is reset every six months. Small investors have been protected under this scheme with an option of exit upto a specified amount. But if investors hold the bond for more than 18 months from the date of allotment, they get additional interest. Call and put options are also available on these bonds. These bonds are targeted at the segment that is sensitive to inflation and wants an additional safety net in the form of exit.

Notes: *Call Option:* This option gives the buyers the right but not the obligation to buy a given quantity of the underlying asset, at a given price on or before a given future date.

Put Option: This option gives the buyers the right but not the obligation to sell a given quantity of the underlying asset, at a given price on or before a given future date.

Regular income bonds: These bonds are issued for a specified period of time. The interest is generally payable half yearly on these bonds. The interest is paid at a pre-determined rate. The bonds also carry option for investors and call option for issuers and an early bird incentive. For example, Industrial Development Bank of India (IDBI) regular income bonds were 10 year bonds issued in 1996, bearing a coupon of 16 per cent, payable half yearly. An additional interest of 0.5 per cent was also paid in this scheme. It brings annualized yield equivalent to 18.2 per cent. The price of each bond was Rs. 5,000. Industrial Finance Corporation of India (IFCI) also issued 5 year tenure bonds with a semi-annual yield of 16 per cent and early bird incentive of 0.75 per cent.

Retirement bonds: These bonds are issued for persons who wish to get fixed installments of a fixed amount after their retirement. Investors get the fixed monthly amount after expiry of the wait period which is at the option of the investors. The investor can also choose the lump sum amount. Also an investor could opt for a nil waiting period in which case he starts getting monthly income immediately, from the next month. These retirement bonds may also carry put and call option. For example, IDBI issued such type of bonds in 1996 with a maturity period of 10 years.

Step-up liquidity bonds: The maturity period of these bonds is generally 5 years. The put option is available every year. The interest rate is stepped up every year. For example, IFCI issued these bonds in 1997. The interest rate offered was 16 per cent, 16.5 per cent, 16.75 per cent and 17 per cent at the end of every consecutive year.

Growth bonds: These bonds generally have a redemption period of 10 years. However, some companies provide put option at the end of five or seven years. A financial institution in India issued such types of bonds in 1996. The face value of each bond was Rs. 20,000 and maturity value was Rs. 1,00,000 after 10 years. If the put option is exercised by an investor, he/she would receive Rs. 43,000 after 5 years and Rs. 60,600 after 7 years.

Index bonds: These bonds provide both security of money invested and the potential of appreciation in the return to the investor. An index bond has two parts, Part A consists of a deep discount bond and Part B consists of a detachable index warrant. Part B gives return in proportion to any increase/decrease in the Bombay Stock Exchange Sensitive Index (BSE – SENSEX).

The face value of the bond will appreciate the same number of times the SENSEX appreciates. The investors' return will be treated as a capital gain. For example ICICI issued index bonds in 1997 at a price of Rs. 6,000. Part A was a 12 year deep discount bond of face value of Rs. 22,000 (initial investment was Rs. 4,000) and Part B was in the form of an index warrant at Rs. 2,000 which gives return in proportion to the increase/decrease in BSE-SENSEX after 12 years.

Capital gain bonds: These bonds are issued with two maturity options – 3 years and 7 years as option I and option II respectively. Rebate of 20 per cent in income tax is allowed on the investment of these bonds. Investment through stock investments will not qualify for rebate. IDBI and ICICI issue such types of bonds. These bonds are beneficial for individuals who are in high tax brackets. These bonds are also called tax-saving bonds.

Encash bonds: Interest on these bonds is stepped up every year. These bonds can be redeemed after one year and eight months. The encashing facility is available only to original holders. These bonds not only offer higher interest but also widen the banking facilities to investors. Improved yield maturity results in favorable secondary market price of bonds.

NEW ISSUES AND INITIAL PUBLIC OFFER (IPO)

When a company needs working capital for expansion of business, diversification and modernizations of its operations, then it either goes to banks for loans or collects money from markets through new issues. However, companies, new as well as old can offer their equity shares to the investors in the primary market. This kind of fund raising process from the investors mainly by new or starting up companies is called Initial Public Offer or IPO. When a company goes public for the first time or issues a fresh stock of shares, it offers it to the public directly. This happens in the primary market.

IPOs are almost invariably an opportunity for existing investors in practicing venture capital firms (discussed later) to make big profits, since for the first time their shares will be given a market value reflecting expectations for the company's future growth.

The Security and Exchange Board of India (SEBI) regulates the way in which companies can make this offering. Companies are allowed to make an IPO if they meet SEBI guidelines in this regard. All the procedures and formalities regarding the size of the initial issue, the exchange on which it can be listed, the merchant bankers' responsibility, the nature and content of the disclosures in the prospectus, are laid down by SEBI and have to be strictly complied with.

In certain cases, exemption may be granted by SEBI for minimum subscription in the case of certain industry sectors like, infrastructure or banking. Several changes have also been introduced in recent years in the procedure under which IPOs are to be marketed. For instance, companies can choose the book building route or they can even choose the secondary market to market their IPOs through brokers or Depository Participants (DPs). All these changes have been made with the objective of making the process more investor friendly by reducing risk, controlling cost, giving greater transparency in the pricing mechanism and protecting liquidity in the hands of investors. Some of the IPOs are available for subscription online. There the bids are made in real time and the information is made available on an instantaneous basis on the screen of a computer. Through DPs, it is possible to subscribe for IPO shares in demat.

Capital Issues (Control) Act, 1947: During the Second World War in 1943, this Act was introduced by the British Government. To support the War effort, was the main the objective of this Act. Government approval was required by companies to raise money from the general public. As a means of controlling the raising of capital by companies and to ensure that national resources were channeled into proper lines, the Act was retained with some modification after India gained independence. The modifications were made for desirable purposes to serve goals and priorities of the government and to protect the interest of the investors. Any company or firm wishing to issue securities had to obtain approval from the Central Government under this Act. The amount, type and price of the issue were fixed by the government. In 1992, this Act was repealed and replaced by SEBI Act.[10]

ELIGIBILITY CRITERIA FOR COMPANIES WHO INTEND TO ISSUE SECURITIES

The companies who intend to issue securities must prepare a transparent offer document, through which they should approach the investing public mainly in the primary market. At the same time, according to a publication of National Stock Exchange, Bombay[11], the companies issuing securities must satisfy the criteria given below when filing the draft offer document with the SEBI as well as at the time of filing the final offer document with the Registrar of Companies (ROC) and designated stock exchange.

A company intending to offer a public issue of securities must file a well prepared prospectus with ROC. But at least 21 days prior to filing the prospectus with the ROC, the company should file a draft prospectus with SEBI through an eligible merchant banker. Further, for a company, which is already listed, issuing securities through a rights issue where the aggregate value of securities, including premium, if any, exceeds Rs. 50 lakh, it is mandatory for the listed company to file the letter of offer with SEBI through an eligible merchant banker at least 21 days prior to the filing of the Letter of Offer (LoC) with the Regional Stock Exchange (RSE).

If a company has been prohibited from accessing the capital market under any order or direction passed by SEBI, the company cannot make an issue.

A company has to make an application for listing those securities with stock exchange(s) which it intends to offer to the investing public. The company should also enter into a

---

[10]Dr. Alok Goyel et al. *Financial Market Operations,* V.K. Publications, New Delhi, India

[11]National Securities Depository, Handbook for NSDL Depository Operations Module', www.india.com or e-mail: nefm@nse.com.in

Memorandum of Understanding (MoU) with the depository before making any public or rights issue. The same steps should also be taken by the company in case of an offer for sale of securities for dematerialization of its securities already issued or proposed to be issued and also the company should give an option to subscribers/shareholders/investors to receive the security certificates or hold securities in dematerialized form with a depository. If an unlisted company meets all the following conditions, it can make public issue of equity shares or any other security convertible into equity shares, at a later date if the following conditions are fulfilled.

❖ In each of the preceding 3 full years (operational year of 12 months each), the company has net tangible assets of at least Rs. 3 crores, of which not more than 50 per cent is held in monetary assets. The company should make firm commitments to deploy excess monetary assets in its business or project if more than 50 per cent of the net tangible assets are held in monetary assets.

❖ The company, in terms of Section 205 of the Companies Act, 1956, has a track record of distributable profits for at least three (3) out of the immediately preceding five (5) years, extraordinary items should not be considered for calculating distributable profits in accordance with Section 205 of the Companies Act, 1956.

❖ In each of the preceding 3 full years, the company has a net worth of at least Rs. 1 crore.

❖ Within the last one year, if the company has changed its name, at least 50 per cent of the revenue for the preceding one full year is earned by the company from the activity suggested by the new name.

❖ All previous issues and the aggregate of the proposed issue made in the same financial year in terms of size (i.e. offer through offer document + firm allotment + promoters' contribution through the offer document), as per the audited balance sheet of the last financial year, does not exceed five (5) times its pre-issue net worth.

The requirement of eligibility norms are exempt for infrastructure companies whose project has been appraised by a public financial institution or infrastructure development finance corporation or infrastructure leasing and financing services and not less than 5 per cent of the project cost is financed by any of the institutions, jointly or severally, by way of loan and/or subscription to equity or a combination of both. The eligibility norms are also exempt for banks and rights issues of listed companies.

It is mandatory to obtain credit rating from a registered credit rating agency for public and rights issues of debt instruments irrespective of their maturities or conversion period, and to disclose the same in the offer document. All the credit ratings, including the rejected ones, need to be disclosed, if the credit rating is obtained from more than one credit rating agency.

Thus the quality of the issue is demonstrated by track record/appraisal by approved financial institutions/credit rating/subscription by qualified institutional buyers.

PRICING OF ISSUES

Eligible companies that intend to make public issues are allowed to freely price their equity shares or any security convertible into equity at a later date in cases of public or rights issues by listed companies and public issue by unlisted companies. In addition, subject to compliance of disclosure of the SEBI norms, eligible infrastructure companies can freely price their equity shares. With the approval of Reserve Bank of India (RBI), the public and private sector banks can also freely price their shares. In the firm allotment category, a company may issue shares to applicants at a higher price than the price at which securities are offered to the public. A listed company making a composite issue of capital may issue securities at differential prices in its public and rights issue. In accordance with the Companies Act, 1956 and SEBI norms, an eligible company can also make a public or rights issue in any denomination determined by it.

In simple words, when a company floats its new issue of equity shares, it fixes a price for its equity. This price is also called the 'issue price'. For a new company this price generally is the face value or at par value. But some established companies may issue their equity at par value or at a higher price than its face value. When the issue price is higher than the par value, it is called premium and when the issue price is lower than par value, it is called discount.

PAR VALUE/AT PAR

Par value is the notional face value of the equity shares which a company issues to investors. In India, par value was fixed at Rs. 10 or Rs. 100 through a Government of India circular in 1983. A company can issue shares above par value, which means at a premium, if it meets profitability criteria laid down by the regulator of capital markets, SEBI. During the second half of 1999, SEBI dispensed with the system of a fixed par value of Rs. 10 or Rs. 100 by withdrawing the 1983 government circular. Par value per se remains. According to the latest regulations, new companies can now issue shares at below Rs. 10 per share. In fact, a company can issue shares to the public at say, Rs. 3, while another company can issue shares at Rs. 5 per share. Shares of the first company will carry a face value of Rs. 3 and in the case of the latter, it will be Rs. 5. Companies can also issue shares with a face value of Rs. 10 as well.

Actually, the latest move of the SEBI will help companies that are planning to float initial public offerings because they will be able to price their offer more realistically than the mandatory Rs. 10 or Rs. 100. Existing companies too can call back their shares and split them into lower denominations.

Though the share premium account remains, the account, however, will vary depending upon a company's par value and the issue price. For example, if a company fixes par value at Rs. 3 but offers shares at Rs. 7, Rs. 3 will be treated as share capital and Rs. 4 as share premium. Had the per value been completely abolished, there would be no premium.

No company can fix any issue price without the approval of SEBI. The offer price cannot be below Re. 1 and must be in multiples of Re 1. This means that no company can price shares in decimals.

All companies are not eligible to fix their own par value. SEBI has restricted freedom only to those companies whose shares have been dematerialized. The reason is that the dematerialization or demat does away with the need to print share certificates leading to savings. If a company prices its own share at Re. 1, the cost of printing a share certificate itself will exceed the Re. 1 face value.

It is easier to do away with Rs. 10 par value of shares. Abolishing the par value altogether may require far too many amendments to the Companies Act, 1956, which may take quite a while. The Companies Act does not have a provision for par value per se; Section 13(4) of the Act provides for a fixed price at which the shares can be issued. SEBI's action ensures that the price fixed in the Act is adhered to.

In the United Kingdom, par value is fixed at one penny even though issues are given the freedom to price. In the United States of America, there is no federal companies act. Some states, however, specify a minimum value for the issuance of shares while most others leave it to companies to issue shares at any value of their choice. Pricing overseas is linked to the underlying business and its future potential.

CALL MONEY, CANCELLATION, LATTER STOCKS AND STAG

In some cases, companies do not ask for full payment from the investors with their applications for allotment of newly issued shares. They allow the investors to pay in installments. The first installment is taken with the application. Later, the companies ask investors to pay the balance amounts in one or more installments. These installments are called 'call money'. The total value of the shares is paid after payment of all installments. Prior to that, the shares are known as half paid shares. After payment of all the installments, payment document and half paid share certificates are sent to the company for endorsement of full payment. Some companies send stickers as proof of payment of the call money or installments. These stickers are pasted in the specified places of the share certificates to make the certificates fully paid ones.

If the shareholders do not pay the total allotment fee for the shares they had applied for or cannot pay the call money in time or fail to pay the call-money with interest in a specified time period, then according to Schedule 1, Table – A Class 29, 30, and 31, those shares are considered for cancellation.

The shares which are distributed to promoters or primary investors are called latter stocks or founder stock. There is no need to register these shares with SEBI. These shares initiate the investment but cannot be traded in the market.

A person who invests in a new issue of established companies and sells the allotment letter before paying the call money is called stag. A person who subscribes to new issue in bulk in the hope of making a killing after listing the company on the stock exchanges, is also known as stag.

CONTRIBUTION OF PROMOTERS AND LOCK-IN

The contribution of the promoters in case of public issues by unlisted companies and their (promoters') shareholding in case of 'offers for sale' should not be less than 20 per cent of the post issue capital. In case of public issues by listed companies, promoters should contribute to the extent of 20 per cent of the proposed issue or should ensure post-issue holding to the extent of 20 per cent of the post-issue capital. The contribution of the promoters should either be 20 per cent of the proposed public issue or 20 per cent of the post-issue capital, for composite issues. At least one day prior to the issue's opening date the promoters should bring in the full amount of the promoters' contribution including the premium. In case of (i) public issue of securities which have been listed on a stock exchange for at least 3 years and have a track record of dividend payment for at least 3 immediate preceding years, (ii) companies where no identifiable promoter or promoter group exists and (iii) rights issues, the requirement of the promoters' contribution is not applicable. The minimum promoters' contribution is locked in for a period of 3 years for any issue of capital to the public. In case the promoters' contribution is in excess of the required minimum contribution, such excess is locked in for a period of one year. Securities allotted in firm allotment basis are also locked in for a period of three years. For sanction of loans by banks or Financial Institutions (FIs), the locked-in securities held by promoters may be pledged with banks or FIs as collateral security.

ISSUE OF SWEAT EQUITY

Earlier we discussed what is meant by sweat equity, now let us see what SEBI has to say regarding the issue of sweat equity. The main provisions laid down in the SEBI Regulations, 2002 for issue of sweat equity are (i) the sweat equity shares can be issued by a company to its employees and directors as well as promoters, under the new guidelines, (ii) the pricing of the sweat equity shares should be as per the formula prescribed for that of preferential allotment, (iii) lock-in period for the sweat equity shares should be 3 years. Lock-in shall be as per the SEBI (DIP) Guidelines 2000, in case of a subsequent public issue being made.

STOCK INVEST

When the investment banks invest in new issues through stock invest scheme then the companies are not entitled to any payment until allotment of shares or bonds are made and investing banks are entitled to get investments at a specified rate till the full allotments are made.

To protect the interest of the general small investors, the State Bank of India along with some other nationalized banks opened the 'stock invest' scheme. If an investor invests in a new issue through this scheme, the invested money is not transferred to the companies' account until the full allotment of shares is made. Prior to this, the investor continues to get interest at a certain rate from the investing bank.

DIFFERENT TERMS OF ISSUES

Mega Issue

If a company floats a large number of shares in a public issue with a particular aim of investment, then that issue is called as 'mega issue'. In the month of July, 1995, Industrial Development Bank of India (IDBI) floated a mega issue of Rs. 2,814 crore which was oversubscribed two times.

Oversubscribed Issue

A company generally floats a new issue to raise a certain amount of money through a specified number of shares. If the number of applications for subscribing to this issue exceeds the specified number of new issue floated then that issue is said to be oversubscribed. A few years back, the new issues of RPPL and RPEL of Reliance Industries group were oversubscribed by 106 times and 90 times respectively. In the Indian capital market these are all time records.

Under-subscribed Issue

When a company floats a new issue which is subscribed to by less than 90 per cent of the issued number, then that issue is considered as under-subscribed and the issue is cancelled and withdrawn. Hence, all the applications along with application money are returned. In the month of March, 1996, the public issue of Mangal Finance Limited was subscribed to by only 85 per cent so the issue was cancelled.

Hot Issue

If the demand for a new issue reaches an unexpected peak, then the issue is called a 'hot issue'. Due to the great demand, after listing in the stock exchanges, the price of these shares also increases very rapidly (see also 'hot stock' below).

Glamour Issue

When an established profit making company floats a new issue in a big way it is termed as a 'glamour issue'.

OBLIGATIONS OF ISSUE

Pre-Issue Obligations

The lead merchant banker plays an important role in the pre-issue obligations of a company. The banker exercises due diligence and satisfies himself about all aspects of the offering, the veracity and adequacy of disclosures in the offer document. A Memorandum of Understanding (MoU) with the lead merchant banker must be signed by each company issuing securities; a MoU specifies their mutual rights, liabilities and obligations relating to the issue. In case of under subscription of an issue, the lead merchant banker responsible for underwriting arrangements has to invoke underwriting obligations and ensure that the underwriters pay the amount of devolvement. A minimum number of collection centers should be ensured by it. For dematerialization of securities, it should also ensure that the issuing company has entered into an agreement with all the depositories. The lead merchant banker should also take care of all the other formalities related to post-issue obligations like, allotment, refund and despatch of certificates.

Post-Issue Obligations

As per prescribed formats, the lead merchant banker should ensure that the post-issue monitoring reports are submitted. These reports should be submitted within 3 working days from the due dates. Along with the company, the lead merchant banker should also take part in post-issue activities namely, allotment, refund and despatch and should regularly monitor redressal of investor grievances arising therefrom. The post-issue lead merchant banker should maintain close co-ordination with the registrars to the issue and arrange to depute its officers to the offices of various intermediaries at regular intervals after the closure of the issue to monitor (i) the flow of applications from bank branches collecting the applications, (ii) processing of the applications including those accompanied by stockinvest, (iii) any other matters till the basis of allotment is finalized, (iv) dispatching of security certificates and refund orders completed and securities listed. The lead merchant banker should ensure that the despatch of share certificates or refund orders and demat credit is completed and the allotment and listing documents submitted to the stock exchanges within 2 working days of finalization of the basis of allotment.

Within 7 working days of finalization of the basis of allotment, the post issue lead manager should ensure that all steps for completion of the necessary formalities for listing and commencement of trading on all stock exchanges where the securities are to be listed are taken. As prescribed in the offer document, the lead merchant banker should ensure payment of interest to the applicants for delayed dispatch of allotment letters, refund orders, etc.

BOOK BUILDING

Book building is a process used for marketing a public offer of equity shares of a company and is a common practice in most developed countries. Book building is so called because the collection of bids from investors is entered in a "book". These bids are based on an indicative price range. The issue price is fixed after the bid closing date.

A company that is planning an initial public offer appoints a category-I merchant banker as a book runner. Initially, the company issues a draft prospectus which does not mention the price, but gives other details about the company with regards to issue size, past history and future plans among other mandatory disclosures. After the draft prospectus is filed with the SEBI, a particular period is fixed as the bid period and the details of the issue are advertised. The book runner builds an order book, that is, collates the bids from various investors, which shows the demand for the shares of the company at various prices. For instance, a bidder may want 50,000 shares at Rs. 500 while another may bid for 25,000 shares at Rs. 600. Prospective investors can revise their bids at anytime during the bid period that is, the quantity of shares or the bid price or any of the bid options. Usually, the bid must be for a minimum of 500 equity shares and in multiples of 100 equity shares thereafter. The book runner appoints a syndicate member, a registered intermediary who garners subscriptions and underwrites the issue.

On closure of the book, the quantum of shares ordered and the respective prices offered are known. The price discovery is a function of demand at various prices, and involves negotiations between those involved in the issue. The book runner and the company conclude the pricing and decide the allocation to each syndicate member.

In other words, it can be said that book building is a process of offering securities in which bids at various prices from investors through syndicate members are collected. Based on bids, the demand for the security is assessed and its price determined. The price is known in advance to investors and the demand is known at the close of the issue in case of normal public issue. In case of public issue through book building, demand can be known at the end of every day but price is known only at the close of issue.

The 75 per cent book building route and 100 per cent book building route are the two options for an issuer company proposing to issue capital through book building. In case the 100 per cent book building route is adopted, (i) not more than 50 per cent of the net offer to the public can be allocated to Qualified Institutional Buyers, (ii) not less than 15 per cent of the net offer to the public can be allocated to non-institutional investors applying for more than 1,000 shares and (iii) not less than 35 per cent of the net offer to public can be allocated to retail investors applying for upto 1,000 shares.

In case 75 per cent of net public offer is made through book building then, (i) in the book built portion, not less than 25 per cent of the net offer to the public, should be available for allocation to non qualified institutional buyers and not more than 50 per cent of the net offer to the public should be available for allocation to qualified institutional buyers, (ii) the balance 25 per cent of the net offer to the public, offered at a price determined through book building, should be available only to retail individual investors who have either not participated or have not received any allocation, in the book built portion. (Provided that 50 per cent of the net profit offered to the public should be mandatorily allotted to the qualified institutional buyers, in case the issuing company is making a public issue under Clause 2.2.2 and 2.3.2 of DIP Guidelines 2000).

Other requirements for book building include: bids should remain open for at least 5 days, only electronic bidding is permitted; bids are submitted through syndicate members; bids can be revised; bidding demand is displayed at the end of every day; allotments are made not later than 15 days from the closure of the issue etc.

According to the publication of the NSE, the Disclosures and Investor Protection (DIP) guidelines for book building provides that the company should be allowed to disclose the floor price, just prior to the bid opening date, instead of in the Red Herring prospectus, which may be done by any means like a public advertisement in newspaper etc. Flexibility should be provided to the issuing company by permitting them to indicate a 20 per cent price band. The issuer may be given the flexibility to revise the price band during the bidding period and the issuers should be allowed to have a closed book building i.e. the book will not be made public. The mandatory requirement of 90 per cent subscription should not be strictly considered, but the prospectus should disclose the minimum subscription required and sources for meeting the shortfall. The Primary Market Advisory Committee recommended the practice of 'green-shoe option' available in markets abroad which is an 'over allotment' option granted by the issuer to the underwriter in a public offering. This helps the syndicate member to over allocate the shares to the extent of option available and to consequently purchase additional shares from the issuer at the original offering price in order to cover the over-allotments.

Unlike international markets, India has a large number of retail investors who actively participate in IPOs. Internationally, the most active investors are the mutual funds and other institutional investors. So the entire issue is book built. But in India, as we already mentioned above, 25 per cent of the issue has to be offered to the general public. Here there are two options to the company. According to the first option, 25 per cent of the issue has to be sold at a fixed price and 75 per cent is through book building. The other option is to split the 25 per cent on offer to the public (small investors) into a fixed price portion of 10 per cent and a reservation in the book built portion amounting to 15 per cent of the issue size. The rest of the book built portion is open to any investor. The book building process allows for price and demand discovery. Also, the costs of the public issue are reduced, and so is the time taken to complete the entire process. Unlike in book building, IPOs are usually marketed at a fixed price. Here the demand cannot be anticipated by the merchant banker and only after the issue is over is the response known. In book building, the demand for the shares is known before the issue closes. The issue may be deferred if the demand is less.

DISCLOSURES AND INVESTOR PROTECTION (DIP)

SEBI governs the primary issuances in terms of SEBI (DIP) guidelines. SEBI framed its DIP guidelines in 1992. Many amendments have been carried out in the same in line with the market dynamics and requirements. In 2000, SEBI issued "Securities and Exchange Board of India (Disclosure and Investor Protection) Guidelines, 2000," which is a compilation of all circulars organized in chapter form. SEBI thereon issues these guidelines and amendments under section 11 of the Securities and Exchange Board of India Act, 1992. SEBI (Disclosure and Investor Protection) guidelines 2000 are called DIP guidelines in short. They provide a comprehensive framework for issuances by the companies.

ON-LINE INITIAL PUBLIC OFFERS (IPO)

A company has to comply with Section 55 to 68A of the Companies Act, 1956 and SEBI (DIP) Guidelines, 2000, if it proposes to issue capital to the public through the on-line system of the stock exchange. The company is required to enter into an agreement with the stock exchange(s) which have the requisite system for on-line offer of securities. The agreement should cover rights, duties, responsibilities and obligations of the company and the stock exchanges interest, with provision for a dispute resolution mechanism between the company and the stock exchange. The issuing company appoints a registrar to the issue having electronic connectivity with the stock exchanges.

Apart from the requirement of listing on the regional stock exchange, the issuer company can apply for listing of its securities at any exchange through which it offers its securities to the public through an on-line system. For the purpose of accepting applications and placing orders with the company, the stock exchange appoints brokers. The lead manager co-ordinates all the activities amongst various intermediaries connected in the system. In addition to the above, the DIP guidelines also provide details of the contents of the offer document and advertisement, and other requirements for issues of securities, like those under Rule 19(2) (b) of SC(R) Rules, 1957. The guidelines also lay down detailed norms for issue of debt instruments, issue of capital by designated financial institutions and preferential and/or bonus issues.

NEW INDEX FOR IPOS

On 24th August, 2009, The Bombay Stock Exchange launched an IPO index to help investors to track the value of companies for two years after their listing in bourses (stock exchanges). The base date of the index is May 3rd, 2004, and base value is 1000 points. The index, which comprises 48 companies, will include only new listings and no follow-on-offers. To be in the index, a scrip must have a minimum free float (non-promoter holding) market capitalization of Rs. 100 crore on its first day of listing. After two years of listing, the scrip will be excluded from the index on the second Monday of the month. Besides, no company will have more than 20 per cent weight.

ENLISTMENT OF SHARES

Enlistment of shares in different stock exchanges gives trading privileges to various companies for various reasons as given below:

1. The SEBI insists on listing
2. Commitment in the prospectus or statement in lieu of prospectus leads to seek listing
3. Compulsion of giving information to the respective Registrar of Companies for Public interest
4. Give awareness regarding safety, security and prospect of the issuing company

Actually, listing means admission of securities of a company on a recognized stock exchange which provides a common forum for dealing of securities. When the securities of a company have been included in the official list of one or more stock exchanges for the purpose of trading, then those securities of the company are considered to be listed.

Listing of securities offered to the general investing public for subscription was not compulsory prior to the Companies (Amendment) Act, 1988. According to Section 73 of that Act of 1988, every company before offering of any security to the public for subscription by issue of prospectus should make an application to a recognized stock exchange or stock exchanges to seek their permission for securities intending to be offered, to be dealt with by stock exchanges.

If it appears in the prospectus that an application has been made for permission for the securities offered to be dealt in one or more stock exchanges, then any allotment made on an application shall be void if the permission by the stock exchange or exchanges is not granted before expiry of ten weeks from the date of closure of subscription list.

Requirements for Listing

1. The minimum issued capital of a company shall be Rs. 3 crores.
2. The minimum public offer of capital of a company shall be Rs. 1.8 crores.
3. Prospectus issued by the company shall be scrutinized by the stock exchange as well as SEBI.
4. Application should be in minimum trading lots of securities.
5. The Memorandum and Article of Association must contain prescribed provisions.
6. Allotment should be fair and unconditional and on equitable basis.
7. If the paid up capital of any company is more than Rs. 5 crores, it is obligatory for the company that listing of its securities should be made on more than one stock exchange.
8. There should be at least a 3 year lock-in period for promoters' contribution.
9. There should be a minimum of ten shareholders for every Rs. 1 lakh of fresh issue capital.
10. There should be a minimum of twenty shareholders for every Rs. 1 lakh of existing capital.
11. In a situation of oversubscription, allotment has to be finalized in consultation with the regional stock exchanges.
12. Equal treatment shall be given to the risk factor and highlights in all public issues of advertisements.

Advantages of Listing

1. It provides liquidity to the securities of the issuing company.
2. It improves the image of the company in the market.

3. Under the Income Tax Act, the listed companies enjoy concessional rates of income tax, because enlisted companies are treated as widely held companies.

4. It gives full access to the issuing company to market its security.

5. It facilitates the company to mobilize savings from all over the country.

6. It provides the maximum collateral value to the securities.

7. The investing public gets regular information about the worth of the securities since the transactions of the listed companies are reported in daily newspapers.

9. Forced disclosure of vital information is beneficial for investors.

Disadvantages of Listing

1. Once the shares are listed, the companies are subjected to various regulatory measures of stock exchanges and SEBI.

2. It is obligatory for the listed companies to submit and disclose vital information to the stock exchanges.

3. The listed companies must send notices of the Annual General Meetings (AGM), annual reports etc. to a large number of shareholders, all this involves considerable expense.

4. The companies have to spend heavily in the process of placing the securities to the public.

UNDERWRITERS

An agreement between the company issuing the security (share or debenture) and a person or an institution is known as underwriting in which the latter gives guarantee to the former that if the issue of securities is not subscribed to fully by the investing public then the unsubscribed portion of the securities will be taken by the underwriter (guarantee providing person or institution). The underwriter renders the service for a commission agreed upon between the securities issuing company and the underwriter subject to the ceiling under the Companies Act. Broker, investment companies, commercial banks and tern lending institutions prove this service. The company that intends to offer an issue to the general investing public appoints an underwriter or underwriters in consultation with merchant bankers/lead managers. Lead managers have to certify that, in their opinion, the underwriters have adequate assets to meet their obligations. This statement should also be included in the prospectus.

An individual, firm or a company/institution who has obtained a certificate of registration from the Securities and Exchange Board of India (SEBI) can act as an underwriter. An idea about underwriters is given in Chart 2.11.

Conditions for Registration

Before granting the certificate of registration SEBI satisfies itself that an applicant:

1. Has the necessary infrastructure, like adequate space and man power

2. Has past experience in underwriting or employs at least 2 persons with experience in underwriting

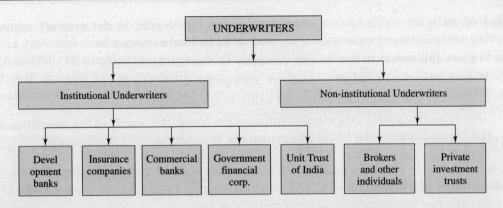

Different Types of Underwriters

3. Meets capital adequacy requirement of net worth of not less than Rs. 20 lakh.
4. Has not been convicted of an offence involving moral turpitude or found guilty of any economic offence
5. Undertakes full obligations under the SEBI Act, rules and regulations
6. Undertakes to abide by the prescribed code of conduct
7. Pays the prescribed fee for grant of registration certificate and for its renewal

Different Types of Underwriting

Full underwriting: It is an agreement under which the underwriter gives a guarantee of buying all the securities (shares or debentures) issued to the public in the event of non-subscription.

Partial underwriting: When the underwriter undertakes the guarantee for only a part of the issue and his liability is limited to that extent.

Joint underwriting: In case of a large issue, the issuing company may enter into an agreement with more than one underwriter. Each underwriter undertakes the guarantee for that entire portion of the issue.

Sub-underwriting: This is when the underwriter enters into an agreement with some other underwriters to undertake guarantee for the issue of whole or part of issue underwritten by him.

Syndicate underwriting: Under this, a number of underwriters enter into an agreement among themselves to undertake the guarantee of buying securities jointly. In syndicate underwriting, there is an agreement between the issuing company and the syndicate.

Firm underwriting: When an underwriter undertakes to buy or subscribe to a certain number of securities irrespective of subscription from the public, it is called firm underwriting. The liability of underwriters in the case of a firm underwriting is both for share underwriter and firm underwriting.

Banker of an issue: The banker of an issue helps functioning in the primary market by accepting applications for securities along with the application money from investors and also refunding the application money to applicants to whom securities could not be allotted. A bank operates as a banker to an issue only after obtaining a certificate of registration from SEBI, which considers the past experience, nature and size of the bank and its overall activities and other conditions for granting such certificates.

FULLY INVESTED

This refers to an investor or a portfolio where funds in cash or cash equivalents are minimum and assets are totally committed to investments, usually in shares. An investor who is fully invested cash has an optimistic view regarding market.

GROWTH STOCKS

This is a stock that pays low dividend but shows faster-than the average gains in earnings over the last five years and is expected to continue to show high profit growth. Over the long run, growth stocks tend to outperform slower growing or stagnant stocks.

Mutual funds that invest in highly risky but potentially rewarding stock are known as go-go stock.

HOT STOCK

This is a newly issued stock that is in great public demand. These stocks rise sharply on listing on stock exchanges. That is, a stock whose price rises quickly the day it goes public. Say you buy a new offering at Rs. 10. What do you do if on the first day of listing on the exchange it is quoted at Rs. 25? Should you sell and make a profit or wait for a while in the hope that the price will go up further?

INACTIVE STOCK AND ONE DECISION STOCK

These are securities that are traded relatively infrequently, either on a stock exchange or Over The Counter (OTC). The low volume makes the securities illiquid and small investors tend to shy away from such an investment. Whereas one decision stock is a stock with good growth potential. Such stocks are ideal to buy or hold.

CAPITALIZATION

Market Capitalization

Market capitalization depends upon the number of shares of a company and the market price of the share. Companies generally increase their capital through new issues. Market capitalization of a company can be determined by multiplying the total number of shares of the company with the market price of that share.

Over Capitalization

When the total value of ordinary shares and debts (secured and unsecured) of a company is more than its net assets then that company is considered as over capitalized. In this situation, the capital of the company remains unutilized. This type of situation is not wanted in a business.

Under Capitalization

When the total value of ordinary shares and debts (secured and unsecured) or loan of a company is less than its net assets, then that company is considered as under capitalized. In this situation, the business of the company is hampered for want of capital and the company fails to gain optimum profit. To overcome this type of situation, the company goes in for a new public issue.

MARKET LOTS AND ODD LOTS

Market lots refer to minimum trading lot of securities on a stock exchange. On compulsorily dematerialized shares for all classes of investors, the market lot is just one share. Odd lots are quite different from market lots. Stocks are sold in quantities of less than a specified minimum number. Odd lots can be sold or bought at a discounted rate at the time of physical share transaction regime.

The shares which are listed in a stock exchange or stock exchanges and are traded on (buy or sell) and appeared in the trading list of that or those stock exchanges are known as quoted shares.

PROGRAMMED TRADING

This is a computer driven buying and selling strategy through programs that constantly monitor securities, giving buy or sell signals as and when instructions are given by the purchasers or sellers. In other words, it is an investment strategy that uses computers programmed to buy or sell large numbers of securities to take advantage of price discrepancies in stock index futures or options and the actual stocks represented in those averages (see Arbitrage). This is probably the nearest you can get to a computer actually trading on the exchange with the cheapest buy and sell to the alternative with the highest price - which, after all, is the objective of any business.

In a stock market, some situations arise when security prices are manipulated to prevent unsuspecting buyers and sellers, that market is known as a pegged market.

BUY BACK OF SHARES

As per insertion of Sections 77A, 77AA and 77B by the Companies (Amendment) Act, 1991 and the respective guidelines issued by SEBI, companies are allowed to purchase their own shares with certain conditions.

Section 77A allows companies to buy their own shares out of their free reserves and securities premium account. If the shares are bought back out of companies' free reserves then a sum equal to the nominal value of the shares bought back shall be transferred to the companies' capital redemption reserve account and shown in the balance sheets. This reserve of the companies shall be used for issue of fully paid shares.

As per Section 77A (2), the buy back is authorized by the articles. The buy back is less than 25 per cent of the total; paid up capital and free reserves of the company provided that the buy back of the equity shares in any financial year shall not exceed 25 per cent of the paid up equity capital of that financial year.

The buy back with respect to listed securities is in accordance with the SEBI regulations in this regard. On the other hand, separate guidelines shall be issued with respect to unlisted specified securities.

In brief, it can be said that it is a process by which a company can buy back its shares from shareholders. A company may buy back its shares in various ways: from existing shareholders on a proportionate basis; through a tender offer from the open market; through a book-building process; from the stock exchange; or from lot holders and odd lot holders. Odd lots stocks are those stocks which are sold in quantities of less than a specified minimum number (round lot). Generally, it costs less to trade in round lots. A company cannot buy back its shares through negotiated deals, whether on or off the stock exchange or through spot transactions or through any private arrangement.

BOOK CLOSURE

Companies keep a register of members (investors) for payment of dividend right issue, bonus issue and to send a notice for annual general meeting and other meetings as prescribed by law. Book closure refers to the closing of that register of the names or investors in the records of a company.

Companies announce book closure dates from time to time. The benefits of dividends, bonus issues, rights issue accruing to investors whose name appears on the company's records as on a given date, is known as the record date. Thus, book closure and record date help a company to exactly determine the shareholders of a company as on a given date. An investor might purchase a share-cum-dividend, cum rights or cum bonus and may therefore expect to receive these benefits as the new shareholder. In order to receive this, the share has to be transferred in the investor's name, or he will stand deprived of the benefits. The buyer of such a share will be a loser. It is important for a buyer of a share to ensure that shares purchased at cum benefits prices are transferred before book-closure. It must be ensured that the price paid for the shares is ex-benefit and not cum benefit.

The company does not close its register of security holders, in case of a record date. Record date is the cut off date for determining the number of registered members who are eligible for corporate benefits. In case of book closure, shares bearing a date on the transfer deed earlier than the book closure cannot be sold on an exchange. This does not hold good for the record date.

The respective exchange sets up a No Delivery (ND) period for that security, whenever a company announces a book closure or record date. During this period only trading is permitted in the security. However, these trades are settled only after the no delivery period is over. This is done to ensure that an investor's entitlement for the corporate benefit is clearly determined.

COMPANY LAW BOARD

As per the Companies Act, 1956, the Ministry of Finance has set up a Department of Company Law Administrator popularly known as the Company Law Board. Formally, the department has set up a three tier control, viz.

1. The Central Office (All India Level)
2. The Zonal Office (Regional Office)
3. Field Officer (Registrar of Companies for all States)

But as per the Companies (Amendment) Act, 1960, the permanent administrative structure of the Company Law Board is as follows:

1. The Central Government (Acts through the Department of Company Affairs), Ministry of Law and Justice and Company Affairs.
2. The Board of Company Law Administrators – As per Companies (Amendment) Act, 2002, the Company Law Board stands dissolved and National Company Law Tribunal and Appellate Tribunal have been constituted.

   (a) A regional office headed by regional directors

   (b) Registrar of Companies stationed in every state capital of India

   The Central Government has appointed a full time officer in each state known as the Registrar of Companies. But as per insertion of Section 55A of the Companies (Amendment) Act, 2002 certain power was transferred to SEBI. The Registrar of Companies has the following duties.

   (a) To decide whether a company submitted the documents and returns in time or not.

   (b) To scrutinize the documents and returns and decide whether they are in conformity with the laws or not.

3. The details of functions and activities of SEBI are discussed in subsequent chapters.
4. The Company Law Advisory Committee has no powers or duties nor is there any obligation on the part of the Central Government or Company Law Board to refer any specific matter for advice. The government and the Company Law board are not bound to constitute an advisory committee nor are they bound to accept any advice.

5. The Public Trustee: As per Section 153-A of the Companies Act, 1956 the Central Government has the power to appoint a public trustee to discharge the function and exercise the rights and powers of shareholders or debenture holders under certain circumstances.

6. The Official Liquidator: The appointment of an official liquidator is made by the Central Government for the purpose of winding up companies by the court. They are attached to the High Court.

7. The Honorable Court: Section 10 states that jurisdiction of the court and the High Court shall be in relation to the place at which the registered office of the company is situated. But as per the Companies (Amendment) Act, 2003 the tribunal will not exercise the jurisdiction to the extent where jurisdiction has been conferred on any direct court. The tribunal will exercise jurisdiction over companies where the registered office is situated within the territorial jurisdiction of the court.

INDIAN DEPOSITORY SYSTEM

Earlier, the share registers of companies constituted the only record of the shareholders' right of ownership. Decades of policies favouring shareholders had cluttered share registers with millions of shareholders and created many small lots which were an obstacle to the rising volume of transactions. Share transfers involved much signing and writing as well as physical transport of shares to companies and back entail procedures which enabled companies to hold up or delay transfers.

These problems were faced in other countries also, and were overcome in one of three ways. In Britain, shares no longer have folio and distinctive numbers. A share certificate may therefore be any number of shares; and upon transfer, the company would be prepared to club together or divide lots. Since the bulk of transactions are between large institutional investors, most share certificates are also of large denomination, and physical share transfer involves little paper work. Since most companies have registries in London, transport of shares is also easy.

In Germany, shareholders commonly lodge their shares with banks. The banks sign agreements whereby they can exercise all the rights of shareholders, including representing them in the AGM of the respective companies. The banks receive dividends etc. and credit them to the shareholders' accounts; similarly they pass on to the shareholders entitlements to right issues, bonus issues etc.

Korea operated with custodian banks until 24th June, 1994. Then at one swoop, the scrips were dematerialized. The depository has updated lists of shareholders which it gives to companies for payment of dividends etc. These are transmitted directly to shareholders or their nominees.

But Americans having been the trend setter, depositories have been functioning smoothly worldwide for last five decades. There is no reason why they should not do so in India. With this expectation, the Government of India, on 22nd September, 1995, announced a Presidential ordinance named 'The Depositories Ordinance, 1995'.

This Presidential Ordinance for setting up a depository system is good news for the average Indian investor. In essence, investors, in the transition period, will retain the option of either joining the depository system or continuing the paper certificate method (this system is gradually being abolished at present). Changes in the ownership in the depository system will be made electronically on the basis of proof of payment/delivery of shares. The tracking will be done continuously by the depository and the companies will be informed accordingly. Some of the main features of the Ordinance are:

Multiple depositories are proposed of which one depository would be designated as the central depository. There will be no regulatory powers for the central depository; its prime function will be clearance of inter-depository trades.

Public institutions like banks, stock exchanges & financial institutions to have 51 per cent stake.

Depository participants can be custodians, FIIs, NBFCs, and brokers. Minimum net worth stipulated for brokers and minimum portfolio for NBFCs.

Depository shall not have voting rights or any other rights.

In simple words, a depository is an organization which holds investors' securities in the form of electronic book entries in the same way a bank holds customers' or account holders' money. Further, a depository transfers securities without actually handling securities, the way a bank transfers funds without actually handling money. There are two depositories, namely, National Securities Depository Ltd. (NSDL) and Central Depository Services (India) Ltd. (CDSL), promoted by Bombay Stock Exchange (BSE), Mumbai, with effect from 1st August,. The system has brought greater transparency and efficiency in capital market transactions besides liberating shareholders from unwanted hassles.

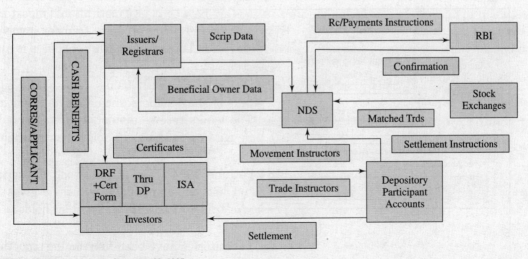

Source: The Telegraph, Calcutta, September 22, 1995.

Chart 2.12   National Depository: Broad Outlines

While the ordinance provides for setting up of one or more depositories, every depository is required to be registered with SEBI. It will also have to obtain a certificate of commencement of business on fulfillment of such conditions as prescribed by SEBI. Investors opting for the system will have to be registered with one or more "participants" (discussed below) who are the agents for the depositories. These may be custodial agencies like banks, financial institutions as well as large corporate brokerage firms.

The steps to be followed to get shares held by the investors, converted into electronic mode i.e. depository mode are given below.

The investor has to approach the DP of his choice and open an account just as we open an account with the bank. On opening an account an investor will get an identification number called 'Client's ID Number' which serves as a reference for all future dealings in the investor's shares.

If an investor still possesses any physical shares then before joining the depository system it is necessary that the concerned shares are held in the name of investor. If the investor has got the market delivery of shares, he has to get the same transferred in his name by sending them to the company.

After the investor has been allotted the Client's ID Number, he can hand over his physical share certificates after duly cancelling or defacing the certificate by writing 'Surrender for Dematerialization' and hand it over to the DP along with the Form for Dematerialization (DRF).

Upon the receipt of the DRF along with the original share certificate(s), the DP will send an electronic request to the registrars for the depository mode through NSDL and CDSL for confirmation of demat and will simultaneously forward the investor's DRF and share certificates to the concerned registrar for confirmation of demat.

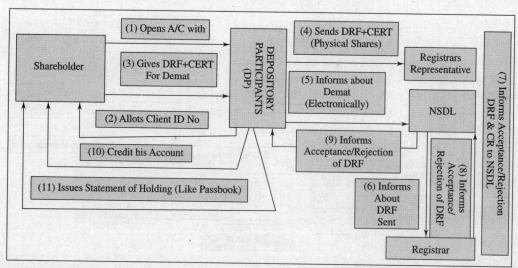

Source: Navneet Publications (India) Limited.

Chart 2.13 Flow Chart of Steps for Converting Physical Shares to Depository Mode

As soon as the registrar confirms the acceptance of the physical shares for dematerialization, NSDL & CDSL will confirm demat to investor's DP.

The DP will credit the investor's account with the number of shares dematerialized and thereafter the investor would hold the shares in electronic form.

The DP will give the investor a statement of holding of shares or a pass book just as in a bank account.

After dematerialization of shares, the investors' names are entered in the books of DP as beneficial owners. The owner's name in the register of companies concerned would be replaced by the name of the DP as the registered owner of the securities. But it is clarified that the investors would continue to be the ultimate owner of the shares and enjoy the economic benefits from the shares as well as voting rights on the shares concerned.

Shares in the depository mode would be fungible and they would cease to have distinctive numbers. Issuers of new securities would give investors the option either to receive physical shares or to join the depository mode. But due to better transparency and operational simplicity, most of the investors, at present, are opting for depository mode.

Ownership changes in the depository system are made automatically on the basis of delivery versus payment. There is a regular, mandatory system of flow of information about the details of ownership in the depository record to the company concerned.

If the company has any reservations about the admissibility of share acquisition by any person on the grounds that the transfer of security conflicts with the provision relating to substantial acquisition of shares and takeovers, or conflicts with the Sick Industrial Companies Special Provisions Act (SICA), the company would be entitled to make an application to the Company Law Board (CLB) for rectification of the ownership records with the depository.

During the pendency of the company's application with the CLB, the transferee would be entitled to all rights and benefits of the shares, except voting rights which would be subject to CLB orders.

The depository bye-laws have been fine-tuned by SEBI, to provide a provision for daily tallying of shares between the depository and the issuer. The bye-laws also envisage that the depository, along with the participant (DP) – normally an institution – will share the responsibility for ensuring that a legitimate sale/purchase order has been executed. The bye-laws contain the modalities for scripless trading, transfer, netting out of trade and settlements, to be operated synchronized with market cycles. The bye-laws also laid down modalities for inter-depository transfer. Details of the bye-laws are given below and the Presidential Ordinance is given in the Appendix.

DEPOSITORY PARTICIPANTS

A Depository Participant (DP) is a representative of the depository in the system. The DP maintains the client's securities account balances and keeps him informed about the status of holdings. According to SEBI regulations, financial institutions, banks, custodians, stockbrokers, etc. can become DPs. They are comparable to a branch of a bank if a depository

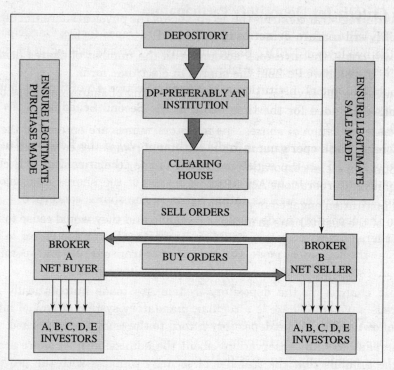

Source: Business Standard, September 26, 1996.

Chart 2.14 Depository Structure in Brief

is likened to a bank. A DP is offered depository services only after it gets proper registration from SEBI.

In fact, the NSDL depository system comprises NSDL and its business partners, i.e., DPs, issuers/Registrar and Transfer (R&T) agents and clearing corporations/stock exchanges.

The relationship between the DPs and NSDL is governed by an agreement made between the two under the Depositories Act. The form of the agreement is specified in the bye-laws of NSDL. Under the Depositories Act, 1996, a DP is described as an agent of the depository. The form of the agreement is specified in the bye-laws of NSDL. A DP is an entity who is registered as such with SEBI under the provisions of the SEBI (Depositories & Participants) Regulations, 1996.

As per the provisions of these regulations, an entity can offer depository-related services only after obtaining a certificate of registration from SEBI as a depository participant. These regulations also define the eligibility criteria for registration with SEBI as a depository participant.

According to an internet publication of a hand book for NSDL, the operational system of a depository is as follows:

Eligibility Criteria for Depository Participation

The eligibility criteria are prescribed by the SEBI (Depository & Participants) Regulations, 1996 and the bye-laws of NSDL. Basic eligibility – Persons belonging to one of the following categories are eligible to become a DP:

1. A public financial institution as defined in Section 4A of the Companies Act.
2. A bank included for the time being in the Second Schedule to the Reserve Bank of India Act, 1934.
3. A foreign bank operating in India with approval of the Reserve Bank of India.
4. A State financial corporation established under the provisions of Section 3 of the State Financial Corporations Act, 1951.
5. An institution engaged in providing financial services, promoted jointly or severally by any of the institutions mentioned in the four above-mentioned clauses.
6. A custodian of securities who has been granted a certificate of registration by SEBI.
7. A clearing corporation or a clearing house of a stock exchange.
8. A stockbroker who has been granted a certificate of registration by SEBI.
9. A non-banking finance company.
10. An R&T agent who has been granted a certificate of registration by SEBI.

SEBI (Depositories & Participants) Regulations, 1996 prescribe a minimum net worth of Rs. 50 lakh for applicants who are stockbrokers or Non-Banking Finance Companies (NBFCs), for granting a certificate of registration to act as a DP. For R & T agents a minimum net worth of Rs. 10 crore is prescribed in addition to a grant of certificate of registration by SEBI. If a stockbroker seeks to act as a DP in more than one depository, he should comply with the specified net worth criterion separately for each such depository. If an NBFC seeks to act as a DP on behalf of any other person, it needs to have a net worth of Rs. 50 crore in addition to the net worth specified by any other authority. No minimum net worth criterion has been prescribed for other categories of DPs.

However, depositories can fix a higher net worth criterion for their DPs. NSDL stipulates a minimum net worth of Rs. 100 lakh for all categories to be eligible to become a DP as against Rs. 50 lakh prescribed by SEBI (D&P) Regulations, 1996, except for R & T agents and NBFCs, as mentioned above.

According to NSDL's bye-laws, an applicant has to submit a net worth certificate certified by a chartered accountant, including the computation of net worth. The certificate, based on the audited books of account, should be in the format specified by NSDL in its bye-laws/ business rules. NSDL has, in its bye-laws, provided for a specific method for calculation of net worth. It is possible that a DP may have different net worth figures for different depositories. The net worth specified under the bye-laws of NSDL has to be maintained by DPs at all times without which NSDL may suspend or terminate their operations. The minimum net worth for a DP prescribed under the bye-laws of NSDL is Rs. 100 lakh.

Restrictions

As per SEBI (Depositories & Participants) Regulations, 1996 the aggregate value of the securities of the beneficial owners, held in dematerialized form through a stockbroker DP cannot be more than 100 times the net worth of the stockbroker. However, where the stock broker has a minimum net worth of Rs. 10 crore, the limits on the aggregate value of the portfolio of securities of the beneficial owners held in dematerialized form in a depository through him, shall not be applicable. NBFCs, having a net worth of less than Rs. 50 crore, may act as DPs only on their own behalf. Only NBFCs having a minimum net worth of above Rs. 50 crore, in addition to the net worth specified by any other authority, may provide depository related services to other persons also.

Application for DP Membership

An entity desirous of becoming a DP of NSDL should make an application to SEBI. The application, complete in all respects should be submitted to NSDL for forwarding to SEBI. NSDL evaluates the application and if it finds that the applicant may be admitted as a depository participant, forwards it to SEBI within 30 days of receiving it, along with its recommendations.

The applicant is required to pay SEBI application fees at this stage. NSDL may reject the application, if it is found to be incomplete or not as per the given instructions. SEBI may require the applicant or NSDL to furnish additional information or clarifications, necessary for considering the application. If the application form is found incomplete, SEBI may also reject the application after giving an opportunity to the applicant for removing the objection(s).

Conditions for Grant of Registration

On being satisfied that the applicant is eligible and has complied with the conditions stipulated in the SEBI (D&P) Regulations, SEBI may grant a registration certificate to the applicant. Before granting a certificate of registration to a DP, SEBI considers, inter alia, whether the applicant has adequate infrastructure and systems. It also takes into account whether it has in place the safeguards and has the trained staff to carry on activities as a DP and the applicant is a fit and proper person. Grant of registration is also subject to the condition that the participant shall redress the grievances of beneficial owners within thirty days of the date of receipt of the complaint and keep the depository informed about the number and nature of redressals. Finally, it examines whether the grant of certificate of registration to such a person is in the interests of investors in the securities market.

NSDL has prescribed the following additional conditions for admission of DPs to its system.

1. The applicant should furnish information and details of its business history for a minimum period of three years.

2. The applicant should not have been convicted in any of the five years immediately preceding the filing of the application in any matter involving misappropriation of funds and securities, theft, embezzlement of funds, fraudulent conversion or forgery.

3. The applicant should not have been expelled, barred or suspended by SEBI, self-regulatory organization or any recognized stock exchange. However, if three years or more have elapsed since the punishment, NSDL may, at its discretion, consider such an application.

4. The applicant should have a minimum net worth of Rs. 1 crore. The net worth is to be calculated as per the method of computation prescribed by NSDL.

5. The applicant should furnish details of its board of directors/authorized officials, who will be responsible for acting on behalf of the DP.

6. NSDL may conduct entrance examinations and/or interviews, to examine the knowledge of the DP (and its staff) related to the operational, functional and technical aspects of the depository. NSDL may also make it mandatory for the DP to appoint a Compliance Officer, who interacts with NSDL on the DP's behalf for compliance with the bye-laws and business rules and resolving investors/clients' grievances.

7. The applicant should have adequate office space exclusively for depository operations. The applicant should also furnish details of his main office, including address, fax and phone number(s). NSDL has the sole discretion to decide whether the applicant has adequate infrastructure facilities at the time of granting admission.

8. The applicant should make adequate arrangements for conducting effective and safe depository operations. These should include security measures, risk containment and insurance requirements, as specified by the depository.

9. For the purpose of satisfying itself regarding the applicants' eligibility, NSDL may carry out an inspection of their office and facilities.

10. In order to ensure availability of qualified personnel in DP service centres, NSDL requires that at least one person in each DP service centre must be qualified in NSE's Certification in Financial Markets (NCFM) – Depository Operations Module.

In short, the steps for joining as a DP are as follows:

Entity eligible and desirous of becoming a DP makes an application to NSDL.

NSDL verifies the application for completeness and confirmity to the requirements NSDL may reject, ask for further information and/or clarifications, or ask the applicant to remove the defects in the application. Upon satisfying the requirements, NSDL grants approval to the application for recommendation to SEBI.

Applicant is required to furnish details in the prescribed forms and procure necessary hardware as per specifications issued by NSDL. Applicant is required to provide the hardware set-up information to NSDL in the prescribed forms. Applicant establishes electronic connectivity with NSDL.

NSDL forwards the application to SEBI for registration along with its recommendation.

SEBI reviews the application and if found satisfactory, grants in principle approval.

The DP pays the registration fees to SEBI within the stipulated period of 15 days. The DP also pays security deposits, insurance charges and other collateral to NSDL.

SEBI grants Certificate of Registration to the applicant.

The DP and NSDL sign an agreement in the prescribed format.

NSDL activates the DP module at the applicant's (now a DP) premises.

DP begins operations.

Validity and Renewal of Registration Certificate

A certificate of registration is valid for a period of five years from the date of issue. The SEBI regulations require the participant to make an application for renewal three months before the expiry date of the validity of the certificate of registration. The application for renewal should be made through the depository. The fees specified for issue of the certificate of registration should accompany the application. It is dealt with in the same manner as if it were a fresh application for grant of certificate of registration. SEBI may reject the application for renewal of a certificate after citing the reasons for refusal in writing. An application for renewal may be submitted to SEBI through NSDL three months before the expiry date of the registration certificate.

1. If the application for renewal is not received at SEBI by the expiry date of the certificate of registration, the intermediary shall:

   (a) Cease to be an intermediary on the date of such expiry.

   (b) Stop carrying on the activities of the intermediary from the date of such expiry.

   (c) Transfer, wherever relevant, the accounts/business of existing clients to another registered intermediary before the date of such expiry.

   If the intermediary fails to comply with all of the above, it will be considered as a violation of Section 12 and may attract action under the relevant provisions of the SEBI Act, 1992 and/or the regulations framed thereunder.

   No application for renewal can be made after the date of expiry of registration. After the expiry of registration, the erstwhile intermediary can apply for registration, which will be considered as a fresh application for registration made under the relevant regulations.

2. If the application for renewal is received by SEBI less than 3 months before the expiry of registration and SEBI has not advised otherwise by the date of expiry of registration, the intermediary shall stop undertaking any fresh business/clients from the date of expiry of the registration.

   SEBI may initiate any action that may be deemed appropriate for late submission of application under the provisions of the SEBI Act, 1992 and the regulations framed there under.

   It is clarified that in the above cases, the application for renewal shall mean the application is complete in all respects. An incomplete application will be treated as no application.

3. If renewal is not granted by SEBI for whatever reason, the intermediary shall:

   (a) Cease to be an intermediary on the date of expiry of registration or the date of receipt of communication of refusal to grant renewal.

   (b) Stop carrying on the activities of the intermediary from the date as at (a) above.

   (c) Transfer, wherever required, the accounts/business of existing clients to another registered intermediary within such period as may be specified.

   If the intermediary fails to comply with all of the above, it will be considered as a violation of Section 12 and shall be liable for action under the relevant provisions of SEBI Act, 1992, and/or the provisions of the rules and regulations framed there under.

Commencement

A DP can commence its operations after complying with the prescribed procedures of the depository for commencing business operations. NSDL has specified the following pre-requisites for DPs for commencing operations:

1. Apply in the prescribed form. Furnish all clarifications and additional documents as may be required by NSDL.

2. NSDL communicates whether or not the application of a DP is accepted.

3. On receiving the approval an application for connectivity with NSDL should be made. Primary connectivity can be by way of V-sat or leased line; full-scale connectivity by way of PSTN line, dial up lines also have to be arranged as a fall back if the primary connectivity fails.

4. Procure the prescribed hardware and communicate the details of the hardware installed to NSDL.

5. NSDL will conduct a pilot test to train the staff on the functions of the depository and to check the systems. The DP has to participate in the pilot test.

6. NSDL conducts training programs for the staff of DPs in its premises. DPs have to have a sufficient number of its employees trained by NSDL.

7. NSDL encourages all DPs to employ staff that is qualified in the Depositories Module of NCFM. NSDL has made it mandatory for all depository participants to appoint at least one NCFM qualified person at all the branches.

8. NSDL depository system application in a live environment is activated in the office of the DP. A DP – ID is issued to the DP.

9. Now the DP can start functioning.

Rights and Obligations

Agreement with beneficial owners: The DP must enter into an agreement with a beneficial owner before acting as a participant on his behalf. A DP, while conducting any business with a client, acts as an agent of NSDL and is liable to the clients for all the acts and deeds performed by it. The agreement has to be made in the form and manner specified by NSDL in its bye-laws. A copy of the agreement should be given to the beneficial owner. Schedule of charges is a part of the agreement. However no agreement is required if:

1. A foreign institutional investor registered with SEBI enters into an agreement with the DP either directly or through its power of attorney holders in accordance with the provisions of sub regulation (1) of Regulation 16 of SEBI (Foreign Institutional Investors) Regulations, 1995. Such an agreement gives the DP the authority to act on behalf of the foreign institutional investors for availing of the services of the depository and such an agreement has already been filed with SEBI.

2. An international multilateral agency, that has entered into an agreement with the DP under Regulation 17 of the SEBI (Custodian of Securities) Regulations 1996, and such agreement states that the custodian will also act as a DP and all provisions pertaining to DP shall be applicable.

Separate accounts: The DP should open a separate account in the name of each beneficial owner. The securities of each beneficial owner should be segregated from the securities of other beneficial owners or from the DP's own securities. For the DP's own securities, he should open a separate account called a 'house account' in the depository system.

Client instructions: Securities should be transferred to or from a beneficial owner's account only on receipt of instructions from the beneficial owner. No entry in the beneficial owner's account should be made unless it is supported by instructions received from the beneficial owner as per the agreement made with him.

Transaction statements: The DP should provide a transaction statement to the beneficial owner as laid down in the agreement with the beneficial owner. NSDL bye-laws require each DP to provide a transaction statement at monthly intervals, or at such lesser interval as may be agreed between the DP and the client. If there is no transaction in the account, the statement should be provided at least once in a quarter. The transaction statement should be dispatched directly to the client's address mentioned in the DPM system of the DP and not through any franchisee/collection centre.

The statement could be provided through the Internet/e-mail, provided an agreement in the prescribed format has been executed with the clients for this and adequate security measures have been taken. SEBI permits the DPs to provide transaction statements and other documents to the Beneficial Owners (BOs) under digital signature, as governed by the Information Technology Act, 2000, subject to entering into a legally enforceable arrangement with the BOs for the said purpose. Providing of transaction statements and other documents in the aforesaid manner would be deemed to be in compliance of the provisions of Regulation 43 of SEBI (Depositories & Participants) Regulations, 1996.

Further, if a client subscribes to Internet-based Demat Account Statement (IDeAS), SEBI has permitted the participants to discontinue providing physical transaction statements to their clients. However, the participants will be required to send a consolidated transaction statement, in physical form, for the entire financial year and the same shall be dispatched before 15th of May every year.

However if the BOs are still desirous of receiving statements in hard copy, the DPs shall be duty bound to provide the same.

Connectivity: The DP should maintain a continuous electronic means of communication with NSDL. In case of failure of primary connectivity the DP should connect to NSDL using a fall back medium of connectivity. The branch offices of DPs handling more than 5,000 accounts should have either direct electronic connectivity with the depository or with the office of the DP directly connected to the depository. The primary connectivity can either be V-Sat or leased line while secondary connectivity can be through a dial-up line.

Monitoring, reviewing and evaluating internal systems and controls: The DP should have an adequate mechanism for the purposes of reviewing, monitoring and evaluating its internal systems and accounting controls. As per NSDL bye-laws, a DP has to get an internal audit done of the depository operations on a quarterly basis by a practicing chartered accountant or company secretary.

Reconciliation: The DP should reconcile its records with NSDL on a daily basis. NSDL system is designed to do this reconciliation automatically every day at the End Of the Day (EOD). In case the DP is using any back-office software it needs to reconcile the same as per the NSDL DPM.

Returns: The DP should submit periodic returns to SEBI and to every depository in which it is a participant in the format specified by SEBI or the bye-laws of the depository. NSDL requires the following returns to be submitted by its DPs:

1. Each participant shall furnish to the depository every year, a copy of its audited financial statement within a period of one month after the balance sheet and profit and loss account have been placed before the company's Annual General Meeting or within 6 months from the end of the participant's financial year, whichever is earlier.

2. Net worth certificate computed in a manner laid down in the business rules, issued by a chartered accountant on the basis of annual audited accounts of the DP.

3. If the DP is a clearing member of the clearing corporation of any exchange, the details regarding any suspension/termination or defaults or any disputes in relation to its dealings with such clearing corporation within two working days of such an event.

4. Number of complaints received from clients, their nature, status and manner of redressal, once a month.

5. Internal audit report and concurrent audit report, once every quarter.

DP to indemnify depository: A DP has to indemnify the depository, its officers and employees for all costs, fees, expenses, liabilities, taxes, actual losses and damages of any nature whatsoever suffered or incurred by any of them for:

1. The failure of the DP to comply with the provision of the bye-laws or the DP agreement or to comply with any directions or procedures of the depository.

2. The acts by the depository or its officers and employees placing reliance upon instructions or communications by the DP. These include giving effect to instructions

or communications by any of them or the failure of the DP to give instructions to the depository as stated in the bye-laws.

3. The acceptance by the depository of eligible securities deposited by the DP and effecting transactions by the depository according to the bye-laws and withdrawal of eligible securities by the DP.

4. The failure of the DP to deliver eligible securities or to perform other duties or obligations set out in the bye-laws.

Prohibition of assignment: No DP can assign or delegate its functions as a depository participant to any other person without prior approval of NSDL. All the DPs are required to provide the details of all places from where they are offering any of the depository services to their clients whether it is called a DPM set-up, head office, main office, branch, franchisee, service centre, collection centre, drop box centre or by any other name and any further updates (addition/deletion/modification) in the information to NSDL within seven days of the change.

Insurance: DPs should take appropriate insurance cover to insure against losses arising from any possible business risk and system failure. However, NSDL takes insurance for itself and on behalf of all DPs. The insurance covers business risk and system failure risk. DPs may additionally take for themselves insurance to cover risks like theft, fire, etc.

Record of services: The DP should maintain and preserve the records and documents for a minimum period of five years. They should also make them available for inspection by the depository whenever required.

1. Forms for opening, closing, freezing and defreezing of accounts given by the clients.

2. Record of all the dematerialization and dematerialization requests received from the clients.

3. Record of all the delivery/receipt instructions given by the clients and clearing members.

4. Copies of correspondence received from clients for updating of client details in DPM.

5. Records of all the actions taken on the exception reports generated by the system.

6. Details of grievances/arbitration proceedings received from the clients, action taken and status of the same.

7. Record of all forms received in respect of pledge, securities lending and transmission of securities.

If a DP has entered into an agreement with more than one depository, the records specified above should be maintained separately for each such depository.

DP has to ensure adherence to guidelines on anti money laundering measures – The Prevention of Money Laundering Act 2002 (PMLA) has come into effect from 1st July, 2005.

As per the provisions of the Act, every banking company, financial institution (which includes a chit fund company, co-operative bank, housing finance institution and a non-banking financial company) and intermediary (which includes a stock-broker, sub-broker, share transfer agent, banker to an issue, trustee to a trust deed, registrar to an issue, merchant banker, underwriter, portfolio manager, investment adviser and any other intermediary associated with securities market and registered under section 12 of the Securities and Exchange Board of India Act, 1992) shall have to maintain a record of all the transactions; the nature and value of which has been prescribed in the rules under the PMLA.

Such transactions include:

❖ All cash transactions of a value more than Rs. 10 lakhs or its equivalent in foreign currency.

❖ All series of cash transactions integrally connected to each other which have been valued below Rs. 10 lakhs or its equivalent in foreign currency where such series of transactions take place within one calendar month.

❖ All suspicious transactions whether or not made in cash.

Broadly, the guidelines on Anti Money Laundering (AML) measures are as under:

1. Participants are to evolve their own guidelines (if not already evolved) so as to comply with the provisions of the PMLA and the rules, guidelines thereof issued by GOI/SEBI, from time to time.

2. Participants to put in place a proper policy framework on AML measures in compliance with relevant laws, rules and instructions.

3. AML procedures should include inter alia, the following three specific parameters which are related to the overall 'Client Due Diligence Process':

    (a) Policy for acceptance of clients

    (b) Procedure for identifying the clients

    (c) Transaction monitoring and reporting especially Suspicious Transactions Reporting (STR).

4. Each participant should appoint a senior management executive to be designated as the Principal Officer, if it has not already done so. The Principal Officer shall be located at the head/corporate office of the participant and shall be responsible for monitoring and reporting of all transactions and sharing of information as required under the law. He will maintain close liaison with the other divisions/departments of the participant, the other participant, the enforcement agencies and other institutions which are involved in similar activities.

5. Monitoring and reporting to Financial Intelligence Unit-India: Participants are required to report information relating to suspicious transactions, in the prescribed format, within seven working days of establishment of suspicion, to the Director, Financial Intelligence Unit-India (FIU-IND) at the following address:

    Director, FIU-IND,

    Financial Intelligence Unit-India,

    6th Floor, Hotel Samrat, Chanakyapuri,

    New Delhi-110021.

6. Maintenance and preservation of records:

   (a) Participants should take appropriate steps to evolve an internal mechanism for proper maintenance and preservation of relevant records and information in a manner that allows easy and quick retrieval of data as and when requested by the competent authorities. Further, the records have to be maintained and preserved for a period of ten years from the date of cessation of the transactions between the client and participant.

   (b) Participants should formulate and implement the client identification program containing the requirements as laid down and such other additional requirements that it considers appropriate. The records of the identity of clients have to be maintained and preserved for a period of ten years from the date of cessation of the transactions between the client and participant.

7. Participants should obtain a certification from their internal auditors that the concerned participant has drawn up a policy on anti money laundering measures in compliance with the relevant laws, rules and instructions. In addition, in every quarterly report, the internal auditor must check and certify whether the participant has complied with the policy so drawn up. Any deficiencies should be specifically pointed out in the report.

8. The Compliance Officer of the participant is required to submit a 'Compliance Certificate' in the prescribed format, at half-yearly intervals (January to June and July to December to be submitted by July 31 and January 31 of every year respectively).

9. Participants should educate the clients about the objectives of the Know Your Customer (KYC) program. The front desk staff needs to be specially trained to handle such situations while dealing with clients.

DP to ensure integrity and back-up of data: DPs who maintain electronic records should ensure the integrity of the data processing systems. All necessary precautions should be taken to ensure that the records are not lost, destroyed or tampered with. In the event of loss or destruction, sufficient back-up of records should have been taken and made available at all times at different places. In order to ensure this, NSDL has prescribed the following back-up policy for its DPs:

1. Business partners have to take back ups every day without fail.

2. Two copies of back-ups have to be taken; one copy has to be preserved at a remote site away from the operations and another on the site itself.

3. Application software generates transaction logs every 15 minutes and writes on to a client machine. DPs should keep the client machine where transaction logs are copied, powered on as long as the DPM server is kept on to have a transaction log written.

4. The back-up tapes should be preserved safely, well protected against fire, theft and manipulation.

5. If the DPs have large business volumes, they may install an additional back-up machine which helps them in continuing the business operation even if the main machine fails.

Suspension of certificate: The certificate of registration granted to a DP may be suspended by SEBI if it is found that the DP has:

1. Contravened any of the provisions of the Depositories Act, the bye-laws, agreements and SEBI (D&P) Regulations, 1996.
2. Failed to furnish any information relating to its activity as a DP required under the regulations.
3. Not furnished the information called for by SEBI under the provisions of the Depositories Act, 1996 or has furnished information which is false or misleading.
4. Not co-operated in any inspection or investigation or enquiry conducted by SEBI.
5. Failed to comply with any direction of SEBI.
6. Failed to pay the annual fee as specified under the SEBI (D&P) Regulations, 1996.

Cancellation of certificate: The certificate of registration granted to a DP may be cancelled by SEBI if it is found that:

1. The DP is guilty of fraud, or has been convicted of an offence involving moral turpitude.
2. The DP has been guilty of repeated defaults specified for suspension of the registration termination by depository – besides these regulatory provisions, each depository may have its own bye-laws for termination or suspension of its DPs. NSDL's bye-laws provide 15 conditions under which it may terminate the operations of a DP.

Termination by DP: A DP may also choose to terminate its participation in the depository by giving a notice of not less than 30 days. On receipt of such a notice, the depository may cease to provide any service or act for the DP. The depository should notify the DP, other participants, clients of the surrendering DP and SEBI within seven days of this action.

CLEARING CORPORATION/CLEARING HOUSE (CC/CH)

This term applies to an entity responsible for clearing and settlement of trades done by clearing members on a recognized stock exchange. A clearing corporation/clearing house of a stock exchange is admitted to the depository system for clearing and settlement of securities traded on their respective stock exchanges. For electronic settlement of securities in demat form, the concerned CC/CH of the stock exchange needs to have electronic connectivity with the depository.

A clearing corporation or a clearing house of a stock exchange may be admitted as a user of NSDL subject to its entering into an agreement with NSDL as laid down in the bye-laws of NSDL. A different agreement has to be drawn up if a clearing house of a stock exchange is not a legal counterparty to the trades on the exchange and the trade/settlement guarantee fund is held and managed by the exchange. A third type of agreement has to be entered into if the members/dealers of the exchange are not the clearing members of the clearing house. A stock exchange may be admitted as a user on the depository, if it conducts the activity of clearing and settlement of trades and if it is not a legal counterparty to the trades thereon and holds and manages the trade/settlement guarantee fund. An agreement, as laid down in the bye-laws of NSDL, has to be entered into.

The provisions of these agreements govern the rights and obligations of the NSDL, the clearing corporation or the clearing house of a stock exchange and the exchange, in respect of transactions entered into in pursuance of such agreements (also see Chapter 3).

Admission Criteria

A clearing corporation of a clearing house of a stock exchange can be admitted as a user on the NSDL only if it fulfills the conditions laid down. These criteria are listed below:

1. The clearing corporation or clearing house of a stock exchange has adequate hardware and software systems to interact with NSDL as specified in the business rules.

2. NSDL is satisfied that the clearing corporation or a clearing house of a stock exchange operates in such a manner that it ensures payment against delivery or guarantees settlement.

3. The clearing corporation or a clearing house of a stock exchange undertakes to co-operate at all times to redress the grievances of clients and DPs in respect of its operation in relation to NSDL.

4. In the opinion of NSDL, the clearing corporation or a clearing house of a stock exchange has the operational capability to provide the services relating to clearing and settlement of transactions pertaining to the securities admitted to the depository to be held in dematerialized form.

A clearing corporation or a clearing house of a stock exchange shall not be permitted to open beneficiary accounts for clients, except where it has been permitted by the RBI to offer constituent SGL account facility to the investors.

A CC or CH of a stock exchange can also be admitted as a full fledged participant including opening beneficiary accounts, provided the following additional conditions are satisfied:

1. The CC/CH applicant has a net worth of Rs. 5 crore. In case it does not have a net worth of Rs. 5 crore, it must undertake to enhance its net worth to Rs. 5 crore within a period of two years.

2. The aggregate value of the client's assets held by a CC/CH participant shall not exceed 20 times its net worth.

Issuers and R&T Agents

The Depositories Act, 1996 gives an option to investors to hold their securities either in physical form or in book entry form with a depository. Issuer of the security i.e. company may offer a facility to hold the securities issued by it in demat form by entering into an agreement with NSDL. The issuers who intend to offer demat facility will have to establish connectivity with NSDL either directly or through a registrar & transfer agent having connectivity with NSDL.

Eligibility Criteria

The following categories of securities are eligible for dematerialization as per SEBI (Depositories & Participants) Regulations, 1996:

1. Shares, scrips, stocks, bonds, debentures, debenture stock or other marketable securities of a like nature in or of any incorporated company or other body corporate.

2. Units of mutual funds, rights under collective investment schemes and venture capital funds, commercial paper, certificates of deposit, securitized debt, money market instruments and government securities, unlisted securities shall also be similarly eligible for being held in dematerialized form in a depository.

All issuers of these securities may make their securities available for dematerialization upon fulfillment of certain criteria. The Executive Committee of NSDL determines the securities that are eligible for dematerialization. Before dematerialization commences, the issuer or its R&T agent, if any, has to comply with the following conditions:

1. The issuer and/or its R&T agent undertake to co-operate at all times to redress the grievances of the client and the DP.

2. The issuer and/or its R&T agent shall have adequate hardware and software systems to interact with depository as specified from time to time in the business rules.

3. The issuer and its R&T agent if any have signed the tripartite agreement as per the bye-laws of NSDL.

The above conditions are not applicable to securities issued by Central or State Government.

NSDL may refuse to accept the admission of securities of an issue as an eligible security or may remove the same from the list of eligible securities if:

1. In the opinion of NSDL, the issuer or its R&T agent does not have or has ceased to have the operational capability to provide services in respect of an issue of securities.

2. The issuer or its R&T agent commits any breach of any terms and/or conditions of the agreement entered into with NSDL,

3. The Board of Directors of NSDL, in its absolute discretion, is satisfied that circumstances exist which render it necessary in the interest of the investors to do so.

Rights and Obligations of Issuers and their R&T Agents

Each issuer whose securities are admitted to NSDL is required to represent and warrant in favour of NSDL that such securities exist at the time of transfer of securities into the depository and thereafter. The issuer also has to warrant that these securities are validly issued and that it is entitled or has full authority to transfer such securities into the depository.

Every issuer has to provide timely information to NSDL about various corporate actions. These include book closure, record dates, dates for payment of interest or dividend, dates for the annual general meeting, dates of redemption of securities, dates of conversion, dates of exercising warrants and such other information as may be specified by the Executive Committee of NSDL from time to time.

The issuer and its R&T agents have to reconcile with records of NSDL, the records in respect of balances of eligible securities with clients and confirm to all the depositories, the total security balances both in physical as well as in electronic holdings in the books. Where a state or the Central Government is the issuer, NSDL reconciles the records of the dematerialized securities with the statement provided by the RBI on a daily basis.

Every issuer or its R&T agent shall issue the certificate of securities against receipt of the Rematerialization Request Form from the client through the DP and on receipt of confirmed instructions from the depository. The issuer or its R&T agent are required to furnish to NSDL allotment details of all clients who have opted for securities to be credited to their account in the electronic form. NSDL electronically provides the details of the clients to the issuer/R&T agent every fortnight. This clause does not apply to government securities.

The depository is responsible for the accuracy/correctness of all such information related to eligible securities intimated by it to the issuer/R&T agent. The issuer/R&T agent is responsible for the accuracy and correctness of all information furnished by it in the prescribed form to NSDL.

The Main Features of the Tripartite Agreement

The rights and obligations of NSDL, the issuer and R&T agent are embodied in the tripartite agreement between them. This agreement has to be signed before the issuer/R&T agent can be admitted in the depository system. Some of the main terms of the agreement are quoted below:

1. The issuer/R&T agent shall furnish a list of authorized officials who shall represent and interact on behalf of the issuer and/or R&T agent with NSDL within 15 days of the execution of this agreement and any changes including additions/deletions thereof shall be communicated to NSDL within 15 days of such change.

2. NSDL shall allocate unique identity codes to the securities issued by an issuer. Such code is called the International Securities Identification Number (ISIN).

3. The issuer/R&T agent shall establish continuous electronic means of communication with NSDL and NSDL shall provide necessary manuals and procedural guidelines to the issuer/R&T agent as is necessary for effective and prompt conduct of the business of the depository. The issuer/R&T agent shall maintain such systems, procedures, means of communication, adequate infrastructure, hardware, software security devices and backup facilities as may be prescribed by NSDL.

4. The issuer/R&T agent shall strictly follow the back-up procedure recommended by NSDL. A copy of the latest back-up of database and subsequently incremental back-up shall be maintained at a designated remote site.

5. The issuer/R&T agent shall comply with all the systems and procedures recommended by NSDL and shall allow access to their systems to an EDP audit team, designated by NSDL for periodic assessment of compliance with systems and procedures.

6. The issuer/R&T agent agree that NSDL shall not be liable to the issuer/R&T agent for any loss arising out of any failure of the issuer/R&T agent to keep full and up-to-date

security copies (back-up) of computer programs and data it uses in accordance with the best computing practice.

7. The issuer shall inform NSDL on the next day on which the information is being sent to the stock exchanges in which the eligible securities are listed, about the dates from which new shares arising out of conversions, further issues, final call payments, etc. become pari passu with its existing shares.

8. The issuer shall furnish information to NSDL of any further issues such as rights, bonus, public offerings with details viz., opening and closing dates, issue size, issue price, record date, book closure, proportion, along with a copy of the offer document.

9. The issuer shall give information to NSDL about book closures, record dates, dates for the payment of interest or dividend, dates for annual general meetings and other meetings, dates for redemption of debentures, dates for conversion of debentures and warrants, call money dates, amalgamation, merger, reduction of capital, reconstruction scheme of arrangement, sub-division, consolidation, and conversion of debentures/loans and such other information relating to any corporate action, on the next day it is being communicated to the relevant stock exchanges, where the eligible security is listed.

10. The issuer and its R&T agent undertakes that the dematerialization and rematerialization requests are processed within 15 and 30 days respectively. However, it is agreed that in case of bulk dematerialization requests, this period may be extended to 30 days.

11. The issuer and its R&T agent undertakes that no dematerialization requests shall be accepted when there are any prohibitory orders, stop transfer, attachment orders, or disputed title, on the day of such request. It is agreed that where a court order has been received by the issuer and/or its R&T agent or where there are court orders against any transfer request if such a request is entertained, the issuer/R&T agent shall be entirely responsible. The issuer/R&T agent agrees to be fully responsible for destruction, mutilation and cancellation of certificates received and accepted by it for dematerialization.

12. It is agreed that the issuer/R&T agent will continue to be responsible for corporate actions. NSDL undertakes to provide the list of beneficial owners with suitable details to the issuer/R&T agent as of the record date. This list shall be provided by the NSDL fifteen days after such request has been received by NSDL. In the event of any loss caused to the issuer/R&T agent, in respect of any incorrect information relating to the client, furnished by NSDL or its participant, NSDL shall indemnify such losses.

13. The issuer/R&T agent shall indemnify NSDL in respect of any loss or liability incurred, or any claim arising in respect of any incorrect information furnished by the issuer/R&T agent in respect of the operations of the depository.

14. Any claims, disputes or liabilities arising in respect of any securities which have been rematerialized under intimation from the issuer/R&T agent to NSDL after the

despatch of such securities' certificates in the manner laid down under the bye-laws shall be settled between the issuer/R&T agent and the owner of such securities.

15. In the case of securities that have been dematerialized and electronically credited to the accounts of the clients in NSDL under intimation from the issuer/R&T agent in the manner laid down under the bye-laws, any claims, disputes or liabilities or cause of action from a third party arising in respect of such securities pertaining to any fake or forged securities shall be settled between the issuer/R&T agent and such third party.

16. NSDL may authorize persons who shall have the right to enter during the regular business hours, on any working day, the premises of such issuer/R&T agent where the records relating to the depository operations are being maintained and inspect, and take copies thereof.

17. NSDL shall provide reports updating details of beneficial owners on a fortnightly basis to the issuer/R&T agent.

18. NSDL shall provide the details of the list of beneficial owners as well as the pending requests for dematerialization and rematerialization that may be required by the issuer/R&T agent from time to time on the payment of such charges as may be provided in the business rules. Such information shall be provided within 15 days from the date of making such a request. where the list of beneficial owners is required as on a particular date, the same shall be provided within a period of 15 days after such date or 15 days from the date of receipt of such request by the NSDL whichever is later.

19. NSDL shall in its discretion provide any other details that may be required by the issuer and/or its R&T agent from time to time on the payment of such charges as it may deem fit.

20. The issuer and/or R&T agent shall inform NSDL of any proposed changes in the address of business partners of NSDL the registered offices, corporate office or of the location where the equipment for communication with NSDL is situated not less than thirty days before the date of such change.

21. NSDL shall inform the issuer and/or its R&T agent of any proposed changes in the address of its registered office or corporate office not less than thirty days before the date of such change.

22. The issuer shall not change, discontinue or substitute its R&T agent unless an alternative arrangement has been agreed to by NSDL.

23. The issuer and/or its R&T agent shall not assign to any other person/entity its functions & obligations, relating to transactions with the depository, without the approval of NSDL.

24. All parties to this agreement shall resolve the grievances of the beneficial owners within a period of 21 days, from the date of receipt of the complaint, concerning NSDL, the issuer and/or its R&T agents.

Role of Issuer/R&T Agent in Dematerialization of Securities

The depository electronically intimates, on a daily basis, all dematerialization (discussed later) requests to the respective issuer or its R&T agent. The issuer or its R&T agent have to verify the validity of the security certificates as well as the fact that the demat request has been made by the person recorded as a member in its register of members. After such verification, the issuer or its R&T agent intimates NSDL and authorizes an electronic credit for that security in favor of the client. On receipt of such intimation, NSDL makes the credit entries in the account of the client concerned. No credit of any securities to the accounts of any client can be made unless NSDL has received intimation from the issuer or its R&T agent.

Where the issuer or its R&T agent rejects any dematerialization request, it has to electronically intimate NSDL regarding such rejection within a period of 15 days. After intimating such rejection to NSDL, the issuer or its R&T agent returns the DRF along with the rejection reason and relevant security certificates, unless the reasons for rejection are any of the following:

1. The security certificates are stolen.
2. The security certificates are fake.
3. In the event of an order from a court or a competent statutory authority prohibiting the transfer of such securities.
4. In case duplicate certificates have been issued in respect of the securities with the same distinctive numbers.

In the event of intimation being received by the depository from issuer or R&T agent to credit the account of the client with securities which do not match with the details of the client or DP, the balance shall be held in a suspense account. In the event of any person making a claim to the securities that are held in the name of the client with NSDL after they are so registered, then such claims must be settled amongst the DPs, clients and issuer or its R&T agent.

The issuer or its R&T agent, after giving intimation as set out in NSDL's bye-laws, represents and warrants to NSDL that such securities exist and are validly issued and the issuer or its R&T agent is entitled or has full authority to transfer such securities with the depository in the name of the client.

Role of Issuer/R&T Agent in Re-materialization of Securities

A client may withdraw its security balances with the depository at any point of time by making an application for re-materialization to the depository through its DP. When the investor submits the Remat Request Form (RRF), the issuer and/or its R&T agent and the NSDL have to take the following steps:

❖ NSDL intimates electronically, details of all accepted rematerialization applications to the issuer or its R&T agent on a daily basis.

❖ The DP forwards the RRF to the issuer or its R&T agent within 7 days of accepting such a request from the client. The issuer/R&T agent, after validating the RRF, confirms to

NSDL electronically that the RRF has been accepted. Thereafter, the issuer/R&T agent dispatch the security certificates arising out of the rematerialization request within a period of 30 days from receipt of such an RRF directly to the client. On receipt of such acceptance from the issuer/R&T agent, NSDL debits the balances from the respective client's account held with the DP's.

Role of Issuer/R&T Agent in Corporate Benefits

It is the function of the issuer/R&T agent to inform NSDL about the corporate actions relating to prescribing dates for book closures, record dates and dates for redemption or maturity of security, dates of conversion of debentures, warrants, call money dates and such other actions from time to time and submit necessary approval documents for the corporate actions. On receiving such intimation, NSDL provides the details of the holdings of the clients electronically to the issuer/R&T agent (as of the relevant cut-off date) for the purpose of corporate actions and distribution of corporate benefits. The issuer/R&T agent distributes dividend, interest or other monetary benefits directly to eligible beneficial owners on the basis of the list provided by the NSDL. The corporate benefits can also be distributed through NSDL with its concurrence.

The issuer/R&T agent may, if the benefits are in the form of securities, distribute such benefits to the clients through NSDL in the following cases:

❖ The newly created security is an eligible security.

❖ The concerned client has consented to receive the benefits through NSDL.

In such a case, the issuer/R&T agent provides allotment details of all clients to the NSDL. On receipt of these details, NSDL makes the necessary credit entries in the account of the client concerned. In certain cases such as splitting of shares, consolidation of shares, mergers, demergers, bonus shares, etc. corporate action is executed automatically as per the fixed ratio defined by the issuer/R&T agent, through the NSDL system. This feature is called "automatic corporate action."

SERVICE STANDARDS

The Depositories Act, 1996 requires that clients avail of the services of a depository through DPs. This requirement has created a new business entity – depository participant. In business, DP has to function in the following circumstances:

❖ Sensitive and demanding clients.

❖ Intense competition on the price front due to which the profit margins are under tremendous pressure.

❖ Thin profit margins require high volume of clients/transactions for operating the DP services profitably.

❖ High volume of business is error prone unless supported by appropriate systems and quality of manpower.

The prerequisites for attracting and retaining a high volume of business are the establishment of service standards in each area of service and consistently adhering to those standards. This chapter attempts to set out some pointers to these service standards, which the DPs may want to establish. The list is indicative and not exhaustive. The service standards may be changed/upgraded in response to client requirements and competitive market demands.

Office Ambience

The front office ambience should be pleasant and should be convenient for clients to conduct their transactions. The waiting space should be proportionate to the number of clients that may visit the office to conduct their business. The type of access to the different areas should match with the specific transaction requirements of the client. The following facilities should be available at every office/branch of DP:

- ❖ Provision to write instructions.
- ❖ Introductory literature/booklets.
- ❖ Display of office timings.
- ❖ Display of a list of services offered from the service centre/branch, i.e. whether opening an account/demat/remat/account transfer/pledge services are available at that branch.
- ❖ Latest list of ISINs available for dematerialization.
- ❖ Compulsory demat list.
- ❖ Display of deadline timings for various transactions.
- ❖ Settlement calendar and settlement numbers, if space for display is available.
- ❖ DP IDs, if possible.
- ❖ Rubber-stamp for cancellation of certificate.
- ❖ Inquiry counter for finding out balances in client account.
- ❖ Forms for nomination, opening an account and all other forms which are not handed over to the client at the time of opening an account.

Branch Office Empowerment

Modern communications technology and IT have made it possible to effectively decentralize operations even while operational reporting and supervision controls are maintained. Such decentralization requires empowerment of branch offices.

The ability of a branch office to give good service to a client is determined by the co-ordination and communication facilities between the head office and the branch. The head office should take care of informational needs of the branch. This should be given extra care if the branch office is not electronically connected to the head office. The head office should provide the following information on a regular/daily basis to the branch office to help the branch achieve customer satisfaction.

❖ ISIN list available for dematerialization.

❖ List of scrips included in the compulsory list.

❖ Adequate supply of account opening forms, nomination forms and other forms.

❖ Settlement calendar, settlement number and other settlement related information.

Regular feedback on transactions as given below:

❖ Status of account opening/account numbers.

❖ Status on demat requests.

❖ Return of rejected demat requests.

❖ Status of transactions executed with particular reference to failed transactions.

❖ Information on balance inquiries.

❖ Statement of transactions and holding.

❖ Information on credits arising out of corporate actions

❖ Address to which demat documents have to be sent if branch office is expected to send the documents directly.

Opening an Account

As in any service industry, the first point of contact is the most important point in customer relationship management. For investors the process of account opening is the first interaction with a DP. This is the stage at which the client interacts with the DP and one that will make a permanent impression about the servicing capabilities of the depository participant. Also, this is the stage at which the client may have several questions that need to be answered and proper guidance provided. The client should be given personal attention and should be helped in completing the account opening formalities without difficulty. The client must be made aware of the structure of fees for the services and other conditions must be explained in detail. Special attention should be given to the points listed below:

❖ Explain the information to be given in the application form. Clarification should be given on items like standing instructions, introduction, nomination, Permanent Account Number (PAN) of the Indian income tax department, importance of correct and complete bank account and address details, special care to be taken in case of joint accounts, Hindu Undivided Family (HUF) accounts, Non-Resident Indian (NRI) accounts, etc.

❖ For ease of operation and elimination of redundancies, the facility of standing instructions has been provided in the account opening form. This facility enables clients to give standing instructions to DPs, at the time of opening the account itself, for receiving securities to the credit of their accounts without any further instruction from them.

❖ Assure the client about the time by which the account will be opened and the account number communicated to him/her.

❖ Hand over the "delivery instructions book" with pre-printed serial number of the slips stamped with client-ID on the slips. The client should be made aware of the need and reasons to take care in preserving and using the book.

❖ Explain various other forms used in the depository system.

❖ Ensure that a copy of the agreement including schedule of charges is given to the client.

Demat Process

The demat process requires defacing of securities which will make the security certificate undeliverable unless the demat formalities are completed. Therefore, the client should be assisted in ascertaining whether the securities in question are available for dematerialization. Clients should be helped in filling up the demat request properly.

Demat rejection causes great inconvenience to the client. The DP should attend to this area with care and caution by ensuring the despatch of DRFs and certificates to R&T agents within seven days. In case of joint holdings, the clients should be informed about the availability of transposition cum demat facility. One of the important reasons for demat rejection is signature mismatch. Taking the following precaution can reduce this:

❖ If the client is aware that the signature with the company and signature of the client at time of opening the account vary significantly, the client should be advised to register the new signature with the company before demat is initiated.

Trading & Settlement

This is an area where the DP must take immense care while accepting and processing requests for transfer of securities from the account of his client to another account. The aspects listed below should be kept in mind:

❖ Ensure that the delivery instruction book given to each client has pre-printed serial numbers and Client-ID.

❖ Inform clients about the pay-in deadline of the stock exchange and the deadline of the DP.

❖ Inform clients about the future-dated instruction facility and encourage them to use this facility.

❖ Each DIS received should be inwarded correctly with the date and time stamp.

❖ Late stamp must be affixed on the instructions received after the expiry of the deadline set by the DP.

❖ Ensure the correctness of execution date on the DIS.

❖ Verify market type and settlement number details for market transfers.

❖ Ensure that the signature on the DIS matches with the records of the DP.

❖ Ensure that the signatures of all holders are obtained in case of joint accounts.

❖ If the client has not issued "standing instructions", he should be made aware that instructions will be required to receive the credits into the account on purchase of shares.

❖ Clients should be made aware of the facility to freeze accounts.

General Services

Since clients are free to choose their DPs depending on criteria like service standards, convenience of location and affordability, providing efficient and timely services is important for all DPs if they have to compete effectively. Factors in general services that they should keep in mind include:

❖ Timely issue of transaction statements.

❖ 30 days notice to clients regarding changes in the structure of fees.

❖ Undertake changes in client master details whenever required and intimate the clients accordingly. This will help the investor in receiving all cash corporate benefits like dividends, interest warrants, redemption payments, etc. at the new address with immediate effect.

❖ Provide the latest list of companies available for demat.

❖ Provide multiple channels of inquiry to help clients obtain answers to their questions relating to their account or to give instructions. For example, enquiries can be handled on the telephone; exclusive inquiry counters can be set up or as a matter of routine, information about the balances in the account after execution of the instructions can be given on the "instruction acknowledgement slip".

❖ Give an acknowledgement for any document that a client submits.

❖ Give the client a feedback on the status of his instructions, especially failed instructions.

❖ Maintain the critical instructions of clients and give them a feedback on each one of them.

❖ Provide complete and timely information to the client about the new services/facilities introduced by the depository and/or DP.

❖ Give notice to the client about any change in the charge structure as prescribed in the DP client agreement.

❖ Provide a list of companies with poor performance in confirming demat requests.

All the operations of a DP should be conducted with transparency and consistent service attitude to foster continuity in the commercial relationship. This is absolutely essential in a competitive environment.

BENEFITS & SAFETY

Until the mid-1990s, the legal and regulatory framework, within which the securities market functioned in India, had weaknesses resulting from fragmentation of authority and multiplicity of rules and regulations. This created inefficiency in enforcement of the regulations. It also led to low efficiency in the allocation and utilization of resources between savers/investors and industrial investment. The formalities in the process of issuing securities kept the cost of issue as well as trading quite high. Also, settlement of trades was cumbersome and marked by delay, as it required physical movement of securities thus reducing liquidity in the hands of investors. The interests of the investors were subjugated to those of the market intermediaries. All these factors hampered the growth and vitality of the capital market as a whole.

To improve efficiency of the market, enhance transparency, check unfair trade practices and ensure international standards in market practices necessitated by the entry of foreign financial institutions, several measures to liberalize, regulate and develop the securities market were introduced during the mid-1990s. These applied to the primary as well as the secondary markets. Additionally, the application of IT has made the task of operations and supervision of the new system possible and efficient.

Prior to the setting up of the NSE, trading on stock exchanges in India took place without the use of information technology for immediate matching or recording of trades. The system was called "out cry" – where bids and offers were matched by voice. The practice of physical trading imposed limits on trading volumes as well as the speed with which the new information was incorporated into prices. Unscrupulous operators used this information asymmetry to manipulate the market. An exploitative practice called "gala" was rampant. Some unscrupulous brokers made a profit by quoting a higher price to their clients than the price at which the securities were actually bought and paying a lesser price than the price at which the securities were actually sold. The client had no means to verify the actual price since there was no access to intra day price changes that were happening at the trading ring, as only brokers and their authorized assistants could enter the ring. The electronic and now fully online trading introduced by the NSE has made such manipulation difficult. It has also improved liquidity and made the entire operation more transparent and efficient.

The system of transfer of ownership of physical securities was grossly inefficient as every transfer involved physical movement of securities to the issuer for registration. The change of ownership was evidenced by an endorsement on the security certificate. In many cases the process of transfer took much longer than the two months stipulated in the Companies Act, 1956, and a significant proportion of transactions ended up as bad delivery due to faulty compliance of paper work, theft, forgery, mutilation of certificates and other irregularities. All this added to costs and delays in settlement restricted liquidity and made redressal of investor grievances time consuming.

The introduction of the depository system was an important step in the reform process. The benefits of the depository system are thus related to removal of many of the inefficiencies and problems of the erstwhile system and also to the various efficiencies created by it. Depository provides instantaneous electronic transfer of securities. This ensures transfer of securities with speed, accuracy and safety. Securities in the depository mode are dematerialized and ownership records are maintained in a book-entry form. In order to streamline both the stages of settlement process, the Depositories Act, 1996 provides for transfer of the ownership of securities by book entry without their physical movement between seller, buyer and issuer. The depository system thus removes some of the physical, structural as well as systemic risks that are inherent to the physical securities based markets.

Benefits

The direct and indirect benefits of the depository system are described in detail below. In the depository system, the ownership and transfer of securities takes place by means of electronic book entries. At the outset, this system rids the capital market of the dangers related to handling of paper.

Elimination of bad deliveries: In the depository environment, once the holdings of an investor are dematerialized, the question of bad delivery does not arise, i.e. their transfer cannot be rejected due to defect in the quality of the security. All possible reasons for objecting to transfer of title due to deficiencies associated with transfer deed and share certificates are completely eliminated since both transfer deed and share certificates are eliminated in depository system.

Elimination of all risks associated with physical certificates: Dealing in physical securities has associated security risks of theft of stocks, mutilation or loss of certificates during movements to and from the registrars. These expose the investor to the cost of obtaining duplicate certificates, advertisements, etc. Such problems do not arise in the depository environment.

No stamp duty: There is no stamp duty for transfer of equity instruments and units of mutual funds in the depository system. In the case of physical shares, stamp duty of 0.5 per cent is payable on transfer of shares.

Immediate transfer and registration of securities: In the depository environment, once the securities are credited to the investor's account on pay out, he/she becomes the legal owner of the securities. There is no further need to send it to the company's registrar for transfer of ownership or registration which is necessary in the case of physical securities. This process normally takes longer than the statutory prescribed period of two months thus exposing the investor to opportunity cost of delay in transfer and to risk of loss in transit. To overcome this, the normally accepted practice is to hold the securities in street names, i.e. not to register the change of ownership. However, if the investors miss a book closure, the securities are not good for delivery and the investor would also stand to lose his corporate entitlements.

Faster settlement cycle: With the introduction of the electronic form of settlement, the Indian capital markets have moved from a 15 day long settlement cycle to T+2 settlement cycle, where the settlement takes place on the second day from the day of trading. This enables faster turnover of stock and enhances liquidity with the investor.

Buyer or seller is secured: In the physical environment, the seller was secured since the sale proceeds were always fully realizable but the buyer was not, since it was not certain whether shares purchased will be transferred or not. The market principle that 'the buyer is king' did not apply to the capital market. This situation has now been corrected. After settlement, pay in or pay out is on the same day for scripless trading, which means the investor gets his securities or the cash/cheque immediately, on purchase or sale of securities as the case may be. Securities stand transferred in the investor's name on the very next day. No courier/postal charges are necessary as there is no need to send the shares for transfer.

Facility for freezing/locking of investor accounts: This enables the investor to make his account non-operational, for instance if the investor is abroad.

Faster disbursement of non-cash corporate benefits: NSDL provides for direct account, thereby ensuring faster disbursement and avoiding the risk of certificates getting lost in transit.

Reduction in rate of interest on loans: Some banks provide this benefit against pledging dematerialized securities. Dematerialized securities eliminate hassles/risks like getting securities registered in their name at the time of book closure if the pledge defaults in repayment. Also eliminated is the risk of stocks coming under objections when they are sent to the company's registrar for registration, if the pledge has to be invoked.

Increase in the maximum limit of advances: This has increased from Rs. 10 lakh to Rs. 20 lakh per borrower. There is also a reduction in the minimum margin from 50 per cent to 25 per cent by banks for advances against dematerialized securities as per the Monetary and Credit Policy of Reserve Bank of India for the first half of 1998-99.

Reduction in brokerage: Since introduction of electronic settlement of securities there has been a significant fall in the brokerage charged for brokers for effecting and settling trades of investors at the stock exchanges. This benefit is given to investors as dealing in dematerialized securities reduces their back office cost of handling paper. It also eliminates the risk of being the introducing broker.

Reduction in handling huge volumes of paper: In the physical environment, every purchase or sale of securities involved handling and passing on papers to the next entity. The amount of paper handled increased with the volume of transactions. However, in the depository environment, except for the delivery instruction to be given by the client/broker, there is no other paper movement. NSDL has permitted the use of CDs to give debit instructions for large volumes of transactions.

NSDL has recently introduced a common internet based platform, SPEED-e, for clients of all DPs so that clients can issue instructions to their DPs through the Internet. Using SPEED-e the client need not write delivery instructions or visit its DP for issuing instructions. Clients can monitor the status of instructions given by them on SPEED-e on Internet.

Periodic status reports: DPs need to provide periodic reports to investors on their holdings and transactions. This leads to better management control on the part of the servicing agency and better information for the investors.

Dematerialized securities can be delivered in the physical segment: Securities forming a part of the SEBI specified compulsory list (wherein delivery in demat form is mandatory for all categories of investors) can be delivered in physical form in the stock exchanges connected to NSDL & CDSL. This requirement is applicable to physical deliveries wherein the number of securities is less than 500.

Elimination of problems related to change of address of investors, transmission, etc.: In the case of change of address or transmission of demat shares, investors are saved from undergoing the entire change procedure with each company or registrar. The investors only have to inform their DP about the change along with all relevant documents. The required changes are effected in the database of all the companies where the investor is a registered holder of securities. The investor will receive all cash corporate benefits like dividends, interest warrants, redemption money, etc. at the new address with immediate effect.

Elimination of problems related to nomination: An account holder can get securities in all companies transmitted/transferred to his account by completing formalities with a single entity i.e. the DP. He need not deal with all companies individually.

Elimination of problems related to selling securities on behalf of a minor: NSDL system provides facilities for opening demat accounts in the names of minors and holding their securities in their own name. Since, under the Contract Act, 1872, minors are not eligible to enter into contracts on their own, the account in the name of minor is required to be operated by their guardian. The guardian may be the natural guardian, guardian appointed by a will or a guardian appointed by an order of the court. The minor's guardian will be eligible to open, operate and close the account on behalf of the minor. The guardian(s) would sign the instruction slips to be given to the depository participant, on behalf of the minor. A minor however cannot be a joint account holder. Non cash corporate benefits arising out of bonus/rights allotment of shares are credited to the account of the minor. Cash corporate benefits will be issued by the concerned issuer of securities in the name of the minor.

Convenient consolidation of accounts: If multiple accounts have been opened by an investor, all the accounts can be consolidated into one account by giving instructions to the DP. In the case of physical certificates, consolidation of folios required correspondence with all the companies individually.

Convenient portfolio monitoring: The client can monitor his/her portfolio by checking a single statement of holding/transaction.

Newer services: Opportunities like pledge/hypothecation and stock lending are given specifically by the depository system.

Increased volumes: Due to ease in transaction and reduced costs, many players have entered/increased their transactions. This helps in improving liquidity.

Safety

NSDL has implemented various checks and measures in the depository system to ensure safety of the investors' holdings. These include:

* ❖ A DP can begin operations only after registration by SEBI. The registration process is based on the recommendation from NSDL after undertaking its own independent assessment and evaluation. SEBI regulations have prescribed fulfillment of several criteria for becoming a DP.

❖ Depository participants are allowed to effect any debit and credit to an account only on the basis of valid instructions from the client.

❖ There are periodic inspections into the activities of both DPs and R&T agents by NSDL. This also includes records based on which the debit/credit is affected.

❖ The data interchange between NSDL and its business partners are protected by standard protection measures such as encryption. This is a SEBI requirement.

❖ There are no direct communication links between two business partners and all communications between two business partners are routed through NSDL.

❖ All investors have a right to receive their transaction statement periodically from the DP.

❖ Every month NSDL forwards a statement of account to a random sample of investors as a counter check.

❖ In the depository, the depository holds the investor accounts on trust. Therefore, if the DP goes bankrupt, the creditors of the DP will have no access to the holdings in the name of the clients of the DP. These investors can then either rematerialize their holdings or transfer them to a different account held with another DP.

❖ NSDL has a complete record of the client's transactions in addition to the records of the DP.

Certification in depository operations: NSDL has introduced a certification program in depository operations. This has been made compulsory for all DPs. Depository participants of NSDL are required to have persons who have passed the NCFM Depository Module Examination at their service centers. NSDL levies a penalty on DPs if NCFM qualified personnel are not appointed in at least 75 per cent of the total service centers (other than drop boxes) of the DPs.

Investor grievances: All grievances of the investors are to be resolved by the concerned business partner within 30 days. If they fail to do so, the investor has the right to approach NSDL at the investor grievance cell of NSDL which would work towards resolution of the grievance.

Insurance cover: NSDL has taken a comprehensive insurance policy to protect the interest of the investors in cases of failure of the DP to resolve a genuine loss.

Computer and communication infrastructure: NSDL and its business partners use hardware, software and communication systems which conform to industry standards. Further, the systems are accepted by NSDL only after a rigorous testing procedure. NSDL's central system comprises an IBM mainframe system with a back-up facility and a remote disaster back-up site. Details with regard to back-up system are given in the following paragraphs.

Machine level back up: The IBM mainframe situated at 'Trade World' (NSDL's office in Mumbai) in which the data are processed has adequate redundancy built into its configuration. There is a standby Central Processing Unit (CPU) to which processing can be switched over if the main system CPU fails. The disk has RAID implementation which ensures that a single point failure will not lead to loss of data. The system has spare disk configuration where data is automatically copied from the main disk when the first failure is encountered (due to RAID implementation – first failure does not result in loss of data). All network components like routers, communication controllers, etc. have on-line redundancy and thus a failure does not result in loss of transaction.

Disaster back up site: In addition, a disaster back up site, equipped with a computer identical to the mainframe computer & computing resources, has been set up at a remote location away from Mumbai. NSDL generally operates from its Mumbai office but often operations are conducted from the disaster back up site to ensure that the disaster site is always in working condition.

Back-up in case of power failure: Continuity in power supply to the main systems is assured by a dual Uninterrupted Power Supply (UPS) for the IBM-mainframe and related components wherein the two UPSs are connected in tandem. In case of failure of the primary UPS, the secondary UPS takes over instantaneously and thus, there is no interruption in operation.

Periodic review: The NSDL hardware, software and communication systems are continuously reviewed in order to make them more secure. These reviews are a part of an ongoing exercise wherein security considerations are given as much importance as operational efficiency. These safety measures taken by NSDL have to be complemented by a similar set of measures at the end of each member of the depository system like the DPs, issuers and R&T agents.

In short, a depository actually refers to an institution registered by the National Securities Depository Limited (NSDL), Central Depository Services (India) Ltd. (CDSL), and SEBI which holds securities in electronic form instead of material form on behalf of investors, such as the Stock Holding Corporation.

In simple terms a depository is an organization which holds securities of investors, on request in electronic form through a registered depository participant. It can be compared with a bank. It holds securities in an account, transfers securities between accounts on the instructions of the account holder, facilitates transfers of ownership without having to handle securities and facilitates safe-keeping of shares. In 2009 the minimum net worth required by SEBI for registering a DP was Rs. 100 crore.

Table 2.1 shows the comparison of costs for an investor selling shares worth Rs. 10,000.

Table 2.1   Cost of an Investor Selling Shares Worth Rs. 10,000

Item	Physical (Rs)	NSDL (Demat) (Rs)	Savings (Rs)
Brokerage	75-100	50-75	25-50
Stamp duty	50	-	50
Postal charges	10-30	-	10-30
Company objection	10-30	-	10-30
Settlement charges	-	5-10	5-10
Custody (5 Years)	-	25-30	25-30
Total			35-100

Though there are some reservations from certain persons and organizations regarding the success of the depository system, generally it is felt that the system has enhanced the efficiency of the Indian securities market and benefits investors by bringing about greater security and safety in share transactions, improved liquidity of the secondary market transactions and better means of ownership.

Most of the above discussions on depositories and Depository Participants (DPs) have been directly taken from an electronic publication of the National Securities Depository Limited (NSDL) titled "Hand Book for NSDL Depository Operations Module." NSDL has also developed application software for scientific and smooth functioning of the depository system. One may refer to the website www.nse-india.com for more details.

*It is mandatory for all participants to install "Server Management Software". Participants may consult NSDL if a specific brand of server/desktop server does not have its own Server Management Software. Besides the above discussions, the charge structure of NSDL for depository participation and procedure for qualifying as DPs are also discussed in the hand-book referred to. Readers are requested to visit the above website for more details. The authors are grateful to NSE and NSDL for allowing them to refer to their publications in this chapter of the book.

Now let us turn to some other aspects of stock related understandings. These aspects are often frequently used in the vocabulary of market operators and the general investor.

RELATIVE STRENGTH INDEX

It is an indicator invented by J. Welles Wilder, which is used to determine overbought or oversold and divergent situations.

Overbought refers to a stock that has risen sharply in price or to the market as a whole after a period of vigorous buying which, it is sometimes said, has left prices "too high".

Oversold situation is the reverse of overbought. It refers to the situation where a single security or a market is believed to have declined to an unreasonable level. Usually, this is where everybody starts screaming "scam" and, if they shriek loud enough, SEBI starts a probe. Sometimes it also applies to overbought situations.

Diversification means the acquisition of a group of assets in which returns on the assets are not directly related over time. Proper investment diversification is intended to reduce the risk inherent in particular securities. An investor seeking diversification for a securities portfolio would purchase securities of firms that are not similarly affected by the same variables. For example, an investor would not want to combine large investment positions in airlines, trucking and automobile manufacturing because each industry is significantly affected by oil prices and interest rates. Of course, diversification is essentially for investors not traders. A lot of thought goes into deciding on investment avenues because one may not look so much at the present status of the industry but at its short- or mid-term future. This, in turn, requires that one takes into an account innumerable factors that could affect the health of the industry. Of course, one can always take an analyst's help, but one should also learn to recognize factors that may impact a particular industry. This calls for clear thinking and common sense.

DIP

A drop in the price of a stock is temporarily makes it the ideal time to buy the stock. A precept common to all businesses: buy low sell high. Never forget, 'highs' and 'lows' are relative not absolute. Any increase over one's purchase price is a gain, and vice versa. One usually gets into trouble when giving in to the thoroughly human instinct for the gap to increase (in case of gains) or decrease (in case of losses). One should book profits (or cut your losses) as one goes; should not allow them to accumulate too long.

DIFFERENTIAL PRICING

Pricing of an issue where one category is offered shares at a price different from the other category is called differential pricing. In the DIP guidelines differential pricing is allowed only if the securities to applicants in the firm allotment category are at a price higher than the price at which the net offer to the public is made. The net offer to the public means the offer made to the Indian public and does not include firm allotments or reservations or promoters' contributions.

STOCK SCREENER

It is a tool investors can use to filter stocks given certain criteria of their choice. According to Inestopedia (a stock market related website), by using a stock screening tool an investor is able to follow a strict set of criteria that he or she requires prior to investing in a company. For example, an investor could screen stocks by entering the following criteria: "listed on the NYSE", "in the telecommunications industry", "has a P/E ratio between 15-25", and "has an annual EPS growth of at least 15 per cent for the past three years". The screener would then produce a list of stocks that display all these attributes. In this example stocks are screened by using only four criteria; however, you can screen stocks by as many criteria as the particular screener you are using will allow. The stock screener has replaced many days' worth of research with a few clicks of a mouse.

SPLIT

A split is book entry wherein the face value of the share is altered to create a greater number of shares outstanding without calling for fresh capital or altering the share capital account. For example, if a company announces a two-way split, it means that a share of face value Rs. 10 is split into two shares of face value of Rs. 5 each and a person holding one share now holds two shares.

In India, the process of splitting equity shares into lower denominations started during the second half of 1999 after withdrawal of the 1983 government circular of issue price guidelines.

Since then, some companies split their shares worth Rs. 100 into shares worth Rs. 10. But the multinational company, Hindustan Lever (HLL) took this even further. On 21st February, 2000, the company told the stock exchanges about its decision of splitting its shares worth Rs. 10 into ten shares with a face value of Re. 1.

GOING PUBLIC

When a company collects money through a first time offering of its equity shares to the general investing public it is known as 'going public.' With the public offering of its equity shares, the company turns into public limited company.

EQUITY FINANCING, ELIGIBLE SECURITY AND DILUTION

The system through which a company collects funds by selling its new equity shares, is called 'equity financing'. According to the regulations of SEBI of 1997, a company should have offered dividend for consecutive three years before going in for equity finance.

When for the purpose of loans, shares, debentures or bonds are mortgaged with banks or loan giving authorities then those securities are called 'eligible securities'. Further, those securities should be listed with share markets and banks.

When new shares or converted shares from other securities of a company are sold in the markets, the Earning Per Share (EPS) and book value (both discussed in Chapter 4) are influenced by those sales. That influence is known as 'dilution'.

TRADING ON EQUITY

Companies generally collect additional required capital by offering new issues to the public. Sometimes, companies without offering public issue offer shares or debenture to the existing shareholders for additional capital requirement. If the profits of the company are more than the rates of interest of the preference shares or debentures, then the ordinary shareholders are entitled to get part of the surplus profit, so the dividend of the ordinary shareholders increases. Generally, this increase in the rate of dividend of the ordinary shareholders is called 'trading on equity'. This can be explained more clearly with the following illustration: Let the equity capital of a company be Rs. 1,000 and the rate of profit is 20 per cent. If the shareholders have paid up fully for the total capital of the company, the shareholders will get dividend at the rate of 20 per cent. But if the shareholders paid Rs. 500 of the capital and the balance Rs. 500 is paid by the preference share shareholders at a rate of 15 per cent interest, then the cost of interest for the preference shareholders will be Rs. 75. Therefore, for ordinary equity shareholders part of the company's profit will be (Rs. 200 − 75) = Rs. 125. Hence, the ordinary shareholders get Rs. 125, and then the rate of dividend will be 25 per cent instead of normal 20 per cent. In this way the ordinary shareholders get additional dividend at the rate of 5 per cent and the process of gaining this additional dividend by the ordinary shareholders is known as 'trading on equity'.

EURO ISSUE AND AMERICAN DEPOSITORY RECEIPTS AND INDIAN DEPOSITORY RECEIPTS

When an Indian company needs to raise its capital, it generally goes to the public with a new issue or bonds within the domestic markets. But after liberalization of the Indian economy during the early nineties, it appears that some companies also float a new issue in the European and American markets especially when a company needs foreign exchange for capital investments or modernization of its plants and equipment. It is now permitted to raise funds from foreign markets through new issues. Earlier, Indian companies used to get these funds from the Reserve Bank of India (RBI) as a long term loan or by purchasing foreign exchange. Since liberalization of Indian economy in 1991, Indian companies have been permitted to raise funds from foreign markets through new issues. These issues when floated in European Markets, are called Euro-issue or Global Depository Receipts (GDR) and when they are floated in the United States of America, they are called American Depository Receipts (ADR).

In an internet article, Lubinisha Saha wrote that 'Indian companies are permitted to raise foreign currency resources through two main sources, the issue of Foreign Currency Convertible Bonds (FCCBs) more commonly known as Euro Issues, and the issue of ordinary equity shares through depository receipts, namely, GDRs or ADRs, from foreign investors. An ADR is a negotiable US Certificate representing ownership of shares in a non-US corporation. ADRs were specifically designed to facilitate the purchase, holding and sale of non-US securities by US investors, and to provide a corporate finance vehicle for non-US companies. GDRs may be defined as a global finance option that allows an issuer to raise capital simultaneously in two or more markets through a global offering.'

Resource mobilization by Indian companies through Euro issues by the way of FCCBs, GDRs and ADRs have free convertibility outside India. In February 2002, the Reserve Bank of India permitted two way fungibles for ADRs/GDRs, which means that investors in any company that has issued ADRs or GDRs can freely convert the ADRs or GDRs into underlying domestic shares. They can also reconvert the domestic shares into ADRs or GDRs, depending on the direction of price change in the stock.'

Euro Issue or GDR Issue

After opening up of the Indian economy in 1991, while the foreign companies started to take an interest in investing in Indian trade and industry, Indian companies started to raise funds from overseas markets through new capital issues for imports of plant and machineries and for other needs of modernization. These capital issues by the Indian companies in overseas markets are called Euro-issues. Euro-issues have two parts, one is known as Global Depository Receipts (GDR) and the other is known as bond issues as we have seen above.

After the liberalization policy of the Indian economy announced by the government in 1991, the government came out with its first regulation policy for Euro-issue in 1992. After that the regulation policy was altered or corrected in favour of the issuing companies. A brief description of the regulation policies is given below:

Policies of Euro issue of 1992

❖ Companies should get prior approval from the Government of India.

❖ Financial performances of the issuing companies should be good for three consecutive years.

❖ There will be no lock-in period for the issuing certificates.

Policies of Euro issue announced in the month of May 1992

❖ There should not be more than two Euro-issue in a year

❖ At least 85 per cent of the funds collected through the Euro-issue should be spent on importing capital goods, purchase of plant and machineries and repayment of foreign exchange etc.

❖ The expenditure accounts for last four months should be published.

Policies of Euro issue announced in the month of October 1999

❖ There is no need to spend the entire amount of funds collected within one year.

❖ The audited report of expenditure should be announced with the GDR issue.

❖ No promised warrants should be announced with the GDR issue.

❖ The funds collected can be invested in foreign markets or in overseas assets.

❖ Companies or organizations can take part in the Euro-issue of specified financial institutions on behalf of small and medium companies.

❖ The basis of the Euro-issue should be Profit Before Tax (PBT) and Earning Per Share (EPS) of the issuing company.

Policies of Euro issue announced in the month of February 2000

❖ No permission is needed for companies making global floatation (GDRs/ADRs). No track record scrutiny.

❖ After issue, companies have to inform the Ministry of Finance and RBI within 30 days.

❖ Employ Stock OPtion (ESOP) by software and information technologies companies (IT Co. S) should also be automatic. Private placement eligible under automatic route.

❖ Automatic approval for the companies expanding capital base.

❖ Approval under Foreign Direct Investment (FDI) policy, Companies Act, limits on overseas investments, the automatic route will not be extended to foreign convertible bond issues, which will continue to be governed by the existing guidelines.

❖ Rules on retention of funds abroad, repatriation and end-use stay.

American Depository Receipts (ADRs)

A significant portion of offerings by non-USA companies in the USA market are in the form of ADRs which are also called American Depository Shares (ADS).

ADRs are negotiable receipts issued to investors by an authorized depository, normally a USA bank or depository, in lieu of shares of the foreign company which are actually held by the depository.

The ADRs can be listed and traded in a USA based stock exchange and help the Indian company to be known in highly liquid USA stock exchanges. The ADRs also help USA based and other foreign investors to reap the twin benefits of having shareholding in a high growth Indian company and the convenience of trading in a highly liquid and well known stock market.

The Indian companies have to go through the depository route as they are prohibited by law from listing rupee denominated shares directly in foreign stock markets. Therefore, they issue such shares to a depository which has an office within India. These shares remain in India with a custodian. Against the underlying shares, the depository issues dollar denominated receipts to the foreign investors. The foreign investors can then sell these receipts in the foreign stock exchanges or bank to the depository and get delivery of the rupee denominated shares which can be sold in Indian markets. This is generally done if institutional investors with a presence in both India and the USA see an arbitrage opportunity arising out of difference in prices on the USA and Indian stock exchanges.

There are some differences between ADRs and GDRs. ADRs are listed on an American stock exchange. Securities and Exchange Commission (SEC) – the market regulator – monitors the issues. GDRs or global depository receipts are listed in a stock exchange other than American stock exchanges, say Luxembourg or London.

A listing in America involves adhering to very strict disclosure and accounting norms. The accounts of the company have to be presented according to the US General Accepted Accounting Principle (GAAP). US GAAP requires representing a combined balance sheet of all group companies, and not just of the company going for the issue. Typically, a good company can expect its reported profits according to Indian accounting rules to be eroded by 20 per cent to 30 per cent under US GAAP. Against this, the disclosure requirements of GDR issues are throughout less stringent.

An ADR listing also allows the famed American retail investors to partake in the offering and leads to wider interest and better valuations of a company's stock, thus enhancing shareholder value.

Also, the Indian company can acquire USA companies against issue of shares. The GDR market is mainly an institutional market, with lower liquidity.

ADRs are quoted in US dollars and are generally structured so that the number of foreign companies' securities will result in a trading price for each ADR in the range of $ 10 to $ 30. The multiple or fraction that an ADR is of the underlying shares is determined with this price range in mind.

The depository receives dividends directly form the Indian company in Indian currency, Rupees, and issues dividend cheques to ADR holders in dollars. When an ADR is sold back to a depository, it is considered as cancelled and the stock of ADRs is not replenished.

The Indian company which wants to go in for an ADR issue must get its group accounts consolidated and audited according to US GAAP by an independent agency. It also has to appoint a team of legal and compliance experts as well as lead managers and investment bankers to the issue. The teams will then have to prepare the draft prospectus or the registration statement which will be submitted to the SEC. The SEC reverts with its comments and requirements, and this goes on till SEC is sufficiently satisfied with the information given.

The ready draft prospectus is to be distributed to prospective investors. Simultaneously, the company will also have to start the application process to list with the particular stock exchange.

With the draft prospectus ready, the company can launch its road show (discussed below) or the setting exercise for getting subscription to the issue. Prospective investors give their price and amount indications to the lead managers to the issue. Based on investors' response, the lead managers fix the price of the issue, which is intimated to the Securities and Exchange Commission (SEC) and the concerned stock exchanges. With their convergence, the issue is listed.

Types of ADR programs

When a company establishes an American Depositary Receipt program, it must decide what exactly it wants out of the program, and how much time, effort and resources it is willing to commit. For this reason, there are different types of programs that a company can choose.

Unsponsored shares

Unsponsored shares are a form of Level I ADRs that trade on the over the counter market. These shares are issued in accordance with market demand, and the foreign company has no formal agreement with a depositary bank. Unsponsored ADRs are often issued by more than one depositary bank. Each depository services only the ADRs it has issued.

Due to a recent change in the SEC rules making it easier to issue Level I depositary receipts, both sponsored and unsponsored, hundreds of new ADRs have been issued since the rule went into effect in October 2008. The majority of these were unsponsored Level I ADRs and now approximately half of all ADR programs in existence are unsponsored.

Level 1

Level 1 depositary receipts are the lowest level of sponsored ADRs that can be issued. When a company issues sponsored ADRs, it has one designated depositary who also acts as its transfer agent. Most transfer agents are banks or trust companies but sometimes a company acts as its own transfer agent.

Transfer agents perform three main functions:

1. Issue and cancel certificates to reflect changes in ownership. For example, when a company declares a stock dividend or stock split, the transfer agent issues new shares. Transfer agents keep records of who owns a company's stocks and bonds and how those stocks and bonds are held – whether by the owner in certificate form, by the company in book-entry form, or by the investor's brokerage firm in street name. They also keep records of how many shares or bonds each investor owns.

2. They act as an intermediary for the company. A transfer agent may also serve as the company's paying agent to pay out interest, cash and stock dividends, or other distributions to stock- and bond-holders. In addition, transfer agents act as a proxy agent (sending out proxy materials), exchange agent (exchanging a company's stock or bonds in a merger), tender agent (tendering shares in a tender offer), and mailing agent (mailing the company's quarterly, annual and other reports).

3. They handle lost, destroyed, or stolen certificates. Transfer agents help shareholders and bond-holders when a stock or bond certificate has been lost, destroyed, or stolen.

A majority of American depositary receipt programs that are currently trading are issued through a Level 1 program. This is the most convenient way for a foreign company to have its equity traded in the United States.

Level 1 shares can only be traded on the OTC market and the company has minimal reporting requirements with the SEC. The company is not required to issue quarterly or annual reports in compliance with US GAAP. However, the company must have a security listed on one or more stock exchanges in a foreign jurisdiction and must publish in English on its website its annual report in the form required by the laws of the country of incorporation, organization or domicile. Companies with shares trading under a Level 1 program may decide to upgrade their program to a Level 2 or Level 3 program for better exposure in the United States markets.

Level 2 (listed)

Level 2 depositary receipt programs are more complicated for a foreign company. When a foreign company wants to set up a Level 2 program, it must file a registration statement with the US SEC and under SEC regulations. In addition, the company is required to file a Form 20-F annually. Form 20-F is the basic equivalent of an annual report (Form 10-K) for a US company. In their filings, the company is required to follow US GAAP standards.

The advantage that the company has by upgrading their program to Level 2 is that the shares can be listed on a US stock exchange. These exchanges include the New York Stock Exchange (NYSE), NASDAQ, and the American Stock Exchange (AMEX).

While listed on these exchanges, the company must meet the exchange's listing requirement. If it fails to do so, it may be delisted and forced to downgrade its ADR program.

Level 3 (offering)

A Level 3 American depositary receipt program is the highest level a foreign company can sponsor. Because of this distinction, the company is required to adhere to stricter rules that are similar to those followed by U.S. companies.

Setting up a Level 3 program means that the foreign company is not only taking steps to permit shares from its home market to be deposited into an ADR program and traded in the U.S.; it is actually issuing shares to raise capital. In accordance with this offering, the company is required to file a Form F-1, which is the format for an offering prospectus for the shares. They must also file a Form 20-F annually and must adhere to US GAAP standards. In addition, any material information given to shareholders in the home market must be filed with the SEC through Form 8K.

Foreign companies with Level 3 programs will often issue material that is more informative and more accommodating to their U.S. shareholders because they rely on them for capital. Overall, foreign companies with a Level 3 program set up are the easiest on which to find information.

Restricted programs

Foreign companies that want their stock to be limited to being traded by only certain individuals may set up a restricted program. There are two SEC rules that allow this type of issuance of shares in the U.S.: Rule 144-A and Regulation S. ADR programs operating under one of these two rules make up approximately 30 per cent of all issued ADRs.

Some foreign companies will set up an ADR program under SEC Rule 144(a). This Form 10-K's provision makes the issuance of shares a private placement. Shares of companies registered under Rule 144-A are restricted stock and may only be issued to or traded by Qualified Institutional Buyers (QIBs).

US public shareholders are generally not permitted to invest in these ADR programs, and most are held exclusively through the Depository Trust & Clearing Corporation, so there is often very little information on these companies.

Regulation S

The other way to restrict the trading of depositary shares to US public investors is to issue them under the terms of SEC Regulation S. This regulation means that the shares are not, and will not be registered with any United States securities regulation authority. Regulation S shares cannot be held or traded by any "US Person" as defined by SEC Regulation S rules. The shares are registered and issued to offshore, non-US residents. Regulation S ADRs can be merged into a Level 1 program after the restriction period has expired, and the foreign issuer elects to do this.

Sourcing ADRs

One can either source new ADRs by depositing the corresponding domestic shares of the company with the depositary bank that administers the ADR program or, instead, one can obtain existing ADRs in the secondary market. The latter can be achieved either by purchasing the ADRs on a US stock exchange or via purchasing the underlying domestic shares of the company on their primary exchange and then swapping them for ADRs; these swaps are called 'crossbook swaps' and on many occasions account for the bulk of ADR secondary trading. This is especially true in the case of trading in ADRs of UK companies where creation of new ADRs attracts a 1.5 per cent Stamp Duty Reserve Tax (SDRT) charge by the UK government; sourcing existing ADRs in the secondary market (either via crossbook swaps or on exchange) instead is not subject to SDRT.

ADR termination

Most ADR programs are subject to possible termination. Termination of the ADR agreement will result in cancellation of all the depositary receipts, and a subsequent delisting from all exchanges where they trade. The termination can be at the discretion of the foreign issuer or the depositary bank, but is typically at the request of the issuer. There may be a number of reasons why ADRs terminate, but in most cases the foreign issuer is undergoing some type of reorganization or merger.

Owners of ADRs are typically notified in writing at least thirty days prior to a termination. Once notified, an owner can surrender the ADRs and take delivery of the foreign securities represented by the receipt, or do nothing. If an ADR holder elects to take possession of the underlying foreign shares, there is no guarantee the shares will trade on any US exchange. The holder of the foreign shares would have to find a broker who has trading authority in the foreign market where those shares trade. If the owner continues to hold the ADR past the effective date of termination, the depositary bank will continue to hold the foreign deposited securities and collect dividends, but will cease distributions to ADR owners. Usually up to one year after the effective date of the termination, the depositary bank will liquidate and allocate the proceeds to those respective clients. Many US brokerages can continue to hold foreign stock, but may lack the ability to trade it overseas.

Road show

When a company plans to float a new issue it calls a press conference where company directors explain all aspects of the issue and answer any questions about the company's past, present and future plans posed by journalists, investors and other related persons.

In the overseas markets, when a company conducts this type of press conference before a Euro-issue or GDR and ADR issue, then the press conference is known as a 'road show'.

ADR is a less popular instrument of raising funds from the foreign market than GDR.

Advantage of Euro-issues (GDRs/ADRs)

It is beneficial to invest in Euro-issues of blue-chip companies. A company can sell its shares at the same price that prevailed in the Indian markets during the time of the Euro-issue. So, the equity capital of the company does not increase, but a fat premium is also available.

Expenditure on dividends happens to be comparatively low as dividends are given on the face value of the shares. That is on value which is inscribed on the share certificate at the time of the initial public offer in India.

Euro-issue has become an easy instrument to draw capital money from the overseas market and has also opened a route for publicity for the Indian companies on foreign soil. The benefits can be illustrated by the following example:

A Rs. 10 share of Reliance Industries is sold at Rs. 300 in a foreign market, that is, it is sold at a premium of Rs. 290. If the dividends are given at the rate of Rs. 50 per cent of the face value of Rs. 10, then the expense on dividend per share turns out to be only Rs. 5. Whereas, if the company takes a loan of Rs. 3,000 at an interest rate of 15 to 20 per cent from a bank or financial institution, then the company would have to pay Rs. 45 to Rs. 60 as the interest. Therefore, the company saves Rs. 40 to Rs. 55 even after giving a dividend at the rate of 50 per cent per share. Therefore, it seems that by a Euro-issue, companies can collect funds at a lower expense as well as increasing its foreign exchange reserves.

Disadvantage of Euro-issues (GDRs/ADRs)

Through the expense of dividend on a Euro-issue will comparatively be low, it will involve expenditure in foreign exchange. If a company issues bonus shares or right shares, the expense on dividend will increase. Sometimes, it can be a problem for a company and if the number of dividend giving companies in foreign exchange become large, then it can be a problem for the country as a whole.

After the government's announcement to allow Euro-issues in 1992, the first two companies who took part in Euro-issues were Reliance Industries and Grasim Industries. In subsequent years the number increased steadily up to the year 2007, but due to the world economic recession in the next two years that is in 2008 and 2009, the number of companies offering Euro-issues declined drastically.

In fact, according to an estimate of Press Trust of India (2nd February, 2009), the total amount of capital raised through equity issues during 2008 was Rs. 49,485 crores recording a 15.7 per cent decline compared to the level in 2007. This decline is believed to be the effect of a great global economic recession that set in after the liquidation of Lehman Brothers and Merril Lynch in 2008.

Indian Depository Receipts (IDRs)

With liberalization and a resultant booming economy in India, foreign companies are also investing in India in every possible way. Indian Depository Receipts (IDRs) are financial instruments that allow foreign companies to mobilize funds from Indian markets by offering equity and getting listed on Indian stock exchanges. IDRs are similar to the GDRs and ADRs, which, as we discussed above, and allow companies to raise funds from European and American markets, respectively.

The government opened this window for foreign companies to raise funds from India as part of its efforts to globalize the Indian capital market and to give local investors exposure in global companies.

Rules and Regulations in India

The provision enabling the issue of IDRs was introduced in the Companies Act, 1956 (the Act) by the Companies (Amendment) Act, 2000 in the form of Section 605A of the Act, which gave power to the Government of India to set the rules for the offer of IDRs and related matters.

In February 2004, the Government of India passed the Companies (Issue of Indian Depository Receipts) Rules 2004 (the IDR Rules), building on the amendments in December 2000 to the Act, to allow foreign companies to sell securities to Indian investors. Under Rule 4(d) of the IDR Rules, SEBI has the power to specify eligibility criteria for IDR issuers, in addition to what is contained in the IDR rules. Under Clause 9 to the Schedule to the IDR rules, SEBI can specify any information to be included in the prospectus from time to time. Accordingly, for companies desirous of coming out with IDR issues, a new Chapter VI A has been added in the SEBI (Disclosure and Investor Protection) Guidelines 2000, containing the guidelines to be followed by an IDR issuer for coming out with such an issue. In an IDR, foreign companies issue shares to an Indian depository, which would, in turn, issue depository receipts to investors in India. The depository receipts would be listed on stock exchanges in India and would be freely transferable. The actual shares underlying the IDRs would be held by an overseas custodian, which would authorize the Indian Depository to issue the IDRs. The overseas custodian is required to be a foreign bank having a place of business in India and needs approval from the finance ministry to act as a custodian, while the Indian depository needs to be registered with SEBI. An IDR issue needs to be approved by SEBI and an application in this regard has to be made a minimum of 90 days before the issue-opening date. The issuing company shall deliver the underlying equity shares or cause them to be delivered to an overseas custodian bank and the custodian bank shall authorize the domestic depository and a merchant banker for the purpose of issue of IDRs. The overseas company also has to file a due diligence report and a Prospectus or Letter of Offer with SEBI and the Registrar of Companies. Furthermore, the overseas company will have to obtain in-principle permission for listing on stock exchanges in India.

To understand the profile of capital market, key indicators of the economy are to be studied. Gross Domestic Product (GDP), growth rate, savings rate, capital formation, per capita national income and foreign exchange reserves are considered as major indicators. India's GDP has doubled from Rs. 42,94,706 crores to Rs. 89,12,178 crores for the period from 2006-07 to 2011-12. Growth has come down from 9.6 per cent to 6.9 per cent due to the global economic meltdown and internal indecision. The savings rate stabilized at around 32 per cent with capital formation rate of 35 per cent. The per capita income has gone up from Rs. 31,206 to Rs. 60,972 almost double keeping 40 per cent of the people below the poverty line. Addition of Foreign Exchange Reserve (FER) went up from $ 119 billion to $ 292 billion in the same period. Table 2.2 shows these facts.

Table 2.2 Growth of Indian Economy

Data Categories and Components	Units	2006-07	2007-08	2008-09	2009-10	2010-11	2011-12
GDP (Current market rate)	Rs Cr.	42,94,706	49,87,090	56,30,063	64,57,352(PE)	76,74,148(BE)	89,12,178(AE)
Growth rate	(%)	9.6	9.3	6.7	8.4	8,4	6.9
Savings rate	(%) GDP	34.6	36.8	32.0	33.8	32.3	NA
Capital formation (Rate)	(%) GDP	35.7	38.1	34.3	36.6	35.1	NA
Per capita national factor cost (at current price)	Rs.	31,206	35,825	40,775	46,117	53,331	60,972
Foreign exchange rate	US$ Billion	119.2	309.7	252.0	279.1	304.8	292.8*

Source: www.deloitte.com (accessed on 24.09.2012)

Table 2.3 depicts resource mobilization through the primary market, which recorded a decrease of 26.68 per cent in 2011 against an increase of 5.74 per cent in 2010. During the period debt collection increased from Rs. 1,500 crore to Rs. 4,791 crore, equity from Rs. 2,082 crore to Rs. 9,683 crore and private placement has gone up from Rs. 1,73,281 to Rs 1,88,530 crore over time in spite of the world over crises.

Table 2.3 Trends in Resource Mobilization

Mode	2008-09	2009-10	2010-11	2011-12 (as on 31.12.11)
1. Debt (Rs. crore)	1,500	2,500	9,451	4,791
2. Equity (Rs. crore)	2,082	46,736	48,654	9,683
of which IPO	2,082	24,696	35,559	5,443
No of IPOs	21	39	53	30
3. Private placement (Rs. crore)	1,73,281	2,12,635	2,18,785	1,88,530
4. Euro Issues (ADR / GDR)	NA	NA	NA	NA
Total (1+2+3+4) (Rs. crore)	1,76,864	2,61,871	2,76,890	2,03,005

Source: SEBI and RBI (for Euro Issues) and www.pwc.com/india (Accessed on 10.10.2012)

The net flow of foreign capital in the form of equity in India in the years 2009-10 and 2011-12 was negative and adversely affected the Indian capital market. But the net debt capital has risen, and as a result total activity in FII first rose and then declined significantly. FII initially preferred the service sector followed by manufacturing, construction, real estate and mining. In 2010-11 the inclination shifted slightly towards manufacturing, overtaking the service sector.

Disinvestment policy after liberalization has witness two methods, from 1991-92 to 1998-99 selling of shares of selected PSUs using various variants of the method and from 1999-2000 to 2003-04 it followed the path of strategic sale of PSUs to private sectors with a process of competitive bidding. But after 2004-05 sale of equity has been the basis of disinvestment. From the period from 1991-92 to 2011-12, government disinvestment was able to mop up

Table 2.4 Net Foreign Capital Inflow   (Figure in Rs. crore)

Transactions of FIIs	2009-10	2010-11	2011-12
Net FIIS (Actual)	1635	1722	1767
Equity market activity (Net)	(−) 47,706	1,10,121	(−) 213
Debt market activity (Net)	1,895	36,317	30,590
Total activity (Net)	1,42,658	1,46,438	30,376
Gross buying	8,46,438	9,92,599	6,64,805
Gross sales	7,93,780	8,46,161	6,34,431

Source: www.rbi.org.in (Accessed on 25.09.2012) and NSE, MCX-SX and UAE

Table 2.5 Sector Wise Equity Inflow   (US $ billion)

Sector	2006-07	2007-08	2008-09	2009-10	2010-11
Manufacturing	1.6 (17.6)	3.7 (19.2)	4.8 (21.0)	5.1 (22.9)	4.8 (32.1)
Services	5.3 (56.9)	8.0 (41.2)	10.2 (45.1)	7.4 (32.8)	4.5 (30.1)
Construction, real estate, mining	1.4 (15.5)	4.3 (22.4)	4.2 (18.6)	6.0 (26.6)	2.6 (17.6)
Others	0.9 (9.9)	3.3 (17.2)	3.4 (15.2)	4.0 (17.7)	3.0 (20 .0)
Total	9.3 (100.0)	19.4 (100.0)	22.7 (100.0)	22.5 (100.0)	14.9 (100.0)

Note: Figures in parentheses indicate percentages of total.
Source: www.rbi.org.in (Accessed on 25.09.2012)

Rs 1,20,426, which was much less than the target. It is alleged that PSU stocks were sold at a low price and could not penetrate the market much.

Table 2.6 Disinvestment in PSUs
(Target Receipts and Actual Receipts)

Year	Target Receipts (Rs. crore)	Actual Receipts (Rs. crore)	Year	Target Receipts (Rs. crore)	Actual Receipts (Rs. crore)
1991-92	2,500	3037.74	2003-04	14,500	15,547.41
1992-93	2,500	1912.51	2004-05	4,000	2,764.87
1993-94	3,500	—	2005-06	No target fixed	1,569.68
1994-95	4,000	4843.10	2006-07	No target fixed	—
1995-96	7,000	168.48	2007-08	No target fixed	4,181.39
1996-97	5,000	379.67	2008-09	No target fixed	—
1997-98	4,800	910.00	2009-10	No target fixed	4,259.00
1998-99	5,000	5,371.11	2010-11	40,000	22,744.00
1999-00	10,000	1,860.14	2011-12	40,000	40,000.00
2000-01	10,000	1871.26	2012-13	30,000	—
2001-02	10,000	5,657.69	20013-14	25,000	—
2002-03	12,000	3,347.98	Total		1,20,426.93

Source: Government of India, Department of Disinvestment, http://divest.nic.in and www.policy bazar.com (24.09.12)

In India the system of trading in shares and other securities, though very old, is not very transparent. So, investors often face huge losses due to dishonest dealing by brokers. Hence, it is necessary for investors to understand the science and mechanism of the ups and down of share trading.

FOR FURTHER READING

1. Rao, Purna Chandra, Purna6232gmail.com
2. Hampton, John J., *Financial Decision Making*, John Wiley and Sons Inc., Third Avenue, USA
3. Rudra, Ashok, *Rates of Growth of Indian Economy*, Economic Development in South Asia, Kandy Conference Proceedings, edited by EAG Robinson and M. Kidron, Macmillan, London, 1970
4. Dey, Amal Krishna, *Readings in Indian Agriculture Development*, E-Book, Published by Cooperyar Limited, London, 1999

Investment, Trading and Transactions in Share Scrips

3

[The whole of this chapter is written on the basis of BSE, NSE, and SEBI guidelines and articles published by them at different times. To make the readers aware of the original ideas of these institutions, we have taken matter from the original publications of these institutions. We are deeply indebted to them for granting permission for us to do so.]

The Indian capital market is going through qualitative as well as quantitative changes. In terms of quality, the overall supervisory authority, the SEBI is implementing several regulatory measures for issuers of capital (shares, debentures, bonds etc.) and intermediaries. Protection of investors' interest has become paramount. The introduction of institutions like the NSE, the OTCEI, credit rating agencies etc., has also started to contribute to the quality of trading in capital market instruments. Still, investment and finance is a nerve wracking field, characterized in the main by high risk. A thorough investor has to go through a large number of alternatives for comparatively risk free investments. Before going deeper into different avenues of investment, it would be better to refresh our ideas about investment itself as well as some market related terms.

INVESTMENT

Investment essentially refers to what one does with their savings. If one keeps their savings in the form of cash, they are certainly going to decrease in value as the value of money is constantly going down due to real inflation. Therefore, if one wants to maintain or increase the value of one's savings they have to keep them in forms other than cash. This is what investment is all about, deployment of one's savings with the intention of preserving or increasing their value. This deployment can be done by using one's savings to buy land, residential property, gold, jewelry, fixed deposits in banks and companies, shares, debentures etc., in fact, anything whose value is likely to remain constant or appreciate with time. For example, by buying a house, one can get monthly income as rent, besides appreciation of the value of the house. Similarly, investment in bank deposits, company deposits, debentures will also give a regular income in the form of interest or dividend. On the other hand, investments in gold and jewelry appreciate in value but do not provide any income.

As an investor one has to decide whether one wants his investment to appreciate in value or to give him a steady and regular income, or a combination of both. Investment in shares of a good company gives a regular income in form of dividends, but if the price or value of those shares appreciates very rapidly in the stock markets, then invested money can increase manifold within a short period of time. But the value of shares can also depreciate in the stock markets. Therefore, investment in the stock market is full of excitements and challenges.

At times, prices of essential commodities remain more or less constant or fluctuate at a low level. During such periods, inflation also remains at a lower level. But nowadays, it is amply clear that inflation is an increasing phenomenon. So, one has not only to make sure that the value of their savings grows with time, but also that the rate of growth is higher than the rate of inflation. If the rate of inflation is 4 per cent, one's post tax income must increase by at least 8 per cent to 10 per cent to maintain a healthy style of living. This is the main reason why it has become essential for every investor to acquire a basic knowledge of investment. It will be much easier to cope with future economic problems if one knows in advance where and when to invest and how to manage these investments efficiently, especially investments made in stock markets. There are two stages of investment and trading in shares; through the primary market and through the secondary market.

PRIMARY MARKET

When a company floats a new issue of securities (shares, debentures or bonds) for the general public, it advertises in the news papers for direct sale of the new issue of securities to the public. The public or general investors can buy these securities by applying for them in the specified application forms with the required part or full payment for them. The process of direct purchase of shares, debentures and other securities from companies or organizations floating new issues are known as procurement shares or debentures or bonds from the primary market.

In fact, the primary market provides the channel for sale of new securities. The primary market provides an opportunity to issuers of securities; government as well as corporate, to raise resources to meet their requirements of investment and/or discharge some obligations. They may issue the securities at face value, or at a discount/premium and these securities may take a variety of forms such as equity, debt etc. They may issue the securities in the domestic market and/or international market.

There are three ways in which a company can raise capital by marketing shares in the primary market, namely: (i) Initial public issue. (ii) Rights issue. (iii) Private placement.

SECONDARY MARKET

According to a publication of NSE (*Financial Markets*), secondary market refers to a market where securities are traded after being initially offered to the public in the primary market and/or listed on the stock exchange. A majority of the trading is carried out in the secondary market. The secondary market comprises equity markets and debt markets. For the general investor, the secondary market provides an efficient platform for trading securities. For the management of a company, secondary equity markets serve as a monitoring and control conduit by facilitating value-enhancing control activities, enabling implementation of incentive-based management contracts, and aggregating information (via price discovery) that guides management decisions.

In the primary market, securities are offered to the public for subscription for the purpose of raising capital or funds. The secondary market is an equity trading venue in which already existing/pre-issued securities are traded among investors. The secondary market could be either an auction or dealer market. While a stock exchange is a part of an auction market, Over-the-Counter (OTC) is a part of the dealer market. Existing share holders sell their holdings to the other investors in the stock exchanges through brokers to make a profit. When the shares of the established profit making companies quote above the face value or above the purchase price, then the shareholders sell their holdings to make good profits.

Sometimes, clever investors buy shares of sick companies at a price below the face value or par value and when those shares show some improvement in the prices in stock exchanges, they sell them without delay and make handsome profits. The trading of shares of a company through a particular stock exchange is only possible when that particular company is listed on that stock exchange. The system or process of trading of shares, debentures, bonds and other securities through stock exchanges is known as trading in the secondary market.

A stock market is an auction market but it is not like a conventional auction market where buyers compete and there is only one seller. Stock exchange delivers a two-way auction. Bidders compete with each other to purchase shares at the lowest possible price and simultaneously, those seeking to sell compete with each other to get the highest price for the shares they are offering. When the buyer and the seller agree on a figure, a transaction or deal is made.

According to a study of the NSE,[1] the past decade in many ways has been remarkable for the securities market in India. It has grown exponentially as measured in terms of amount raised from the market, number of stock exchanges and other intermediaries, the number of listed stocks, market capitalization, trading volumes and turnover on stock exchanges, and investor population. Along with this growth, the profiles of the investors, issuers and intermediaries have changed significantly. The market has witnessed several institutional changes resulting in a drastic reduction in transaction costs and significant improvements in efficiency, transparency, liquidity and safety. In a short span of time, the Indian derivatives market has found a place in the lists of top global exchanges. Market capitalization has grown over this period indicating that more companies are using the trading platform of the stock exchange.

Reforms in the securities market, particularly the establishment and empowerment of SEBI, a determined allocation of resources, screen based nation-wide trading, dematerialization and

---

[1]National Securities Depository, *Handbook for NSDL Depository Operations Module*, www.nsdl-india.com, e-mail: nefm@nse.com.in

electronic transfer of securities, rolling settlement and a ban on deferral products, sophisticated risk management and derivatives trading, have greatly improved the regulatory framework and efficiency of trading and settlement. According to the National Stock Exchange, Mumbai, the Indian market is now comparable to many developed markets in terms of a number of qualitative parameters. In short, it can be said that the secondary market is mainly an equity trading venue in which already existing/pre-issued securities are traded among investors. The secondary market could be either auction or dealer market. While a stock exchange is a part of an auction market, Over-the-Counter (OTC) is a part of the dealer market as has been discussed in detail in the previous two chapters.

There is a common belief that the stock exchange is a place where people indulge only in speculation and try to reap quick profits. This is partially true. Because of the wide fluctuations in share prices, share markets are prone to speculation. But, then, no stock market can function efficiently without some sort of speculation as it affords the essential liquidity to stock prices.

Table 3.1 Amount of Capital Raised by Regions and Categories   (In Rs. crore)

Year	By Different Regions				All Total	Total		IPOs
	Eastern	Western	Northern	Southern		Public	Rights	
1993-94	1352	14559	5828	2633	24372	15449	8923	7864
1994-95	2216	10824	6654	8039	27633	21045	6558	16572
1995-96	1416	10811	5109	3467	20804	14240	6564	10924
1996-97	767	9041	3381	1087	14284	7565	6719	5959
1997-98	1164	2391	302	713	4570	1862	1708	1048
1998-99	266	4856	171	293	5587	5019	568	404
1999-2000	106	5235	1900	577	7817	6257	1560	2719
2000-01	240	4105	207	1555	6108	5378	729	2722
2001-02	180	5942	1002	419	7543	6502	1041	1202
2002-03	117	3358	78	588	4070	3639	431	1039
2003-04	636	6826	14576	1235	23272	22265	1007	3434
2004-05	204	17951	8725	1377	28256	24640	3617	13749
2005-06	1495	14969	5389	5535	27382	23294	4088	10936
2006-07	165	22964	3673	6706	33508	29696	3710	18504
2007-08	1093	64139	16526	5270	87029	54511	32518	42595
2008-09	315	11202	2902	1800	16220	3582	12637	2082
2009-10	4175	15796	24714	12870	57555	49236	8319	24696

Source: Securities and Exchange Board of India Bulletins.

Stock markets owe their breadth and liquidity – both essential features for smooth functioning – to speculators. However excessive and undisciplined speculation can lead to artificial price levels and payment defaults by operators. Such a situation can have a disastrous effect on stock markets. To control the activities of the stock exchanges, the government has passed an act known as the Securities Contracts (Regulation) Act, 1956, which lays down the broad guidelines for recognized stock exchanges. Using this as the basis, each stock exchange frames its bye-laws, regulations and rules to conduct the various functions relating to the sale and purchase of shares and other securities. The act deals with all aspects of the securities markets, including the procedure for granting recognition to stock exchanges, the manner of applying for membership of stock exchanges and the levy of fees, details of reports to be furnished to the government by each stock exchange, the procedure for inquiries to be made by the governing board of stock exchanges and the procedure and fees payable for granting licenses by dealers in securities on the stock exchange.

The highest authority of the stock exchange is the governing board; it consists of a majority of elected members along with public and government nominees. The board is assisted in its day-to-day functions by an administrative department of the exchange which is generally headed by an executive director. This department is responsible for functions such as processing applications from companies for listing, publication of daily quotations, fixation and realisation of margin money from members, reconciliation and clearing of business transactions, maintenance of security deposits of members, arbitration in matters of dispute and differences and other related functions.

All the excitement, joys and sorrows of investors revolve around stock exchanges which are known as the secondary market, and persons who play major roles in all this excitement are the members of stock exchanges who are commonly known as share brokers.

Share Broker

In exercise of the powers conferred by Section 29 of SEBI Act, 1992, the Central Government has made SEBI (Stock-brokers and Sub-brokers) Rules, 1992. In terms of Rule 2(e), "Stock-broker" means a member of a stock exchange.

It is known that a stock exchange is a market for dealing in equities and other securities. The investor must employ the services of a registered member of a recognized stock exchange, who is commonly known as a stock-broker or share broker. These stock brokers buy and sell shares in a stock market on behalf of an investor, who is known to them as a client, but cannot trade in shares in their own name. A client gives instructions (an order) to buy or sell to his broker, who charges a commission or brokerage for his services and executes the order on the floor of the exchange through the jobbers. It is also important to know that brokers merely act as agents for their clients and deal with another class of stock exchange professionals known as jobbers. A jobber has no direct contact with the investing public – he deals only with his own account. The stock exchange does not recognize any party to bargain in shares, other than its registered members. So, an investor's broker must be a registered member of the stock exchange through which he performs the trading.

Thus, the broker is an intermediary who arranges to buy and sell securities on behalf of clients (the actual buyer and the seller). According to Rule 2 (e) of SEBI (Stock-brokers and Sub-brokers) Rules, 1992, a stock-broker must be a member of a recognized stock exchange. No stock-broker is allowed to buy, sell or deal in securities, unless he or she holds a certificate of registration granted by SEBI. A stock-broker applies for registration to SEBI through a stock exchange or stock exchanges of which he or she is admitted as a member. SEBI may grant a certificate to a stockbroker [as per SEBI (Stock-brokers and Sub-brokers) Rules, 1992] subject to the conditions that:

1. He/She holds a membership of any stock exchange.
2. He/She shall abide by the rules, regulations and bye-laws of the stock exchange or stock exchanges of which he/she is a member.
3. In case of any change in the status and constitution, he/she shall obtain prior permission of SEBI to continue to buy, sell or deal in securities in any stock exchange.
4. He/She shall pay the amount of fees for registration in the prescribed manner.
5. He/She shall take adequate steps for redressal of grievances of the investors within one month of the date of receipt of the complaint and keep SEBI informed about the number, nature and other particulars of the complaints.

While considering an application of an entity for grant of registration as a stock-broker, SEBI shall take into account the following, namely, whether the stock-broker applicant –

1. Is eligible to be admitted as a member of a stock exchange.
2. Has the necessary infrastructure like adequate office space, equipment and man power to effectively discharge his activities.
3. Has any past experience in the business of buying, selling or dealing in securities.
4. Is being subjected to any disciplinary proceedings under the rules, regulations and bye-laws of a stock exchange with respect to his business as a stock-broke involving either himself or any of his partners, directors or employees [*'Financial Markets'*, NSE]

Membership Criteria of NSE

There are no entry/exit barriers to membership in the NSE. Anybody can become member by complying with the prescribed eligibility criteria and exit by surrendering membership without any hidden/overt costs. The members are admitted to the different segments of the exchange subject to the provisions of the Securities Contracts (Regulation) Act, 1956, the Securities and Exchange Board of India Act, 1992, the rules, circulars, notifications, guidelines, etc., issued thereunder and the bye laws, rules and regulations of the exchange.

The standards for admission of members are laid down by the exchange and stress on factors such as corporate structure, capital adequacy, track record, education, experience, etc. and reflect a conscious effort on the part of NSE to ensure quality broking services so as to build and sustain confidence among investors in the exchange's operations. Benefits to the trading membership of NSE include:

1. Access to a nation-wide trading facility for equities, derivatives, debt and hybrid instruments/products.
2. The ability to provide a fair, efficient and transparent securities market to the investors.

3. Use of state-of-the-art electronic trading systems and technology.

4. Dealing with an organization which follows strict standards for trading and settlement at par with those available at the top international bourses.

5. A demutualised exchange which is managed by independent and experienced professionals.

6. Dealing with an organization which is constantly striving to move towards a global marketplace in the securities industry.

New membership of the NSE is open to all persons desirous of becoming trading members, subject to meeting requirements/criteria as laid down by SEBI and the exchange. These can be obtained directly from SEBI.

The different segments currently available on the exchange for trading are:

❖ Capital market (equities and retail debt)

❖ Wholesale debt market

❖ Derivatives i.e., futures and options market (discussed in Chapter 8).

Admission to membership of the segments of the exchange is currently open and available. Persons or institutions desirous of securing admission as trading members (stock brokers) on the exchange may apply for any one of the following segment groups:

1. Wholesale Debt Market (WDM) segment

2. Capital Market (CM) and Wholesale Debt Market (WDM) segments

3. Capital Market (CM) and Futures & Options (F&O) segments

4. Capital Market (CM), Wholesale Debt Market (WDM) and Futures & Options (F&O) segments

5. Clearing membership of the National Securities Clearing Corporation Ltd. (NSCCL) as a Professional Clearing Member (PCM)

Eligibility for Acquiring New Membership of NSE

1. The following persons are eligible to become trading members:

(a) Individuals

(b) Partnership firms registered under the Indian Partnership Act, 1932. Individual and partnership firms are not eligible to apply for membership in the WDM segment.

(c) Institutions, including subsidiaries of banks engaged in financial services.

(d) Body corporate including companies as defined in the Companies Act, 1956.

A company shall be eligible to be admitted as a member if:

(a) Such company is formed in compliance with the provisions of Section 12 of the said Act.

(b) Such company undertakes to comply with such financial requirements and norms as may be specified by the Securities and Exchange Board of India for the registration of such company.

(c) The directors of such company are not disqualified for being members of a stock exchange and have not held the offices of the directors in any company which had been a member of the stock exchange and had been declared defaulter or expelled by the stock exchange.

(d) Such other persons or entities as may be permitted from time to time by RBI/SEBI under the Securities Contracts (Regulations) Rules, 1957.

2. No person shall be admitted as a trading member if:

(a) He has been adjudged bankrupt or a receiver order in bankruptcy has been made against him or he has been proved to be insolvent even though he has obtained his final discharge.

(b) He has compounded with his creditors for less than full discharge of debts.

(c) He has been convicted of an offence involving a fraud or dishonesty.

(d) He is engaged as a principal or employee in any business other than that of securities, except as a broker or agent not involving any personal financial liability or for providing merchant banking, underwriting or corporate or investment advisory services, unless he undertakes to sever its connections with such business on admission, if admitted.

(e) He has been at any time expelled or declared a defaulter by any other stock exchange or he has been debarred from trading in securities by any regulatory authorities like SEBI, RBI etc;

(f) He has been previously refused admission to trading membership by NSE unless a period of one year has elapsed since the date of such rejection.

(g) He incurs such disqualification under the provisions of the Securities Contract (Regulations) Act, 1956 or rules made there under so as to disentitle him from seeking membership of a stock exchange.

(h) He incurs such disqualification consequent to which NSE determines it to be not in the public interest to admit him as a member on the exchange. Provided that in case of registered firms, body corporates and companies, the conditions from (a) to (h) above will apply to all partners in case of partnership firms, and all directors in case of companies.

(i) It is a body corporate which has committed any act which renders it liable to be wound up under the provisions of the law.

(j) It is a body corporate or a company in respect of which a provisional liquidator or receiver or official liquidator has been appointed by a competent court.

SHAREHOLDING PATTERN

Securities markets have an inherent tendency to be volatile and risky. Therefore, there should be adequate risk containment mechanisms in place for the stock exchanges. One such risk containment tool is the concept of 'dominant promoter/shareholder group' which is very unique for applicants acquiring membership on the NSE. Though membership on the NSE is granted to the entity applying for it, for all practical purposes the entity is managed by a few shareholders who have controlling interest in the company. The shareholders holding the majority of shares have a dominant role in the affairs of the company. In case of any default by the broking entity, the exchange should be able to identify and take action against the persons who are behind the company. The exchange, therefore, needs to know the background, financial soundness and integrity of these shareholders holding such controlling interest. Hence, during the admission process the dominant shareholders are called for an interview with the membership recommendation committee.

DOMINANT PROMOTER/SHAREHOLDER GROUP (DPG)

Dominant promoter norms are applicable to all the corporate trading members. The norms relating to a dominant promoter are given as under:

1. Unlisted corporate trading member. A corporate trading member will identify a group of shareholders (Dominant Promoter Group – DPG), who would normally be individuals, not exceeding 4, who jointly and/or severally hold not less than 51 per cent of the shares in the trading member corporate at the time of admission as well as subsequently at all relevant points of time.

   The shareholding/interest of close relatives of the DPG viz., parents, spouse, children, brothers and sisters would also be counted for arriving at the total dominant holding/ interest, if such relative(s) give unqualified and irrevocable support in writing to the individual concerned in respect of such holding/interest.

2. Listed characteristics of corporate trading member:

   (a) A corporate trading member with net worth of less than Rs. 50 crores, will identify a group of shareholders (Dominant Promoter Group – DPG), who would normally be individuals, not exceeding 4, who jointly and/or severally hold not less than 40 per cent of the shares in the trading member corporate at the time of admission as well as subsequently at all relevant points of time.

   (b) A corporate trading member with net worth of Rs. 50 crores and above, will identify a group of shareholders (Dominant Promoter Group – DPG), who normally would be individuals, not exceeding 4, who jointly and/or severally hold not less than 26 per cent of shares in the trading member corporate at the time of admission as well as subsequently at all relevant points of time.

   The shareholding/interest of close relatives of the DPG viz., parents, spouse, children, brothers and sisters would also be counted for arriving at total dominant holding/interest, if such relative(s) give unqualified and irrevocable support in writing to the individual concerned in respect of such holding/interest.

   Existing unlisted trading member corporate proposing to get listed should continue to have their dominant promoters holding not less than 40 per cent or 26 per cent as the case may be, of the share capital post listing. If there is a change in the promoter group through a take over process and a new group acquires controlling interest, the changes shall be treated as reconstitution of the trading member corporate tantamounting to transfer of membership.

3. Corporate shareholders to be identified as dominant shareholders:

   (a) Corporate shareholders are allowed to be identified as dominant shareholders (Dominant Promoter Group – DPG), if they are listed corporates each having a net worth of Rs. 50 crores and above and the promoter group of the listed corporate holds at least 26 per cent of the share capital.

   (b) Corporate shareholders not meeting the above norm can still be brought into the dominant shareholders group (DPG) provided:

   The trading member corporate is a wholly owned subsidiary of another company.

   The identifiable individual dominant promoter(s) (not more than 4) (Dominant Promoter Group) hold at least 51 per cent of the share capital of the holding company or promoter group holding not less than 40 per cent in case of a listed holding company and/or there are two or more listed corporate shareholders jointly holding at least 51 per cent of the share capital of the holding company and the promoter group holding in the listed corporates (independently) is at least 40 per cent and/or one or more listed corporate shareholders along with individual shareholders (belonging to the promoter group) together, not exceeding four in number, jointly hold at least 51 per cent of the shares of the holding company, and the promoter group holding in the listed corporate is at least 40 per cent.

   Provided that in none of the above instances the holding company of the trading member corporate becomes the subsidiary of another corporate. Existing unlisted corporate shareholder(s) of the trading member entity, proposing to get listed should continue to have their dominant promoters holding not less than 40 per cent or 26 per cent as the case may, of the share capital post listing. The said dominant promoters undertake in writing, not to dilute their shareholding in the holding company without prior consent of the exchange. If there is a change in the promoter group of such dominant corporate shareholders through a take over process and a new group acquires controlling interest in such dominant corporate shareholder, the changes may be treated as reconstitution of the trading member corporate tantamounting to transfer of membership.

4. Banks, central or state government/owned finance and/or development institutions:

   Scheduled banks, central or state government owned finance and/or development institutions etc. are also allowed to be identified as dominant shareholder(s) even if they are not listed, provided they have a net worth of at least Rs. 50 crores.

5. Foreign entities: For foreign entities taking trading membership of the exchange through their Indian subsidiary under the automatic approval route permitted by the government (i.e., without approaching the FIPB), subject to compliance with the guidelines of the RBI in this regard:

   (a) The promoting foreign entity should be either a bank or insurance organization regulated by the Central Bank or such other appropriate regulatory authority of that country, and/or the promoting foreign entity should be a broking house/

participant in the securities market that is registered or regulated by the relevant regulatory authority of that country. The entity should have a sound track record, and/or the promoting foreign entity is one whose domestic arm or subsidiary is registered with SEBI for participation in any domestic venture for custodial or asset management services.

(b) The promoting foreign entity shall hold, directly or indirectly not less than 51 per cent of the controlling stake in the applicant company proposing to take the trading membership of the exchange.

(c) The net worth of the entity having a controlling stake in the applicant company or the promoting foreign entity should be at least Rs. 50 crores.

Corporate shareholders of the trading member company can also extend their support to the DPG, provided the shareholding of the dominant promoter group along with the support of their specified relatives in the corporate shareholder is not less than 51 per cent or 40 per cent if it is a listed corporate as the case may be. The indirect shareholding shall be calculated proportionately by reckoning the direct shareholding of the DPG along with the support of their specified relatives in the corporate shareholder of the trading member company. Corporate trading members will also be allowed to change their shareholding pattern so long as such change is within the above norms as specified in 1 to 3 above and existing dominant promoter group continues to hold controlling interest and prior approval from the exchange is obtained. Once a DPG is identified during admission, the same has to be maintained at all points of time. Any change in the DPG will require the trading member to seek fresh approval of the exchange as if for admission of a new trading member and rules relating to the same will apply. However, inter-se transfer of shareholding among the dominant promoters will be exempt for the same.

Trading members are also requested to note that any change in shareholding requires prior approval from the exchange, except in the case of shareholding changes related to public shareholding in a listed company. If none of the dominant promoters/shareholders is a director on the board of the trading member company, then at least two other directors having the requisite experience and qualification shall hold a minimum of 5 per cent shares (each) in the paid up equity capital of the trading member company. Failure to maintain the required level of shareholding will be treated as a breach of the continuing membership norms, which would be tantamount to a reconstitution of the trading member corporate as the existing DPG would no longer hold controlling interest in the trading member corporate or alternatively a new group would have emerged with controlling stake. In such a case the exchange may initiate disciplinary action including withdrawal of trading facility of such trading members.

ONLINE EXAMINATION

At any point of time the applicant has to ensure that at least the sole proprietor/one of the designated partners/one of the designated directors/compliance officers has a valid certificate for at least one of the following NCFM modules:

1. Securities market (basic) module
2. Compliance officer (broker) module
3. Capital market (dealers) module
4. Derivatives market (dealers) module

The dealers on the CM segment are required to clear the capital market (dealers) module of NCFM while dealers on the futures & options segment are required to clear the derivatives market (dealers) module of NCFM. This is a pre-requisite without which user-IDs are not issued.

BROKER CLIENT RELATIONSHIP

The Trading Member (TM) shall enter into an agreement in the specified format provided by the NSE with the client before accepting orders on the latter's behalf. The said agreement shall be executed on non-judicial stamp paper of adequate value, duly signed by both the parties on all the pages. A copy of the said agreement is to be kept with the TM permanently. In addition to the agreement, the TM shall seek information from the client in the 'client registration application form' obtaining information like: investor risk profile, financial profile, investor identification details, address details, income, PAN number, employment, age, investments, other assets and financial liabilities. The TM shall obtain recent passport size photographs of each of their clients in case of individual clients and of all partners in case of partnership firms and of the dominant promoter in case of corporate clients. The TM shall also take proof of identification and address of the client.

A trading member shall make the constituent aware of the trading segment to which the trading member is admitted, particulars of SEBI registration number, employee primarily responsible for the constituents affairs, the precise nature of the trading member's liability for business to be conducted, basic risks involved in trading on the exchange (equity and other instruments) including any limitations on the liability and the capacity in which the trading member acts and the constituent's liability thereon, investors' rights and obligations, etc. by issuing to the constituent a risk disclosure document in such format, as may be prescribed by the exchange from time to time and shall obtain the same from his constituents duly signed.

Execution of client registration form, member constituent agreement and risk disclosure document is optional in the case of institutional clients.

A stock broker shall not deal knowingly, directly or indirectly, with a client who defaults to another stock broker. There is no limit on the number of clients for a TM.

UNIQUE CLIENT CODE

SEBI made it mandatory for all brokers to use unique client codes for all clients. Brokers shall collect and maintain in their back office the PAN allotted by the income tax department for all their clients.

Brokers shall verify the documents with respect to the unique code and retain a copy of the document. They shall also be required to furnish the above particulars of their clients to the stock exchanges/clearing corporations and the same would be updated before placing orders for the clients. The stock exchanges shall be required to maintain a database of client details submitted by brokers.

Margins from the Clients

Members should have a prudent system of risk management to protect themselves from client default. Margins are likely to be an important element of such a system. The same shall be well documented and be made accessible to the clients and the stock exchanges. However, the quantum of these margins and the form and mode of collection are left to the discretion of the members (SEBI/MRD/DoP/SE/Cir–07/2005 dated February 23, 2005). The margin so collected shall be kept separately in the client bank account and utilized for making payment to the clearing house for margin and settlement with respect to that client.

Execution of Orders

Where the constituent requires an order to be placed or any of his orders to be modified after the order has entered the system but has not been traded, the trading member may, if it so desires, obtain order placement/modification details in writing from the constituent. The trading member shall accordingly provide the constituent with the relevant order confirmation/ modification slip or copy thereof, forthwith, if so required by the constituent.

Where the constituent requires any of his orders to be cancelled after the order has been entered in the system but has not been executed, the trading member may, if it so desires, obtain the order cancellation details in writing from the constituent. The trading member shall accordingly provide the constituent with the relevant order cancellation details, forthwith, if so required by the constituent. The trading member may, if it so desires, obtain in writing, the delivery and payment requirement in any instructions of an order that it receives from the constituent. Where a trading member receives a request for order modification or order cancellation from the constituent, it shall duly bring it to their notice that if the order results in a trade in the meantime, the requests for modification or cancellation cannot be executed.

Contract Note

A contract note is a confirmation of trade(s) done on a particular day for and on behalf of a client. A stock broker shall issue a contract note to his clients for trades (purchase/sale of securities) executed with all relevant details as required therein to be filled in (refer to SEBI circular no. SMD/SED/CIR/23321 dated November 18, 1993). A contract note shall be issued to a client within 24 hours of the execution of the contract duly signed by the TM or his authorized signatory.

As per Regulation 18 of SEBI (Stock-Brokers & Sub-Brokers) Regulations, 1992, the TM shall preserve the duplicate copy of the contract notes issued for a minimum of five years.

The TM shall ensure that:

1. Contract notes are in the prescribed format.
2. Stamp duty is paid.
3. All statutory levies are shown separately in the contract note.
4. Contract notes are signed by the TM or by an authorised signatory TM. The contract note should contain the name and address (registered office address as well as dealing office address) of the TM, the SEBI registration number of the TM, details of trade viz. order number, trade number, order time, trade time, security name, quantity, trade price, brokerage, settlement number and details of other levies.

Payments/Delivery of Securities to Clients

Every TM shall make payments to his clients or deliver the securities purchased within one working day of pay-out unless the client has requested otherwise.

Brokerage

The maximum brokerage chargeable by a TM in respect of trades effected in the securities admitted to dealing on the CM segment of the exchange is fixed at 2.5 per cent of the contract price, exclusive of statutory levies. This maximum brokerage is inclusive of sub-brokerage. The brokerage shall be indicated separately from the price, in the contract note. The TM may not share brokerage with a person who is a TM or in employment of another TM.

Segregation of Bank Accounts

The TM should maintain separate bank accounts for his client's funds and his own funds. It shall be compulsory for all TMs to keep the money of the clients in a separate account and their own money in a separate account. Funds shall be transferred from the client's account to the clearing account for the purpose of funds pay-in obligations on behalf of the clients and *vice versa* in case of funds pay-out. No payment for transaction in which the TM is taking position as a principal will be allowed to be made from the client's account.

Segregation of Demat (Beneficiary) Accounts

The trading members shall keep the dematerialized securities of constituents in a separate beneficiary account distinct from the beneficiary account maintained for holding their own dematerialized securities. No delivery towards the own transactions of the trading members shall be allowed to be made from the account meant for constituents. For this purpose, every trading member is required to open a beneficiary account in the name of the trading member exclusively for the securities of the constituents (to be referred to as "constituent's beneficiary account"). A trading member may keep one consolidated constituents' beneficiary account for all its constituents or different accounts for each of its constituents as it may deem fit.

The relationship between a broker and his client is governed by the bye-laws of the stock exchange concerned and also by the customs of the trade.

For instance, as a general rule, a broker is liable to third parties for acts done on behalf of his clients. However, if it becomes manifest that a client intends to default on his bargain, the broker need not wait for the client to actually default, but he can buy or sell other shares in the market and claim the difference. Thus a broker enjoys a right to indemnification from his client.

Apart from this, a broker also has a right of lien in relation to the client's property that has come into his hands. All securities and assets, including cash, held by the broker for his client are subject to the broker's lien for any 'on account' balance or margin money including interest, commission, brokerage and other expenses that may be due from the client.

Further, the broker is at liberty to sell, pledge or borrow money against such securities and assets. He cannot only reimburse himself from these but can also pay out any money payable by him on behalf of his clients.

When the broker of a client defaults, the client may lodge a complaint with the governing board of the exchange of which he is a member. The board will investigate the complaint and take suitable action against the broker.

If, in an extreme case, the broker is declared a defaulter, the defaulter's committee of the exchange will take charge of all his books of accounts and papers. It will also recover all money, securities and other assets of the defaulter and distribute them prorata among the creditor members and the clients.

A client may also seek redressal in a civil or criminal court against a defaulter broker. However, this is a time consuming and expensive procedure which a smart client would prefer to avoid.

SUB-BROKERS

In terms of Rule 2(f) of Section 29 of SEBI Act, 1992, 'Sub-broker' means any person not being a member of a stock exchange who acts on behalf of a stock broker as an agent or otherwise for assisting the investors in buying, selling or dealing in securities through such stock brokers. A stock broker or sub-broker shall not buy, sell, and deal in securities, unless he holds a certificate granted by SEBI (Rule 3). This means that the trading members of the exchange may appoint sub-brokers to act as agents of the concerned trading member for assisting the investors in buying, selling or dealing in securities. The sub-broker would be affiliated to the trading members and are required to be registered with SEBI. A sub-broker would be allowed to be associated with only one trading member of the exchange.

Trading members desirous of appointing sub-brokers are required to submit the following documents to the membership department of the exchange:

❖ Copy of sub-broker - broker agreement duly certified by the trading members.

❖ Application form for registration as a sub-broker with Securities and Exchange Board of India (Form B).

❖ Recommendation letter to be given by the trading member with whom the sub-broker is affiliated (Form C).

Eligibility

A sub-broker may be an individual, a partnership firm or a corporate. In case of a corporate or partnership firm, the directors or partners and in the case of an individual sub-broker applicant, shall each comply with the following requirements:

1. They shall not be less than 21 years of age.
2. They shall not have been convicted of any offence involving fraud or dishonesty.
3. They shall have at least passed the 12th standard or any equivalent examination from an institution recognized by the government.
4. They should not have been debarred by SEBI.
5. The corporate entities applying for sub-brokership shall have a minimum paid up capital of Rs. 5 lakhs and it shall identify a dominant shareholder who holds a minimum of 51 per cent shares either singly or with the unconditional support of his/her spouse.

Registration

No sub-broker is allowed to buy, sell or deal in securities, unless he or she holds a certificate of registration granted by SEBI.

Sub-brokers are required to obtain a certificate of registration from SEBI in accordance with SEBI (Stock Brokers & Sub-brokers) Rules and Regulations, 1992, without which they are not permitted to buy, sell or deal in securities. SEBI may grant a certificate to a sub-broker, subject to the conditions that:

1. He shall pay the fees in the prescribed manner.
2. He shall take adequate steps for redressal of grievances of the investors within one month of the date of the receipt of the complaint and keep SEBI informed about the number, nature and other particulars of the complaints received.
3. In case of any change in the status and constitution, the sub-broker shall obtain prior permission of SEBI to continue to buy, sell or deal in securities in any stock exchange.
4. He is authorized in writing by a stock-broker, who is a member of a stock exchange for affiliating himself in buying, selling or dealing in securities.

The applicant sub-broker shall submit the required documents to the stock exchange with the recommendation of a trading member. After verifying the documents, the stock exchange may forward the documents of the applicant sub-broker to SEBI for registration. A sub-broker can trade in that capacity after getting himself registered with SEBI. The exchange may not forward the said application of the sub-broker to SEBI for registration if the applicant is found to have introduced or otherwise dealt with fake, forged, stolen, counterfeit etc. shares and securities in the market.

Other Requirements

The trading member has to issue contract notes for all trades in respect of its sub-broker in the name of the sub-broker and the sub-broker shall, in turn issue purchase/sale notes to his clients as per the format prescribed by the exchange.

The trading member with whom the sub-broker is affiliated is responsible for:

1. Ensuring the compliance by a sub-broker of the rules, bye-laws and regulations of the exchange
2. Inspecting that the sub-brokers are registered and recognized.
3. Ensuring that the sub-brokers function in accordance with the scheme, rules, bye-laws, regulations etc. of the exchange/NSCCL and the SEBI regulations etc.
4. Informing the sub-broker and keeping him apprised about trading/settlement cycles, delivery/payment schedules and any changes therein from time to time.
5. Reporting any default or delay in carrying out obligations by any of the sub-brokers affiliated to him, to all other stock brokers with whom the said sub-broker is affiliated.

Cancellation of Registration

In case a trading member/sub-broker intends to cancel the registration as a sub-broker, the sub-broker is required to submit the original SEBI registration certificate through their affiliated trading member. While applying for cancellation of registration, the affiliated trading member needs to give a public notification to this effect.

For further details, Circular No. 199, dated June 15, 2001 (Ref. No.: NSE/MEM/2618) may be referred to.

Sub-broker - Client Relations

A sub-broker is an important intermediary between stock broker and client. In the capital market segment "sub-broker" means any person not being a member of a stock exchange who acts on behalf of a stock broker as an agent or otherwise for assisting the investors in buying, selling or dealing in securities through such stock brokers.

Registration

A broker shall deal with a person who is acting as a sub-broker only if such a person is registered with SEBI as a sub-broker. It is the responsibility of a broker to ensure that none of its clients is acting as a sub-broker unless it is registered with SEBI.

A broker of the exchange executing transactions on behalf of its clients through a broker of another stock exchange is also required to be registered with SEBI as a sub-broker of respective broker.

Application of a sub-broker registration has to be submitted to the exchange with recommendation of the associated stock broker, in a prescribed format.

Relationship with Clients/Role

A sub-broker shall have to enter into a tripartite agreement with his clients and the stock broker specifying the scope of rights and obligations of the sub broker, stock broker and such clients of the sub-broker as per the format prescribed by SEBI for dealing in securities in the cash segment. There shall be privacy of contract between the stock broker and the sub-broker's client. A separate agreement has to be executed for each exchange.

A sub-broker will help the client in redressal of grievances in respect of transactions executed through its associated broker. A sub-broker will also assist and co-operate in ensuring faster settlement of any arbitration proceedings arising out of the transaction entered through its associated broker and shall be jointly/severally liable to implement the arbitration award.

A sub-broker will provide assistance to a stock broker and clients introduced to it to reconcile their accounts at the end of each quarter with reference to all the settlements where payouts have been declared during the quarter.

Contract Notes: Role of a Sub-Broker

A stock broker shall issue a contract note as per the format prescribed by the exchange to a client introduced through a sub-broker. A sub-broker shall render necessary assistance to its client in obtaining the contract note from the stock broker. A sub-broker shall not issue any purchase/sale note or confirmation memo to its client.

Securities/Funds

Transactions in securities executed on behalf of a client introduced through the sub-broker shall be settled by delivery/payment between the stock broker and the client directly, in accordance with the rules, regulations and bye-laws of the exchange and such settlements shall not take place through a sub-broker. Delivery of securities and payment of funds relating to the transactions of a client introduced by the sub-broker shall be directly between the stock broker and the client of the sub broker.

Placing an Order

An investor or a client has two options when instructing his broker to transact business.

- ❖ He may tell the broker to buy or sell 'at a best fixed rate' and leave the matter to the broker's judgment.
- ❖ He may specify reasonable price limits. For instance, the client may tell the broker to buy a specified quantity of shares at a specified rate of Rs. 102 per share maximum of a specified company

However, in such a situation, the broker may have been unable to execute the order as the share may not have been traded at the specified rate. Too strict an adherence to limits can result in an opportunity being missed, especially when the market is changing rapidly. In a bull market (discussed later) a clever investor avoids strict buying limits to ensure a purchase, otherwise he could be trailing a share for days together without buying it.

Similarly, in a bear market (discussed later), the same intelligent investor places sell orders at 'market rates'. By restricting the selling price limit, the opportunity of selling of shares may be lost on that day.

CONTRACT NOTE IN GENERAL

We have already discussed above the NSE/SEBI criteria regarding contract notes and the role of a broker and sub-broker in making a contract note. In general, it can briefly be said that a contract note describes the rate, date, time at which the trade was transacted and the brokerage rate. A contract note issued in the prescribed format establishes a legally enforceable relationship between the client and the member (registered broker) in respect of trades stated in the contract note. These are made in duplicate and the member and the client both keep a copy each. A client should receive the contract note within 24 hours of the executed trade.

TRANSFER DEED

This is an official document which records the transfer of ownership of securities. Before dematerialization (computer screen based trading), the transfer deed was attached with the share certificate at the time of transfer of ownership of securities. In the UK it is called a transfer form.

PAYMENT TO BROKER

As a seller, in order to ensure smooth settlement one has to deliver the shares to the broker immediately after getting the contract note for sale but in any case before the pay-in day. Similarly, as a buyer, one should pay immediately on the receipt of the contract note for purchase but in any case before the pay-in day.

PAY-IN AND PAY-OUT

Pay-in is the day on which brokers deposit shares sold by them and make payments to the clearing house for shares bought during the settlement period (discussed later). Pay-out is the day on which brokers receive shares for which they have made the payment and receive funds for shares sold by them earlier. The NSE has a weekly settlement for which trading begins on Wednesday and ends on the subsequent Tuesday. For this settlement, the pay-in is on the Monday of the following week and pay-out is on Wednesday. For BSE, the weekly settlement begins on Monday and ends on Friday. The pay-in for this settlement is on Thursday of the subsequent week and pay-out on Saturday.

JOBBERS

Members of a stock exchange that can trade, that is, can buy or sell in their own name are known as jobbers. Jobbers specialize in one or more listed securities. By trading in out of the market for a small difference in price, they help in maintaining a liquid and continuous market in stocks they specialize in. For active shares, there may be several jobbers trading in them. On the other hand, for active shares, a lone jobber may deal in several of them. To help brokers and the authorized clerks to locate the jobbers dealing with individual securities, trading takes place at the spot where the security is posted. Thus the floor of the exchange is roughly divided into a series of small markets for government securities, debentures, non-specified shares and specified shares, and each of these markets is further divided into sub-markets for one or more securities.

Jobbers specialize in some counters, that is, a place where particular shares are traded. Even at one counter, there may be more than one jobber and the price quoted by them may differ according to their individual judgments. However, all jobbers try to keep their books clean at the end of the day. This means that whatever they purchase is sold by them, and whatever they have sold earlier is purchased by them. They do not keep any outstanding business to carry forward to the next day. In the London stock market, jobbers are trend makers in the market, while in the US stock markets, they are known as market specialists.

JOBBERS' SPREAD

Usually, when a broker approaches a jobber, he will quote two prices. The higher price or offer price represents the figure at which the jobber will sell. The lower price or bid price represents the price at which he will buy. The difference of these two prices is known as jobbers' spread. For a share which is not active there is only one jobber, the jobber concerned is not faced with any competition and, therefore, his spread can be large. The concept of jobbers' spread can be explained by considering an illustration.

Assume an investor has given his broker an order to buy 100 equity shares of a company, say, Telco at not more than Rs. 220 per share. On receiving the order, his broker or one of his authorized persons goes to that part of the trading floor where jobbers dealing in the company Telco counter are to be found. Approaching one of them, the broker's representative shouts, 'What price Telco?' or simply, 'Telco.' Actually, he will not disclose whether he wants to buy or sell, he will just ask for a quotation.

The jobber could reply '218-220' or '18-20'. This means he is prepared to buy at Rs. 218 and sell at Rs. 220. The difference between the two quotations is called the jobbers' spread and represents the profit the jobber hopes to make if the deal gets through. On getting a quotation of '218-220' from the jobber, the broker or his representative has three options. Since he has been asked to purchase at a price of Rs. 220 maximum, he may accept the offer and complete the deal, or he may approach another jobber to find out if he quotes anything less. As Telco is an actively traded and popular share, during the time of transaction, it will not be difficult for the jobber, who may quote slightly differently, say, '217-219' or '218.5-219.5'. The third option the broker can exercise is to make a counter-bid, and buy at '218.5'. If he fails to get a response, he may raise his bid to '219'.

At this stage, a jobber, who perhaps, had purchased 100 shares of Telco at '218' finds the offer attractive and comes forward and shouts in return, 'Bought 100 Telco at 219' and the deal is struck. The broker and jobber will then make penciled notes in their books. No documents are exchanged at this stage and the deal is concluded only on the basis of the spoken word. However, at the end of the day, the brokers and jobbers will check their entries to find out if there had been any mistakes due to rush of business and settle them amicably and in good faith. At present, major stock exchanges have introduced computer-aided tally sheets.

Prices of actively traded shares change almost from minute to minute depending upon demand and supply. If there are more buyers than sellers, jobbers will raise prices to attract sellers and discourage buyers. The process will be reversed if sellers outnumber buyers. The objective of every jobber will be to balance his purchases and sales. Every time a jobber deals with a broker, he knows how much stock he has on his books and the price at which different lots have been purchased. Therefore, he always quotes a price which enables him to neutralise his outstanding purchases or sales and leave him a profit.

Jobbers ensure liquidity for the shares in which they trade. The two way prices which they quote are the source of their profit. However, it is not always possible for a jobber to earn a profit at the end of the day. Even if a jobber is careful to keep a spread between buying and selling prices, the ruling price may move below the price at which he had bought the shares. In that case, he will suffer a loss.

Actually, a jobber is performing a crucial function – he is helping to make an active continuous market in the shares in which he specializes.

In some case, the spread could be 5 per cent to 7 per cent of the price. It is, therefore, advisable that, other things being equal, the investors should prefer active shares so that their transaction costs do not have large element of jobbers' spread. However, the operations of jobbers are not adequately regulated and it is not uncommon for jobbers to refuse to buy or sell or to quote large spreads. In financial news papers, which print daily share prices, a typical entry of a particular day may be published as Tisco (139), 142, and 145. The entry in parenthesis (139) refers to the closing price on the previous day.

If the broker of an investor bought shares of Tisco for him at 145, the investor might get the impression that the broker bought at the peak of the market and did not get you a good bargain. This is not necessarily so. It is possible that as soon as trading started the jobber's quote was '139 - 142' and the first transaction was a sale to the jobber at 139. At that time the broker might not have realized that he was oversold, that is, he had too many sales undercover on his books.

Therefore, in order to attract more sellers, he could have raised his bid to '139-145'. Again it is possible that the second transaction at mid-session was also a purchase by the jobber at '142' and only the last transaction toward the end of the session was a sale by the jobber to the investor's broker at '145'. In such a situation, the broker could not have got the investor a better deal that day by buying at '145' because throughout most of the session, that was the only price at which the jobber was willing to sell.

It is important for an investor to understand the reality of the jobbers' spread, over which brokers have no control. A lack of its understanding may cause several misunderstandings between clients and brokers and often dilute their mutual trust. Once considered crucial as market-makers, the jobbers had been marginalized with the introduction of screen-based online trading on the Bombay Stock Exchange. But later, they came back in business through a circular form of trading in low-priced, illiquid stocks. Jobbers operating as a cartel, systematically push up the prices of several scrips, especially in non-specified group.

Jobbers have also been linked to the regular hammering of share prices of companies likely to make public or right issues. The promoters of these issues have, then, no option but to start trading and pick up shares to boost the scrip price. In market circles, these illiquid stocks are known as *Kalbadevi brand* scrips, named after a middle-class Mumbai locality, implying that they lack the fundamentals to justify the interest. Most of these scrips are generally placed in the spot category or have been suspended by the Bombay Stock Exchange in the near past. Market operators believe that the criterion, in these cases, is volume and not the scrip's fundamentals or price movements.

The *modus operandi* is as follows: Within the cartel, broker A after a verbal agreement with broker B, makes a sells quote of Rs. 50,000 for the scrip at an absurdly low price of, say, Rs. 8. Broker B buys and sells on the same day to broker C at a slightly higher price. Broker C, at the end of the day, or early next day, buys further stocks to drive up their price, before pulling out quickly. In other cases, the cartel operates to pull down the share price of companies whose public or rights issues are expected to hit the market. According to a leading broker of Mumbai, the price is pulled down so fast that the promoter has no option but to buy the shares from these brokers at a higher price.

These types of situations created by jobbers are very harmful to promoters as well as general investors. To ensure market safety from circular trading and price rigging the exchange authorities implement stringent surveillance systems from time to time. SEBI also imposes strict rules by replacing the existing rules.

TARAWANI WALAS

Tarawani walas are like jobbers and often handle transactions on a commission basis for other brokers. They make transactions on their own account and may act as brokers on behalf of the public.

CLEARING HOUSE OR CORPORATION

A clearing house or clearing corporation is an agency which settles trades among brokers. It nets out broker positions pertaining to payment of funds and delivery of shares. The clearing house of the Bombay Stock Exchange is the Bank of India Shareholding Limited, a joint venture between the exchange and the Bank of India (BOI). Individual investors do not come in contact with clearing houses. The National Securities Clearing Corporation Limited (NSCCL) which is a hundred per cent subsidiary of the NSE handles clearing functions of the exchange (also see Chapter 2 for more details).

LIQUIDITY

Liquidity reflects the quantum of transactions in a particular counter. Counter refers to the counter in a stock exchange where shares of a particular company are generally traded. The larger the volume of trading, the higher the level of liquidity. In the case of highly liquid shares, the spread between the buy and sell quotes is extremely narrow because of the larger volumes. Normally, higher liquidity is seen in stocks which have a relatively large capital and large shareholders' base, as well as large market capitalization. Illiquid stocks are those in which trades do not take place frequently.

Liquidity can be said to be a measure of the number of shares, or money value of shares traded daily. Mutual funds and other institutional buyers prefer high liquidity stocks so they can easily move in and out of positions. The market must also adapt quickly to new information and incorporate that information into the stock's price. Liquidity is one of the most important characteristics.

LISTING AND CATEGORIES OF SHARES

A stock exchange is a place where securities can be bought or sold. However, it is wrong to presume that shares and debentures issued by any company can be freely purchased or sold on any stock exchange.

Dealing in a particular stock exchange can take place only in those securities which are listed on that particular stock exchange. A security is listed when it is added to the list of securities in which trading is permitted on that exchange. Listing is generally done through an application to a particular stock exchange or different stock exchanges with a fee for listing. There is no legal obligation on any public limited company to get its shares or debentures listed on a recognized stock exchange. However, there are situations which make it difficult for a widely held public limited company to avoid listing.

The Bombay Stock Exchange (BSE) and other regional stock exchanges have classified the shares listed with them into various categories. The BSE has three categories, namely A, B1 and B2 for equities. The A group consists of a certain number scrips for which carry forward or *badla* (discussed later in this chapter) facility is provided. In other words, traders or investors can carry forward their transactions from one settlement period (discussed later) to another settlement period, only in the specified number of shares belonging to the A group, which is also known as the specified group. B1 and B2 are cash groups which means carry forward is not allowed, and an investor has to take delivery of shares compulsorily after the settlement is over. These are also called non-specified ones. Group B1 consists of good quality, high volume shares while Group B2 is low-market capitalization thinly traded stocks. The governing body of an exchange has the power to notify, from time to time, the securities which shall be included in or excluded from specified or non-specified list.

This move is generally aimed at extending the carry forward facility to move liquid scrips in the non-specified or cash group. The move is expected to result in greater volatility and increased turnover in the scrips promoted and also the specified group as whole. Investors are allowed to carry forward their positions in scrips, paying *badla* charges but without taking delivery of shares. A prominent exchange like the Bombay Stock Exchange does use some parameters for specification of the scrips for reshuffling of A group.

First, market capitalization[1]: The scrip should be among the top 300 scrips ranked by market capitalization.

Second, liquidity[2]: It includes trading volumes, number of trades and trading frequency of the scrips. The average trading turnover in the scrip over the last six months should have been in the top 75 per cent of 300-scrip universe. The selected scrips should form part of the BSE 500 index (to be discussed later).

The floating stock[3]: This should be adequate in the market. The index committee takes into account parameters such as promoter's holding, number of shares, quality of management and image and background of the promoters while deciding on this factor.

This scrip is expected to offer dematerialization facility within three months from the date of shifting to A group. The specified list is subject to review by an index committee every quarter.

The Bombay Stock Exchange decides to make changes in its reshuffling plan following the Securities & Exchange Board of India (SEBI) order asking it to look into criteria for selection of the scrips. The SEBI from time to time, constitutes a committee for recommendation of the scrips to be shifted from one group to another. The committee takes into account various parameters such as floating stock, liquidity, profitability, and the size of the capital.

Notes:

[1] **Market capitalization** is the total market value of company scrip at current stock exchange price. This is arrived at by multiplying the total number of shares issued by a company by the current price of that share in the stock exchange (see Chapter 2).

[2] **Liquidity** means an asset must be convertible into cash at its fair price. That is, a large number of shares of the company can quickly be converted into cash without a drop in the price (also discussed earlier).

[3] **Floating stock** is the number of shares of a company that is traded on the stock exchange; usually a fraction of the total number issued and outstanding.

'Z' GROUP OF SHARES

On July 26th 1999, the Bombay Stock Exchange introduced a new group of shares called Z group in addition to the existing A, B1 and B2 groups, to separately classify errant companies. The exchange so far has shifted nearly 300 companies to the Z group mostly from B2 group. The move of the BSE to separately classify the companies as Z group companies forms part of its plan to protect investors' interests. The companies which do not comply with the clauses of the exchange's listing agreement and fail to redress investors' complaints are generally shifted to the Z group. The move aims at alerting prospective investors against these companies so that they desist from putting their money into stocks of these companies.

It can be easily understood that the companies are not queuing up to be selected for Z group. More seriously, the BSE comes out with a blacklist on the basis of companies' compliance levels. The exchange considers whether the companies are following its rules and regulations as stated in the listing agreement, such as payment of listing fees, timely announcement of quarterly, half-yearly and annual accounts, announcement of book closure, submission of some important documents such as annual reports, share holding pattern and so on. Redressal of investor grievances is also an important criterion for the selection of the companies.

Prior notice is also sent to them advising remedial action. Shifting an errant company is a regular process. A precautionary message appears on the Bombay on line trading terminal if any investor places orders for Z group stock.

BOOK CLOSURE

Book closure is the period during which the company entertains transfer of shares (discussed later). The company announces book closure dates for entitlement of dividend or bonus and right shares and entitlement of other securities. So, if an investor wants to get the benefits of these issues, he should enlist his name with the company much before the date of book closure, which is announced or published in different news papers by different companies in different times.

In other words it can be said that book closure and record date help a company to exactly determine the shareholders of a company as on a given date. Book closure refers to the closing in the register of the names or investors in the records of a company. Companies announce book closure dates from time to time. The benefits of dividends, bonus issues, rights issue accruing to investors whose name appears on the company's records as on a given date, is known as the record date. An investor might purchase a share-cum-dividend, cum rights or cum bonus and may therefore expect to receive these benefits as the new shareholder. In order to receive them, the shares have to be transferred in the investor's name, or he would stand deprived of the benefits. The buyer of such shares will be a loser. It is important for a buyer of shares to ensure that shares purchased at cum benefits prices are transferred before book-closure. It must be ensured that the price paid for the shares is ex-benefit and not cum benefit.

In case of a record date, the company does not close its register of security holders. The record date is the cut off date for determining the number of registered members who are eligible for corporate benefits. In case of book closure, shares bearing a date on the transfer deed earlier than the book closure cannot be sold on an exchange. This does not hold good for the record date.

NO-DELIVERY PERIOD

Whenever any company announces a book closure or record date, the exchange sets up a No-Delivery (ND) period for that security. During this period only trading is permitted in the security. However, these trades are settled only after the no-delivery period is over. This is done to ensure that an investor's entitlement for the corporate benefit is clearly determined.

EX-DATE

The first day of the no-delivery period is the ex-date. If there are any corporate benefits such as rights, bonus or dividends announced for which book closure/record date is fixed, the buyer of the shares on or after the ex-date will not be eligible for the benefits.

EX-DIVIDEND DATE

This is the date on or after which a security begins trading without the dividend (cash or stock) included in the contract price.

CIRCUIT FILTER

The circuit filter is the maximum permissible limit for fluctuation of a share price – upward or downward – during a session. Earlier, it was eight per cent in A group stocks and B1 group stocks. But with effect from July 3rd 2000 the SEBI has relaxed the price bands to 8+4 and finally to 8+8 per cent totaling 16 per cent, for the 200 top scrips and those in the compulsory rolling settlement mode (rolling settlement will be discussed later). Circuit filter remained 25 per cent in certain B2 stocks.

PUBLISHING RATES OR QUOTATIONS

The prices of shares of the specified and non-specified groups are compiled in a daily list by the recording clerks of different stock exchanges. These clerks are employees of the stock exchanges who go around obtaining rates at which the shares of different companies (listed respectively in the stock exchanges in which they work) were traded on a particular day. They obtain these rates from jobbers. These rates or prices of shares are reproduced by the different news papers and are commonly known as daily quotations.

MARKET PRICE

The market price of an equity share is the price at which it is being traded on the bourses. However, this price depends on various factors like liquidity, the demand and supply of the share and investors' perception. It is well accepted that the market price of an equity share is determined by interaction of demand and supply of that share. Supply and demand are, in turn, governed by many rational and irrational factors. Irrespective of minor fluctuations in the stock market, share prices tend to move in trends which persist for an appreciable length of time. Changes of such trends are caused by shifts in the demand and supply position of shares.

CHANGING MARKET PRICES OF SHARES

The market price or values of actively traded equity shares seldom remain constant. They keep fluctuating – some moderately and some violently due to a variety of reasons to be discussed in later chapters. These fluctuations in the market prices always cause anxiety and discomfort for general investors. Many market watchers feel that price movements of stocks are totally unpredictable. They can go up, stay steady, or come down. It is just not possible to make any predictions about price movements. They are like mathematical random numbers, which have an equal chance of occurrence. Many academicians have raised a basic doubt about any proof behind the historical data on share prices, which can help in predicting future prices. After a great deal of research they have come to the conclusion that share prices fluctuate randomly and expert knowledge is required for success in investment.

This behavior of stock prices has come to be known as the 'Random Walk Theory.' It is perhaps one of the most publicized stock market theories in recent years. In simple language, the 'Random Walk Theory' runs somewhat along these lines: The share prices on a given day, are already a fair reflection of their value. They do not change in any systematic manner. They change only if an unexpected event occurs, such as a change in the political scenario, an increase in prices of petroleum products, any drastic change in the Companies Acts or monetary policies etc. Since the investors do not know what may happen tomorrow, the academics' view is that no one can predict whether the next price change will be favorable or unfavorable. Therefore, they argue, share prices move randomly over a period of time.

According to the Random Walk hypothesis, the value or price of a share cannot be determined precisely. The price in the marketplace tends to vary randomly around the intrinsic value of the shares. As new information is received, it is transmitted to the marketplace and a new value is established. In the process, the prices over-adjust and there may be a lag in the adjustment process. In addition, the adjustment process assumes that any change in the price is independent of the previous ones, which is really the definition of a random market. What is more, the sequences of share price changes have no memory and so past sequences cannot be used to predict the future.

MARKETABILITY

Equity shares which are listed and activity quoted and traded on stock exchanges can be disposed of easily. Whenever one requires funds, one can simply ring up a broker and dispose of one's shares at the prevailing market prices.

Marketability of shares means the shares in one's portfolio which can be marketed without difficulty. If there are too many unlisted or inactive shares in one's portfolio, one may face problems in marketing or encashing them and switching from one investment to another. A good portfolio should appreciate in value in order to protect the investor from any erosion in purchasing power due to inflation. In other words, a balanced portfolio must consist of investments which can sustain inflation as well as be easily marketable.

BULLS AND BEARS

Most stock exchange speculators can broadly be grouped into two categories: the bulls and bears. A bull is a speculator who takes an optimistic view of the future. He expects the price of a particular share to rise in the immediate future. Therefore, he buys these shares at their current prices in hope of selling them later at higher prices. He is a speculator because he buys with the short-term objective of making quick profits out of price fluctuations. When a lot of bull activities dominate the stock market there is a general all-round rise in share prices. Such a market is commonly referred to as a 'bull market'. Bull is thus a term used to describe a rising market.

A bear, on the other hand, is a speculator who takes a pessimistic view of the future. He expects share prices to fall in the immediate future. He makes his money by selling shares at the current price with the hope of buying them later at a lower price. He usually sells shares which he does not own with the intention of buying them later for delivery to the actual buyer. This, in stock market parlance, is referred to as 'short selling.'

SHORT SELLING

Short selling is a legitimate trading strategy. It is the sale of a security that the seller does not own, or any sale that is completed by the delivery of a security borrowed by the seller. Short sellers take the risk that they will be able to buy the stock at a more favorable price than the price at which they "sold short."

If a bear operator wants to carry forward his transaction from one settlement period to the next, he must find someone who will loan him the shares which he has to deliver on the settlement day. Or, he can find a bull operator who cannot pay for his purchase and wants his business also to be carried forward (discussed below).

Usually, a bear does not have to pay interest on his carried forward business. On the contrary, he receives a payment identical to that paid by the bull operator. This is because a bull, who purchased shares but cannot pay for them, is glad to pay a small charge to a bear who has sold shares but cannot deliver them.

However, at times, the seller (bear) who usually gets paid contango on his sales may have to pay the buyer a charge called 'backwardation' or *undhabadla*. This happens when the shares are oversold and buyers are in a demanding position.

In these types of dealings, *budliwalas* play important role. *Budliwala* is an intermediary who provides the necessary finance for taking delivery of shares or lends the required shares for making delivery at the end of clearing (discussed later in this chapter). They usually give fully secured loans for a short period of two or three weeks. The *budliwalas* charge fees (as we have already mentioned above) called contango or *sidhabadla* and *undhabadla*, for granting credit facilities to the buyer and the sellers.

Short sales are very disturbing transactions for most sections of the market associates for various reasons. Investors hate short sales because they think that short selling triggers the downtrend in prices which, in turn, erode their wealth. Traders and stock exchanges are apprehensive of imminent erosion in volumes, brought about by a modification of the ruling practice. The regulatory authority faces tremendous pressure from a section of the market community to check the excessive speculative activity during a bear phase. Sometime ago, SEBI appointed a committee under the chairmanship of B.D. Shah, former chairman and managing director of New India Assurance Company and former managing director of General

Insurance Corporation of India, to look into the issue of regulating short sales on the stock exchanges.

Among other things, the committee recommended that brokers of stock exchanges should mandatorily declare, scrip-wise, their net short sales and net long purchases at the end of each trading day, and that this information should be further verified and compiled on a cumulative basis by each stock exchange. The committee also suggested that stock exchanges should levy differential margins on sales and purchases, depending on market conditions. It also suggested a stock-lending scheme. The committee ruled that disclosure of outstanding positions should be made regularly. SEBI issued norms and guidelines on stock lending on 6th February 1997.

There have been frequent demands from the market operators to ban short sales temporarily whenever the market is engulfed by a bear phase for a considerably long period of time. However, SEBI usually does not take any drastic step like banning short sales, even for a short duration, despite mounting pressure on it to do so. But from time to time it assigns a committee the task of looking into the issue of regulating short sales. One such committee, the B.D. Shah Committee opined against any ban on short selling on 27th November, 1998. Some market analysts feel that as they are universally known and accepted, short sales not only provide liquidity to the markets, but also aid in the price discovery process by providing competitive bids. Thus, the greater the number of transactions, the better is the price discovery and liquidity, which are considered to be the two attributes of vibrant stock markets. Hence, regulating short sales by banning them could be suicidal because volumes will shrink.

General investors think that while a ban on short sales may be undesirable, excessive short sales for any unrestricted speculation have to be checked. Excessive short sales are bound to manifest their ill effects of undue depression of share prices, which erodes investors' wealth.

Short sales in the Indian markets have a wider connotation. The B.D. Shah Committee has defined a short sale as a sale of shares without having physical possession of them unless it is for either squaring up an earlier purchase in the same settlement period of the same stock exchange or against pending deliveries (from the same stock exchange) pertaining to a previous settlement. Thus, short sales encompass a host of sales transactions like sales for a subsequent squaring during the same day or during the same settlement, selling for carry forward to the next settlement and selling to take advantage of the price differential of the same stock on two different stock exchanges called arbitrage. Sales of these types are also sometimes termed naked short sales. A broker who purchases security in one market and sells the same in another market to get opportunistic profit is also known as an arbitrageur. Dealers who deal with different securities in different stock exchanges at the same time are called arbitrageurs. They simultaneously make attempts to acquire the same or equivalent securities to take advantage of price differences in the same or different markets.

Considered as one of the instruments for short sales, the carry forward system, or *badla* as it is widely known, has come under criticism from a section of the market operators. Some market analysts say that the carry forward system favors short sellers or bears because they get *badla* charges for going short in a scrip, and this gives them an undue advantage over bulls or long buyers. This drags down prices further in a falling market. In a time-tested system like carry forward, wherein market forces determine the *badla* rates during every screen-based trading session, can operators on any side (here the short sellers) continue to be in an advantageous position for a long time? The reason why bears or short sellers get *badla* charges for selling short is that a substantially higher risk component is involved in short selling. A short seller trades against the long-term secular uptrend of the market and he is always prone to be squeezed by the buyer who can insist on delivery of shares which are difficult to procure. Borrowing shares is always more difficult than borrowing money. A short seller is paid for the risk he takes in this respect.

Whenever there are excessive short sale positions for carry forward in any settlement, the long buyer steps into the shoes of the short seller as the latter has to pay *badla* charges called backwardation charges, or *undha badla*, to the buyer. 'The larger the component of short sales in the market, the weaker is the short seller and the system is self-corrective,' says M.R. Mayya, former executive director of the Bombay Stock Exchange. Thus, to say that sellers are always in an advantageous position over buyers in a carry forward or *badla* system would not be appropriate.

While it is impossible for short sellers to dictate a downward trend in the market because the latter adjusts to fundamentals in the long run, bears can take advantage of depressed market conditions to accentuate a further fall by hammering and thus make quick money in the short run.

According to brokers, the modus operandi of the operators was simple: hammer down the prices of a few pivotal shares simultaneously through programmed trading. Then spread some rumours to create panic in the market. And, as prices come down (when deliveries are offloaded by investors in panic), cover the short positions and make a killing in the short term.

The settlement system on the Indian bourses leaves scope for traders/operators to take advantage of the seven-day cycle by effecting transactions like those in the case above to make quick gains in the short run. The country's largest stock exchange is often blamed for inculcating what is known as a casino culture among investors. Traders/Operators indulge in large-scale speculation on a daily basis, also known as day trades.

Given that speculators rule the roost in Indian stock exchanges, as is evident in the small percentage of delivery trades to total trades, the existence of rampant short sales on a daily or on a settlement basis is obvious. But SEBI seems to be reluctant to impose a ban fearing a drastic fall in volumes and a consequent fall in liquidity. During a temporary ban by SEBI on daily short sales in order to check volatility in prices in a few trading sessions in June-July, 1998, the volumes on both the BSE and NSE had in fact declined substantially in a few trading sessions during that period. Stock lending or securities lending is one of the ways by which naked short sales on the exchanges could be regulated, according to market participants. In fact, the B.D. Shah Committee on short sales recommended stock lending as a measure to regulate short sales. Subsequently, SEBI issued norms and guidelines for a stock-lending scheme in February 1997.

An analyst explains that under the stock-lending scheme, the temporary needs of borrowers, like brokers, can be met by the lenders – usually by an institutional investor holding the stock as a long-term portfolio investment – to support trading activities like short sales or to meet short-term delivery obligations of the borrowers like meeting the shortfall in deliveries. Thus, a lender can loan the securities to the borrower through an Approved Intermediary (AI) under an agreement which states that the borrower will return an equivalent number of securities of the same type and class at the end of the specified period along with the corporate benefits accruing on the borrowed securities. While operators/traders can use stock lending as a tool for trading, institutional investors can use it for earning extra income by way of fees or charges for lending from shares held as long-term investments. There were two vital bottlenecks due to which stock lending did not make much headway initially. SEBI's norms and guidelines on stock lending stated that the risk of default by the borrower will be borne by the AI. Not all AIs, however, were willing to take such a principal risk because they preferred to act only as agents in stock-lending transactions. It was subsequently clarified by SEBI that AIs can act merely as agents in stock-lending transactions provided all the parties to the contract agreed. The second important issue related to the levy of tax on stock-lending transactions: whether such transactions should be considered as regular buy-sale transactions or treated separately. The tax officials clarified that lending and borrowing of shares under the stock-lending scheme will be free from capital gains tax.

Some other operational bottlenecks in stock lending, however, remain. One is the high degree of principal risk involved for the lender (say an institutional investor) in lending the securities, like failure of the borrower (usually a broker or an individual investor) to return the securities lent. Second is the possibility of bad title of the shares returned by the borrower to the lender. While the former risk is the intrinsic business risk in stock-lending activity, the latter is related to the ills of dealing in physical shares like bad delivery, delay in transfer, etc. Market operators feel that while the intrinsic risk (like the quality of the borrowers) will be taken care of as the market matures, the risk associated with dealing in physical shares can be done away with total dematerialization.

According to the authorities of the SHCIL, the problems associated with paper-based securities, i.e., the possibility of their getting stolen, benami, fake and bogus certificates, both as collateral and as repayment of loans, can be eliminated by popularising the concept of dematerialisation and trading in the demat segment. Authorities of National Securities Depository Limited (NSDL) have already made available to its members the computer module so that they can participate in stock lending. Market operators feel that though *badla* and stock lending will co-exist for some time, the latter could outpace the former over a period of time.

Stock lending, nonetheless, is expected to better the liquidity in the market as shares which are lying idle with institutions (in their long-term investment portfolio) would come to the stock exchanges for trading. An increase in liquidity will lead to a better price discovery. In fact, stock lending has become an integral part of the smooth functioning of markets in many countries. Besides helping in addressing the problems of settlement failures, stock lending also aids in increasing the delivery ratio on the stock exchanges, which is all the more necessary in the Indian markets where deliveries constitute only a small portion of trades.

The operational guidelines and norms for stock lending issued by SEBI provide substantial freedom to market participants in stock lending. Things like tenure of the loan, the fees payable by the borrower and the amount and type of collateral have all been left to the market participants to decide.

Once a proper stock-lending scheme is in place, short sales on a daily basis or those indulged in for squaring in the same settlement can be checked by banning such sales on a downtick, i.e., at a price below the last closing price. Thus, as is the practice in the US, short sales could be permitted only on an up tick, i.e., at a price above the last closing price. This will help check depression in share prices due to excessive short sales or hammering. One way in which, short sales could be controlled is by reducing the circuit breaker ceiling on the stock exchanges. In our country, it is high when compared to limits in the developed markets like the US, the UK and Germany.

Nonetheless, SEBI's recent initiatives to tighten the margin system and strengthen the disclosure norms are steps in the right direction and can help check excessive speculative trades, including short sales. Thus, the requirement of scrip-wise disclosure of gross outstanding positions at the end of every day by a broker, without setting off purchases of one client with sales of another client, will mean a better disclosure of the outstanding position per scrip. This will also help check excessive speculation in scrip. While brokers were hitherto required to disclose, scrip-wise, their net outstanding positions separately on trades done on their own account and those on their client's account, the latter was disclosed after squaring of inter-client positions in the same scrip. On the margins front, it is now mandatory for the broker to collect margins upfront from the clients and deposit the same in a separate account.

It would be helpful if institutional investors like domestic investment institutions, FIIs and mutual funds take part in short sell. It is felt that this could generate a lot of demand for stock lending and will be the proper way to regulate short sales. If adverse developments like the economic slowdown, fears of a widening fiscal deficit, turmoil in leading international economies like Russia and Japan and the US-64 imbroglio usually depress stock markets, new developments in the political scenario, assembly elections and the resultant uncertainty over the fate of vital economic issues may drag the market down. On the other hand, sound economic policies of the government may fuel the stock market in a better way. The rally, however, does not mean that SEBI should put the issue of regulating short sales on the backburner. Regulating short sales, nonetheless, is a complex issue and care is needed to regulate short selling.

While discussing 'Performance Attribution with Short Position' in the *Journal of Performance Measurement* (Winter 2002/2003), Dr. Jose Menchero[2] quickly reviewed the basics of selling short or purchasing on margin in a USA stock market.

According to Dr. Menchero, when an investor places an order to sell a security short, the investor in effect borrows the security from a broker and agrees to repay the loan at some

---

[2]Jose Menchero, Performance Attribution with Short Position, *Journal of Performance Measurement*, Winter 2002, USA, p. 203

later date by delivery of the security, thus closing out the short position. If the price of the security falls, the investor certainly stands to profit from such a trade. As collateral for the loan, the broker gives not only the cash proceeds from the short sale but also an *initial margin requirement,* which typically amounts to 50 per cent of the value of short sale. The investor is entitled to earn interest on both cash proceeds and the initial margin requirement. Although in practice these two cash sources may earn different interest rates, for simplicity Dr. Menchero assumes that they earn the same rate (corresponding to the margin lending rates). For instance, suppose that an investor shorts one share of stock XYZ at $100, then the cash proceeds together with the $50 initial margin requirement are placed into the margin account (for a total of $150). Suppose the margin account earns 4 per cent interest for the period, and that the price of XYZ drops to $90. The value of margin account thus increases to $156. The investor purchases the stock at $90, closes out the short position, and is left with $66. Since the initial capital put forward was $50 (margin requirement), the investor has thus earned a profit of $16. Of this, $10 came from a drop in price of XYZ, and $6 came from interest earned on the margin account.

In the case of an investor purchasing a security on margin, the investor is not required to pay the full value of the security up front but rather borrows part of the amount from the broker. The amount that the investor is required to pay up front is determined by the initial margin requirement, which again is typically 50 per cent. For instance, suppose that an investor purchases on margin one share of stock ABC at $100. The investor is required to pay $50 up front, and borrows the remaining $50 from the broker. Let the borrowing rate in the margin account be 6 per cent and the price of ABC rises to $110. The investor sells ABC for $110 at the end of the period, uses $53 to pay off the loan, and is left with $57 (for a $7 profit). In this instance, the $7 profit was due to the $10 earned on stock ABC, less the $3 interest paid on the borrowed funds. Note that if the investor had simply purchased $50 of stock (without margin), the profit would have been only $5. By purchasing the stock on margin, and thereby using leverage, the investor was able to earn a higher return.

In order to develop a rigorous sector-based attribution analysis that incorporates short positions, Dr. Jose Menchero[3] derived a methodology. He opined that, it is first necessary to establish how security-level weights and returns are computed. In what follows, he assumed a single period buy-and-hold scenario. After establishing the framework for a single period, it is a simple matter to extend the analysis to multiple periods.

Let $v_0(j)$ be the beginning-of-period market value for security j within the portfolio. It is important to stress that if the portfolio contains cash position, then these positions must be explicitly treated as securities for analytical purposes. The beginning-of-period market value V_0 for the entire portfolio is simply the sum of the individual market value,

$$V_0 = \Sigma \, v_0(j) \tag{1}$$

It should be noted that since some securities are held short, individual $v_0(j)$ may be negative. The portfolio marked V_0, by contrast, must be positive (i.e. in net long position) for the fund to remain solvent. Dr. Menchero defined the portfolio weight $w(j)$ of the security j in the standard way,

---

[3]ibid

$$\omega(j) = \frac{v_0(j)}{V_0} \tag{2}$$

Using this definition, it is clear that short positions have negative weights. It is also clear that the weights defined by Equation (2) are normalized to unity, i.e.

$$\Sigma w(j) = (1/V_0) \Sigma v_0(j) = 1 \tag{3}$$

The portfolio return R is also given by standard definition,

$$R = \frac{\Delta V}{V_0} \tag{4}$$

Here, ΔV is the change in the market value of the portfolio over the period, which is simply given by the sum of changes in the market values $\Delta v(j)$ of the individual securities,

$$\Delta V = \sum_j \Delta v(j) \tag{5}$$

The return $r(j)$ on an individual security j is also defined in the standard way,

$$r(j) = \frac{\Delta v(j)}{v_0(j)} \tag{6}$$

The return defined in this way has the nice property that it is independent of whether the security is held long or short. For instance, if the price of a stock changes from \$50 to \$55 over a period of time, then the return of the stock is simply 10 per cent (irrespective of the stock held long or short). The contribution that the stock makes to the portfolio returns, obviously, will depend on whether it was held long or short.

This observation was also mentioned by another analyst, Damien Laker[4]. Substituting Equations (5) and (6) into Equation (4), the portfolio return can be written as

$$R = \frac{1}{V_0} \sum_j \Delta v(j) = \frac{1}{V_0} \sum_j v_0(j) r(j) \tag{7}$$

Using the definition of weight from Equation (2), this can be written as

$$R = \sum_j w(j) r(j) \tag{8}$$

Equation (8) expresses the portfolio return as a sum of contributions from individual securities. The results from this section show that all the standard definitions and relationships for security-level weights and returns continue to apply for the case in which some securities are held short.

Example: Let us now refer to Table 3.2(a) and consider a concrete example. Suppose that a portfolio manager begins the period with \$1,000 and makes the following transactions: (i) The portfolio manager purchases \$800 of stock ABC, thus leaving \$200 available cash. (ii) The manager shorts \$400 of stock XYZ, using the \$200 in available cash as the initial

---

[4]Damien Laker, Performance Measurement for Short Position, *Journal of Performance Measurement*, Spring, 2002, USA, pp 6-8

Table 3.2(a)   Market Value of Each Security in the Portfolio after Each Transaction

Security	Transaction (0)	(1)	(2)
ABC	$0	$800	$800
XYZ	0	0	(400)
Margin Cash	0	0	600
Available Cash	1000	200	0
Total	$1000	$1000	$1000

Note: In Transaction(1), the portfolio manager puchases $ 800 portfolio ABC. In Transaction (2), the manager shorts $ 400 of stock of XYZ. It may be noted that the market value of the portfolio is unchanged after each transaction.

margin requirement. It may be noted that the net amount in the margin account is therefore $600 ($400 from the proceeds of short sale, and $200 from the margin requirement).

Suppose the stock ABC raises by 10 per cent and that XYZ falls by 10 per cent. The market value of the long position in ABC thus increases to $880, whereas the market value of the short position in XYZ decreases to $360. Assuming that the portfolio manager earns 4 per cent in interest for the period on $600 in cash, the market value of this position grows to $624. Adding up all of the assets and liabilities, an end-of-period market value for the portfolio of $1,144 can be obtained. The portfolio return for the period is therefore 14.4 per cent. The security-level weights and returns for this example are tabulated in Table 3.2(b) below, and show that sum of contributions indeed gives the investor the portfolio return of 14.4 per cent.

Table 3.2(b)   Security-Level Weights and Returns. The Portfolio Return is given by the Sum of the Contributions.

Security	Begin Value	End Value	Weight (%)	Return(%)	Contribution(%)
ABC	$800	$880	80.0	10.0	8.0
XYZ	(400)	(360)	−40.0	−10.0	4.0
Cash	600	624	60.0	4.0	2.4
Total	$1000	$1144	100.0	14.4	14.4

Note: For further details of weights, returns and attributes analysis of short positions, please refer to the article of Dr. Jose Menchero [26].

SECURITIES LENDING

In securities lending, the legal right of a security is temporarily transferred from a lender to a borrower. The lender retains all the benefits of ownership, other than the voting rights. The borrower is entitled to utilize the securities as required but is liable to the lender for all benefits, e.g. dividends, interest or rights.

Securities lending began as a means to cover short sales (discussed above), but has since evolved as a means of facilitating sophisticated trading strategies. Securities lending occurs when a holder of securities or his agents lends eligible securities to borrowers in return for a fee. The absence of a formal market for securities lending had been felt for a while. Responding to market needs SEBI introduced a scheme for securities lending and borrowing in 1997. It is quite well known in the market that a securities lending program is used by the lenders to maximize yields on their portfolio. Borrowers use the securities lending program to avoid settlement failures.

Securities lending provides income opportunities for securities holders and creates liquidity to facilitate trading strategies for borrowers. Securities lending is particularly attractive for large institutional holders of securities, as it is an easy way of generating income to offset custody fees and requires little, if any, of their involvement or time. Securities lending gives borrowers access to the lender's portfolios, which provide the flexibility necessary when borrowing for strategic positioning and financing inventories. From the point of view of markets, securities lending and borrowing facilitates timely settlement, increases the settlements, reduces market volatility and improves liquidity.

The lender receives a guarantee for his securities as the borrower has to deposit collateral securities, which could be cash bank guarantees, government securities or certificates of deposit or other securities, with an approved intermediary. In case the borrower fails to return the securities, he will be declared a defaulter and the approved intermediary will liquidate the collateral deposited with it. In the event of default, the approved intermediary is liable to making good the loss caused to the lender. The borrower cannot discharge his liabilities of returning the equivalent securities through payment in cash or kind.

The main approved intermediaries registered with SEBI are: the National Securities Clearing Corporation Ltd. (NSCCL), Stock Holding Corporation of India (SHCIL), Deutsche Bank, and Reliance Capital etc. NSCCL proposes to offer a number of schemes including the Automated Lending and Borrowing Mechanism (ALBM), automatic borrowing for settlement failures and case by case borrowing.

Organizations that can participate in securities lending/borrowing are: clearing and trading members of stock exchanges, corporates, financial institutes, foreign individual investors, mutual funds and individuals. Depending upon the constituent's own internal statutory guidelines and the eligibility criteria set by the approved intermediary for different schemes, these entities may act as lenders, borrowers or both. Income from securities lending and borrowings is exempted from capital gains tax vide CBDT Circular 751 dated February 10th 1997.

Auction

An auction is conducted for those securities that members fail to deliver/short deliver during pay-in. Three factors primarily give rise to an auction: short deliveries, un-rectified bad deliveries, and un-rectified company objections.

Market for Auctions

The buy/sell auction for a capital market security is managed through the auction market. As opposed to the normal market where trade matching is an on-going process, the trade matching process for an auction starts after the auction period is over. If the shares are not bought at the auction i.e. if the shares are not offered for sale, the exchange squares up the transaction as per SEBI guidelines. The transaction is squared up at the highest price from the relevant trading period till the auction day or at 20 per cent above the last available closing price whichever is higher. The pay-in and pay-out of funds for auction square up is held along with the pay-out for the relevant auction.

LEVERAGE

Leverage is any means of increasing the value and return by borrowing funds or committing less of one's own money. For corporations, it refers to the ratio of debt (in the form of bonds and preferred stock outstanding) to equity (in the form of common stock outstanding) in the company's capital structure.

The more long-term debt there is, the greater is the financial leverage. Shareholders benefit from this financial leverage to the extent that the return on the borrowed money exceeds the interest costs of borrowing it. The market value of the company rises and so does its shares. Because of this effect, financial leverage is popularly called trading on the equity. For individuals, leverage can involve debt, as when an investor borrows money from his broker on margin and so is able to buy more stock than he otherwise could. If the stock goes up, he repays the broker the loan amount and keeps the profit for himself. By borrowing money he has achieved a higher return on his investment than if he had paid for all the stock himself. Rights, warrants, futures and option contracts also provide leverage, not through debt but by offering the prospect of a high return for little or no investment.

The downside is that most individuals pledge existing stocks with their bankers or brokers for the loan, which is a percentage of the market value of the stocks pledged. Say you have pledged stocks worth Rs. 100 on the market against which you are given a loan of Rs. 50 (50 per cent). Now suppose the market value of the pledged stocks goes down to Rs. 75. The lender is immediately going to ask you to pledge more stocks (or pay cash) to bring the level up to 200 per cent of the loan.

Multiply this instance by thousands and you can imagine the margin pressure that is exerted on the market. This is when the market falls and turns into what is known as a bear market.

If a company, which has been financed by taking a debt and equity fund, has more than one-third of debt capitalization, it is considered as a highly leveraged company. Such companies may also show poor results during an economic slowdown. Take over of a public corporation using borrowed funds is known as leveraged buy out. Leverage, in short, can be said to be a company's long-term debt in relation to equity in its capital structure. The longer the long-term debt, the higher is the leverage.

When the amount of total assets of a company is divided by the equity, one gets the leverage ratio; it indicates the amount of assets the company employs on a unit of equity.

DIFFERENT SYSTEMS OF SHARE TRADING

Trading or transactions on a stock exchange are carried out mainly on either a cash basis or carry over basis. Carry over is permitted only in respect of group-A securities. Types of transactions on a cash basis according to arrangement for delivery are given below.

Spot Delivery

When the delivery of shares (in case of buying order) or payment of shares (in case of selling order) is made on which the order is placed by an investor to the broker, then that delivery is called a spot delivery. Sometimes spot delivery is also shifted to the next day according to mutual understanding between investors and brokers. This system is also known as spot basis trading or forward trading.

Hand Delivery

For hand delivery of shares that is for delivery and payment within the time or date stipulated while entering into a bargain which, however, shall not be more than 14 days following the date of placing the order. This also is known as clearing delivery or cash basis trading.

Special Delivery

Special delivery is the delivery under which payment for shares sold or delivery of shares purchased is made within the time or the date stipulated while entering into a bargain. This time generally exceeds 14 days following the date of contract (order) with the broker. The contract has to be permitted by the governing board or president of the stock exchange in which the deal is done. This system is also called settlement basis trading or carry forward trading and rolling settlement basis trading (introduced in the late 1990s with some modifications by SEBI).

In this system, trading or bargain can be done without ready-money in hand or without ready share-scrips in possession. By paying the differences of share prices, a deal can be continued for these settlement periods in this system. Finally, the deal can be completed after three settlement periods. In this system, all categories of shares, i.e., A, B1, or B2, can be traded. But comparatively rich and cash rich investors participate in this system of trading rather than small investors. With the introduction of computer based trading better liquidity has started to appear in this system.

Bargains for spot delivery, hand delivery and special delivery can be made in any security in which dealings are permitted on the exchange. However, bargains for clearing are allowed to be made only in specified securities.

After the introduction of computer based trading, settlement based trading was streamlined and complaints of late settlement and most of the earlier irregularities seemed to be removed. The settlement cycles of different exchanges are described in Charts 3.1 - 3.3.

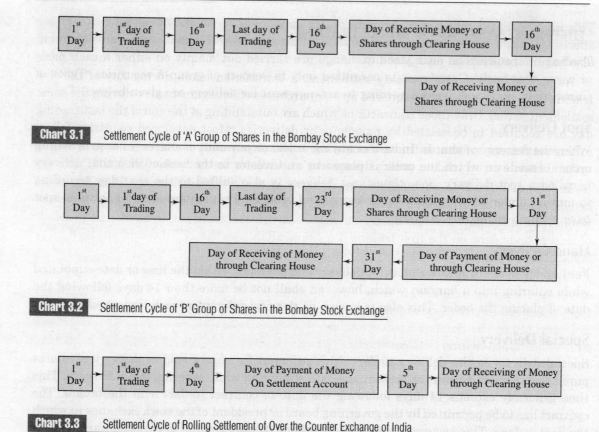

Chart 3.1 Settlement Cycle of 'A' Group of Shares in the Bombay Stock Exchange

Chart 3.2 Settlement Cycle of 'B' Group of Shares in the Bombay Stock Exchange

Chart 3.3 Settlement Cycle of Rolling Settlement of Over the Counter Exchange of India

Rolling Settlement

After the introduction of screen-based trading and dematerialization of stocks (paperless trading), rolling settlement and daily *badla* system have been introduced in India phase by phase (scrips wise) by the Indian regulatory authorities during late 1990s. From July 2nd, 2001, the finance minister made all the scrips included in the Borrowing and Lending Securities Scheme (BLESS), Automated Lending and Borrowing Mechanism (ALMB) and MCFS and others comprising the BSE 200 index (discussed later), to be traded in rolling settlement mode, compulsorily across all Indian exchanges. This has been done with a view to make it difficult for anybody to manipulate the prices in scrips and to bring Indian settlement systems and procedures on par with the international standards.

Rolling settlement implies that any outstanding transaction at the end of the day will necessarily result in settlement (payments made for purchases or deliveries in the case of sale of securities). If one has purchased, say 1,000 shares of a big Indian company such as Reliance, and the transaction remains outstanding at the end of the day, he would have to make payment on the settlement day. The settlement day would be T+5, as specified by SEBI.

This implies that if shares were brought on Monday, the settlement, that is payment for the shares bought, would be done on next Monday. If the shares were sold instead, delivery would also have to be given on next Monday.

As opposed to this, in a weekly settlement, a transaction made during any of the five trading days is permitted to be squared up – or purchases offset against sale – during the same settlement period. Only those transactions which are outstanding at the end of the last trading day are required to be settled by payments or deliveries. Most developed countries follow rolling settlement system. In India though, the broker community is not very happy with the system. Institutional traders prefer the system as it allows faster rotation of funds.

In rolling settlements, payments are quicker than in the weekly settlements. Thus, investors benefit from faster turnaround times. For example, in a rolling settlement system, investors would receive the payments on the day after the sale. In the weekly settlement, sale proceeds of transactions done on the first trading day are available on the 12th day and on the 8th day if the trade takes place on the last day of the trading cycle.

In India, the rolling settlement is a separate segment. The trading volumes in this segment are insignificant as compared to those seen in the normal or weekly trading segment. So far Carry Forward for scrips in Rolling Settlement (CFRS) has been permitted by SEBI and was implemented by the Bombay Stock Exchange from November 21, 2000. But the NSE was the first to introduce Rolling Settlement (RS) in India. It could not be introduced earlier because the country did not have depositories. This is because the rolling settlements necessarily require electronic transfers of funds and demat facilities in respect of securities being traded. Handling large volumes of paper on a daily basis is extremely difficult for the clearing houses of stock exchanges. It is only now that India has adequate facilities for electronic delivery of shares (demat shares), which facilitates trading and clearing large volumes on a daily basis.

The main drawback is that it results in a drop in liquidity on the bourses. This is because in India the cash market has been used as a *de facto* futures market by speculators and day traders. Rolling settlements forces this segment, which accounts for nearly 80 per cent of exchange volumes, to either square up their positions by the end of the day or pay cash and take delivery of stock.

ROLE OF SPECULATORS AND DISCUSSION ON RELATIONS AMONG THE SYSTEMS OF BADLA OR CARRY FORWARD TRADING AND ASSOCIATED SHORT SELLING POSITION

There is a long history of carry forward trading system in India. Forty-six years ago when one of the most remembered personalities of the Indian stock market scenario, P.J. Jeejeebhoy introduced the carry forward system, commonly known as the *badla* system in the Indian stock market, it converted an essentially spot market into a forward market.

The concept of the *badla* system can be expressed as follows: If A is buyer who does not wish to pay and take delivery and B is a seller, with or without possession of scrips, a *badla* financier C would have to take delivery and thus pay up. In this case A would pay an interest cost or *badla* on the amount he borrows from C. This *badla* amount is determined by the demand and supply of money and the particular scrip on the day of *badla* trading. Let us take a macro view, in a situation; the *badla* rate would depend on the number of purchases which have to be financed and the number of scrips that can be delivered. If the number of shares that sellers can deliver is high or if the number of buyers not willing to take delivery is high, then the *badla* rate too will be high and will be paid by the purchaser. In another situation, the volumes of purchases for delivery outnumber the volume of shares physically delivered, the process is reversed and the seller has to borrow money to buy the shares to be delivered. There is then a premium on the scrip and what is earned is *undha badla* (also discussed above) by the purchaser.

Futures trading was considered speculative and therefore was not allowed during that period (early sixties to early nineties) under the Securities Regulation Contract Act, the *badla* system allowed Indian investors to take a shot at future expectations. Forward trading allowed in specified shares enhanced liquidity, increased market capitalization and pushed up the index. It worked well on Indian bourses till the early 1990s.

With the stock market index refusing to look up despite a very positive Central Government budget in February 1993, many market persons were of the view that it was the trading system and not trading sentiment that was keeping share prices depressed. Taking advantage of the widespread attention the crash in share prices attracted, certain broking houses sought to bring the issue to the forefront, i.e. the need to either alter or scrap the current system of *badla*. Not just the broking community, but everybody concerned even remotely with financial markets, whether they were in the government, the Reserve Bank of India, financial institutions or academia, opined a view on *badla*. And more often than not, it was derogatory. In fact *badla* financiers, who put in an estimated average of Rs. 400 crore every fortnight, were castigated for their greed and lucre. With *badla* rates known to be as high as 90 per cent per annum, *badla* in the Indian capital market had become a dirty word (*Business Standard*, April 8, 1993).

In reality, *badla* was only the price of money. A person who buys shares for a particular settlement would normally have to take delivery at the end of the settlement period that was 14 days. The carry forward system enabled him to postpone this to the next settlement, if he so desired, by paying *badla* or carry forward to the *badla* financier. Thus *badla* essentially represents interest payable by the buyer for postponing payment by one settlement period. The then executive director of the Bombay Stock Exchange, M.R. Mayya, opined that the system followed in India was an amalgam of cash and futures, which was unique but carried an element of a foreign concept. Stock broker Nemish Shah also observed that this was not unique to India. The world over share purchasers who do not wish to take delivery pay the sellers an interest cost. While what Shah said was true, there was, in India, a variation from worldwide practices. On the Indian bourses there was no restriction on the short sales or blank sales as opposed to a genuine hedge. Shorn of jargon, all this meant was that just as a purchaser wished to buy without having money, a seller could also sell without having the security and earn *badla* or interest without any investment.

So, although the *badla* system was essentially designed to help investors hedge themselves against a future change in price, in India it soon came to be abused for short selling or selling without physical position of shares. Many market analysts observed that there was very heavy speculation in the Indian market. Annual trading volumes in some of the leading scrips were 10 times that of their market capitalization. Less than 10 per cent of the total transactions in these scrips were registered. In the UK and the USA, the trading is only 0.5 times the market capitalization of a particular company. In India, there was a heavy concentration of trading in a few scrips. As a result speculation had become a destabilizing factor and degenerated into manipulation. *Badla* started to encourage speculation by people who were not genuine. So, market watchers felt that there should be a total ban on transactions which were not backed by the person making transaction. In fact, the phenomenon of short sellers earning an interest without any investment was a reason why there were more sellers than buyers on the stock markets during early 1990s.

Short sales, in those days, were disconcerting transactions for most sections of the market fraternity and for different reasons. Investors abhorred short sales because they were thought to have triggered the downtrend in prices during that period, which in turn eroded their wealth. Traders and stock exchanges were apprehensive of imminent erosion in volumes brought about by a modification of the existing practice. For the regulatory authority, there is tremendous pressure from a section of the market community to check the excessive speculative activity due to the long-extended bear phase.

Some years ago, SEBI appointed a committee under the chairmanship of B.D. Shah, former chairman and managing director of New India Assurance Company and former managing director of General Insurance Corporation of India, to look into the issue of regulating short sales on the bourses.

The committee recommended, among other things, that brokers/members of stock exchanges should mandatorily declare, scrip-wise, their net short sales and net long purchases at the end of each day, and that this information should be further verified and compiled on a cumulative basis by each stock exchange. The committee also suggested that stock exchanges should levy differential margins on sales and purchases, depending on market conditions. It also suggested a stock-lending scheme. The committee ruled that disclosure of outstanding positions should be made with immediate effect. Even while the committee was deliberating on the issue of short sales, SEBI directed brokers to disclose their outstanding positions from 29th November 1996. Consequent to the submission of the report by the committee on 21st January 1997 (and as suggested by it), SEBI issued norms and guidelines on stock lending on 6th February 1997.

A need for regulating short sales further was felt when the investing community was disillusioned by sinking share prices over a four-year long bear phase. There have been frequent demands from the market fraternity to ban short sales temporarily in light of the falling share prices. Though SEBI did not take any drastic steps, like banning short sales, even for a short duration, despite mounting pressure on it to do so, it once again assigned the B.D. Shah Committee the task of looking into the issue of regulating short sales.

It is universally known and accepted that short sales not only provide liquidity to the markets, but aid in the price discovery process by providing competitive bids also. Thus, the greater the number of transactions, the better is the price discovery and liquidity, which are considered to be the two attributes of vibrant stock markets. Hence, regulating short sales by banning them could be suicidal because volumes will shrink. The B.D. Shah Committee, too, ruled out a ban in its meeting on 27th November 1998. A number of market analysts opined against a ban on short sales. While a ban on short sales may be undesirable, excessive short sale for any unbridled speculation has to be checked. Excessive short sales are bound to manifest their ill effects of undue depression of share prices, which erodes investors' wealth.

Short sales in the Indian markets have a wider connotation. The B.D. Shah Committee has defined short sale as a sale of shares without having physical possession of them unless it is for either squaring up an earlier purchase in the same settlement of the same stock exchange or against pending deliveries (from the same stock exchange) pertaining to a previous settlement. Thus, short sales encompass a host of sales transactions like sales for a subsequent squaring during the same day or during the same settlement, selling for carry forward to the next settlement and selling to take advantage of the price differential of the same stock on two different stock exchanges called arbitrage. Sales of these types are sometimes also termed naked short sales.

Considered as one of the instruments for short sales, the carry forward system, or *badla* as it is widely known, has come under criticism from a section of the market fraternity. Critics say that the existing carryforward system favours short sellers or bears because they get contango or *badla* charges for going short in scrip, and this gives them an undue advantage over bulls or long buyers. This drags down prices further in a falling market. In a time-tested system like carryforward, wherein market forces determine the *badla* rates during every screen-based trading session (held on Saturday), can an operator on any side (here the short seller) continue to be in an advantageous position for a long time? The reason why bears or short sellers get *badla* charges for selling short is that a substantially higher risk component is involved in short selling. A short seller trades against the long-term secular uptrend of the market and he is always prone to be squeezed by the buyer who can insist on delivery of shares which are difficult to procure. Borrowing of shares is always more difficult than borrowing of money. A short seller is paid for the risk he takes in this respect.

Besides, whenever there are excessive short sale positions for carry forward in any settlement, the long buyer steps into the shoes of the short seller as the latter has to pay badla charges called backwardation charges, or *undha badla*, to the buyer. 'The larger the component of short sales in the market, weaker is the short seller and the system is self-corrective,' says M.R. Mayya, former executive director of the BSE. Thus, to say that sellers are always in an advantageous position over buyers in a carry forward or *badla* system would be inappropriate.

What's more, a study conducted by the BSE on the fall in the market during the period from 17th April 1998 to 6th November 1998 (the 30-share BSE Sensex declined from 4186 to 2884) shows that the average long buy position of Rs. 923 crore for carry forward in a settlement far outweighed the average short sale position of Rs. 241 crore. This puts to rest the claim of some that bears/short sellers have accentuated the fall in the market by hammering scrips using the carry forward system.

While it is impossible for short sellers to dictate a downward trend in the market because the latter adjusts to fundamentals in the long run, bears can take advantage of depressed market conditions to accentuate a further fall by hammering and thus make a lot of money in the short run. In fact, market persons were taken by surprise, when, during a few trading sessions in early October 1998, prices of pivotals fell like nine pins as a few operators resorted to programmed trading methods to hammer down the prices.

According to brokers, the modus operandi of the operators was simple: hammer down the prices of a few pivotals simultaneously through programmed trading. Then spread some rumours to create panic in the market. And, as prices come down (when deliveries are offloaded by investors in panic), cover the short positions and make a killing in the short term. At different times, the Indian regulatory authority made changes in regulations in the settlement system. But the settlement system on the Indian bourses left scope for traders/operators to take advantage of the seven-day cycle by effecting transactions like those in the case above to make quick gains in the short run. The country's largest stock exchange is often blamed for inculcating what is known as a 'casino' culture among investors. Traders/Operators indulge in large-scale speculation on a daily basis, also known as day trades.

Given that speculators rule the roost in Indian bourses, as is evident in the small percentage of delivery trades to total trades, the existence of rampant short sales on a daily or on a settlement basis is obvious. But SEBI seems to be reluctant to ban even this type of short sales (i.e. short sales related to a day or a settlement) fearing a drastic fall in volumes and a consequent fall in liquidity. In fact, volumes on both the BSE and NSE had declined substantially in a few trading sessions in June - July 1998 (17th June to 6th July 1998) when SEBI had put a temporary ban on daily short sales in order to check volatility in prices. Thus, the volume of business on the NSE fell to a record level low in the late June 1998.

Stock lending or securities lending is one of the ways by which naked short sales on the bourses could be regulated, according to market participants. In fact, the B.D. Shah Committee on short sales recommended stock lending as a measure to regulate short sales. Subsequently, SEBI issued norms and guidelines for a stock-lending scheme in February 1997.

Under the stock-lending scheme, the temporary needs of borrowers, like brokers, can be met by the lenders – usually by an institutional investor holding the stock as a long-term portfolio investment – to support trading activities like short sales or to meet short-term delivery obligations of the borrowers like meeting the shortfall in deliveries. Thus, a lender can loan the securities to the borrower through an approved intermediary under an agreement which states that the borrower will return an equivalent number of securities of the same type and class at the end of the specified period along with the corporate benefits accruing on the borrowed securities. While operators/traders can use stock lending as a tool for trading, institutional investors can use it to earn an extra income by way of fees or charges for lending from shares held as long-term investments. There were two vital bottlenecks due to which stock lending did not make much headway initially. SEBI's norms and guidelines on stock lending stated that the risk of default by the borrower will be borne by the AI.

Not all AIs, however, were willing to take such a principal risk because they preferred to act only as agents in stock-lending transactions. It was subsequently clarified by SEBI that AIs can act merely as agents in stock-lending transactions provided all the parties to the contract agreed. The second important issue related to the levy of tax on stock-lending transactions was whether such transactions should be considered as regular buy-sale transactions or treated separately. The CBDT clarified that lending and borrowing of shares under the stock-lending scheme will be free from capital gains tax.

Some other operational bottlenecks in stock lending, however, remain. One is the high degree of principal risk involved in lending the securities for the lender (say an institutional investor) like failure of the borrower (usually a broker or an individual investor) to return the securities lent. The second is the possibility of bad title of the shares returned by the borrower to the lender. While the former risk is the intrinsic business risk in stock-lending activity, the latter is related to the ills of dealing in physical shares like bad delivery, delay in transfer, etc. Market persons feel that while the intrinsic risk (like the quality of the borrowers) will be taken care of as the market matures, the risk associated with dealing in physical shares can be done away with once dematerialization is largely in place.

In fact, market persons feel that stock lending is unlikely to make much headway if the shares are in physical form and it is only after NSDL achieves a critical mass in dematerialization that stock lending may really take off. 'The problems associated with paper-based securities, i.e. the possibility of their getting stolen, *benami*, fake and bogus certificates, both as collateral and as repayment of loan, can be eliminated by popularizing the concept of dematerialization (see Chapter 10) and trading in the demat segment,' says B.V. Goud, former managing director, SHCIL.

SEBI's initiatives on dematerialization augur well in this respect. 'SEBI's first priority is to get rid of paper and the associated ills. I am sure they will expand the list for compulsory demat for retail investors gradually,' says C.B. Bhave, former managing director, NSDL. Meanwhile, NSDL has already made available to its members the computer module so that they can participate in stock lending.

Will *badla* or carry forward be the major hindrance to the growth of stock lending? 'We don't fear *badla*. The market has, in fact, learned stock lending through *badla*. Now, only the rules are changing,' says Thomas Sasse, former custody services head, India, Deutsche Bank. Market persons felt that though badla and stock lending will co-exist for sometime, the latter could outpace the former over a period of time. For one, institutional investors like mutual funds are not allowed to lend stock in the *badla* system. Second, among the leading stock exchanges, the NSE does not have the *badla* system. 'Though lending of shares already exists in the *badla* system, we have a regulated and more transparent form in stock lending where players are clear about the rules of the game and there are certain compliances for reporting. It is the transparencies inherent in stock lending which will help our business grow,' said Sasse.

According to Sasse, leading brokers of NSE and institutions like UTI, besides Association of Mutual Funds in India (AMFI) members, have shown substantial interest in borrowing and lending securities. Though mutual funds in India are not allowed to lend securities, SEBI is in the process of allowing them to do so and detailed guidelines for the same are expected shortly.

Stock lending, nonetheless, is expected to better the liquidity in the market, as shares which are lying idle with institutions (in their long-term investment portfolio) would come to the bourses for trading. An increase in liquidity will lead to a better price discovery.

In fact, stock lending has become an integral part of the smooth functioning of markets in many countries. Besides helping in addressing the problems of settlement failures, stock lending also aids in increasing the delivery ratio on the bourses, which is all the more necessary in the Indian markets where deliveries constitute only a small portion of trades.

The operational guidelines and norms for stock lending issued by SEBI provide substantial freedom to market participants in stock lending. Things like tenure of the loan, the fees payable by the borrower and the amount and type of collateral have all been left to the market participants to decide. 'SEBI has created a framework for stock lending which is a step towards having modern capital markets. Stock lending will take off gradually,' said L.K. Singhvi, former senior executive director (investigation, enforcement, surveillance), SEBI.

The OTCEI and the NSE started screen based trading on November 4th, 1994 while the BSE introduced on-line screen based Trading System (BOLT) on March 14th, 1995.

ROLE OF DIFFERENT MARKET AND STOCK INDICES IN UNDERSTANDING MOVEMENTS OF PRICES OF STOCKS

To understand the use and functioning of the index derivatives markets, it is necessary to understand the underlying index. In this section of the chapter, we take a look at index related issues. Traditionally, indices have been used as information sources. By looking at an index, we know how the market is faring. In recent years, indices have come to the forefront owing to direct applications in finance in the form of index funds and index derivatives. Index derivatives allow people to easily alter their risk exposure to an index (hedging) and to implement forecasts about index movements (speculation). Hedging using index derivatives has become a central part of risk management in the modern economy.

Traditionally, indices have been used as benchmarks to monitor markets and judge performance. Modern indices were first proposed by two 19th Century mathematicians: Etienne Laspeyres and Hermann Paasche. The grandfather of all equity indices is the Dow Jones Industrial Average (USA) which was first published in 1896; since then indices have come a long way – not only in their sophistication – but also in the variety. There are three main types of indices, namely price index, quantity index and value index. The price index is most widely used. It measures changes in the levels of prices of products in the financial, commodities or any other markets from one period to another. The indices in financial markets measure changes in prices of securities like equities, debentures, government securities, etc.

The most popular index in the financial market is the stock or share (equity) index which uses a set of stocks that are representative of the whole market, or a specified sector, to measure the change in overall behaviour of the markets or sector over a period of time. A stock index is important for its use:

1. As the lead indicator of the performance of the overall economy or a sector of the economy: A good index tells us how much richer or poorer investors have become.

2. As a barometer for market behaviour: It is used to monitor and measure market movements, whether in real time, daily, or over decades, helping us to understand economic conditions and prospects.

3. As a benchmark for portfolio performance: A managed fund can communicate its objectives and target universe by stating which index or indices serve as the standard against which its performance should be judged.

4. As an underlying for derivatives like index futures and options. It also underpins products such as, exchange-traded funds, index funds etc. These index-related products form a several trillion dollar business and are used widely in investment, hedging and risk management.

5. As it supports research (for example, as benchmarks for evaluating trading rules, technical analysis systems and analysts' forecasts); risk measurement and management; and asset allocation.

In addition to the above functional use, a stock index reflects the changing expectations of the market about the future of the corporate sector. The index rises if the market expects the future to be better than previously expected and drops if the expectations about the future become pessimistic.

The price of a stock moves for two reasons, namely, company specific development (product launch, improved financial performance, closure of a factory, arrest of chief executive) and development affecting the general environment (nuclear bombs, election result, budget announcement, growth in GDP of the economy), which affects the stock market as a whole. The stock index captures the second part, that is, the impact of environmental change on the stock market as a whole. This is achieved by averaging which cancels out changes in prices of individual stocks.

Actually, an index is a summary measure that indicates changes in value(s) of a variable or a set of variables over time or space. It is usually computed by finding the ratio of current values(s) to a reference (base) value(s) and multiplying the resulting number by 100 or 1000. For instance, a stock market index is a number that indicates the relative level of prices or value of securities in a market on a particular day compared with a base-day price or value figure, which is usually 100 or 1000.

There are several market indices in India, before discussion of the other indices, first let us discuss the most popular stock index of the country, Bombay Stock Exchange Sensitive Index or BSE 30 or most popularly known as the SENSEX (Sens taken from Sensitive and ex taken from Index).

The BSE Sensex or Bombay Stock Exchange Sensitive Index is a value-weighted index composed of 30 stocks with the base April 1979 = 100 (as adopted on 1st April, 1979). It consists of the 30 large and most actively traded stocks, representative of various sectors, on the Bombay Stock Exchange. These companies account for more than one-fifth of the market capitalization of the BSE.

First compiled on 1st January 1986, SENSEX is a basket of 30 constituent stocks representing a sample of large, liquid and representative companies. The SENSEX is not only scientifically designed but also based on internationally accepted construction and review methodology. The base year of SENSEX is 1978-79 and the base value is 100. The index is widely reported in both domestic and international markets through print as well as electronic media.

The BSE authorities at irregular intervals review and modify its composition to make sure it reflects current market conditions. More importantly, the BSE Index Committee meets every quarter to discuss index related issues. In case of a revision in the index constituents, the announcement of the incoming and outgoing scrips is made six weeks in advance of the actual implementation of the revision of the index.

Since its inception, SENSEX has received wide acceptance amongst the Indian investors; and hence it is regarded to be the pulse of the Indian stock market. As the oldest index in the country, it provides the time series data over a fairly long period of time (from 1979 onwards). It is a small wonder, then that the SENSEX has over the years become one of the most prominent brands in the country.

Table 3.3   Some Specifications of the SENSEX

Base year	1978-79
Base index value	100
Date of launch	01-01-1986
Method of calculation	Launched on full market capitalization method and effective September 01, 2003, calculation method shifted to free-float market capitalization (discussed below).
Number of scrips	30 (Any of the included scrip or scrips are likely to be replaced according to specified criterion).

Source: BSE, Mumbai

Before entering into the details of the construction of the SENSEX, it may be noted that till 31st August 2003, this index was constructed on the basis of full market capitalization but from the 1st September 2003, SENSEX is being calculated/constructed on the basis of free float market capitalization. Free float market capitalization stands for non-promoter, non-strategic shareholding.

The criteria for selection of constituents in SENSEX are as follows:

1. The selected scrip should have a listing history of at least 3 months at BSE. An exception may be made if full market capitalization of a newly listed company ranks among the top 10 in the list of BSE universe. In case, a company is listed on account of merger/demerger/amalgamation, minimum listing history would not be required.

2. The selected scrip should have been traded on each and every trading day in the last three months at the BSE. Exceptions can be made for extreme reasons like scrip suspension etc.

3. The selected scrip should figure in the top 100 companies listed by final rank. The final rank is arrived at by assigning 75 per cent weightage to the rank on the basis of three-month average full market capitalization and 25 per cent weightage to the liquidity rank based on a three-month average daily turnover and three-month average impact cost.

4. The weightage of each scrip in the SENSEX, based on the three-month average free-float market capitalization (discussed below), should be at least 0.5 per cent of the index.

5. Scrip selection would generally take into account a balanced representation of the listed companies in the universe of BSE.

According to the opinion of the BSE Index Committee, the company should have an acceptable track record.

Free-float Methodology

Understanding Free-float Methodology

Free-float methodology refers to an index construction methodology that takes into consideration only the free-float market capitalization of a company for the purpose of index calculation and assigning weight to stocks in the index. Free-float market capitalization takes into consideration only those shares issued by the company that are readily available for trading in the market. It generally excludes promoters' holding, government holding, strategic holding and other locked-in shares that will not come on to the market for trading in the normal course. In other words, the market capitalization of each company in a free-float index is reduced to the extent of its readily available shares in the market.

The country's equity benchmark SENSEX has been calculated based on the free-float methodology since 1st September 2003. Earlier, the SENSEX was calculated based on the full market capitalization methodology.

Globally, the free-float methodology of index construction is considered to be an industry best practice and all major index providers like MSCI, FTSE, S&P and STOXX (all these indices are discussed later) have adopted the same. The MSCI India Standard Index is also based on the free-float methodology.

In India, BSE pioneered the concept of free-float with the launch of the country's first free-float based index – BSE TEC*k* in July 2001 and BANKEX in June 2003. The shifting of the SENSEX to this methodology is a culmination of successful experiences with these two indices and a series of debates and discussions in the last few years. In order to generate a nationwide debate on the issue of free-float, BSE had organized a "Roundtable on Free-float Index" in March 2002, which was chaired by Mr. Mark Makepeace, President and CEO – FTSE Group. The Roundtable was followed by a series of discussions with a cross section of market participants. The feedback was overwhelming for shifting benchmark indices to the free-float methodology.

The new methodology has aligned the SENSEX with the best global practice in index construction. A smooth transition from full market capitalization to free-float market capitalization methodology ensured that the basic characteristics of SENSEX are retained. Importantly, the free-float methodology has further improved the benchmarking qualities of SENSEX while maintaining its historical continuity.

The following free-float factors have been applied to the SENSEX companies. A free-float factor of say 0.9 means that only 90 per cent of the total market capitalization of that company would be taken into consideration for index calculation.

Table 3.4   Free-float Bands

% Free-float	Free-float Factor	% Free-float	Free-float Factor
>0 - 5%	0.05	>50 - 55%	0.55
>5 - 10%	0.10	>55 - 60%	0.60
>10 - 15%	0.15	>60 - 65%	0.65
>15 - 20%	0.20	>65 - 70%	0.70
>20 - 25%	0.25	>70 - 75%	0.75
>25 - 30%	0.30	>75 - 80%	0.80
>30 - 35%	0.35	>80 - 85%	0.85
>35 - 40%	0.40	>85 - 90%	0.90
>40 - 45%	0.45	>90 - 95%	0.95
>45 - 50%	0.50	>95 - 100%	1.00

Source: BSE, Mumbai

More elaborately it can be said that the BSE has designed a free-float format, which is filled and submitted by all index companies on a quarterly basis. The BSE determines the free-float factor for each company based on the detailed information submitted by the companies in the prescribed format. Free-float factor is a multiple with which the total market capitalization of a company is adjusted to arrive at the free-float market capitalization. Once the free-float of a company is determined, it is rounded-off to the higher multiple of 5 and each company is categorized into one of the 20 bands given in Table 3.5. A free-float factor of say 0.55 means that only 55 per cent of the market capitalization of the company will be considered for index calculation.

Shareholding of investors that would not, in the normal course come into the open market for trading are treated as 'controlling/strategic holdings' and hence are not included in free-float. Specifically, the following categories of holding are generally excluded from the definition of free-float:

1. Shares held by founders/directors/ acquirers which has control element
2. Shares held by persons/bodies with "controlling interest"
3. Shares held by the government as promoter/acquirer
4. Holdings through the FDI route
5. Strategic stakes by private corporate bodies/individuals
6. Equity held by associate/group companies (cross-holdings)

7. Equity held by employee welfare trusts

8. Locked-in shares and shares which would not be sold in the open market in the normal course.

Advantages of Free-float Methodology

A free-float index reflects the market trends more rationally as it takes into consideration only those shares that are available for trading in the market.

Free-float methodology makes the index more broad-based by reducing the concentration of the top few companies in the index.

A free-float index aids both active and passive investing styles. It aids active managers by enabling them to benchmark their fund returns *vis-à-vis* an investible index. This enables an apple-to-apple comparison thereby facilitating better evaluation of performance of active managers. Being a perfectly replicable portfolio of stocks, a free-float adjusted index is best suited for passive managers as it enables them to track the index with the least tracking error.

Free-float methodology improves index flexibility in terms of including any stock from the universe of listed stocks. This improves market coverage and sector coverage of the index. For example, under the full-market capitalization methodology, companies with large market capitalization and low free-float cannot generally be included in the index because they tend to distort the index by having an undue influence on the index movement.

However, under the free-float methodology, since only the free-float market capitalization of each company is considered for index calculation, it becomes possible to include such closely-held companies in the index while at the same time preventing their undue influence on the index movement.

Globally, as we mentioned above, the free-float methodology of index construction is considered to be an industry best practice and all major index providers like MSCI, FTSE, S&P and STOXX have adopted the same. MSCI, a leading global index provider, shifted all its indices to the free-float methodology in 2002. The MSCI India Standard Index, which is followed by Foreign Institutional Investors (FIIs) to track Indian equities, is also based on the free-float methodology. NASDAQ-100, the underlying index to the famous Exchange Traded Fund (ETF) - QQQ is based on the free-float methodology.

METHODOLOGY FOR CALCULATION OF SENSEX

The SENSEX is calculated using the "free-float market capitalization" methodology (discussed below), wherein, the level of the index at any point of time reflects the free-float market value of 30 component stocks relative to a base period. The market capitalization of a company is determined by multiplying the price of its stock by the number of shares issued by the company. This market capitalization is further multiplied by the free-float factor to determine the free-float market capitalization (discussed below).

That is, Market Capitalization (MC) of the selected company = Market price of the selected stock multiplied by the total number of shares issued by the company.

Free-float market capitalization = MC multiplied by free-float factor of the selected company.

We have already mentioned above that the base period of the SENSEX is 1978-79 and the base value is 100 index points. This is often indicated by the notation 1978-79 = 100. The calculation of SENSEX involves dividing the free-float market capitalization of 30 companies in the index by a number called the index divisor. The divisor is the only link to the original base period value of the SENSEX. It keeps the index comparable over time and is the adjustment point for all index adjustments arising out of corporate actions, replacement of scrips etc. During market hours, prices of the index scrips, at which latest trades are executed, are used by the trading system to calculate the SENSEX on a continuous basis.

The closing SENSEX on any trading day is computed taking the weighted average of all the trades on SENSEX constituents in the last 30 minutes of the trading session. If a SENSEX constituent has not traded in the last 30 minutes, the last traded price is taken for computation of the index closure. If a SENSEX constituent has not traded at all in a day, then its last day's closing price is taken for computation of index closure. The use of an index closure algorithm prevents any intentional manipulation of the closing index value.

SCRIP SELECTION CRITERIA FOR SENSEX

The general guidelines for selection of constituents in SENSEX are as follows:

Listed history: The scrip should have a listing history of at least 3 months on the BSE. Exceptions may be considered if full market capitalization of a newly listed company ranks among the top 10 in the list of the BSE universe. In case, a company is listed on account of merger/demerger/amalgamation, minimum listing history would not be required.

Trading frequency: The scrip should have been traded on each and every trading day in the last three months at the BSE. Exceptions can be made for extreme reasons like scrip suspension etc.

Final rank: The scrip should figure in the top 100 companies listed by final rank. The final rank is arrived at by assigning 75 per cent weightage to the rank on the basis of three-month average full market capitalization and 25 per cent weightage to the liquidity rank based on three-month average daily turnover & three-month average impact cost.

Market capitalization weightage: The weightage of each scrip in the SENSEX based on a three-month average free-float market capitalization should be at least 0.5 per cent of the index.

Industry/Sector representation: Scrip selection would generally take into account a balanced representation of the listed companies in the universe of the BSE.

Track record: In the opinion of the BSE Index Committee, the company should have an acceptable track record.

At present, the list of 30 companies selected for calculation of the SENSEX are furnished in Table 3.5.

Table 3.5 List of Companies Selected for the SENSEX

SENSEX Constituents		Composition Revised from 03/05/2010 Free-float Adjustment Factor Revised from 10/05/2010	
Code	Name	Sector	Adj. Factor
500410	ACC Ltd.	Housing related	0.55
500103	Bharat Heavy Electricals Ltd.	Capital goods	0.35
532454	Bharti Airtel Ltd.	Telecom	0.35
500087	Cipla Ltd.	Healthcare	0.65
532868	DLF Ltd.	Housing related	0.25
500300	Grasim Industries Ltd.	Diversified	0.75
500010	HDFC	Finance	0.90
500180	HDFC Bank Ltd.	Finance	0.80
500182	Hero Honda Motors Ltd.	Transport equipment	0.50
500440	Hindalco Industries Ltd.	Metal, metal products & mining	0.70
500696	Hindustan Unilever Ltd.	FMCG	0.50
532174	ICICI Bank Ltd.	Finance	1.00
500209	Infosys Technologies Ltd.	Information technology	0.85
500875	ITC Ltd.	FMCG	0.70
532532	Jaiprakash Associates Ltd.	Housing related	0.55
500510	Larsen & Toubro Limited	Capital goods	0.90
500520	Mahindra & Mahindra Ltd.	Transport equipment	0.75
532500	Maruti Suzuki India Ltd.	Transport equipment	0.50
532555	NTPC Ltd.	Power	0.20
500312	ONGC Ltd.	Oil & gas	0.20
532712	Reliance Communications Limited	Telecom	0.35
500325	Reliance Industries Ltd.	Oil & gas	0.55
500390	Reliance Infrastructure Ltd.	Power	0.60
500112	State Bank of India	Finance	0.45
500900	Sterlite Industries (India) Ltd.	Metal, metal products & mining	0.45
532540	Tata Consultancy Services Limited	Information technology	0.30
500570	Tata Motors Ltd.	Transport equipment	0.65
500400	Tata Power Company Ltd.	Power	0.70
500470	Tata Steel Ltd.	Metal, metal products & mining	0.70
507685	Wipro Ltd.	Information technology	0.20

Source: Bombay Stock Exchange, Mumbai.

The methodology and maintenance of different indices are described in a tabular form which is directly taken from BSE publications. In fact most of the write ups in this chapter are taken from different publications of the BSE.

Example: Suppose the index consists of only 2 stocks: Stock A and Stock B.

Suppose company A has 1,000 shares, of which 200 are held by the promoters, so that only 800 shares are available for trading to the general public. These 800 shares are the so-called 'free-floating' shares.

Similarly, company B has 2,000 shares, of which 1,000 are held by the promoters and the remaining 1,000 are free-floating.

Now suppose the current market price of stock A is Rs. 120. Thus, the 'total' market capitalization of company A is Rs. 1,20,000 (1,000 × 120), but its free-float market capitalization is Rs. 96,000 (800 × 120).

Similarly, suppose the current market price of stock B is Rs. 200. The total market capitalization of company B will thus be Rs. 4,00,000 (2,000 × 200), but its free-float market cap is only Rs. 2,00,000 (1,000 × 200). So as of today the market capitalization of the index (i.e. stocks A and B) is Rs. 5,20,000 (Rs. 1,20,000 + Rs. 4,00,000); while the free-float market capitalization of the index is Rs. 2,96,000. (Rs. 96,000 + Rs. 2,00,000).

The year 1978-79 is considered the base year of the index with a value set to 100. What this means is that suppose at that time the market capitalization of the stocks that comprised the index then was, say, 60,000 (remember at that time there may have been some other stocks in the index, not only A and B, but that does not matter), then we assume that an index market cap of 60,000 is equal to an index-value of 100. Thus the value of the index today is = 296,000 × 100/60,000 = 493.33, and this is how the SENSEX is calculated. Generally, stock market indices differ from one another basically in their sampling and/or weighting methods.

Sampling Method

Unlike market indices such as the American Stock Market Index and the Hong Kong Stock Exchange All-Ordinaries Index that comprise all the stocks listed in a market, under the sampling method, an index is based on a fraction or a certain percentage of select stocks which is highly representative of the total stocks listed in a market.

Weighting

In a value-weighted index, the weight of each constituent stock is proportional to its market share in terms of market capitalization. In an index portfolio, we can assume that the amount of money invested in each constituent stock is proportional to its percentage of the total value of all constituent stocks. Examples include all major stock market indices like S&P, CNX and Nifty.

There are three commonly used methods for constructing indices:

    Price weighted method
    Equally weighted method
    Market capitalization weighted method

A price-weighted index is computed by summing up the prices, of the various securities included in the index, at time 1 (current period), and dividing it by the sum of prices of the securities at time 0 (base period) multiplied by base index value. Each stock is assigned a weight proportional to its price.

INDEX CALCULATION & MAINTENANCE

Formula for Calculation of Index

All BSE indices, SENSEX and others, (except BSE-PSU index) are calculated using the following formula:

Free-float market capitalization of index constituents/Base market capitalization * Base index value

For calculation of the BSE-PSU index, full market capitalization of index constituents is considered instead of free-float market capitalization. Dollex-30, Dollex-100 and Dollex-200 are dollar-linked versions of the SENSEX (discussed below), BSE-100 and BSE-200 index. For more details see *www.bseindia.com*.

The BSE IPO index is calculated using the following formula:

$$\frac{\text{Capped market capitalization of index constituents}}{\text{Base market capitalization}} \times \text{Base index value}$$

Where capped market capitalization for scrips in the BSE IPO index is arrived at by multiplying the free-float adjusted market capitalization of an individual scrip with its respective capping factor. Such capping factor is assigned to the index constituent to ensure that no single scrip based on its free-float market capitalization exceeds weightage of 20 per cent at the time of rebalancing. In case, weightage of all the constituents in the index is below 20 per cent, each company would be assigned a capping factor of 1.

Index Closure Algorithm

The closing index value on any trading day is computed by taking the weighted average of all the trades of index constituents in the last 30 minutes of the trading session. If an index constituent has not traded in the last 30 minutes, the last traded price is taken for computation of the index closure. If an index constituent has not traded at all in a day, then its last day's closing price is taken for computation of index closure. The use of an index closure algorithm prevents any intentional manipulation of the closing index value.

Maintenance of BSE Indices

One of the important aspects of maintaining continuity with the past is to update the base year average. The base year value adjustment ensures that replacement of stocks in the index, additional issue of capital and other corporate announcements like 'rights issue' etc. do not destroy the historical value of the index. The beauty of maintenance lies in the fact that adjustments for corporate actions in the index should not per se affect the index values.

The BSE Index Cell does the day-to-day maintenance of the index within the broad index policy framework set by the BSE Index Committee. The BSE Index Cell ensures that all BSE indices maintain their benchmark properties by striking a delicate balance between frequent replacements in the index and maintaining its historical continuity. The BSE Index Committee comprises capital market experts, fund managers, market participants, and members of the BSE Governing Board.

On - Line Computation of the Index

During trading hours, the value of the indices is calculated and disseminated on a real time basis. This is done automatically on the basis of prices at which trades in index constituents are executed.

Adjustment for Bonus, Rights and Newly Issued Capital

Index calculation needs to be adjusted for issue of bonus and rights issue. If no adjustments were made, a discontinuity would arise between the current value of the index and its previous value despite the non-occurrence of any economic activity of substance. At the BSE Index Cell, the base value is adjusted, which is used to alter market capitalization of the component stocks to arrive at the index value.

The BSE Index Cell keeps a close watch on the events that might affect the index on a regular basis and carries out daily maintenance of all BSE indices.

Adjustments for rights issues: When a company, included in the compilation of the index, issues right shares, the free-float market capitalization of that company is increased by the number of additional shares issued based on the theoretical (ex-right) price. An offsetting or proportionate adjustment is then made to the base market capitalization.

Adjustments for bonus issue: When a company, included in the compilation of the index, issues bonus shares, the market capitalization of that company does not undergo any change. Therefore, there is no change in the base market capitalization; only the 'number of shares' in the formula is updated.

Other issues: Base market capitalization adjustment is required when new shares are issued by way of conversion of debentures, mergers, spin-offs etc. or when equity is reduced by way of buy-back of shares, corporate restructuring etc.

Base market capitalization adjustment: The formula for adjusting base market capitalization is as follows:

New base market capitalization

$$= \text{Old base market capitalization} \times \frac{\text{New market capitalization}}{\text{Old market capitalization}}$$

To illustrate, suppose a company issues additional shares, which increases the market capitalization of the shares of that company by say, Rs. 100 crore. The existing base market capitalization (old base market capitalization), say, is Rs. 2,450 crore and the aggregate market capitalization of all the shares included in the index before this issue is made is, say Rs. 4,781 crore. The "new base market capitalization" will then be:

$$\frac{2450 \times (4781 + 100)}{4781} = \text{Rs. } 2501.24 \text{ crores}$$

This figure of Rs. 2,501.24 crore will be used as the base market capitalization for calculating the index number from then onwards till the next base change becomes necessary.

Index Review Frequency

The BSE Index Committee meets every quarter to discuss index related issues. In case of a revision in the index constituents, the announcement of the incoming and outgoing scrips is made six weeks in advance of the actual implementation of the revision of the Index.

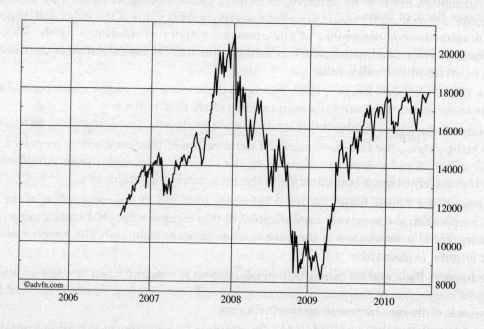

Source: www.advfn.com

Chart 3.4   BSE SENSEX Historical Chart (July 2006 to July 2010)

DOLLEX SERIES OF BSE INDIA*

We have already discussed that all BSE indices reflect the growth in market value of constituent stocks over the base period in Rupee terms. A need was felt to design a yardstick by which these growth values are also measured in Dollar terms. Such an index would reflect, in one value, the changes in both the stock prices and the foreign exchange variation.

*Reproduced from BSE publication

This was facilitated by the introduction of a dollar-linked index in which the formula for calculation of the index is suitably modified to express the current and base market values in dollar terms. The scope for a dollar-linked index emerged due to Indian equity markets becoming increasingly integrated with global capital markets and the need to assess the market movements in terms of international benchmarks. Dollar-linked indices are useful to overseas investors, as they help them measure their 'real returns' after providing for exchange rate fluctuations.

Dollex-30, is a dollar-linked version of the SENSEX, that was launched on July 25th, 2001 whereas **Dollex-200**, a dollar-linked version of BSE-200 was launched on May 27th, 1994. These indices were initially calculated at the end of the trading session by taking into consideration the day's Rupee/US$ reference rate as announced by India's central bank i.e. the Reserve Bank of India.

BSE introduced **Dollex-100**, a dollar linked version of BSE-100, on May 22nd, 2006.

Dollex-30, Dollex-100 and Dollex-200 are calculated and displayed through the BSE On-line Trading Terminals (BOLT) by taking into account the real-time Rs./US$ exchange rate. The formula for calculating the index is:

$$\text{Dollex} = \frac{\text{Index value (in local currency)* based on Rupee-US\$ rate}}{\text{Current Rupee-US\$ rate}}$$

More precisely, it can be said that the Stock Exchange, Mumbai launched the index 'Dollex-30' to track the performance of SENSEX scrips in Dollar terms.

Like SENSEX, the base-year for Dollex-30 has been fixed in 1978-79 with the base value at 100 points. The exchange has computed historical index values of 'Dollex-30' since 1979.

It is quite evident from Chart 3.5 of the BSE that the SENSEX and Dollex-30 are maintaining a high and positive correlation between them since the inception of the two indices.

The vast difference between the SENSEX and Dollex-30 in respect of points became more evident and wider in the decade of the 1990s, owing to steep depreciation of the Rupee against the Dollar. The Rs. US$ conversion rate which was about Rs. 8.21 in 1980 rose to about Rs. 47.15 in July 2001 showing a six fold depreciation over two decades. This variation also explains the wide difference in the returns from both these indices.

The level of SENSEX: In rupee terms the index increased around 34 times whereas in US$ terms it increased by only 5.8 times. A foreign investor with a investment of US$ 1,000 in India in 1979 would have made US$ 6,033 at the end of June 2001 (at an annualized return of 8.5 percent in US$ terms), whereas a domestic investor with an investment of Rs. 8,210 in 1979 (equivalent to US$ 1,000 in 1979) would have got a return of Rs. 2,83,802 at the end of June 2001 (at an annualized return of 17.5 percent in rupee terms).

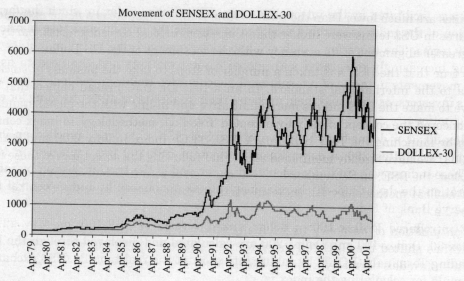

Movement of SENSEX and DOLLEX-30

Source: BSE, Mumbai

| **Chart 3.5** | Movement of SENSEX and Dollex-30 |

Table 3.6 Performance of Emerging Market Country Indices in Terms of both Local Currency and US Dollar (Performance Since January 1988)

Sr.No.	Country	Index	% Increase in Local Currency since Jan 1988	% Increase in US Dollar since Jan 1988
1	India	SENSEX	668%	110%
2	Indonesia	MSCI Indonesia Index	417%	−25%
3	Korea	MSCI Korea Index	50%	−8%
4	Malaysia	MSCI Malaysia Index	110%	38%
5	Thailand	MSCI Thailand Index	17%	−35%
6	Singapore	MSCI Singapore Index	106%	126%
7	Philippines	MSCI Philippines Index	231%	31.50%

Source: BSE, Mumbai

A comparative study (BSE) of returns of major emerging economic indices measured in terms of domestic currency and US$ reveals that India tops among Asian majors. The returns are compared on the basis of SENSEX returns in the case of India with MSCI country indices in respect of Asian countries. Dollex-30, has a very high correlation of 0.96 with the MSCI India Standard Index. Since January 1988 till June end 2001, returns from the SENSEX were to the tune of 668 per cent in respect of local currency and 110 per cent in US$ terms. Three of the major Asian countries namely Korea, Thailand and Indonesia in fact yielded negative returns in US$ terms during this period, whereas the positive returns of Malaysia and the

Philippines are much lower than the returns from India. Singapore is a major exception where the returns in US$ terms were higher than the return in local currency terms, partly because of the greater alignment of its currency with the movement of the US Dollar.

It is true that the BSE has taken a number of steps to take the business of stock trading in India to the international standard. In an article Dr. B.R. Prasad opined that 'with an objective to make the BSE indices more qualitative and in-line with the global standards, the BSE pioneered the concept of globally accepted 'free-float methodology' in index construction in India by launching the TMT benchmark 'BSE-TEC*k* Index' in July 2001 and BANKEX in June 2003.' We have already mentioned above that following the acceptance of these indices in the market, the BSE, on September 1st 2003, shifted the country's bellwether index 'SENSEX' to the free-float methodology. All the above indices are widely reported in the electronic and print media.

In continuation of its policy to gradually shift all indices to the free-float methodology, the BSE has shifted the BSE-100 index to the 'free-float methodology' w.e.f. April 5th 2004. The BSE-100 index (formerly known as BSE National Index) was launched on January 3rd 1989 and it was calculated taking prices of constituents from five major stock exchanges viz. Mumbai, Kolkata, Delhi, Chennai and Ahmedabad. An average of the prices quoted on two or more exchanges was considered for index compilation. Later in 1996, BSE National Index was re-designated as BSE-100 Index and only prices quoted on BSE were taken into account for compilation of the index.

The shifting of BSE-100 to the free-float methodology has greatly enhanced the quality of the index and brings it at par with international standards. The BSE-100 weighted on free-float has started reflecting authentically the investment opportunity of the constituent stocks thereby making the index a more reliable benchmark for the broad market performance.

BSE TEC*k* INDEX

After Dollex-30, another recent innovation was the introduction of the BSE TEC*k* index, the first free float index in India. These two indices enable greater cohesion and convergence of Indian capital markets with international markets in respect of products and practices.

To make it comparable to the global standards in equity index construction methodology and leading the way in responding to the market demand for a Technology, Media and Telecommunications (TMT) benchmark, The Stock Exchange, Mumbai (BSE) launched the country's first free-float based Index – BSE TEC*k* index. The new index marks a paradigm shift in the Indian equity indexing scenario by introducing the concept of free-float adjustment – a globally accepted index construction methodology. 'TEC*k*' stands for the following:

T - Technology (BSE Sector: Information Technology)

E - Entertainment (BSE Sector: Media & Publishing)

C - Communication (BSE Sector: Telecom)

k - Other knowledge based companies not falling in any of the above three sectors

We have already discussed the fact that a free-float based index construction methodology (also called modified market capitalization method) takes into consideration only the non-promoter holding for the purpose of calculating the index. In case of the BSE TEC*k* index, the market capitalization of a company is adjusted to reflect the free-float portion only. For example if a company has 35 per cent non-promoter-holding, then only 35 per cent of the total market capitalizations of the company would be considered for the purpose of calculating the BSE-TEC*k* index.

The innovative BSE TEC*k* index has been produced specifically as a benchmark that would reflect the dynamic and unique characteristics of the TMT industries in India. With 21 constituents covering around 90 per cent of the market capitalization of the entire listed TMT universe, the new index ensures a very liquid, tradable index. The base value for the new index has been set as 1000 points as on the base date of April 2nd 2001.

The market capitalization and trading pattern of the TMT sectors on the bourses, coupled with the relevance of a sector specific product, qualifies the BSE TEC*k* index as an appropriate benchmark for funds tracking these industries.

"The BSE-TECk Index has been launched in line with the international best practices and involved a lot of research in devising the construction methodology for the adjustment of free-float. The outcome is a quality equity benchmark for the TMT sectors which would find great utility in the market place both with retail and institutional investors." (Ref: BSE, Mumbai).

BANKEX: A FREE FLOAT WEIGHTED INDEX ON THE BANKING SECTOR

BSE launched Bank Index, Bankex on 16th June 2003. Indian banking is considered to be an important service sector industry in Asia both in terms of strength and soundness. In the year 2002, return on assets in Indian banking was higher compared to many emerging economies and the Moody's Bank Financial Strength Index (2002) placed India at 27.5, which is much better than 16.7 of Korea, 15.8 of Thailand and 12.5 of Japan. Similar to the experiences in other rapidly growing countries, India is making sizeable gains in expanding into consumer credit with tightening of credit administration procedures. Major policy actions that led to a sharp fall in the interest rates enabled banks to post significant rise in operational profits. The enactment of the Securitization Bill offered great opportunities to step up loan recoveries that could further enhance the scope of greater profitability.

These developments impacted the performance of bank stocks significantly. Since bank stocks have emerged as a major segment in the equity markets, BSE considered it important to design an index exclusively for bank stocks. The index is computed on the basis of the globally accepted free float methodology.

A few important features of the BSE Bank Index, which is known as BANKEX, are given below:

❖ BANKEX is based on the free float methodology of index construction
❖ The base date for BANKEX is 1st January 2002
❖ The base value is 1000 points

❖ BSE has calculated the historical index values of BANKEX since 1st January 2002

❖ 12 stocks which represent 90 per cent of the total market capitalization of all banking sector stocks listed on BSE are included in the Index

❖ The index is disseminated on a real-time basis through BSE Online Trading (BOLT) terminals

❖ BANKEX tracks the performance of the leading banking sector stocks listed on the BSE

Stocks forming part of the BANKEX along with the particulars of their free float adjusted market capitalization during its inception are listed in Table 3.7.

Table 3.7 List of Banks Selected for Construction of BANKEX (At the time of inception, 16 June 2003)

Sr. No.	Code	Name of the Banks	Full Mkt. Cap. (Rs. cr.)	Free-float Adj. Factor	Free-float Mkt. Cap. (Rs. cr.)
(1)	(2)	(3)	(4)	(5)	Col(4)xCol(5)=(6)
1	532418	Andhra Bank	1226.00	0.40	490.40
2	532134	Bank of Baroda	3062.12	0.40	1224.85
3	532149	Bank of India	2283.44	0.40	913.38
4	532483	Canara Bank	3864.25	0.30	1159.28
5	532179	Corporation Bank	2353.13	0.50	1176.57
6	500180	HDFC Bank	7104.29	0.80	5683.43
7	532174	ICICI Bank Ltd.	8732.68	1.00	8732.68
8	531807	ING Vysya Bank	638.44	0.50	319.22
9	500315	Oriental Bank of Commerce	2419.26	0.40	967.70
10	532461	Punjab National Bank	3846.89	0.20	769.38
11	500112	State Bank of India	18236.26	0.50	9118.13
12	532477	Union Bank of India Ltd.	1516.09	0.40	606.44
		BANKEX Mkt. Cap.	**55282.85**		**31161.44**

Source: BSE, Mumbai.

BANKEX, which is comparatively new entrant in BSE's current portfolio of 13 indices, has enhanced BSE's ability in reflecting both the broad market and specific sector movements in the Indian equity markets.

UNDERSTANDING S&P CNX NIFTY

S&P CNX and Nifty (Nifty 50 or simply Nifty), the most popular and widely used indicators of the stock market in the country, is a 50-stock index comprising the largest and the most liquid stocks from about 25 sectors in India. These stocks have a Market Capitalization (MC) of over 50 per cent of the total MC of the Indian stock market. The index was introduced in 1995 by the National Stock Exchange (NSE), Mumbai, keeping in mind that it would be used for modern applications such as index funds and index derivatives besides reflecting the stock market behaviour. NSE maintained it till July 1998, after which the ownership and management rights were transferred to India Index Services & Products Ltd. (IISL), the only professional company in India which provides index services. IISL is a joint venture between the NSE and CSISIL. Nifty is one of the most significant stock indices in India and the other is SENSEX.

India Index Services & Products Ltd. (IISL)

IISL is jointly promoted by NSE, the country's leading stock exchange and The Credit Rating and Information Services of India Ltd. (CRISIL), the leading credit rating agency in India. IISL has a licensing and marketing agreement with Standard & Poor's (S&P), the leading index services provider in the world.

S&P CNX Nifty, the most popular and widely used indicator of the stock market in India, is owned and managed by IISL, which also maintains over 80 indices comprising broad based benchmark indices, sectoral indices and customized indices.

Actually, Nifty was developed by the economists Ajay Shah and Susan Thomas, then at IGIDR. Later on, it came to be owned and managed by India Index Services and Products Ltd., which is a joint venture between NSE and CRISIL. IISL is India's first specialized company focused upon the index as a core product. IISL have a consulting and licensing agreement with Standard & Poor's (who are world leaders in index services). It is a simplified tool that helps investors and ordinary people alike to understand what is happening in the stock market and by extension, the economy. If the Nifty index performs well, it is a signal that companies in India are performing well and consequently that the country is doing well.

An upbeat economy is usually reflected in a strong performance of the Nifty index. A rising index is also indicative that the investors are gung-ho about the future. The Nifty index is based upon solid economic research. It is internationally respected and recognized as a pioneering effort in providing simpler understanding of stock market complexities Nifty is the flagship index of NSE, the third largest stock exchange in the world in terms of number of transactions (stock futures).

CNX stands for CRISIL NSE indices. CNX ensures common branding of indices, to reflect the identities of both the promoters, i.e. NSE and CRISIL. Thus, 'C' stands for CRISIL, 'N' stands for NSE and X stands for Exchange or Index. The S&P prefix belongs to the US-based Standard & Poor's Financial Information Services. It is calculated as a weighted average, so changes in the share prices of larger companies have a greater effect. The base is defined as 1000 at the price level of November 3rd, 1995.

Criteria for Inclusion of Stock in Nifty50

❖ Average market capitalization of Rs. 5,000 million or more during the last six months.

❖ Liquidity: Cost of transaction (impact cost) of less than 0.75 per cent for more than 90 per cent of trades, over six months.

❖ At least 12 per cent floating stock (not held by promoters of the company or their associates).

Choice of Index Set Size

While trying to construct Nifty, a number of calculations were done to arrive at the ideal number of stocks. A simple index construction algorithm was implemented which did not pre-specify the size of the index set, but added and deleted stocks based on criteria of MC and liquidity. Ten index time series (from 1990 to 1995) were generated by using various thresholds for addition and deletion of stocks from/into the index set.

These index sets turned out to range from 69 to 182 stocks as of the end of 1995, indicating that the ideal number of stocks for the index could be somewhere in the range 69 to 182. For each of these ten index time-series, the correlation between the index time-series and thousands of randomly chosen portfolios was calculated. This gave a quantitative sense of how increasing the index set size helps improve the extent to which the index reflects the behaviour of the market. It was observed that the gain from increasing the number of stocks from 69 to 182 was quite insignificant. It was corroborated by the theory on portfolio diversification, which suggests that diversifying from 10 to 20 stocks results in considerable reductions in risk, while the gains from further diversification are smaller. An analysis of liquidity further suggested that the Indian market had comfortable liquidity of around 50 stocks. Beyond 50, the liquidity levels became increasingly lower. Hence the index set size of 50 stocks was chosen.

Selection of Stocks

From early 1996 onwards, the eligibility criteria for inclusion of stocks in S&P CNX Nifty are based on the criteria of market capitalization, liquidity and floating stock.

Market capitalization: Stocks eligible for inclusion in Nifty must have a six monthly average market capitalization of Rs. 500 crore or more during the last six months.

Liquidity (Impact cost): Liquidity can be measured in two ways: Traditionally liquidity is measured by volume and number of trades. The new international practice of measuring liquidity is in terms of impact cost. An ideal stock can be traded at its ruling market price. However practically, when one tries to buy a stock, one pays a price higher than the ruling price for purchase, or receives a price lower than the ruling price from sale, due to sufficient quantity not being available at the ruling price. This difference from the ruling price in percentage terms is the impact cost. It is defined as the percentage degradation suffered in the price for purchase or sale of a specified quantity of shares, when compared to the ideal price.

It can be computed for each individual stock based on order book snapshots. It can also be computed for a market index based on the impact cost of constituent stocks, using their respective index weights. The impact cost of a market index is effectively the cost incurred when simultaneously placing market orders for all constituents of the index, in the proportion of their weights in the index. A highly liquid market index is one where the impact cost of buying or selling the entire index is low.

It is the percentage mark up suffered while buying/selling the desired quantity of a stock compared to its ideal price, that is, (best buy + best sell)/2.

In short, the main features on the S&P CNX Nifty can be written as follows:

The S&P CNX Nifty is a market capitalization index based upon solid economic research. It was designed not only as a barometer of market movement but also to be a foundation of the new world of financial products based on the index like index futures, index options and index funds. A trillion calculations were expended to evolve the rules inside the S&P CNX Nifty index. The results of this work are remarkably simple:

1. The correct size to use is 50

2. Stocks considered for the S&P CNX Nifty must be liquid by the 'impact cost' criterion

3. The highest 50 stocks that meet the criterion go into the index. S&P CNX Nifty is a contrast to the adhoc methods that have gone into index construction in the preceding years, where indices were made out of intuition and lacked a scientific basis. The research that led up to S&P CNX Nifty is well-respected internationally as a pioneering effort in better understanding how to make a stock market index.

The Nifty is uniquely equipped as an index for the index derivatives market owing to:

1. Its low market impact cost.

2. High hedging effectiveness. The good diversification of Nifty generates low initial margin requirement. Finally, Nifty is calculated using NSE prices, the most liquid exchange in India, thus making it easier to do arbitrage for index derivatives.

Significance of Index Movements

It is quite well known that the movements of an index reflect the changing expectations of the stock market about future dividends of the corporate sector. The index goes up if the stock market thinks that the prospective dividends in the future will be better than previously thought. When the prospects of dividends in the future become pessimistic, the index drops. The ideal index gives us instant readings about how the stock market perceives the future of the corporate sector.

Every stock price moves for two possible reasons:

1. News about the company (e.g. a product launch, or the closure of a factory)

2. News about the country (e.g. budget announcements)

The job of an index is purely to capture the second part, the movements of the stock market as a whole (i.e. news about the country). This is achieved by averaging. Each stock contains a mixture of two elements - stock news and index news. When we take an average of returns on many stocks, the individual stock news tends to cancel out and the only thing left is news that is common to all stocks. The news that is common to all stocks is news about the economy. That is what a good index captures. The correct method of averaging is that of taking a weighted average, giving each stock a weight proportional to its market capitalization.

Example: Suppose an index contains two stocks, A and B. A has a market capitalization of Rs. 1,000 crore and B has a market capitalization of Rs. 3,000 crore. Then we attach a weight of 1/4 to movements in A and 3/4 to movements in B. Besides serving as a barometer of the economy/market, the index also has other applications in finance.

Index Derivatives

Index derivatives are derivative contracts which have the index as the underlying. The most popular index derivatives contract the world over is index futures and index options. NSE's market index, the S&P CNX Nifty was scientifically designed to enable the launch of index-based products like index derivatives and index funds. The first derivative contract to be traded on NSE's market was the index futures contract with the Nifty as the underlying.

This was followed by Nifty options, derivative contracts on sectoral indices like CNX IT and BANK Nifty contracts. Trading on index derivatives were further introduced on CNX Nifty Junior, CNX 100, Nifty Midcap 50 and Mini Nifty 50.

Index Funds

An index fund is a fund that tries to replicate the index returns. It does so by investing in index stocks in the proportions in which these stocks exist in the index. The goal of the index fund is to achieve the same performance as the index it tracks.

For instance, a Nifty index fund would seek to get the same return as the Nifty index. Since the Nifty has 50 stocks, the fund would buy all 50 stocks in the proportion in which they exist in the Nifty. Once invested, the fund will track the index, i.e. if the Nifty goes up, the value of the fund will go up to the same extent as the Nifty. If the Nifty falls, the value of the index fund will fall to the same extent as the Nifty. The most useful kind of market index is one where the weight attached to a stock is proportional to its market capitalization, as in the case of Nifty. Index funds are easy to construct for this kind of index since the index fund does not need to trade in response to price fluctuations. Trading is only required in response to issuance of shares, mergers, etc.

Exchange Traded Funds

Exchange Traded Funds (ETFs) are innovative products, which first came into existence in the USA in 1993. They have gained prominence over the last few years with over $300 billion invested as of end 2001 in about 360 ETFs globally. About 60 per cent of the trading volume on the American Stock Exchange is from ETFs. Among the popular ones are SPDRs (Spiders) based on the S&P 500 Index, QQQs (Cubes) based on the Nasdaq-100 Index, iSHARES based on MSCI Indices and TRAHK (Tracks) based on the Hang Seng Index. ETFs provide exposure to an index or a basket of securities that trade on the exchange like a single stock. They have a number of advantages over traditional open-ended funds as they can be bought and sold on the exchange at prices that are usually close to the actual intra-day NAV of the scheme. They are an innovation to traditional mutual funds as they provide investors with a fund that closely tracks the performance of an index with the ability to buy/sell on an intra-day basis. Unlike listed closed-ended funds, which trade at substantial premia or more frequently at discounts to NAV, ETFs are structured in a manner which allows the creation of new units and redemption of outstanding units directly with the fund, thereby ensuring that ETFs trade close to their actual NAVs.

The first ETF in India, the Nifty Benchmark Exchange Traded Scheme (Nifty BeEs) based on S&P CNX Nifty, was launched in December 2001 by Benchmark Mutual Fund. It is bought and sold like any other stock on the NSE and has all the characteristics of an index fund. It provides returns that closely correspond to the total return of stocks included in Nifty.

Futures markets can be used for creating synthetic index funds. Synthetic index funds created using futures contracts have advantages of simplicity and low costs. The simplicity stems from the fact that index futures automatically track the index. The cost advantages stem from the fact that the costs of establishing and re-balancing the fund are substantially reduced because commissions and bid-ask spreads are lower in the futures markets than in the equity markets.

The methodology for creating a synthetic index fund is to combine index futures contracts with bank deposits or treasury bills. The index fund uses part of its money as margin on the futures market and the rest is invested at the risk-free rate of return. This methodology however does require frequent roll-over as futures contracts expire. Index funds can also use the futures market for the purpose of spreading index sales or purchases over a period of time. Take the case of an index fund which has raised Rs. 100 crore from the market. To reduce the tracking error, this money must be invested in the index immediately. However large trades face large impact costs. What the fund can do is, the moment it receives the subscriptions it can buy index futures. Then gradually over a period of say a month, it can keep acquiring the underlying index stocks. As it acquires the index stocks, it should unwind its position on the futures market by selling futures to the extent of stock acquired. This should continue till the fund is fully invested in the index.

Capturing Behavior of Portfolios

A good market index should accurately reflect the behavior of the overall market as well as of different portfolios. This is achieved by diversification in such a manner that a portfolio is not vulnerable to any individual stock or industry risk. A well-diversified index is more representative of the market.

However there are diminishing returns from diversification. There is very little gain by diversifying beyond a point. The more serious problem lies in the stocks that are included in the index when it is diversified. We end up including illiquid stocks, which actually worsens the index. Since an illiquid stock does not reflect the current price behavior of the market, its inclusion in an index results in an index, which reflects delayed or stale price behavior rather than current price behavior of the market.

Including Liquid Stocks

Liquidity is much more than trading frequency. It is about the ability to transact at a price, which is very close to the current market price. For example, a stock is considered liquid if one can buy some shares at around Rs. 320.05 and sell at around Rs. 319.95, when the market price is ruling at Rs. 320. A liquid stock has very tight bid-ask spread.

Impact Cost

Market impact cost is a measure of the liquidity of the market. It reflects the costs faced when actually trading an index. For a stock to qualify for possible inclusion into the Nifty, it has to have market impact cost of below 0.75 per cent when doing Nifty trades of half a crore rupees. The market impact cost on a trade of Rs. 3 million of the full Nifty works out to be about 0.05 per cent. This means that if Nifty is at 2000, a buy order goes through at 2001, i.e. 2000 + (2000*0.0005) and a sell order gets 1999, i.e. 2000 – (2000*0.0005)

Hedging Effectiveness

Hedging effectiveness is a measure of the extent to which an index correlates with a portfolio, whatever the portfolio may be. Nifty correlates better with all kinds of portfolios in India as compared to other indices. This holds good for all kinds of portfolios, not just those that contain index stocks. Similarly, the CNX IT and BANK Nifty contracts which NSE trades in correlate well with information technology and banking sector portfolios.

Nifty, CNX IT, BANK Nifty, CNX Nifty Junior, CNX 100, Nifty Midcap 50 and Mini Nifty 50 indices are owned, computed and maintained by IISL, a company setup by NSE and CRISIL with technical assistance from Standard & Poor's.

With reference to different articles published by the Bombay Stock Exchanges we have discussed some of indices of our country. There are other indices as well in our country which are maintained by the BSE and NSE as well other stock exchanges and different financial news papers of the country. The total list of different indices of India is furnished in Table 3.8 and a list of indices of different countries is given in Table 3.9.

Brief introductions for some of the world's important indexes are furnished below:

International

- ❖ BBC Global 30 – World stock market index of 30 of the largest companies by stock market value in Europe, Asia and the Americas.
- ❖ iShares MSCI EAFE Index (EFA) – Provides investment results generally equivalent to publicly traded securities in the European, Australasian and Far Eastern markets Maintained by Morgan Stanley Capital International.
- ❖ MSCI World – Free-float weighted equity index. Index includes stocks of all the developed markets be consider as Common benchmark for world stock funds.
- ❖ S&P Global 1200 – Global stocks index covering 31 countries and around 70 percent of global market capitalization.

Table 3.8 Different Share Indices of India

Bombay Stock Exchange Indices	National Stock Exchange Indices (NSE), Mumbai (Formerly Bombay)	Other Indices
BSE 30 (SENSEX)	S&P CNX Nifty 50-stock large MC Index (CNX stands for CRISIL NSE Indices)	CALCUTTA SENSITIVE INDEX: Initiated in 1996 by Calcutta Stock Exchange with 50 selected shares.
AUTO INDEX	S&P CNX 500 A broad based 500 stock Index	BUSINESS STANDARDINDEX: Initiated in 1980-81
BANKEX	S&P CNX Defty US $ denominated Index of S&P CNX Nifty	ECONOMIC TIMES INDEX: Initiated in 1984-85
BSE - 100	S&P CNX Industry indices The S&P CNX 500 in classified in 72 industry sectors. Each such sector forms an Index by itself.	OVER THE COUNTER INDEX
BSE - 200	CNX Nifty Junior 50-stock Index which comprise the next rung of large and liquid stocks after S&P CNX Nifty	
BSE - 500	CNX Midcap A midcap Index of 100 stocks	
BSE - CAPITAL GOODS	CNX PSE Index Public Sector Enterprises Index	
BSE - CONS. DURABLES	CNX MNC Index Multinational Companies Index	
BSE - FMCG	CNX IT Index Information Technology Index	
BSE - HEALTHCARE	CNX FMCG Index Fast Moving Consumer Goods Index	
BSE - INFOTECH	CNX Bank Index	
BSE Mid-Cap	CNX Energy Index	
BSE PUBLIC SECTOR	CNX Pharma Index	
BSE Small-Cap		
BSE TECK INDEX		
METAL INDEX		
OIL & GAS INDEX		

Source: Bombay Stock Exchange

UNITED STATES

Dow Jones Indexes - Leading global indexes provider.

Overview

The Dow Jones Total Stock Market Index family is a clear, comprehensive mirror to the global equity market. Anchored by the Dow Jones Global Total Stock Market Index, the Dow Jones Total Stock Market Index family includes more than 12,000 securities from 65 countries – providing near-exhaustive coverage of both developed and emerging markets. As its U.S. component, the family features the Dow Jones U.S. Total Stock Market Index, which comprises all U.S. equity securities with readily available prices.

Table 3.9 Different Share Indices of the World

		ASIA / PACIFIC AND AFRICA			
Country	*Name of Index*	*Stock Exch.*	*Country*	*Name of Index*	*Stock Exch.*
Japan	Nikkei 225*	Tokyo	Australia	S&P/ASX 200	Sydney
China	Songhai Composite (SSE)	Songhai	South Korea	Seoul Composite KOSPI	Seoul
Hong Kong	Hang Seng (33)	Exch. Stockware bn	New Zealand	NZX50	NZ Exchange
Indonesia	Jakarta Composite (JSX)	Jakarta	Taiwan	Taiwan Weighted TSEC	Taiwan
Malaysia	KLSE Composite		South	Johannesburg	Johannesburg
	FTSE Busra Malaysia Index	Kualalampore	Africa	All Share Index	
Thailand	SETI	Bangkok	Morocco	MASI Index	Casablanca
Singapore	Straight Times	Singapore	Oman	MSM-30	Oman
Philippines	Composite PSEi Index	Philippines	Egypt	CMA Case-30	Cairo & Alexandria
Pakistan	KSE-100	Karachi	Jordan	ASE Market Cap.	Amman
Israel	TA-100 & TA-25	Tel Aviv	Asia & Pacific	S&P Asia 50	-
		EUROPE			
Country	*Name of Index*	*Stock Exch.*	*Country*	*Name of Index*	*Stock Exch.*
England	FTSE – 100*	London	France	CAC 40	Paris
Germany	GDAXI (30)	Frankfurt	Netherland	AEX General	Amsterdam
Norway	OSEAX	Oslo	Denmark	OMX – 20	Copenhagen
Finland	OMX Helsinki-20	Helsinki	Austria	ATX	Vienna
Belgium	BEL – 20	-	Italy	MIB Tel	Milan
Turkey	ISE National-100(IXX)	Istanbul	Czech Repub.	PX Index	Prague
Spain	SMSI, IBEX 35	Madrid	Switzerland	SSMI Swiss Market	Geneva
Sweden	OMXSPI (30)	Stockholm	Poland	WIG	Warsaw.
Portugal	PSI – 20	Lisbon	-	-	-
		NORTH AMERICA			
Country	*Name of Index*	*Stock Exch.*	*Country*	*Name of Index*	*Stock Exch.*
USA	GSPC-500 Index	-	USA	AMEX Composite	-
USA	Dow Jones Indexes	New York	USA	Dow Jones Index30	New York
USA	Dow Jones Wilshare – 5000	New York	USA	Russell-3000 Indexes	-
USA	NASDAQ Compo.	New York	USA	NYSE Composite	New York
USA	Russell Indexes	-	Canada	GSPTSE, S&PTSX	Toronto
		SOUTH AMERICA			
Argentina	MARVAL	Buenos Aires	Brazil	Bovespa Index	Sao Paulo
Mexico	Indice de Preciosy Cotizaciones (IPC)	Bolsa Mexicana De Valores	Latin America	iShare S&P Latin America 40 Index	ILF

Notes: Accompanied and bracketed figures with respective indexes are the composition of companies selected in the respective index.

U.S. Indices

Global Indices

Real Estate Indices

These can be elaborated as:

The Dow Jones U.S. Total Stock Market Indexes are designed to provide comprehensive coverage of the U.S. equity market. The flagship index of the family, the Dow Jones U.S. Total Stock Market Index, is an all-inclusive measure composed of all U.S. equity securities with readily available prices. This broad index is sliced according to stock-size segment, style and sector to create distinct sub indices that track every major segment of the market. All the indices are created and maintained according to an objective and transparent methodology with the fundamental aim of providing reliable, accurate measures of U.S. equity performance.

Dow Jones U.S. Total Stock Market Index: Measures all U.S. equity securities that have readily available prices.

Dow Jones U.S. Completion Total Stock Market Index: A subset of the Dow Jones U.S. Total Stock Market Index that excludes components of the S&P 500.

Dow Jones Broad Stock Market Index: The largest 2,500 stocks within the Dow Jones U.S. Total Stock Market Index.

Size-Segment Indices

Dow Jones U.S. Large-Cap Total Stock Market Index

Dow Jones U.S. Mid-Cap Total Stock Market Index

Dow Jones U.S. Small-Cap Total Stock Market Index

Dow Jones U.S. Micro-Cap Total Stock Market Index

Style Indices

Dow Jones U.S. Large-Cap Growth Total Stock Market Index

Dow Jones U.S. Large-Cap Value Total Stock Market Index

Dow Jones U.S. Mid-Cap Growth Total Stock Market Index

Dow Jones U.S. Mid-Cap Value Total Stock Market Index

Dow Jones U.S. Small-Cap Growth Total Stock Market Index

Dow Jones U.S. Small-Cap Value Total Stock Market Index

Dow Jones Industrial Average – one of the most widely quoted of all the market indicators consists of 30 of the largest publicly traded firms in the U.S. (NYSE).

Dow Jones Wilshire 5000 – designed to track the performance of all publicly traded companies based in the U.S.

Sector Indices

Indices constitute 10 Industries, 19 Super sectors, 41 Sectors and 114 Subsectors as defined by ICB.

AMEX Composite – Composite value of all of the stocks traded on the American Stock Exchange.

NASDAQ Composite – With over 3,000 components, the NASDAQ Composite is a stock market index comprising all the common stocks and similar securities listed on the NASDAQ stock market. In terms of indicating the performance of technological companies and growth companies, the NASDAQ Composite is the most followed in the United States, although is it not solely a U.S. index.

The NSYE is the world's largest stock exchange in terms of market capitalization. NASDAQ is the largest exchange of the world in terms of turnover.

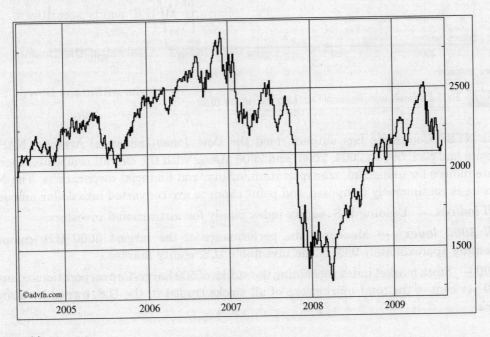

Source: www. advfn.com

Chart 3.6   NASDAQ Composite Index Historical Chart (July 2005 to July 2010)

NYSE Composite – Covers all common stocks listed on the New York Stock Exchange. There are over 2,000 stocks listed on the NYSE Composite, which are all common stock listed on the New York Stock Exchange. Of that 2,000, over 1,600 are from the United States and there are more then 360 foreign listings as well. Using a value of 5,000 points and a market-value weighted number of shares listed for each issue, the NYSE composite uses a free-float market cap weighting.

Source: www. advfn.com

Chart 3.7 NYSE Composite Index Historical Chart (July 2005 to July 2010)

This NYSE Composite has outperformed the Dow Jones Industrial Average, NASDAQ Composite and S&P 500 in 2004, 2005, and 2006. Along with the overall composite, there are separate indices for industrial, transportation, utility, and financial corporations. The NYSE Composite is continuously computed and point changes are converted into dollar amount.

Russell Indices – Leading U.S. equity index family for institutional investors.

Russell 3000 Index – Measures the performance of the largest 3000 U.S. companies representing approximately 98% of the investable U.S. equity market.

S&P 500 – Stock market index containing the stocks of 500 Large-Cap corporations comprises over 70 per cent of the total market cap of all stocks traded in the U.S. owned by Standard & Poor's.

Egypt

Case 30 – Index of the Cairo & Alexandria Stock Exchange; includes the top 30 companies in terms of liquidity and activity.

Morocco

MASI Index – Stock index of the Casablanca Stock Exchange.

South Africa

Johannesburg All Share Index

Australia

All Ordinaries – Index of shares listed on the Australian Stock Exchange (ASX).

S&P/ASX 200 – Index of 200 largest and most liquid companies.

China

SSE Composite – Index of all listed stocks (A shares and B shares) at Shanghai Stock Exchange.

Hong Kong

Hang Seng Indexes – Record daily changes of the 30 largest companies of the Hong Kong stock market (represent about 67 per cent of capitalization of the Hong Kong Stock Exchange). On the Hong Kong Stock Exchange, a capitalization-weighted stock market index called the Hang Seng Index is used to record and monitor daily changes of the largest companies on the Hong Kong Stock Market.

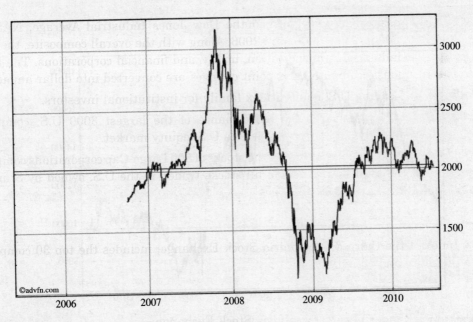

©advfn.com

Chart 3.8 Hang Seng Index Historical Chart (July 2005 to July 2010)

Source: www. advfn.com

The Hang Seng is used as the main indicator of the overall market performance in Hong Kong and the 38 companies represent about per cent of the capitalization of the Hong Kong Stock Exchange. Compiled and maintained by HIS Services Limited, a subsidiary of the second largest bank listed in terms of market capitalization Hang Seng Bank, it is responsible for compiling, publishing and managing the Hang Seng Index.

India (All have been discussed above)

BSE SENSEX 30 – Includes the 30 highest and most actively traded stocks on the Bombay Stock Exchange.

S&P CNX Nifty – Index for 50 large companies on the National Stock Exchange of India.

Indonesia

JSX Composite – Index of all stocks traded on the Jakarta Stock Exchange.

Japan

Nikkei 225 – Stock market index of the 225 largest companies listed on the Tokyo Stock Exchange. As the stock market index for the Tokyo Stock Exchange, the Nikkei 225 is the most followed index of Asian stocks. It is calculated daily and reviewed once a year by the Nihon Keizai Shimbun (Nikkei) newspaper using a price-weighted average. Equal weighting based on a par value of 50 Yen/share is given to stocks in the Nikkei 225 and certain events, such as stock splits, affect the weighting of stocks and the divisor.

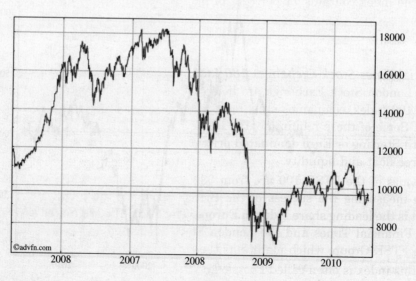

Source: www. advfn.com

Chart 3.9 Nikkei 225 Index Historical Chart (July 2005 to July 2010)

Malaysia

FTSE Bursa Malaysia Index

Pakistan

KSE 100 – Index acting as a benchmark to compare prices on the Karachi Stock Exchange.

Philippines

PSEi Index – Index acting as a benchmark to compare prices on the Manila Stock Exchange.

Korea

KOSPI – Index of all common shares on the Korean Stock Exchanges.

Taiwan

TSEC – Capitalization-weighted index of all listed common shares traded on the Taiwan Stock Exchange.

Canada

S&P/TSX Composite – Made up of the largest companies on the Toronto Stock Exchange, the S&P/TSX Composite Index is measured by market capitalization. Of all companies listed on the TSX, the index contains 71 per cent of market capitalization for all Canadian-based companies.

Europe

FTSE (Financial Times Stock Exchange) 100 Index – The most highly capitalized companies listed on the London Stock Exchange are listed on the FTSE 100 index. In order to appear on the FTSE 100 Index, companies must meet a number of requirements put in place by the FTSE Group. Some of these requirements include having a full listing on the London Stock Exchange with Sterling or Euro dominated price on SETS as well as meeting certain tests on nationality, free float and liquidity.

Trading hours of the FTSE 100 are from 0800-1629, which is when the closing auction starts. When measuring the success of the British economy, the FTSE 100 is used as an indicator as it is the leading share index in Europe. The FTSE 100 originated as a joint venture between the Financial Times and the London Stock Exchange and is now an independent company, the FTSE Group, which maintains the share index.

In short, this index is often called Footsie and the composition of this index is 100 largest companies.

Dow Jones Euro Stoxx 50 – Free-float market capitalization-weighted index of 50 Euro zone stocks provides a blue-chip representation of Super sector leaders in the Euro zone.

FTSEurofirst Index Series – Provides pan-European indices Joint product of FTSE Group, the leading global index provider, and Euronext, an integrated cross border European exchange.

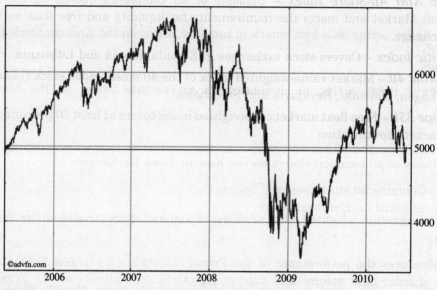

Source: www. advfn.com

Chart 3.10   FTSE 100 Index Historical Chart (July 2005 to July 2010)

Source: www. advfn.com

Chart 3.11   FTSE AIM All Share Index Historical Chart (July 2005 to July 2010)

FTSEurofirst 300 Index – Free-float capitalization-weighted price index measures the performance of Europe's largest 300 companies by market capitalization; covers 70 per cent of Europe's market cap.

The FTSE AIM All-Share Index – Consists of all companies quoted on the Alternative Investment Market and meets the requirements for liquidity and free float on the London Stock Exchange.

OMX Baltic Index – Covers stock exchanges in Estonia, Latvia and Lithuania.

OMX Nordic 40 – Market value-weighted index of the 40 most-traded stock classes of shares in Copenhagen, Helsinki, Reykjavik and Stockholm.

S&P Europe 350 – Free float market cap weighted index covers at least 70 per cent of European equity market capitalization.

France

CAC 40 – Contains 40 stocks selected among the top 100 market capitalization and the most active stocks listed on Euronext Paris.

Germany

DAX – Measures the performance of the Prime Standard's 30 largest German companies in terms of order book volume and market capitalization. Actually, on the Frankfurt Stock Exchange, 30 large German companies make up the DAX 30. Prices for this Blue Chip stock market index are taken from the electronic trading system Xetra.

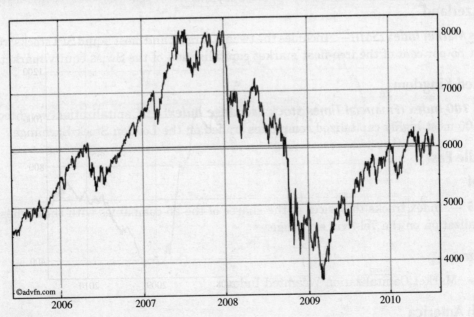

Source: www. advfn.com

Chart 3.12   DAX Index Historical Chart (July 2005 to July 2010)

Ireland

ISEQ 20 – Represents the 20 most liquid and largest capped equities quoted on the Irish Stock Exchange.

Italy

S&P/MIB Index – Capitalization weighted index developed by S&P and Borsa Italiana.

Mibtel Index – This Milan blue-chip index is an all-share index for the Italian Stock Market which is used as a benchmark.

Netherlands

AEX Index – Index of Euronext Amsterdam, consists of the 25 most active securities in the Netherlands.

Poland

WIG Index – Index of the Warsaw Stock Exchange

Russia

MICEX Index – Capital-weighted price index of the 30 major and most liquid Russian stocks traded at the Moscow Interbank Currency Exchange.

RTS Index – Index of 50 Russian stocks traded on the RTS Stock Exchange.

Switzerland

Swiss Market Index (SMI) – Includes the twenty largest and most liquid SPI stocks; represents about 85 per cent of the free-float market capitalization of the Swiss equity market.

United Kingdom

FTSE 100 Index (Financial Times Stock Exchange Index) – Capitalization-weighted index of the 100 most highly capitalized companies traded on the London Stock Exchange.

Middle East

Israel

TA-25 – Index tracks the prices of the shares of the 25 companies with the highest market capitalization on the Tel-Aviv exchange.

Jordan

ASE – Market Capitalization Weighted Index

South America

iShares S&P Latin America 40 Index (ILF)

Argentina

MERVAL – Index of the Buenos Aires Stock Exchange.

Brazil

Bovespa Index – About 50 stocks on the Sao Paulo Stock Exchange are listed on the Bovespa Index. This index is made up of a theoretical portfolio with stocks that account for 80 per cent of the volume traded in the last 20 months and were traded on at least 80 per cent of the trading days. Every quarter the Bovespa Index is revised quarterly to ensure an accurate representation of the volume traded and on average the companies in the Bovespa Index represent 70 per cent of all the stock value traded.

Source: www. advfn.com

Chart 3.13 | Bovespa Index Historical Chart (July 2005 to July 2010)

Mexico

Indice de Preciosy Cotizaciones (IPC) – Index of 35 stocks traded on the Bolsa Mexicana de Valores.

There are a number of factors that influence the movements of share prices, which will be discussed in the next chapter.

FOR FURTHER READING

1. Panchal, Salil, Jobbers Back in Business, *Business Standard*, October 6, 1995

Movements of Share Prices

4

REASONS FOR MOVEMENTS OF SHARE PRICES

In the bourses (different stock markets), prices of companies' stocks fluctuate every day. In other commodities markets the prices of commodities also fluctuate, but unlike the commodities market, where prices more or less always keep upward trends and seldom show a downward trend, in the stock market prices can maintain an upward trend (commonly known as bullish trend) on a particular day and on the very next day the price can show a downward trend (commonly known as bearish trend).

The market price of an equity share is the price at which it is being traded on the bourses. Many factors influence the movement of the price at which a company's equity share trades, such as liquidity, the demand and supply of the share and investors' perception. It is well accepted that the market price of an equity share is determined by the demand and supply of that share. Demand and supply are, in turn, governed by many rational and irrational factors. Irrespective of minor fluctuations in the stock market, share prices tend to move in trends which persist for an appreciable length of time. Changes in such trends are caused by shifts in the demand and supply position of shares. It is a well accepted fact that according to the general law of economics, in a perfect market the price of a commodity tends to go up if the supply of that commodity fails to meet the demand of that commodity. Similarly, if the supply is plenty but demand is less, price of that commodity will witness an obvious fall. The share market also follows the same pattern. Here, if the buyers of a particular share are more than sellers, the price of that share will rise and if the situation is reversed, the price will fall. In theory, it sounds very simple, but in practice it is not so. The changes in demand and supply or fluctuations in share prices are influenced by some very important factors as given below.

If banks and other financial institutes reduce the interest rates on deposits, the general public with funds to invest will turn to the share market for better returns and if the banks' interest rates on deposits increase, the investments on shares will decrease. If the government offers better and more favorable investment opportunities to foreign investors and to the representatives of foreign financial institutes, the share markets will follow a bullish trend. When the government relaxes any stringent rules and introduces some favorable rules for certain industries, then share prices of the companies belonging to those industries will increase in the markets. When some companies announce encouraging or discouraging financial results of their companies, the share price of those companies will also behave accordingly in the markets.

As in the past, the prices of shares are today also influenced significantly by the political atmosphere of the country. If the political situation of the country becomes unstable for one reason or another, the bourses also stumble and share prices are likely to crash. During March, 1996, some of the leading Indian politicians were arrested due to money laundering and for taking bribes. As a result, the share markets of India witnessed a great fall in share prices. During election time, if the political situation of the country gives rise to doubts about the formation of a stable government in the country, a fall in share prices will be observed in the share markets. During the second week of May, 1998, when the Atal Behari Vajpayee government conducted two nuclear tests at Pokhran in the state of Rajasthan in India, the share index nose dived by more than 150 points. Similarly, in the last week of May of the same year, Pakistan conducted six nuclear tests at Chaghai in Baluchistan and the share market of Karachi reflected these tests with a crash in share prices. According to some market specialists, the USA and developed countries of G-8 sometimes threaten other countries with an economic blockade and curtailing foreign investments; these fears can also invite a recession in the share markets of the concerned countries.

When the agricultural and industrial situations of a country improve, companies' profits and dividends increase, inflation remains controlled, deposits and investments increase, trade surpluses arise, that is, when the overall economic situation of the country improves, bourses also react accordingly and so share prices increase. If a country experiences an overall good rainfall, then an agriculture based country like India expects a good harvest and so an overall improvement in the economy. In these situations, the share market of the country moves upwards. In fact, when the gross domestic income of the country increases, the investable fund of the people also increases, this phenomenon is reflected in the share market.

Some times bullish and bearish situations arise in the stock market due to speculative activities. The actual meaning of speculation is deep observation or intensive analysis, but in India, the meaning of speculation is entirely different. Here, one who takes the highest risk to achieve the highest gain is called a speculator. They take risks for a short period. The shorter the period, the higher the speculation. When the stock market falls under the influences of bull operators, speculation appears with a rise in share prices and when the share market falls under the influences of bear operators, speculation appears with the fall of share prices.

In the stock markets, prices of shares can take flight or can nose dive in a short period of time and hence there is always excitement among investors, market observers and market players. Ironically, a rise in share price is not a welcome situation to some investors, similarly a fall in prices is not a matter of grief to other investors. In a rising trend, bull operators make good profits and in a downward trend, bear operators make good harvests. In a year, there are several seasons, some are more important some less. But in the stock market there are no seasons, all the twelve months are important here. There is no seasonal change only two seasons work here, (i) When the market is under bull operators, it is summer and (ii) when it is under bear operators, it is considered winter in the market. Changes of summer and winter happen according to a mathematical rule (popularly known as fundamental and technical analysis); similarly, changes of share prices follow some mathematical rules. It is necessary for investors to understand these basic rules which are not very simple.

In general, then we see that the market prices of values of actively traded equity shares seldom remain constant. They keep fluctuating – some moderately and some violently due to a variety of reasons discussed above and in different relevant chapters of this book. These fluctuations in the market prices of stocks always cause anxiety and discomfort for general investors.

Many market watchers feel that the price movements of stocks are totally unpredictable. They can go up, stay steady, or come down. It is just not possible to make any predictions about price movements. They are like mathematical random numbers, which have an equal chance of occurrence. Many academics have raised a basic question, namely, that historical data on share prices can help in predicting future prices. After a great deal of research they have come to the conclusion that stock prices indeed fluctuate randomly and that no expertise is required for success in investments based purely on trying to predict short-term price movements.

This point of view regarding the behavior of stock prices has come to be known as the 'Random Walk Theory'. In 1953, Maurice G. Kendall, a distinguished Professor of Statistics of University of London, presented an extraordinary paper before the Royal Statistical Society in London. The professor examined the behaviour of stock and commodity prices to determine a regular cycles. Instead of discovering any regular price cycle, he found each series to be "a wandering one, almost as if once a week the Demon of Chance drew a random number......... and added it to current price to determine the next week's price." It can be said that prices appeared to follow a random walk, implying that successive price changes are independent of one another and have the same probability distribution but over the passage of time prices show an upward trend.

In support of the random walk hypothesis, two other highly significant papers were published in 1959. In one of these two papers, Harry Roberts established that a series obtained by cumulating random numbers bore resemblance to a time series of stock prices. In another paper, the renowned physicist, Osborne, observed that the behavior of stock prices was similar to the movement of very small particles suspended in a liquid medium - such movement is referred to as Brownian motion.

In his book on *Investment Analysis and Portfolio Management*, Prasanna Chandra[1], opined that a random walk means that successive stock prices are independent and identically

[1]Prasanna Chandra, *Investment Analysis and Portfolio Management*, Tata McGraw-Hill Publishing Company Limited, New Delhi, 2008, p. 277

distributed. Therefore, in the true sense, the behavior of stock prices should be characterized as a sub martingale, implying that the expected change in price can be positive because investors expect to be compensated for time and risk. Further, the expected return may change over time in response to a change in risk.

Following the paths of M.G. Kendall, Harry Roberts and Osborne, a considerable number of research analysts employed ingenious methods to the randomness of stock price behaviour. Most of these tests have vindicated the random walk hypothesis. Overwhelming empirical evidence proved that the random walk hypothesis was a sound economic idea. In 1973 Burton Malkiel[2] wrote the classic investment book, *A Random Walk Down Wall Street*, based on the random walk theory. Malkiel opined that study of fundamental and technical analysis is nothing but a waste of time and cannot be tested in real life. He believed that long-term buy and hold is by far the best strategy and investors should not waste their time in the market.

A number of academicians, researchers and market analysts tried to get the answer to the question of finding the economic process which leads to a random walk. Through a lot of research work, they observed that the prices of stocks change only in response to ever changing information which has great influence on the movement of market prices but does not have any relation to previous information. As information cannot be predicted, changes in market prices cannot be predicted and hence market prices behave like a random walk. Finally, they came to the conclusion that the randomness of stock prices was a result of an efficient market. According to Prof. Prasanna Chandra, an efficient market is one in which the market price of a security is an unbiased estimate of its intrinsic value. This means that they will impound all available information.

The random walk theory is perhaps one of the most publicized stock market theories in the recent past. In simple language, the random walk theory runs somewhat along these lines: The stock prices on any given day are already a fair reflection of their value. They do not change in a systematic manner. They only change if an unexpected event occurs, such as a change in the political scenario, an increase in prices of petroleum products, any drastic change in the Company's Act or monetary policies, prospects of agricultural production etc. Since investors do not know what may happen tomorrow, academicians claim that no one can predict whether the next price change will be favorable or unfavorable. Therefore, they argue, share prices move randomly over time.

According to the random walk hypothesis, the value or prices of a stock cannot be determined precisely. The price in the market place tends to vary randomly around the intrinsic value of the shares. As new information is received, it is transmitted to the market place and a new value is established. In the process, the prices over-adjust and there may be a lag in the adjustment process. In addition, the adjustment process assumes that any price change is independent of the previous ones, which is really the definition of a random market. What is more, the sequence in which the share price changes has no memory, and so the past sequence cannot be used to predict the future.

---

[2]Burton G. Malkiel, *A Random Walk Down Wall Street*, W.W. Norton, 1999

In his book, *Investment Analysis and Portfolio Management,* Prasanna Chandra[3] said that sometimes greed and euphoria influence the general investors and pushes the market price of stocks to unsteady heights. On the other hand, stock prices nose dive to a low level when fear and despair develop in market circles. The father of modern economic theories, J.M. Keynes[4], described this phenomenon more lucidly in his book *The General Theory of Employment, Interest and Money.*

According to Keynes, "A conventional valuation which is established as an outcome of the mass psychology of a large number of ignorant individuals is liable to change violently as a result of a sudden fluctuation of opinion due to factors which do not really make much difference to the prospective yield." Another author, Burton G. Malkiel, described any type of psychological approach towards the market as a 'castle-in-the-air' theory which is likely to collapse within a short period. So, instead of any type of psychological approach, it is always preferable to approach the market with scientific reasoning and analyze the market accordingly.

In two articles entitled "Random Walk in Stock Market Prices", published in *Financial Analysts* in 1965 and "Efficient Capital Markets: A Review of Theory and Empirical Work," published in 1970, Eugene F. Fama[5,6] coined the concept of an efficient market hypothesis and stated that intense competition in the capital market establishes the idea of fair pricing of a security. Fama classified efficient stock markets in three levels of efficiency as weak form, semi-strong form and event form on the basis of availability of information as an efficient stock market has been reflected in the security prices on the degree of information. There are five conditions of market efficiency; free flow of information, unbiased information, cost free information, cost free transaction and all investors' views will be the same regarding the implication of information for current and future prices of stock.

Weak Form

As per weak form the efficient market hypothesis states that as the random walk hypothesis prevails in the stock market it is not possible to state the current prices of securities based on past prices and volumes. Serial correction test, filter rule test etc., based on the empirical test satisfy the weak form efficiency hypothesis.

Semi-strong Form

As per the semi-strong efficient market hypothesis prices of securities rapidly absorb all publicly available information like annual announcement of financial results, issue of securities etc.

---

[3] Op.cit.

[4] J.M. Keynes, *The General Theory of Employment, Interest and Money*, Macmillan, for Royal Economic Society, Third Edition, 1973, New York, p. 158

[5] Eugene F. Fama, 'Random Walk in Stock Market Prices', *Financial Analyst Journal*, 21, No.5 (September-October 1965), pp 55-59

[6] Eugene F. Fama, 'Efficient Capital Markets: A Review of Theory and Empirical Work', *Journal of Finance*, 25, No.2 (May 1970), pp 383-417

Event studies, portfolio studies tests satisfy the hypothesis. Event study examines events like declaration of dividend, split of securities and how far they influence the market. Portfolio study observes the characteristics of P/E ratio, EPS on the market. However, the results of an event study and portfolio are found to be mixed.

Strong Form

As per the strong form efficient market hypothesis all available public or private information has been reflected through security prices. Empirical evidence does not satisfy that. Several research studies based on the American and other European markets reveal that the outcome of the efficient market hypothesis is inconsistent and is termed as efficient stock market anomalies.

January Effect

Stock performs relatively well during the month of January in comparison with other months of the year. This is nothing but the violation of the weak form of efficient market.

Week-end Effect

Stock returns are relatively low in comparison with Monday's opening to Friday's closing. The US market shows this historically. European and North American markets show low average returns on Monday due to geographical proximity with the USA.

P/E Ratio Anomaly

Stocks with low P/E ratio out-perform stocks with a high P/E ratio. If investing in low P/E ratio stocks be the profitable investment strategy then it will put the efficient market hypothesis in doubt.

ANALYSIS OF SHARE MARKETS

Influences of Political and Economic Parameters on the Movement of Share Prices

In general, there are three main reasons which influence the movements of stock prices, which are given below.

1. The macro-economic changes of the country
2. Overall performance of the companies as well as the industry of which they are a part
3. Technical analysis (Analysis of share indexes and fluctuations in share prices)

Commonly the analysis of the above two factors i.e., (1) and (2) are known as fundamental analysis.

According to market researchers, the above three factors are the ones that influence the movement of stock prices significantly.

1. Macro-economic changes of the country

To keep the country's economic health safe and sound, the rulers and policy makers introduce economic policies or amend the existing policies from time to time. These policies are very important for the country's economic growth, the stock market is naturally influenced by these policies or changes in the existing policies. In India, the government's policies which mainly influence the stock market are: Five year plans, annual budget, annual economic reviews, agricultural and industrial policies, different monetary and fiscal policies of the Reserve Bank of India and other banks, and different policies of non banking financial institutions.

Five year plans: In view of the overall economic development of the country, India, adopts a well structured plan for every five year period. These plans are known as five year plans. The Planning Commission of the country is responsible for formulating and developing these plans. The Prime Minister of India is the Chairman of this Planning Commission and the responsibility of Deputy Chairmanship is generally entrusted to a reputed economist or renowned politician or appropriate bureaucrat.

A proposal for establishing the Planning Commission was first made by the great freedom fighter of India, Netaji Subhash Chandra Bose, in the summit of the National Congress at Haripura in 1938. After independence (1947), the first five plan was finalized and started in 1951-52 and ended in 1955-56. Then gradually the second five year plan (1956-57 to 1960-61) and the third five year plan (1961-62 to 1965-66) were chalked out and implemented in the country. In the next three years, that is in 1966-67, 1967-68 and 1968-69 only annual plans were adopted as during those periods the India-Pakistan wars and the freedom movement in Bangladesh (formerly East Pakistan) took place. Hence, India faced tremendous economic pressure during those periods. To overcome an economic meltdown, they again turned to forming five year plans. The fourth five year plan was adopted from 1969-70 to 1973-74. During the latter part of the fifth five year plan (1974-75 to 1978-79) the political situation of the country changed with the fall of the Congress government and the rise of the Janata Party (JP) government. So, the last year (1979-80) of the fifth five year plan turned out to be an unplanned year or a year of 'plan holiday' after the JP government took over the reins of the country.

Though the JP government restarted the formation of five year plans under the Planning Commission and adopted the sixth plan (1978-79 to 1982-83), due to conflicts among the party leaders of the JP regarding dual membership, the government collapsed and the sixth plan could not be implemented. After formation of a fresh government by the Congress party, the sixth five year plan (1980-81 to 1984-85) was freshly drawn up and implemented. In the seventh five year plan, instead of implementing the plan proposals on the basis of the financial year, it was proposed that the total calendar time periods from 1985 to 1990 should be considered for implementation of the seventh five year plan proposals. Due to general elections, only yearly plans were recommended for 1991 and 1992. After the elections, the eighth five year plan was formulated for 1993 to 1997, then the ninth five plan (1997-2002) and subsequently other plans were formulated as well as implemented in the country without any obstruction. In 2004, the UPA government came to power headed by the Congress party and ruled the country after the fall of the NDA government without any major disturbance. In 2009, UPA again came to power for a second time and preparation of the twelfth five year plan was started.

The reasons for discussing the history of five year plans is to make the readers aware of the fact that though the five year plans do not influence the share prices directly, the economic policies of the government and the process of implementing them sometimes directly or indirectly influence the movement of share prices in the bourses. To understand the implementation of economic policies in India, one should understand the five year plans of the country. The adoption of the country's annual budgets is based on the relevant five year plans and the policies announced in the annual budgets have a direct and significant relation with the movement of share prices.

Annual Budgets and Economic Policies

Government annual budgets: Almost all the governments in the world formulate and implement an annual budget every year to run the economic affairs and development works in the country for the next year. India is one of them. In the annual budget (both central and state budgets), the income or revenue, expenditure and deficit or surplus of the government is carefully prepared. Most of the revenues of the government are collected through indirect taxes, i.e., excise duty and customs duty and central sales tax; a small portion of the revenue is collected through direct taxes like income tax and wealth tax. A large portion of the governmental revenue is used for administrational expenditure, interest payments, defense requirements and payment of different subsidies.

After all these expenditures, very little revenue is left for plan development or public investment, but every government has to allot a significant amount of money for public investment and this leads to excess of governmental expenditure over governmental revenues and hence the fiscal deficit arises. So, the government has to borrow to meet this deficit and this measure of the government is popularly known as fiscal policy.

There are usually three ways in which the government finances this fiscal deficit. First, the government can borrow from the Reserve Bank of India, second, the government can borrow from the domestic capital market and third, the government can borrow from aboard. All these borrowings affect the country's economy. The first is likely to lead to an increase in the money supply which has an inflationary impact on the economy, the second is likely to push up domestic interest rates and may hamper private sector investment and the third prevents flow of the foreign exchange reserve of the country. These measures of the government have a direct impact on the stock exchanges of the country.

According to market analysts, favorable and unfavorable budgets can be classified as described in Table 4.1.

Table 4.1 Favorable and Unfavorable Budgets for Stock Price Movement

Favorable	Unfavorable
A balanced budget with manageable deficit.	A budget with unfavorable surplus or deficit.
Both the internal and external level of debt can be serviced without much difficulty.	Both the internal and external level of debt can be difficult to service.
An income tax structure which can provide excess investable money with the public.	An income tax structure which may prove to be unfavorable to the general investors.
A favorable corporate tax structure.	An unfavorable corporate tax structure.

Source: Investment Analysis and Portfolio Management, Prasanna Chandra.

We have already mentioned above that the budgets are prepared for one financial year and tabled before the parliament for approval as provided by Article 112 to 116 of the Indian Constitution. But in certain years, due to forthcoming elections or other political reasons, the government does not have sufficient time to prepare a full-fledged budget. So, to continue the economic activities of the government, the finance minister or minister in charge of finance ministry, furnishes a financial proposal for a few months, which is known as 'vote on account.' This 'vote on account' does not influence the stock prices significantly.

Economic survey and economic review: Prior to submission of annual budget proposals, a report on 'Economic Survey' is published every year. Last year's performances of the agricultural and other sectors, economic rates and industrial growth, as well as fluctuations in foreign reserves etc., are reflected in this report. So, a general idea for the current year can be obtained from this report, which ultimately influences the movement of share prices. State governments also publish similar reports known as 'Economic Reviews'. But these have very little or no effect on stock prices.

Industrial and agricultural policies: Industrial policies have a direct relation with the movement of share prices and agricultural policies influence it indirectly. In the nineties, the contribution of the agricultural sector to gross national income was much higher than that of the industrial sector. But in recent years, the contribution of the agricultural sector is decreasing and that of the industrial sector is increasing. Hence, it is quite obvious that the recent phenomenon of significant industrial growth in India has helped the growth of the Indian share market significantly in recent years. It is also true that government procurement prices of different agricultural commodities and selling prices of those procured commodities through the public distribution system is likely to influence the movements of stock prices indirectly.

Monetary policy of the Reserve Bank of India (RBI):   The RBI is the principal authority for launching monetary policies in India. Generally, this central bank decides the rates of interest for industrial investment loans, company loans and interest on public deposits. All banks (nationalized banks and private banks) are liable to follow the RBI rules or policies. The RBI does not invest in agriculture or industry directly. But according to its policies, all the nationalized and private banks invest money in industrial, agricultural and service sectors of economy.

Prior to 1961, except for the RBI and the State Bank of India, all other banks in India were under private ownership. During that period, certain large industrialists of the country opened a number of banks and invested all the depositors' money in their own industry or business. Besides this, other irregularities also occurred in these private banks. Mainly due to these reasons and to regulate these banks, the Government of India socialized some of these private banks through an Ordinance. But this Ordinance was not able to regulate the irregularities of these banks to a desired level. So, in the month of November 1969, Indian government decided to nationalize 14 private banks and later more banks were also taken over by the government. At present, these nationalized banks are the main medium for investment in agriculture and industry. We shall discuss later, how the loan distribution systems of these banks influence the trade, industry and commerce and ultimately the share market of the country.

Policies of non-banking financial institutions: The various policies issued by the RBI are also applicable to other financial organizations. The working systems of financial institutions are different from those of commercial banks. Commercial banks can directly receive deposits from depositors and can invest in the agricultural, industrial and corporate sectors. Financial institutions can neither take direct deposits from depositors nor can they invest in any economic sector directly. Financial institutions can only collect money from general investors through different schemes and plans and invest that money in shares and stocks of different companies. In return, these financial institutions give interest or a share of their profits to the investors. These institutions collect a large amount of money from small investors and invest it in the share market, which can influence the price trend of different shares directly if they invest a massive amount of money in the share market.

2. Overall performance of the companies as well as the industry of which they are a part

A number of market analysts think that share price of a company can be forecast by accurate analysis of its financial performances (on the basis of evaluations of the income statement and balance sheet) and potential of the industry to which it belongs. A fundamental analyst analyzes the Earning Per Share (EPS), current market price, Price Earning ratio (P/E ratio) and probable earnings of share investors. It is known that EPS x P/E ratio = Market price of the share. If the market price of the targeted company's shares is found to be higher than that of the fundamental analysis, then the investors are advised to sell their shares of the company. If the share price is less than the results of the fundamental analysis then investors are advised to buy shares of that company. The basis of the fundamental analysis is the analysis of the necessary financial ratios and system of company management. To understand the fundamental analysis (company analysis), one should know which different companies function in the market and how these companies are managed and should have a perfect knowledge of the income statement and the balance sheet, in short the financial statements.

A Brief Discussion on Different Types of Companies

Private company: As per section 3(1)(iii) of the Companies Act, 1956 as amended by the Companies (Amendment) Act, 2000 a private company is a company which has a minimum paid up capital of Rupees one lakh in case of new companies incorporated after commencement of the Companies (Amendment) Act, 2000 i.e. 13.12.2000, provided the existing private companies raise their capital to Rupees one lakh within two years from the date of commencement. The word 'Private Limited' must be added to the name of a private company.

If the company be a default company u/s 560, the Registrar of companies has the right to strike its name from the Register. An Article restricts the right to transfer shares and the number of members varies from 2 or 3 to 50. An article also prohibits public subscription and acceptance of deposits from persons other than its members' directors or their relatives as included by the Companies (Amendment) Act, 2000.

Public company: As per Section 3(1) (iv) of the Companies Act, 1956 as amended by the Companies (Amendment) Act, 2000 a public company is defined as one which is not a private company and the minimum paid up capital is Rupees five lakhs or more. A company registered u/s 25 before or after the commencement of the Companies (Amendment) Act, 2000 shall not maintain minimum paid up capital as per specification. This type of company is known as a Public Sector Unit or PSU as the majority of the equity shares are held by the government.

If a private company is a subsidiary of a public company it will be considered as a public company from the date of commencement of the Companies (Amendment) Act, 2000. Sometimes, due to some economic reasons, the government sells its holdings (shares) of a PSU in the share market. This is known as privatization of the PSU.

Privatization: The principal motivation for privatization, especially in developing countries, has been an awareness born of budgetary crises that public enterprises are usually 'white elephants' that incur heavy losses on a sustained basis. Instead of accumulating surpluses or supplying services efficiently, these enterprises have become a drain on the national exchequer. Privatization seems to be a very convenient way of raising resources for reducing the fiscal deficit. Many governments may not find privatization ideologically very palatable, yet they find it appealing as a practical device to cope with fiscal problems. So, it can be said that privatization or the disinvestment process is quite popular in the investment world. It may be relevant to mention that disinvestment is the process of transferring public ownership partially or fully to private ownership through sale of equities. This is a very important form of privatization since ownership is transferred. It refers to sale parts of a public firm. In effect, disinvestment is the opposite of acquisition or merger.

Since the beginning of the 1980s, privatization has been resorted to by more than 50 countries, both developed as well as developing, around the world. This process has gathered momentum due to the debt trap overtaking Latin America, political restructuring in Eastern Europe, and economic reforms in the Asia-Pacific region. The most conspicuous example of privatization in the developed countries is that of the United Kingdom. It began in 1979 when Mrs. Thatcher came to power. The salient aspects of the British privatization program are as follows: (i) By 1991, barring certain enterprises operating in sensitive areas like nuclear energy, defense and railways, the privatization cycle in the United Kingdom was nearly complete. (ii) While the British government sold the majority equity holding to the public, it retained a minority equity holding with substantial power to intervene through the instrumentality of what is called the 'golden cause'. (iii) A ceiling of 15 per cent on foreign equity participation was imposed. The regulations after privatization has been a very contentious issue. It appears that there is an escalating war between privatized utilities and their regulators.

The French privatization began when Jacques Chirac became the prime minister in 1986. He announced a five year privatization plan which was meant to cover 65 enterprises. But the programme lasted for barely two years and was terminated with the changed majority in the French parliament. However, the companies that were privatized continue to remain in private hands. Despite various problems in implementation, the British and French privatization programs have been fairly successful in (i) reducing the pressure on the public budget, (ii) improving economic performance, (iii) broadening the base of shareholders, and (iv) the increasing the importance of London and Paris on the international financial markets.

In developing countries like Brazil, Turkey, Chile, Malaysia, Philippines, South Korea, Sri Lanka, and Pakistan, privatization has been directed towards the transfer of public sector enterprises engaged in the manufacture of consumer and industrial products (like textiles, processed foods, chemicals, fertilizers, and so on) into private hands. Financially and administratively over-stretched, the governments in many developing countries are resorting to privatization to reduce budgetary deficits and improve efficiency.

Privatization programs have been initiated in a number of planned economies of Eastern Europe, members of the erstwhile Soviet Union, China, Vietnam. The compulsions of privatization in these countries appear very strong. However, the privatization program in these countries has suffered for want of well-defined property rights, developed capital market, and a wide entrepreneurial base.

India declared its intention to 'disinvest' in 1991, and has had a Disinvestment Commission to draw a roadmap for over a number of years. An attempt in the direction of disinvestment was made by the Government of India in the financial year 1991-92. During that year the Government of India sold equity shares of about 30 public sector undertakings and realized over Rs. 30,000 million. Enthused by the experience, the Committee on Economic Affairs approved a proposal to disinvest shares up to 49 per cent of the equity in public sector undertakings. So, even after two decades of that policy, not one public sector undertaking has yet moved out of government control through the process of disinvestment.

Registered company: A company registered under the Companies Act, 1956 is known as a registered company. A registered company may be incorporated as a private company, public company, limited company and unlimited company. As per section 12(2) of the Companies act, 1956 a registered company may be:

1. A company limited by shares
2. A company limited by guarantee
3. An unlimited company

1. ***Company limited by shares:*** As per section 12(2)(a) of the Companies Act, 1956 a company has the liability of its members limited by the Memorandum. If any amount of money is not paid up on the shares held by them, then it is called a limited liability company. Truly the liability of the company is never limited only the liability of its members is limited as the company has a separate entity.

2. ***Company limited by guarantee:*** As per section 12(2) (b) of the Companies Act, 1956 a company having the liability of its members limited by the memorandum may undertake by the memorandum to contribute to the assets of the company at the time of wind-up is called a company limited by guarantee.

   As per section 426(2) of the Companies Act, 1956 a company whose liability of a member is not only limited to the amount of guarantee but he has to contribute to the extent of any sum remaining unpaid on the shares held by him as if the company were a company limited by shares.

3. ***Unlimited companies:*** As per Section 12(2)(c) of the Companies Act, 1956 a company having no limit on the liability of its members is an unlimited company. The company has a separate legal entity and its claims can be enforced only against the company. The members may be called upon to discharge the liabilities without claim.

Holding company: As per Section 4 of the Companies Act, 1956 if a company controls the policy matters of another company by holding ownership of more than 50 per cent of its equity shares capital and enjoys more than 50 per cent of its voting right or has control over the composition of its board of directors, the controlling company is called a holding company and the controlled company is called a subsidiary company.

Statutory company: A statutory company may be incorporated by means of a special Act of Parliament or any State Legislature. They do not require any memorandum of association or articles of association. A statutory corporation although owned by the government has a separate entity.

Government company: As per Section 617 of the Companies Act, 1956 a government company is defined to mean a company formed and registered under the Companies Act, 1956 as defined in Section 3 of the said Act. A government company is a company in which not less than 51 per cent of the paid up share capital is held by the central government or any state government or partly by the central government and partly by one or more state governments.

Foreign company: A foreign company is a company incorporated outside India and having a place of business in India. A foreign company may be a private company or a public company. A foreign company has to file the necessary documents within 30 days of the establishment of the place of business in India.

Joint venture: A joint venture, also referred to as strategic alliance, represents a partnership between two or more independent companies, sometimes between two entities one of which is in the private and the other in the public sector, which join hands to achieve a common purpose. It is usually organized as a newly created company, though the partners may choose any other form of organization. Typically, the partners partake in the equity of the common enterprise, contribute resources (technology, facilities, distribution networks, brands, key manpower, and so on), and share management and control. Very popular abroad, joint ventures are becoming fashionable in India as well, particularly between foreign and local companies.

Companies Emerging from Companies (Second Amendment) Act, 2002

Producer company: If ten or more individual producers or two or more institutional producers or a combination of ten or more individual and institutional producers form and incorporate a company as a producer company that may be considered as a limited liability company. The status of such a company shall be that of a private company having no limit on the number of members.

Industrial company: As per Clause 19AA this type of company owns one, or more than one, industrial undertakings.

Industrial undertakings: If any undertaking pertaining to any industry has one or more factories or units, it falls under the definition given in clause (aa) of Section 3 of the Industries (Development and Regulation) Act, 1951 but does not include Small Scale Undertakings (SSI Units) as defined in Clause (j) of Section 3.

Sick industrial company: As per Clause 46AA an industrial company whose accumulated losses in any financial year is equal to 50 per cent or more of its average net worth during the four years immediately preceding the financial year or which has failed to repay its debts within any three consecutive quarters as per written demand for repayment made by the creditors of such company is called a sick company.

Sick industries: A specter has for some time been haunting the Indian industrial scene – the specter of industrial sickness. The phenomenon of 'sick units' (an Indian contribution to the Lexicon) has entailed huge economic wastage on the one hand and untold human sufferings on the other hand. For about three decades, the problems have been somehow tackled from crises to crises by an implicit process of social welfare. From the mid-1980s, the problem was acknowledged to be a necrosis and a frame work for salvage operations was put in place in the shape of the Board for Industrial and Financial Reconstruction (BIFR) under the purview of the Sick Industrial Companies (Special Provision) Act, 1985 which was subsequently amended in the Sick Industrial Companies (Special Provision) Amendment Act, 1993 and ultimately repealed in 2003 by the Sick Industrial Companies (Special Provision) Repeal Act, 2003.

As per the Repeal Act, 2003 of SICA a "sick industrial company" means an industrial company (being a company registered for not less than five years) which has at the end of any financial year accumulated losses equal to or exceeding its entire net worth. The Steel Authority of India Limited (SAIL) has been out of the red since the beginning of the 21st century by right sizing and 45,000 employees received a golden handshake as a part of the revival package.

The new act diluted certain provisions of SICA and plugged some of the loopholes. It not only combated industrial sickness but saw to it that companies could not use it as an escape route by using legal provisions and try to derive benefits or concessions from financial institutions. Under the new provision, the BIFR and the Appellate Authority for Industrial and Financial Reconstruction (AAIFR) were dissolved and replaced by the National Company Law Tribunal (NCLT) and National Law Appellate Tribunal (NCLAT) respectively.

By compiling data of the RBI and the All India Census of Micro, Small and Medium Enterprises (MSMEs) made by its nodal agency, Indian Industries Association (IAA) it was found that 4.8 lakh enterprises were closed by the end of March, 2010 out of which 79,778 units were closed in Tamil Nadu, 75,659 in Uttar Pradesh and 8,881 in West Bengal. The MSME sector accounts for 8 per cent of the country's GDP, 45 per cent of India's manufacturing output and 40 per cent of the total exports. The sector also relates 6 crore jobs for over 4 crore MSMEs currently engaged in operations across the country.

In 2008, the all India figure of sick units dropped to 85,000 (UP accounts for 16,820 sick units) and in 2010 the number again dropped to 77,723 sick units (UP had 17,217 sick units, and the other worse performer is WB with 16,813 sick units).

BSE and NSE data reveal that once reputed companies like Aditya Gears (public holding 83 per cent), Assam Brook (public holding 64 per cent), Dunlop India, DSQ Software, India Foil, Ispat Profiles, LCC InfoTech, Standard Batteries (public holding 60 per cent), Usha India, NEPC Agro (public holding 81 per cent) along with over 1,750 companies have been delisted for non-compliance and near about Rs. 10,000 crores of public wealth is locked up in these suspended companies. Holdings of public and financial institutions is more than 40 per cent in over 1,400 companies and in some cases public holding along with financial institutions goes up to 80 per cent. It is expected that the government should take appropriate steps and the promoters should be penalized if they avoid exchange appointed valuers by misusing non-compliance tools.

DISCUSSION ON THE USE OF COMPANIES' ANNUAL REPORTS FOR FUNDAMENTAL ANALYSIS

Fundamental Analysis

Fundamental analysis covers the entire economic activities of a country including performance of the industrial and corporate sectors (more commonly known as financial performance of companies). But in stock market circles fundamental analysis means periodical analysis of financial results of different companies. It is quite well known that financial results of a company directly influence the movement of share prices of that company in a normal share market. Hence, some companies try to paint a bright picture of their company in their financial statements and predict a bright future of growth. To know how far these financial statements are true, it is necessary to correctly read the balance sheet and income statement of the company as well as to properly understand the subject matters related with the balance sheet. Profit and loss accounts (income statement) of the company, analysis of the financial parameters are also very necessary. If after proper analysis of financial parameters of the balance sheet and profit and loss account of a company, investors decide to invest in the shares of that company, then it is most likely that they will be able to make a significant profit in the near future.

In most countries, general investors invest their money in company shares without perfect knowledge of the financial performance of the company and management system of that company. These investors often lose money in share markets. To get a healthy return from share market investments, general investors must know how to read and understand the financial parameters of the balance sheet and profit and loss accounts of a company as well as properly understand the subject matters related with the balance sheet and profit and loss account.

Reading a Company's Balance Sheet, Profit and Loss Accounts or Annual Report

For those general investors who have only a nodding acquaintance with finance, reading financial statements may appear daunting and may be by no means an agreeable task. But once one knows what to look for, reading balance sheets, profit and loss accounts or annual report could be a rewarding exercise, and is valuable to know whether all the claims which the company is making are actually true.

Let us take the balance sheet first. A balance sheet is one of the most important documents, which reveals the financial health of a company at a particular time. On the other hand, the income statements present the operational details for a particular operational period i.e. over a period of time. The balance sheet is prepared on the last day of the company's financial year. A balance sheet, published in the annual report of a company, mainly comprises the source of funds and application of funds. This is represented by the Fund Flow Statement. Along with that preparation and incorporation of a Cash Flow Statement in the Annual Report is mandatory as per Accounting Standard 3 (AS 3) with effect from 1st April, 2001.

Source of Funds

Source of funds are liabilities of the companies. The source of funds includes share holders' funds and loan funds. Together, they constitute the company's capital. Shareholders' funds consist of share capital and reserve and surpluses. Loan funds consist of secured and unsecured loans.

Share Capital (Capital)

Share capital shows the paid-up share capital, which is the total money invested by shareholders. It consists of share capital and preference share capital.

Reserve and Surplus

The portion of profits, which is not distributed as dividend forms the reserve and surplus. Reserves can be broadly classified into revenue reserves and capital reserve. Revenue reserve is the accumulation of retained earnings from normal business operations like general reserve, and investment allowance reserves. The capital reserves are formed by gains other than normal business operations. For example, gains on revaluation of assets and securities premium on issue of shares. Sometimes revaluation of assets creates suspicions as they could be arbitrary and depend totally on the method of valuation adopted. Net profits retained after distribution of dividend and tax on distributed dividends are appropriated to different reserve accounts as required. The amount left after the allocations from the surplus could be carried forward to the next year and used again for appropriation. This is why it is called ploughing back of profit.

Capital redemption reserve is created during the time of redemption of preference shares out of profit. Similarly, companies may form a debenture redemption reserve account while redeeming debentures out of profit. The capital redemption reserve account is utilized for issuing fully paid bonus shares. The general reserve is the free reserve which could be used for all purposes.

According to SEBI guidelines no bonus shares will be issued within 12 months of public or rights issue and bonus shares can only be issued out of the profit or securities premium collected in the form of cash. In addition, the residual reserve after capitalization will be equal to at least 40 per cent of the increased paid up capital. On revealing a firm's assets, the value of fixed assets goes up resulting in increased weightage on the asset side of the balance sheet. It is balanced by transferring an amount equivalent to that by which the value of assets has gone up, to the asset revaluation reserve account on the liability side. Asset revaluation reserves should be excluded from any kind of analysis. That is because revaluation of assets is highly subjective and can be controversial.

Growth in reserves is free reserves and surplus mirrors the growth of the firm. The reserve and surplus grows only when there is retained profit, which is deployed for growth of the company. A company with a limited growth avenue is likely to retain less profit and opt for distributing it as dividend to its shareholders. For a firm with a low return on investment it is always advisable and better to distribute profit rather than retain it.

Loan Funds

Loan is debt capital and comprises secured loans and unsecured loans. Secured loans are those, which are taken against some collateral securities, whereas unsecured loans are not. Loans may be long-term for say, financing fixed assets or short-term like a working capital loan. Working capital loans are generally payable within one operating cycle of the company. Loans are obviously a source of funds.

The long-term loan and shareholders' fund together form the capital structure of the company. The capital structure depicts the risk associated with the company in terms of gearing the company's long-term liquidity. The loan could prove risky. First, the risk involved is in the repayment of the loan, which is often gauged by the debt-equity ratio and debt-asset ratio. The second is the risk involved in the operational front in servicing debt. This is measured by the ratio of Earnings Before Depreciation Interest and Tax (EBDIT) to the interest payment, the interest coverage ratio. On the flip side, Debt Service Coverage Ratio (DSCR) is the ratio between (PAT + Depreciation + Interest) to (Installment + Interest) measures the debt repayment ability of the company. For any company, DSCR must be more than 1.33. But the financial expert, Prasanna Chandra, in one of his books opined that it should be 2.

An increase in the loan amount is not something to worry about if the company has the ability to make handsome returns from it, which is more than the returns necessary to serve the interest. That ability is often revealed by the return on capital employed (ROCE = EBDIT/ Total capital). The return excess of the interest rate goes to the shareholders. The practice is known as trading on equity.

Application of Funds

Application of funds comprises a company's assets where capital or funds raised are invested. Fixed assets, investments, net current assets, and miscellaneous expenditure comprise the application of funds.

Fixed assets: Fixed assets are assets like land, buildings, plant and machinery, which are acquired for use over a long period of time to conduct operations of a firm. Fixed assets are always presented as a gross block, from which the accumulated depreciation is deducted to get the net block.

Depreciation: Section 205 and Section 350 of the Companies Act, 1956 lay down that depreciation on all fixed assets, except land, is a must. It should also be noted that the rate and method of depreciation cannot change frequently. This depreciation is actually not outgoing funds but a notional charge, made so as to keep funds aside for replacing the asset when its life runs out. There are many reasons for depreciation of fixes asset, such as wear and tear, change of technology, and passage of time. Natural resources cannot be replaced and depreciation for these types of assets is called amortization. According to Section 205 of the Companies Act it is mandatory to calculate depreciations of fixed assets. There are depreciations for every asset but not land assets, which only appreciate.

Utilized assets represent unproductive assets that lock in the shareholders value without return. Such assets should be disposed of and utilized for productive purposes. Asset utilization is measured by the ratio of total turnover of the asset and return on assets. Apart from these, one can look at the capacity utilization as an easy measure to gauge asset utilization. An analysis of capacity utilization should be accompanied by market analysis. Utilized capacity, in the context of a company' expanding market could be viewed as a potential for growth without bothering about the capacity utilization.

Capital work-in-progress: Any costs incurred towards fixed assets, which is incomplete, like a building under construction or a machine under installation, are treated as capital in progress. Once the on going job or jobs are completed, the amount is transferred to fixed assets.

Investments: Investment represents the company's investments in securities like shares of other companies, mutual funds, other companies' debentures and government securities. Some of these investments are quoted (that is their current market price is available) while others are not quoted like shares of an unlisted company.

It is important for the investors to know the returns from an investment. Returns generated by investments contribute to the total return as *other income* in the income statement. But, it is imperative to carry out a subjective analysis, as the companies do not keep investments solely for the purpose of returns. The purpose of maintaining such investments could be manifold. Idle cash generates nothing. A firm may temporarily lodge its large amount of cash arising from a capital issue in a liquid instrument with good returns, before deploying it into the main business. Funds, earmarked for redemption of debentures or preference shares in the near future, could be maintained in the form of investments. Companies also strategically invest in shares of other companies, like its subsidiaries, to retain control over the company. We have already discussed long-term assets and liabilities earlier. Now let us focus on the current assets less current liabilities which give the net current assets. Net current assets are financed by a working capital loan and a portion of the long term fund.

Current assets, loans and advances: These are short tern assets, which are transformed into cash in a single operating circle. Examples of such assets are inventories of raw materials, work-in-progress, finished goods, and other stocks, sundry debtors, cash and bank balance. Inventories are nothing but the stocks' position. Work-in-progress is the unfinished product. The value of work-in-progress is the total amount spent till that stage of the product. Sundry debtors represent the total amount owed by the debtors (principally the buyer of the company's products) to the company. It is quite often compared with sales figures, which give an idea about what percentage of the sales, are in credit. It also highlights the market situation. In a competitive market, companies are compelled to go in for high credit sales.

Current liabilities and provisions: Current liabilities are short-term obligations of the company like credit purchases. These obligations are generally expected to mature within a year. Provisions are maintained to temporarily lodge funds for obligations, which will be due within a year like provision for tax and dividends. Current liabilities which include sundry creditors are another source of funds. Such trade credit is usually one of the cheapest sources of funding.

Miscellaneous expenditure: This expenditure is not written off in a particular year. For example, it is difficult to show the entire amount of huge advertisement expenditure in a particular year. There are two reasons: first, owing to the amount of the expenditure, the company may end up registering a loss in a financial year. Second, the benefit of a big advertisement is generally realized over a long period of time. Hence, companies first transfer the entire amount to the miscellaneous expenditure account as an asset, and then a predetermined percentage of it is written off every year from the company's annual income. Thus, the amount under miscellaneous expenditure reduces gradually over time to zero. If the profit and loss account is not written off due to amount of the expenditure and the benefit derived for the particular year, it should be shown on the asset side of the balance sheet under the head 'miscellaneous expenses' and be called as fictitious assets.

Till now we have mainly discussed the definitions of different parameters of a balance sheet. Now, to understand clearly the functions of these parameters let us discuss them in the light of a balance sheet of an imaginary company. The balance sheet of an imaginary, large (according to sales turnover) Indian manufacturing company as on March 31st 2011, is given in Table 4.2, as an example.

Table 4.2 Balance Sheet of a Manufacturing Company as on 31st March, 2011

	Schedule	As at 31-03-2011 (Rs. in lakhs)	Total	As at 31-03-2010 (Rs. in lakhs)	Total
I. Source of Funds:					
1. Shareholders' funds:					
(a) Capital	1	5,202.03		5,178.79	
Share suspense		-		- 1.43	
(b) Reserve and surplus	2	60,763.92		60,664.13	
			65,965.95		65,844.35
2. Loan funds:					
(a) Secured loans	3	37,314.66		43,064.09	
(b) Unsecured loans	3	19,962.49		16,363.95	
			57,227.15		59,428.04
TOTAL			**1,23,243.10**		**1,25,272.39**
II. Application of Funds:					
1. Fixed assets	4				
(a) Gross block		96,363.95		1,01,192.30	
(b) Less: depreciation		36,628.12		36,685.16	
(c) Net block		59,735.83		64,507.14	
(d) Capital work-in-progress		4,722.04		12,142.00	
			64,457.87		76,649.14
2. Investments:	5		26,262.65		19,749.64
3. Current assets, loans and advances	6				
(a) Income accrued on investment and fixed deposits		38.71		139.72	
(b) Inventories		15,352.38		19,198.33	
(c) Sundry debtors		9,481.93		14,957.29	
(d) Cash and bank balances		3,869.42		3,077.93	
(e) Loans and advances		26,165.04		14,912.64	
			54,907.48		53,285.91
Less: Current liabilities and provisions:	7		24,111.80		24,942.42
Net current assets			30,795.68		28,343.67
4. Miscellaneous expenditure: (To the extent not written off or adjusted)	8	1,726.90		529.94	
TOTAL			**1,23,243.10**		**1,25,272.39**

The balance sheet shows the source of funds which a business has and the uses to which these funds have been applied. In the case of our selected manufacturing company, for example, the share holders' fund, consisting of capital and reserves and surplus, amounts to Rs. 659.66 crores as on March 31st 2011. As on that date, Rs. 963.64 crores stood invested by the company in gross fixed assets, 'gross' meaning that the accumulated depreciation charged every year is not subtracted from it.

Sources and uses of funds: Now let us make a distinction between long and short term sources and uses of funds. For example, current assets are short term uses, current liabilities are short-term sources. Loans for working capital are usually taken as short-term sources of funds. According to a well known market analyst, Manas Chakraborty, it is debatable to what extent a cash credit limit can be said to be short-term, since they are hardly ever repaid. Shareholders' funds are obviously a long-term source of funds, while fixed assets are a long-term use. Investments need to be divided between those which can be immediately sold and longer term investments, especially in group companies and its subsidiaries, which are long term in nature.

The schedules to the balance sheet need to be looked at in order to make up one's mind regarding how to classify them. The whole purpose of such classification is to find out whether long-term uses are being met by long-term sources. If they are not and short-term sources are being used for long-term purposes, you have a mismatch, which is what an Indian alcoholic beverage manufacturing company had when it relied excessively on short-term inter-corporate deposits.

One of the most interesting, yet simple, ways of looking at the balance sheet is to figure out how the company used the funds available to it during the course of year. Let us look at the balance sheet of the manufacturing company furnished in Table 4.2. During 2010-11, the company's outstanding loan declined by Rs. 21 crores compared to 2009-10, and its level of current liabilities went down by Rs. 8 crores. The level of miscellaneous expenditure increased by Rs. 12 crores. Most importantly, it increased its investments by Rs. 66 crores (see Table 4.3).

Table 4.3   Raising and Spending Funds

Sources		Applications	
Shareholders' Funds:	2	Loans	21
Fixed assets	121	Investments	66
		Current assets	16
		Current liabilities	8
		Miscellaneous expenditure	12
Total	**123**		**123**

All these examples are applications of funds which the company made during the year. How did the company get the money to do all this? The level of fixed assets shows that while the gross block was Rs. 1011.92 crores as on April 1st 2010, they amounted to Rs. 963.64 crores a year later. Sales and disposals during the year were higher than additions. Further, while there was a large amount of capital work-in progress as on March 31st 2010, that amount was substantially less a year later. Particularly all of the company's use of funds during 2010-11 was made drawing down the level of fixed assets, hardly a healthy or sustainable situation.

A look at the investments and loans and advances of a company will enable one to determine whether the company has siphoned off money or not. Many companies use these avenues to siphon off funds to investment companies, which in turn invest in other group companies. When the level of inventory is considered, especially finished goods inventory, and is calculated as a percentage of sales, a mere increase in inventory is not enough to cause worry. But a substantial increase in the proportion of finished goods inventory to sales could indicate that finished goods of the company are not selling. This could also be indicated by a high proportion of sundry debtors to sales, which is a measure of the credit period allowed on sales.

Though we have discussed the meaning of different ratios in the paragraphs below, it may be relevant to discuss some related ones here itself. To judge whether a company's borrowing is within limits, bankers use a ratio called the debt-equity ratio. This ratio also called the total debt-equity ratio, can be calculated by:

$$\text{Total-debt-to-equity} = \frac{\text{Current liabilities + long-term debt}}{\text{Total common equity (shareholders' equity)}}$$

If this ratio is 2.5: 1, then the company is considered to be in good health. The smaller the ratio, the less is the outside dependence. Financial institutions that are long-term debtors, use the long-term debt to equity ratio, while commercial banks use the total outside liabilities by Tangible Net Worth (TNW) ratio. To arrive at the figure of tangible net worth, the intangible items are to be deducted. Intangible items are: goodwill, patents and trade marks, development expenditure etc. The ratio can be calculated by:

$$\text{Tangible net worth ratio} = \frac{\text{Total current (outside) liabilities}}{\text{Tangible net worth}}$$

When this ratio is high, the working capital will be inadequate as a result of which outside borrowings will have to be resorted to. This ratio indicates the financial soundness of a company. The smaller the tangible net worth and larger the liabilities, the less security the creditor can have.

Total outside liabilities are the sum of liabilities which the company owes to outside parties, which means loans plus current liabilities. Revaluation reserves are not included in TNW. The net worth figure can also be used to calculate the return on net worth. Many companies raise a lot of funds from the market very cheaply, and the sheer weight of these funds alone is enough to show higher profits and higher earnings per share. Whether these funds are being used efficiently will be shown by dividing the net profit by the average net worth, which will give the return on net worth.

Understanding Profit and Loss Account

Now let us discuss the parameters of a profit and loss account. It is well known that the account summarizes the performance of the company for the accounting period, which is usually a year. Everyone knows what the net profit, or bottom line is. But there are different types of profits.

Table 4.4 Profit & Loss Account of a Company for the Year Ending 31st March, 2011

	As at 31-03-2011 (Rs. in lakhs)	As at 31-03-2011 (Rs. in lakhs)
INCOME		
Sales	1314.97	1130.44
Other income	71.47	47.93
Increase/Decrease in stocks	(12.37)	25.03
TOTAL	**1374.07**	**1203.73**
EXPENDITURE		
Manufacturing expenses	847.27	722.18
Purchases	39.16	32.70
Payment and provisions for employees	87.01	75.51
Administration, selling and miscellaneous expenses	94.66	76.00
Interest and finance charges (Net)	67.39	81.65
Excise duty (Net)	142.41	129.79
Depreciation	33.28	33.40
TOTAL	**1311.18**	**1151.24**
Profit before taxation	62.90	62.90
Provision for taxation	-	-
Profit after taxation	62.90	52.49

Turnover: Let us start from the top line or sales. This is also called turnover. Some large companies add the inter-divisional sales to arrive at the total sales figure. For purposes of comparison with those companies who do not follow this practice, these inter-divisional sales must be deducted from the total sales figure. Net sales are gross sales less excise duty. Since excise duty varies for different products, it is the net sales figure which should be used for comparison between different companies.

Total income has two components – sales and other income. The income which a company earns from non-operational activities or income which does not form part of the company's normal revenue is known as other income. For example, income from investments is the most common component of 'other income' for a manufacturing company. For an investment company, income from investments would not be other income, as investments are what the company is set up for.

While a lot of controversy surrounds other income, all that one needs to know at this elementary level is that a higher other income may conceal a drop in profit. For example, in the profit and loss account of the manufacturing company given in Table 4.4, other income during 2010-11 was Rs. 23.54 crores more than such income in 2009-10. At the same time, profit after tax of the company increased by Rs. 10.41 crores. This means that had the increase in other income not come about during the year, the company would actually have recorded a lower profit than the previous year.

This does not necessarily mean that 'other income' is something which should be looked at doubtfully. But analysts who talk of companies sticking to core competencies are of the opinion that is not the business of a manufacturing company to earn income from investments, and an investor would actually be better served if the amount were to be distributed to the shareholders.

Operating profit: To get an operating profit, one should deduct all expenditures except interest, depreciation and tax, from net sales and the value of the increase or decrease in stock. To arrive at a precise figure, one should also deduct 'other expenses' which go towards earning 'other income'. But much of accounting is convention, and it is difficult to locate the figure of other expenses.

By deducting interest from operating profit, one gets gross profit. Some companies give only the net interest figure in the profit & loss account, that is, the interest paid by the company less the interest earned by it on its investments. In case, the company is not a financial company, one will have to add the interest earned to other income, to arrive at the actual figure for other income. Gross profit less depreciation is profit before tax. Since depreciation is only notional, one must add back the depreciation to the net profit to arrive at what is called the cash profit. After paying taxes, the figure arrived at is called the net profit which is also called the bottom-line.

To get the EPS, the net profit should be divided by the number of shares outstanding. This is not however, how much one's share earned during the year, which is known as dividend. The dividend distribution is made out of net profits, and the balance of profit carried forward is added to the company's reserves. One should also check whether dividends have been paid out of current profits, as paying dividend out of the company's reserves would speedily erode them. The price earning ratio, which is a measure of market sentiment about scrip, is calculated by dividing the price of the scrip by earning per share.

Margin: Anybody who wants to understand the health of any company, should know what is meant by margins. The operating profit divided by net sales would be the operating margin. One may also decide to deduct other income from operating profit before calculating this margin. Similarly, gross margin is the gross profit as a percentage of net sales, and net margin is the proportion of net profit to net sales. The different ratios will tell you different things. For example, a company's operating margin may increase compared to the previous year, while its gross margin may decline. This could be because hefty interest payments have been made during the year.

Thus if operating margins go up one can safely conclude that the company's operations – that is manufacturing, sales etc. – have become more efficient. Margins will tell the unit difference between income and expenditure. If margins come down, for example, it could mean a fall in prices of the product or an increase in costs. It would also mean that the company would have to go in for higher volumes in order to get the same profits as before. Ratios carry little meaning if they are not compared with the same ones of the last year. It is important for the investors to know whether the company they have invested in has performed better than others. If it has not, one could consider switching investments. But care should be taken in a decision to switch. Balance sheets and profit & loss accounts are based on historical data, while what actually matters to an investor is how the company will perform in the future.

As regards ratios, one could compute any number of ratios, but the point is to compare them and interpret them perfectly (later, in this chapter we have discussed the methods of calculating different ratios and interpreting them). One could also compare the profit and loss accounts of different companies in the same line of business, which would enable one to determine whether the company invested in has performed better than others.

Window dressing: Almost all business organizations have a tendency to cover up the ugly patches of their financial statements in an attempt to make these statements look attractive to shareholders and investors who are not cautious. This process of cosmetic surgery of financial statements by companies is known as window dressing of financial statements. Investors should be careful about this phenomenon. The process of interpreting the financial statement in the form of face lifting is called cosmetic accounting, which is prohibited by the Company Act.

Besides taking recourse to other income, as we discussed earlier, there are several ways of dressing up profit and loss account. One of the most commonly used by companies is to change the method of depreciation. If this is done, the auditor's notes to the accounts in the annual report will not only point out that it has been done but will also tell you the effect the change has had on the profit or loss. Similarly, companies may change the method of valuing closing stock. The auditor's notes will tell you the effect this has on the profit. Another area which one should check out carefully is the figures of expenditure. Uninitiated investors may be effortlessly misled as it is easy for a company to show a higher profit by suppressing essential expenditure. For example, a company can cut back expenses on advertising in a particular year but this will be bad from a long-term point of view.

More skilled examples of padding profits arise in the sale and lease back of assets. A company may on paper sell its assets and shortly after lease back the assets, thus generating cash from the sale of asset in the process. But in doing so it has also lost an asset and at the same time has taken on a recurring expenditure. Furthermore, there is a class of expenditure called miscellaneous expenditure which is written off to the profit & loss account, as the jargon has it, only in installments. This is on the rationale that such expenditure yields benefits over a period of time. Some companies' expenditure on the voluntary retirement scheme, project expenses, product launches etc. show they have all been written off in this fashion. If profit and loss is not written off it is carried to the balance sheet, where it forms what is called a fictitious asset.

There are some other methods of reporting the financial statements of the companies in different countries of the world. The International Financial Reporting Standard is one of them.

The concept of the International Financial Reporting Standards (IFRS) as issued by International Accounting Standard Boards has emerged after the occurrence of a series of financial scams, viz. Enron, WorldCom, Global Crossing, Satyam, Xerox along with others. Nearly 120 countries have accepted IFRS and this number will soon touch 150. The Institute of Chartered Accountants of India and Ministry of Company Affairs have toiled endlessly for convergence with the IFRS (Indian Accounting Standard) w.e.f from 1st April 2012. There are 38 International Accounting Standards (IASs) and IFRSs but the ICAI has issued 35 Indian ASs converged with IFRSs after a final decision by the National Advisory Committee on Accounting Standards (NACAS) and thereafter notified by the Ministry of Company Affairs (MCA).

Infosys and Wipro have already prepared their balance sheet as per the Indian Accounting Standard and as per International Accounting Standard for listing in the New York Stock Exchange. Infosys prepared its financial results for the financial year 2000-11 in compliance with International Financial Reporting Standards as issued by International Accounting Standards.

Table 4.5 Consolidated Financial Results of Infosys Technologies Limited as per IFRS
(in Rs. crores, expected per share data)

Particulars	As on 31.03.2010	As on 31.03.2011
Revenues	22,742	27,501
Cost of sales	13,020	15,916
Gross profit	9,722	11,585
Selling and marketing expenses	1,184	1,512
Administrative expenses	1,628	1,971
Operating profit	6,910	8,102
Other income	990	1,211
Profit before income taxes	7,900	9,313
Income tax expense	1,681	2,490
Net profit	6,219	6,823
Paid-up equity share capital (Par value Rs.5/- each, fully paid)	286	286
Share premium, retained earnings and other components	23,787	23, 787
Earnings per share (per value Rs.5/- each) Basic	109.02	119.45

Source: Infosys Annual Report 2010-11

Auditors report: As important as the balance sheet or the profit and loss account, are the auditors' report and notes to these accounts. These give the auditor's comments on the financial statements, and expose the company's attempts at creative accounting for a cover up. They also tell, for example, whether the company has made provision for doubtful debts or the amount of grants which the company has given on behalf of loss making subsidiaries.

Table 4.6   Statement of Assets and Liabilities (IFRS Consolidated): Infosys

(in Rs. crores)

Particulars	As on 31.03.2010	As on 31.03.2011
Cash and cash equivalents	12,111	16,666
Other current assets	1,577	2,226
Trade receivables	3,494	4,653
Investments		
Available for sale financial assets, current	2,518	21
Investments in certificate of deposits	1,190	123
Property, plant and equipment	4,439	4,844
Other non- current assets	2,283	2,730
TOTAL	**27,612**	**31,263**
Liabilities and equity		
Liabilities	82	88
Provisions	3,111	3,553
Other current liabilities	346	319
Non-current liabilities attributable to equity holders of the company		
Share capital	286	286
Reserves and surplus		
Share premium	3,047	3,082
Liabilities and equity		
Retained earnings	20,668	23,826
Other component of equity	72	109
Retained earnings	20,668	23,826
TOTAL	**27,612**	**31,263**

Source: Infosys Annual Report 2010-11

When investors read the financial statements of a company, they should keep in mind that a company's financial statements usually show what the company wants to show. There are innumerable small ways of fudging a balance sheet. What is unveiled to the public is what cannot be concealed. Nevertheless, used intelligently, these statements can still be used as tools for investors. The auditor's opinion may be unqualified, qualified, adverse or negative and disclaimer which is in compliance with Auditing and Assurance Standard 28 (AAS28). In case of an unqualified opinion, the auditor expresses his opinion without reservations. On the other hand, in case of a qualified opinion the auditor express his opinion with reservations. If the financial statements are not prepared as per accounting standards, later on as per IFRS an auditor gives an adverse opinion. If an auditor fails to get sufficient information to express his opinion, he may give disclaimer of opinion.

Cash flow: Some market analysts feel that only the balance sheet cannot be a gauge of the financial health of a company and the cash flow statement should also be analyzed. But, not many investors refer to the 'cash flow statement' before taking an investment decision. Most people look only at the balance sheet. The cash flow statement may not reveal any insider information or any magic figure. It is one of the simplest and most efficient ways of analyzing a company's performance. The cash flow statement is a simple recording of all activities made in cash by a firm. It records all cash receipts and cash expenditures of the company. It gives a bird's eye view of what is left after the company has paid for everything, be it the CEO's salary or stationery expenses. The net amount of the statement is called free cash, this free cash can be distributed to shareholders in the form of dividend, repurchase of shares, or just as an investment for future use.

A cash flow statement has many advantages over the normal conventional profit and loss statement of earning summary. It is the best tool to assess a company's financial health because it considers all the accounting assumptions built into the net profit or earnings. A company's profit figure may be high and growing but until one looks at its free cash flow, one does not know if the company has generated money which is being stated in the profit figure. Unlike earnings, free cash flows represent real cash and does not consider non-cash items like debtors, creditors, depreciation, valuation changes and book entries.

Another reason why investors all over the world prefer free cash flow is because it is difficult for companies to gloss over the figures, the way they do with earnings. Companies can push around expenses; can focus on specific ratios like earnings before interest, operating earnings, gross earnings, or other factors to make earnings look better. They can window dress by treating some operational expenses as capital expenditure, capitalizing or deferring some expenses and many other tactics. But cold facts all show up in a free cash flow statement. Free cash flow can also be considered as another bottom-line. It is important to understand that a negative free cash flow is not necessarily bad but it does suggest that one is dealing with either a speculative investment (which is spending heavily) or an underperformer. A negative cash flow raises other questions. If the company is spending so much money; is it at least earning a high return on that capital? And is all that spending resulting in a rapid sales and profit growth? As an investor, one should know the answers to all these questions before letting the company spend your money.

The cash flow parameter is also important as it eliminates the effects of depreciation and deferred taxes from accounting practice. So, it allows easy comparison across countries and industries, and makes free cash flow the ideal benchmarking metric for corporate valuation and is useful while comparing multinational companies. There are several methods for preparing

```
                        ┌─────────────────────────┐
                        │    OPERATING PROFIT     │
                        └─────────────────────────┘

        ┌─────────────────────┐          ┌─────────────────────┐
        │        ADD          │          │        LESS         │
        └─────────────────────┘          └─────────────────────┘
        ┌─────────────────────┐          ┌─────────────────────┐
        │ Other income        │          │ Interest paid       │
        │ Decrease in current │          │ Tax paid            │
        │  assets             │          │ Increase in current │
        │ Increase in current │          │  assets             │
        │  liability          │          │ Decrease in current │
        │                     │          │  liability          │
        └─────────────────────┘          └─────────────────────┘

              ┌────────────────────────────────────────┐
              │    NET CASH FLOW FROM OPERATORS         │
              └────────────────────────────────────────┘

        ┌─────────────────────┐          ┌─────────────────────┐
        │ Decrease in fixed   │          │ Increase in fixed   │
        │  assets             │          │  assets             │
        │ Decrease in         │          │ Increase in         │
        │  investments        │          │  investments        │
        │                     │          │ Capital expenditure │
        └─────────────────────┘          └─────────────────────┘

           ┌────────────────────────────────────────────┐
           │  NET CASH FLOW FROM INVESTMENT ACTIVITIES   │
           └────────────────────────────────────────────┘

        ┌─────────────────────┐          ┌─────────────────────┐
        │ Issue of equity     │          │ Redemption of debt  │
        │ Issue of debt       │          │ Non operating       │
        │ Non operating income│          │  expenditure        │
        └─────────────────────┘          └─────────────────────┘

           ┌────────────────────────────────────────────┐
           │  NET CASH FLOW FROM FINANCING ACTIVITIES    │
           └────────────────────────────────────────────┘
                              │
                              ▼
                   ┌─────────────────────┐
                   │      FREE CASH      │
                   └─────────────────────┘
```

Source: *Figuring out the Maze,* Aman Chowhan, *Business Standard,* 5th March 2001

Chart 4.1 Determination of Free Cash

the cash statements. The widely used method involves three stages. In the first stage, cash flows from operating activities equal net profit after tax + extraordinary receipts.

Non cash activities like depreciation, debtors, creditors, inventory, and increase in current assets are deducted from the figure or added in case of reduction. The final figure arrived at is termed net cash from operations. In the second stage, cash flows from investing activities are ascertained by considering investments for fixed assets, increase/decrease in investments and adjustments for other income. In the third stage, the net cash position from financing activities is ascertained. This can be in the form of new capital issuance, capital receipts/ payment from assets, redemption or issuance of debt and adjustments for intangible assets like goodwill and asset revaluations. The net result is the net cash position from the financing activities. The sum total of all these three stages gives the net cash position of the company for the year. A positive figure indicates cash generated by the company and vice versa.

It is considered to be good if the company has generated cash from operating activities itself since it indicates that revenues are generated from the core business activities. But, it is not necessarily a bad sign if the company has failed to do so. The company may have generated cash by judicial use of operating capital.

Briefly, it can be said that when analyzing cash one should look at how much cash was generated from operating activities. Then from the cash that was generated, one should also look at how much was used in investing activities like, capital expenditure and how much additional debt was needed or whether any was used to pay down debt. It will add a new angle to the financial analysis and help to form an exact judgment about the creation of profits. Though the industry specific analysis of cash flow statements for some cases does not follow the above norm, it is a well accepted method to judge a company's financial health.

Leverage: It is needless to say that positive growth of a company drives the share value of that company. It is obvious that growth comes from profits (bottom-line) and profits come from sales or revenue (top-line). Thus, for better understanding of a company, it is necessary to understand how changes in the top-line affect the bottom-line. In other words, one needs to understand how net profit is influenced by the changes in revenue.

In the world of finance, the relationship between the top-line and bottom-line is often defined through a concept called leverage. Conventionally in business, leverage sometimes denotes loans and borrowings or debt. According to the Oxford Dictionary, leverage stands for 'influence' or 'power of lever'. So, it can be said that anything that can be used like a lever to lift the net profit of a company could be considered as leveraging. It is true that loans or other kinds of debts that are borrowed at rates less than the total return on investments of the company can act as a lever and help push up the net profit. The leverage attained with debt is referred to as financial leverage.

There is another kind of leverage called operating leverage which takes into account the cost structure of the company. Both the financial leverage and the operating leverage together form the total leverage or combined leverage. The effect of the operating leverage is reflected on the gross profit that is, EBIT. Let us take a small company ABP. Let us assume that the company produces electric bulbs and sells them at a price of Rs. 10 each. In the year 2011, it produced and sold 1,00,000 bulbs. While the variable cost per bulb is Rs. 8, the fixed cost is Rs. 40,000. Variable cost varies with the quantity of output whereas fixed costs remain fixed regardless of the quantity of output. The total revenue of the company is Rs. 10,00,000, and variable cost for one lakh bulbs is Rs. 8,00,000. The EBIT or gross profit of the company is worked out by deducting the total variable costs and fixed costs from the total revenue of the company. Thus, the gross profit or EBIT of the company is:

$$EBIT = Rs.\ 10,00,000 - 8,00,000 - 40,000 = Rs.\ 1,60,000$$

Now let us consider the first case, where it is estimated that the market price of bulbs will rise by 20 per cent in the year 2012. Then the total quantity sold will be 1,20,000. The total revenue, at the rate of Rs. 10 per piece, will be Rs. 12,00,000. Variable costs, at eight rupees per unit, will be Rs. 9,60,000. The fixed costs will remain unchanged at Rs. 40,000. Thus the gross profit turns to be

$$EBIT = Rs.\ 12,00,000 - 9,60,000 - 40,000 = Rs.\ 2,00,000$$

It may be noticed here that a 20 per cent increase in revenues led to a 25 per cent increase in gross profit. It is obvious from the above calculations that, a rise in the revenues results in a bigger rise in the gross profit. This is the effect of leverage and is called operating profit.

Now, let us consider the second case, where the quantity sold during the year 2012 falls by 20 per cent. So, while total quantity sold becomes 80,000 units, revenues will add up to Rs. 8,00,000. Total variable costs amount to Rs. 6,40,000. Total fixed costs remain at Rs. 40,000. The gross profit turns out to be

$$EBIT = Rs. 8,00,000 - 6,40,000 - 40,000 = Rs. 1,20,000$$

This is 25 per cent less than what was sold the previous year. This proves that, based on the company's current operational structure, if the revenues increase or decrease by 20 per cent, the gross profit increases or decreases by 25 per cent.

Financially, operating leverage is defined as the change in gross profit due to change in revenue. By definition,

$$\text{Degree of Operating Leverage (DOL)} = \frac{\text{Percentage change in gross profit}}{\text{Percentage change in revenue}}$$

$$\text{So, DOL} = \frac{25}{20} = 1.25 \text{ per cent.}$$

Because of fixed costs, companies get the benefit of operating leverage. The higher the fixed costs, the higher the leverage. A company with no fixed costs gets no operating leverage. When fixed costs are higher, the leverage of the company is higher but the gross profit realized is lower. Let two companies have the same total costs but different cost structures. While one of them has fixed costs and lower variable costs, the other has just the opposite structure. The former possesses high DOL and, is consequently, also more risky. If the demand increases, with every increase in revenue, the company with higher DOL will be able to register higher growth in gross profit. On the other side, if demands fall, the company with higher DOL will register a steeper decline in gross profit.

Thus, DOL is a measure of the risks associated with company operations and its cost structure. In favorable market conditions, it is advisable to invest in a company with high DOL. If market conditions are unfavorable, investment should be made companies with low DOL. Similarly, financial leverage is the percentage change in net profit (PAT) due to percentage change in the gross profit (EBIT). Thus

$$\text{The degree of financial leverage (DFL)} = \frac{\text{Percentage change in PAT}}{\text{Percentage change in EBIT}}$$

It is important to note that, DOL and DFL do not remain constant. Both the leverages are functions of units produced and sold, fixed costs and variable costs. As the scale of operations changes, leverage of a company changes as well.

Leveraged buyout: A leveraged buyout involves a transfer of ownership consummated mainly with the help of debt. Generally, a leveraged buyout involves acquisition of a division or unit of a company; occasionally it entails the purchase of an entire company.

A leveraged buyout entails considerable dependence on debt. The sponsors of a leveraged buyout are lured by the prospect of wholly (or largely) owning a company or a division, with the help of substantial debt finance. They assume considerable risks in the hope of reaping handsome rewards. The success of the entire operation depends on their ability to improve the performance of the unit. Above, we have discussed most of the criteria that are involved in fundamental analysis. Actually, there are two schools of thought. One believes that fundamental analysis is sufficient to determine the movements of share prices and the other school believes that technical analysis can do it more efficiently.

Not only is technical analysis more short term in nature that fundamental analysis, but the goals of a purchase (or sale) of a stock are usually different for each approach. In general, technical analysis is used for a trade, whereas fundamental analysis is used to make an investment. Investors buy assets they believe can increase in value, while traders buy assets they believe they can sell to somebody else at a greater price. The line between a trade and an investment can be blurred, but it does characterize a difference between the two schools.

Now we shall discuss the most important tool of the market action, which is commonly known as the Technical Analysis.

3. Technical analysis

The history of technical analysis is considered to be more than a hundred years old. Technical analysts believe that the principles of technical analysis derive from the observation of the financial market over hundreds of years. The oldest known hints of technical analysis appear in Joseph de la Vega's accounts of the Dutch markets in the 17th century. In Asia, the oldest example of technical analysis is thought to be a method developed by Homma Munehisa during the early 18th century which evolved into the use of candlestick techniques, and is today a main charting tool. In the 1920s and 1930s Richard W. Schabacker published several books which continued the work of Dow and William Peter Hamilton in his books *Stock Market Theory and Practice* and *Technical Market Analysis*. At the end of his life he was joined by his brother-in-law, Robert D. Edwards who finished his last book. In 1948 Edwards and John Magee published *Technical Analysis of Stock Trends* which is widely considered to be one of the seminal works of the discipline. It is exclusively concerned with trend analysis and chart patterns and remains in use to the present day. It is now in its 9th edition. As is obvious, early technical analysis was almost exclusively the analysis of charts, because the processing power of computers was not available for statistical analysis. Charles Dow reportedly originated a form of chart analysis used by technicians, namely point and figure analysis.

Dow Theory is based on the collected writings of Dow Jones, co-founder and editor of Dow Jones and Co. and inspired the use and development of modern technical analysis from the end of the 19th century. He constructed two indices – one is the 'industrial average' and the other is the 'rail average.' Later on they became familiar as the Dow Jones Industrial Average (DJIA) and Dow Jones Transportation Average (DJTA) respectively. As per Dow the averages will reflect three kinds of trends. The primary trend is the long-range cycle reflected by ups and downs of the market; the secondary trend is working as a restraining force over primary trends and the minor trends shows day to day movement of markets. On 19th December, 1900

Dow wrote in the *Wall Street Journal*, "The market is always considered as having three movements, all going at the same time. The first is the narrow movement from day to day. The second is the short swing, running from two weeks to a month or more; the third is the main movement, covering at least four years in its duration." Interestingly Dow came to this conclusion by observing the wave length of ocean tides, waves and ripples. The Dow Jones Industrial Average (DJIA) incorporates 30 blue chip corporations of the USA based on price weighted index. The BSE 30 (Base 1978-79) of India is a close comparison of DJIA with wide content. The improvement of Dow Theory leads to the development of the 'Random Walk Theory.' Other pioneers of analysis techniques include Ralph Nelson Elliott, William Delbert Gann, Wells Wilder and Richard Wyckoff who developed their respective techniques in the early 20th century.

During the period from 1929-1937, Ralph Nelson Elliot, in a series of articles, accurately explained the Wall Street crash of 1929 and subsequent movements stock prices and a number of cyclical phenomena that move in waves with patterns that repeat themselves. Therefore, future moves can be predicted in terms of time, direction and amplitude. The Elliot Wave theory has become one of the most popular tools of technical analysis. One of its advantages is that although it predates chaos theory, it can be applied across any timeframe whatsoever since this is a fractal system. Each pattern of waves forms a subset of a larger pattern of waves which in turn forms another subset of yet a larger pattern of waves. Elliot himself classified eight time-frames ranging from subminuette to the grand super cycle – a range from minutes to centuries. In fact, Elliot Wave theorists use cycles to analyze all sorts of periodic data and they are perfectly comfortable making predictions over very long periods of time.

Wells Wilder is considered the first technical analyst who used silicon power to the hilt by performing complicated mathematical calculations. He created many indicators that have later become industry standards like the Relative Strength Index (RSI). With the help of RSI, he defined a rigorous philosophy for measuring market momentum in terms of over bought and over sold stocks and divergent situations. His book, *New Concepts in Technical Trading System*, is considered as the Bible of the trading community. Another technical analyst, John Murphy defines technical analysis, as the study of market action, primarily through the use of charts, for the purpose of forecasting future trends of stock prices. But before we enter into a detailed discussion and explanation of techniques and tools used in technical analysis, we think, it may be necessary to discuss some logical situations on which technical analysis is based. We have also tried to draw some clear distinctions between technical analysis and fundamental analysis. The investment community is drawn from a wide spectrum of different professional community clusters in Wall Street, who used their highly developed quantitative skills and computer programs based on Chaos Theory to analyze the movements of stock prices.

The behavior of price and volume of trading will act as price indicator over a passage of time. The advance (NSE Adv) and decline (NSE Dec) of NSE stock reveal the fluctuation of the SENSEX. The most popular measure is to calculate the daily net difference between the numbers of NSE stock which advance in comparison with those that decline. The net difference is added to the difference of the next day to calculate the breadth or continuous cumulative difference. The continuous difference is plotted and compared with the SENSEX. Here we are making a comparison of the cumulative difference with the SENSEX during the period from 18th July to 22nd July, 2011. The technical analyst stresses on the change of breadth instead of absolute change. The breadth and SENSEX will move in the same direction. If it is contradictory, it will indicate the new direction of the market. The SENSEX cannot defy the market in the long run. If the resistance is longer, the chance of reversal is also greater.

Table 4.7   Behavior Price and Volume of Trading

(Figures in number of shares)

Date (Up/Down)	Day	Advance	Decline	Net Advance or Decline	Breadth	SENSEX
18.07.2011	Monday	779	657	122	122	+55
19.07.2011	Tuesday	909	525	374	496	+147
20.07.2011	Wednesday	493	955	−462	34	−151
21.07.2011	Thursday	515	935	−419	−385	−66
22.07.2011	Friday	935	517	418	33	+286

Source: Information compiled from NDTV Profit.

Fundamental analysis involves researching to see if the market in general, as well as the stock in particular, is currently undervalued or overpriced. In fact, the fundamental approach examines all the relevant factors affecting the price of a stock in order to determine its intrinsic value. The intrinsic value is what the fundamental stock is actually worth. If the value is below the current market price, then the stock is overpriced and should be sold, and *vice versa*. The fundamental analyst carries out the analysis by comparing the current stock price with what they think is the fair value. To gauge a stock's fair value, the fundamental analyst will look at the "basics" of a company. He will check the company's management practice, cash flow, total assets, earnings and revenue, debt, paid-up capital and so forth, to determine exactly how much the company's stock should be worth. Once he has that value, he will compare it with the current stock price. If the stock price is cheaper than his estimation of its fair value, he will conclude that the stock is undervalued and worth buying. We have already discussed earlier, that fundamental analysis involves analyzing the characteristics of a company in order to estimate its value.

On the other hand, **technical analysis** involves trying to predict a stock's price movement by looking at how it has previously performed, and how people might act in the future. To a technical analyst, a stock price's past movement tells them a lot about how it will move in the future. A technical analyst is not interested in what a stock is really worth, i.e. about the "value" of a company or a commodity. Technicians (sometimes called chartists) are only interested in the price movements in the market and whether the public will buy the stock or not. He will use various charts and indicators to monitor the trend and momentum of a stock as well as investors' behavior.

If a stock is on a roll and investors appear greedy, the technical analyst will probably decide that the price will continue to rise, and will invest in the stock. On the other hand, if the stock is losing steam, the technical analyst will probably conclude that investors are starting to lose interest in the stock, and he will avoid buying it since the price trend might reverse.

Technical analysts examine what investors fear or think about those developments and whether or not investors have the wherewithal to back up their opinions; these two concepts are called psych (psychology) and supply/demand. Technicians employ many techniques, one of which is the use of charts. Using charts, technical analysts seek to identify price patterns and market trends in financial markets and attempt to exploit those patterns.

Technicians using charts search for archetypal price chart patterns, such as the well-known head and shoulders or double top/bottom reversal patterns; study technical indicators and moving averages; and look for forms such as lines of support, resistance, channels and more obscure formations such as flags, pennants, balance days and cup and handle patterns. Technical analysts also widely use market indicators of many sorts, some of which are mathematical transformations of price, often including up and down volume, advance/decline data and other inputs. These indicators are used to help assess whether an asset is trending, and if it is, the probability of its direction and of continuation. Technicians also look for relationships between price/volume indices and market indicators. Examples include the relative strength index, and Moving Average Convergence/Divergence (MACD). Other avenues of study include correlations between changes in options (implied volatility) and put/call ratios with price. Also important are sentiment indicators such as bull/bear ratios, short interest, implied volatility, etc.

There are many techniques in technical analysis. Adherents of different techniques (for example, candlestick charting, Dow Theory, and Elliott wave theory) may ignore the other approaches, yet many traders combine elements from more than one technique. Some technical analysts use subjective judgment to decide which pattern(s) a particular instrument reflects at a given time and what the interpretation of that pattern should be. Others employ a strictly mechanical or systematic approach to pattern identification and interpretation. Technical analysts believe that the historical performance of stocks and markets are indications of future performance.

However, one should be cautious as neither method (fundamental or technical) is 100 per cent accurate in predicting a stock's movement, long-term or short-term. Stock and market levels are easily affected by external forces such as global terrorism, oil prices, inflation and political change, as well as news that is directly related to the stock in question. Therefore, caution must always be used when trying to predict a stock's movement, whichever method one chooses to utilize. Both technical and fundamental approaches, to market forecasting, attempt to determine the direction in which prices are likely to move; it is just that the approach is from different directions. Most traders classify them as either technicians or fundamentalists. But the work of both classes overlaps most of the time. While most of the fundamentalists have knowledge of basis price trends and chart analysis, technical analysts have at least a passing awareness of the fundamentals. If a market operator has to choose between the two approaches, the choice would logically have to be the technical one. By definition, the fundamentals are already reflected in the price. The reverse, however, is not true.

In recent decades, many more technical tools and theories have been developed and enhanced with an increasing emphasis on computer-assisted techniques using technical analysis software. All these are discussed in the latter parts of this chapter.

Market discounts everything: It is a common belief amongst technical analysts that the market price can be affected by any incident which may be fundamental, political or psychological that is reflected in the price of stocks. So, to understand the market one has to study the activity of price movements of stocks. The classical theory of supply and demand also rules the stock market. If supply exceeds demand, price will fall and if demand exceeds supply, price will rise.

This classical theory of supply and demand is the basis for all economic and fundamental forecasting. Thus, the technical analyst assumes that if prices are rising, for whatever reasons, the demand must exceed supply and the fundamentals are bullish. If the market situation is reverse, fundamentals are bearish. It may apparently seem irrelevant in the context of the discussion on technical analysis, but it is not so, because, the technical analyst also indirectly studies fundamentals during his study of technicals. Generally, chartists do not concern themselves with reasons why prices fluctuate in the market, but they know that there are reasons why markets go up and down. The chartist does not believe that knowing those reasons is necessary in the forecasting process with technical indicators. The chartist, with the help of his study of price charts and host of supporting technical indicators, determines the way in which the market is most likely to move. In fact, the chartist or technical analyst only takes the help of technical tools and techniques in the process of studying market action.

Trends in movement of prices: In the study of technicals, it is absolutely necessary to understand the trend. It is quite well known that the basis of technical analysis is the statistical analysis of a time series data. In the study of movement of price of stocks, the price series of concerned stock is considered. A trend in the motion of a price series, with ups and downs, is more likely to continue in the same direction than to reverse. Nair observed that this corollary is an adaption of Newton's first law of motion. This corollary can be stated another way, that is, a trend in motion will continue in the same direction until it reverses. It is statistically possible to predict future trends following the existing trend in a series of price data over a period of time. So, the whole purpose of charting price action is to understand the future market in the light of the present trend in the movement of a stock price.

History tends to repeat itself: According to Cory Janssen, Chad Langager and Casey Murphy, another important idea in technical analysis is that history tends to repeat itself, mainly in terms of price movement. The repetitive nature of price movements is attributed to market psychology; in other words, market participants tend to provide a consistent reaction to similar market stimuli over time. Technical analysis uses chart patterns to analyze market movements and understand trends.

Although many of these charts have been used for more than 100 years, they are still believed to be relevant because they illustrate patterns in price movements that often repeat themselves. Analysis can be used on any security with historical trading data. This includes stocks, futures and commodities, fixed-income securities, forex, etc. These concepts can be applied to any type of security. In fact, technical analysis is more frequently associated with the study of future trends in the light of repetition of events in the past.

Timing the market: For successful trading, timing is very important. In the forecasting process, both the technical and fundamental approach can be used. However, the question of timing in determination of specific entry and exit points is almost purely technical. So, the correct application of technical analysis is absolutely necessary before making a market commitment. One should consider appropriate steps of technical analysis before approaching the market even if one has gone through some fundamental analysis in earlier stages of a decision. Timing the market is a very sensitive task. For this purpose daily and intra-day charts are more useful than long-term charts. Long-term charts or long-term trend analysis are not meant for daily trading purpose. A distinction has to be made between analysis for forecasting purposes and the timing of market commitments. Long-term charts are useful in the analytical process to help determine the major trend and price objectives. They are not suitable for the timing of entry and exit points.

Utility and advantage: Different tools of technical analysis are very flexible and well accepted among researchers in different fields for their adaptability to virtually any medium and time dimension involving any type of time series data, including any type of trading parameters. Technical analysis can be applied with great advantage to determine the behavior of stocks, commodities, interest rate markets, foreign currencies, spread and options trading.

Unlike the fundamental analyst, the technical analyst can easily follow as many markets as desired. Most of the fundamental analysts have to deal with a tremendous amount data of different economic fields, so, they tend to specialize in one or a few sectors. Also, markets and sectors go through active and dormant periods, trending and non-trending stages. The technical analyst can concentrate his attention and resources in those that display strong trending tendencies while choosing to ignore the rest. A fundamentalist, who may be a specialist in his field, does not have that flexibility. There is a misconception that charting is useful only in the short term. It has been suggested that fundamental analysis should be used for long term forecasting with technical factors limited to short term timing. The fact is that longer range forecasting, using weekly and monthly charts going back several years, has proven to be an extremely useful application of these techniques.

There are two very important indicators in technical analysis, one of them is price-charts and the other is volume. Charts are similar to the charts that you see in any business setting. A chart is simply a graphical representation of a series of prices over a set time frame. Before discussing the role of volume in technical analysis, let us discuss the different types of charts, their characteristics and applications over different time frames.

Daily bar charts: It is also known as the daily bar diagram and it is the most popular of all charts utilized by the technical analyst for forecasting and trading. It has gained wide acceptance as a primary working tool amongst most traders and analysts as they confine their interest to relatively short-term market action. The chart usually covers a period of only six to nine months in the life of stock trading history. As each day's market action is represented by a vertical bar, this chart is called a daily bar chart. This chart shows the opening price, the high and low for a specific day and closing price. The high and low for the day are represented by the high and low of the vertical bar respectively.

The chart is made up of a series of vertical lines that represent each data point. This vertical line represents the high and low for the trading period, along with the closing price. The close and open are represented on the vertical line by a horizontal dash. The opening price on a bar chart is illustrated by a dash that is located on the left side of the vertical bar. Conversely, the close is represented by a dash on the right.

Candlestick charts: The candlestick chart is similar to a bar chart, but it differs in the way that it is visually constructed. Similar to the bar chart, the candlestick chart also has a thin vertical line showing the period's trading range. The difference comes in the formation of a wide bar on the vertical line, which illustrates the difference between the open and close.

Line charts: A line chart is a chart where only the closing price for each successive day is plotted. This type of chart is also widely used by technical analysts. It is not as popular as the daily bar chart among the market analysts, but, a considerable number of chartists or technical analysts believe that the closing price of any stock in a trading day is important in studying the price behavior of that stock and hence a line chart is a more valid measure of price activity of a stock. Further, according to a specific requirement of the analyst, some techniques used in chart analysis are easier to perform on a line chart than on a bar chart. In other words, it can be said that the line is formed by connecting the closing prices over the time frame. Line charts do not provide visual information of the trading range for individual points such as the high, low and opening prices. However, the closing price is often considered to be the most important price in stock data compared to the high and low for the day and this is why it is the only value used in line charts.

Intra-day charts: A number of traders as well as investors want to know intra day activities of the price of different stocks. The daily charts can indicate the open, high, low and closing prices of the trading day. But, the daily chart fails to capture the entire amount of trading activity that takes place during the trading session, so, an enormous amount of trading activity of a trading session is lost on daily charts. In fact, it is possible to capture the intra-day activity by conventional daily charts for short intervals. For example, bar charts can be obtained for time periods of five minutes, fifteen minutes, one hour and so on. For day traders, especially for short-term traders, intra-day data have proved to be very useful. So, the intra-day chart is becoming increasingly popular with the advancement of computer technology and increasing daily use of computers.

Point and figure charts: The point and figure chart is not well known or used much by the average investor but it has had a long history of use dating back to the first technical traders. This type of chart reflects price movements and is not as concerned about time and volume in the formulation of the points. The point and figure chart removes the noise, or insignificant price movements, in the stock, which can distort traders' views of the price trends. These types of charts also try to neutralize the skewing effect that time has on chart analysis.

Charts for longer periods: It is true that average traders depend on daily charts and are interested in short term market behavior. But for portfolio investment, price charting with weekly and monthly price data can be considered as a very useful and rewarding area. To study the movement of stock prices over a much longer period of time, the prices of a daily trading session are compressed in such a way that it indicates the direction of the movement of prices. So that it can be observed on a weekly chart, the price activity of a stock during the entire week is represented by one bar chart. Similarly, on a monthly chart, each bar shows the price action that took place during an entire month.

The principles of technical analysis – including trend analysis, support and resistance levels, trend lines and channels, percentage retracements, and price patterns – lend themselves quite well to the analysis of long-range price movements. Actually, almost all the charting techniques that are applied to daily bar charts can also be applied to weekly and monthly charts. The chartists believe that long-term forecasting can sometimes be easier than short-term forecasting.

Macro to micro: Among the technical analysts, long-term trend is known as 'macro' trend and short-term trend is known as 'micro' trend. It is always advisable in order to understand chart analysis that one should start with long-term trends and gradually work to the short-term. If one starts with only the short-term trends, he may face some confusion as daily data are continuously changing and drawing any conclusions appears to be difficult. A thorough analysis of a daily chart may have to be completely redone after looking at the long-range charts. By starting with the long-range charts, all data to be considered are already included in the chart and a proper perspective is achieved. Once the analyst understands the market movement from a long-term perspective, he can easily understand short-term perspective from that market movement. So, for the analyst it is always easier to move from 'macro' to 'micro'.

Trading volume: Volume is one of the important factors for understanding the behavior of market movement. In a stock market, volume represents the total number of shares that changed hands on a given day. In the commodity market, it refers to the number of contracts traded. It is quite obvious that each transaction is the result of meeting a demand, on the one hand, with supply on the other. Prices are likely to rise if demand exceeds supply and if supply exceeds demand, prices are likely to fall. So, also in the stock market, the classical rule of demand and supply exists. If one wants to measure the supply and demand, he must study the trading volume.

The volume for a particular stock is usually recorded by a vertical bar at the bottom of the chart under that day's price bar. Heavier trading volume is represented by a higher volume bar and a smaller bar represents lighter volume. Volume can be plotted for weekly charts as well, in which case, total volume for the week would simply be plotted under the bar representing that week's price action. Volumes are not normally shown in the monthly charts. Well known market analysts, Curtis M. Arnold and Dan Rahfeldt in their book *'Timing Market'* outlined some basic rules of volume analysis. They are:

❖ When prices are rising and volume is increasing, the present trend will continue, that is, prices will continue to rise.

❖ When prices are rising and volume is decreasing, the present trend is not likely to continue, that is, prices will decelerate and then turn downward.

❖ When prices are falling and volume is increasing, the present trend will continue, that is, prices will continue to fall.

❖ When prices are falling and volume is decreasing, the present trend is not likely to continue, that is, prices decline will decelerate and then price will turn upward

❖ When volume is not rising or falling the effect on price is neutral.

Sentiment Indicators

❖ Short interest ratio = Number of shares short sale/Average daily trading volume

❖ Short interest ratio means a number of shares that are in short demand and short sale will be covered up with the help of new buying and it will affect the price accordingly. If the short interest ratio is high it indicates the market sentiment.

❖ Pull/Call ratio = Number of 'put' purchased/Number of 'calls' purchased

❖ When the Pull/Call ratio is rising, speculators are pessimistic and when it is falling speculators are optimistic.

❖ Trin Statistic = Volume of declining/No of declining by volume of advances/No of advances

❖ If the trin is more than 1 it indicates a bearish trend as declining stock has a higher average volume than that of advancing stock. If it is less than 1, it indicates a bullish trend as the advancing stock has a higher average volume than that of declining stock.

Now let us discuss some practical applications in the light of the above concept. Let us assume a company stock has been in the trading range for several weeks with average daily volume of 1,00,000 shares changing hands. Prices now tend to move higher and daily volume picks up to 1,50,000 shares. In this situation, one is justified in believing that the price will continue to move higher, fueled by 'demand volume.' One can be sure that due to strong volume, prices will continue to move higher over the next three weeks.

In the fourth week, it is observed that prices tumble and lose 25 per cent of their previous gains. Then an investor may be confused in deciding whether to hold or sell the stock. Here also one can take a decision after analyzing the volume picture. It is noticed in the fourth week that the said stock has been trading only 50,000 shares per day. According to volume rules, this phenomenon can be considered as a temporary reaction. So, early buyers could be taking profits or any new buyer could be waiting for a set back before buying. This is a normal situation, and the market is paused for a correction. Hence, there is no reason to abandon one's position in this situation, unless it is noticed that volume is beginning to increase on a down day.

In the fifth week, according to expectations, prices start shooting up again on the volume averaging 1,00,000 shares per day. In the sixth week, the market behaves in the same way. In the seventh week, a reaction in the prices of the said stock is noticed, but volume is reduced to 50,000 shares per day. In this situation, one should hold his stock. In the eighth week, prices move to new heights, but volume rises to a daily average of only 60,000 shares. This is an obvious signal of alarm as the demand volume is drying up.

If any fundamental economic situation encourages the market condition both prices and volume are likely to go up. If prices fail to get that extra boost, they can fall under their own weight, even on heavy volume – and one should sell their stock.

Now let us apply the concepts we have discussed above to key patterns which appear on the charts furnished below.

To understand the technical approaches to market analysis, the concept trend is absolutely essential. It is one of the most important concepts in technical analysis. The meaning in finance is not all that different from the general definition of the term – a trend is really nothing more than the general direction in which a security or market is headed. The sole purpose of all the tools like 'support and resistance level,' 'price patterns,' 'moving averages' and 'trend lines' used by the market analyst, is to help in determining the market trend for the purpose of participating in that trend. In simple words, a trend can be said to be the direction of the market or the way in which the market is moving. Like other economic indicators, stock prices do not generally move in a straight line in any direction. In stock markets, prices of stocks move in a zigzag path. These zigzags resemble a series of successive waves with fairly obvious peaks and troughs. It is the direction of these peaks and troughs that constitute the market trend.

It is not difficult to see that the trend in Chart 4.2 is up; however, it is not always this easy to see a trend from a chart alone. Consider Chart 4.3, There are lots of peaks and troughs i.e. lots of ups and downs in this chart, but there is no clear indication of which direction the price of this security is headed. Unfortunately, trends are not always easy to see. In other words, defining a trend goes well beyond the obvious. In any given chart, you will probably notice that prices do not tend to move in a straight line in any direction, but rather in a series of highs (peaks) and lows (troughs). In technical analysis, it is the movement of the highs and lows that constitutes a trend.

Meaning of Trend

In stock market circles, trend is represented by the movement of peaks and troughs or highs and lows, which generally move in three directions. They can move up, down or side ways. When successive higher peaks and troughs are observed, the trend can be defined as an upward trend. If the picture is opposite, that is, if the successive peaks and troughs are declining, the trend is to be considered as a downward trend, and if the successive peaks and troughs are found to be horizontal, then it is considered as a sideways trend (see Charts 4.4, 4.5 and 4.6).

There is a common belief among general investors that the price trend is always either upwards or downwards. Actually, trend commonly known as market trend moves in three directions, that is, up, down, and sideways or flat. As the sideways trend looks like a flat

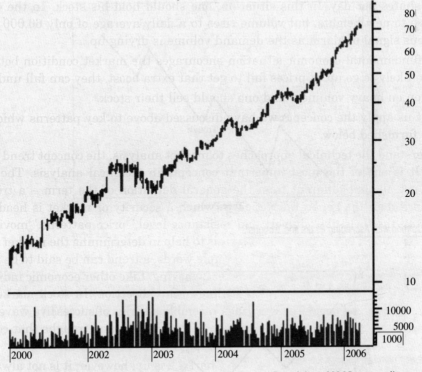

Copyright © 2006 Investopedia.com

Chart 4.2   Peaks and Troughs of Market Trends

Note: We are thankful to Investopedia.com

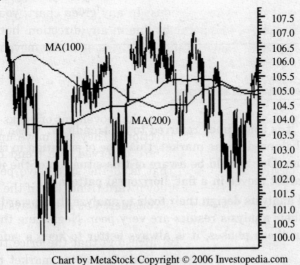

Chart by MetaStock Copyright © 2006 Investopedia.com

Chart 4.3   Uptrend with Ascending Peaks and Troughs

Note: We are thankful to Investopedia.com & Meta Stock.

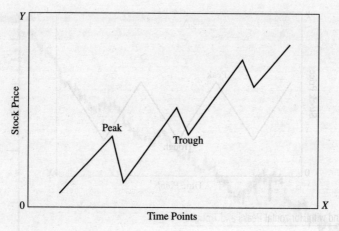

Uptrend with Ascending Peaks and Troughs

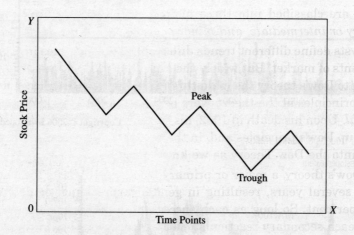

Downtrend with Descending Peaks and Troughs

and horizontal pattern, it is sometimes referred to as 'trendless'. When demand and supply positions are relatively balanced in the market, this type of situation in the market is known as a period of equilibrium. One should be aware of this situation of the market as at least a third of the time the market moves in a flat, horizontal pattern.

Most of the technical analysts design their tools to analyze the upward or downward trend and hence, sometimes their analysis results are very poor. Neglecting the 'trendless' phases can prove very costly. In these phases, it is always better to keep a safe distance from the market.

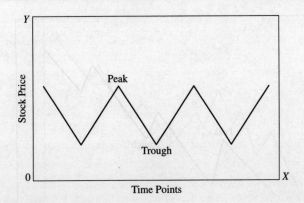

| **Chart 4.6** | Sideways Trend with Horizontal Peaks and Troughs |

Classifications of Trend

Generally, trends are classified into three main categories. They are termed as *major or primary, secondary or intermediate, and minor or near term or day-to-day trend.*

Different analysts define different trends differently. So, sometimes investors feel confused about the movements of market. But widely the excepted ones are those suggested by Charles H. Dow. According to Dow's theory the main three classifications are those we have mentioned above. The basic principles of the theory were outlined by him in editorials he wrote for the *Wall Street Journal.* Upon his death in 1902, his successor as editor of the newspaper, William P. Hamilton, took up Dow's principles and, in the course of 27 years of writing on the market, formulated them into the Dow Theory as we know today.

According to Dow's theory, a major or primary trend usually lasts for more than one year and may run for several years, resulting in general appreciation or depreciation in value of more than 20 per cent. So long as each successive rally reaches a higher level than the one before it and each secondary reaction stops at a higher level than the previous reaction, the primary trend is up and we are in a *bull market.* In the reverse situation, when each intermediate decline carries prices to successive lower levels and each intervening rally fails to exceed the top of the previous rally, the *primary or major trend* is down and we are in a *bear market.*

Curtis M. Arnold and Dan Rahfeldt in their book '*Timing Market*' expressed that *the secondary trend or intermediate trend are reactions occurring in a bull market and rallies occurring in a bear market.* In general, they last from a few weeks to a few months and retrace from one-third to two-thirds of the gain or loss registered by preceding swing in the *major trend.*

Minor or near term trends are usually defined as anything that last less than six days but may last up to three weeks. Actually, the *secondary trend* is composed of *minor trends* or day-to-day fluctuations but the Dow's theorist considers them as unimportant.

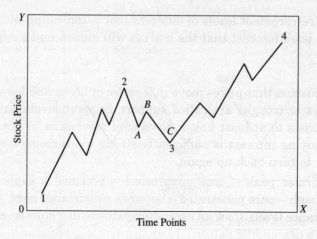

Source: A Trendy Approach, BS (25.05.01 to 16.07.01), Rajesh Nair

Chart 4.7   Minor or Near Term Trend

Each trend is part of the next larger trend and is itself comprised of smaller trends. It can be seen in Chart 4.7 that the major trend is up as reflected by the rising peaks and troughs (points 1, 2, 3, 4). The corrective phase, that is, from 2 to 3 represents an intermediate correction within the major uptrend. So also, wave 2-3 breaks down into smaller waves (A, B, C). At point C, the analyst would say that the *primary* or *major trend* is still up, but the *secondary* or *intermediate* and *minor trends* are down. However, at point 4, all three trends would be up.

Retracement Theory

It is quite well known that the market never moves steadily up or steadily down. In each primary direction, each movement is followed by a reaction, which can, in turn, be followed by another thrust. Each thrust, measured from bottom to top or top to bottom, is known as a 'swing' or 'move'. Each reaction or rally retraces part of the move and therefore, is known as 'retracement'. When the reaction is greater than the move, it is considered that the trend has changed, at least, for the near term or minor. Retracement theory sets predetermined target levels for these moves, which can easily be determined by computer applications.

In this theory, the first problem is to determine the primary trend. But once it is reasonably assured that the market is a downtrend or an uptrend, the key is to how far a move is likely to be retraced before the market resumes that trend. Knowing that, one could better judge an appropriate point to enter the market on a reaction. Apart from judging the correct primary trend, the most important aspect of trading is probably correctly timing entries on reactions. Market analysts have long debated regarding the definition of 'normal retracement'. The general consensus is that a normal retracement'. recaptures between one-third and two-thirds of the previous move. Another group of analysts say it is between 40 and 60 per cent. Most agree that 50 per cent retracement is the most likely.

Often, one can find key retracement levels of different moves coinciding with one another, lending more credibility to one's forecast that the market will indeed find a support level.

Support and Resistance

We see from the above discussion that prices move in a series of highs and lows or peaks and troughs. The reactions lows or troughs are called support. Support level is a price level at which sufficient demand exists to at least halt a downward movement in prices. This is an area on the chart where buying interest is sufficiently strong to overcome selling pressure; from here prices are likely to turn back up again.

In an uptrend, each former peak – once suppressed – becomes a support level. In a downtrend, each former trough – once penetrated – becomes a resistance level. Actually, in an uptrend, support and resistance levels show an ascending pattern, in a downtrend, the support and resistance levels show a descending pattern. In an uptrend, the resistance levels pause in that uptrend and are usually exceeded at some point. In a downtrend, support levels are not sufficient to stop the decline permanently, but are liable to check them at least temporarily. It is to be remembered that when a support level is broken, it becomes resistance, and when resistance level is broken, it becomes support.

Normally, a support level is identified beforehand by a previous reaction. In Chart 4.8, point 2 and point 4 represent support levels and the resistance level is identified by the previous peak. In the same chart, points 1 and 3 are resistance levels.

For an uptrend to continue, each successive low (support level) must be higher than the one preceding it. Each resistance level must be higher than the one preceding it. If the corrective dip in a trend comes all the way down to the previous low, it may be an early warning that the uptrend is ending or at least moving from an uptrend to a sideways trend. If the support level is violated, then a trend reversal from up to down is likely. Failure to exceed a previous peak in an uptrend, or the inability of prices to violate the previous support low in a downtrend, is usually the first warning that the existing trend is changing.

In Chart 4.9, the failure of prices at point 5 to exceed the previous peak at point 3 followed by a downside violation of the previous low at point 4 constitutes a downside trend reversal. This pattern is also called a double top.

In Chart 4.10, usually the first sign of a bottom is the ability of prices at point 5 to hold above the previous low at point 3. The bottom is confirmed when the peak at 4 is overcome.

Until now, we have defined 'support' as previous low and 'resistance' as previous high. But this is not always true. Whenever a support or resistance level is penetrated by a significant amount, they reverse their roles and become the opposite. Actually, it can be said that a resistance level becomes a support level and a support level becomes resistance level. In part A of Chart 4.11, the reaction at point 4 stops at or above the top peak at point 1. The previous peak at point 1 had been resistance level. But once it was decisively penetrated by wave 3, the previous resistance peak became the support level. All of the previous selling was near the top wave 1 creating the resistance level, which has now become buying. If in part B of

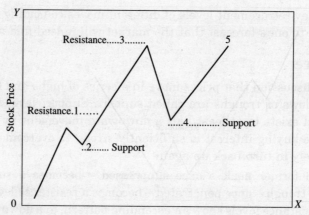

Source: *A Trendy Approach, BS,* Rajesh Nair

Chart 4.8 Support and Resistance Level

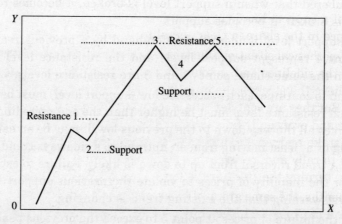

Chart 4.9 Reversal of Trend

the same chart, showing declining prices, point 2, which had been a previous support level, has now become a resistance level acting as a ceiling at point 5.

In simple words it can be said that investors should be careful not to start buying before the upturn in case the support line loses its quality. It is not to unknown for the curve to penetrate it. Another feature about it is that an investor should not expect the curve to bounce up too many times. If it has bounced off the support line five or six times, there is a high possibility of adverse movement in the share. Investors should be watchful for the moments when a resistance line turns itself into a support line. This happens when the curve penetrates the former and keeps bouncing upwards of this line. If an investor can sense this opportunity – of a share breaking past its resistance line – it is a clear indication of a good buy.

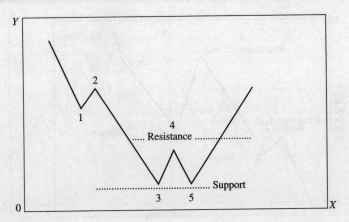

Source: *A Trendy Approach, BS,* Rajesh Nair

Chart 4.10   Bottom Reversal Pattern

Penetration of a support line is of course bad news and is recognized as a break down of investor confidence in the share, a clear signal to sell.

Consider a hypothetical situation illustrated in part B of Chart 4.11. A group of buyers has been waiting on the sidelines and watching a stock decline from 1 to 2. At the given price at point 2, they believe the stock is cheap so they buy. The stock begins to rise and eventually reaches point 3. But they are confident the stock will go much higher. Unfortunately, the stock begins to decline and eventually falls to point 4. At this point, the investors begin to feel they have made a mistake and vow to dump the stock if they can get their money back. Luckily, the stock begins to rally and as it reaches point 5, the same level as point 2, these investors sell their shares, turning the stock prices down once again.

After some months, the same group of investors finds a new hot stock of Company X. In the situation of part A of Chart 4.11, they buy it at point 1, and after a few weeks, the stock has risen to point 2. This time without repeating the same mistake they made earlier, they sell the stock and pocket a considerable profit. A week later, the stock dropped to point 3 and they feel proud for having their profit at 2. But a month later, the price of the stock of Company X has risen to point 4. Now they do not feel so smart. They decide that if they get another chance to buy the stock at point 1 level, they will hold the stock for a longer time. This is an example of how previous tops can act as support.

The simplest technical tool employed by the technical analyst is the basic trend line. The basic trend line though very simple to draw is very important and most valuable. In an upward movement, successive peaks or tops are getting higher and successive troughs or bottoms are also getting higher and the trend line is a straight line drawn with an upward angle (see Figure-A of Chart 4.12). We have discussed earlier that the up trend line is drawn under the rising bottoms by joining 1, 3 and 5. When there is an upward trend, we start drawing a line connecting the bottoms on the chart, because the buyers are in control of the market

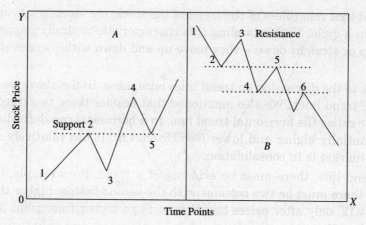

Chart 4.11 Support and Resistance

and driving prices higher. Then one identifies the top of the trend by drawing a line that is parallel to the bottom.

Similarly, in an upward movement, successive peaks or tops are getting lower and successive troughs or bottoms are also getting lower and the trend line is a straight line drawn with a downward angle (see Figure-B of the Chart 4.12). The down trend line is drawn under the descending peaks or tops by joining 1, 3 and 5. We have a downward trend, start by drawing a line connecting the tops on the chart, because the sellers are in control of the market and driving prices lower. Then one attempts to identify the bottom of the trend by drawing a line that is parallel to the tops. So, it is easier for an investor to indentify the trading zone between two parallel lines.

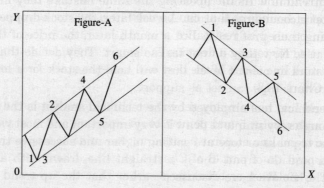

Chart 4.12 Basic Trend Lines

It can be noted that regardless of the trend of the stock, the stock is moving upwards and downwards within a cycle. Understanding this characteristic is vitally important. Stocks do not go straight up or straight down – they move up and down within cycles characterized by parallel lines.

Let us go back to the discussion on trend lines once more. In the above we have discussed the two shapes of trend lines. We also mentioned that besides those two trend lines, there is another trend line called the horizontal trend line. In a horizontal trend, the tops and bottoms do not get substantially higher and lower (see Chart 4.6). It has relatively stable tops and bottoms and the market is in consolidation.

To draw a trend line, there must be evidence of a trend. For example, for an up trend line to be drawn there must be two bottoms with the second bottom higher than the first. In part A of Chart 4.12, only after prices have begun to go higher from point 3 is the chartist reasonably confident that a reaction bottom has been formed, and only then can a tentative up trend line be drawn under points 1 and 3.

One group of chartists requires that the peak or top at point 2 be penetrated to confirm the uptrend before drawing the trend line. Other group only requires a 50 per cent retracement of wave 2-3, or prices to approach the top wave 2. Once two ascending bottoms have been identified, a straight line is drawn connecting the bottoms and projected up and to the right. While a tentative trend line is found so far, in order to confirm its validity, that the line should be touched a third time with prices bouncing off it. In part A of the Chart 4.12, the successful test of the trend line occurs at point 5. In the case of a down trend line also all these rules and conditions remain the same.

One must be careful about the use of trend. The fundamental concept of trend is that a moving trend tends to remain moving with certain speed maintaining a certain slope, represented by a trend line. Then the trend line helps to determine the end points of the corrective phases and tells the investors the time of changing of the trend, which is very important for the purpose of investment.

For example, during the uptrend, the most probable corrective dip will often touch or come very close to the uptrend line. As the investors intend to buy on dips in an uptrend, the trend line provides a support boundary that can be used as a buying area. For selling purposes, a down trend line can be used as resistance area. As long as the trend line shows no sign of violation, it can be used for taking a decision in favor of buying or selling areas. The violation or breaking of the trend line is one of the best early warnings of a change in trend (see Figure A and Figure B of Chart 4.13).

When the uptrend line has already set in (see part A), subsequent dips near the line can be used as buying areas, point 5 and point 7 could be used for new or additional acquisition. The violation of the trend line at point 9 called for disposing of all belongings by indicating a downside trend. In position of part B of Chart 4.13, point 5 and point 7 could be considered as selling areas. The violation or breaking of the trend line at point 9 indicates an upside trend.

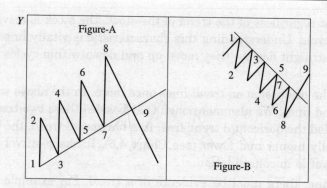

Chart 4.13 Upward and Downward Trends

There are certain thumb rules for testing the significance of a trend line. Significance can be determined by the time period for which it is intact and the number of times it has been tested. A trend line is obviously more significant that is successfully tested eight times than a trend line that has been touched only three times. Further, it can be said that the trend line which has been effectedly continued for one year is of more importance than the trend line has been in effect for only three months. A sound and more significant trend line inspires the trading people to take the right decision and its penetration is also more important. Generally, if the violation of a trend line is relatively minor and is only on an intra-day basis, and prices close back above the trend line, then it may be best to stay with the trend without paying any attention to the violation or breaking of the line.

Close beyond the trend line is more significant than just an intra-day penetration. A variety of time and price filters are used to isolate valid penetrations and estimate bad signals or *whipsaws*. One example of the price filter is the three per cent penetration criteria, which is used mainly for breaking of longer-term trend lines. It requires the trend line to be broken, on a closing basis, at three per cent. For shorter-term trading, however, a one per cent criterion would serve better. If the filter is too small, it will not be very useful in reducing the impact of *whipsaws*. If it is too big, then much of the initial move will be missed before a valid signal is given. The trader must determine what type of filter is best suited to the degree of trend being followed.

A time filter is an alternative to a price filter. The two-day rule is a very common time filter. Prices must close beyond the trend line for two successive days to have a valid breaking of the trend line. To break important support and resistance levels, the three per cent rule and two-day rule are also applicable.

Earlier, during the discussion of support and resistance levels it was mentioned that support and resistance levels become opposite once violated. This principle holds true of trend lines also. Usually, on subsequent rallies, a support line will function as a resistance barrier after it has broken on the down-side (see Chart 4.14). Similarly, a down trend line will become a support line once it has been broken on the upside. Price objective can also be

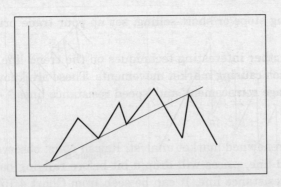

Chart 4.14 Reversal of Role

determined by using the trend lines. If a trend line is violated or broken, prices will move a distance beyond the trend line equal to the vertical distance that prices achieved on the other side of the line, prior to trend reversal. With an example it can be said that if in the prior uptrend, prices moved Rs. 50 above the up trend line when measured vertically, then prices would be expected to drop by that same Rs. 50 below the trend line after it is broken.

The Importance of Support and Resistance

In brief, it can be said that support and resistance analysis is an important part of trends because it can be used to make trading decisions and identify when a trend is reversing. For example, if a trader identifies an important level of resistance that has been tested several times but never broken, he or she may decide to take profits as the security moves toward this point because it is unlikely that it will move past this level.

Support and resistance levels both test and confirm trends and need to be monitored by anyone who uses technical analysis. As long as the price of the share remains between these levels of support and resistance, the trend is likely to continue. It is important to note, however, that a break beyond a level of support or resistance does not always have to be a reversal. For example, if a price moved above the resistance levels of an upward trending channel the trend has accelerated, not reversed. This means that the price appreciation is expected to be faster than it was in the channel.

Being aware of these important support and resistance points should affect the way that you trade a stock. Traders should avoid placing orders at these major points, as the area around them is usually marked by a lot of volatility. If you feel confident about making a trade near a support or resistance level, it is important that you follow this simple rule: do not place orders directly at the support or resistance level. This is because in many cases, the price never actually reaches the whole number, but flirts with it instead. So if you are bullish on a stock that is moving toward an important support level, do not place the trade at the support level. Instead, place it above the support level, but within a few points. On the other hand, if you are placing stops or short selling, set up your trade price at or below the level of support.

Now let us turn to other interesting techniques on the trend line which can also be used to judge the phenomenon causing market movements. These are known as the 'fan principle,' 'channel line,' 'percentage retracement' and 'speed resistance lines.'

The Fan Principle

In a series of articles, renowned market analyst, Rajesh Nair[7] observed that sometimes after violation of an uptrend line, prices will drop a bit before rallying back to the bottom of the old trade line, now a resistance line. It can be seen from Chart 4.15 that prices rallied, but failed to penetrate line 1. Now a second trend line, line 2 can be drawn, which is also broken. After another failed rally attempt, a third line is drawn. The breaking of that third trend line is usually an indication that the prices are headed lower.

It may be noticed that the trend line 1 and trend line 2, that is the broken support lines became resistance lines. In the case of the 'fan principle' at a bottom, the breaking of the third trend line signals the upside trend reversal. The earlier broken resistance lines become support levels. The term 'fan principle' is derived from the appearance of the lines that gradually flatten out, resembling a fan.

During the first half of the 20th century, the legendary stock and commodity trader, William D. Gann, favored a technique of where up trend lines tend to approximate an average slope of about 45 degrees. This type of line reflects a situation where prices are ascending or descending at such a rate that price and time are in perfect balance. A too steep trend line indicates that prices are ascending too rapidly and this situation will not be sustained. The breaking of that steep trend line would be to revert to a more sustainable slope closer to the 45 degree line. If the trend line is too flat, it indicates that the uptrend is too weak and no action is advisable in such a situation.

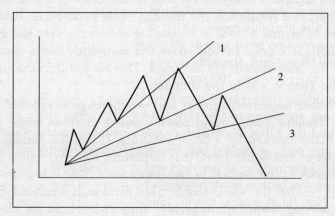

| **Chart 4.15** | Trend Lines of Fan Principle |

[7]Rajesh Nair, A series of articles on Technical Analysis published every week during March 25 to July 16, 2001 in *Business Standard*

Channel Lines

A channel, or channel lines, is the addition of two parallel trend lines that act as strong areas of support and resistance. The upper trend line connects a series of highs, while the lower trend line connects a series of lows. A channel can slope upward, downward or sideways but, regardless of the direction, the interpretation remains the same. Traders will expect a given security to trade between the two levels of support and resistance until it breaks beyond one of the levels, in which case traders can expect a sharp move in the direction of the break. Along with clearly displaying the trend, channels are mainly used to illustrate important areas of support and resistance.

Part B of Chart 4.12 illustrates a descending channel on a stock chart; the upper trend line has been placed on the highs and the lower trend line is on the lows. The price has bounced off of these lines several times, and has remained range-bound for several months. As long as the price does not fall below the lower line or move beyond the upper resistance, the range-bound downtrend is expected to continue. Once the break out occurs from an existing price channel, prices usually travel a distance equal to the width of the channel. The analyst, therefore, has to simply measure the width of the channel and then project that amount from the point at which either trend line is broken.

Percentage Retracement

From our earlier illustrations, it can be noticed that in all uptrends and downtrends, prices retrace a portion of the previous trend before resuming the move in the original direction. The best known application of the phenomenon is the 50 per cent retracement. For example, in an uptrend, a stock moves from Rs. 100 to Rs. 200. The subsequent reaction is expected to retrace 50 per cent of the prior move to the Rs. 150 level. Besides the 50 per cent retracement, which is more or less tentative, there are the minimum and maximum percentage parameters, also widely recognized as the 1/3rd and the 2/3rd retracements.

What this means is that, in a correction of a strong trend, the market usually retraces at least a third of the previous move, which is 33 per cent, and a maximum of 66 per cent (Chart 4.16). The correction must stop at 66 per cent, if the prior trend is to be maintained. If prices move beyond 66 per cent, the odds favour a trend reversal rather than just retracement. Usually, the move, then retraces 100 per cent of the prior trend.

The three percentage retracement parameters – 50 per cent, 33 per cent, and 66 per cent, referred to here are according to the Dow Theory. However, there are other opinions also. Fibonacci ratios and the Elliot Wave Theory use percentage retracements of 38 per cent and 62 per cant. So, any serious analyst can use both approaches by combining for a minimum retracement zone 33 per cent to 38 per cent and maximum zone of 62 per cent to 66 per cent. The trend structure was broken down into eighths by W. D. Gann, namely 1/8, 2/8, 3/8, 4/8, 5/8, 6/8, 7/8, and 8/8. But, he also gave special importance to 3/8 (38 per cent), 4/8 (50 per cent), and 5/8 (62 per cent) retracement numbers and also opined that it was important to divide the trend into thirds, that is 1/3 (33 per cent) and 2/3 (66 per cent). Now before discussing speed resistance lines, let us discuss some basics of the Elliot Wave Theory.

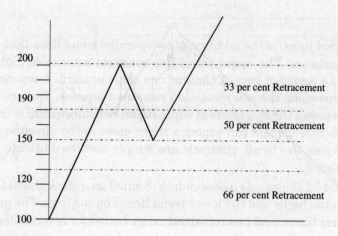

200 — ....

190 —   33 per cent Retracement

150 —   50 per cent Retracement

120 —

100 —   66 per cent Retracement

Chart 4.16 Retracement Levels

Elliot Wave Theory

Elliot Wave Theory is the most controversial as well as the most popular technical analysis tool available so far. Besides stock market moves, this wave theory provides a complete framework for any in-depth repetitive phenomenon across any given timeframe.

A series of uncanny predictions made by Ralph Nelson Elliot about the great depression of 1919-1937, helped him to achieve prominence. Elliot used the mathematical basis of the Fibonacci Ratios of 0.618 and 1.61 that are evident in a Fibonacci series. Long after Elliot's death, the development of modern chaos theory suggests that there was also underlying fractal logic in some of his border interpretation. A number of followers of Elliot have since modified his methods to yield more sophisticated interpretations of the basic theory.

Let us discuss now some basic interpretations of Elliot Wave theory. Elliot observed that stock market actions occurred in waves. He believed that those waves usually come in predictable patterns of 5 up (action) followed by 3 down (reaction). Occasionally the 5-wave trend will be down, followed by a 3-wave uptrend. Each wave can be decomposed into smaller waves. Each wave in a pattern – 1, 2, 3, 4 and 5 should posses certain characteristics. While 1, 3 and 5 will move in the direction of the long term trend, 2 and 4 will be corrections. A five-wave advance is always followed by a three-wave correction or downtrend. The Fibonacci ratios apply in determining the relationships between the waves. Depending on the way in which the wave count is categorized, Elliot Wave Theory can make predictions about the direction, amplitude and duration of the next wave. These relationships are independent of scale and hence the Elliot Wave theory can make predictions ranging over centuries. It can also make predictions about price moves in the next minute, if sufficient detailed data are available.

We have already mentioned that the action waves are conventionally numbered 1 to 5. Similarly, reaction waves are usually labeled a, b, c. It is obvious that there is subjectivity in

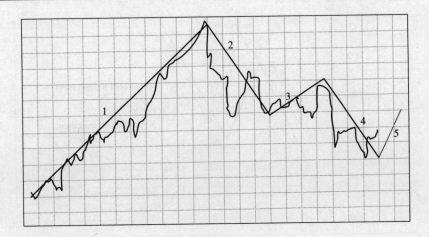

Chart 4.17   Interpretation of Elliot Wave Theory (1)

the picking of the scale and interpretation of pattern. Though there is much confusion among a number of Elliot theorists regarding interpretation of the same pattern, there is general agreement about a few things.

Inside the 5 to 3 pattern itself, some of the waves will be strong vertical moves, while others will be flat or failures as we have discussed above. That is 1, 3, and 5 may be strong uptrend when 2 and 4 will corrections. The second reaction wave 'b' will be a 'correction within correction' and this could move in the basic direction of the previous 5-wave trend.

In an analytical article, eminent market analyst Devansu Datta[8] opined that to understand the basic pattern one must look at the 'Elliot Wave Count. Projections for the next wave's duration and magnitude are made according to the Fibonacci ratios. If it is a reaction phase, the likeliest pattern is down until some Fibonacci retracement level of the previous move while in an uptrend wave the move will rise to some Fibonacci multiple. Quite often the Elliot Wave theorist will attempt to superimpose the wave pattern on a stock that he is interested in then derive likely projections. In practice, wave counts are rarely clear cut and this is where the problems arise. In Charts 4.17, 4.18 and 4.19 we have presented three possible interpretations of the movements of the SENSEX between considerable periods of time. In the first interpretation (Chart 14.17), we observed a 5th wave failure. This wave ought to have been an uptrend that drove the market up further than the 3rd wave peak. Proceeding further, with this interpretation, we are now in the 5th wave of a downtrend and could expect a three-wave corrective uptrend when this current wave 5 ends.

The next 3-wave reaction will be a weak up move that will not take the market back to its earlier peak levels although it would definitely be a bull market. According to the next or second interpretation (Chart 4.18), we are in the second 'b' wave of the 3-wave corrective after a 5-wave impulse or uptrend that also ended with a failure. In this case, we can expect another

---

[8]Devansu Datta, Wave Theory, *Business Standard*, December 10, 2001

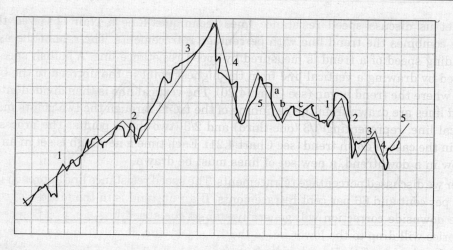

Chart 4.18   Interpretation of Elliot Wave Theory (2)

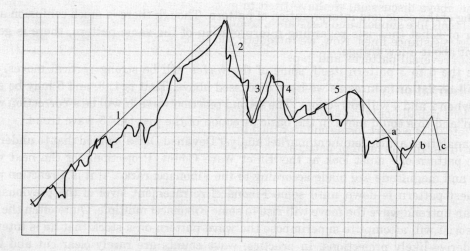

Chart 4.19   Interpretation of Elliot Wave Theory (3)

downtrend when the 'd' wave ends and the 'c' wave starts. Here the expectations would be a continuing bear market after this the temporary 'b' wave uptrend concludes.

According to the third interpretation (Chart 4.19), we are in the fourth wave of a 5-wave cycle and a strong up move should come if the 5th wave is an impulse uptrend. It is obvious that this would mean a totally different outlook from the first two interpretations. If one wishes to use Elliot Wave Theory, he should take care in studying this system, as the subjectivity of the wave count is what makes Elliot Wave Theory difficult to handle. If one uses it without proper understanding, it is possible to make errors in interpretation.

Now let us discuss speed resistance lines technique. Rajesh Nair observed that this technique combines the trend line with percentage retracements. The rate of the ascending or descending speed of a trend is measured by speed resistance line. A bullish speed line is constructed by drawing a vertical line from the highest point in the uptrend to the bottom of the chart where the trend began (see Chart 4.20). The vertical line is then divided into thirds. Two trend lines are drawn from the beginning of the trend through the two points marked on the vertical line, representing 1/3 (one-third) and 2/3 (two-third) points. The process is just reversed in the case of down trend (see Chart 4.21). Each time a new high is set in an uptrend or new low in a downtrend, a new set of lines must be drawn.

Earlier we discussed percentage retracements. The speed resistance line approach is similar to the 33 per cent and 66 per cent retracements. If an uptrend is in the process of correcting itself, the downside correction will generally stop at the speed line, i.e. at 2/3 speed line. If not, the price will drop to the lower i.e. to the 1/3 speed line. It will likely to continue all the way to the beginning of the trend, if the lower line is also broken. Once they are broken, as with all trend lines, speed lines reverse roles.

In the above discussion, we have tried to give an insight into a number of introductory technical tools like support and resistance, trend lines and channels, percentage retracements, and speed resistance lines. Now, we introduce you to be other important tools such as wedge formation, reversal patterns and gaps.

Wedge Formation

The wedges usually only reverse a minor trend and should typically take three weeks or so to complete. It is a chart formation in which price fluctuations are confined within converging straight lines. In this form of pattern, the wedges may have a rising or falling slant.

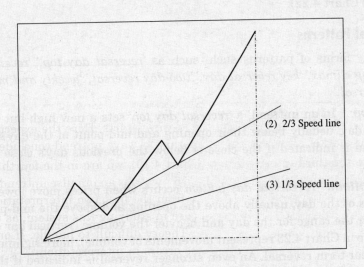

(2) 2/3 Speed line

(3) 1/3 Speed line

Chart 4.20 Bullish Speed Lines

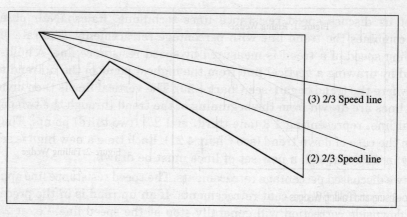

(3) 2/3 Speed line

(2) 2/3 Speed line

Chart 4.21 Bearish Speed Lines

In a *rising wedge*, both boundary lines slant up from left to right but lower line rises at a steeper angle than the upper line. After breaking the lower line boundary, prices usually decline sharply.

In the rising stage, each wave up or fresh price advance, is weaker than the last one, implying that at higher price levels, demand for investment is weakening. In a bear market, when rising wedges are found, they are considered to be more reliable (see Figure-1 of Chart 4.22).

In a *falling wedge*, both boundary lines slant down from left to right but the upper line falls at a steeper angle than the lower line. Unlike the rising wedge, once prices move out of a falling wedge, they are more apt to drift sidewise and 'saucer out' before beginning to rise (see Figure-2 of Chart 4.22).

Minor Reversal Patterns

There are many forms of patterns such. such as 'reversal day top,' 'reversal day bottom,' 'buying or selling climax,' 'key reversal day,' 'two-day reversal,' 'weekly and monthly reversals' and 'island reversal.'

Reversal day top: In an uptrend, a 'reversal day top' sets a new high but then closes near the lows of the day, usually below their opening and mid-point of the day's range. An even stronger reversal is indicated if the close is below the previous day's close (see Figure-A of Chart 4.23).

Reversal day bottom: A *reversal day bottom* occurs when prices move lower but then close near the heights of the day, usually above the opening and above the mid-point of the day's range. The wider the range for the day and heavier the volume (vertical bar diagrams shown below each figure in Chart 4.23 represent movements of volume), more significant is the signal for a possible near-term reversal. An even stronger reversal is indicated if the close is above the previous day's close (see Figure-B of Chart 4.23). The bottom reversal day is sometimes

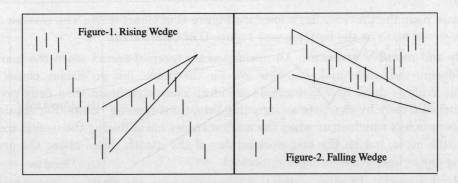

Chart 4.22   Rising and Falling Wedges

also referred to as a *selling climax*. It is to be noted that in Figures-A and B, while volume is heavier on the reversal day, also high and low exceed the range of the previous day, thus forming an *outside day*. Though outside day is a requirement for a reversal day, it does carry more significance.

Key reversal days: All one-day reversals can be considered as potential *key reversal days*, but only a few actually become *key reversal days*. Actually, most of the one-day reversals represent nothing more than temporary stoppage in the existing trend after which the trend resumes its course. The true *key reversal day* marks an important turning point, but cannot be correctly identified as such until well after the prices have moved significantly in the opposite direction of the prior trend.

Two-day reversal: A reversal which takes two days to form is known as a *two-day reversal*. In an uptrend, this is a situation where prices set a new high for a move and close near the day's high. On the following day, instead of continuing higher, prices remain unchanged and

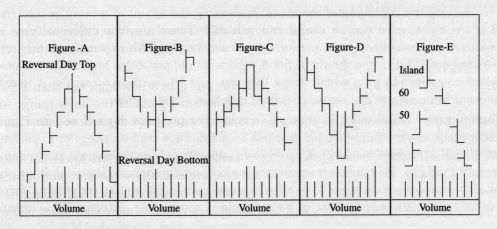

Chart 4.23   Reversal Tops and Bottoms

then close near the previous day's low (see Figure-C of Chart 4.23). The reverse or opposite picture would occur at the bottoms (see Figure-D of Chart 4.23).

Weekly and monthly reversal: An *upside weekly reversal* occurs when the market trades lower during the week, makes a new low for the move, but on Friday closes above the previous Friday's close. *Weekly reversals* are much more significant than daily reversals and are watched closely by chartists as signaling important turning points. For similar reasons, *monthly reversals* which occur when the market trades lower during the month, makes a new low for the move, but on the last working day of the month closes above the previous last working day's close, are even more important.

The island reversal: Imagine a situation where the price of a stock in a rising market closes at its high of 50 and then on the following day, opens at its low of 60, leaving a *gap* of 10 points (*gaps* are discussed later). Some days later, the market moves back down and forms another gap in approximately the same 50-60 area (see Figure-E of Chart 4.23). Thus, all the trading above 60 will appear on the chart to be isolated, like an island, from all previous and subsequent fluctuations. This is known as *island reversal*. Island reversals are extremely good indicators of a reversal in the trend, though they happen quite rarely. But when they appear, their appearance indicates that an extreme change in sentiment has occurred.

Gaps: *Gaps* represent an area on the bar chart where no trading takes place. For example, if a stock reaches a highest price of, say, 50 on Monday, but then opens at or above that price, say, 60 on Tuesday, moving straight up from the opening, it is obvious that no trading occurred in the area between 50 to 60. This no-trading zone appears on the bar chart as a hole or *gap*. So, in an up trending market, a gap is produced when the highest price of any one day is lower than the lowest price of the following day. In a downtrend, the day's highest price is below the previous day's low. Upside gaps are signs of market strength, while downside gaps are usually signs of weakness. The gaps are more commonly seen on daily bar charts. In fact, they can also appear on long-term weekly as well as monthly charts and, when they do, are usually significant.

In spotting the beginning of the move, measuring the extent of a move or confirming the end of the move, gaps can be useful and valuable. There are four different types of gaps: *Common gaps, breakaway gaps, measuring or runway gaps.* While some *gaps* are important, others are not. While some should be filled, others should not. *Gaps* have different forecasting implications depending on which types they are and where they occur. So, it is extremely important to be able to distinguish between different types of gaps.

Common gaps: These are also known as *temporary gaps, pattern gaps,* and *area gaps.* They usually occur in very thinly traded markets in a sideways trading range or price congestion area. Usually, the price moves back up or down subsequently as the market returns to the gap area to 'fill the gap.' It is the least important for forecasting purpose. However, it may be noted that *common gaps* are more apt to develop in consolidation rather than in reversal formations. In other words, the appearance of gaps within consolidation patterns (like rectangles or symmetrical triangles) is a signal that the breakout should be in the same direction as that of the preceding trend (see Figure-1 of Chart 4.24).

The breakaway gap: Usually, the *breakaway gap* occurs at the completion of an important price pattern and signals the beginning of a significant market move. In fact, the breakaway gap occurs as prices break away from an area of congestion. Typically, prices will break away from an ascending or descending triangle with a gap. This gap indicates that the change in sentiment has been strong and that the ensuing move will be powerful. Often the market does not return to fill the gap, especially if volume is heavy after the gap is formed. If the volume is thin or not significantly heavy, there is a reasonable chance that the gap will be filled before prices resume their trend (see Figure-2 of Chart 4.24). *Upside gaps* usually act as support areas on subsequent market corrections, and *downside gaps* as resistance areas on subsequent bounces.

The measuring or runaway gap: As this gap occurs in the middle or halfway point of a price trend and can be used to measure how far the price trend will move, it is called the *measuring gap*. By measuring how the trend has already travelled, from the original trend signal or beak-out, an estimate of the probable extent of the measuring move can be determined by doubling the amount already achieved. Rather than being associated with a congestion area, it is more likely to occur in the course of a rapid, straight-line advance or decline, usually at approximately the halfway point (see Figure-3 of Chart 4.24). This gap is also called a *runaway gap* because after the move has been underway for while, somewhere around the middle of the move, prices will leap forward to form a second type of gap or a series of gaps. In this situation, the market moves smoothly on a moderate volume. In an uptrend, it is a sign of market strength, in a downtrend, weakness.

The exhaustion gap: This gap signals the end of a market move. Like *measuring gaps*, *exhaustion gaps* are associated with rapid, extensive advances or declines. One may find it difficult to differentiate an *exhaustion gap* from a *measuring gap*. A clue may be found in the volume. An *exhaustion gap* is often accompanied by particularly high volume. Another clue for detecting an *exhaustion gap* is with a 'reversal day' (see Figure-4 of Chart 4.24). Near the end of an uptrend, prices leap forward in a last gasp. However, this fades quickly, and the prices turn lower. When prices close under that gap, it is a dead giveaway that the *exhaustion gap* has made its appearance. This is a classic example where the filling of a gap in an uptrend has very bearish implications.

Reversal Formation or Reversal Patterns

Earlier, we discussed some minor reversal patterns. Now we will try to explain some major reversal formations or reversal patterns. It can be said that the price pattern belongs to either a reversal or continuation pattern. Justifying its name, a reversal pattern indicates that an important reversal in trend is taking place, while, a continuation pattern suggests that the market is only pausing for a while, probably to correct a near-term overbought or oversold condition. The term 'continuation pattern' may be unfamiliar to some, but earlier we have discussed *triangles*, *wedges* as well as some other related terms; all these constitute the

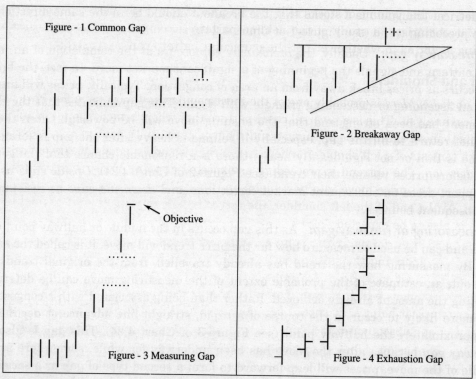

Figure - 1 Common Gap

Figure - 2 Breakaway Gap

Figure - 3 Measuring Gap

Objective

Figure - 4 Exhaustion Gap

Ref: *Timing Market*- Arnold, Rahfeldt, Weiss Research, Vision Books, New Delhi

Chart 4.24 Market Timings

study of continuation patterns. Some other continuation patterns will be discussed in later paragraphs.

In a number of write-ups it is expressed that a continuation pattern has a distinct difference from a reversal pattern (one in which the trend changes) in that the former is often very short in the time that it takes to setup, or more simply, its duration. This is very true and should make the continuation pattern much easier to see and act upon – especially for new technical analysts. What the new analyst needs to always remember is that a continuation pattern is never set in stone. It may end up being a reversal pattern, and we would not recognize this for a long time. All patterns that may initially appear to be continuation patterns may end up being reversal patterns and *vice versa*. So, extreme caution is needed in the analysis of continuation and reversal patterns.

As we have already discussed some continuation patterns earlier, here we have confined ourselves to the discussion of some important reversal patterns. The most common reversal patterns are different forms of *head and shoulders*, *double tops and bottoms*, *triple tops and bottoms, and rounding* (saucer or cup and handle and rounding bottom etc.) patterns. It is to be noted that the volume of stocks sold plays a pivotal role in all these types of price patterns. If any doubt arises, a study of the volume pattern accompanying the price data can be a deciding factor as to whether or not the particular pattern can be trusted.

Head and Shoulders

Head and shoulders is probably one of the most popular and most reliable chart patterns in technical analysis. This is a reversal chart pattern that when formed, signals that the security is likely to move against the previous trend. This pattern can be explained by Chart 4.25. This pattern consists of a left shoulder, a head and a right shoulder and is also known as *head and shoulders top*. The uptrend is proceeding as expected at point A with signs of a top. Volume expands on the price move into new highs and this is normal and here the left shoulder is formed. At the end of the left shoulder, the corrective dip to point B is on the lighter volume, which is also to be expected.

The head then forms at the point C with heavy volume on the upside and with lesser volume accompanying the subsequent reaction. At this point, in order to conform to proper form, prices must come down somewhere below the top of the left shoulder to point D, and something happens which is even more disturbing. The decline reaches below the top of the previous week at point A. It should be remembered that, a penetrated peak should function as support on subsequent corrections.

When the market rallies again to point E on usually less volume than any previous rallies, the right shoulder forms at this point. Here, the price is not able to reach the top of the previous peak at point C. The failure of the rally at point E to reach the previous peak at point C fulfils half of the requirement for a new downtrend which can be termed as a descending trend. At this point, one may notice that the trend is shifted from up to sideways. So, this situation sufficiently alerts the investors to liquidate long held positions, but not necessarily enough to justify new short sales.

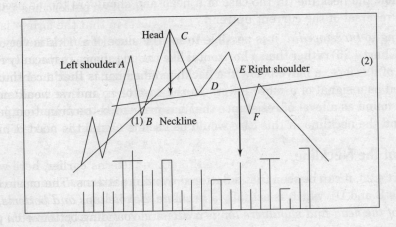

Chart 4.25   Head and Shoulders (1)

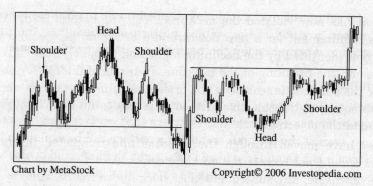

Chart by MetaStock   Copyright© 2006 Investopedia.com

On the left, head and shoulder tops are shown. Head and shoulders bottom, or inverse head and shoulders, is on the right.

| **Chart 4.26** | Head and Shoulders (2) |

In brief, it can be said that both of these head and shoulder patterns are similar in that there are four main parts: two shoulders, a head and a neckline. Also, each individual head and shoulder comprises a high and a low. For example, in the head and shoulders top image shown on the left side in Chart 4.26, the left shoulder is made up of a high followed by a low. In this pattern, the neckline is a level of support or resistance. Remember that an upward trend is a period of successive rising highs and rising lows. The head and shoulders chart pattern, therefore, illustrates a weakening in a trend by showing the deterioration in successive movements of the highs and lows.

Neckline

To determine strategic areas to place orders, a level of support or resistance found on a head and shoulders pattern is used by traders. Each peak of a regular head and shoulders pattern falls toward a support level, also known as a neckline, before it rises to create the next peak. A move below the neckline (in the case of a head and shoulders top) is used by traders as a signal of a reversal of the current uptrend.

According to *Investopedia*, it is possible to see the slope of a neckline be drawn at a slight angle (see Chart 4.25) rather than a horizontal like the one shown in the image above. However, regardless of its slope, a move below the neckline of a regular head and shoulders pattern is always used as a signal of a move lower. In the case of an inverse head and shoulders, the neckline is found as a level of resistance that has prevented the price from heading higher. A move beyond the neckline in this case would be used to signal the start of an uptrend.

Breaking of the Neckline

In the Chart 4.25, it can be seen that a flattered trendline is drawn under the last two reaction lows (points B and D), which is actually a neckline that is line (2). *The deciding factor in the resolution of the head and shoulders top is a decisive closing violation of the neckline.* (The 3 per cent penetration criterion or the two day rule can be used for added confirmation. The price movement has now violated the neckline along the bottom points B and D, and has completed the requirement for a new downtrend – descending peak and troughs. The new downtrend is now identified by the declining highs and lows at points C, D, E and F. Volume should increase on the breaking of the neckline. In terms of finding a price objective, prices travel roughly the same distance below the broken neckline as they do above it. However, it is important to note that the objective arrived at is only a minimum target. Prices will often move well beyond the objective.

Once prices have moved through the neckline and completed the head and shoulder pattern, *prices should not recross the neckline again.* At a top, once the neckline has been broken on the downside, any subsequent close back above the neckline is a serious warning that the initial breakdown was probably a bad signal, and creates what is often called, a failed head and shoulders.

Double Tops and Bottoms

This chart pattern is another well-known pattern that signals a trend reversal – it is considered to be one of the most reliable and is commonly used and recognized after the *head and shoulder*. The general characteristics of a *double top* are similar to that of *head and shoulders*. It can be seen from Chart 4.27, that the price sets a new high at point A, usually on increased volume. The next rally to point C, however, is unable to penetrate the previous peak at A on a closing basis and begins to fall back again. A potential *double top* has been set up. The ideal top has two prominent peaks at about the same price level. During the first peak, volume tends to be heavier and lighter on the second. A decisive close under the middle trough at point B on heavier volume completes the pattern and signals a reversal trend to the downside. A return move to the breakout point is not usual prior to resumption of the downtrend.

Usually these patterns are formed after a sustained trend and signal to analysts that the trend is about to reverse. The pattern is created when a price movement tests support or resistance levels twice and is unable to break through. This pattern is often used to signal

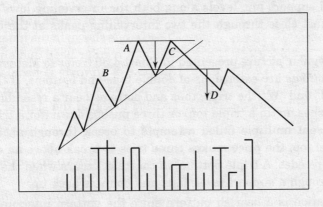

Chart 4.27   Double Tops and Bottoms (1)

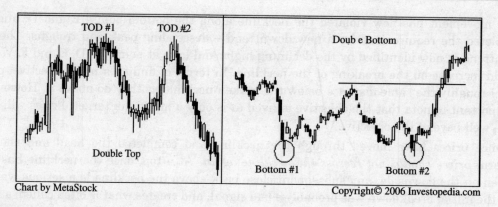

Chart 4.28 Double Tops and Bottoms (2)

intermediate and long-term trend reversals. A more common picture of double top and double bottom is reproduced in the Chart 4.28 below from *Metastock*.

In the case of the *double top* pattern in Chart 4.28, the price movement has twice tried to move above a certain price level. After two unsuccessful attempts at pushing the price higher, the trend reverses and the price heads lower. In the case of a *double bottom* (shown on the right), the price movement has tried to go lower twice, but has found support each time. After the second bounce off of the support, the security enters a new trend and heads upward.

Triple Tops and Bottoms

Most of the points covered in the treatment of *head and shoulders* are also applicable to other reversal patterns. The triple top or bottom, which occurs very rarely, is a slight variation of that pattern. The main difference is that the three peaks or troughs in the triple top or triple bottom are about the same level (see Chart 4.29). The volume tends to decline with each successive peak at the top and should increase at the breakdown point. The triple top is not complete until support line levels along both the intervening lows have been broken. Conversely, prices must close through the two intervening peaks at the bottom to complete a triple bottom.

Citing the most regular picture presented in Chart 4.30 (refer to Metastock), it can be said that *triple top* and *bottoms* are extensions of double tops and bottoms. If the double tops and bottoms resemble "M" and "W," the triple tops and bottoms bear a resemblance to the cursive "M" or "W": three pushes up (in a triple top) or three pushes down (for a triple bottom). These price patterns represent multiple failed attempts to break through an area of support or resistance. In a triple top, the price makes three tries to break above an established area of resistance, fails and recedes. A triple bottom, in contrast, occurs when the price makes three stabs at breaking through a support level, fails and bounces back up.

A triple top formation is a bearish pattern since the pattern interrupts an uptrend and results in a trend change to the downside. Its formation is as follows:

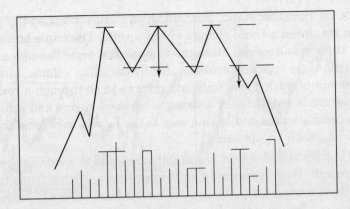

Chart 4.29   Triple Tops and Bottoms (1)

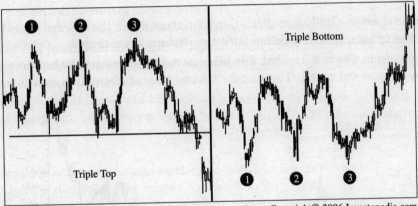

Triple Bottom

Triple Top

Chart by MetaStock

Copyright© 2006 Investopedia.com

Chart 4.30   Triple Tops and Bottoms (2)

❖ Prices move higher and higher and eventually hit a level of resistance, falling back to an area of support.

❖ Price tries again to test the resistance levels, fails and returns towards the support level.

❖ Price tries once more, unsuccessfully, to break through resistance, falls back and through the support level.

This price action represents a duel between buyers and sellers; the buyers try to lift prices higher, while the sellers try to push prices lower. Each test of resistance is typically accompanied by decreasing volume, until the price falls through the support level with increased participation and corresponding volume. When three attempts to break through an established level of resistance have failed, the buyers generally become exhausted, the sellers take over and price falls, resulting in a trend change.

Triple bottoms, on the other hand, are bullish in nature because the pattern interrupts a downtrend, and results in a trend change to the upside. The triple bottom price pattern is characterized by three unsuccessful attempts to push the price through an area of support. Each successive attempt is typically accompanied by declining volume, until the price finally makes its last attempt to push down, fails and returns to go through a resistance level. Like triple tops, this pattern is indicative of a struggle between buyers and sellers. In this case, it is the sellers who become exhausted, giving way to the buyers to reverse the prevailing trend and become victorious with an uptrend.

A triple top or bottom signifies that an established trend is weakening, and that the other side is gaining strength. Both represent a shift in pressure. With a triple top, there is a shift from buyers to sellers; a triple bottom indicates a shift from sellers to buyers. These patterns provide a visual representation of the changing of the guard, so to speak, when power switches hands.

Cup and Handle

A cup and handle chart is a bullish continuation pattern in which the upward trend has paused but will continue in an upward direction once the pattern is confirmed.

It can be seen from Chart 4.31, that this price pattern forms what looks like a cup, which is preceded by an upward trend. The handle follows the cup formation and is formed by a

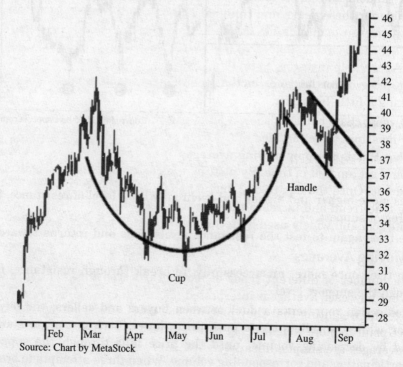

Source: Chart by MetaStock

Chart 4.31 Cup and Handle

generally downward/sideways movement in the security's price. Once the price movement pushes above the resistance lines formed in the handle, the upward trend can continue. There is a wide ranging time frame for this type of pattern, with the span ranging from several months to more than a year.

Rounding Bottom

A rounding bottom, also referred to as a saucer bottom, is a long-term reversal pattern that signals a shift from a downward trend to an upward trend. This pattern is traditionally thought to last anywhere from several months to several years. A rounding bottom chart pattern looks similar to a cup and handle pattern but without the handle. The long-term nature of this pattern and the lack of a confirmation trigger, such as the handle in the cup and handle, make it a difficult pattern to trade.

One should now be able to recognize each chart pattern as well as the signal it can form for analysts. We will now move on to other technical techniques and examine how they are used by technical traders to gauge price movements.

MOVING AVERAGES

We have already discussed that stock prices do not follow a well defined track. On the contrary, they exhibit random movement and produce numerous peaks and troughs. A host of factors are responsible for these peaks and troughs. These factors may be good fundamentals, stock specific news or even manipulation by market players. So, more often general investors feel confused under these circumstances. In this situation one mathematical tool known as Moving Average (MA) can help investors to understand the market movements better. It can be used to minimize price distortion and fluctuations and bring out a board trend that can make decision taking a little bit easier.

Actually, most chart patterns show a lot of variation in price movement. This can make it difficult for investors to get an idea of a security's overall trend. One simple method traders use to combat this is to apply moving averages. A moving average is the average price of a security over a set amount of time. By plotting a security's average price, the price movement is smoothed out. Once the day-to-day fluctuations are removed, investors are better able to identify the true trend and increase the probability that it will work in their favor. It is the most favorite tool and widely used by technical analysts across the world.

Types of Moving Averages

There are a number of different types of moving averages that vary in the way they are calculated, but how each average is interpreted remains the same. The calculations only differ in regards to the weighting that they place on the price data, shifting from equal weighting of each price point to more weight being placed on recent data. The three most common types of moving averages are simple, linear weighted and exponential.

Simple Moving Average (SMA): This is the most common method used to calculate the moving average of prices. It simply takes the sum of all of the past closing prices over the time period and divides the result by the number of prices used in the calculation. For example, in a 5-day moving average, the last 5 closing prices are added together and then divided by 5 (the simple arithmetic mean). As you can see from Table 4.5, an investor is able to make the average less responsive to changing prices by increasing the number of periods used in the calculation. Increasing the number of time periods in the calculation is one of the best ways to gauge the strength of the long-term trend and the likelihood that it will reverse. A case of SMA is illustrated in Chart 4.32

Many researchers are doubtful regarding the usefulness of this type of average which is limited because each point in the data series has the same impact on the result regardless of where it occurs in the sequence. They also argue that the most recent data are more important and, therefore, they should have a higher weighting. This type of debate has been one of the main factors leading to the invention of other forms of moving averages, like weighted moving average or linear weighted moving average.

Linear weighted average: Weighted moving average is a variation of the simple moving average. This moving average indicator is the least common out of the three and is used to address the problem of equal weighting. It can be seen from Table 4.6 and Chart 4.33 that the linear weighted moving average is calculated by taking the sum of all the closing prices over a certain time period and multiplying them by the position of the data point and then dividing by the sum of the number of periods. For example, in a five-day linear weighted average,

Table 4.5   Calculation of 5-Days Simple Moving Average of a Selected Company

Date	Closing Price	5-days Total	Col.3/5=
(1)	(in Rs.0.00) (2)	(3)	(4)
1-July-2011	25.50		
4-July-2011	30.60		
↓5-July-2011	32.95		
6-July-2011	33.70		
7-July-2011	32.10	154.85	30.97
8-July-2011	35.50	164.85	32.97
11-July-2011	34.80	169.05	33.81
12-July-2011	36.80	172.90	34.58
13-July-2011	37.75	176.95	35.39
14-July-2011	35.95	180.80	36.16
15-July-2011	34.80	180.10	36.02
18-July-2011	33.95	179.25	35.85

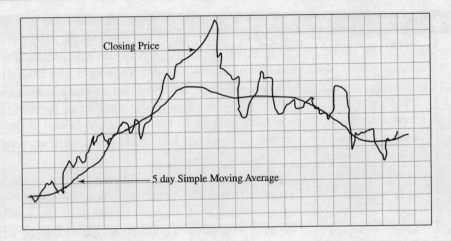

Closing Price

5 day Simple Moving Average

Chart 4.32   Five Day Simple Moving Average

today's closing price is multiplied by five; yesterday's by four and so on until the first day in the period range is reached. These numbers are then added together and divided by the sum of the multipliers. In our example the total weights (multipliers) is (5+4+3+2+1=15).

Exponential Moving Average (EMA): According to *investopedia.com*, this moving average calculation uses a smoothing factor to place a higher weight on recent data points and is regarded as much more efficient than the linear weighted average. Having an understanding of the calculation is not generally required for most traders because most charting packages do the calculation for you. The most important thing to remember about the exponential moving average is that it is more responsive to new information relative to the simple moving average. This responsiveness is one of the key factors why this is the moving average of choice among many technical traders. A 15-period EMA rises and falls faster than a 15-period SMA. This slight difference does not seem like much, but it is an important factor to be aware of since it can affect returns.

Below we reproduce some of the observations done by *investopedia.com* for further clarification of the readers (for this we thankfully acknowledge our indebtness to *Investopedia*).

Major Uses of Moving Averages

Moving averages are used to identify current trends and trend reversals as well as to set up support and resistance levels. Moving averages can be used to quickly identify whether a security is moving in an uptrend or a downtrend depending on the direction of the moving average. As can be seen from Chart 4.34, when a moving average is heading upward and the price is above it, the security is in an uptrend. Conversely, a downward sloping moving average with the price below can be used to signal a downtrend.

Another method of determining momentum is to look at the order of a pair of moving averages. When a short-term average is above a longer-term average, the trend is up. On the

Table 4.6 Calculation of 5-Days Weighted Moving Average of a Selected Company

Date	Closing price (Rs.0.00)	5 X Col.(2)	4 X Price of one day ago in Col.(2)	3 X Price of one day ago in Col.(2)	2 X Price of one day ago in Col.(2)	1 X Price of one day ago in Col.(2)	Total of col.(3) to (7)	Weighted Moving. Avg. Col.(8)/5
'(1)	'(2)	'(3)	'(4)	'(5)	'(6)	'(7)	'(8)	
1-July-2011	25.50							
4-July-2011	30.60							
5-July-2011	32.95							
6-July-2011	33.70							
7-July-2011	32.10	160.50	134.80	98.85	61.20	25.50	480.85	32.06
8-July-2011	35.50	177.50	128.40	101.10	65.90	30.60	503.50	33.57
11-July-2011	34.80	174.00	142.00	96.30	67.40	32.95	512.65	34.18
12-July-2011	36.80	184.00	139.20	106.50	64.20	33.70	527.60	35.17
13-July-2011	37.75	188.75	147.20	104.40	71.00	32.10	543.45	36.23
14-July-2011	35.95	179.75	151.00	110.40	69.60	35.50	546.25	36.42
15-July-2011	34.80	174.00	143.80	113.25	73.60	34.80	539.45	35.96
18-July-2011	33.95	169.75	139.20	107.85	75.50	36.80	529.10	35.27

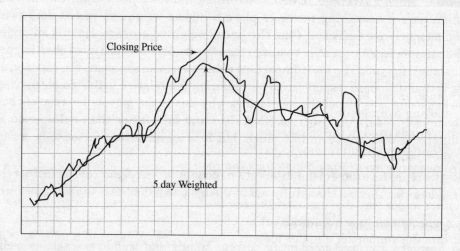

Chart 4.33 Five Day Weighted Moving Average

other hand, a long-term average above a shorter-term average signals a downward movement in the trend.

Moving average trend reversals are formed in two main ways: when the price moves through a moving average and when it moves through moving average crossovers. The first common signal is when the price moves through an important moving average. For example,

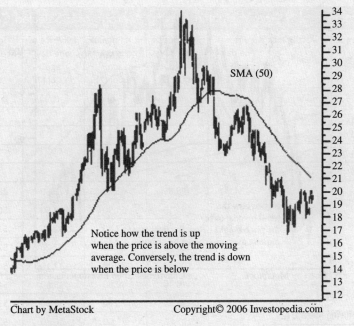

Notice how the trend is up
when the price is above the moving
average. Conversely, the trend is down
when the price is below

SMA (50)

Chart by MetaStock   Copyright© 2006 Investopedia.com

Chart 4.34 | Simple Moving Average (1)

when the price of a security that was in an uptrend falls below a 50-period moving average, as in Chart 4.35, it is a sign that the uptrend may be reversing.

The other signal of a trend reversal is when one moving average crosses through another. For example, as can be seen from Chart 4.36, if the 15-day moving average crosses above the 50-day moving average, it is a positive sign that the price will start to increase.

If the periods used in the calculation are relatively short, for example 15 and 35, this could signal a short-term trend reversal. On the other hand, when two averages with relatively long time frames cross over (50 and 200, for example), this is used to suggest a long-term shift in trend.

Another major way moving averages are used is to identify support and resistance levels. It is not uncommon to see a stock that has been falling stop its decline and reverse direction once it hits the support of a major moving average. A move through a major moving average is often used as a signal by technical traders that the trend is reversing. For example, if the price breaks through the 200-day moving average in a downward direction, it is a signal that the uptrend is reversing.

Moving averages are a powerful tool for analyzing the trend in a security. They provide useful support and resistance points and are very easy to use. The most common time frames that are used when creating moving averages are the 200-day, 100-day, 50-day, 20-day and 10-day. The 200-day average is thought to be a good measure of a trading year, a 100-day

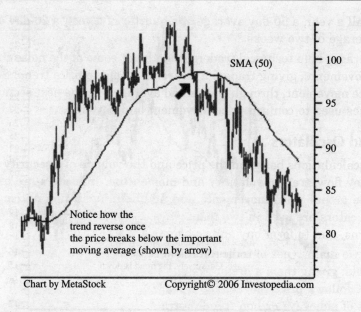

Notice how the
trend reverse once
the price breaks below the important
moving average (shown by arrow)

SMA (50)

Chart by MetaStock   Copyright© 2006 Investopedia.com

Chart 4.35   Simple Moving Average (2)

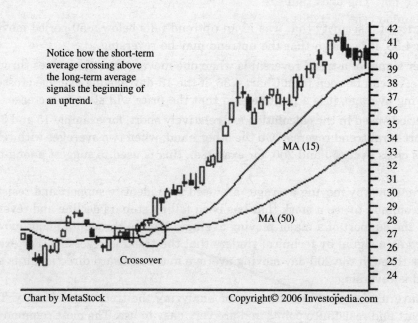

Notice how the short-term
average crossing above
the long-term average
signals the beginning of
an uptrend.

MA (15)

MA (50)

Crossover

Chart by MetaStock   Copyright© 2006 Investopedia.com

Chart 4.36   Short Term Upward Moving Average

average of a half a year, a 50-day average of a quarter of a year, a 20-day average of a month and 10-day average of two weeks.

Moving averages help technical traders smooth out some of the noise that is found in day-to-day price movements, giving traders a clearer view of the price trend. So far we have been focused on price movement, through charts and averages. In the next section, we look at some other techniques used to confirm price movement and patterns.

Indicators and Oscillators

Indicators are calculations based on the price and the volume of a security that measure such things as money flow, trends, volatility and momentum. Indicators are used as a secondary measure to the actual price movements and add additional information to the analysis of securities. Indicators are used in two main ways: to confirm price movement and the quality of chart patterns, and to form buy and sell signals.

There are two main types of indicators: leading and lagging. A leading indicator precedes price movements, giving them a predictive quality, while a lagging indicator is a confirmation tool because it follows price movement. A leading indicator is thought to be the strongest during periods of sideways or non-trending trading ranges, while the lagging indicators are still useful during trending periods.

There are also two types of indicator constructions: those that fall in a bounded range and those that do not. The ones that are bound within a range are called oscillators - these are the most common type of indicators. Oscillator indicators have a range, for example between zero and 100, and signal periods where the security is overbought (near 100) or oversold (near

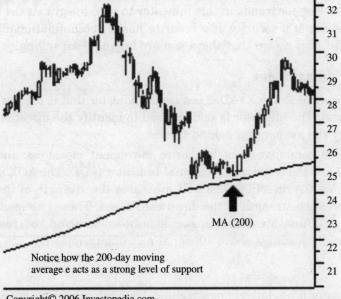

Notice how the 200-day moving average e acts as a strong level of support

MA (200)

Copyright© 2006 Investopedia.com

Chart 4.37   Moving Average Showing Strong Level of Support

zero). Non-bounded indicators still form buy and sell signals along with displaying strength or weakness, but they vary in the way they do this.

The two main ways that indicators are used to form buy and sell signals in technical analysis is through crossovers and divergence. Crossovers are the most popular and are reflected when either the price moves through the moving average, or when two different moving averages cross over each other. The second way indicators are used is through divergence, which happens when the direction of the price trend and the direction of the indicator trend are moving in the opposite direction. This signals to indicator users that the direction of the price trend is weakening.

Indicators that are used in technical analysis provide an extremely useful source of additional information. These indicators help identify momentum, trends, volatility and various other aspects in a security to aid in the technical analysis of trends. It is important to note that while some traders use a single indicator solely for buy and sell signals, they are best used in conjunction with price movement, chart patterns and other indicators.

Accumulation/Distribution Line

The accumulation/distribution line is one of the more popular volume indicators that measures money flows in a security. This indicator attempts to measure the ratio of buying to selling by comparing the price movement of a period to the volume of that period.
Calculated:

$$Acc/Dist = ((Close - Low) - (High - Close))/(High - Low) * Period's Volume$$

This is a non-bounded indicator that simply keeps a running sum over the period of the security. Traders look for trends in this indicator to gain insight on the amount of purchasing compared to selling of a security. If a security has an accumulation/distribution line that is trending upward, it is a sign that there is more buying than selling.

Average Directional Index

The Average Directional indeX (ADX) is a trend indicator that is used to measure the strength of a current trend. The indicator is seldom used to identify the direction of the current trend, but can identify the momentum behind trends.

The ADX is a combination of two price movement measures: the positive Directional Indicator (+DI) and the negative Directional Indicator (–DI). The ADX measures the strength of a trend but not the direction. The +DI measures the strength of the upward trend while the –DI measures the strength of the downward trend. These two measures are also plotted along with the ADX line. Measured on a scale between zero and 100, readings below 20 signal a weak trend while readings above 40 signal a strong trend.

Aroon

The Aroon indicator is a relatively new technical indicator that was created in 1995. The Aroon is a trending indicator used to measure whether a security is in an uptrend or downtrend and the magnitude of that trend. The indicator is also used to predict when a new trend is beginning.

The indicator comprises two lines, an "Aroon up" line (black line) and an "Aroon down" line (dotted line). The Aroon up line measures the amount of time it has been since the highest price during the time period. The Aroon down line, on the other hand, measures the amount of time since the lowest price during the time period. The number of periods that are used in the calculation is dependent on the time frame that the user wants to analyze.

Aroon Oscillator

An expansion of the Aroon is the oscillator, which simply plots the difference between the Aroon up and down lines by subtracting the two lines. This line is then plotted between a range of −100 and 100. The centerline at zero in the oscillator is considered to be a major signal line determining the trend. The higher the value of the oscillator from the centerline point, the more upward strength there is in the security; the lower the oscillator's value is from the centerline, the more downward pressure. A trend reversal is signaled when the oscillator crosses through the centerline. For example, when the oscillator goes from positive to negative, a downward trend is confirmed. Divergence is also used in the oscillator to predict trend reversals. A reversal warning is formed when the oscillator and the price trend are moving in an opposite direction.

The Aroon lines and Aroon oscillators are fairly simple concepts to understand but yield powerful information about trends. This is another great indicator to add to any technical trader's arsenal.

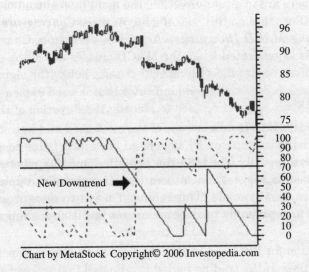

New Downtrend →

Chart by MetaStock Copyright© 2006 Investopedia.com

Chart 4.38   Aroon Up and Aroon Down Lines

Moving Average Convergence

The Moving Average Convergence Divergence (MACD) is one of the most well known and used indicators in technical analysis. This indicator is comprised of two exponential moving averages, which help to measure momentum in the security. The MACD is simply the difference between these two moving averages plotted against a centerline. The centerline is the point at which the two moving averages are equal. Along with the MACD and the centerline, an exponential moving average of the MACD itself is plotted on the chart. The idea behind this momentum indicator is to measure short-term momentum compared to longer term momentum to help signal the current direction of momentum.

MACD = shorter term moving average - longer term moving average

When the MACD is positive, it signals that the shorter term moving average is above the longer term moving average and suggests upward momentum. The opposite holds true when the MACD is negative – this signals that the shorter term is below the longer and suggests downward momentum. When the MACD line crosses over the centerline, it signals a crossing in the moving averages. The most common moving average values used in the calculation are the 26-day and 12-day exponential moving averages. The signal line is commonly created by using a nine-day exponential moving average of the MACD values. These values can be adjusted to meet the needs of the technician and the security. For more volatile securities, shorter term averages are used while less volatile securities should have longer averages.

Another aspect to the MACD indicator that is often found on charts is the MACD histogram. The histogram is plotted on the centerline and represented by bars. Each bar is the difference between the MACD and the signal line or, in most cases, the nine-day exponential moving average. The higher the bars are in either direction, the more momentum behind the direction in which the bars point. (For more on this, see *Moving Average Convergence Divergence - Part 1 and Part 2*, and *Trading MACD Divergence*). As can be seen from Chart 4.39, one of the most common buy signals is generated when the MACD crosses above the signal line (dotted line), while sell signals often occur when the MACD crosses below the signal.

Relative Strength Index

The Relative Strength Index (RSI) is another one of the most used and well-known momentum indicators in technical analysis proposed by Robert A. Levy. RSI helps to signal overbought and oversold conditions in a security. The indicator is plotted in a range between zero and 100. A reading above 70 is used to suggest that a security is overbought, while a reading below 30 is used to suggest that it is oversold. This indicator helps traders to identify whether a security's price has been unreasonably pushed to current levels and whether a reversal may be on the way.

The standard calculation for RSI uses 14 trading days as the basis, which can be adjusted to meet the needs of the user. If the trading period is adjusted to use fewer days, the RSI will be more volatile and will be used for shorter term trades.

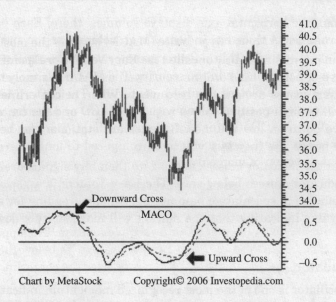

Chart by MetaStock   Copyright© 2006 Investopedia.com

Chart 4.39   Convergence and Divergence Lines

Relative Strength (RS) = Average of × days up − closings/Average of × days down − closing

Relative Strength Index (RSI) = 100-100/1+RS

On-Balance Volume

The On-Balance Volume (OBV) indicator is a well-known technical indicator that reflects movements in volume. It is also one of the simplest volume indicators to compute and understand.

The OBV is calculated by taking the total volume for the trading period and assigning it a positive or negative value depending on whether the price is up or down during the trading period. When price is up during the trading period, the volume is assigned a positive value, while a negative value is assigned when the price is down for the period. The positive or negative volume total for the period is then added to a total that is accumulated from the start of the measure. It is important to focus on the trend in the OBV – this is more important than the actual value of the OBV measure. This measure expands on the basic volume measure by combining volume and price movement.

Many technical analysts use OBV as a useful if crude indicator of volumes following into or out of a stock. This indicator simply assumes that a price rise is indicative of rising demand that accompanies price rises. If the prices fall, volumes are subtracted. The direction of the line is supposed to indicate rising or falling demand. Some other volume indicators can be useful even to other than expert general investors. One of the couple of interesting indicators designed by Richard Arms is Equivolume which requires a special charting option. Here the volumes are incorporated into the price bar graph. While the vertical axis is meant to display high-low as normal, the horizontal axis displays volumes, there. Each bar's thickness varies according to the volumes. A thick bar indicates high volumes at the specific price range.

There is also an interesting indicator called the Easy Volume or Ease of Movement indicator, which is indicative of both critical order size as well as the likely movement of a stock. This is an oscillator that moves around the zero mark. When prices can be moved up on light volumes there will be high positive values registered. Low or negative values are registered when prices move down on low volumes. If prices are stationary or heavy volumes will be required to move prices, the indicator will be zero.

Actually, when the indicator crosses above zero then buy signals are generated and a sell is given when indicator crosses below zero. The Easy Volume is especially useful for a bear who is about to indulge in speculative hammering. An ideal reading for such a bear would be a high negative value indicating that the market will move sharply downwards if a big sell order is placed.

Stochastic Oscillator

The stochastic oscillator is one of the most recognized momentum indicators used in technical analysis. The idea behind this indicator is that in an uptrend, the price should be closing near the highs of the trading range, signaling upward momentum in the security. In downtrends, the price should be closing near the lows of the trading range, signaling downward momentum.

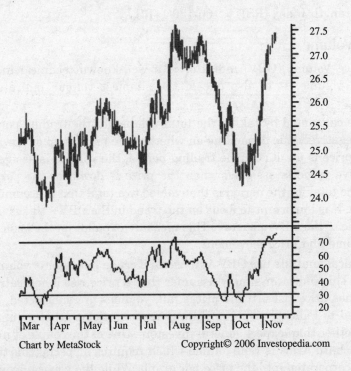

Chart by MetaStock   Copyright© 2006 Investopedia.com

Chart 4.40 Relative Strength Index Line

The stochastic oscillator is plotted within a range of zero and 100 and signals overbought conditions above 80 and oversold conditions below 20. The stochastic oscillator contains two lines. The first line is the %K, which is essentially the raw measure used to formulate the idea of momentum behind the oscillator. The second line is the %D, which is simply a moving average of the %K. The %D line is considered to be the more important of the two lines as it is seen to produce better signals. The stochastic oscillator generally uses the past 14 trading periods in its calculation but can be adjusted to meet the needs of the user.

In the next chapter we will discuss some legal aspects of stock trading, which are equally important for the readers as well as traders and general investors.

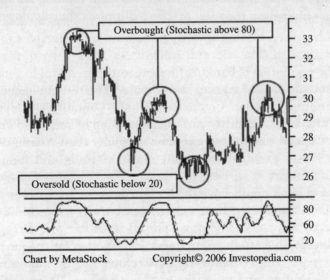

Chart by MetaStock   Copyright© 2006 Investopedia.com

Chart 4.41   Stochastic Oscillator Line

Role of Different Financial Institutions in the Capital Market

5

COMMITTEES ON BANKING REGULATIONS

For the purpose of restoring discipline among industrial borrowers, the Reserve Bank of India (RBI) has been issuing several guidelines and directives to the banking sector from time to time. Several committees have been formed in India dealing with the regulation of banking finance, working capital in general and the money market and capital market in particular. The recommendations of the Dehejia Committee, Tandon Committee, Chore Committee, Marathe Committee and Chakrobarty Committee are the foundation of such guidelines. The National Credit Council constituted a committee under the Chairmanship of V.T. Dehejia in 1968 to examine the credit needs of trade and industry and suggest ways and means of curbing this factor. The committee observed that the requirement of bank credit for industry was growing at a faster pace than that of the industrial output, which was the reason why such credit was diverted for position of fixed assets and other purposes. In the year 1974, the Reserve Bank of India set up a study group under P.L. Tandon for the purpose of regulating bank credit. The recommendations related to the quantum of bank finance, style of lending and reporting system there on. To review the performance of regional rural banks, the RBI constituted a committee under the Chairmanship of Prof M.L. Dantwala in June, 1977, which submitted its report in February, 1978. The committee opined that by adjusting their organization and functions, regional rural bank will be a very useful component in the rural credit structure. The Reserve Bank of India constituted another working group headed by K.B. Chore in 1979. The committee made numerous recommendations relating to cash credit; loans and bills. The Reserve Bank of India appointed another committee in the year 1982 under the chairmanship of Marathe to review the Credit Authorization Scheme (CAS). The committee recommended that the commercial banks be given the discretion to deploy credit in the CAS with the fulfillment of certain requirements without taking prior approval from the RBI. In the year 1985, the Reserve Bank of India appointed a high-power committee under the chairmanship of Sukhamoy Chakaraborty to review the working of the monetary system of India. The committee made the following recommendations regarding the working capital finance by the bank: (i) inclusion of penalty clause for delayed payment; (ii) division of total credit limit into three parts viz., (a) Cash Credit I to cover supplies to government with minimum lending rate, (b) Cash Credit II to cover special circumstances with a maximum prevailing lending rate of the bank and (c) normal working capital limit for the loan portion rate between minimum and maximum bill finance, at 2 per cent below the normal rate and for the cash credit portion the maximum prevailing lending rate of the bank.

The Government of India had appointed a committee under the headship of Shri M. Narasimham in the year 1991 to examine the structure, organization, functions and procedures of the financial system prevailing in the changing economic scenario of India. The committee submitted its report on 16th November, 1991. The salient points are: (i) substantial and accelerated liberalization of the Indian capital market; (ii) SEBI should formulate guidelines to protect investors; (iii) SEBI should function as a market regulator; (iv) to improve the depth of the market efforts should be taken to introduce new type types of equities and innovative debt instrument. As per the recommendations of the Narasimham Committee, the Department of Supervision (DOS) was created on 22nd November, 1993 to supervise the RBI's functions. Apart from that the Board for Financial Supervision (BFS) was set up on 16th November, 1994 to supervise the banking and non-banking financial institution in the post securities scam regime. Needless to say, in spite of DOS and BFS, the RBI is unable to control massive frauds and irregularities prevailing in the banking sector of India. The Narasimham Committee II on Banking was set up in 1998 to examine the second generation reforms in three interrelated areas: measures should be taken to (i) strengthen the foundation of the banking system; (ii) streamline the procedure, upgrade the technology and human resource development; (iii) introduce structural changes in the system, (iv) cover different aspects of banking policy and legislative dimensions, (v) set up a tribunal to expedite the recovery of Non-Performing Assets (NPA) and substantially adjust the Statutory Liquidity Ratio (SLR) and Cash Reserve Ratio (CRR) as a part of financial sector reform.

In the post liberalization period of 1991 and with the rules of the World Trade Organization (WTO), the reform of the insurance sector was the need of the hour. For this a committee was formed under the chairmanship of the former governor of the Reserve Bank of India, Shri R.N. Malhotra to consider the possibility of reforms in the insurance sector, which submitted its report in 1994. By following the recommendations of the Malhotra Committee, the Insurance Regulatory and Development Authority (IRDA) was set up on 19th April, 1999 by the Government of India under the control of the Ministry of Finance. Later on, the Insurance Regulatory and Development Authority (IRDA) Act was enacted in 1999 and the IRDA was set up on 19th April, 2000. After that many private players apart from LIC, GIC and its subsidiaries entered the Indian insurance industry, such as Tata AIG Life Insurance, ICICI Prudential Life Insurance, Max New York Life Insurance etc.

The term bank comes from the Italian word *'banca',* which means bench. At that time traders used to offer loans sitting on a bench in Venice, Italy. As a result the first bank came into existence in Italy with the formation of the Bank of Venice in the year 1157. As in other countries, an effort was made in India to establish a central bank in the middle of the 17th century. (Some central banks in other countries are: the Federal Bank of America (1913), European Central Bank (ECB), Bank of Japan, Bank of England (1694) – but the entire stock was acquired by the State by the Bank of England Act, (1946), Swedish National Bank etc.)

Before the Battle of Plassey (23rd June, 1757), Jagat Seth was the Banker of Bengal. In 1773 the then Governor of Bengal Warren Hastings made a recommendation to form the *General Bank of Bengal and Bihar*. By forming the Bank of Bengal in 1807 the organized banking system started its journey in India. In 1940 the Bank of Bombay and in 1943 the Bank of Madras were set up. All the three banks were known as Presidency banks and were partly financed by the East India Company. In 1881 the Oudh Commercial Bank came into existence as the first purely Indian bank followed by the Punjab National Bank in 1894, People's Bank in 1901 and so on and so forth. In 1905, the *Swadeshi* movement got momentum by declaration of *Bango –bhango*. This is one of the reasons why so many banks were established; during 1913 to 1948 nearly 1,100 banks failed and security of investors became a priority of the newly born independent country. In 1913, the Chamberlain Commission also highlighted the necessity of forming a central bank in India. In 1921, the Imperial Bank of India was set up by amalgamating the Presidency Bank of Bengal, the Bank of Bombay and the Bank of Madras. In 1926, the Hilton Young Commission (also known as the Royal Commission of Indian Currency and Finance) again stressed the need of a central bank and proposed the name *Reserve Bank of India*. In 1931, the Indian Central Banking Enquiry Committee also opined in favor of the Reserve Bank of India. In 1933, a White Paper published on Indian Constitutional Reforms, again stressed the necessity of forming of a central bank. The Reserve Bank of India Bill was placed in the Indian Legislative Assembly on 8th September, 1933 and passed on 22nd December, 1933. The bill was also passed by the Council of State on 16th February, 1934 and received the assent of the Governor General on 5th March 1934. At last, the Reserve Bank of India came into operation from 1st April, 1935. After World War II, 44 nations sat together to form two international institutions, the International Monetary Fund (IMF) to overcome the balance of payment crisis and the International Bank for Reconstruction and Development (IBRD) to restructure war affected countries. As per the requirement of the IMF, the RBI was nationalized as per the Reserve Bank of India Act, 1948 i.e. January, 1949. R. S. Sayers identified the role of *the central bank as an organ of government*. In the words of Sayers, "The central bank is an organ of the government that undertakes the major financial operations of the government and by its conduct of these operations and by other means, influences the behavior of financial institutions so as to support the economic policy of the government."

The growth of public sector banks in India took place in three stages. The establishment of the State Bank of India and its subsidiaries lies in the recommendation of the Rural Credit Survey Committee report. In 1955, the Imperial Bank of India was converted into the State Bank of India and later on eight states were associated with it. Schedule banks were converted as subsidiaries of the State Bank of India between October, 1959 and May, 1960 as per the

State Bank of India (Subsidiary Banks) Act, 1959. One of the subsidiaries later merged with another subsidiary.

Fourteen major banks were nationalized on 19th July, 1969. In 1980, a further six banks were nationalized. Primarily, twenty-eight banks laid the foundation of public sector banking. In 1965, the Monopolies Enquiry Commission headed by Justice K.C. Das Gupta observed that big business houses had an advantage over small business houses for getting assistance from banks because of the reasons for which advances were made. The commission also observed that big enterprises have a better risk factor which gives them an advantage in getting advances and could take part in the growth process as an economic power. The genesis of bank nationalization is to be found in the then Prime Minister Indira Gandhi's note on economic policy endorsed by the All India Congress Committee (AICC) at the Bangalore session of its plenary session held in July 1969. The Ordinance of nationalization of fourteen major banks was mooted on 19th July, 1969 with an objective 'to serve better the needs of development of the economy in conformity with national priorities and objectives'. The then Prime Minister Indira Gandhi expressed the broad objective of nationalization in Parliament on 21st July, 1969 by saying, 'The Government felt that the public ownership of major banks will help in the most effective mobilization and development of national resources so that our objectives can be realized with a great degree of assurance.' A comprehensive list of the fourteen nationalized banks is: The Central Bank of India Ltd., The Bank of India Ltd., The Punjab National Bank Ltd., The Bank of Baroda Ltd., The United Commercial Bank Ltd., Canara Bank Ltd., United Bank of India Ltd., Dena Bank Ltd., Syndicate Bank Ltd., The Union Bank of India Ltd., Allahabad Bank Ltd., The Indian Bank Ltd., The Bank of Maharashtra Ltd. and The Indian Overseas Bank Ltd. The Banking Companies (Acquisition and Transfer of Undertakings) Act, 1969 was challenged in the Supreme Court for violating the constitutional validity as, 'the Act violates the guarantee of compensation under Article 31(2) in that it provides for giving certain amounts determined according to principles which are not relevant in the determination of compensation of the undertakings of the named banks and by the method prescribed the amount which cannot be regarded as compensation.' The President of India promulgated another ordinance on 14th February, 1970 by eliminating the discrimination and compensation clause with fourteen banks ultimately re-nationalized. On 15th April, 1980 the Government of India took over six more commercial banks by an ordinance issued by the President of India. These banks were: Andhra Bank Ltd., Corporation Bank Ltd., New Bank of India Ltd., Oriental Bank of Commerce Ltd., Punjab and Sind Bank Ltd. and Vijaya Bank.

As per the statistics of the Indian Bankers' Association, the number of members of public, private, foreign and cooperative sector banks was 158 as on 1st October, 2010.

The Reserve Bank of India issues currency, is the banker of the government, banker of banks, promoter of the financial system, controller, regulator and monitor of the banking system including publications, in India. Commercial banks comprise scheduled banks, non-scheduled banks, private banks, public banks, foreign banks, regional rural banks and co-operative banks.

Table 5.1   Existing Players in the Indian Banking Sector

Bank Group	No of Banks	Deposit Market Share (per cent)	Advance Market Share (per cent)
SBI	7	22.32	22.50
Nationalized banks	20	49.83	49.80
Old private banks	15	4.52	4.60
New private banks	7	12.25	12.90
Foreign banks	32	5.06	4.90
Schedule state co-operatives	16	1.40	1.29
Schedule urban co-operatives	53	1.60	1.48
Regional rural banks	82	2.90	2.36

Source: The Times of India, August 30th 2011

Profitability and liquidity are the motto of banks with safety and welfare as principals. After the 65th Independence Day it was observed that more than 70 per cent of advances and deposits came from PSU banks (SBI and its subsidiaries along with other nationalized banks). Private banks (in terms of the same parameters) contribute more than 15 per cent, and the foreign banks are trailing behind with 5 per cent on the said basis. With globalization, Indian banks have adopted capital adequacy norms and manage non-performing assets by obeying the financial health code along with transparency and disclosure principals considered the basic inertia of globalization.

In India Public Sector Banks (PSBs) comprise nineteen nationalized banks, the State Bank of India and its seven subsidiaries and other public sector banks like IDBI Bank Ltd. etc. Private sector banks can be divided in two groups; old private sector banks and newly established private sector banks. Besides these banks, there are around thirty-six foreign banks' offices in India.

As the commercial banks provide short-term and working capital finance, for medium-term and long-term finance (term-finance), equity capital, judging techno-economic viability of the project on the basis of the loan repayment ability and sustainability, promoting enterprises with technical know-how, the corporate world has to depend on Financial Institutions (FIs). Since FIs have to perform multidimensional roles regarding development of industry and the corporate world, these institutions are commonly known as development financial institutions or development banks as used by William Diamond in his book, *Development Banks* and by Shirley Boskey in her book *Problems and Practices of Development Banks,* both published by the World Bank.

The first government sponsored Direct Financial Institution (DFI) started its operations in the Netherlands in the year 1822. The long-term financing in France took place with the establishment of French Credit Mobilier in 1852. Nearly five decades after the Second World War Japan was rebuilt with the help of the state owned Japan Development Bank (JDB) and later on a new financial institution was set up with new objectives. Since 1960,

Table 5.2 Distribution Banks in India by Different Sectors

Sectors	Public Sector Banks (PSBs)
I. Nationalized Banks	1. Allahabad Bank 2. Andhra Bank 3. Bank of Baroda 4. Bank of India 5. Bank of Maharashtra 6. Canara Bank 7. Central Bank of India 8.Corporation Bank 9. Dena Bank 10. Indian Bank 11. Indian Overseas Bank 12. Oriental Bank of Commerce 13. Punjab and Sind Bank 14. Punjab National Bank 15. Syndicate Bank 16.United Commercial Bank (UCO) 17.Union Bank of India 18. United Bank of India 19. Vijaya Bank
II. State Bank of India	State Bank of India. From 1st October, 2010 State Bank of Indore merged with State Bank of India
III. Associates of State Bank of India	1. State Bank of Bikaner and Jaipur 2. State Bank of Hyderabad 3. State Bank of Indore 4. State Bank of Mysore 5. State Bank of Patiala 6. State Bank of Travancore
IV. Other Public Sector Banks	1. IDBI Bank Ltd.
	Private Sector Banks
I. Old Private Sector Banks	1. City Union Bank Ltd 2. ING Vysya Bank Ltd 3. SBI Commercial and International Bank Ltd 4. Tamilnad Mercantile Bank Ltd. 5. The Bank of Rajasthan Ltd. 6. The Catholic Syrian Bank Ltd 7. The Dhanalakshmi Bank Ltd 8. The Federal Bank Ltd 9. The Jammu and Kashmir Bank Ltd. 10. The Karnataka Bank Ltd 11. The Karur Vysya Bank Ltd. 12. The Laxmi Vilas Bank Ltd 13. The Nainital Bank Ltd. 14. The Ratnakar Bank Ltd. 15. The South Indian Bank Ltd.
II. New Private Sector Banks	1. Axis Bank Ltd. (03.12.93) 2. Development Credit Bank Ltd. 3. HDFC Bank Ltd. (30.08.1994) 4. ICICI Bank Ltd.(05.01.94) 5. IndusInd Bank (31.01.94) 6. Kotak Mahindra Bank (21.11.1985) 7. Yes Bank (21.11.2003)
III. Foreign Bank Offices in India	1. AB Bank Ltd. 2. Abu Dhabi Commercial Bank Limited 3. American Express Banking Corporation 4. Antwerp Express Banking Corporation 5. Bank International Indonesia 6. Bank of America 7. Bank of Bahrain and Kuwait BSC 8. Bank of Ceylon 9. Barclays Bank PLC 10. BNP Paribas 11. Chinatrust Commercial Bank 12. Citi Bank 13. Commonwealth Bank of Australia 14. Credit Agricole Corporate and Investment Bank 15. Credit Suisse AG 16. DBS Bank Ltd 17. Deutsche Bank AG 18. First Rand Bank Ltd 19. JP Morgan Chase Bank 20. JSC VTB Bank 21. Krung Thai Public Company Ltd 22. Mashreqbank 23. MIZUHO Corporate Bank Ltd 24. Oman International Bank 25. Serbbank 26. Shinhan Bank 27. Societe Generale 28. Sonali Bank 29. Standard chartered Bank 30. State Bank of Mauritius Ltd 31. The Bank of Nova Scotia 32. The Bank of Tokyo –Mitsubishi UFJ Ltd 33. HSBC Ltd 34.The Royal Bank of Scotland 35. UBS 36. United Overseas Bank

Source: Indian Banking Year Book, published by Indian Association of Bankers

the Korean Development Bank (KDB) has contributed significantly to the implementation of government projects. In India, eleven national level financial institutions (including six All India Development Banks, two specialized financial institutions and three investment institutions) and forty-six state level institutions (including eighteen state financial corporations and twenty-eight state industrial development corporations) played a large role in the development of the industrial and service sector on one hand and the development of the capital market on the other.

Among the All India Development Banks (AIDBs), Industrial Finance Corporation of India (IFCI) was first established by the then Industrial Minister Dr. Shyama Prasad Mukherjee in the year 1948. This laid the foundation of industrial development of the newly independent nation. It was followed by the National Industrial Corporation in October, 1954, National Small Industries Corporation in 1955, Industrial Credit and Investment Corporation of India (ICICI) in 1955, (ICICI Bank promoted in the year 1994 and in April, 2002 by way of backward merger ICICI Bank Ltd. took over ICICI Personal Services and ICICI Capital Services Ltd. and reduced its role as an AIFI), Industrial Development Bank of India (1964), Agriculture Finance Consultants Ltd. (1968), Industrial Investment Bank of India (IIBI) in 1997 (erstwhile it was the Industrial Reconstruction Corporation of India in 1971 and was re-named as the Industrial Reconstruction Bank of India i.e. IRBI in 1985), Shipping Credit and Investment Corporation of India (1986), Risk Capital and Technology Finance Corporation Ltd. in January, 1988, Infrastructure Leasing and Finance Services Ltd. in May, 1988, Technology Development and Information Company of India Ltd. (TDICI) in July 1988, Tourism Finance Corporation of India on 1st February, 1989, Infrastructure Development Finance Company (IDFC) on June 30th, 1997 following the recommendation of the Expert Group formed by the Department of Economic Affairs, Ministry of Finance under the Chairmanship of Dr. Rakesh Mohan and Small Industries Development Bank of India (SIDBI) in 1990.

There are two Specialized Financial Institutions (SFIs) comprising the Export and Import Bank of India (EXIM Bank), which was set up in the year 1981 and the National Bank for Agriculture and Rural Development (NABARD), set up in the year 1982. Three investment institutions consisting of IFCI Venture Capital Funds Ltd., ICICI Venture Funds Management Company Ltd. and Tourism Finance Corporation of India Ltd. were primarily included in the list but on the basis of their nature of activities, they were delisted from the category.

There are twenty-four State Financial Corporations (SFCs) out of which twenty-one SFCs were established as per the State Finance Corporation Act, 1951. The Tamil Nadu Industrial Investment Corporation (TIIC) was formed in 1949 as the Madras Industrial Investment Corporation (MIIC). The Punjab Government played a pioneering role by establishing the Punjab State Financial Corporation (PSFC) in the year 1953. The Maharashtra State Financial Corporation (MSFC), Gujarat State Financial Corporation (GSFC), Uttar Pradesh Financial Corporation (UPFC), Tamilnadu Industrial Investment Corporation (TIIC), Karnataka State Financial Corporation (KSFC), Kerala Financial Corporation (KFC), Andhra Pradesh State Financial Corporation (APSFC), West Bengal State Financial Corporation (WBSFC) followed afterwards.

The insertion of Section of 4A of the Companies Act, 1956 in 1974, gave power to the Central Government to notify certain institutions such as Public Financial Institutions (PFIs). Some of the Public Financial Institutions are: EXIM Bank (1981), NABARD (1982), Power Finance Corporation Ltd (1986) National Housing Bank Ltd. (1988), SIDBI (1989), India Infrastructure Finance Company Limited (IIFCL) incorporated on January 5th 2006 and PFI started on January 14th 2009, the Infrastructure Development Finance Corporation (IDFC) started in 2000 and the National Housing Bank (NHB) started in 1988 for promoting and developing housing finance institutions at the regional and local level. As a result of this, the Housing and Urban Development Corporation Ltd. (HUDCO) and the Housing Development Finance Corporation of India Ltd. (HDFC), were constituted.

The first investment trust Financial Association of India and China was established in the year 1869. Real investment started in the year 1933 with the establishment of the Industrial Investment Trust by M/s Premchand Roychand in Bombay, which was followed by Bird and

Co., Calcutta, Investment and Finance Co., Calcutta, General Investment and Trust Co. Calcutta. All these were organized by Bird and Co. The New India Investment Corporation, Calcutta was promoted by M/s Ramdutta Ramkrishnadas. Tata Investment Trust Bombay and Consolidated Investment Trust Bombay, played path breaking roles later.

During World War II, acceleration of investment trust was made due to initatives taken by managing agency firms. Pioneering managing agents have their own investment companies: Tata (Investment Corporation of India Ltd. and Investment Industrial Corporation Ltd.), Birla (New India Investment Corporation Ltd. and Hindustan Investment Corporation Ltd.), Goenka (Jaipur Investment Co. Ltd. and Calcutta Investment Co. Ltd.)

On 16th March, 1963 the then Finance Minister T.T. Krishnamachari announced in the Lok Sabha during the budget discussion that the government was seriously considering the proposal for formation of an Investment Trust for generating savings and investment habits among the people.

He said, "We are wedded to the establishment of a socialist society in which the people will own the means of production, and distribution of the product will be equitable. In furtherance of that idea, we want people's ownership of the means of production through the Unit Trust, of the devices which we adopted from the Western countries to suit our own economic and social objectives." The Unit Trust of India Bill was passed in the Lok Sabha on 5th December, 1963 and the Rajya Sabha on 12th December, 1963 and received the assent of the President of India on 30th December, 1963. The Unit Trust of India Act, 1963 came into effect from 1st February 1964. As stated by Krishnamachari, "The basic idea of the proposal is to afford the common man a means to acquire a share in the widening prosperity based on industrial growth of the country which combines the advantages of maximum security and reasonable return."

Since its inception, the UTI has launched the unique scheme Unit-64 for mobilizing the savings of millions of small investors and channelizing that fund for the betterment of the country's economy during its first thirty years. From the very beginning, UTI was managed mainly by the RBI. In 1976 the UTI was delinked from the RBI and came under the control of IDBI. No control of SEBI existed till 30th June, 1994 as SEBI was yet to be formed. In conformity with the Vaghul Committee recommendations, all the new schemes launched by the UTI henceforth, required to take prior permission from SEBI. After the UTI scam in 2000, the government bailed it out with a package of Rs. 3,500 – Rs. 4,000 crore on August 31st 2002. The restructuring of UTI took place on 1st February, 2003 in which the UTI was bifurcated into two parts without diluting the government's commitment to protect the interests of investors, especially small investors. The two parts are: UTI-I (cannot launch any new scheme, monitored by the Government of India and comes under the purview of Mutual Fund) and UTI-II (popularly known as UTI Mutual Fund Limited, which has been privatized and is sponsored by SBI, PNB, BOB and LIC and is fully in conformity with the SEBI rules) by the Unit Trust of India (Transfer of Undertaking and Repeal) Act, 2002.

The journey of the life insurance business started in Calcutta in 1818 with the Oriental Life Insurance Company covering the life of Europeans first. Later on, eminent Indians came into the fold of life insurance coverage at a different premium rate. The Bombay Mutual Life

Assurance Society came into existence in 1870. Other insurance companies that followed later were, the National Insurance Company Ltd. and United India Insurance Company. After the Life Insurance Companies Act, 1912, the Insurance Act, 1938 made a provision for both life and non-life insurance. The Life Insurance Corporation of India (LIC) was established in the year 1956 by taking over the management through an ordinance and by passing the act in Parliament on 19th June, 1956, effective from 1st September, 1956 to spread the message of life insurance (*jeevan ka sath bhi jeevan ka bad bhi*) with mobilization of savings for nation building.

In 1968, the Insurance Act was amended to extend social control over the general insurance business and its subsequent amendment General Insurance Business (Nationalization) Amendment Act, 2002. Following the Malhotra Committee recommendations in the post-liberalization era, enactment of the Insurance Regulatory and Development Authority (IRDA) was made in 1999, which came into existence from April 19th, 2000 to give scope to private players. Important private insurance players are ICICI Prudential Life Insurance, Kotak Mahindra, Old Mutual Life Insurance, Max New York Life Insurance and Tata AIG Life Insurance, which have played significant roles in the post-privatization era in the insurance field.

The non-life insurance company i.e. General Insurance Corporation (GIC) was formed in November, 1972. In total, 107 Indian and Foreign Insurance Companies were functioning in India, which came under the fold of four subsidiaries of GIC with effect from 1st January, 1973. According to the General Insurance Business (Nationalization) Act, 1972 (GIBNA), the subsidiaries of GIC are the National Insurance Company Limited, New India Insurance Company Limited, Oriental Insurance Company Limited and United India Insurance Company Limited which are working throughout the country. In the IRDA regime, GIC got the status of Indian Reinsurer and its supervisory role over subsidiaries came to an end.

The money market is the formal financial market and provides short-term or working capital finance. On the turn over side, the capital market provides medium-term and long-term finance. The government, central bank, commercial banks, private banks, foreign banks, financial institutions, mutual fund houses, foreign institutional investors, discount houses along with others are involved in the money market of the country. There are many risks associated with the money market viz., market risk, inflation risk, interest risk, currency risk and certainly political risk. In India the money market is mainly controlled by the RBI and with the help of the Cash Reserve Ratio (CRR), Statutory Liquidity Ratio (SLR), open market operation, monitoring bank rate, repo rate (rate at which banks borrow from the RBI) and the reverse repo rate (the rate at which banks park surplus funds with the RBI).

Considering the macro economic situation of the country, the RBI has consistently increased the repo rate and reverse repo rate thirteen times during the 18 months from January 31st 2010 to October 25th 2011 (the repo rate was increased from 4.75 per cent on January 31st 2010 to 8.5 per cent on October 25th 2011 and the reverse repo rate from 3.25 per cent to 7.5 per cent during the same period), for controlling unmanageable inflation (the wholesale price index rose from 8.68 per cent to 9.72 per cent with fluctuations in spite of a straight increase of repo and reverse repo rates). The Reserve Bank of India has also deregulated savings banks' interest rates after 1978 which helped those banks having small savings bank account deposits, like Yes Bank, IDBI Bank and Kotak Mahendra Bank.

Table 5.3 Distribution of Banks by Share of Current Saving Account (CASA) in Total Deposit

Name of the Bank	CASB Share (per cent)	Change of Share Price (per cent)*
State Bank of India (SBI)	48	(-) 3.52
HDFC Bank	48	(-) 3.71
Axis Bank	41	(-) 4.52
Punjab National Bank (PNB)	38	(-) 4.36
Kotak Mahendra Bank	26	+ 5.23
IDBI Bank	19	+ 3.29
Yes Bank	13	+ 8.81

*Rise and fall of share price for deregulating SB interest rate in BSE
Source: The Times of India, 26.10.2011

In India, the RBI acts as a promoter, monitor and developer of the prevailing financial system. Nevertheless, in the post-liberalization period the RBI has come up with a new instrument known as the Interim Liquidity Adjustment Facility (ILAF) instead of General Refinance Facility (GRF), in tandem on the recommendation of the Narasimham Committee II. As ILAF was functioning well, the RBI introduced the second generation of ILAF on 19th April, 2001 comprising operating procedures and liquidity support facilities. Trading of Government Bonds has been started through stock exchanges right from January 16th 2003 as a land mark in the bond market.

Capital market finance mainly comes from FIs, financial intermediaries, industrial securities market (both equity and debt market), government securities market (debt market), FDIs, FIIs (in particular), Foreign Portfolio Investments (FPIs), NRI deposits etc. But, a disciplinary and development role has been initiated, mainly by SEBI, for both the primary and secondary markets with special emphasis on protection of investors' interest, promotion and development of the capital market, by forming laws and regulations and implementation of the regulations as and when required. SEBI has taken the major role in capital market regulation but the other wings of the Government of India, namely, the Department of Company Affairs, Department of Economic Affairs and RBI are all acting on behalf of the Ministry of Finance, Government of India. SEBI looks after the activities with the help of the Primary Market Department, Market Intermediaries Registration and Supervision Department, Market Regulation Department and Derivatives and New Products Department.

The banking industry has shown tremendous growth in India in spite of the global meltdown situation initiated in 2008. This growth will continue with little exception, and competition will intensify in the changing scenario. But the contribution of Public Sector Undertakings Banks (PSU Banks) in terms of the number of branches, number of employees, deposit and advances is well ahead of private banks and foreign banks.

Table 5.4   Growth in the Indian Banking Sector

Parameters	P S U Banks		Private Banks		Foreign Banks	
	2008-09	*2009-10*	*2008-09*	*2009-10*	*2008-09*	*2009-10*
Number of offices	57,732	61,301	9,236	10,387	295	310
Number of employees (lakhs)	7.32	7.35	1.76	1.82	0.30	0.28
Deposits (Rs. crores)	31,12,747	36,91,802	7,36,378	8,22,801	2,14,076	2,37,853
Advances (Rs. crores)	22,59,212	27,01,300	5,75,328	6,32,494	1,65,385	1,63,260

Source: RBI Banks Profile, 2009-10 cited in The Times of India, 1st October, 2010

Sayers has rightly pointed out in his banking classic, *Modern Banking* that, "Historically the term 'merchant banker' was used of a wealthy merchant who developed a banking side to his business; in London this banking business would often be connected with foreign trade. In general merchant bankers in London do not now engage in commodity trade, but have a miscellaneous financial business, including a little banking and a lot of work in connection with the issue and placing of securities. The Accepting Houses are merchant banking firms that have acquired a very high repute as acceptors of bills of exchange, and submit themselves to informal surveillance by the Bank of England."[1]

Merchant banking or investment banking started its operation in Italy in the 15th century and later spread to France and the UK in the 18th century. The term merchant banking comes from the fact that Dutch and Scottish traders or merchants carried out banking activities with innovative ideas in the 19th century. Reccardi of Lucca Medici and Fugger are the pioneers in the field. Merchant banking has been developed and professionalized in the UK. In the UK, Barings Brothers was the oldest merchant bank. Other merchant banks of the UK were Rothschilds, Kleinwort, Erlanger, Lizards who did small business in comparison with the big banks of the UK but were very powerful in their own line of business. The modern concept of merchant banking has its origin in Accepting House of the UK and Investment Bank of the USA. In the USA, merchant banks were effective from 1880; Brown Brothers, Drexel and Morgan and Co. were active in the beginning of the 19th century.

However, after the great depression in the USA in 1929 the government, by introducing the Glass–Steagall Banking Act, 1933 segregated merchant banking activities from commercial banking. Over time merchant bankers have become Multinational Companies (MNCs) and have a presence in almost all countries of the world.

Some of the world famous merchant banking firms are J. P. Morgan, Morgan Stanley, Dean Witter, Merrill Lynch, Goldman Sachs, and Lehman Brothers. It is cited that the collapse of Lehman Brothers led to the crisis in the US at the end of 2008.

Due to a legal challenge on the part of investment bankers, the US Government has allowed banks to do merchant banking and investment banking as subsidiary functions right from 1988. In India Grindlays Bank played a pioneering role in merchant banking under the regime of the Controller of Capital Issue in the year 1967 by opening ANZ Grindlays Merchant

---

[1]R.S. Sayers, *Modern Banking,* Oxford University Press, 1976, Delhi, p. 66

Banking. Following the Banking Commission Report (1972) the State Bank of India introduced SBI Capital Market Limited in the year 1973. Under the helm of development banks, the ICICI opened up a merchant banking division in 1974 by way of ICICI Merchant Banking Services. JP Finance was set up in 1973 to provide indigenous merchant banking services in India; after this many private, public and development banks came forward in the field to open their respective operations. Unfortunately, the growth of merchant banking services during the eighties was very slow. The nineties witnessed rapid growth in the merchant banking arena. In 1992 the share scam saw the involvement of many private and public merchant banking firms. Later on many Foreign Investment Banks (FIBs) entered the Indian capital market. FIBs had a massive capital base and global experience but lacked knowledge regarding the Indian capital market in particular. A Strength-Weakness-Opportunity-Threat (SWOT) study indicates that Indian merchant banking has a strong domestic base and has also entered into joint ventures with foreign banks which can be considered as a strength; lack of expansion of expected growth can be considered as a weakness; availing of the opportunity of the emerging market can be considered as an opportunity and merchant bankers facing stiff competition from the foreign players can be considered as a threat.

A few examples of successful and failed tie-ups are cited below:

Successful tie-ups

1. SBI Capital Markets – Lehman Brothers
2. Kotak Mahindra – Goldman Sachs
3. DSP Financial Consultants – Merrill Lynch
4. JP Finance – Morgan Stanley

Failed tie-ups:

1. IDBI – Asian Capital Partners
2. ICICI Securities – JP Morgan

Merchant Banking Divisions of Commercial Banks

1. SBI Capital Market Ltd. (1972)
2. PNB Capital Services Ltd.
3. Bank of Baroda Financial Services Ltd. (1978)
4. Can Bank Financial Services Ltd.
5. Indian Bank Merchant Banking Services
6. Andhra Bank Financial Services
7. Central Bank of India Merchant Banking Division (1977)
8. Syndicate Bank Merchant Banking Divisions (1977)
9. Indian Overseas Bank Merchant Banking Division

Merchant Banking Divisions of All India Financial Institutions

1. ICICI Merchant Banking Services Ltd. (1974)
2. IFCI Merchant Banking Services (1986)
3. IDBI Merchant Banking Services (1991)

Merchant Banking Divisions of Private Firms

1. DSP Blackrock Investment Managers Private Limited
2. JM Financial and Investment Services Ltd.
3. L and T Finance Ltd.
4. Kotak Mahindra Capital Co.

Merchant Banking Divisions of Foreign Banks

1. Grindlays Bank Merchant Banking Services (1967)
2. Standard Chartered Bank Merchant Banking Services (1978)
3. Citi Bank Merchant Banking Services
4. HSBC Merchant Banking Services

The introduction of SEBI was a land mark in the history of merchant banking in India, which made registration of merchant banking mandatory. The original registration of merchant bankers was valid for three years and thereafter they have to approach SEBI for renewal three months before the expiry of registration. Merchant bankers have to pay registration fees, annual fees and renewal fees as per the provision of SEBI.

As per the Securities and Exchange Board of India (Merchant Bankers) Rules, 1992 Regulation 2 merchant banker means, "Any person who is engaged in the business of issue management either by making arrangements regarding selling, buying or subscribing to securities or acting as a manager, consultant, advisor or rendering corporate advisory service in relation to such issue management."[2]

Investment bankers or merchant bankers act as a catalyst between the issuing house and the ultimate purchaser of securities. Merchant bankers perform the issue management regarding selling, buying, subscribing, consulting, underwriting and rendering advisory services regarding the specific issue.

SEBI has issued stringent guidelines regarding net worth requirement and fee structure to control the mushrooming merchant bankers' activities in India. Securities and Exchange Board of India (Merchant Bankers) Regulations, 1992 and SEBI (Merchant Bankers) Amendment Regulation, 1996 played a pioneering role in this regard. Before 8th December, 1997 merchant banks were categorized into four categories on the basis of net worth and registration fees that were imposed accordingly. With effect from 9th December, 1997 multi categories has been abolished and a single category has come into existence. SEBI will provide a certificate of registration for three years. The applicant merchant bankers must possess Rs. 5 crore as their minimum net worth. They have to pay Rs. 5 lakhs as registration fees for the first three years and Rs. 2.5 lakhs as renewal charges for every three years effective from the fourth year. The RBI has relaxed these norms for Non Banking Financial Companies (NBFCs) who have registered their name with SEBI as merchant bankers. But they have to perform their operations in accordance with the rules and regulations of SEBI. As per SEBI (Portfolio Managers) Rules and Regulations 1993 read with Securities and Exchange Board of India

---

[2]SEBI Manual, *SEBI (Merchant Bankers) Rule, 1992*, Bharat Law House Pvt. Ltd., New Delhi, 2000, p.III 244

Table 5.5 Categories of Merchant Bankers: Valid till 8th December, 1997

Categories	Capital Adequacy	Registration Fees
Category I	Minimum net worth Rs. 5 crore	Rs. 2.5 lakhs for the first two years and Rs. 1 lakh for the third year
Category II	Minimum net worth Rs. 50 lakhs	Rs. 1.5 lakhs for the first two years and Rs. 50,000 for the third year
Category III	Minimum net worth Rs. 20 lakhs	Rs. 1 lakh for the first two years and Rs. 25,000 for the third year
Category IV	Net worth is required	Rs. 5,000 for first two years and Rs. 1,000 for the third year

Source: SEBI

(Underwriters) Rules and Regulations, 1993, merchant bankers have to be registered and with these provisions will perform as underwriter.

It is to be noted that the minimum registration fees for merchant bankers have been raised to Rs. 5 lakhs and the minimum net worth has been fixed up to Rs. 5 crore, from 9th December, 1997 and its subsequent amendments up to August 16th 2011. The merchant bankers that carry out issue management related services fall under Category I. Merchant bankers that act as co-managers, advisors, consultants, underwriters or portfolio managers belong to Category II. Merchant bankers who function as underwriters, advisors or consultants fall under Category III.

Merchant bankers who only act as consultants or advisors fall in Category IV. From 9th December, 1997, issue of licenses will be restricted to Category I only. Categories II, III and IV have been abolished with effect from 9th December, 1997 as per SEBI guidelines.

The different regulations of merchant bankers are as follows:

> Regulation 3-12: Registration of Merchant Bankers
>
> Regulation 13: Code of Conduct of Merchant Bankers
>
> Regulation 14: Maintenance of Books of Accounts, Records
>
> Regulation 18: Appointment of Lead Merchant Bankers
>
> Regulation 19: Restriction on Appointment of Lead Managers
>
> Regulation 24: Documents to be Furnished to the Board
>
> Regulation 26: Acquisition of Shares Prohibited
>
> Regulation 27: Information to the Board (SEBI)
>
> Regulation 28: Disclosures to the Board
>
> Regulation 29-34: Procedure for Inspection
>
> Regulation 35-43: Procedure for Action in Case of Default

The main task of merchant bankers is to act as skilled financial advisors, who charge fees for the services rendered. Additionally, they provide consultancy services, administrative services, investment management services, distribution services, services for merger and acquisition, underwriting services, broking services and other related financial services. In no circumstances, do merchant bankers provide retail banking services. If the issuing company does not have enough expertise and infrastructure for raising funds from the market, merchant bankers come forward and use their skills and diligent expertise to perform those duties. They will enhance investors' confidence and help the company to mobilize resources for the company in particular and the national economy in general.

For new and risky projects, introduction of new generation technology in tandem with mobilization of venture capital or innovation of new product lines is the expertise of merchant bankers. Deriving a better scale of operations and economy of scale synergy in the form of mergers, acquisition amalgamation is the need of the hour. In such cases merchant bankers take up the responsibility in the area with specialized aims by following the Securities and Exchange Board of India (Substantial Acquisition of Shares and Takeovers) Regulations, 1997. The first billion dollar mega merger took place in 1897 between US Steel and Carnegie Steel in the US. In India, the strategic merger of IDBI with its subsidiary IDBI Bank was made in the year 2005. VSNL acquired Tata Power Broadband Ltd. from Tata Power Company in the same year.

The entry barriers and bargaining power of merchant banking are low, but competition and bargaining power of users are high. Merchant banking is also facing competition from within and from substitute services.

Universal banking is a new word in banking terminology consisting of commercial banking and merchant banking. This comprises activities right from depositing, lending, underwriting, broking, stock trading, trading of financial instruments, foreign exchange dealing, investment management, insurance and many similar activities. The Reserve Bank of India has come up to the conclusion that, 'universal banking is desirable from the point of view of efficiency of resource use, both banks and DFIs should be cautious in moving towards such a system.' Outstanding of banks are mounting day by day. The National Democratic Alliance (NDA) headed by the then Prime Minister, Atal Bihari Vajpayee, had taken harsh decisions for acquiring the property in case of default of repayment of dues. They authorized officers of a bank under the Securitization and Reconstruction of Financial Assets Act, 2002 and in exercise of powers conferred under section 13(12) read with the Rule 8 of the Security Interest (Enforcement) Rules, 2002.

Apart from the money market and the capital market, the Clearing Corporation of India was set up on April 30th 2001 for clearing government securities (G. sec) transactions and repos by the Negotiated Dealing System (NDS) by the end of May, 2002 for facilitating on-line dealings through electronic auction and transaction of government securities in the secondary market by dissemination of trade information.

Table 5.6 Holding of US Treasury Securities by Top 5 Holders

Country	Amount (US$ billions)	Per cent of Holding of US Securities
China	1,159.8	25.7 per cent
Japan	912.4	20.2 per cent
UK	346.5	7.7 per cent
Oil exporters	229.8	5.1 per cent
Brazil	211.4	4.7 per cent

The world famous rating agency Standard & Poor's (S & P) cut the US sovereign rating from AAA to AA+, which has also made a negative impact on the world stock market.

Foreign Institutional Investors (FIIs) have been allowed to enter the Indian capital market by the Securities and Exchange Board of India (Foreign Institutional Investors) Regulations, 1995 and its subsequent amendment SEBI (FIIS) Amendments Regulations, 1997, SEBI (FIIs) (Second Amendment) Regulations, 1999, SEBI (FIIs) (Third Amendment) 1997 and Indian investors are allowed to raise from funds through American Depository Receipts (ADR)/ Global Depository Receipts (GDR) issues, by a notification made by the Investment Division, Department of Economic Affairs, Ministry of Finance, Government of India, on November 14th 1995 and its subsequent modifications. SEBI has introduced guidelines for shelf discloser documents on October 15th, 2012 on the plea that some of the firms are manipulating share prices after issuing GDRs.

By implementing Basel II as a part of the disclosure requirement, the RBI introduced 'capital adequacy and market discipline,' norms on April 27th 2007. Foreign banks operating in India and Indian banks operating abroad for implementing credit risk and a basic indicator approach were adopted as a part of the revised framework on and from March 31st 2008.

One of the recent studies made by PWC, titled *Quest for Growth Destination India 2012: An Overview of Tax and Regulatory Framework in India* (published in July 2012) has mentioned the minimum capitalisation norms for foreign equity furnished in Table 5.7.

For NBFCs, the minimum capitalisation norm has been fixed at US$ 0.5 million.

Table 5.7 Minimum Capitalization Norms (Foreign Equity): Fund-Based Activities

Per cent FDI	Minimum Capitalization
Foreign capital up to 51 per cent	US$ 0.5 million to be bought upfront
Foreign capital > 51 per cent and up to 75 per cent	US$ 5 million to be bought upfront
Foreign capital > 75 per cent	US$ 7.5 million to be bought upfront and the balance of US$ 42.5 million in 24 months

Source: PWC

Minimum Capitalization Norms (Foreign Equity): Non-Fund-Based Activities

For NBFCS the minimum capitalization norm has been fixed at US$ 0.5 million.

The following activities are classified as non-fund-based activities:

- ❖ Investment advisory services
- ❖ Financial consultancy
- ❖ Forex broking
- ❖ Money changing
- ❖ Credit rating

MUTUAL FUNDS (MFs)

Victor Hugo was the pioneer of the concept of mutual funds in the US. The Investment Trust of the UK is quite different from the Unit Trust. It consists of open-ended investment companies similar to those of the US and Canada. L.M. Bhole has rightly differentiated investment trust and unit trust by saying, "Investment trusts (in the UK, for example) are different from unit trusts. An investment trust is an investment-holding company that is now being increasingly known as an investment trust company. It is incorporated under the Companies Act and has the same type of capital structure as an industrial or commercial company. Only a unit trust is a trust at law."[3] He added that in the nomenclature of investment trust vis-à-vis unit trusts, "while open-ended investment companies (in the US and Canada) are like unit trusts, the close-ended investment companies are different from unit trusts."[4] India's path breaking mutual fund, UTI was set up by the UTI Act, 1963 passed in parliament, but other mutual funds were set up by the Indian Trust Act, 1882. The origin of investment trusts can be identified with the formation of the Societe Generale de Belgique in Belgium in 1922 by the then Royal Family of Holland.

In India, the journey of mutual funds started with the incorporation of the Unit Trust of India in 1964 by the UTI Act, 1963, with the launching of its unique product, Unit 64. It was set up and regulated by the Reserve Bank of India, SBI, LIC and other FIs and banks. In 1978 controlling and regulatory power was passed from the RBI to IDB after the amendment of the Public Financial Institutions Law (Amendment) Act, 1975. The UTI Act, 1964 was amended in 1985 to widen the scope of the business of the UTI. To create global links, UTI floated the close ended India Fund in 1986, which was converted to a multi class open ended fund in 1994 followed by India Growth Fund in 1988, Columbus India Fund in 1994 and India Access Fund in 1996. UTI has also extended support for development of unit trusts in Sri Lanka and Egypt. Till 1987, the Unit Trust of India was the only mutual fund operating in the country. Thereafter, the State Bank of India appeared in the market as a Non-UTI Mutual Fund in June 1987 followed by Canbank Mutual Fund in December 1987, LIC Mutual Fund in June 1989, Punjab National Bank Mutual Fund in August 1989, Indian Bank Mutual Fund in November 1989, Bank of India Mutual Fund in June 1990, GIC Mutual Fund in December in 1990, and Bank of Baroda Mutual Fund in October 1992, who floated their mutual fund products.

The UTI's Asset Under Management (AUM) was Rs. 6,700 crores by the end of 1988. The AUM of MFs stood at Rs. 47,004 crores by the end of 1993 (including UTI). But in 2003, the AUM of 33 MF houses touched Rs. 1,21,805 crores (UTI's contribution to this AUM was Rs. 44,541 crores). At the end of June, 2011 the quarterly average AUM of the UTI touched Rs. 69,105 crores.

The Dave Committee submitted its report in 1991 indicating the need for mutual funds and subsequently the Ministry of Finance, SEBI Comprehensive Mutual Fund Regulation SEBI (Mutual Fund) Regulations, 1993 opened up the market for private sector mutual funds and accordingly, Kothari Pioneer was the first to appear in the market. Later, Kothari Pioneer merged with Franklin Templeton. After this the Indian mutual fund industry (except UTI)

---

[3]L.M. Bhole, *Financial Institutions and Markets - Structure, Growth and Innovations,* Tata McGraw-Hill Publishing Company Pvt. Ltd., 2005, New Delhi, p.121

[4]*Ibid*

came under the purview of SEBI according to SEBI (Mutual Fund) Regulation, 1996 and its subsequent amendments, SEBI (Mutual Fund) Amendment Regulation, 1998, 1999, etc.

The definition of a mutual fund was given by the Securities and Exchange Board of India (Mutual Funds) Regulations, 1996, as follows: "A mutual fund means a fund established in the form of a trust to raise monies through the sale of units to the public or a section of the public under one or more schemes for investing in securities, including money market instruments."

A mutual fund is formed as a trust under the Indian Trust Act, 1882. It is formed as a trust consisting of a sponsor, trustees, an asset management company and custodians. In the case of the SBI Mutual Fund, the State Bank of India is the sponsor of the fund. SBI Mutual has been set up as a trust under the Indian Trust Act, 1882. SBI Funds Management Private limited is working as the asset management company. The SBI Mutual Fund Trustee Company Private Limited is the custodian of the fund. Asset Management Companies (AMCs) are separate companies that act as key players on behalf of the mutual fund industry. They are appointed by the trustees and mobilize funds from investors and provide portfolio investment management, technical and advisory services against fees. AMCs have to collect a registration certificate from SEBI as per SEBI (Portfolio Managers) Rules and Regulations, 1993, SEBI (Portfolio Management) Amendment Regulations, 1998 and 1999. Every mutual fund industry possesses its own asset management company. The success and failure of a mutual fund mostly depends on the success and failure of its AMC.

A list of some AMCs of MFs is as follows: UTI Asset Management Co. Ltd. acts as an investment manager of the UTI, SBI Fund Management Private Limited (a joint venture between SBI and AMUNDI) AMC partner of SBI Mutual Fund, HDFC Asset Management Company is the AMC of HDFC Mutual Fund, DSP Black Rock Investment Managers Private Ltd., act as AMC of DSP Black Rock Mutual Fund, Fidelity Fund Management Private Limited acts on behalf of Fidelity Mutual Fund.

Needless to say a financial advisor performs a pivotal role for creating wealth on behalf of investors. Fund managers diversify portfolios and minimize the risk with an economic scale of operation. Low brokerage and transaction costs, adequate return, liquidity, flexibility, variety of schemes with the advantage of tax benefits, make mutual funds an attractive prospect to invest in, especially for small investors.

The schemes launched by MFs are broadly classified into two parts: open ended funds and close ended funds. Open ended funds are purchased and redeemed every day on the basis of the closing Net Asset Value (NAV) on a daily basis. In the case of close ended funds a fixed number of units can be sold for a stipulated period of time until the issue is open for subscription. It is to be noted that 'investment in all mutual funds and securities are subject to market risks and there can be no assurance that the objectives of the scheme will be achieved.' The NAV of the scheme may go up or down depending on the factors and forces affecting the capital market in general and composition of stock in particular.

Calculation of the NAV by the mutual fund house as per valuation norms is a must according to SEBI guidelines and is published in at least two newspapers within an interval not exceeding one week. NAV is calculated by dividing the net assets of the scheme by the number of units outstanding at the date of valuation. Investment valuation of mutual funds will be done by obeying the valuation norms falling into four categories: traded securities (based on the last quoted closing price of the stock exchange), non-traded securities (those securities that have not been traded 30 days prior to the date of valuation will be valued on good faith), right shares (based on renunciation value) and expenses and income (all expenses and incomes are made on an accrual basis till the date of valuation but admissible recurring expenses of a MF can be 2.5 per cent for first Rs. 100 crores, 2.25 per cent for next Rs. 300 crores, 2 per cent on the next Rs. 300 crores and 1.75 per cent on the balance amount based on the weekly average of the NAV.

AMCs monitor daily administration of fund activities and also act as fund managers. During the 1990s, the UTI and LIC jointly held more than 10 per cent of L & T's stake and tried to see that Dhirubhai Ambani stepped down as Chairman of L & T through an Extra Ordinary General Meeting.

Ambanis raised the question, as to whether FIs control the corporate world or the corporate world uses the funds of FIs. Specified undertakings of the Unit Trust of India (formed in the year 2002 after the UTI scam), the government, ITC and Axis Bank had a stake in L & T, amounting to Rs. 36,000 crores as on 21st October 2011.

Table 5.8   Value of Shares Possessed by SSUTI in Three Blue Chip Companies

Company	Stake (per cent)	Value (Rs. crores)
L & T	8.27	6,756
ITC	11. 54	18,262
Axis Bank	23.58	10,930

Source: BSE (Value based on 21.10.2011 closing price) cited in The Times of India on 24.10.2011

MFs can be classified into different schemes like, sectoral funds, equity funds, balance funds and income funds on the basis of risk and return. Investors who are willing to take higher risks prefer sectoral funds, while those preferring lower risks will go in for income schemes. Balanced funds have a higher risk than income funds but a lower risk than equity funds. Risk and return from income funds, balance funds, equity funds and sectoral funds, have a positive correlation in ascending order. This classification varies from fund house to fund house. On the basis of product variety, mutual fund schemes can be classified as: equity funds, debt funds, hybrid funds and money market funds. Equity funds can again be classified as: growth, large cap, large and mid-cap, multi cap, mid and small cap, sector, tax planning, income, index, elss and etfs. Debt funds are corporate funds and can be classified as: gilt, bond index and floating rate, hybrid equity oriented, debt oriented and arbitrage.

Equity funds: Those that invest in equity shares.

Equity diversified funds: Most popular among the equity fund category investment concreted on the equity market with potential return with risk aversion. DSPBR small and mid cap,

UTI Master Value, Reliance Regular Savings Equity, IDFC Premier Equity, Sundaram India Leadership Fund and Reliance Equity Fund fall in this category.

Growth fund: Growth funds face better return than equity oriented funds. Growth funds attract moderate to high risk provided the dividend is re-invested for capital appreciation. SBI Blue Chip Fund, SBI One India Fund, Magnum Multicap, Reliance Growth Fund, Reliance Vision Fund, HDFC Growth Fund, HDFC Equity Fund HDFC and Top 200 Fund are well-known funds that fall into this category.

Large cap/Mid cap fund: Generally these are growth oriented but have a more than average profit earning ratio for value creation. Magnum Midcap Fund, UTI Opportunities, UTI Dividend Yield, HDFC Top 200, Fidelity Education Fund have a consistent performance in the market.

Tax planning fund: It attracts rebate as per Section 88 of the Income Tax Act, 1961 and at the same time provides a gain to investors. Sundaram Tax Save and Fidelity Tax Advantage Fund (ELSS) are representative of this category.

Income fund: Portfolios are normally based on dividend yield, mainly on blue chip shares. Reliance MIP, HDFC MIP Long Term Plan, Sundaram Ultra Short-Term Fund and L & T MIP are examples of income funds.

Index fund: Funds are invested in stocks included for index calculation. Inclusion or exclusion depends on the performance of the stocks, which is highly sensitive to fluctuation of index. Some are fully replicated or some are partly replicated and risk associated accordingly. Magnum Index Fund, HDFC Index Fund are well reputed index funds.

Equity Linked Savings Scheme (ELLS): Funds are invested in equity or equity related instruments for long-term capital appreciation. It includes attachment of tax rebates as per Section 88, provided there is a 3 years lock-in period. Reliance Tax Saver (ELSS) Fund, HDFC TaxSaver, HDFC Long Term Advantage Fund, Magnum Tax Gain Scheme are examples of Exchange Traded Funds (ETFs). ETFs are funds that are traded in the stock exchanges with the inter-day closing NAV of the fund. ETF Gold fund has become very attractive due to the increase in gold prices, which is expected to touch $2,200 per ounce by the end of 2013 from the present level of $1,650 per ounce. Gold ETFs shine in a jittery market. Quantum Gold, Kotak Gold ETF, UTI Gold ETF and Reliance Gold ETF are examples of such schemes.

Debt funds: These funds are invested in debt securities.

Corporate funds: These funds are invested in bonds issued by companies to generate a fixed income with low risk. Magnum Monthly Income Plan Floater and HDFC MF Monthly Income Plan are some examples.

Gilt fund: Funds are invested in Government Securities (G-Sec) bearing no credit risk associated interest rate risk. Magnum Gilt Fund (Short term fund), Magnum Gilt Fund (Long term plan) are some examples.

Bond index funds: Bond index funds are similar to equity index funds that are associated with a bond related index. Risk and return are both moderate. SBI Dynamic Bond Fund is one such example.

Floating rate fund: Funds are invested in floating rate debt instruments with fixed interest rate security against volatility of interest rate. Some examples are: Magnum Income Fund Floating Rate Plan (Savings plus Bond Plan) and Magnum Income Fund (Floating rate plan).

Hybrid funds: These funds are an admixture of equity and debt funds.

Equity oriented fund/balance: Equity exposure is more than 60 per cent and the rest is debt exposure. HDFC Balance, HDFC Prudence, Reliance Regular Savings Balance, Canara Robeco Balance and Magnum Balanced Fund fall into this category.

Debt oriented fund: Average equity exposure lies between 25 to 60 per cent and rest is in debt funds. DSP Black Rock Bond Fund, DSP Black Rock Strategic Bond Fund, DSP Black Rock Money Manager Fund are strictly confined to this group.

Arbitrage fund: Derived arbitrage benefit between equity and derivatives, e.g. SBI Arbitrage Opportunities Fund.

The premier mutual fund of India, UTI has a vision, 'to be the highest performing mutual fund.' Their schemes are classified as: equity funds, index funds, balance funds, income funds and liquid funds. SBI Mutual Fund calls itself a 'partner for life' and has the following schemes: equity scheme, growth scheme, balanced scheme and equity linked savings scheme. Private fund house ICICI Prudential Mutual Fund, Tarakki Karein has equity funds, balanced funds, income funds and gift funds. HDFC Mutual offers schemes like growth funds, balanced funds, equity linked savings schemes, indexed linked schemes and monthly income schemes. Reliance Mutual Fund (Anil Dhirubhai Ambani Group) has growth schemes, sector schemes, indexed linked schemes and equity linked savings schemes. Thirty-nine other fund houses have many more schemes. ET Wealth in collaboration with Value Research has identified 100 funds falling into 10 categories. The methodology for choosing the top 100 includes funds having a 5- or 4-star rating from value research. The rating is based on subtracting a fund's risk score from its respective return score. The ratings are ***** for the top 10 per cent and **** for the next 22.5 per cent.

Table 5.9   Rating Scenario of Different Types of Funds

Type of Fund and Name of the Scheme	Value Research Fund Rating
Equity: Large–cap	
Franklin India Blue-chip	*****
IDFC Imperial Equity	*****
DSPBR Top 100 Equity Regular	****
ICICI Prudential Growth	****
ICICI Prudential Index Retail	****
Nifty Benchmark ETS	****
Reliance Equity Advantage Retail	****
Sahara Growth	****

Equity: Large and Mid–cap	
HDFC Top 200	*****
UTI Opportunities	*****
Contra Robeco Equity Diversified	*****
Fidelity India Growth	*****
Reliance NRI Equity	*****
Birla Sun Life Frontline Equity	*****
Baroda Pioneer Growth	****
DSPBR Opportunity	****
Franklin India Flexi-cap	****
Franklin India Prime Plus	****
Fidelity Equity	****
ICICI Prudential Indo Asia Equity Retail	****
Magnum Equity	****
Principal Large Cap	****
Tata Equity Management	****
UTI Equity	****
Equity: Multi–cap	
HDFC Equity	*****
Quantum Long Term Equity	*****
Templeton India Equity Income	*****
DSPBR Equity	****
Fidelity International Opportunities	****
Fidelity India Special Situations	****
HDFC Growth	****
ICICI Prudential Dynamic	****
Reliance Equity Opportunities	****
Reliance Regular Savings Equity	****
Templeton India Growth	****
UTI Dividend Yield	****
Equity: Mid- and Small–cap	
DSPBR Micro Cap Regular	*****
DSPBR Small and Mid Cap Regular	*****
HDFC Mid-cap Opportunities	*****
Religare Contra	*****
Birla Sun Life Dividend Plus	****
Birla Sun Life Small and Mid Cap	***
ING Contra	****

ING Dividend Yield	****
IDFC Premier Equity	****
ING Dividend Yield	****
L and T Mid-cap	****
Reliance Long Term Equity	****
Religare Mid-cap	****
Sundaram Select Mid Cap Regular	****
Tata Dividend Yield	****
UTI Master Value	****
Equity: Infrastructure	
Canara Robeco Infrastructure	*****
Taurus Infrastructure	****
Birla Sun Life Infrastructure	****
DSPBR JIDER Reg	****
ICICI Prudential Infrastructure	****
Tata Infrastructure	****
Equity: Tax Planning	
Canera Robeco Equity Tax Saver	*****
HDFC Tax Saver	*****
Religare Tax Plan	*****
Franklin India Tax Shield	****
Fidelity Tax Advantage	****
HDFC LT Advantage	****
ICICI Prudential Tax Plan	****
Sahara Tax Gain	****
Taurus Tax Shield	****
Hybrid: Equity–oriented	
HDFC Balance	*****
HDFC Prudence	*****
Reliance Regular Savings Balance	*****
Birla Sun Life '95	****
Canara Robeco Balance	****
DSPBR Balanced	****
Hybrid: Arbitrage	
UTI SPREAD	*****
HDFC Arbitrage Retail	****
Kotak Equity Arbitrage	****
SBI Arbitrage Opportunities	****

Hybrid: Debt-oriented Conservative	
Birla Sun Life MP II Savings 5	*****
DWS Money Plus Advantage Regular	*****
HDFC MP Long Term	*****
Reliance MIP	*****
Birla Sun Life Monthly Income	****
Canara Robeco MIP	****
DSPBR Savings Manager	****
UTI Monthly Income Scheme	****
Debt: Income	
Birla Sun Life Medium – Term Retail	*****
BNP Paribus Bond Regular	*****
IDFC SSI Medium – Term Plan A	*****
IDFC SSI medium – Term Plan B	*****
Birla Sun Life Dynamic Bond Retail	****
Canara Robeco Income	****
DWS Premium Bond Regular	****
HSBC Flexi Debt Regular	****
ICICI Prudential Medium – Term Regular	****
ING Income	****
LIC MP Bond	****
Principal Income Long–term	****
Reliance Regular Savings Retail	****
Sahara Income	****

Source: www. Wealth. economictimes. com

The strong NAV of the UTI came tumbling down in September – October, 1998 due to an internal crisis in particular and depression of the stock market in general. The Deepak Parekh Committee recommended infusion of additional funds in the year 1999. In August, 2002 the Cabinet Committee of Economic Affairs, Ministry of Finance and Government of India announced a bailout package for the UTI. In February 2003, UTI was bifurcated by repealing the UTI Act, 1964. Assets of Unit 64 assured return and remained as a Specified Undertaking of UTI (popularly known as UTI–I) under the control and monitoring of the Government of India. The remaining part was formulated as UTI Mutual Fund Ltd. (familiarly known as UTI-II) under the sponsorship of SBI, PNB, BOB and LIC and came under the purview of SEBI.

Since inception till July, 2011, apart from Unit 64, UTI has launched 47 schemes.

Table 5.10 Different UTI Schemes Launched After the Inaugural Scheme, Unit-64

A. Inception Date	
Equity Fund Category	
Diversified Funds:	
UTI Master Share Unit Scheme	15 October, 1986
UTI Master Plus Unit Scheme	31 December, 1991
UTI Equity Fund	18 May, 1992
UTI Contra Fund	22 March, 2006
UTI Wealth Builder Fund (not open for sale)	11 October, 2006
UTI Top2100 Fund	20 May, 2009
Speciality/Theme Based Funds:	
UTI MNC Fund	29 May, 1998
UTI Master Value Fund	1 July, 1998
UTI Service Industries Fund	28 June, 1999
UTI Infrastructure Fund	7 April, 2004
UTI Mid Cap Fund	7 April, 2004
UTI Dividend Yield Fund	3 May, 2005
UTI Opportunities Fund	20 July, 2005
UTI Leadership Equity Fund	30 January, 2006
UTI India Lifestyle Fund	30 July, 2007
UTI Wealth Builder Fund Series II	19 November, 2008
Sector Funds:	
UTI Pharma and Health Care Fund	28 June, 1999
UTI Banking Sector Fund	7 April, 2004
UTI Energy Fund	12 November, 2007
UTI Transportation and Logistics Fund	11 April, 2008
Tax Planning Funds:	
UTI Equity Tax Savings Plan	15 December, 1999
UTI MEPUS (not open for sale)	31 March, 2003
UTI Long Term Advantage Fund Ser I (not open for sale)	20 March, 2007
UTI Long Term Advantage Fund Ser II (not open for sale)	19 March, 2008
Arbitrage Funds:	
UTI Spread Fund	22 June, 2006
B. Index Fund Category	
Pure Index Funds:	
UTI Master Index Fund	1 July, 1998
UTI Nifty Index Fund	6 March, 2000
Exchange Index Funds:	

UTI Sender	11 July, 2003
C. Balanced Fund Category	
Pure Balanced Funds:	
UTI Balanced Fund	2 January, 1995
Segment Focused Funds:	
UTI Unit Linked Insurance Plan	1 October, 1971
UTI Charitable and Religious Trust and Registered Society	1 October, 1981
UTI Children's Career Balanced Plant	12 July, 1993
UTI Retirement Benefit Pension Plan	26 December, 1994
UTI Mahila Unit Scheme	8 March, 2001
UTI CCP Advantage Fund	30 January, 2008
Monthly Income Schemes:	
UTI Monthly Income Scheme	12 September, 2002
UTI MIS Advantage Plan	16 December, 2003
D. Income Fund Category	
Segment Focused Funds:	
UTI Bond Fund	4 May, 1998
UTI Treasury Advantage Fund	12 July, 1999
UTI G-Sec Fund Investment Plan	23 August 1999
UTI Gift Advantage Fund – LTP	21 January, 2002
UTI Short Term Income Fund	23 June, 2003
UTI Floating Rate Fund	29 August, 2003
UTI G-Sec Fund Short Term Plan	24 November, 2003
UTI Dynamic Bond Fund	16 June, 2010
E. Liquid Fund Category	
UTI Money Market Fund	23 April, 1997
UTI Liquid Fund Cash Plan	23 June, 2003

Source: UTI FUND WATCH, July, 2011

Another leading mutual fund, SBI Mutual Fund has been actively managing investors' assets since 1987 and providing consistently delivered value to their investors through equity schemes.

Table 5.11 Different Mutual Fund Schemes of the State Bank of India

Equity Scheme	Type of Scheme	Date of Inception
Magnum Equity Fund	An open ended equity fund	01.01.1991
Magnum Multiplier Plus Scheme	An open ended equity scheme	28.02.1993
Magnum Tax Gain Scheme	An open ended equity linked savings scheme	31.03.1993

Magnum Global fund	An open ended equity fund	30.09.1994
Magnum Balanced Fund	An open ended balanced scheme	31.12.1995
MSFU – Contra Fund	An open ended equity fund	14.07.1999
MSFU-FMCG Fund	An open ended equity fund	14.07.1999
MSFU-IT Fund	An open ended equity fund	14.07.1999
MSFU-Pharma Fund	An open ended equity fund	14.07.1999
Magnum Index Fund	An open ended growth scheme	04.02.2002
Magnum NRI Investment Fund – FAP	An open ended scheme	09.02.2004
MSFU – Emerging Business Fund	An open ended equity fund	11.10.2004
Magnum Midcap Fund	An open ended growth scheme	29.03.2005
Magnum COMMA Fund	An open ended growth scheme	08.08.2005
Magnum Multicap Fund	An open ended growth scheme	29.09.2005
SBI Blue-chip Fund	An open ended growth scheme	14.02.2006
SBI Arbitrage Opportunities Fund	An open ended equity scheme	03.11.2006
SBI One India Fund	An open ended growth scheme	17.01.2007
SBI Infrastructure Fund - Series I	An open ended equity fund	06.07.2007
SBI PSU Fund	An open ended growth scheme	07.07.2010

Source: SBI

SBI Mutual Fund Investment update –September 2011

Global mutual funds outperform Indian mutual funds in the short-term situation but not in the long-term situation, due to a number of factors. On one hand, investment in global mutual funds diversifies an investment portfolio but it should be restricted to 10-15 per cent of the investment of a total 20 per cent investment of the corpus and it will attach currency risk along with country-specific risks.

Table 5.12 Yield of Global Funds on the Basis of One Year Return

Schemes	One Year Return (per cent)
AIG World Gold Fund	S38.64
DSP BR World Gold Fund	28.99
DSP BR World Energy Fund	26.20
Birla Sun Life CEF –Global PMP	26.07
Fidelity Global Real Assets Fund	25.93
ING OptiMix Global Commodities Fund	25.16
DSP BR World Mining Fund	22.33
Birla Sun Life CEF –Global MCP	21.06
Mirae Asset China Advantage Fund	20.54
Birla Sun Life CEF – Global Agri Fund	18.41

Source: The Economic Times Wealth March 14, 2011 cited in an article written by Shobhana Chandra – Should *You* Invest in Global Funds?

The century old mutual fund house, Morgan Stanley, entered the Indian market just after liberalization in 1994. Morgan Stanley Investment Management Pvt. Ltd performs the role of investment manager on behalf of Morgan Stanley Mutual Fund.

Table 5.13 An Overview of Morgan Stanley Funds

Name of the Fund	Nature of the Fund	Date of Incorporation
Morgan Stanley Growth Fund	Open ended equity fund from 19.01.2009	18.02.1994
Morgan Stanley A.C.E. Fund	Open ended across capitalization equity fund	03.04.2008
Morgan Stanley Short		
Term Bond Fund	An open ended debt fund	26.05.2009
Morgan Stanley Active Bond Fund	An open ended debt fund	28.05.2009

Source: Morgan Stanley Mutual Fund Fact Sheet, September, 2011 Website

Investment in mutual funds is subject to market risk apart from other risks. A one-time investment does not minimize risk factors and thus, financial planners prefer Systematic Investment Plans (SIPs) for risk adjustment by averaging cost. SIPs will also help in inculcating financial discipline and decrease the time required for generating investable surplus. A Value Averaging Investment (VIP) plan provides the benefits of an SIP with high return at comparatively lower cost. The principle of an SIP is based on cost averaging but a VIP is based on value averaging technique. Acquisition cost of a VIP mode is lower than that of a SIP mode due to the fact that the average cost per unit of a VIP is slightly lower than that of an SIP. A Systematic Withdrawal Plan (SWP) is the reverse of a SIP, in which investors withdraw a fixed amount of money periodically over a period of time that will average the return and minimize the risk factor.

Table 5.14 Comparison of Return and Cost under SIP and VIP Mode

Month	SIP Mode			VIP Mode			
					Target	Actual	
	NAV	Investment (Rs)	Units	NAV	Investment (Rs)	Investment (Rs)	Units
1	10.50	1,000	100	10.00	1,000	1,000	100
2	10.50	1,000	92.238	10.50	2,000	949.998	90.475
3	11.00	1,000	90.90	11.00	3,000	904.461	82.251
4	11.50	1,000	86.956	11.50	4,000	863.6385	75.099
5	12.00	1,000	83.33	12.00	5,000	826.08	68.840
6	12.50	1,000	80.00	12.00	6,000	791.675	63.334
	Total units purchased 533.424			Total units purchased 480			
	Total investment Rs. 6,000			Total investment Rs. 5336.1525			
	Average cost per unit Rs. 11.24			Average cost per unit Rs. 11.11			
	Market value of portfolio Rs. 6,667.8			Market value of portfolio Rs. 6,000			
	Return from SIP (11.3 per cent)			Return from VIP (per cent) 12.44			

Table 5.15 Average Asset Under Management (AUM): Ten Top Mutual Fund Houses (as on 30th September, 2011) (Rs. crores)

Name of Mutual Fund	Asset Under Management (Corpus)
HDFC Mutual Fund	92,557
Reliance Mutual Fund	79,552
ICICI Prudential MF	72,044
Birla Sun Life MF	65,265
UTI Mutual Fund	60,076
SBI Mutual Fund	47,882
Franklin Templeton MF	40,195
Kotak Mahindra MF	30,739
DSP Black Rock MF	29,653
IDFC Mutual Fund	26,623

Source: (www. hdfcsec. com/ Mutual Fund/MF Fund HouseList.apsx).

Up to 30th November, 2011, mutual funds mobilized Rs. 1,00,338 crores in corporations with Rs. 49,406 crores in the year 2010-11 and thus, market mobilization shot up by 103 per cent. The market value of asset under management reached Rs. 6,81,655 crores as on 30th November, 2011 in comparison with Rs. 6,65,282 crores as on 31st March 2011 indicating marginal appreciation of 2.5 per cent. It is to be noted that fund mobilization more than doubled, whereas the appreciation of asset under management grew at a crippling rate of 2.5 per cent.

Considering the holding pattern, on one hand 97 per cent of individual investors hold about 40 per cent of the mutual fund assets, and on the other hand, 1 per cent corporate/institutional investors hold 55 per cent of the assets as shown in Table 5.15.

Table 5.16 Holding Pattern of Mutual Fund Industry as on 31st March, 2010

Category	Number of Investors Accounts	Per cent of Total Investors Accounts	Net Assets (Rs. Crores)	Per cent of Total Net Assets
Individuals	4,63,27,683	97.07	2,45,390.28	39.77
NRIs	9,43,482	1.88	27,428.86	4.45
FIIs	216	0.00	6,335.00	1.03
Corporate/Institutions	4,52,330	0.95	3,37,812.58	54.75
Total	4,77,23,711	100.00	6,16,966.72	100.00

Source: Indian Financial System-Markets, Institutions and Services, Bharati V. Pathak, 3rd Ed., 2011, Pearson, Delhi (pp.578).

Tax Benefit from Mutual Fund Investments

Income received by the holders in respect of the units of a MF will be exempted from income tax under section 10(35) of the Income Tax Act, 1961. However, dividend distribution tax will be payable by the MF. No tax will be deducted at source on any income distributed by the MF under the provision of sections 194K and 196A of the Income Tax Act, 1961.

Table 5.17 Capital Gains		
Nature of Capital Gains	*Indian Equity Scheme*	*Debt Scheme or Non-Equity Scheme*
Indian Mutual Fund	Minimum 65 per cent investment in Indian equities	
Long Term Capital Gains (More than 12 months holding period)	0 per cent	10 per cent without indexation or 20 per cent with indexation
Short Term Capital Gains (Less than or equal to 12 months holding period)	15 per cent	Capital gains added to income and total income taxed as per tax slab
Foreign Mutual Fund	100 per cent in foreign equities	
In both the cases of long term and short term	Investor has to pay tax as usual	

Source: NSE, Mumbai.

FOR FURTHER READING

1. Indian Banking Year Book 2010
2. For a detailed history of Investment Trust refer the book written by Kuchhal, S.C., *Corporation Finance – Principles and Problems*, Chaitanya Publishing House, Allahabad, 1982, pp. 358-384,
3. Speech of T. T. Krishnamachari on 16th March, 1963
4. Speech of T.T. Krishnamachari on 5th December, 1963
5. Verma Meenu, Can AMCs Sustain Their Big Gains, *Portfolio Organizer*, the ICFAI University Press, December, Hyderabad, India, 2000
6. SEBI Manual, *SEBI (Mutual Fund) Regulations, 1996*, Bharat Law House Pvt. Ltd., New Delhi, India, p III 467.

Laws and Regulations Affecting the Capital Market

6

To review the stock market performance after the First World War, during the slump in the Colonial Indian Economy (1923-24) an enquiry committee was formed on 14th September, 1923 under the Chairmanship of Wilfred Atlay. After considering the report of the Atlay Committee, the Bombay Legislative Assembly passed the Bombay Securities Contract Act, 1925 to regulate the functioning of the Bombay Stock Exchange. The Indian stock market was deeply influenced by the world economic crises during the time of great depression (1929-33). On 24th August, 1921 The Dow Jones Industrial Average (DJIA) was at the 63.9 mark but from 3rd September, 1929 it increased six fold touching the 381.2 mark. The crisis originated on Wall Street on 29th October, 1929, known as black Tuesday when the DJIA dipped 38 points nearly by 12.8 per cent and came down to the 260 mark and the crisis ended with the beginning of the Second World War in 1939. In the year 1935-36, the Bombay Stock Exchange constituted an enquiry committee under the Chairmanship of W.B. Morrison. The Morrison Committee report recognized the necessity of speculative action legislation. In order to check speculative activities, the Defense of India Rules 94A and the Act were promulgated on 17th May, 1943. These rules prohibited both forward trading and carryover of pending security transactions from one period to another, and made the delivery of shares with a time of seven days from the contract mandatory.

After the Second World War, the provisions of the Defense of India Rules relating to stock market operations were replaced by the Capital Issues (Control) Act, on 18th April, 1947. The main objective of this act was to introduce control over capital and lay down some directives of the Government of India relating to the issues. Afterwards the Indian Government passed the Capital Issues (Exemption) Order, 1969.

For the purpose of reviewing prevailing stock exchanges and make suitable suggestions and to regulate and control them a committee was formed in May, 1948 under the chairmanship of Dr. P.J. Thomas. On the basis of the report of the Thomas Committee, the Government of India formulated the Forward Contracts (Regulation) Bill, 1950 and referred it to the A.D. Garwale

Committee. On the basis of the Garwale Committee report the Indian Government drafted the Securities Contract (Regulation) Bill, 1954, and this bill was later renamed as the Securities Contract (Regulation) Act, 1956 and the act came into effect from 20th February, 1957. The act empowered the government to license the dealers (brokers) of the securities to lay out conditions for dealing in securities.

For the purpose of reviewing the organization and management of stock exchanges a high power committee was constituted in 1984 under the Chairmanship of G.S. Patel. Patel made a remarkable statement that, 'It may be highlighted that out of 1400 active brokers in the country, not more than 100, at best, may be considered to be fit and proper in terms of general or professional knowledge, adequacy of education, skill in business, availability of infrastructure facilities etc., to render any worthwhile integrated services to investors."[1]

In October, 1988, the Bhansali Committee's recommendation of share transfer procedures was implemented whereby the newly allotted shares have to be treated at par with the old shares for delivery purposes, subject to the adjustment of the dividend depending on time of allotment. The minimum capital of listing has been raised to Rs. 3 crores out of which Rs. 1.8 crores should have been issued to the public with effect from February, 1989. This was further raised to Rs. 5 crores from October, 1995 and Rs. 10 crores and above on the NSE, BSE, DSE etc.[2]

The Prerwani Committee was formed in December, 1991 to review the operation of the stock exchange. The committee has recommended the setting up of a permanent Financial Instruments Review Committee within the Ministry of Finance or within SEBI.[3]

By following the Securities and Exchange Commission of the USA and the Securities and Investment Board of the UK, the Government of India abolished the Capital Issues Control Act, 1947; which was the basic legislation of the capital market in India after independence. This act was repealed on 4th April, 1992 by the Securities and Exchange Board of India by following the recommendation of the Patel Committee formed in the year 1988.

The Government of India set up the SEBI on 12th April, 1988 but for almost four years it never enjoyed any statutory power and after the Harshad Mehta scam there was a hue and cry within and outside parliament. The Joint Parliamentary Committee (JPC) was formed in 1992 with 20 members from the Lok Sabha and 10 members from Rajya Sabha from a wide political spectrum, under the chairmanship of Ram Nivash Midhya, to identify the share scam which was officially admitted at Rs. 8,000 crores and unofficially acknowledged at Rs. 40,000 crores led by the broker Harshad Mehta on the basis of bank receipts. The then government in an overnight decision, conferred SEBI with statutory powers. Afterwards, the SEBI Act, 1992 was passed in parliament and got the ascent of the President of India. Now the SEBI acts as the regulatory authority of India. The board of SEBI consists of a chairman, two officials from

---

[1]Prasanna Chandra, *Fundamentals of Financial Management,* Tata McGraw-Hill Publishing Company Ltd., 1993, p.453

[2]V.A. Avadhani, *Marketing of Financial Services and Markets,* Himalayan Publishing House, 1999, p.463

[3]Ishwar C. Dhingra, *The Indian Economy - Resources, Planning, Development and Problems,* Sultan Chand and Sons, 1995, p.632

the Central Government from the Ministry of Company Affairs and two from the Ministry of Law and Justice and one member from the RBI, comprising a total of six members along with the chairman. Out of the five members, at least three shall be full time members appointed by the Central Government.

Although more than 20 years have passed since the formation of the SEBI, unfortunately, back-door entry still continues despite a constant vigil by SEBI, the Ministry of Finance, the Government of India, the Reserve Bank of India and Ministry of Company Affairs. There have been a number of problems on the stock markets, e.g. in 2001 Dinesh Singhania was involved in a payment crisis in the Kolkata Stock Exchange; activities of Ketan Parekh were banned by SEBI in 2003, alleging a profit sharing arrangement with brokers; in 2010 Sanjay Dalal was charged with manipulation of stock prices, and Nirmal Kotecha, investor of Bangalore Real State drew regulatory attention for price manipulation of Pyramid Saimara Stock, to mention a few. In the *Times of India*, dated 22nd August, 2012 there was a cover story under the headline *Back-door Entry*, in which stories of more manipulative incidents came out and which had shocked the investing communities of India as a whole.

In spite of taking efforts to develop the Indian financial system; due to inefficient management, no accountability and responsibility, no quick redressal mechanism and lack of punishment clauses, the efforts are fatally faulted. The cloud of the scam cover-up in the financial sector leads to huge loss from the public exchequer and hard earned public money is looted by unscrupulous people, who have delayed the reform procedure. The Top 10 investment scams are listed in Table 6.1.

Table 6.1 Top 10 Investment Scams

Name of the Scam	Year of Occurrence	Key Accused	Volume of Scam in (Rs. crores)
The Securities Scam	1992	Harshad Mehta	8,000
The IPO Scam	1993-1996		
Favored Share Scam			550
Chain Roop Bhansali Card Board Scam	Mid-90s		1,000
Plantation Firms' Scam	Mid-90s		8,000
The 1998 Scam	1998	Harshad Mehta	NA
Mutual Fund Scam	1999 and 2000	UTI	4,800
DSQ Software Scam	2000 and 2001	Dinesh Dalmia	595
Home Trade Scam	2000	Sanjoy Agarwal	82
Satyam Scam	2008*	Ramalingam Raju	700

Source: http://business.mapsofindia.com/investment-industry/top-10-investment-scams.html

The preamble of the act stated that the board is entrusted to protect the interests of the investors and to promote the development of the capital market and regulate the securities market. Even after formation of SEBI there were share scams in 1993 by Hiten Dalal and in 1999 by Ketan Parikh, the former by way of preferential allotment and the latter by way of pay order. The banks offered a huge amount of unauthorized advances to Ketan Parikh knowing fully well that the funds used in the stock market operation by way of pay order amounted to a total loss Rs. 5,000 crores. The banks involved were: MMCB, Bank of India (BOI), Punjab National Bank (PNB), Standard Chartered Bank, Global Trust Bank (GTB). In tandem with the Global Standard Financial Sector Assessment Program made by the IMF and World Bank "Bretton Woods Twins," SEBI has appointed an expert group on 5th August, 2004 headed by Justice Kanoria, Former Chief Justice of India to seek suggestions regarding amendments to the SEBI Act, 1992. The terms of reference of the Kanoria Committee were as follows:

1. To identify the inconsistencies prevailing in the existing SEBI Act.
2. To give suggestions to improve the SEBI Act in the light of investor friendly concepts.
3. To take into account the recommendations of the Joint Parliamentary Committee (JPC) and other expert groups formed from time to time.

The functions of SEBI are as follows:

1. To collect information and give advice to the government regarding the capital market.
2. To issue licenses and lay out regulations for merchant banks and mutual funds.
3. To prepare legal drafts in favor of SEBI.
4. To perform any other function as may be prescribed by the Central Government.

The SEBI has been entrusted with both regulatory and developmental powers. Section 11 of the SEBI Act, 1992 specifies those dual functions.

Regulatory Role Played by SEBI

1. Regulate the business of the stock exchanges and any other securities market.
2. Registration of brokers and sub-brokers and other players of the market.
3. Registration of collective investment schemes and mutual funds.
4. Regulation of stock exchanges and other stock regulatory organizations, merchant banks, portfolio managers.
5. Prohibition of all fraudulent and unfair trade practices of the securities market.
6. Controlling insider trading of securities and imposing penalties thereon.

Developmental Role Played by SEBI

1. Promote investors' awareness education programs.
2. Arrangement of training programs for intermediaries of the securities market.
3. Promotion of fair practices and code of conduct for all SROs.
4. Conduct research and publish information useful to all market participants.
5. Encourage fair trading activities.
6. Create a transparent atmosphere in tandem with the global scenario.

SEBI GUIDELINES ON NEW ISSUES

On 12th June, 1992 SEBI released guidelines relating to new issues of the securities market. Under the new regime there is virtually no restriction on the types of securities that can be issued, moreover there is substantial freedom of pricing of securities and no ceiling of payment of dividend and interest. The new regime provides additional safeguards regarding price and product control, additional safeguards relating to interest to investors, emphasis on prudential control along with disclosure principal. In 1994 FFIs and FBFs were licensed to enter the primary market. The Central Government had raised the investment limit from $5 billion to $25 billion for FIIs in the budget in the year 2011-12.

Public Issues and Rights Issues as per SEBI (ICDR) Regulations, 2009 were amended on 7th February, 2012.

The related prescribed fees of public and rights issues are given in Table 6.2 and Table 6.3.

Table 6.2 Size of Public Issue and Related Fees

Size of the Issue	Rate of Fees
Less than Rs. 50 lakhs	Not permitted
Less than or equal to Rs. 10 crores	Flat charge Rs. 25,000
More than Rs. 10 crores but less than or equal to Rs. 5,000 crores	0.025 per cent of the issue size
More than Rs. 5,000 crores but less than or equal to Rs. 25,000 crores.	Rs. 1,25,00,000 + 0.00625 per cent of the portion of the issue size in excess of Rs. 5,000 crores
More than Rs. 25,000 crores	A flat charge of Rs. 3 crores

Source: SEBI

Table 6.3 Size of Rights Issue and Related Fees

Size of the Issue	Rate of Fees
Less than Rs. 50 lakhs	Not permitted
Less than or equal to Rs. 10 crores	Flat charge Rs. 25,000
More than Rs. 10 crores but less than or equal to Rs. 500 crores	0.005 per cent of the issue size
More than Rs. 500 crores	A flat charge of Rs. 5 lakhs

Source: SEBI

SEBI Guidelines for the Capital Market

1. The Board of Directors of stock exchanges has to be reconstituted so that 50 per cent of the total number of members must be non-members, public representatives and government representatives.

2. *Badla* and carry forward business, which was banned in early 1995 was reintroduced in October, 1996.

3. Twelve months should elapse between public issue, right issue and bonus issue.

4. Issues to the public by existing companies can be priced differently as compared to rights issue.

5. If the total issue exceeds Rs. 250 crores, disclosure is voluntary and if it exceeds Rs. 500 crores, disclosure is compulsory.

6. The employees' stock option scheme should not exceed 10 per cent subject to a maximum allotment of 200 shares per employee and this quota is non-transferable for three years, which has now been abolished.

7. Bonus shares are to be issued out of free reserves, securities premium account, development rebate reserve account and invest allowance reserve. As per recent guidelines the residual reserve after the proposed capitalization should be at least 40 per cent of the enhanced capital (that means old capital plus new capital). 30 per cent of the average Profit Before Tax (PAT) for a period of 3 years should yield a rate of dividend of 10 per cent on the expanded capital.

8. Mutual funds related primarily to the capital market and also related to the money market instruments have to be regulated by SEBI. All schemes floated by mutual funds have to be registered with SEBI.

The SEBI finalized the code for new takeover guidelines based on the Report of Justice P.N. Bhagwati constituted in August, 1996, and submitted it in January, 1997.

Securities Market Regulations and Guidelines of SEBI

The SEBI Act, 1992 has undergone several changes and amendments along with setting up new rules over the passage of time, as follows:

1. SEBI (Stock broker and sub-broker) Rules, 1992 — No broker or sub-broker shall be entitled to deal with securities unless they hold a certificate issued by the board. SEBI (Stock brokers and sub-brokers) Regulation, 1992 and its subsequent (Second Amendment) Regulations, 2011 held on 17th August, 2011.

2. SEBI (Prohibition of Insider Trading) Regulations, 1992.

3. SEBI (Merchant Bankers) Regulations, 1992 and SEBI Merchants Bankers (Amended) Regulations, 2012 held on 29th March, 2012.

4. SEBI (Disclosure and Investor Protection) Guidelines, 1992 – Several amendments have been made. These amendments are made as per Section 11 of the SEBI Act, 1992.

5. SEBI (Bonus Share) was issued first on 11th June, 1992 with further amendments on 13th April, 1994.

6. SEBI (Portfolio Managers) Regulations, 1993 and SEBI (Portfolio Managers) (Amendment) Regulations, 2012 held on 10th February, 2012.

7. SEBI (Underwriters) Regulations, 1993.

8. SEBI (Registrars to an Issue and Share Transfer Agents) Regulations, 1993.

9. SEBI (Debenture Trustees) Regulations, 1993 and SEBI (Debenture Trustees). (Second Amendment Regulations), 2011 held on 14th December, 2011.

10. SEBI (Bankers to an Issue) Regulations, 1994.

11. SEBI (Prohibition of Fraudulent and Unfair Trade Practices Relating to Securities Markets) Regulations, 1995.

12. SEBI (Foreign Institutional Investors) Regulation, 1995. SEBI has registered FIIs. As on 31st March, 2006 country wise FII registrations with SEBI are: US (342), UK (148), Luxembourg (64), Singapore (47), Hong Kong (30), Canada (26), Australia (23), Ireland (23), the Netherlands (23) and Mauritius (22).

13. SEBI (Custodian of Securities) Regulations, 1996 – As on 31st March, 2006 eleven 2012 Custodians were registered with SEBI. Nine were banking entities and two were non-banking institutions.

14. SEBI (Depositories and Participants) Regulations, 1996 and SEBI (Depositories and Participants) (Amendment) Regulations, held on 11th September, 2012.

15. SEBI (Venture Capital Funds) Regulations, 1996.

16. SEBI (Mutual Funds) Regulations, 1996: As on 31st March, 2006 and SEBI (Mutual Funds) (Second Amendment) Regulations, 2012 held on 26th September, 2012.

17. SEBI (Substantial Acquisition of Shares and Takeovers) Regulations, 1997.

18. SEBI (Buy Back of Securities) Regulation, 1998 and SEBI (Buy Back of Securities) (Amendment) Regulation, 2012, held on 7th February, 2012.

19. SEBI (Credit Rating Agencies) Regulation, 1999 SEBI (Credit Rating Agencies) (Second Amendment Regulations), 2011 held on 27th December, 2011.

20. SEBI (Collective Investment Schemes) Regulation, 1999 – No CIS entry is registered with SEBI as on March, 2006.

21. SEBI (Employee Stock Option Scheme and Employee Stock Purchase Scheme) Guidelines, 1999.

22. SEBI (Foreign Venture Capital Investors) Regulations, 2000.

23. SEBI (Issue of Sweat Equity) Regulation, 2002.

24. SEBI (Procedure for Holding Equity by Equity Officer and Imposing Penalty) Regulations, 2002.

25. SEBI (Control Listing Authority) Regulations, 2003.

26. SEBI (Ombudsman) Regulations, 2003.

27. SEBI (Central Database of Market Participants) Regulations, 2003.

28. SEBI (Issue of Capital and Disclosure Requirements) Regulations, 2009 and SEBI (Issue of Capital and Disclosure Requirements) (Third Amendment) Regulations, 2012 held on 24th August, 2012.

29. SEBI [Know Your Client (KYC) Registration Agency], 2011 passed on 2nd December, 2011.

The Companies (Amendment) Act, 2000 has inducted Section 55A for transferring specific powers to SEBI. The provisions of Sections 55 to 58, 59 to 84, 108 to 110, 112, 113, 116 to 122, 206, 206A and 207 relating to issue of securities, transfer of securities and non-payment of dividend by the listed public companies or public companies that intend to get their securities listed on recognized stock exchanges of India or companies administered by the Central Government. All powers relating to prospectus, statement in lieu of prospectus, return of allotment, issues of shares and redemption of irredeemable preference shares shall be exercised by the Central Government, Company Law Board along with Company Law Tribunal or the Registrar of Companies as per provision.

According to the SEBI Act, 1992 amended on 29th October, 2002 the functions of SEBI are as follows:

1. Recognizing and regulating of stock exchanges.
2. Regulating substantial acquisition of shares and takeover of companies.
3. Regulating the business of the secondary market.
4. Prohibiting insider trading of securities.
5. Promoting and regulating the self regulatory organization.
6. Prohibiting fraudulent and unfair trade practices relating to the securities market.
7. Registration and regulation of working of stock brokers, sub-brokers, banks relating to issues, merchant banks, underwriters, portfolio managers, investment advisors etc.
8. Levying fees or any other charges as mentioned in Section 11.
9. Calling for information, undertaking inspections, conducting inquiries or audits of stock exchanges, mutual funds, intermediaries, self-regulatory organizations of stock market and any other persons associated with the securities market.
10. Registering and regulating the function of depositories custodians and depository participants; registration of FIIs.
11. Conducting research relating to securities market:
    - Promoting investor education and training of intermediaries.
    - Discharging any other functions as may be prescribed by the law.

Table 6.4	Powers of SEBI	Prior to the SEBI Act, 1992, the Government of India Exercised this Power as per the Securities Contract (Regulation) Act, 1956.
Sections Under SEBI Act, 1992	**Power of SEBI**
Section 6(1)	Power to call for periodical returns of stock exchanges.
Section 6(2)	Power to give instructions for maintenance of certain documents by the stock exchanges.
Section 6(3)	Power to call upon exchanges or any member to furnish explanations or information relating to affairs of stock exchanges.
Section 9	Power to approve bye-laws of stock exchanges for regulation and control of contracts.
Section 10	Power to amend bye-laws of the stock exchanges.
Section 17	Licensing of dealers of securities in stock exchanges.
Section 21	Power to compel a public company to list its shares.
Section 30	Power to issue certificates to brokers or sub-brokers.

Source: SEBI

SEBI executed their power with 13 arms, that is, through 13 committees.

Table 6.5   SEBI Committees

1. Technical Advisory Committee
2. Committees for Review of Structure of Market Infrastructure Institutions
3. Member of the Advisory Committee for the SEBI Investor Protection and Education Fund
4. Takeover Regulations Advisory Committee
5. Primary Market Advisory Committee (PMAC)
6. Secondary Market Advisory Committee (SMAC)
7. Mutual Fund Advisory Committee
8. Corporate Bond and Securitization Advisory Committee
9. Takeover Panel
10. SEBI Committee on Disclosures and Accounting Standards (SCODA)
11. High Power Advisory Committee on Consent Orders and Compounding of Offences
12. Derivatives Market Review Committee
13. Committee on Infrastructure Funds

Source: www.sebi.in

The different departments of SEBI take into account the following activities:

1. ***Market Intermediaries Registration and Supervision Department (MIRSD):*** Registration, supervision, inspection and compliance with monitoring of all market intermediaries in respect of all market segments, viz. equity, derivatives, debt and debt related derivatives.

2. ***Market Regulation Department (MRD):*** Formulating policies and operations of securities exchanges, their subsidiaries and institutions such as clearing and settlement organizations and depositories.

3. ***Derivatives and New Product Department (DNPO):*** Supervising trading of derivatives segments of stock exchanges including new products and their respective policies.

4. ***Legal Department:*** This department takes care of legal matters.

5. ***Institutional Investment Department (IID):*** Looks after mergers and acquisitions.

6. ***Research and Publication and International Relations:*** This department frames policies for foreign institutional investors and mutual funds.

7. ***Investigation Department:*** Conducts investigations and inspections of various activities of stock exchanges and intermediaries regarding scams.

8. ***Listing Department:*** The primary function of the department is to establish the securities of companies for trading purposes on different stock exchanges.

9. ***Investor Service Department:*** Its objective is to provide services to investors and to attend to complaints against brokers and sub-broker members and listed companies.

10. ***Public Relations Department:*** Liaison between intermediary investors and the government.

11. SEBI has two advisory committees for the primary market and secondary market. The function of these committees is non-statutory and their advice is only recommendatory by nature.

COMPANY LAW AND ITS AMENDMENTS

The first Companies Act was marked by the Joint Stock Companies Act, 1850 in which the separate entity concept came into force. The Joint Stock Companies Act, 1857 replaced the Act of 1850, and the concept of limited liability was recognized. In 1860, 1866, 1882, 1895, 1910 and 1913 different acts were introduced. The Companies Act of 1913 was amended in the years 1936 and 1951. To reform the Companies Act and to cope with the rapid expansion of trade, industry and commerce, a committee was formed under the Chairmanship of C.H. Bhabha (Bhabha Committee) in the year 1950, which submitted its report in March, 1952. The bill was moved by the then Finance Minister Mr. C.D. Deshmukh in the year 1955. In 1956 a new Companies Act, 1956 replaced The Companies Act, 1913. The Companies Act, 1956 consists of 658 sections, 15 schedules along with different sub-sections, clauses and sub-clauses. The Companies Act, 1956 has been amended several times in 1960, 1962, 1963, 1965, 1966, 1969, 1977, 1988, 1996, 1999, 2000 and 2002. The Companies Bill of 1993 was placed before parliament but due to political turmoil it was not translated into an act. The political scenario of 1997 was primarily responsible for not converting the Companies Bill of 1997 into an act. The Companies Bill of 1997 consisted of 458 sections by excluding 200 sections, again the political scenario was primarily responsible for the premature death of the Company Bill.

The Company Bill was again introduced in the *Lok Sabha* in 2008, but it automatically lapsed because of a change of government and it was re-introduced in 2009. The Company Bill, 2011 has replaced the half century old Company Act, 1956 with several changes in the light of the Rs. 14,000 crore accounting fraud of Satyam (popularly known as the Satyam scam), which exposed the weakness of the corporate governance framework, role of the auditor and independent directors and compelled the government to put the process of redrafting the Company Bill on the fast track. The salient features of the bill are as follows:

1. Two per cent of the average profit for the last 3 years be mandatorily spent above a certain threshold for Corporate Social Responsibility (CSR). (Introduced in the Company Bill, 2011).

2. Bill also tightens the laws for raising money from the public.

3. Insider trading by company directors or by key managerial personnel is considered a criminal offence.

4. Serious fraud investigation office given more power with more teeth.

5. Fixed term of independent directors and class action suits is provided.

6. SEBI regulation will be a greater force in case of conflict with any other laws.

This Act will provide the minimum standard of business integrity and standard of management behavior. It also opens up the horizon of disclosure environment exploring the framework of accounting to Accounting Standard (AS) and from AS to International Financial Reporting Standard (IFRS). It upholds corporate democracy by ensuring that shareholders have effective participation and control with legitimate interest. It also empowers the government to investigate matters and intervene in the daily affairs of the company in the line of law of the land.

Table 6.6 Provisions of the Companies Act, 1956 Regarding the Capital Market

Sections	Contents
Section 11-54	Incorporation of company and matters related to it
Section 55-68B	Prospectus
Sections 69-75	Allotment of securities
Sections 78-79	Issue of securities at premium and discount
Section 80	Issue and redemption of preference shares
Section 81	Issue of right shares
Sections 82-84	Nature numbering and certificate of shares
Sections 85-90	Kinds of share capital
Sections 91-99	Miscellaneous provisions regarding share capital
Sections 100-105	Reduction of share capital
Sections 106-107	Variation of shareholders' right
Sections 108-112	Transfer of share and debentures
Section 113	Limitation of time for issue of share certificate
Sections 114-115	Share warrants
Section 116	Penalty for personation of shareholders
Sections 117-123	Special provisions as to shareholders
Sections 150-156	Registers of members and debenture holders
Section 181	Restriction on exercise of voting rights of members who have not paid calls
Section 182	Restriction on exercise of voting rights of other group that is void.
Section 205	Dividend to be paid only out of profit
Section 425	Modes of winding up
Section 448	Appointment of official liquidator
Section 457	Powers of liquidator

Source: Companies Act, 1956.

Relevant changes in the Companies Act, 1956 as per Companies (Amendment) Act, 1999, Companies (Amendment) Act, 2000 and Companies (Amendment) Act, 2002 apart from Companies (Amendment) Act, 1996 in the post liberalized era.

Section 3	: Minimum paid up capital requirement for private company is Rs.1 lakh and in case of a public company is Rs.5 lakh as per (Companies) Amendment Act, 2000
Section 10E	: The Company Law Board will stand dissolved by virtue of new inclusion of section 10FA as per Companies (Second Amendment) Act, 2002
Section 10FB	: Formation of National Company Law Tribunal as per Companies (Second Amendment) Act, 2002
Section 10FC	: Composition of National Company Law Tribunal with a maximum of sixty-two members with judicial and technical members as the Central Government deemed fit as per Companies (Second Amendment) Act, 2002, along with New Sections 10FC, 10FD, 10FE, 10FF, 10FH, 10FI, 10FJ, 10FL, 10FM, 10FR, 10FQ, 10FS, 10FT, 10FV related to the newly constituted National Company Law Tribunal
Section 17	: Power of confirmation of alteration of objective clause was vested in the Central Government instead of the Company Law Board as per Companies (Second Amendment) Act, 2002
Section 17A	: Shifting of registered address be made only after prior permission as per Companies (Amendment) Act, 2000
Section 43A	: A private company will not be consider as a deemed public company as per Companies (Amendment) Act, 2000
Section 55A	: SEBI will monitor the administration relating to prospectus, issue of shares, payment of dividend and accounting disclosure of listed companies as per Companies (Amendment) Act, 2000
Sections 58AA and 58AAA	: Introduced to grant protection to investors as per provision of the Companies (Amendment) Act, 2002
Section 60(1)	: Registration of prospectus before application and allotment as per Companies (Amendment) Act, 2000
Section 67	: If the company makes the offer of securities to more than 50 persons in any financial year it will be deemed to be a public company as per Companies (Amendment) Act, 2000
Sections 77A and 77B	: A company can buy back its own securities provided the company complies with the provisions made in Sections 159, 207 and 211 as per the Companies (Amendment) Act, 1999
Section 79A	: Issue of sweat equity shares as per Companies (Amendment) Act, 1999
Section 86	: Public companies are allowed to issue non-voting equity shares as per Companies (Amendment) Act, 2002

Section 100 : Power of capital reduction by the court was conferred to the National Company Law Tribunal as per Companies (Second Amendment) Act, 2002

Section 109A : Every shareholder or debenture holder has the power to nominate on his death as per Companies (Amendment) Act, 1999

Section 109B : Transmission of shares to nominee as per Companies (Amendment) Act, 1999

Sections 153A and 153B : No further appointment of public trustees, as per Companies (Amendment) Act, 2000

Section 192A : Postal ballot is compulsory as per notification of the Central Government for taking resolutions as per Companies (Amendment) Act, 2000

Section 205A(5): New provision relating to unclaimed/unpaid dividend for five years from the date of its transfer to unpaid dividend account, the company has to transfer to the Investor Education and Protection Fund as per Companies (Amendment) Act, 1999

Section 205C : Establishment of Investor Education and Protection Fund for promotion of investor awareness and also for the protection of interest of investors in accordance with the rule as per Companies (Amendment) Act, 1999

Section 207 : Payment of dividend within 30 days from the date of declaration of dividend and a penalty of Rs. 1,000 per day of default apart from 18 per cent interest paid by the company as per Companies (Amendment) Act, 2000

Section 210A : National Committee on Accounting Standards be formed with a chairman along with seven members including one from SEBI to advise on accounting policies and standards as per Companies (Amendment) Act, 1999

Section 211 : Form and contents of balance sheet and profit and loss account as per Companies (Amendment) Act, 1999

Section 224(1B): Number of public limited companies of which a person can be the auditor as per existing ceiling; in addition to that he may be the auditor of any number of private and foreign companies as per Companies (Amendment) Act, 2000

Section 227 : Audit report stated whether the profit and loss account and balance sheet complied with accounting standards or not as per Companies (Amendment) Act, 1999 and audit report to state certain matters in thick type or italics on adverse comments or observations as per Companies (Amendment) Act, 2000

Section 275 : Person can be the director of a maximum of 15 companies as per Companies (Amendment) Act, 2000

Section 292A : Every public company having paid up capital of Rs. 5 crore or more will have to appoint an audit committee as per Companies (Amendment) Act, 2000

Section 372A : Inter-corporate loans and advances may be provided by what company by what type of Board and where it is not applicable as per Companies (Amendment) Act, 1999

Section 383A : Company secretary's report in compliance with the Companies Act, 1956 is mandatory for companies having paid up capital of Rs. 10 lakh and above as per Companies (Amendment) Act, 2000

Section 605A : Companies incorporated outside India whether doing business in India or not may have depository receipts in India and raise capital funds from the Indian public as per the Companies (Amendment) Act, 2000.

Companies emerging from Companies (Second Amendment) Act, 2002 include Clause 19AA – definition of Industrial Company, Clause 19AB – definition of Industrial Undertaking, Clause 46AA – definition of Sick Industrial Company.

CONSUMER PROTECTION ACT, 1986

The first consumer movement originated from England. As a result, the International Organization for Standardization (ISO) was established in 1947. Ralph Nader is the father of the consumer movement. Every year, 15th March is observed as World Consumers' Rights Day. The Consumer Protection Act, 1986 was passed in parliament and received the assent of the President of India on 24th December, 1986. In the same year the Bureau of Indian Standards Act, 1986 was also passed which has taken the responsibility of the ISI mark and hallmark for gold jewelers. The Consumer Protection (Amendment) Act, 1993 extended facilities in connection with banking, finance and insurance under the purview of service as per Section 2(1) (o) and widen the definition of consumer as per Section 2(1) (d). The Consumer Protection Act was amended in the year 2002. The Consumer Protection (Amendment) Act, 2002 empowers the District Forum, State Commission and National Commission, as the case may be, with the powers of a First Class Judicial Magistrate for summary trial not withstanding anything contained in the Indian Penal Code. The Consumer Protection (Amendment) Act, 2002 has also empowered the District Forum, the State Commission or the National Commission to attach the property of a person who does not comply with the interim order.

The Consumer Protection Rule 1987 and the Consumer Protection Regulations were passed and accepted for better compliance of the law and redress of consumers' grievances.

The following categories of persons may file a complaint under the Consumer Protection Act, 1986:

1. A consumer
2. Any voluntary consumer association, registered under the Companies Act, 1956
3. The Central Government
4. Any State Government
5. One or more consumers, where there are numerous consumers having the same interests

The maximum limit to the amount in the cases filed at the district, state and national level as per the Consumer Protection (Amendment) Act, 2002 is as follows:

District level courts up to Rs. 20 lakhs

State level court Rs. 20 lakhs to Rs. 1 crore

National level court Rs. 1 crore and above

Investors' Protection and Consumer Protection Act

As per the Consumer Protection Act, 1986 six consumer rights are laid down as follows:

1. The right to be protected against the marketing of hazardous goods.
2. The right to protect the consumer against unfair trade practices regarding quality, quantity, potency, standards of purity and price.
3. The right to get a variety of products at competitive prices.
4. The right to be heard and to address the consumers' interest at the appropriate forums.
5. The right to seek redressal mechanism against unfair or unscrupulous trade practices by the manufacturer and which goes against the interest of the consumers.
6. The right to consumer education.

The Rights of an Investor

Shareholders or debenture holders of a company enjoy the following rights:

1. To receive share or debenture certificates or preference share certificates bearing the paid up value. After dematerialization investors do not hold certificates in physical form, rather they maintain their details of holding in electronic format viz; in d-mat form.
2. To receive dividend or interest in due course of time.
3. To receive the right of getting bonus shares or right shares as per the decision of the board of directors and as approved by the annual general meeting of the respective companies.
4. The right to receive the annual report containing income statement, balance sheet and cash flow statement along with audited report, attendance slip and proxy form.
5. The right to apply to NCLT to call or direct an AGM.
6. The right to attend an AGM and cast a vote in the AGM personally or by proxy, provided the proxy is entitled to vote only on a poll and not on a vote by show of hands as per section 176(1) (c) of the Companies Act, 1956.

The NSE has published a booklet for awareness and education of investors under the name: *'Guiding Light for Investors,'* stating the investor's obligation and rights, which are given below:

The obligation to:

1. Sign a proper member-constituent agreement

2. Possess a valid contract note
3. Deliver securities with valid documents and proper signature

The obligation to ensure:

1. Payment is made on time
2. Shares are delivered on time
3. Securities are sent for transfer to the company on time
4. All papers received from the company under objections to the Trading Member (TM) are forwarded on time
5. Payment is made by cheque, with the investor's the purpose of payment, written on the back of the cheque. Also a Xerox copy of the cheque should be preserved if possible.

Investor's Rights

The right to get:

1. The best price
2. Proof of price/brokerage charged
3. Money/Shares on time
4. Shares through auction where delivery is not received
5. The amount squared up where delivery not received in an auction.

The right for redresses against:

1. Fraudulent price
2. Unfair brokerage
3. Delays in receipt of money or shares
4. Investor unfriendly companies

SEBI has taken regulatory action under Section 11B debarring companies for taking access from the capital market and under Section 15C empowering SEBI to impose penalty clauses.

The Companies (Amendment) Ordinance, 1999 be repealed and the Companies (Amendment) Act, 1999 further amended the Companies Act, 1956. Finally the Central Government has brought about certain changes in the Companies Act, 1956 by this amendment by providing certain measures of good corporate governance and investors' protection. The Investors' Education and Protection Fund (IEPF) has been created as per Section 205C of the Companies (Amendment) Act, 1999 for awareness and protection of investors.

As the 'amount in unpaid dividend,' 'application money received by the companies for allotment of any securities and due for refund', 'matured deposits with the companies', 'matured debentures with the companies' and 'interest accrued on the amount of refund' are accumulated in the RBI's custody, a portion of that fund is to be transferred to IEPF by the Central Government for the purpose of investor awareness and also for protection of the interests of investors. Apart from this, different NGOs, magazines (*Money Life*), business newspapers (*The Economic Times*), consumer affairs departments of the Central and State

Governments (Consumer Affairs Department, Government of West Bengal) have taken the initiative to impart awareness to consumers, especially small investors.

The Central Government established the Investors' Education and Protection Fund on 1st October, 2001 to protect the interests of general investors. All payment unclaimed or unpaid after 30th October, 1991 to 31st October, 1998 shall be transferred to the fund, provided such amount was paid to the parties prior to the enactment of Companies (Amendment) Act, 1999.

Sections 58AA and 58AAA were introduced to grant protection to investors. Investors who have invested up to Rs. 20,000 in a financial year in a company will be protected by the provisions laid down by the Companies (Amendment) Act, 2000.

The Government of India has set up a committee under the Chairmanship of Dr. N.L. Mitra to consider investors' protection. The committee felt that there was a need of a special act for investors' protection. A judicial form is also needed for redressal of investor grievances. The consumer court should be activated for providing redressal to small investors.

The Consumer Protection (Amendment) Act, 2002 extended the services to include financing, banking and insurance services. The cabinet of the former NDA government took up a comprehensive investors' awareness program on 17th January, 2003 by utilizing a portion of unclaimed dividend lying idle in the hands of the Reserve Bank of India. As a result, workshops were organized throughout the country. A booklet on investors' awareness and material was also distributed in the workshops. Audio-visual clippings, launching of a dedicated investor website, advertisements in leading daily newspapers and on All India Radio in English and Hindi along with local language were made part of the campaign. The fund is also utilized to protect distressed individual investors. For the purpose of administering this fund an Investors' Grievance Forum (IGF) was set up as an independent trust consisting of a governing council and a regional council. In the Governing Council the Finance Minister acts as Chairman, other members are the Governor of the RBI, a representative from the Department of Company Affairs (DCA), Ministry of Finance, one member from SEBI and one representative from NGO. The council meets once in six months to decide policy and action regarding the fund.

In his budget speech of 2005-06, the then Finance Minister authorized SEBI to form a National Institute of Securities Market (NISM) for the purpose of educating and training intermediaries of the stock market and promoting research and consultancy in related areas.

Investors' Grievance Cell (IGS)

Every stock exchange has to establish an Investors' Service Cell (ISC) to redress the complaints and grievances made against the listed companies or member companies. After receiving the complaint, the ISC gives directives to the company to resolve the matter within 15 days and clear up the pending complaints on a priority basis. If the pending complaints exceed 25 days but not more than 45 days, the ISC issues a show cause notice within 7 days to the company and finally either the respective scrip is suspended or transferred to Z category for non-compliance to ISC directives. The ISC may even call a representative of the company, register and the transfer agent to resolve the matter on an urgent basis. If the complaints are regarding non-delivery of shares, non-receipts of payment, dividend, bonus shares or right shares, a complaint may be lodged against the member and after receiving the complaints ISC refers the matter to the member within 7 days for response and redressal. If a response or satisfactory response is not received, the matter is placed before the Investors' Grievance Redressal Cell (IGRC). The IGRC, which is headed by a retired judge of the High Court, tries to resolve the matter after hearing both the parties. If the complaint cannot be resolved by the IGRC the matter is referred for arbitration. Finally, the arbitrator closes the reference after giving the award or decision. If the complainant is not satisfied with the award, he may appeal to the stock exchange within 15 days from the date of the award. There after an appeal bench comprising 5 arbitrators hears the matter again and a final award is made. A complaint being made against the defaulter member of the respective exchange can be filed directly for arbitration within 6 months from the date on which the member was declared as a defaulter by the stock exchange. If the award goes against the defaulter member the matter is scrutinized by a standing committee viz. the Defaulters Committee (DC) for judging the originality.

Grievances against brokers and sub-brokers are scrutinized by the grievance cells of the respective stock exchanges. Grievances against mutual funds are to be considered by the compliance officer of the mutual fund. Grievances relating to depository services go to the investor relation cell or the concerned depository. The investor information center of the respective stock exchange will take up all complaints relating to traded or listed securities. Aggrieved investors may also seek redressal of their complaints either from the Consumers' Disputes Redressal Forum (CDRF) or may file a suit in a court of law as per the Indian Penal Code, 1976, for appropriate relief.

Penalty Clause as Prescribed by SEBI

Penalties are levied by the Securities and Exchange Board India Act, 1992 and its subsequent amendments as per Section 15A(a) for failure to furnish any document or report to SEBI when required to do so. Under the rules and regulations of the act the maximum penalty is Rs. 1,00,000 per day in the case of default or Rs. 1 crore, whichever is less provided whoever made the failure. As per Section 15A(b) failure to file any return or furnish any information, books etc. under the regulations has a maximum penalty of Rs. 1,00,000 per day of default or Rs. 1 crore, whichever is less provided whoever commits the failure.

As per Section 15A(c) failure to maintain books of accounts or records has a maximum penalty of Rs. 1,00,000 per day of default or Rs. 1 crore, whichever is less provided whoever commits the failure, as per Section 15B, failure by an intermediary to enter into any agreement with his client attracts a maximum penalty of Rs. 1,00,000 per day of default or Rs. 1 crore, whichever is less provided the intermediary is required under the Act, rules or regulations to enter into such agreement, but fails to do so. As per Section 15C failure by a listed company or an intermediary to redress grievances of the investors attracts a maximum penalty of Rs. 1,00,000 per day of default or Rs. 1 crore, whichever is less provided the listed company or intermediary is required by the Board to redress the grievances, but fails to do so. As per section 15D(a) failure to obtain a certificate of registration from SEBI for sponsoring or carrying on any collective investment scheme including mutual funds, attracts a maximum penalty Rs. 1,00,000 per day of default or Rs. 1 crore, whichever is less provided whoever commits the default. As per section 15D(b) failure to comply with the terms and conditions of registration for any collective investment scheme, including mutual funds, attracts a maximum penalty Rs. 1,00,000 per day of default or Rs. 1 crore, whichever is less provided any registered collective investment scheme, including mutual funds for sponsoring or carrying on any investment scheme defaulted. As per Section 15D(c) failures to make an application for listing of a collective investment scheme as provided for in the concerned regulation maximum has a penalty Rs. 1,00,000 per day of default or Rs. 1 crore provided any registered collective investment scheme including mutual funds, committed the default. As per Section 15D(d) failures to dispatch unit certificates to the holders of the units under any scheme, including mutual funds in the manner provided for in the concerned regulations has a maximum penalty of Rs. 1,00,000 per day of default or Rs. 1 crore, whichever is less provided any registered collective investment scheme committed the failure. As per Section 15D(e) failure to refund application money to the investors within the prescribed period has a penalty of Rs. 1,00,000 per day of default or Rs. 1 crore, whichever is less provided the company committed the default. As per section 15D(f) failures to invest money collected in the manner or within the period prescribed by the concerned regulation have a maximum penalty of Rs. 1,00,000 per day of default or Rs. 1 crore whichever is less provided any registered collective investment scheme, including mutual fund committed the default. As per Section 15E failure by an Asset Management Company (AMC) of a mutual fund to comply with any regulations governing its activities has a maximum penalty Rs. 1,00,000 per day of default or Rs. 1 crore whichever is less provided the asset management company committed the default. As per Section 15F(a) failure by a registered stock broker to issue contract notes in the form and manner specified by the stock exchange has a maximum penalty equal to five times the amount for which the contract note was required to be issued provided the stock broker committed the default. As per Section 15F(b) failure by a registered stock broker to deliver to the investor, any security or make payment of the amount due to him has a maximum penalty Rs. 1,00,000 or Rs. 1 crore provided the stock broker committed the default. As per Section 15F(c) any registered stock broker, charging brokerage in excess of the rate prescribed by the regulation is liable for a maximum penalty of Rs. 1,00,000 or 5 times of the excess brokerage charged, whichever is higher provided the stock broker committing the default.

Sections 15G (i), 15G (ii) and 15G (iii) pertaining to insider trading impose a maximum penalty of Rs. 25 crore or 3 times the amount of profits made, whichever is higher provided the concerned insider is held liable. Sections 15H (i), 15H (ii), 15H (iii) and 15H (iv) pertaining to substantial acquisition of shares and takeover impose a maximum penalty of Rs. 25 crore or 3 times the amount of profit made, whichever is higher provided the person who is required under the act, rules or regulations is liable to make such disclosure. As per section 15HA for indulging in fraudulent and unfair trade practices, the maximum penalty is Rs. 25 crore or 3 times the amount of profits, whichever is higher provided any person indulges in fraudulent and unfair practices. As per section 15HB failure to comply with any provisions of the act, rules, regulations or directions where no separate penalty is provided, has a maximum penalty is Rs. 1 crore provided any person contravenes the law.

It is to be noted that more than two decades have elapsed since the enactment of the SEBI Act and there have been lot of changes in the securities' laws by the Securities (Amendment) Act, 1995, Depositories Act, 1996, Securities Laws (Amendment) Act, 1999, Securities Laws (Second Amendment) Act, 1999 and Securities and Exchange Board of India (Amendment) Act, 2002. The government continuously reviews and strengthens the securities laws from time to time. A large number of judicial and quasi-judicial norms have been passed so far in conformity with the changing stock market scenario. The Foreign Exchange Management Act, (FEMA) 1999 also has to be considered in the context of global investment, foreign direct investment, foreign institutional investments, global depository receipts or American depository receipts.

Role of Income Tax Laws in the Capital Market

7

The book, 'Arthashastra' on public administration, which was written by Kautilya gave an idea of taxation during Maurya period. The British Government faced a financial crunch as a result of the sepoy mutiny of 1857, which led to the enactment of the Income Tax Act in 1860 by Sir James Wilson. Between 1939 and 1956, the Income Tax Act was amended twenty-nine times. In 1956, the government referred the act to the Law Commission and the Law Commission drafted the bill and referred it back to the Government of India in 1958. Meanwhile, the government appointed a Direct Taxes Administrative Enquiry Committee under the Chairmanship of Sri Mahavir Tyagi and the committee submitted its report in the year 1959, and in April, 1961 the Income Tax bill was presented in the Lok Sabha (Parliament). The bill received the assent of the President of India on 13th September, 1961 and was enacted in our country on 1st April, 1962. Nani Palkiwala and Congo have rightly stated that, 'The provisions of the Income Tax Act are like a railway ticket – good only for one journey in time from 1st April to 31st March of the next and sometimes not even for the whole of that journey.' Income tax is dynamic because of the following reasons, (i) due to changes in the finance bill, (ii) due to changes in the Central Board of Direct Taxes (CBDT) circulars and (iii) due to the judgment on cases with the Commissioner of Income Tax (CIT).

India has a well-defined and diverse tax structure with the authority to levy taxes by the Central Government or State Government or both. Taxes are also classified into two broad categories: direct taxes and indirect taxes. There are also certain state government taxes.

Under the Direct Tax Code (DTC), the government is preparing new legislation to refine existing tax laws in the country. In the original DTC released in August 2009, the government had proposed to replace the existing system of Exempt-Exempt-Exempt (EEE) with Exempt-Exempt-Tax (EET) in case of pension funds, provident funds and life insurance schemes. Later on DTC draft notes stated that 'approved pure life insurance products and annuity schemes will also be subject to EEE method of tax treatment.' Meanwhile the Union Finance Minister, at that time, Mr. Pranab Mukherjee advocated in favor of a

Table 7.1 Structure of Taxes

Nature of Central Taxes	Examples	Act	Authority	Imposed on
Direct Tax	Income Tax	*Income Tax Act, 1961	CBDT	Imposed on or paid by person on which it is levied
	Wealth Tax	*Wealth Tax Act, 1957	CBDT	
Indirect Tax	Central Excise	Central Excise Tax,1944	CBEC	
	Custom Duty	Customs Act, 1962	CBEC	Imposed on a person but liability shifted to others
	Central Sales Tax	Central Sales Act, 1956	Govt. of India	
Nature of State Taxes	Sales Tax	Respected State's Act	State Govt.	Imposed on a firm but liability shifted to others
	Value added Tax	Respected State's Act	State Govt.	

*To be repealed by DTC; CBDT = Central Board of Direct Taxes; CBEC = Central Board of Excise & Customs.

moderate tax regime for individuals by lowering the tax slabs proposed in the original draft of the Direct Tax Code (DTC). The first draft of the DTC released in August 2009 had proposed the following structure: up to Rs. 1.6 lakh will be exempted from tax, tax on income up to Rs. 10 lakh per annum @ 10 per cent, income above Rs. 10 lakh and up to Rs. 25 lakh @ 20 per cent and income beyond Rs. 25 lakh @ 30 per cent. The company tax rate will be 20 per cent. The finance minister opined that the DTC will come as a big relief to the middle class, which was currently paying 10 per cent tax on an income up to Rs. 5 lakh, 20 per cent between Rs. 5 lakh and Rs. 8 lakh and 30 per cent beyond that. On 26th August, 2010 the cabinet cleared a heavily diluted DTC and there was no revolution in the process of direct taxes as proposed by Dr. Raja J. Chelliah, in the name of tax reforms, i.e. up to Rs. 2 lakh tax free, Rs. 2 lakh to Rs. 5 lakh @ 10 per cent, Rs. 5 lakh to Rs. 10 lakh @ 20 per cent and Rs. 10 lakh and above @ 30 per cent. Corporate tax rate will be 30 per cent.

DTC has withdrawn education cess and surcharge which gives marginal relief. Proposed investment level has gone up from Rs. 1.2 lakh to Rs. 1.5 lakh.

There are three steps of income tax assessment:

1. Determination of tax
2. Computation of tax liability
3. Filing of returns, payment of advance tax and final payment of tax

As per Sec 14 of IT Act 1961 there are five heads of income:

1. Income from salary; Section 15-17
2. Income from house property; Section 22-27
3. Income from profits and gains of business or profession; Section 28-44
4. Income from capital gains; Section 45-55
5. Income from other sources; Section 56-59

Capital Gains

As per Section 2(42A) of the IT Act, an asset will be termed as a short-term capital asset if it is held for not more than 12 months in case of shares or not more than 36 months in case of depreciable assets.

On the other hand, as per Section 2(29A) an asset held by an assessee for more than 12 months or 36 months (as the case may be) will be termed as a long term capital asset. Short term capital gains arise on transfer of short term capital assets. Similarly, long term capital gains arise from transfer of long term capital assets. Short term capital gains are taxed as per the tax slab, i.e. at a marginal rate and long term capital gains are taxed at a concessional rate of 10 per cent without indexation and @ 20 per cent with indexation for debt schemes. As per Section 111A, tax on short term capital gains should be charged @ 15 per cent plus surcharge and education cess but in case of long term capital gains it will come down to zero for equity schemes. In the case of short term capital gains certain conditions have to be followed:

1. Short term capital gains arise from transfer of equity shares of a company or unit of a mutual fund.
2. Transaction takes place after 1st October, 2004.
3. Security transaction tax has already been paid.

As per SEBI regulations, if a scheme maintains 65 per cent of its average weekly net assets invested in Indian equities it will be consider as equity scheme and an investor will not pay any tax on such investments on a long term basis. On the other hand, if an investor invests 100 per cent in foreign equity even on a long term basis, the investor will not have to pay tax on the basis of the equity scheme.

Tax implications for FII and FDI investments are a major concern in today's context. One of the recent studies made by the PWC, titled *Quest for Growth Destination India 2012: An Overview of Tax and Regulatory Framework in India* (published in July 2012) mentions the minimum corporate tax rates for Indian and foreign companies furnished in Table 7.2.

Table 7.2 Minimum Corporate Tax Rates for Indian and Foreign Companies

Company	Where Taxable Income Exceeds INR 10 million	Other Cases
Domestic company	32.45 per cent	30.9 per cent
	(30 per cent plus surcharge of 5 per cent plus education cess of 3 per cent)	(30 per cent plus education cess of 3 per cent)
Foreign company	42.02 per cent	41.2 per cent
	(40 per cent plus surcharge of 2 per cent and education cess of 3 per cent)	(40 per cent plus education cess

Source: PWC

Dividends

Payment of dividends will be made after the payment of dividend distribution tax by the Indian company. Remittance of dividends will be possible subject to compliance of specific requirements but RBI permission is not mandatory in this regard.

Dividend Distribution Tax (DDT)

Income from dividends will be exempted in the case of shareholders. But DDT is levied on companies declaring dividends. The effective rate of DDT will be 16.22 per cent (15 per cent plus 5 per cent surcharge and education cess of 3 per cent). The exemption privilege for companies developing Special Economic Zones (SEZs) regarding DDT has been withdrawn from 1st June, 2011. In order to tone down the cascading effect of DDT, dividend received by a domestic company from its subsidiary during the financial year will be reduced from the dividend paid or declared by the domestic company for the computation of DDT. It is also to be noted that the subsidiary company complied with DDT norms as per the provisions of Indian tax laws.

As per the Income Tax Act, 1961 deductions from capital gains are shown in Table 7.3.

Table 7.3 Deduction from Capital Gains

Sections	Types of Capital Gains	Content
54	LTCG	Deduction available from capital gains on sale of residential property
54B	STCG/LTCG	Deduction available from capital gains from transfer of land used for agriculture purpose
54D	STCG/LTCG	Deduction available from capital gains on compulsory acquisition of land
54EA		Whole or net consideration has to be invested within six months from the date of transfer or sale in specific assets
54EB		Total capital gains have to be invested in specific securities within six months from the date of transfer or sale of long-term capital assets
54EC	LTCG	Deduction available from capital gains on acquisition of certain bonds
54F	LTCG	Deduction available from capital gains on transfer of capital assets other than residential property
54G	STCG/LTCG	Deduction from capital gains on transfer of capital assets in case of shifting of industrial undertakings from an urban area to any other area
54G	STCG/LTCG	Deduction available from capital assets in case of shifting an industrial undertaking from urban area to SEZ

Cost Inflation Index

The Central Government by an official gazette notification announced the cost inflation index for different financial years on the consumer price index.

Computation of Tax on Long Term Capital Gains Section 112

As both short term and long term capital gains are indispensible parts of the taxable income of assessees, the tax orbit will be different for two components of income falling under the head of 'income from capital gains.' While short term capital gains are taxed at the normal rate, long term capital gains will be charged at a concessional rate.

Expenditure incurred by the assessee before 1st April, 1981 indexation is not required as expenditure and can be completely ignored. But for expenditure incurred after 1st April, 1981 indexed cost of acquisition is useful.

Table 7.4 Cost Inflation Index (CII)

Financial Year	Cost Inflation Index	Financial Year	Cost Inflation Index
1981-82	100	1997-98	331
1982-83	109	1998-99	351
1983-84	116	1999-2000	389
1984-85	125	2000-01	406
1985-86	133	2001-02	426
1986-87	140	2002-03	447
1987-88	150	2003-04	463
1988-89	161	2004-05	480
1989-90	172	2005-06	497
1990-91	182	2006-07	519
1991-92	199	2007-08	551
1992-93	223	2008-09	582
1993-94	244	2009-10	632
1994-95	259	2010-11	711
1995-96	281	2011-12	785
1996-97	305	2012-13	852

A high inflation index will bring down the liability of capital gains tax using the cost inflation index number in case of long-term capital gains.

Treatment of short term capital loss and long term capital loss:

1. From the assessment year 2003-04, short term capital loss is set off against capital gains from any other capital assets (short term or long term) as per Section 70(2).
2. Loss on transfer of long term capital assets can be set off against long term capital gains from transfer of other long term capital assets as per Section 70(3).

Table 7.5 Concessional Rate of Tax on Long Term Capital Gains

Section(sub-sec) (clause)	Nature of Assessee	Taxable Income	Rate of Tax
Section 112(1) (a)	Individual	Entire	20 per cent
Section 112(1) (b)	Domestic company	Exceeding Rs. 1 crore	20 per cent
Section 112(1) (c)	NRI or foreign company	Exceeding Rs. 1 crore	20 per cent
Section 112(1) (d)	Any other resident assessee	Entire	20 per cent
Section 115AB	Overseas financial organization	For long term capital gains	10 per cent
Section 115AC	Non-resident	For long term capital gains arising from global depository receipts	10 per cent
Section 115AD	Foreign institutional investors		10 per cent

LONG TERM CAPITAL GAINS ARISING FROM SECURITIES

Income arising from sale or transfer of capital assets is considered as income from capital assets and taxed in a different manner than that of the other five heads. For the purpose of computation of short term and long term capital gains consider hypothetical cases. Let, Mr. A sell 100 shares of Infosys in March, 2012 @ Rs. 3,200 which he had acquired in July, 2011 @ Rs. 2,100 considering brokerage @ 2 per cent on the sale. Since the holding period of shares is less than one year and is liable for short-term capital gains the calculation will be made in the following manner as shown in Table 7.6.

Table 7.6 Calculation of Short Capital Gains (Illustration)

	Rs.
Sale Price	3,20,000
Less:	
Brokerage @ 2.5 per cent (Maximum as per SEBI Guidelines)	7,000
Cost of acquisition Rs 2,100 × 100	2,10,000
Total Cost	2,17,000
Short term capital gains	1,03,000
Income tax thereon @ 20 per cent	20,600
Tax Rate	20 per cent

If the assessee holds the same security for more than one year he can avoid the tax. If the investor purchased Infosys shares in 2005-06 and sold them in 2012-13 considering the same price of purchase and sale for the same unit.

Table 7.7 Calculation of Long Capital Gains (Illustration)

Cost of inflation index in FY 2005-06	497
Cost of inflation index in FY 2012-13	852
	Rs.
Sale price	3,79,578
Less brokerage	7,000
Less indexed cost of acquisition 2,10,000 × 852/497	3,60,000
Total cost	3,67,000
Long term capital gains	12,578
Income tax thereon	2,516
Tax Rate	20 per cent

TAX BENEFITS FROM MUTUAL FUND INVESTMENTS

Income received in respect of the units of MFs will be exempted from income tax in the case of unit holders under Section 10(35) of the Act. However, dividend distribution tax will be payable by the MF. No tax will be deducted at source on any income distributed by the MF under the provisions of Sections 194K 196A of the Act.

Capital Gains

Long term capital gains arising on sale/repurchase of units will be chargeable under Section 112 of the Act, under Section 205 (plus surcharge and education cess) subject to the exemption of long term capital gains provided in Section 10(38) of the Act.

Short term capital gains arising on sale or repurchase of such units shall be taxed @ 30 per cent plus 10 per cent surcharge in case of corporate or firm unit holders where the total income exceeds Rs. 10,00,000. Further, an additional surcharge of 3 per cent by way of education cess is payable on amount of tax inclusive of surcharge.

Short term capital gains arising on sale/repurchase of such units shall be taxed at @ 30 per cent in case of local authorities. Further, an additional surcharge of 3 per cent by way of education cess is payable on amount of tax.

In case of short term capital gains arising to individuals and HUFs are clubbed with the income under the remaining four heads and taxed as per the Finance Act by considering 'income tax is one tax.' Short term capital gain income of domestic companies is taxed @ 30 per cent, in case of foreign companies @ 40 per cent, and in case of FIIs @ 30 per cent as per section 115AD of the Act.

In case of equity oriented funds as per section 111A of the Act, the short term capital gains arising from the sale (redemption) of a unit, where such sale (redemption) affects STT is taxable @ 10 per cent. However, at the time of sale (redemption) of units the unit holder will have to pay STT @ 0.25 per cent on the value of sale of the MF, which will be calculated by the MF and deposited in the government treasury.

In terms of the provisions of Section 80C of the Act, an individual or HUF is entitled to claim a deduction in respect of specified investment made in any FY of up to Rs. 1,00,000 provided subscription be made to any unit of any MF notified under clause (23A) of Section 10 of the Act or any scheme notified by the Central Gazette.

As per Circular No 75 dated 8th August, 1995 issued by the Central Board of Direct Taxes (CBDT) in case of a residential unit holder no tax is deducted at source from capital gains arising at the time of repurchase or redemption of the units.

As per Section 196D of the IT Act, no tax is required to be deducted at source on incomes by way of capital gains earned by a FIIs.

Relative Tax Advantage of Public Provident Fund and Fixed Deposit (PPF vs FDs)

Suppose an investor invests his money in Fixed Deposit (FD) @ 8 per cent return, then people in the higher tax bracket will have to earn less. If the assessee belongs to the 10 per cent tax bracket, actual return = $r(1 - i) = 8(1 - 10/100) = 8 \times 0.9 = 7.2$ per cent

If the assessee belongs to the 20 per cent tax bracket, actual return = $r(1-i) = 8(1-20/100)$ = $8 \times 0.8 = 6.4$ per cent

If the assessee belongs to the 30 per cent tax bracket, actual return = $r(1-i) = 8(1-30/100)$ = $8 \times 0.7 = 5.6$ per cent

Table 7.8 Maximization of Return by using Tax Free Instruments: (Individual Belongs to High Tax Bracket)

Investor belongs to Tax Bracket	Return from PPF	Return from FD After Tax	Tax Haven
10 per cent	8.8 per cent	7.2 per cent	1.6 per cent
20 per cent	8.8 per cent	6.4 per cent	2.4 per cent
30 per cent	8.8 per cent	5.6 per cent	3.2 per cent

Maximize the Return from PPF Investments by Exercising the Art of Finance

If investors invest their money in PPF getting an 8.8 per cent return, the actual return in their hand will be calculated as per tax bracket.

Investor belongs to 10 per cent tax bracket, actual return = $r/(1-t) = 8.8/1 - 10/100$
$$= 8.8/1 - 0.1 = 8.8/0.9 = 9.77 \text{ per cent}$$

Investor belongs to 20 per cent tax bracket, actual return = $r/(1-t) = 8.8/1 - 20/100$
$$= 8.8/1 - 0.2 = 8.8/0.8 = 11 \text{ per cent}$$

Investor belongs to 30 per cent tax bracket, actual return = $r/(1-t) = 8.8/1 - 30/100$
$$= 8.8/1 - 0.3 = 8.8/0.7 = 12.57 \text{ per cent}$$

An investor in the high tax bracket will enjoy greater benefits.

It is also to be noted that up to the financial year 2010-11, if an investor invested Rs. 70,000 per year @ 8 per cent tax free interest, the cumulative amount after 16 years will be Rs. 22,92,516 including Rs. 11,72,516 tax free interest. By investing in the PPF every year, tax savings will be Rs. 21,630 considering that the tax payer belongs to the 30.9 per cent tax bracket. In 16 years, the accumulated tax savings will be Rs. 3,62,307 from investment. In 16 years the investor will have a tax free corpus of Rs. 22,92,516. With tax savings the total gains in 16 years will be Rs. 26,54,823 after investing Rs. 70,000 carrying interest @ 8 per cent.

If an investor belongs to the 10.3 per cent tax bracket, actual return = $r/(1-i) = 10,87,614/(1-0.103) = 11,72,516/0.897 = 13,07,152$ (Rs.)

If an investor belongs to the 20.6 per cent tax bracket, actual return = $r/(1-i) = 10,87,614/(1-0.206) = 11,72,516/0.794 = 14,76,720$ (Rs.).

If an investor belongs to the 30.9 per cent tax bracket, actual return = $r/(1-i) = 10,87,614/(1-0.309) = 11,72,516/0.691 = 16,96,839$ (Rs.).

An investor can open a PPF account in any branch of the SBI or GPO. The maximum investment is Rs. 1,00,000 with a minimum investment in any year of Rs. 500 bearing 8.8 per cent annual interest and attracting tax deduction under Section 80C of IT Act. PPF matures in 15 years but can be extended twice in a period of 5 years.

Table 7.9 Comparative Analysis of an Investment of Rs. 70,000 in EPF, PPF, FD and LIC

Investment Avenues	Interest Rate (per cent)	Return (After Tax)	Real Income (per cent)
EPF	9.50	9,500	9.50
PPF	8.80	8,800	8.80
FD	9.50	6594.5	6.56
LIC	7.00	7,000	7.00

(Provided the investor belongs to the 30.9 per cent tax shield including cess.)

However, a proposed investment in PPF of Rs. 1,00,000 every year for 15 years @ 8.8 per cent steady interest rate will create a corpus of Rs. 31 lakhs (approx). Whereas, if the interest remains the same as before @ 8 per cent by the same investment, the corpus will be Rs. 29.32 lakhs and tax haven and real income will vary accordingly.

Any investment decision depends on risk, return, liquidity and tax shelter. Moreover, dividend from Indian companies and mutual funds are to be considered as tax free as per Section 10(34) and Section 10(35) respectively as per the IT Act.

Investment in mutual funds is by far the best investment in the volatile situation. These are broadly categorized as equity funds, debt funds and hybrid funds. Taxation is also dynamic in relation to the variety of funds. Apart from risk, return and liquidity, tax is a yardstick on which an investor can balance earnings and maximize wealth.

Equity Diversified Funds

Average equity investment of more than 60 per cent is made in blue chip shares, large cap, mid cap and small cap. It yields medium to long term capital appreciation and tax benefits accordingly. As per studies made by the IFMF in 2010, Indian diversified mutual funds performed well globally in comparison with their counterparts in advanced countries. The best performing Indian mutual funds are DSP Black Rock Small and Mid Cap, Reliance Equity Opportunities, UTI MID Cap Fund (Growth).

Large cap funds: More than 80 per cent of the corpus invested in large cap companies.

Large and mid cap funds: 60-80 per cent of the corpus invested in large cap companies.

Multi cap funds: 40-60 per cent of corpus invested in large cap companies.

Mid and small cap funds: At least 60 per cent of the corpus invested in small and mid cap companies.

If an investor sells equity funds within a year he will have to pay 15 per cent capital gains tax. Moreover, dividend received from such a fund does not attract any tax obligation. Presently long-term capital gains from equity funds are not be taxable. This will make the growth option more attractive. In the case of the dividend reinvestment option, the amount invested in the form of units is the dividend amount and in future it will not be considered as capital gains and so the question of capital gains tax does not arise. In addition, dividend reinvested qualify for exemption as per Section 80C. Forthcoming DTC dividend may attract 5 per cent tax.

Equity Link Savings Scheme (ELSS)

The investment objective is the same as equity diversified funds but attracts tax benefits under Section 80C along with employee's provident fund, public provident funds, national savings schemes, five year tax of different banks, tax savings schemes of mutual funds etc., subject to a lock in period of three years. Financial discipline can be imposed if an investor opts for a Systematic Investment Plan (SIP). Before investing five years trend should be observed.

Dividend Yield Funds

This fund will provide a regular income with steady capital appreciation by investing in stock having high dividend yield with less volatility and risk.

Equity Index Funds

This type of fund provides similar returns to that of bench mark funds like S and P CNX Nifty, BSE 100 and has market and systematic risk.

Contra Funds

These are also equity diversified funds, which are undervalued but have long-term potentiality.

Hybrid-equity oriented: Average equity exposure of more than 60 per cent of the corpus.

Hybrid-debt oriented aggressive: Average equity exposure varies from 25-60 per cent.

Hybrid-debt oriented conservative: Average equity exposure must not exceed 25 per cent of the corpus.

Hybrid-arbitrage: Investment of the corpus between equity and derivatives.

If redemption of debt fund be made within a year capital gains tax will arise. For the 10 per cent tax bracket the benefit will be marginal; if the tax payer belongs to the 20 per cent or 30 per cent tax bracket he will have to opt for dividend option for tax benefit. Debt funds held for more than a year will provide more benefit for growth option as long term gains from debt funds will be taxed subject to inflation indexation benefit which is high in the inflation regime.

ETF Funds

The popularity of gold exchange traded funds has increased day by day due to the fact that funds are invested in a non-material form rather than in the form of jewelry, coins or bars. Gold ETF unit, equivalent to 1 gram of gold can be held in the demat form and traded on recognized stock exchanges. Security, convenience and liquidity are the triple benefits that investors can enjoy. Gold ETFs are open-ended fund schemes that invest in the bullion market. There are nine ETFs available on the NSE, including: Benchmark Gold BSE, UTI Gold ETF, SBI Gold ETF, Kotak Gold ETF, RIL Gold. SIP is not available for ETFs but there are no front loading fees. However, to invest in a Gold ETF (GTEF) costs Rs. 500 per year apart from fund management cost of 1 per cent per year and brokerage charge per transaction of

Table 7.10 Evaluations of Various Investment Avenues

Financial Instruments	Types	Risk	Return	Liquidity	Tax Shelter	Convenience
Financial Securities	Equity shares	High	High	Fairly high	Tax free: Dividends, but capital gains tax	High
	Fixed deposit/ Debentures of company	Medium	High	Average	Nil	High
	Savings bank accounts	Negligible	Moderate	High	Taxable	Very high
	PO savings bank accounts	Negligible	Moderate	High	Tax free	Very high
Non-Securitized Financial Assets	Public provident fund	Nil	High	Average	Qualified U/S 80C	Very high
	Life insurance policy	Nil	Medium	Average	Qualified U/S 80C	Very high
	Equity fund	High	Significantly high	High	Qualified U/S 80C	Very high
	Growth scheme (Equity 80-100 per cent)	High	High	High		Very high
Mutual Fund Schemes	Income scheme (Equity 0 per cent)	Low to medium		Significantly high		Very high
	Balanced (Equity 0-60 per cent)	Medium to high	Medium			
	Equity link savings scheme (ELSS)	Moderate to high	Long-term capital appreciation	3-year lock-in period	Qualified U/S 80C	
	Value fund	Risky	Potential growth	As per fund house	Attracts capital gains tax	
Exchange Traded Fund (ETF)	Indexed fund	Risky	Compare with benchmark return	As per fund house	Attract capital gains tax	
	Large-cap (More than 80 per cent in large-cap companies)	High	High	High	Qualified U/S 80C	Very high
	Large and mid-cap (60-80 per cent is invested in large-cap Companies)	High	High	High	Qualified U/S 80C	High
Equities:	Multi-cap (40-60 per cent assets deploy in large cap assets)	Moderate	Moderate	Moderate	Not qualified	Moderate

	Fund	Risk tolerance	Returns	Dividend / Income	Tax rebate U/S 80C	Moderate (80-100 per cent)
	Mid and small cap (At least 60 per cent assets in small & mid-cap tax savings)	High	High	High		Moderate (80-100 per cent)
Debt Fund	Corporate bond funds	High	High	As per fund house	Attracts capital gains tax	
	Floating Rates Funds (FRFs)	Protected capital loss	Average	Varies as per fund house	Attracts capital gains tax	
	Balance fund	Low risk	Moderate	Varies as per fund house	Attracts capital gains tax	
Hybrid Fund	Money market mutual/liquid or safer fund	Low	Moderate	High	No tax benefit	
Real Assets	Real estate (Land and residences)	Negligible	Medium to high	Low	Some	Fair
	Gold and Silver	Average	Moderate	Average	Nil	Average

Table 7.11 Calculation of Taxable Income

Income from salary	Rs
[Subject to deductions available regarding HRA u/s 10(13A) least of HRA received; rent paid minus 10 per cent of basic; and 50 per cent salary (40 per cent in case of Kolkata, Mumbai, Delhi and Chennai); MA, LTA and conveyance allowance]	-------
Income from house property	-------
As per 24 (a) Subject to standard deduction 30 PControl Act maximum rent will be the standard rent. Municipal tax and interest paid on loan for construction, reconstruction and repair of the house will be admissible as deduction provided interest on loan u/s 24(b) is up to Rs. 1,50,000. In case of joint loan ceiling of interest will be Rs. 3,00,000 for self occupied only interest on loan will be admissible as deduction. With effect from 1st April, 2012 standard deduction came down 20 per cent with introduction of DTC but taxpayers have to pay 1 per cent wealth tax if the property value including luxury car and gold jewelry exceeds.Income from business or profession (Subject to adjustment of expenditure for business or profession and losses of the profession and losses of the previous year)	-------
Income from capital gains	
[Subject to indexation, losses carried forward and investment in specified cases. Short term capital gains from non-equity assets added with income, short term capital gains from equity taxed @ 15 per cent. Long term capital gains from non-equity assets taxed @ 10 per cent]	-------
Income from other sources	
(Interest, dividend from foreign companies, gifts, etc.)	
Gross Total Income	-------
Less Deduction u/s 80CCC to u/s 80U	
(Except that of Section 80G)	
Less Tax Savings u/s 80C, 80CCC and 80CCD	Maximum Rs. 1,00,000
Less Medical Insurance u/s 80D	
Family and self Maximum Rs 15,000	
Parents Maximum Rs 15,000	
Senior citizen Maximum Rs 5,000	
Less medical treatment of dependent disabled u/s 80DD	Depends on illness
Less medical treatment of some special disease u/s 80 DDB	Depends on illness
Less interest on education loan u/s 80E	No Limit
Less donation u/s 80G 50-100 per cent of donation less deduction u/s 80GG Rs. 2,000 per month or 25 per cent of total income or actual rent paid in excess of 10 per cent of total income provided taxpayer, spouse or minor children do not hold any residential accommodation where they reside, employed or carry out business or profession.	
Less deduction u/s 80T Savings Bank Interest	Maximum Rs.10,000

0.25-0.5 per cent. Purchase of gold in the physical form attracts short-term capital gains if held for up to three years. On the other hand short-term capital gains are liable for ETFs held for less than one year and holding the ETFs for more than one year comes under the purview of long-term capital gains. It is found from observations that the dollar price and gold price move in opposite direction. Moreover, Indian investors must bear in mind the behavior of the Rupee vs. the US$.

Any increase in international gold prices will not be translated into gains if the Indian rupee appreciates significantly against the US dollar. Today, a speculator in the bullion market plays a significant role specially in the case of silver or gold.

If the tax payer falls in the tax bracket of 10.3 per cent, 20.6 per cent and 30.9 per cent respectively, tax savings will be Rs. 2,060, Rs. 4,120 and Rs. 6,180 respectively. If buyback is after 5 years, the effective return will be 9.39 per cent, in all cases and if the bonds are held for 10 years the effective return will be 11.58 per cent.

The calculation is as follows: $20,000 - 2,060 = 17,940$ and return = Rs. 9,388 will be 10.46 per cent and in the 10.3 per cent tax bracket it comes as 9.395 per cent. Similar calculations can be carried out in the other cases.

If the assessee donates Rs. 50,000, out of which Rs. 10,000 is to the Prime Minister's National Relief Fund and National Foundation for Communal Harmony where there is no maximum limit of donation, then deduction as a percentage of the net qualifying amount is 100 per cent. Whereas the rest, i.e. Rs. 40,000 was donated to a public charitable institution a deduction of 50 per cent of donated amount is admissible, i.e. Rs. 20,000, but this is limited to 10 per cent of gross total income. With rising medical expenditure, education expenditure, building loan or rental housing expenses a taxpayer can go beyond section 80C to reduce taxes.

Income of Other Persons Included in Assessee's Total Income

As per Section 64 of the Income Tax Act, 1961 income of other persons are to be clubbed with the income of the individual under the following circumstances:

- Section 64(1) (ii): Remuneration received by spouse in cash or kind are to be attached with the income of the individual.
- Section 64 Explanation 1: When the husband and wife have substantial interest in the concern or both of them are in respect of remuneration, the remuneration shall be clubbed with the total income of the husband or wife, whose total income excluding this income is higher.
- Section 64(1) (iv): Income arising to the spouse by way of asset transferred other than adequate consideration is added to the individual effecting such transfer.
- Section 64(1) (vi): Income arising from the asset transferred to the son's wife of an individual other than the adequate consideration is added to the income of the individual effecting such transfer.
- Section 64 (1A): In computing the total income of an individual, all income raised or accrued to minor children shall be clubbed with the total income of the individual.

- Section 6 Explanation 3: When the assets are transferred directly or indirectly by an individual to his spouse or son's wife are invested by the transferee, income arising from such investment shall be clubbed with the total income of an individual.
- The income of minor children shall not be included in the total income of the parent of the minor when:
  1. The minor child is suffering from any of the disabilities specified in section 80U such as permanent physical disability.
  2. The income arises to such minor on account of any manual work done by him.
  3. The income arises to the minor from activity involving skill talent or specialized knowledge and experience.

Table 7.12 Comparison of Different Tax Savings Schemes

Type	Lock in Period	Rate of Return	Tax Status	Maximum Investment	Risk
PPF	15 years	8.8 per cent	Tax free	Rs. 1,00,000	No
EPF		9.5 per cent	Tax free	Rs. 1,00,000	No
NSC	6 years	8.6 per cent	Taxable	Rs. 1,00,000	No
Senior Citizen Savings Scheme (SCSS)	5 years	9 per cent	Taxable	Rs. 1,00,000	No
Tax Savings FD	Time varies	6-8 per cent	Taxable	Rs. 1,00,000	No
Infrastructure Bond	Time span depends on option	8 per cent	Taxable	Rs. 20,000	Withdrawn from the FY 2012-13
ULIP	3-5 years	Market link	Tax free	Rs. 1,00,000	Yes
ELSS	3 years	Market link	Tax free	Rs. 1,00,000	Yes

Source: www.indiapost.gov.in and www.indiappf.gov.in

It is necessary to know who will be exempted from filing returns and who are liable to file returns. Salaried person will be exempted from filing returns from the financial year 2010-11 if the assessee fulfils the following conditions:

1. Total income after admissible deductions is up to Rs. 5,00,000
2. Income is restricted to salary and savings bank interest
3. Salary is only from one employer
4. Savings bank interest must not exceed Rs. 10,000 and is included in Form 16.

Tax Implication of NCD in Relation with FD and PPF

Non-Convertible Debentures (NCDs) have always provided a higher interest rate to investors than traditional bank deposits. Due to weakness in the stock market on one hand and higher interest rate on the other, investors are turning towards the safety of a fixed income option. Apart from fixed deposits and fixed monthly pension, non-convertible debentures attract investors. Fixed deposits of a bank are insured up to Rs. 1,00,000, whereas non-convertible debentures are not backed by any such insurance or guarantee. Liquidity of non-convertible debentures varies along with the listing of the NCDs of different stock exchanges.

Independent assessment of issuer's ability is reflected by credit rating, which varies from AAA (Highest safety), AA (High safety), A (Adequate safety), BBB (Moderate safety), BB (Moderate risk), B (High risk), C (Very high risk) to D (Default). This is equally true in the case of a country. When Standard and Poor's downgraded the rating of bonds of the US Government from AAA to AA+, the Dow Jones Industrial index along with the world's capital market came tumbling down. Since any income from NCDs is added to the total income and taxed accordingly, for the 10.3 per cent tax bracket, 11.5 per cent return from NCD comes down to 10.31 per cent; for the 20.6 per cent tax bracket it falls to 9.13 and for the 30.9 per cent tax bracket it will come down to 7.95 per cent compared with 8 per cent tax free return of PPF.

At the time of tax planning age and gender consideration is vital in India. Men and women below 60, senior citizens above 60 or very senior citizens above 80, all have to abide by the tax slabs.

Table 7.13 Distribution of Tax Rate by Category and Tax Slab

Men below 60 years:

Tax slab		Tax rate
Up to Rs. 2 lakh	----------	Nil
Next Rs. 3 lakh	----------	10 per cent
Next Rs. 5 lakh	----------	20 per cent
Over Rs. 10 lakh	----------	30 per cent

Women below 60 years:

Tax slab		Tax rate
Up to Rs.2 lakh	----------	Nil
Next Rs. 3 lakh	----------	10 per cent
Next Rs. 5 lakh	----------	20 per cent
Over Rs. 10 lakh	----------	30 per cent

Senior citizens above 60 years but below 80 years:

Tax Slab		Tax rate
Up to Rs. 2.5 lakh	----------	Nil
Next Rs. 2.5 lakh	----------	10 per cent
Next Rs. 5 lakh	----------	20 per cent
Over Rs. 10 lakh	----------	30 per cent

Very senior citizen above 80 years:

Tax slab		Tax rate
Up to Rs. 5 lakh	---------------	Nil
Next Rs. 5 lakh	---------------	20 per cent
Over Rs. 10 lakh	-------------	30 per cent

As per their study, McKinsey International identified that those who can earn Rs. 10,00,000 or more includes senior corporate executives, large business owners, high end professionals and big agricultural land owners will be ear marked as global Indians. If we assume taxable income is Rs. 10,00,000, which is arrived at after availing of all deductions and exemptions but includes surcharges and cesses on tax then from the Financial Year 2007-08 to 2011-12 the tax burden came down to Rs. 1.56 lakh from Rs. 2.56 lakh over four years indicating they have a tax savings of Rs. 1,00,000.

Table 7.14 Advance Tax Schedule for Any Financial Year

Advance Tax	Tax Payment Deadline
30 per cent of tax assessed	15th Sept., of every year
60 per cent of tax assessed	15th Dec., of every year
100 per cent of tax assessed	31st March of every year
Tax assessed on taxable income including cess.	

Tax planning in the case of men below 60 years:	
	Rs.
Gross total income	10,00,000
Savings under section 80C	1,00,000
Medical insurance section 80D	
Family and self	15,000
Parents	15,000
Interest on education loan section 80E	50,000
Net taxable income	8,20,000
Income exempted from tax	2,00,000
10 per cent tax on income up to Rs. 5,00,000	30,000
20 per cent tax between Rs. 5,00,000 to Rs. 8,20,000	64,000
Tax payable	94,000
Education cess @ 3 per cent on tax	2,820
Total tax payable	96,820
Effective tax rate	9.682 per cent

If the assessee took Rs. 15,00,000 as house loan interest @ 15 per cent, then a maximum of Rs. 1,50,000 interest will be admissible as deduction as per Section 24(b) under the head income from house property and gross total income come down to Rs. 8,50,000 and the tax burden is reduced by Rs. 30,900 in this case and the ultimate tax liability will be Rs. 65,920. In that case effective tax rate will be 6.592 per cent.

By taking a home loan the assessee is entitled to get tax benefit under section 80C from repayment of the principal amount to a maximum of Rs. 1,00,000 including other long term investments that fall in that category and Section 24(b) for payment of interest to a maximum of Rs. 1,50,000 of the Income Tax Act. Co-owners are entitled to get tax benefits subject to the fact they are co-borrower of the home loan and the limit is applicable for each borrower. It is to be noted that if the co-owner is not a co-borrower, then he or she is not entitled to any tax benefit. Similarly, if the co-borrower is not a co-owner the question of tax benefit does not arise.

Consider the situation when an assessee has a corpus fund of Rs. 15,00,000 in GPF or PPF but has taken a house loan of equal amount. In this situation he is enjoying Rs. 1,32,000 as tax free interest and enjoying tax relief on Rs. 1,50,000 interest paid (considering the situation he is taking Rs. 15,00,000 home loan @ 10 per cent and the amount paid as interest is Rs. 1,50,000) depending on the tax orbit to which the assessee belongs. In the 10 per cent tax bracket it will be Rs. 15,450, for the 20 per cent tax bracket it will be Rs. 30,900 and for the 30 per cent tax bracket it will be Rs. 46,350. But interest of Rs. 20,000 will be earned from GPF or PPF and tax savings in the 10 per cent tax bracket is Rs. 12,360, for the 20 per cent tax bracket it is Rs. 24,720 and in the 30 per cent tax bracket it will be Rs. 37,080. Loss in the 10 per cent tax bracket from interest earned and interest paid is Rs. 2,190 but gain from the 20 per cent tax bracket is Rs. 25,620 and from the 30 per cent tax bracket it will be Rs. 53,430. So if the tax payer falls in the high tax bracket he will gain more.

Table 7.15 Gains from Housing Loan by Different Categories of Tax Payers

Home loan of	Individual	on Different Tax	Bracket
Rs. 15,00,000 @ 10 per cent	@ 10 per cent	@ 20 per cent	@ 30 per cent
Interest paid	Rs. 1,50,000	Rs. 1,50,000	Rs. 1,50,000
Less: Interest earned (from GPF/PPF) Tax saved on interest earned Tax saved on interest paid	Rs. 1,20,000 Rs. 12,360 Rs. 15,450	Rs. 1,20,000 Rs. 24,720 Rs. 30,900	Rs. 1,20,000 Rs. 37,080 Rs. 46,350
Gain /(Loss)	(Rs. 2,190)	Rs. 25,620	Rs. 53,430

What Amount of Tax is Paid on Global Income?

As the world is treated as a global hub the Indian investor is hunting for global earnings. Any gains from overseas investments are taxed in India. Interest earned from bonds and deposits, dividend from foreign companies doing business in India and abroad, earnings from foreign funds and short-term capital gains thereof are added to the original income and taxed at the usual rate.

Long-term capital gains from global investments will be taxed @ 20 per cent. Rental income from house property situated outside India will be added to income after 30 per cent standard deduction and taxed at the usual rate. As the Direct Tax Code (DTC) came into effect from 1st April, 2012, the distinctions between short-term and long-term capital with respect to time were abolished. It is also to be noted that standard deduction for rental income came down from 30 per cent to 20 per cent. Investment in global funds diversifies an investor's portfolio, so he can derive the benefit from the rise in the foreign market. The global stock market performance of 15 countries is considered in this regard.

Table 7.16 Global Stock Market Performance in 2010 ($ return)

Gainers	Per cent	Gainers	Per cent
Russia	49.0	China	3.3
Denmark	29.9	Greece	43.8
Sweden	29.4	Spain	25.8
India	14.8	Ireland	21.5
USA	11.8	Italy	20.5
Japan	9.8	France	8.5
Germany	5.1	Brazil	0.9
UK	3.5		

Source: The Economic Times 5th January, 2011

In a portfolio, global equities must not make up more than 10 to 15 per cent of your incremental investment. After fulfilling domestic investment prospective, an investor must look to global diversification. Fund houses that invest 65 per cent or more in foreign stocks are not entitled to get tax relief from the point of view of long-term capital gains. Moreover, this type of investment contains exchange rate risk. If the money invested depreciated against the rupee, return will be lower and vice versa. Country specific risk is also associated with foreign investments. Crises in the global market change the direction of foreign market investment by potential investors.

Many global mutual funds out perform domestic mutual funds as investments in the bullion market mainly in silver, gold and oil. Global funds are good on a short-term basis as multidimensional factors are involved in them. From a long-term perspective, returns from Indian mutual funds are supposed to be better than those of global mutual funds.

The orbit of taxation changes with the residential status of the tax payer. A resident and ordinary resident has to pay tax on any one of the five sources of income earned worldwide. Long-term capital gains earned from world-wide assets are to be taxed @ 20.6 per cent, while short-term capital gains are to be taxed @ between 10.3 per cent to 30.9 per cent depending upon the level of income of the individual. A resident individual who earns income in the form of dividend or interest from overseas investment is to be taxed @ varying from 10.3 per cent to 30.9 per cent. With the introduction of the Direct Tax Code (DTC) from 1st April, 2012 overseas income is taxable where it is earned as per the law of the country where it arises. To avoid double taxation, a taxpayer can use the beneficial provision of the Double Taxation Avoidance Agreement (DTAA) between India and the income generating country of the individual depending on tax laws of both countries considering the natural income, the tax bracket and status of the employee, bearing in mind the Foreign Exchange Management Act, 1999 (FEMA) and the power given to the Reserve Bank of India in this regard.

Presently each component of income will have to be examined in respect of the provisions laid down in the Double Taxation Avoidance Agreements for relief.

Why Should One Invest in the New Pension Scheme (NPS)?

The New Pension Scheme (NPS) was introduced on 1st May, 2009. The one time fee for opening an account is Rs. 350 and there is a registration fee of Rs. 40. Rs. 9 per Rs. 10 lakh are the fund management charges, i.e. fund management charges are only 0.0009 per cent compared to annual mutual fund charges of up to Rs. 22,500 i.e. 2.25 per cent. Rs. 20 is the transaction fee for every fresh contribution. As per SEBI's recent circular, the entry load is free for mutual fund contribution. The low cost will be applicable if and only if the number of members subscribing to the scheme is sufficient. A Permanent Retirement Account Number is allotted against an NPS account with a fees of Rs. 50 and annual maintenance charge of Rs. 350. NPS accounts are of two types: Tier I and Tier II. In Tier I pension account, the minimum deposit is Rs. 6,000 per year, and the account holder cannot withdraw any money before he is 60 years. After the age of 60 years, contributions are stopped and withdrawals begin. Sixty per cent of the corpus can be withdrawn in turn or by phase over the next 10 years i.e. up to the age of 70 years. This means 40 per cent is retained. At the age of 70, the entire balance can be withdrawn.

It is to be noted a Tier II account is like a mutual fund from which you can withdraw any amount at any time. But opening a Tier II account is allowed only if one has a Tier I account. A Tier II account must have a balance of Rs. 2,000. From the Financial Year 2011-12 employers' contribution to NPS accounts are treated as business expenses. As the contribution to NPS by employer is not taxable, the employer's contribution will be considered as a tax free benefit.

Table 7.17 New Pension Scheme of the Central Government

Tier I	Tier II
(Mandatory)	(Optional)
Employee's contribution is 10 per cent of basic pay + dearness pay + dearness allowance	No ceiling of contribution by employees
Government matches contribution	No contribution by the government
Full amount cannot be withdrawn during service	Any amount can be withdrawn at any time

Regulator: Pension Fund Regulatory and Development Authority (PFRDA)

Fund houses: Six fund houses handle the NPS corpus till date: SBI Pension Fund, UTI Retirement Solution, IDFC Pension Fund, ICICI Prudential Pension Fund, Kotak Pension Fund and Reliance Pension Fund. There is a misconception regarding LIC's Pension Plus Scheme, LIC's Pension Plus (a Unit Linked Pension Plan in Table 7.14) which does not come under the purview of NPS.

Investment Horizon

By using four yardsticks of risk, return, liquidity and tax haven, golden harvesting is possible. Wealth creation, on one hand and an increased corpus on the other, leads to financial health. Five per cent (5 per cent) directly invested in equity, 10 per cent in equity linked mutual funds, a portion in commodity futures and passive investors seeking commodity exposure or active investors go for low yield government securities. Risk-return criteria and the age of the investor are very important factors when considering investments. At a young age an investor generates a small investment surplus or may even have negative net worth due to a home loan, car loan or education loan, but risk taking ability may be high. With passage of time the corpus may be high but risk taking ability is low. It may be said that at 25 years, bond related investments are 25 per cent and equity related investments are 75 per cent, at age 60 years bond related investment is 60 per cent and equity related investment is 40 per cent. Tax haven and liquidity must also be kept in mind according to one's needs in life.

Financial Tips for Investors

1. A career is the greatest financial asset. Invest intellect, energy and money to build your prospective career. This will fetch good returns on your time, money and energy invested. Remember the *sutras* of Chanakya, the mentor of Indian public administration:

   (a) Equip yourself fully with worldly knowledge

   (b) One who has acquired knowledge becomes one who has conquered himself

   (c) The self-conquered shall endow upon all resources

2. Insurance is not to be considered as a protection plan alone, it will also fulfill financial goals and wealth creation.

   (a) Risk coverage for early death, huge medical expenses and loss of income. Due to any disability which may eventually happen, plan for term insurance, health insurance and accident and disability insurances respectively.

   (b) Savings for children's education, daughter or son's marriage and retirement plans; opt for Child ULIP and endowment plan.

   (c) Wealth creation for long-term, tax efficient savings and investment by way of ULIP.

   To decrease the premium go for online insurance instead of offline insurance.

   More life coverage is possible at a lower cost through term insurance policys.

3. The former Chairman of the Administrative Reform Committee, L.K. Jha once said 'tax evasion is a fine art of evading tax.' The honest investor and tax payer end up evading tax due to ignorance. But ignorance is not an excuse. Some common mistakes which investors make are:

   (a) Ignoring the income of their spouse and children

   (b) Ending life insurance policy before three years, which attracts tax

   (c) Selling a house bought on loan before five years, increases the tax burden

(d) Not including interest income as income from other sources at the time of filing returns

(e) Receiving gifts and cash from unrelated persons enhances tax obligation

(f) Withdrawing PF within five years attracts tax as per slab.

4. Education loans cut the tax burden. Use the option if required.

5. House loans also reduce the tax burden. It is better to opt for a home loan after building a reasonable corpus in GPF or PPF. In this case it will help to be in the lower tax orbit. Creation of wealth and owning a flat or house is possible with loan capital. Home loans attract full interest exemption if the property is rented.

6. Financial planning is required to maintain some standard ratios:

   (a) Six months emergency funds should be kept as liquid

   (b) Pay one third of income as house building loan

   (c) Assets should be twice the debts

   (d) Standard savings should be 20 per cent of income

   (e) Debt payment to be restricted to 10 per cent

7. Lock in to long term deposit before rate cut which is next to debt fund.

8. Debt mutual fund investments can be more advantageous than FDs, they are more tax efficient than FDs, return may be higher in five star rated funds, there is no day loss regarding growth and they have greater flexibility.

9. Investment in the stock market or commodity trading should be through registered members of the exchange only. Filling of KYC form, collecting periodical statements and payments should be made by cheque or bank channels in case any legal steps are necessary in the future.

10. Investments in mutual funds are the beginning of equity investment. Wealth can be created gradually by investing NFO in SIP option i.e. with dividend reinvestment option. This spreads the risk by diversifying in several funds.

11. An investment portfolio must contain Gold ETFs because of liquidity, transparency in pricing, tax attractiveness, affordability, assurance of purity, safety and convenience and quick conversion into physical gold. Gold ETFs are the best way to invest in gold as compared to gold jewelry, bars, biscuits or coins. E-gold is available through the National Spot Exchange Limited (NSEL) Gold Fund or Gold Future.

12. At the time of filing returns, it should be borne in mind that deductions like loss of stock, house rent allowance, expenses for chronic illness, disabilities, donations, interest from a second home loan, child allowance and residing in one's parent's house as a tenant attract tax benefits.

13. Government considered Navaratna PSUs as milk cows. The investor was milked at will in the form of high dividends as selected PSUs retained enormous cash balance in their balance sheet.

14. Indexation inflation brings down capital gains tax.

15. By using reverse mortgage (opposite of a home loan) pension from one's home can be derived as tax-free pension.

16. Cultivating the art of saving and investment right from an early age gives one an edge.

17. Don't put all your eggs in one basket. Diversify the portfolio. Concentrate on blue chip stocks. But here also invest in different companies. Investing in blue chips from a long-term investment point of view creates wealth.

18. Rs. 22,000 crores of investors' money is lying idle in insurance companies, banks, mutual funds and the government without interest. Follow the rules for nomination, operation in due course of time, change of address, year-end paper work with the bank, KYC in case of banks, mutual funds, PPF etc.

19. When purchasing a car try to avail of dealer discount, corporate discount, exchange bonus, loyalty bonus, free insurance and discount on loan to borrow less money and pay less interest. A professional or business person can avail of a discount on a car loan, chauffeur's salary, insurance cost, maintenance cost and even fuel costs, to reduce tax and save more.

20. Do not make financial mistakes by hiding crucial information on finance from your spouse, borrowing beyond your limit. Cut your suit according to the cloth and set aside an emergency fund.

21. Do not be greedy at the time of investment, be wise regarding finance.

22. According to Charbak, an ancient, Indian Philosopher, *'rinang kritta ghitam pribet,'* i.e. borrowing brings sorrowing. When using credit cards do not exceed your budget, make full payment of bill, maintain credit limit, avoid cash advance and above all secure the credit card.

23. Five golden rules for new investors:
    (a) Start with small investments.
    (b) Be realistic regarding returns.
    (c) Learn from failure i.e. experience is the best teacher and that comes from bad experiences.
    (d) Try to invest in known areas.
    (e) Do not let your emotions get in the way as far as finance is concerned.

24. In the case of short-term investments stress on technical analysis and in the case of long-term investments rely on fundamental analysis.

25. Arrange portfolios on the basis of four factors: risk, return, liquidity and tax bracket. Avoid investing in chit funds as it is high risk, even though it shows high returns. Investing in GPF and EPF are mandatory but a portfolio must incorporate PPF for reasonable risk with absolute return. Savings rate does not cover inflation, this is why people rush to invest in fixed deposits. From 1992 to March 2011 annualized returns on fixed deposits was 10.28 percent in comparison with the SENSEX appropriation of 7.26 per cent. A portfolio must contain FDs. But considering the tax slab, return from

a debt fund is higher than that from a fixed deposit. Investment in equity funds is more risky than in debt and balance funds.

26. Monitor the date of renewal of life insurance policies, medical claim policies, car insurance policies. Remember the date of maturity of FDs otherwise they will be automatically renewed and stem the liquidity of the investor.

27. Savings bank interest is by far the highest in case of Yes Bank and Kotak Mahindra Bank. A maximum limit of Rs. 2 lakhs can be maintained in a savings bank account to get insurance coverage from RBI.

28. A new investor should first enter into debt funds, and then venture into balance funds and equity funds. The ratio between debt fund, balance fund and equity fund varies from the point of view of an investor's age and risk taking capacity. Investing in equity funds is better than investing in debt and balance funds from the point of view of taxation. Dividends are the best option for generating liquid cash, and reinvestment for wealth creation.

Role of Derivatives, Futures and Options

8

HISTORY OF DERIVATIVES

There is a very long history of derivatives trading. Evidence of derivatives in some form or the other was found in Greece. In modern times the concept of derivatives was evolved to protect farmers. The first *future* contracted was held in the Yodoya Rice Market in Osaka in Japan around 1650. Chicago Board of Trade (CBOT) was established in 1848 to felicitate forward contract of different commodities. Derivatives trading began 1865 when the CBOT listed the first "exchange traded" derivatives contract in the USA. They named these contracts as *future contracts*. In 1919, the Chicago Butter and Egg Board, a spin-off of CBOT, was reorganized to allow futures trading. Its name was changed to the Chicago Mercantile Exchange (CME). The first stock index futures contract was traded at the Kansas City Board of Trade. Currently the most popular stock index futures contract in the world is based on the Standard & Poor's 500 Index traded on the CME. In April 1973, the Chicago Board of Options Exchange was set up specifically for the purpose of trading in options. The market for options developed so rapidly that by the early '80s the number of shares underlying the option contract sold each day exceeded the daily volume of shares traded on the New York Stock Exchange. And there has been no looking back ever since (S.S. Nair, 2009).

INTRODUCTION OF DERIVATIVES IN INDIA

The nineteenth century was witness to the organized trading of derivatives with the establishment of the Cotton Trade Association in 1875. But for a long time, derivatives markets have been in existence in India in some form or the other. In the commodities market, the Bombay Cotton Trade Association started futures trading in 1875 and, by the early 1900s India had one of the world's largest futures industries. In 1952 the government banned cash settlement and options trading and derivatives trading shifted to informal forwards markets. During the late the '90s, government policy changed, allowing for an increased role for market-based pricing and less suspicion of derivatives trading. The ban on futures trading of many commodities was lifted starting in early 2000, and national electronic commodity exchanges were created (Nair, 2009). Derivatives trading in India formally started on 12th June, 2000. The National Stock Exchange acts as the biggest exchange in India of its kind for traded derivatives, viz. stock options, stock futures, index options and index futures.

In Indian equity markets, for decades there was a system of forward trading which was commonly known as *badla*. But this developed some undesirable practices that were against the aspirations of general investors. So, SEBI prohibited this system of trading a number of times and finally banned it for good in 2001.

Between 1993 and 1996, a series of reforms took place in the stock market that cleared the way for equity traded derivatives markets in India. With the collaboration of state owned financial institutions, the government of India established the NSE in 1993. This exchange initiated a totally computer screen based stock trading system with greater efficiency and much needed transparency. The ban on trading in options was lifted in 1995 and in 1996 the NSE sent a proposal to SEBI for derivatives trading through this exchange.

DEFINITION OF DERIVATIVES AND THEIR ROLE IN CAPITAL MARKET

According to Dr. Manoj Vaish, CEO of the BSE Derivatives Segment, a derivative is an instrument whose value is derived from the value of one or more underlying instruments, which can be commodities, precious metals, currency, bonds, stocks, stocks indices, etc. The four most common examples of derivative instruments are forwards, futures, options and swaps.

The word 'derivative' is very common in mathematics, it is more frequent in algebra, where it refers to a variable, which has been derived from another variable. Actually, derivatives have no value of their own and hence the name. They derive their value from the value of some other asset, which is known as the underlying (S.S. Nair, 2009).

It can be said that derivatives allow investors to trade instruments derived from the cash market, where typically buyers take delivery on payment of cash. For instance, instruments such as futures and options allow investors to hedge their risk or even take speculative positions.

Generally, it can be said that it is a financial instrument and its value depends on the value of other, more basic underlying assets. Underlying assets can be commodities, currency, equity or stocks, stock indices, precious metals and foreign exchange rates or interest rates.

In short, it can be said that *"Derivatives are specialized contracts which signify an agreement or an option to buy or sell the underlying asset of the derivate up to a certain time in the future at a prearranged price, the exercise price."*

With the help of derivatives, institutional investors and corporations are able to manage their portfolio of assets and liabilities more effectively through the instruments, stock index futures or index options.

In Table 8.1, a chronological picture of derivatives is presented more clearly.

Table 8.1   Chronological Picture of Introduction of Derivatives in India

Dates	Events
November 18, 1996	The NSE sought SEBI's permission to trade index futures.
May 11, 1998	The L.C. Gupta Committee was set up to draft a policy framework for index futures.
July 7, 1999	The L.C. Gupta Committee submitted a report on the policy framework for index futures.
May 24, 2000	The Reserve Bank of India gave permission for OTC forward rate agreements and interest rate swaps.
May 25, 2000	SIMEX chose Nifty for trading futures and options on an Indian index.
June 1, 2000	BSE commenced trading in Index options on SENSEX
June 9, 2000	SEBI allowed the NSE and the BSE to trade in index futures. Exchange traded index derivatives contracts – BSE Sensex.
June 12, 2000	Trading of the BSE Sensex futures commenced on the BSE.
September 25, 2000	Nifty futures trading commenced on the SGX.
July 2, 2001	In India, stock index options were introduced.
July 9, 2001	Stock options were introduced.
November 9, 2002	Single stock futures were launched.
September 13, 2004	BSE launched weekly options in the derivatives market.
August 29, 2008	Trading of currency derivatives commenced in NSE.
August 31, 2009	Trading of interest rate derivatives commenced in NSE.
February, 2010	Launching of currency futures as additional currency pairs.
October 28, 2010	Introduction of European style stock options.
October 29, 2010	Introduction of currency options

Source: 1. "http://www.articlesbase.com/human-resources-articles/future-of-derivatives-in-india-999592.html"
(Accessed on 27.12.2011)

2. BSE CERTIFICATION ON SECURITIES MARKETS, Publication of BSE Training Institute Ltd., p. 105

3. Equity Derivatives: A Beginner's Module Curriculum, NSE's Certification in Financial Markets, Mumbai, 2011, p. 6

The contract for derivatives has a fixed expiry period generally in the range of 3 to 12 months from the date of commencement of the contract. According to Nair, the value of the contract depends on the expiry period and also on the price of the underlying asset. There are many types of financial instruments that are grouped under the term derivatives, but options/futures and swaps are among the most common. Options or futures are different kinds of contracts where one party agrees to pay a fee to another for the right to buy or sell something to the other.

In the world of capital market, more particularly in financial transactions, there are a number of risks. Derivatives allow investors to manage these risks more efficiently by underlying the risks and allowing either hedging or taking only one or more risks at a time. To make it clearer we consider the following:

If an investor buys a share of TISCO from his broker, the investor takes the following risks:

1. The risk that the price of TISCO shares may go up or down due to company specific reasons (unsystematic risk).
2. The risk that the price of TISCO shares may go up or down due to reasons affecting the sentiments of the whole market (systematic risk).
3. Liquidity risk, if investor's position is very large, he may not be able to cover his position at a prevailing price (called impact cost).
4. Counterparty (credit) risk on the broker in case he takes money from the investor but before giving delivery of shares goes bankrupt.
5. Counterparty (credit) risk on the exchange, in case of default of the broker, an investor may get partial or full compensation from the exchange.
6. Cash out-flow risk that the investor may not able to arrange the full settlement value at the time of delivery, resulting in default, auction and subsequent losses.
7. Operating risks, like errors, omissions, loss of important documents, fraud, forgeries, delays in settlement, loss dividends and other corporate actions etc.

Once the investor goes long on TISCO he can hedge the systematic risk by going short on index futures. On the other hand, if he does not want unsystematic risk on any one share, but wishes to take only systematic risk – he can go long on index futures, without buying individual shares. The credit risk, cash outflow risk and operating risks are much easier to manage in this case.

FUTURES CONTRACT

It is an agreement between two parties to buy and sell an asset (financial instrument/ commodity) at a certain future time and sure price. Simply, a futures contract is a contract to take delivery of an instrument or product in the future, at a price set now. For example, if a farmer decides in April to buy 5 kg of tomatoes for Rs. 10 from a tomato trader to be delivered when ripe in July, the farmer is said to have entered into a futures contract (F.E. Jan. 25, 2000). Futures are traded on exchanges where the terms of the contract are standardized by exchange with respect to the quantity of the underlying, quality of the underlying (not required in financial futures), the date and month of delivery, the units of price quotation (not price itself) and minimum change in price (tick-size) and location of settlement.

Though future markets have their roots in agriculture, today futures and options are traded on a wide range of products right from rice and wheat to natural gas, the stock indices, precious metals and currencies. Among the financial futures, the most popular are the stock index futures. Futures in individual stocks exist in some countries (e.g. Sydney Futures Exchange, Australia) but in general are not very popular. In the United States trading in individual stock futures is not permitted. Price volatility in individual stocks is much higher than the index. This results in higher risk of clearing corporation and margin requirement. In addition, such instruments suffer from lack of depth and liquidity in trading. In most cases, futures based on individual stocks often have a physical settlement, resulting in more complex regulatory requirements. Further, it is much more difficult to manipulate an index than individual stock, resulting in price manipulations. In India, the Dr. L.C. Gupta Committee has not mentioned futures on individual stocks as possible derivative contracts.

INDIVIDUAL SECURITIES FUTURES

In India, futures on individual securities were introduced in 2001. Futures on all the listed securities are not permitted till now. SEBI has specified a list of securities in which future contracts are permitted. Both the stock exchanges of Mumbai that is, the BSE and NSE have introduced futures on individual securities.

The salient features of futures on individual securities on the NSE (National Stock Exchange) are as follows (Prasanna Chandra, 2008):

❖ The underlying for the futures on individual securities contracts shall be the underlying security available for trading in the capital market segment of the exchange.

❖ Futures contracts on individual securities will have a maximum of three-month trading cycle. New contracts will be introduce on the trading day following the expiry of near month contract.

❖ Futures contracts on individual securities shall expire on the last Thursday of the expiry month. If the last Thursday happens to be a trading holiday, the contracts shall expire on the previous day.

❖ The permitted lot size of future contracts on individual securities shall be multiples of 100 and fractions, if, any, shall be rounded off to next higher multiple of 100 or size of the lot may be stipulated by the exchange from time to time.

❖ In respect of all futures contracts, the price steps admitted to the dealings of the exchange shall be Rs. 0.05.

❖ On introduction of new contracts, the base price of future contracts shall be the previous day's closing price of the underlying security. On the subsequent trading days, the base price of contract will be the settlement price of the future contracts.

❖ On individual securities, futures contracts shall be initially cash settled and would be settled as follows:

   (a) Daily mark-to market settlement

   (b) Final mark-to market settlement on expiry of a future contract

❖ The pay-on and pay-out mark-to-market settlement is on trading day + 1 day (T + 1 day).

The trading system of futures and options of the NSE is called NEAT-F&O. It is a nationwide fully automated screen-based trading arrangement for Nifty futures and options and stock futures and options, with online monitoring and surveillance mechanism. This trading system can be accessed by two types of users, the trading members and the clearing members. The users have all the flexibility in terms of kinds of orders that they can place on the system.

STOCK INDEX FUTURES

Index futures trading commenced on the BSE in the year 2000. It is needless to say that index is an indicator of the status of the market. By tracking the changes in the indices, one can effectively gauge stock market moods in the country. The most popular stock indices in India are the BSE Sensex and NSE Nifty. The Sensex is the most popular index and is considered as the pulse of the Indian stock market. Index futures are future contracts where the underlying asset is the index itself, which may be the Sensex or Nifty. It is a great help when one wants to punt on the movements of the market. Assume that a person feels the market is very bullish and Sensex would rally crossing 20,000 points. Instead of buying shares that may make up the index, he can buy the entire market by taking a position on the index future and thus take advantage of Sensex movements. One could either take a long or short position similar to individual shares. Long and short positions indicate whether one has bought or sold the index. For instance, if one has bought 50 Sensex futures then he is long on the Sensex and if he has sold 50 Sensex futures, he is short. In brief, it can be said that long and short positions indicate whether you have a net over-bought position termed as long or over-sold position termed as short.

The stock index futures contracts of the National Stock Exchange is based on S&P CNX Nifty Index and those of Bombay Stock Exchange on the Sensex. The following are features of S&P CNX Nifty futures contracts:

❖ On the NSE F&O segment the Nifty futures contracts (FUTDIX) is traded.

❖ Clearing and settling agency for all deals done on the NSE F&O segment is the National Securities Clearing Corporation (NSCCL) and NSCCL guarantees all F&O settlement.

❖ S&P CNX Nifty index futures contracts have a maximum of 3-month trading cycle— the near month (one), the next month (two), and the far month (three). After the expiry of the near month contract, a new contract will be introduced.

❖ On the last Thursday of the expiry month S&P CNX Nifty Index futures contracts expire. If that Thursday happens to be a trading holiday, the contracts will expire on the previous trading day.

❖ The lot size of S&P CNX Nifty index futures contracts is permitted to be 200 or multiples thereof.

Index futures can be used as hedging, speculating, arbitrage, cash flow management and asset allocation.

HEDGING

A person who combines derivatives with a business risk is known as a hedger. Derivatives allow risk related to the price of the underlying asset to be transferred from one party to another. For example, a wheat farmer and a miller could sign a futures contract to exchange a specified amount of cash for a specified amount of wheat in the future. Both parties have reduced a future risk: for the wheat farmer, the uncertainty of the price, and for the miller, the

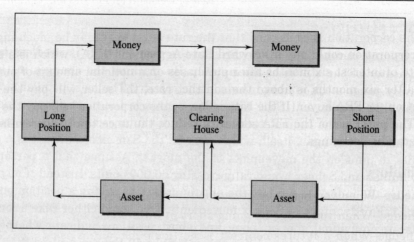

Chart 8.1 The Role of Clearing Houses in Futures Contracts Trading

Note: Short position commits the seller to deliver an item at contracted price on maturity; and *Long position* commits the buyer to purchase an item at the contracted price on maturity.

Source: Prasanna Chandra, 2008, Investment Analysis and Portfolio Management, 3rd Edition, Tata McGraw-Hill Publishing Co. Ltd. New Delhi.

availability of wheat. However, there is still the risk that no wheat will be available because of events unspecified by the contract, such as the weather, or that one party will renege on the contract. Although a third party, called a clearing house, insures futures contracts, not all derivatives are insured against counter-party risk.

From another perspective, the farmer and the miller both reduce a risk and acquire a risk when they sign the futures contract: the farmer reduces the risk that the price of wheat will fall below the price specified in the contract and acquires the risk that the price of wheat will rise above the price specified in the contract (thereby losing additional income that he could have earned). The miller, on the other hand, acquires the risk that the price of wheat will fall below the price specified in the contract (thereby paying more in the future than he otherwise would have) and reduces the risk that the price of wheat will rise above the price specified in the contract. In this sense, one party is the insurer (risk taker) for one type of risk, and the counter-party is the insurer (risk taker) for another type of risk.

Hedging also occurs when an individual or institution buys an asset (such as a commodity, a bond that has coupon payments, a stock that pays dividends, and so on) and sells it using a futures contract. The individual or institution has access to the asset for a specified amount of time, and can then sell it in the future at a specified price according to the futures contract. Of course, this allows the individual or institution the benefit of holding the asset, while reducing the risk that the future selling price will deviate unexpectedly from the market's current assessment of the future value of the asset.

Derivatives can serve legitimate business purposes. For example, a corporation borrows a large sum of money at a specific interest rate. The rate of interest on the loan resets every six months. The corporation is concerned that the rate of interest may be much higher in six months. The corporation could buy a Forward Rate Agreement (FRA), which is a contract to pay a fixed rate of interest six months after purchases on a notional amount of money. If the interest rate after six months is above the contract rate, the seller will pay the difference to the corporation, or FRA buyer. If the rate is lower, the corporation will pay the difference to the seller. The purchase of the FRA serves to reduce the uncertainty concerning the rate increase and stabilize earnings.

Hedge Terminology

❖ Long hedge–When you hedge by going long in futures market.

❖ Short hedge–When you hedge by going short in futures market.

❖ Cross hedge–When a futures contract is not available on an asset, you hedge your position in cash market on this asset by going long or short on the futures for another' asset whose prices are closely associated with that of your underlying.

❖ Hedge contract month–Maturity month of the contract through which hedge is accomplished.

❖ Hedge ratio–Number of future contracts required to hedge the position.

Swaps

A swap is a flexible, private, forward-based contract or agreement, generally between two counter parties to exchange streams of cash flows based on an agreed on (or notional) principal amount over a specified period of time in the future.

Swaps are usually entered into at-the-money (i.e. with minimal initial cash payments because the fair value is zero), through brokers or dealers who take an up-front cash payment or who adjust the rate to bear default risk. The two most prevalent swaps are interest rate swaps and foreign currency swaps, while others include equity swaps, commodity swaps, and swaptions.

❖ Swaptions are options on swaps that provide the holder with the right to enter into a swap at a specified future date on specified terms (stand-alone option in a swap) or to extend or terminate the life of an existing swap (embedded option on a swap).

Swap contracts are used to hedge entire price changes (symmetrically) related to an identified hedged risk, such as interest rate or foreign currency risk, since both counter parties gain or lose equally.[1]

SPECULATION AND ARBITRAGE

Derivatives can be used to acquire risk, rather than to insure or hedge against risk. Thus, some individuals and institutions will enter into a derivative contract to speculate on the value of the underlying asset, betting that the party seeking insurance will be wrong about

---

[1]Devangshu Dutta, Play it Safe, *Intelligent Investor*, July 31, 2001, pp 43-45 and June 30, 2001, pp 38-39

the future value of the underlying asset. Speculators look to buy an asset in the future at a low price according to a derivative contract when the future market price is high, or to sell an asset in the future at a high price according to a derivative contract when the future market price is low.

Individuals and institutions may also look for arbitrage opportunities, as when the current buying price of an asset falls below the price specified in a futures contract to sell the asset.

Speculative trading in derivatives gained a great deal of notoriety in 1995 when Nick Leeson, a trader at Barings Bank made poor and unauthorized investments in futures contracts. Through a combination of poor judgment, lack of oversight by the bank's management and regulators and unfortunate events like the Kobe earthquake, Leeson incurred a US$1.3 billion loss that bankrupted the centuries-old institution.[2]

According to Dr. Vaish (12th July, 2000), hedging is a mechanism to reduce price risk inherent in open positions. Derivatives are widely used for hedging. A hedge can help lock in existing profits. Its purpose is to reduce the volatility of a portfolio, by reducing the risk. The basic logic is, "If long on cash underlying: short future and if short in cash underlying: long future." It can be made clearer by a simple example.

If one has bought 100 shares of Company A and wants to hedge against market movements, he should short an appropriate amount of index futures. This will reduce his overall exposure to events affecting the whole market (systematic risk). In case a war breaks out or divesting natural calamity occurs, the entire market will fall (including Company A). So his loss in Company A would be offset by gains in his short position in index futures. In the following cases hedging strategies are useful:

❖ Reducing the equity exposure of a mutual fund by selling index futures.

❖ Investing funds raised by new schemes in index futures so that market exposure is immediately taken.

❖ Partial liquidation of portfolio by selling the index future instead of actual shares where the cost of transaction is higher.

As indicated earlier, there are some differences between Hedgers, Speculators and Arbitrageurs. Hedgers wish to eliminate or reduce the price risk to which they are already exposed. The classes of investors who willingly take price risk to profit from changes in the underlying are known as speculators. Arbitrageurs profit from a price differential existing in two markets simultaneously operating in two different markets. Hedgers and investors provide the economic substance to any financial market. Speculators provide liquidity and depth to the market. Arbitrageurs bring price uniformity and help price discovery.

Besides index futures and commodity futures or physical assets futures, there are other future contracts also such as interest rate futures and foreign exchange futures. Interest rate futures is a contract, which sets a purchase yield or rate of interest on a specified debt security or deposit effective at a future date agreed on at the time of the transaction. Foreign

[2]Arup Chattapadhya, *Scientific Analysis and Portfolio Management*, Study Material for Distant Education, Burdwan University, pp 40-43.

exchange futures is a contract which involves booking or swapping of currencies at future dates, depending on perception of whether the currencies are going to strengthen or weaken.

ROLE OF THE EXCHANGES

Stock exchanges play very important roles by acting as a market maker in case of index futures by offering two way quotes for buying and selling the index. The exchanges will clear the trades daily and match the deals. The exchange, this way brings the buyers and sellers together and lends liquidity in the system by making trading feasible. The exchange's most important function is to reconcile sales and purchases and keep account of margin payments. The clearing house of each exchange will stand between each counter-party of a futures contract to ensure that every contract is honoured.

A clearing house (or clearing corporation) is also responsible for risk management of its members and carries out inspection and surveillance, besides collection of margins, capital etc. It also monitors the net-worth requirements of the members. The clearing house will only guarantee fulfillment of the contract to a clearing member of the exchange. It ensures the fulfillment of every contract in two ways. One way is that the clearing house imposes itself between two counter-parties thereby replacing the original contract (say between A and B) by two new contracts (say between A and the clearing house and B and the clearing house) thereby itself becoming counter-party to every trade. This is called full Novation. The other way is to guarantee performance of all the contracts made on the exchange (Vaish, 2000).

A non-clearing member, such as broker's client, will not be guaranteed by the clearing house. Every client will, in turn, have to sign an agreement with his broker, which will enable him to understand and assume all the risks involved in futures trading.

In India, there are three national level multi-commodities exchanges offering on-line futures trading in commodities. These are National Commodity & Derivatives Exchange Limited (NCDEX), Multi Commodities Exchange of India Limited (MCX), and National Multi Commodity Exchange (NMCE). Among these, NCDEX and MCX are most active and popular commodity exchanges promoted by leading banks and financial institutions established in Mumbai (Bombay) in 2003.

PRICING OF FUTURES CONTRACTS

The theoretical procedure of calculating any future is to factor in the current or spot price and all holding costs, that is, interest expenses. The general model of future price is known as cost-of-carry model, which simply can be written as:

$$\text{Future price} = \text{Spot price} + \text{Costs of carry}$$

Cost of carry is the equivalent of interest costs or carry costs. This depends on opportunity cost, cost of storage, insurance etc. (R. Chopra, 2000). The largest component is opportunity cost of capital, which is the equivalent of interest costs. So, in general it is obvious that

Futures price > Spot price

Futures price – Spot price = Basis.

Basis is not constant, it will decrease with time and on expiry the basis becomes zero. So, ultimately it turns out to be:

Futures price = Spot price

The 'cost of carry' model provides the foundation for pricing in all types of futures. The 'cost of carry model' for a perfect market with unrestricted short selling can be written as:

$$F_{0,t} = S_0 (1 + C) \text{ where,}$$

$F_{0,t}$ is the futures price at $t = 0$ for delivery at time t, S_0 is the spot price at $t = 0$, C represents the cost of carrying the underlying asset from $t = 0$ to time t (M. Philipose, 2000).

It can also be given as $F_{0,t} = S_0 (1 + r_f)^t$ where, $S_0 = 500$ risk for interest rate is 1 per cent per month. Then one month future contract should be $F_{0,1} = 500(1 + 0.01) = 500 \times 1.01$;

For 2 months, $F_{0,2} = 500(1 + 0.01) = 500(1.01)^2$; for 3 months $F_{0,3} = 500(1.01)^3$ and so on.

In case of financial assets, cost of carry would include the cost of financing the spot purchase and for non-financial assets, it would also include the cost of transporting and storing non-financial assets (such as commodity futures).

APPLICATION OF COST OF CARRY MODEL TO STOCK INDEX FUTURES

It is understood that by holding the stock of a company, the owner gets dividends. It is quite well known that the stock market index is generally a price index and the value of the index at given time depends absolutely on the price of stocks, and not on the dividends the underlying companies might pay.

As the futures prices are directly associated with the values of index, the future prices should also not include dividends. So, during pricing stock index futures, the basic question must be adjusted to include the dividends that would be received between present (spot) and expiration of the futures. In brief, it can be said that the chance to receive dividends lowers the cost of carrying the stocks.

Trading in index futures, like the Sensex or Nifty futures is like trading in any other security. Just like normal shares, an investor will be able to buy or sell futures on the BSE BOLT terminal of the NSE NEAT screen through his broker. The orders will have to be punched into the system and the confirmation will be immediate just as in the existing system. Since the tick size, market lot in futures will be similar to individual stocks; trading in futures is similar to trading in individual stocks. Just as for shares, investors get separate buy and sell quotations that are available in the stock exchanges.

FAIR PRICE MODEL FOR STOCK INDEX FUTURES

A fair price model and modified 'cost of carry' model should be consistent with one another. It implies that the value of dividend receipts must be deducted while arriving at the cost of carry.

A well known stock analyst, Mobis Philipose in one of his articles (*BS*, 27th Nov., 2000) gave an example of fair value of a stock index futures contract, which is updated as follows:

Assume an index consisting of only two stocks each having only one share outstanding. Before starting calculations, let us name this index as Futurex. The calculations are based on the Futurex December contract which closes on December 28th (the last Thursday of the month). Hence, there are 32 days until the contract expires. Annual interest rates are assumed to be 12 per cent.

Let two stocks say, X and Y be priced currently at Rs. 500 and Rs. 1,000 respectively. The companies incidentally would pay dividends of Rs. 5 and Rs. 10 respectively, payment dates of dividends being December 4th for X and December 9th for Y. As December 28th happens to be the closing date of contract, the dividend receipts can be invested for 25 and 20 days respectively. For the sake of convenience, finally let us assume that both the original market value and base value of the index is 1,000. This simply means that the sum of two prices is also the value of index.

Now on the basis of the above data, the present value of the index can be calculated as:

$$500(X) + 1000(Y)/1000 \times 1000 = 1500$$

The cost of buying the stocks in the index is simply the sum of the prices of two stocks, that is, Rs. 1,500.

The interest cost for carrying the stocks till expiration, will be 12 per cent for 32 days, or 1.05 per cent.

$$\{(12/100)\,(32/365)100\} = 1.052.$$

Thus the cost of buying and carrying the stocks to expiration will be

$$\text{Rs. } 1500 \times 1.052 = \text{Rs. } 1578.00$$

Offsetting this cost will be dividends received and interest earned on the dividends, which would be:

For the stock X, it means Rs. 3 + (25/365 × 0.12 × 3) = Rs. 3.025

For the stock Y, it means Rs. 5 + (20/365 × 0.12 × 5) = Rs. 5.033

So, the net cost of buying the stocks and carrying them to expiration will be:

$$\text{Rs. } 1578.00 - \text{Rs. } 3.025 - \text{Rs. } 5.033 = \text{Rs. } 1569.94$$

In the cost of carry model, the future price must equal this entire cost of carry. Hence, the fair value of the Futurex December contract is 1569.94. As the price conforms to cost of carry model, this value precludes arbitrage opportunities.

INDEX ARBITRAGE

Deviations from the theoretical price of the cost of carry gives rise to arbitrage opportunities. If the futures price exceeds its fair value, traders or investors will engage in cash-and-carry arbitrage. Under this, the traders will buy the underlying stocks and sell the index futures contract at the same time.

If the futures price falls below its fair value, traders can exploit the pricing discrepancy through a reverse cash-and-carry strategy. At this stage, the trader buys the index future and shorts the underlying stocks. These strategies in stock index futures are called index arbitrage. Because index arbitrage may require the trading of many stocks, index arbitrage is often implemented by using computer programs to automate the trading. Computer directed index arbitrage is known as program trading.

CASH-AND-CARRY STRATEGY

In his article, Mobis Philipose (*BS*, 27th Nov., 2000) further illustrated cash-and-carry index arbitrage, considering both arbitrage strategies using the same example with present value of index at 1500 and fair value for the future contract at 1569.94.

Assume that all the previous data holds, but the Futurex December contract is trading at 1520. The arbitrageur, to exploit this discrepancy in prices, will carry the stocks underlying the index till expiration and at the same time will also sell a future contract. During the period, assume that the stock prices increased. That is, stock price of X increased to 510 and that of Y increased to 1100, there would be profit in cash market, but at the same time there would be loss on the future market. In the cash market, cash flows will come from the sale of the shares, and future value of the dividends, say:

$$(Rs.\ 510 + Rs.\ 1100 + Rs.\ 3.025 + Rs.\ 5.033) = Rs.\ 1618.06.$$

The profit on cash market works out to Rs. 102.28, after consideration of the debt payment to Rs. 1515.78. On the futures transaction, the index value at expiration will then equal

$$1610\ (510 + 1100)$$

This gives the futures loss of 90 (1610 − 1520).

Taking all these cash flows together, the profit will be Rs. 12.28. The profit will be the same, no matter what happens to stock prices as the figure is simply the difference between the prevailing futures position (1520) and the fair value (1507.78).

REVERSE CASH-AND-CARRY STRATEGY

Similarly, arbitrageurs can engage in reverse cash-and-carry transactions, if the futures price is too low relative to a fair value. That is, assume that the futures is trading at 1500, well below the fair value of 1507.78. Essentially, the arbitrageur will take positions just the opposite of those under the cash and carry strategy.

Thus, the arbitrageur will sell both the stocks short and will lend the amount for remaining period of 32 days at 12 per cent for a cash inflow of Rs. 1515.78 at expiration. Besides, since he is foregoing the dividend payments he would have received had he held on to his stock, these will be considered as part of his cost. This equals a cost of about Rs. 8.058. Irrespective of price prevailing on the closing date, the trader will make a profit equal to the difference between the fair value of the future contract (1507.78) and the current value (Philipose).

In the above paragraph, the cash-and-carry and the reverse cash-and-carry transactions are illustrated with a hypothetical two-stock index futures contract, real stock futures trading involves many more stocks. The BSE Sensex is the smallest with 30 stocks, while the NSE Nifty contains 50 stocks. To exploit index arbitrage opportunities with actual stock index futures, not only requires futures, but also simultaneously buying or selling the entire collection of stocks underlying the index.

To execute large and complicated stock market orders through the use of a computer is called program trading. While computers are also used for other kinds of stock market transactions, index arbitrage is the main application of program trading. Often, the terms "index arbitrage" and "program trading" are used interchangeably.

An Alternate Example: Actual Trading in Futures

Now let us give another example of actual trading of futures as described by Rishi Chopra in *The Economic Times*, 17th January, 2000:

Assume that on 1st January, 2012, there are three contracts open for trading on the BSE. There are one month January futures maturing on 26th January, 2012, two month February futures maturing on 23rd February, 2012 and a three month March futures maturing on 29th March, 2012.

Also assume that on 1st January, 2012 the Sensex is at 16500 and the one-month January future maturing on 26th January, 2012 is quoting at 16568. Now, an investor buys 50 Sensex January futures and the value of this contract is

$$(16568 \times 50) = \text{Rs. } 8,28,400$$

Assuming a daily margin at 5 per cent, the investor has to pay an initial margin of

$$(5 \text{ per cent of } 16568 \times 50) = \text{Rs. } 41,420$$

i.e. 5 per cent of Rs. 8,28,400

If at the end of trading on 1st January, 2012 the January futures close at 16535, then the investor will have to pay a marking to market loss of

$$\{(16568 - 16535) \times 50)\} = (-) \text{ Rs. } 1,650$$

Similarly, if at the end of 2nd January, 2012 the January futures close at 16590 then the investor will get the difference of the following sum credited to his account.

$$\{(16590 - 16535) \times 50)\} = \text{Rs. } 2,750$$

On 3rd January if the January futures close at 16570, then the investor will again be debited with

$$\{(16590 - 16570) \times 50)\} = \text{Rs. } 1,000$$

In this way the profit and loss at the end of the day will be marked to the market and debited or credited to the investors' account on a daily basis in addition to the initial margin ensuring the safety of the brokers as well as the market. This directly amounts to automatic squaring of positions since marking to market of the positions takes care that at the of the day, the investor has already received or paid the full profit/loss on his position.

CLOSING OUT POSITION

The investor now has two options, either to hold the contract till maturity or to simply square it at any time just like the normal market. In case he chooses to square off a buy position, he simply has to sell the future and reverse his position. In our case, if the January futures quotes at 16600 on 4th January, then the investor may sell his 50 futures at 16600 and get the difference of the following sum credited to his account.

$$\{(16600 - 16570) \times 50)\} = \text{Rs. } 1,500$$

The actual profit he would have made would be the difference between his contracted price of 16568 and his squaring price of 16600 which would result in a net profit of

$$\{(16600 - 16568) \times 50)\} = \text{Rs. } 1,600$$

Even, the netting of the daily debit and credit of his account for the four days will confirm this net profit of

$$(-1650 + 2750 - 1000 + 1500) = \text{Rs. } 1,600$$

On the other hand, if the investor decides to hold his position till maturity on 26th January 2012 (the last Thursday of the month), then the investor will get the difference between the contracted value and the closing index value and not the futures price as on 26th January since the futures price will equal the spot value of the Sensex. Assuming the Sensex closes at 16700 on 26th January, 2012, the investor will end up making the following as profit (Chopra 2000).

$$\{(16700 - 16568) \times 50)\} = \text{Rs. } 6,600$$

It was already mentioned earlier that the lifetime of each series will be three months. At any point of time, there will be three series open for trading. In this way, investors will have one-month futures, two-month futures or three-month futures. The contract will mature on the last Thursday of the respective month. A new series will come into existence on the immediately succeeding day, which is Friday. For instance, if the BSE introduces trading in Sensex futures from 1st January, 2012, then investors will have three contracts open for trading.

Investors will have one month January futures maturing on 26th January, 2012, two month February futures maturing on 23rd February, 2012 and three month March futures maturing on 29th March, 2012. On expiry of the one month January futures on 26th January, 2012, a new April three month futures will come into existence on 27th January, 2012 and will mature on 26th April, 2012.

The two month February futures will now automatically become the one month February futures while the three month March futures will now become two month March futures. Hence, every future will be replaced by a new three month futures on its expiry and the remaining two futures will automatically change to one month and two month futures respectively.

Just like individual shares have a tick size of five paisa, here the tick size will be ten paisa of a point. Index contracts are valued at contract multiplier times the index value. The multiplier plays a role similar to lot size in the normal market where the total value of shares bought or sold is compared after multiplying the value of each share by the lot size.

Since the underlying asset, that is, the index cannot be purchased or delivered the settlement is thus made in cash. SEBI has recommended a minimum contract value of Rs. 2,00,000. Just as shares have a minimum lot size of 10, 50 or 100, for BSE index futures, each contract would have a minimum lot of 50 while Nifty will have a minimum lot of 100.

This minimum lot is required to achieve the minimum prescribed contract value of Rs. 2 lakhs. Assuming, the Sensex futures price is 16500 and the minimum lot is 50, the value of a minimum 50 BSE futures will be Rs. 2.25 lakhs. Hence, any investor would be required to keep a minimum exposure of Rs. 2.25 lakhs if he wants to take a position on Sensex futures.

If the contract is held until expiry the open positions are closed out on the last date of trading at a price determined by the spot 'cash' value of the index, since on expiry the futures price equals the spot price. It has already been mentioned earlier that an index cannot be delivered, an index futures contract is settled in cash. Cash settlement means, there will be no physical delivery of securities.

TRADING EXCHANGES OF FUTURES

In the international market, there are broadly two types of futures: commodity futures and financial futures: A commodity futures is a futures contract in commodities like metals, agricultural and manufacturing commodities, while a financial futures is a futures contract like treasury bills, stock index, foreign currencies etc.

Forward Contract

A forward contract is a contract between two parties to buy or sell an asset at a certain future date at a certain predetermined price. Future date may be called expiry date and predetermined price means the forward price. Forward contract means a private contract and terms of reference determined by parties.

Forward contract is only traded in the Over the Counter (OTC) exchange and not on any other stock exchange. As OTC is a private exchange, private players negotiate on a one to one basis either by parties, individuals or institutions.

Table 8.2   Futures and their Exchanges

Commodity Futures	Exchanges	Financial Futures	Exchanges
Cotton, wheat, potatoes etc.	New York Cotton Exchange, Multi Commodities Exchange of India Limited (MCX),	U.S. treasury bills, Indian treasury bills	International Monetary Market (IMM) at CME, Chicago,
Gold, aluminium etc.	London Metal Exchange,	Standard & Poor Index, Sensex, Nifty	IMM, BSE,NSE etc.
Crude oil, soya bean oil etc.	Chicago Board of Trade, Int. Petroleum Exchange	Eurodollar deposit, Sterling	IMM, London Int. Financial Future Exch.

Source: The Investment Game, Prasanna Chandra

Settlement of Forward Contracts

After expiry of forward contracts there are two types of settlements that can be made: physical settlement and cash settlement.

Physical settlement: Forward contract settled by the physical delivery of contract of underlying assets between the seller and the buyer i.e. by a short investor to long investor and payment of forward price by buyer to seller to be made on the agreed settlement date.

Let, the spot price at the expiry date be St and forward price be Ft where $St > Ft$ and the number of shares be n.

Short position investor of underlying asset makes a loss = $(Ft - St)n$

Long position of investor of underlying asset makes a profit = $(St - Ft)n$

Cash settlement: Cash settlement is not related with actual delivery or receipts of the security. Each party either pay or receives cash equal to net loss as per their position involved in the contract.

Case 1: $Se > Ft$, for short position investor has to pay an amount equal to loss

Case 2: $St < Ft$, for long position investor has to pay an amount equal to loss

Case 3: $St = Ft$ no need to pay to any one

Table 8.3   Difference between Forwards and Futures

Forwards	Futures
Private negotiation of contract	Exchange negotiated contract
Non-standardized	Standardized
Settlement date fixed by the parties	Settlement date fixed by the parties
Counter party risk is high	Counter party risk is nil

Source: NSE

Derivatives Trading on the NSE

1. Index future
2. Index option

3. Stock future

4. Stock option

1. *Index Futures*

Index futures is a future contract considering index as the underlying asset. Nifty, Bank Nifty and CNX IT that are traded on the NSE are examples.

Table 8.4 S and P Nifty Index

Underlying Asset	S and P CNX Index
Exchange of trading	NSE
Contract size	Lot of 50, minimum value Rs. 2 lakhs
Trading cycle	Maximum period of three months. Near month one, next month two and far month three. New contract may be introduced after expiry of near month contract.
Expiry date	Last Thursday or one day before, if last Thursday is a holiday.
Settlement basis	Cash settlement T+1
Settlement Price	Daily settlement on the basis of the closing price of the contract for settlement date. Final settlement on the basis of price of the underlying index on the last trading date.

Source: NSE

2. *Index Option*

Sanjiv Mehta of BSE (*ET*, 4th June, 2001) explained that the stock index options are options where the underlying asset is a stock index for example, options on BSE Sensex, options on S&P 500 index etc. Index options were first introduced by the Chicago Board of Options Exchange (CBOE) in 1983 on its index S&P 100. As opposed to options on individual stocks, index options give an investor the right to buy or sell the value of an index, which represents a group of stocks.

Table 8.5 S and P CNX Nifty Options

Underlying Index	S and P CNX Index
Contract price	Lot of 50, minimum value Rs. 2 lakhs.
Trading cycle	Maximum period of three months. Near month one, next month two and far month three. New contract may be introduce after expiry of near month contract.
Expiry date	Last Thursday or one day before, if the last Thursday is a holiday.
Settlement basis	Cash settlement T+1
Exchange of trading	NSE
Settlement price	Daily settlement not applicable. Closing value of the index on the last working day.

3. Stock Future

Stock futures are based on future individual stocks considered as an underlying asset. The cycle of the stock future is the same as the index future.

Table 8.6   Stock Future

Underlying Asset	Individual Securities
Contract price	As specified by the exchange and a minimum value of Rs. 2 lakhs.
Trading cycle	Maximum period of three months. Near month one, next month two and far month three. New contract may be introduce after expiry of near month contract.
Expiry date	Last Thursday or one day before, if the last Thursday is a holiday
Settlement basis	Market to market and cash settlement T+1
Exchange of trading	NSE
Settlement price	Daily settlement is the closing price of the contract. Closing value of securities on the last working day.

4. Stock Option

Stock option considers individual stock as the underlying asset. The NSE considers stock options with European style settlement.

Table 8.7   Stock Option

Underlying Asset	Individual Securities
Contract price	As specified by the exchange and a minimum value Rs. 2 lakhs
Trading cycle	Maximum period of three months. Near month one, next month two and far month three. New contract may be introduce after expiry of near month contract.
Expiry date	Last Thursday or one day before, if the last Thursday is a holiday.
Settlement basis	Both daily and final settlement on T+1 basis.
Exchange of trading	NSE
Settlement price	Closing date of underlying asset on expiry of exercise day.

Source: NSE

DEFINITION OF OPTIONS AND THEIR ROLE IN THE CAPITAL MARKET

Options are contracts which go a step further than futures contracts in the sense that they provide the buyer of the option the right, without obligation, to buy or sell a specified quantity of underlying asset, at an agreed price, on or up to a particular date. The underlying assets may be commodities like wheat/rice/cotton/gold/oil or financial instruments like equity stocks/stock index/bonds etc. To acquire this right, the buyer has to pay a premium to the seller.

The seller, on the other hand, has the obligation to buy or sell that specified asset at that agreed price. This makes options more of an insurance product where the downside risk is covered for the payment of a certain fixed premium. So the loss will be minimized to the extent of the premium paid, like an insurance product.

The premium is the price negotiated and set when the option is bought or sold. A person who buys the option is said to be the long in the option. A person who sells (writes) the option is said to be the short in the option. Options contracts are entered into between two parties wherein the buyer receives a privilege for which he pays a fee called the premium and the seller accepts an obligation for which he gets a fee.

In India regulators have allowed the American types of options in stocks and European style in indexes. An American style option is one which can be exercised by the buyer on or before the expiration date, that is, anytime between the day of purchase of the option and the day of expiry. The most exchanged traded options are American. The European kind of option is one which can be exercised by the buyer on the expiration day or before that. The properties of American options are frequently deduced from their European counterpart.

In an earlier chapter we have given a short definition of 'call option' and 'put option'. Here we discuss these two types of options in detail.

CALL OPTIONS

According to Sanjiv Mehta of BSE (*ET*, 4th June, 2001), a call option gives the holder/buyer (one who is long put), the right to sell a specified quantity of the underlying asset at the strike price on or before the expiration date. The seller (one who is short call) however, has the obligation to sell the underlying asset if the buyer of the call option decides to exercise his option to buy.

Let an investor buy one European call option on Company A at a strike price of Rs. 3,500 at a premium of Rs. 100. If the market price of Company A on the day of expiry is more than Rs. 3,500, the option will be exercised. The investor will earn a profit once the share prices cross Rs. 3,600 (Strike price + Premium, that is, 3,500 + 100). Let the stock price be Rs. 3,800, the option will be exercised and the investor will buy one share of Company A from the seller of the option at Rs. 3,500 and sell it in the market at Rs. 3,800 making a profit of Rs. 200.

{(Spot price – Strike price) – Premium paid}

In another scenario, if at the time of expiry, stock price falls below Rs. 3,500 to say Rs. 3,000, the buyer of the call option will choose not to exercise his option. In this case the investor loses the premium (Rs. 100), paid which shall be the profit earned by the seller of the call option.

PUT OPTION

A put option gives the security holder, the right to sell a specified quantity of the underlying asset at the strike price on or before the expiration date. The seller of the put option (who is short put) however, has the obligation to buy the underlying asset at the striking price if the buyer decides to exercise his option to sell.

Let an investor buy one European put option of Company *B* at a strike price of Rs. 300 at a premium of Rs. 25. If the market price of Company B on the day of expiry is less than Rs. 300, the option can be exercised as it is 'in the money.' The investor's breakeven point is Rs. 275 (Strike price - Premium paid), that is, the investor will earn a profit if the market falls below Rs. 275. Let the stock price be Rs. 260, the buyer of the put option immediately buys shares of Company B in the market at a rate of Rs. 260 and exercises his option of selling the share of Company B at Rs. 300 to the option writer thus making a net profit of Rs. 15.

{(Strike price – Spot price) – Premium paid}

In another scenario, if at the time of expiry, the market price of a share of Company B is Rs. 320, the buyer of the put option will choose not to exercise his option to sell in the market at a higher rate. In this case the investor loses the premium (Rs. 25), paid which shall be the profit earned by seller of the put option (see Table 8.8).

Both the call and put options have time value. The OTM or ATM has only time value. The maximum time value exists when the option is ATM. The price specified in the option contract is known as *strike price*. The price at which the underlying asset trades, if the *spot-market ITM option* is an option, generates positive cash flow for the holder who has exercised it immediately on an urgent basis. ATM option is an option that leads to zero cash flow if it is exercised immediately on urgent basis. OTM option is an option that leads to negative cash flow if it is exercised immediately on an urgent basis.

Table 8.8 Trading of Options in India

	Striking the Price	
	Call Option	Put Option
In-The-Money (ITM)	Strike price < Spot price	Strike price > Spot price
At-The-Money (ATM)	Strike price = Spot price	Strike price = Spot price
Out-of-The-Money (OTM)	Strike price > Spot price	Strike price < Spot price
	The Option Game	
	Call Option	Put Option
Option Buyer or Option Holder	Buys the right to buy the underlying asset at a specified price.	Buys the right to sell the underlying asset at a specified price.
Option Seller or Option Writer	Has the obligation to sell the underlying asset (to the option holder) at a specified price.	Has the obligation to buy the underlying asset (from the option holder) at a specified price.

Note: Strike price and spot price of underlying asset be considered in all cases
Source: Sanjiv Mehta of Bombay Stock Exchange (*Economic Times*, Calcutta, 4th June, 2001)

IN THE MONEY, AT THE MONEY AND OUT OF THE MONEY OPTIONS

When the option's

Strike price = Underlying asset price, then that option is said to be 'at the money'. This is true for both puts and calls.

When the call option's

Strike price < Underlying asset price, then that option is said to be 'in the money'.

Example: A Sensex call option with a strike of 16800 is 'in-the-money,' when the spot Sensex is at 17000 as the call option has value. The call holder has the right to buy a Sensex at 16800, no matter how much the spot market price has risen.

Further, When the call option's

Strike price > Underlying asset price, then that option is said to be 'out-of-the-money'.

Now, if the Sensex falls to 16600, the call option no longer has positive exercise value. The call holder will not exercise the option to buy Sensex at 16800 when the current price is at 16600.

When the put option's

Strike price > Spot price of the underlying asset, then that option is said to be 'in-the-money'.

A Sensex put at strike of 17300 is in-the-money when the Sensex is at 17000. In this case, the put option has value because put holder can sell the Sensex at 17300, at an amount greater than the current Sensex of 17000.

Similarly, when the put option's

Strike price < Spot price of the underlying asset price, then that option is said to be 'out-of-the money'.

Now, the buyer of a Sensex put option will not exercise the option when the spot is at 17700. The put no longer has a positive exercise value.

Options are said to be deep in-the-money or deep out-of-the-money, if the exercise price is at significant variance with the underlying asset price.

COVERED CALLS AND NAKED CALLS

When a call position is covered by an opposite position in the underlying assets like shares or commodities etc. it is called a covered call. Writing (selling) covered calls involves call options when the shares that might have to be delivered (when option holder exercises his right to buy), are already owned. That is, a writer writes a call on Company A so that if the call is exercised by the buyer, he can deliver the stocks.

The covered call technique involves the use of call options only. Options trade exactly the same way that stocks do. There are investors who want to buy options and there are investors who want to sell, or write, option. When these two investors reach an agreement on price, the contract trades. This trade happens in exactly the same way as stocks are bought and sold on the stock market (Hooper and Zalewski 2006).

All stock exchange-traded options have certain standard characteristics. To be a successful covered call writer (seller), one must recognize from the outset what one's objectives are and the mind-set one requires in order to achieve them.

Covered calls are far less risky than naked calls (where there is no opposite position in the underlying assets), since the worst that can that happen is that the investor is required to sell shares he already owns below their market value.

When a physical delivery uncovered/naked call is assigned an exercise, the writer will have to purchase the underlying asset to meet his call obligation and his loss will be the excess of the purchase price over the exercise price of the call reduced by the premium received for writing the call.

INTRINSIC VALUE AND TIME VALUE OF AN OPTION

The **intrinsic value** of an option is defined as the amount by which an option is in-the-money, or the immediate exercise of the option when the underlying option is market-to-market.

For a call option:

Intrinsic Value = Spot price – Strike price

For a put option:

Intrinsic Value = Strike price – Spot price

The intrinsic value of an option can be positive or 0, but cannot be negative. For a call option, the strike price must be less than the price of the underlying asset for the call to have an intrinsic value greater than 0. For a put option, the strike price must be greater than the underlying asset price for it to have intrinsic value.

Time value is the amount option buyers are willing to pay for the possibility that they may become profitable prior to expiration due to a favorable change in the price of the underlying asset. An option loses its time value as its expiration date nears. At expiration, an option is worth only its intrinsic value. Time value cannot be negative.

FACTORS THAT AFFECT THE VALUE OF AN OPTION PREMIUM

There are two types of factors that affect the value of an option premium:

Quantifiable factors

❖ Underlying stock price
❖ The stock price of the option
❖ The volatility of the underlying stock
❖ Time for expiry
❖ The risk free interest rate

Non-quantifiable factors

❖ Market participants' varying estimates of the underlying asset's future volatility.
❖ Individuals' varying estimates of futures performance of the underlying asset, based on fundamental or technical analysis.

❖ The effects of supply and demand both in the case of the options market place and for the underlying asset.

❖ The depth of market for that option – the number of transactions and contract volume on any given day.

PRICING MODELS FOR OPTIONS

On the basis of the above mentioned influencing factors, the theoretical option pricing models are used by option traders for calculating the fair value of the option. An option pricing model assists the trader in keeping the prices of calls and puts them in a proper numerical relationship to each other, helping the trader make bids and offers quickly. The most popular option pricing models are:

❖ *Black-Scholes model:* Fisher Black and Myron Scholes developed this model, which assumes that percentage change in the price of the underlying asset follows a normal distribution. This most popular for pricing option model was published in 1973, in the same year when the world's first organized options exchange, Chicago Board of Options Exchange (CBOE), was set up.

❖ *Binomial model:* This assumes that the percentage change in the price of the underlying asset follows a binomial distribution.

The Black-Schloes model can be applied in the following manner: Suppose there is a situation where stock-prices change more or less continuously, leading to a continuum of possible prices at the end of the year. Theoretically, in this situation an investor could set up a portfolio which has a payoff identical to that of a call option. However, the composition of this portfolio will have to be changed continuously as the situation changes.

The Black-Schloes model (B.S. Model) for calculating the value of such a portfolio is:

$$C_0 = \{S_0 N (d_1) - (E/e^{rt}) N (d_2)\}$$

Where C_0 is the present equilibrium value of the call option, S_0 is the present price of the stock now, E is the exercise price, e is the base of natural logarithms, r is the annualized continuously compound risk free interest rate, t is the length of time in years to the expiration date, and $N(d)$ is the value of the cumulative normal density function.

$$d_1 = \frac{\ln\left[\dfrac{S_0}{E}\right] + \left[r + \dfrac{1}{2}\,\sigma^2\right]}{\sigma\sqrt{t}} \text{ and } d_2 = d_1 - \sigma\sqrt{t}$$

Where ln is the natural logarithm and σ is the standard deviation of the annualized continuously compounded return on stock.

Example: Let the current price of a stock be Rs. 90 per share, the risk free interest rate is 8 per cent (annualized continuously compound rate). If the volatility of the stock is 23 per cent p.a, what is the expected price of the Rs. 80 call option in 6 months? Given N (1.0517) = 0.8535; and N (0.8891) = 0.8130.

Solution: Performing the above mentioned steps,

1. $\ln = (90/80) = 0.117783$

2. $\left[r + \dfrac{\sigma^2}{2}\right] = \left[0.08 + \dfrac{0.23 \times 0.23}{2}\right] = 0.08 + \dfrac{0.0529}{2} = 0.10645$

3. $\sigma\sqrt{t} = 0.23\sqrt{0.5} = 0.23 \times 0.707106781 = 0.162634559$

4. $d_1 = \dfrac{ln\left[\dfrac{S_0}{E}\right] + \left[r + \dfrac{1}{2}\sigma^2\right]}{\sigma\sqrt{t}} = \dfrac{0.117783 + (0.10645 \times 0.5)}{0.162634559} = 1.0517$

5. $d_2 = d_1 - \sigma\sqrt{t} = 1.0517 - 0.162634559 = 0.8891$

6. $C_0 = \{S_0 N (d_1) - (E/e^{rt}) N (d_2)\}$

           $= 90 \times 0.8535 - 80 \times e^{-0.08 \times 0.5} \times 0.8131$

           $= \text{Rs. } 14.33$

European Put Option Pricing

The B.S. model initially provided the formula for pricing European style call option on assets without any immediate income. Simultaneously, in an article in *Bell Journal of Economics and Management Science*, Roster Merton provided an elegant analysis in which he provided explicit formulas for pricing put option, expressed as:

$$P = Ee^{-rt} N(-d_2) - S_0 N(-d_1)$$

It can be noted that $N(-d_2)$ is the same as $1 - N(-d_2)$ and $N(-d_1)$ is the same as $1 - N(-d_1)$

So, the put option valuation in the earlier example would be:

$$P = 80 \times e^{-0.08 \times 0.5} \times (1 - 0.8130) - 90 \times (1 - 0.8535) = 1,1884 = 1.19$$

There is one more way to calculate the put option value, once the value of the call option is known:

$$P = C_0 + Ee^{-rt} - S_0$$

$$= 14.33 + 80\, e^{-0.08 \times 0.5} - 90$$

$$= 14.33 + 80 \times (0.96979) - 90$$

$$= 14.33 + 76.863 - 90 = 1.193.$$

Assumptions and Limitations of the B.S. Model

Just as with any other models in finance, the Black Scholes Option Pricing Model (BSOPM) is also based on some assumptions, which are as follows:

1. Frictionless market: The B.S. model assumes, (i) no transaction cost (ii) similar borrowing and lending rates and (iii) infinitely devisable assets. It permitted short selling. B.S.'s intention was to separate market forces on option prices.

2. The asset pays zero dividends.

3. The option is European style. However, the B.S. model can be applied to American style options too.

4. Asset returns are normal and stationary. Many critics found this assumption the biggest hole in the B.S. formula. Even Prof. Fisher Black (the inventor of the Black Scholes model) admitted it in an influential article in the *Journal of Applied Corporate Finance* in 1989.

The assumption may seen quite unrealistic but the real utility of BSOPM is that it provides a mechanism to hedge an option and the cost of hedging gives insights into the likely price of the option. In the B.S. model all the data inputs are directly observable except volatility.

The **Binomial model** for calculating the value of a portfolio consisting of Δ shares and B debt that has the same payoff as that of a call option is:

$$C = \Delta S - B$$

Where, $\Delta = \{(C_u - C_d)/S(u - d)\}$

$\qquad$ = spread of the possible option price/spread of the possible share price

and $\quad B = \{(dC_u - uC_d)/(u - d)R$

The stock, currently selling for S, can have two possible values next year, uS or dS ($uS > dS$).

An amount of B can be borrowed or lent at the rate of r the risk free rate. The interest factor $(1 + r)$ may be represented, simply as R.

The value of R is such that $d < R < u$. This condition ensures that there is no risk-free arbitrage opportunity.

The exercise price is E.

The value of the call option, before expiration, if the stock price goes up to uS, is

$$C_u = \text{Max} (dS - E, 0)$$

Similarly, the value of the call option, before expiration, if the stock price goes down to dS, is

$$C_d = \text{Max} (uS - E, 0)$$

Now if the stock price rises, $\Delta uS - RB = C_u$ and if the stock price falls $\Delta dS - RB = C_d$

Option Greeks

There are certain factors on which the price of options depends, such as price and volatility of the underlying assets, time to expiry etc. Sensitivity of the option price to the above mentioned factors are measured by tools known as option Greeks. Professional traders use these tools for trading and managing the risk of the large positions and stocks. Some of the common option Greeks are described below:

Delta: It is the option Greek that measures the estimated change in option price or premium for a change in the price of the underlying asset.

Gamma: It measures the estimated change in the Delta of an option for a change in the price of the underlying asset.

Vega: It measures the estimated change in the option price for a change in the volatility of the underlying asset.

Theta: It measures the estimated change in the option price for a change in the option expiry.

Rho: It measures the estimated change in the option price for a change in the risk free interest rate.

Table 8.9 Summary Table of the Formulae for the Greeks

	Call Option	Put Option
Delta	$N(d_1)$	$N(-d_1)$
Gamma	$\dfrac{e^{-d_1^2/2}}{S_0 \sigma \sqrt{2\pi t}}$	$\dfrac{e^{-d_1^2/2}}{S_0 \sigma \sqrt{2\pi t}}$
Theta	$\dfrac{S_0 \sigma e^{-d_1^2/2}}{2\sqrt{2\pi t}} - r . E e^{-rt} N(d_2)$	$\dfrac{S_0 \sigma e^{-d_1^2/2}}{2\sqrt{2\pi t}} - r . E e^{-rt} (1 - 4N(d_2))$
Vega	$\dfrac{S_0 \sqrt{t} \, e^{-d_1^2/2}}{\sqrt{2\pi}}$	$\dfrac{S_0 \sqrt{t} \, e^{-d_1^2/2}}{\sqrt{2\pi}}$
Rho	$t \, E e^{-rt} N(d_2)$	$-t \, E e^{-rt} \{1 - N(d_2)\}$

Illustrated Calculation of Option Greeks

Let the current price of the share (S_0) = Rs. 486

Exercise price (E) = Rs. 500

Time to expiration = 65 days

Standard deviation (σ) = 0.54

Continuously compound rate of interest = 9 per cent p.a

Dividend expected = Nil

From the earlier calculation of examples it is observed that:

$$d_1 = 0.06 \text{ and } d_2 = -0.17$$

For Delta

$$N(d_1) = N(0.06) \text{ and } N(d_2) = N(-0.17) = 0.4325$$

For call option Delta = $N(d_1) = 0.5239$

For put option Delta = $N(d_1) - 1 = 0.5239 - 1 = -0.4761$

This implies that if the price of the underlying share increases by Rs. 1, the price of the call option would rise by approximately 52 paisa while the put option price would fall by 48 paisa.

For Gamma

It can be observed from Table 8.9 that formulae for calculations of Gamma for both call and put option are the same:

$$\frac{e^{-d_1^2/2}}{S_0\sigma\sqrt{2\Pi t}}$$

$$= \frac{e^{-(0.06)2/2}}{486(0.54)\sqrt{2(22/7)(65/365)}}$$

$$= \frac{1.001801621}{262.44\sqrt{2860/(7 \times 365)65}}$$

$$= \frac{1.001801621}{277.6627} = 0.0036$$

So, it appears that if the share price increases by Re. 1, the call Gamma would change from 0.5239 to 0.5239 + 0.0036 = 0.5275 approximately, and similarly it is likely that put option Gamma would change to $-0.4761 + 0.0036 = 0.4625$.

For Theta

Call option for theta is $\dfrac{S_0\sigma e^{-d_1^2/2}}{2\sqrt{2\Pi t}} - r. Ee^{-rt}N(d_2)$

$$= \frac{486(0.54)e^{-(0.06)22}}{2\sqrt{2(22/7)(65/365)}} - 0.09 \times 500e^{-0.09(65/365)}(0.17)$$

$$= -142.97$$

Now, put option for Theta is $\dfrac{S_0\sigma e^{-d_1^2/2}}{2\sqrt{2t}} + r. Ee^{-rt}(1 - N(d_2))$

$$= \frac{-486\,(0.54)\,e^{-(0.06)2/2}}{2\sqrt{2}(22/7)(65/365)} - 0.09 \times 500e^{-0.09(65/365)}\,(1 - 0.4325)$$

$$= -98.69$$

Theta indicates that there are changes in the option value for small changes of time. For call option, the time decay is 142.97/365 = 0.39 or 39 paisa per day. Similarly, for put option, it is found to be equal to 98.69/365 = 0.27 that is, 27 paisa per day. Thus a nearer to expiry would cause a fall of about 39 paisa for call option and about 27 paisa for the put option.

For Vega

Like Gamma, Vega is the same for both call and put option, that is,

$$\frac{S_0\sqrt{t}\,e^{-d_1{}^2/2}}{\sqrt{2\Pi}} = \frac{486\,\sqrt{(65/365)}\,e^{-(0.06)2/2}}{2\sqrt{2}\,(22/7)} = \text{Rs. } 81.67$$

This implies that 0.1 change in σ would cause a change of $\approx$ Rs. 8.17 (= 81.67/10) in the values of call and put option alike. Greater σ would increase and smaller σ would reduce these values.

For Rho

For call option Rho = $t\,Ee^{-rt}\,N(d_2)$ = (65/365)(500) $\times\,e^{-0.09(65/365)} \times 0.4325$ = 37.89

For put option Rho = $-t\,Ee^{-rt}\,\{1 - N(d_2)\}$ = (65/365)(−500) $\times\,e^{-0.09(65/365)} \times 0.5675$ = − 49.73

From the Rho values, it is evident that an increase of 1 per cent in the risk-free rate of interest will increase the value of call option by 38 paisa, while value of put option would reduce by 0.4973 or 50 paisa. A decrease of 1 per cent would have the effect of reducing the call premium by that amount respectively.

OPTION CALCULATOR

An option calculator is a tool to calculate the price of an option on the basis of various influencing factors like the price of the underlying asset and its volatility, time to expiry, risk free interest rate etc. It also helps the user to understand how the change in one or more of the factors will affect the option price. This calculator can be viewed by any interested investors at *http://www.cboe.com/software/toolbox/toolbox.exe*

OPTION STRATEGIES

Option Pay-offs

Option pay-offs imply probable profits or losses found by an option trader under different market conditions. There are four types of option traders namely,

❖ Holder of call option

❖ Writer of call option

❖ Holder of put option

❖ Writer of put option

To derive the pay-off line for each of these four types of trades, it can be assumed that in the option in European style and at the time of maturity of the option, the prevailing spot price of the underlying asset is S_T. In regard to other notations to be used here, K denotes strike price, C is the price of the call option and P implies the price of the put option. K, C and P are all fixed, but S_T is a variable. It must be noted that S_T is not the last transaction price of the underlying asset, rather it is the weighted average of the prices of all the transactions that take place for the underlying asset during the last few minutes (30 minutes in India) in the transaction day (last Thursday of the concerned month).

A holder of call option earns positive gross profit when $S_T > (K + C)$ and here net profit is likely to be $[(S_T - K) - C]$. The breakeven point is achieved when $S_T = (K + C)$. If $S_T < K$, the call option will not be exercised, the holder incurs losses to the amount of 'C'. Incorporating all this information, the pay off line of the call option holder is shown in Figure 8.1.

Pay-off line of the put option holder would be the mirror image of that in Figure 8.1.

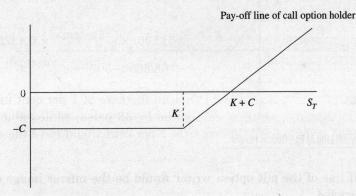

Figure 8.1   Pay-off Line of Call Option Holder

From Figure 8.1 it is evident that a call option holder can lose a maximum amount equal to the price of the option (i.e. C) but there is no limit of profit, depending of course on the rising value of S_T.

On the other hand, from the Figure 8.2 it is evident that there is a limit to earning profit by the call option writer (up to C) but there is no limit of his incurring loss.

A put option holder's pay-off also varies due to variation in S_T as depicted in Figure 8.3.

When the market price (S_T) of the underlying asset is greater than its contract price (K) as per option, put option will not be exercised by the holder and loss in that situation will be to the amount of 'P' (i.e., option price).

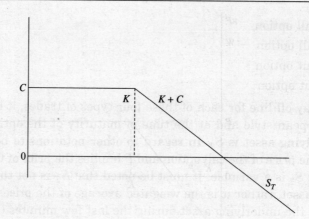

Figure 8.2   Pay-off Line of Call Option Writer

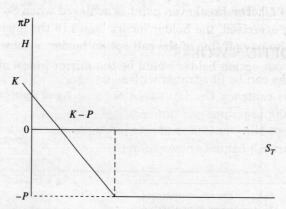

Figure 8.3   Pay-off Line of Put Option Holder

The pay-off line of the put option writer would be the mirror image of the Figure 8.3, as shown in Figure 8.4.

From Figure 8.4, it is seen that $S_T < K$. It is profitable to sell the asset to the writer as per the contract and the holder's gross and net profit in this situation will be $(K - S_T)$ and $[(K - S_T) - P]$ respectively. So, a no profit no loss situation will arise here when

$$K - S_T - P = 0 \text{ or } S_T = K - P$$

From Figure 8.3 and Figure 8.4 it can be observed that a put option holder can earn a maximum profit of amount K, which is the maximum possibility of incurring loss by a put option writer. Similarly, the put option writer can earn maximum profit to the amount of 'P' which is the maximum possibility of incurring loss by a put option holder. It should be noted that the value of 'P' is much less than the value of 'K'.

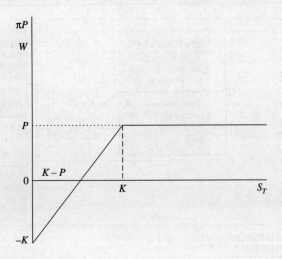

Figure 8.4   Pay-off Line of Put Option Holder

HOW THE CALL OPTION WORKS

How a call option works can be illustrated with some figures with similar possibility after 90 days. Let it be 90 days contract. On day 1 spot Nifty is 1100; strike price 1150; the number of options bought is 100; premium per option is Rs. 10. After the expiry of 90 days there are two alternatives, (i) spot Nifty is 1200 and (ii) spot Nifty is 1000. Chart 8.2 exhibits how call option works and Chart 8.3 exhibits how put option works.

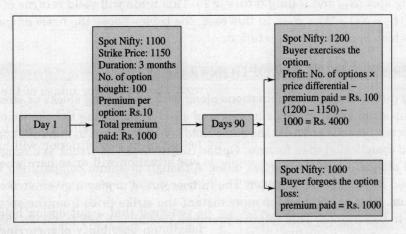

Chart 8.2   How Call Option Works

Concept of Spread in Option Trading

Assume a trader buys one spot Nifty (S_0) and sells one future Nifty (F_0) on day 0. On day T, the day he closes these trades, (which may or may not be the expiry day) but for simplicity

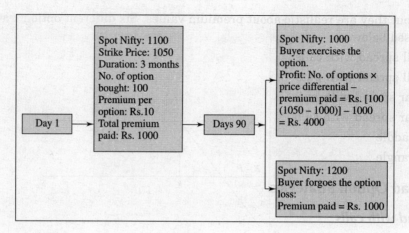

Day 1	→	Spot Nifty: 1100 Strike Price: 1050 Duration: 3 months No. of option bought: 100 Premium per option: Rs.10 Total premium paid: Rs. 1000	→	Days 90	→	Spot Nifty: 1000 Buyer exercises the option. Profit: No. of options × price differential – premium paid = Rs. [100 (1050 – 1000)] – 1000 = Rs. 4000

Spot Nifty: 1200
Buyer forgoes the option
loss:
Premium paid = Rs. 1000

Chart 8.3   How Put Option Works

let us assume it to be the same day, he reverses these trades by selling one spot Nifty (S_T) and buying the future Nifty back (F_T). His total return constitutes the return from the spot transaction and return from the future transaction, or $[(S_T - S_0) + (F_0 - F_T)]$.

By rearranging signs, the above equation can be written as $[(F_T - S_0) - (F_T - S_T)]$. But $(F_0 - S_0)$ is the difference between the future price and the spot price on day zero while $(F_T - S_T)$ is the difference on day T. The difference between the spot prices is called the spread or basis.

The opposite hedge is to sell spot (S_0) and buy future (F_0) on day zero; square off on day T by buying spot (S_T) and selling future (FT). This trade will yield returns of $[(S_0 - S_T) - (F_0 - F_T)]$ or $[(F_T - S_T) - (F_0 - S_0)]$. In this case, the trader hopes the basis or spread will widen by day T which is a bearish expectation.

FURTHER STRATEGIES ON OPTION TRADING

By holding different option combinations along with underlying stocks or stock portfolio, one can build up strategy for minimizing risk and also for increasing the chance of earning profit in the expected new situation. At the same time it could be kept in mind that options are more flexible and complicated than futures. Option contracts can be struck at a range of prices, plus rights and obligations of the parties differ. Although premium computation is complex it is not essential knowledge for a trader. The further out of money a given strike price, lower is the premium. That is because the more distant the strike price from the spot price, the less likely it is to be attained. This relative premium pricing is a key factor. In the simplest case, a buyer's loss on a naked call or put option is restricted to the premium paid.

However, by using a combination of hedges, losses can be restricted further. As stated earlier, it is dangerous to write naked options. But when the position is covered, writing an option generates cash and it is a useful hedge. By combining covered writes with buying puts and calls, traders can construct complex strategies. The following examples use imaginary numbers, but they are realistic about premium values. Six different option trading strategies are discussed below.

- ❖ Bull spread with calls
- ❖ Bull spread with puts
- ❖ Bear spread with puts
- ❖ Bear spread with calls
- ❖ Straddle
- ❖ Strangle

Bull Spread Option Strategies

Bull spread with calls

With spot at Rs. 200, buy a call at Rs. 220 and write a call at Rs. 250. One pays Rs. 6 and receives Rs. 2 as premium. So, total cost is Rs. 4. If the stock moves to Rs. 236, by exercising options, one makes Rs. 16, which works out to a profit of Rs. 12. However, if stock moves to Rs. 250, the second is exercised and profit is capped at Rs. 26 [(250 − 220) − 4].

Bull spread with puts

With spot at Rs. 200 one writes a put at Rs. 190 receiving Rs. 6 and buys a put at Rs. 180 paying Rs. 2 – one has Rs. 4 in hand. If the price stays above Rs. 190, he keeps the cash. If the price drops to Rs. 190 and put is exercised against the trader, then at Rs. 180, one's puts covers the position. The maximum loss is Rs. 6 [(19 − 180) − 4].

Bear Spread Option Strategies

Bear spread with puts

With spot at Rs. 200, one buys a put at Rs. 190 paying a premium of Rs. 6 and writes a put at Rs. 160 receiving Rs. 2 as premium. One's maximum loss is the premium difference of Rs. 4 and his potential gain is capped at Rs. 26 [(190 − 160) − 4].

Bear spread with calls

With spot at Rs. 200 one writes a put at Rs. 220 receiving Rs. 6 as premium and buys a call at Rs. 250 paying Rs. 2 upfront. He gets a maximum profit of Rs. 4 upfront and maximum loss of Rs. 26[(250 − 220) − 4]. Again the cash in hand may be utilized elsewhere.

Straddle

Straddle is when one feels that volatility in a stock or market will be high, but is not sure of the direction. In the case of stock, this applies typically to takeovers and in the run up to financial results.

The straddle involves buying both a put and a call at the same price and expiry date. This is an expensive strategy, as the trader pays two premiums. But the price swing in open direction will compensate.

With spot at Rs. 200, one buys a put and call for Rs. 8 each (total cost Rs. 16) at the strike price of Rs. 200. On any price change whatsoever, some pay-off reduces the maximum loss. The straddle writer has the opposite profile – a maximum profit equal to the sum of the two premiums and an unlimited loss.

Strangle

A strangle combines put-call with different strike price to sandwich the spot. It is cheaper because of out of money premiums are lower. With spot at Rs. 200, one buys a put at Rs. 190 and a call at Rs. 210, paying Rs. 6 for cash. There is a likely profit only if the stock moves out of the Rs. 178 – 222 range.

Stock Index Options

Index options enable investors to gain exposure to a board market, with trading decision and frequently with one transaction. To obtain the same level of diversification using individual stocks or individual equity options, numerous decisions and trades would be necessary. Since, board exposure can be gained with one trade; the transaction cost is also reduced by using index options. As a percentage of the underlying value, premiums of index options are usually lower than those of equity options as equity options are more volatile than the index. Index options are effective enough to appeal to a broad spectrum of users, from conservative investors to more aggressive stock market traders. Individual investors might wish to capitalize on market options (bullish, bearish or neutral) by acting on their views of the broad market or one of its sectors. The more sophisticated market professionals might find the variety of index option contracts excellent tools for enhancing market timing decisions and adjusting asset mixes for asset allocation.

Large equity positions may mean using index options to either reduce risk or increase market exposure.

The underlying for index options is the BSE 30 Sensex, which is the benchmark of Indian capital markets, comprising 30 scrips of different companies significant to construction of the index. The Sensex options of the European style of options, that is. The options would be exercised only on the day of expiry. They will be premium style that is, the buyer of the option will pay a premium to the option writer (seller) in cash at the time of entering into the contract. Generally, the premium is settled on $T + 1$ basis.

Like stocks, options and futures are also traded on any exchange. In the Bombay Stock Exchange stocks are traded on BSE On Line Trading (BOLT) system and options and futures are traded on Derivatives Trading and Settlement System (DTSS).

In the equity derivative segment, the BSE witnessed a decrease in total turnover from Rs. 2,42,308 crore in 2007-08 to Rs. 58,173 crore in 2011-12 (considering the figures for 9 months). Meanwhile, the NSE witnessed a considerable increase from Rs. 1,30,90,478 crore in 2007-08 to Rs. 2,37,15,138 crore in 2011-12 (considering the figures for 9 months). During the same period cash turnover witnessed a decrease from Rs. 15,78,670 crore to Rs. 4,88,133 crore in the BSE and from Rs. 35,51,038 crore to Rs. 19,79,730 crore in the NSE due to a worldwide crisis.

Table 8.10 Contract Specifications for the Options on SENSEX

Underlying Index		BSE 30 SENSEX
Contract Multiplier	:	INR 100
Strike price Intervals	:	50 SENSEX points. There shall be minimum of 5 strikes (two In-the-Money, one Near-the-Money and two Out-the-Money)
Premium Quotation	:	SENSEX points
Last Trading Day	:	Last Thursday of the contract month. If it is a holiday, the immediately preceding business day.
Expiration Day	:	Last Thursday of the contract month. If it is a holiday, the immediately preceding business day. Note: Business day is a day during which the underlying stock market is open for trading.
Contract Month	:	1, 2 and 3 months
Exercise Style	:	European
Settlement Style	:	Cash
Trading Hours	:	9:30 a.m. to 3:30 p.m.
Tick Size	:	0.1 SENSEX points (INR 10).
Settlement Value	:	Closing value of the SENSEX on the expiry day.
Exercise Notice Time	:	It would be a specified time (Exercise Session) on the last trading day of the contract. All In-the-Money options would be deemed to be exercised unless the participant communicates otherwise in the manner specified by the derivatives segment.

Source: Sandeep Singhal, Project Manager, Derivatives Segment, Bombay Stock Exchange

Table 8.11 Some Significant Differences between Futures and Options

Futures	Options
Futures are agreement/contracts to buy or sell a specified quantity of the underlying assets at a price agreed upon by the buyer and seller, on or before a specified time. Both buyer and sellers are obliged to buy or sell the underlying asset.	Buyers of the options enjoy the right and not the obligation, to buy/sell the underlying asset.
Future contracts have a symmetric risk profile for both buyers as well as sellers.	Options have an asymmetric risk profile. For a buyer (or holder), the downside is limited to the premium (option price) he has paid while the profits may be unlimited. For a seller or writer, however, the downside is unlimited and not connected to the premium he has received from the buyer.
The futures contract prices are affected mainly by the price of the underlying asset.	Prices of options are however, affected mainly by the price of the underlying asset, time remaining for expiry of the contract and volatility of the underlying asset.
It costs nothing to enter into a futures contract.	There is a cost of entering into an options contract, termed as premium.

Souce: NSE & BSE

Table 8.12   NSE Derivatives Segment Turnover: How it Accelerates

| Year | Index Futures | | Stock Futures | | Indexed Options | | Stock Options | |
	No of contract	Turnover Rs. (Cr)	No of contract	TurnoverRs. (Cr)	No of contract	Turnover Rs. (Cr)	No of contract	Turnover Rs. (Cr)
2001-02	1025588	21483	1957856	51515	175900	3765	1037529	25163
2002-03	2126763	43952	10676843	286533	442241	9246	3523062	100131
2003-04	17191668	554446	32368842	1305939	1732414	52816	5583071	217207
2004-05	21635449	772147	47043066	1484056	3293558	121943	5045112	168836
2005-06	58537886	1513755	80905493	2791697	12935116	338469	5240776	180253
2006-07	81487424	2539574	104955401	3830967	25157438	791906	5283310	193795
2007-08	156598579	3820667	203587952	7548563	55366038	1362110	9460631	359136
2008-09	210428103	3570111	221577980	3479642	212088444	3731501	13295970	229226
2009-10	178306889	3934388	14591240	5195246	341379523	8027964	14016270	506065
2010-11	165023653	4356754	186041459	5495756	650638557	18365365	32508393	1030344
2011-12	146188740	3577998	158344617	4074670	864017736	22720031	36494371	977031
2012-13	53758304	1315507	67378326	1761781	396624665	10342805	25986507	715717

Source: www.nseindia.com (Accessed on 22.09.12)

Tax Haven of Derivatives Instrument

Prior to 2005, the Income Tax Act, 1961 did not provide any specific provision for taxability of derivatives. Sections 43(5) and 73(1) consider derivatives transactions as speculative transactions which come under the head *Income from Other Sources.* Any loss incurred on derivatives transactions would be set off against any such other transactions. As a result derivatives transactions attract a high tax rate.

Table 8.13   Market Turnover (Rs. crores)

Market	2007-08	2008-09	2009-10	2010-11	2011-12 (as on 31.12.11)
BSE :	15,78,670	11,00,074	13,78,809	1,105,027	4,88,133
Cash Equity Derivatives	2,42,308	12,268	53,323	9,582	58,173
NSE :	35,51,038	27,52,023	41,38,024	3,577,410	19,73,730
Cash Equity Derivatives	1,30,90,478	1,10,10,482	1,76,63,665	29,248,221	2,37,15,138

Source: BSE, NSE and www.sebi.gov.in (Accessed on 10.10.2012)

After amending Section 43(5) in the year 2005 derivative transactions taking place in recognized stock exchanges are not taxed as *speculative transactions.* The income from derivative transactions is considered as business income under the head *Profits and Gains of Business or Profession.* Any loss arising from derivative trading is either adjusted as a business loss of the current year or carried forward and set off against any other business loss over the next eight years.

INVESTMENT RELATED WEBSITES

1. http://www.savvysoft.com/framewk.htm
2. http://beginnersinvest.about.com/od/stocksoptionswarrants/qt/putoptions.htm
3. http://beginnersinvest.about.com/od/stocksoptionswarrants/a/aa012305.htm
4. http://www.magportal.com/cgi/search.cgi?q=derivatives&c=216&x=33&y=16
5. http://www.fdic.gov/bank/analytical/fyi/2003/032603fyi.html
6. http://www.cfo.com/article.cfm/3010251
7. http://www.findarticles.com/p/articles/mi_m3301/is_11_106/ai_n15883978
8. http://www.erivativesreview.com/content/content.cfm?ID=04F019E5-EA22-4A2B-8487
   90B83AD2EBE6&SectionID=7E15D8B1-3F72-4F46-93A2EF580430CA80&IssueID=E
   54B92A3-C290-448E-867D4424EF81ED41
9. http://www.time.com/time/europe/magazine/article/1,13005,901040531-641106,00.html
10. http://www.findarticles.com/p/articles/mi_m4070/is_195/ai_114050444
11. http://www.findarticles.com/p/articles/mi_mEIN/is_2005_Nov_23/ai_n15867778
12. http://www.findarticles.com/p/articles/mi_qa3743/is_200507/ai_n14685366
13. http://www.time.com/time/magazine/article/0,9171,981587,00.html
14. http://www.findarticles.com/p/articles/mi_qa3715/is_200309/ai_n9301074
15. http://links.jstor.org/sici?sici=0022-1082(199303)48:1<65:RTBWAS>2.0.CO;2-Y
16. http://www.iop.org/EJ/abstract/-search=17677498.8/0295-5075/66/6/909
17. http://links.jstor.org/sici?sici=0022-1082(198507)40:3<793:DTSMO>2.0.CO;2-
   Q&origin=repec
18. http://www.hkex.com.hk/research/dmtrsur/DMTS04_E.pdf
19. http://www.blackwell-synergy.com/doi/abs/10.1111/j.1369-412X.2003.00044.x?prevSear
   ch=allfield:(indian+stock+market)
20. http://www.iop.org/EJ/abstract/-search=17677657.2/0295-5075/77/2/28001

Computer Screen Based Trading

9

THE ROLE OF COMPUTERS IN STOCK TRADING

In today's situation of the communication revolution, the world has become smaller and the market has become bigger. By following the communication revolution trading is no more a local activity, it has become an international one considering the globe as a hub. In Europe, due to the introduction of a single currency, major investors have stopped looking at individual countries within the European Economic Community (EEC). A consolidation of European stock exchanges is inevitable. The first move was taken by the merger of the Paris, Brussels and Amsterdam stock exchanges in March, 2000 by forming Euro next. The next move was taken by the two largest stock exchanges of the European Union of London and Frankfurt which joined together for settlement and clearing services and subsequently for joint ventures with NASDAQ of the USA. The new stock exchange is called iX with its headquarters in London and the price is quoted and traded in Euros and Pounds as a compromise, instead of only the Euro.

Stock exchanges across the Atlantic face a stiffer competition from Electronic Communication Networks (ECNs). As per a rough estimate, up to 50 per cent of equity trades in the USA take place outside the recognized stock exchanges. Competition between NYSE and NASDAQ relating to pertaining territory is very keen. The NYSE has floated ECN for trade but NASDAQ lists stocks and has opened up a trading facility of NYSE stocks for their member brokers. The competition is no more confined to the domestic market. On one hand NASDAQ is considered as more international than that of Tokyo and Europe and on the other hand the NYSE is exploring a 24 hour Global Equity Market (GEM) in collaboration with Tokyo, Euro next, Australia, Toronto and Hong Kong. The Asian tiger China is growing by merging its two premier stock exchanges in Shanghai and Shenzhen.

Massive changes have been made in the arena of the stock market. Internet has opened up the horizon for exploring the information in favor of investors and uses the same for their benefit. By replacing the physical trading floor, the NSE introduced automated screen based trading in India using Very Small Aperture Terminals (VSATs), for the first time. In fact, in order to provide efficiency, liquidity and transparency, NSE introduced a nation-wide on-line fully automated Screen Based Trading System (SBTS) where a member can punch the quantities of securities and his transaction prices into the computer and the transaction is executed as soon as it finds a matching sale or buy order from a counter party. SBTS electronically matches orders on a strict price/time priority and hence cuts down on time, cost and risk of error, as well as on fraud resulting in improved operational efficiency. It allows faster incorporation of price sensitive information into prevailing prices, thus increasing the informational efficiency of markets. It

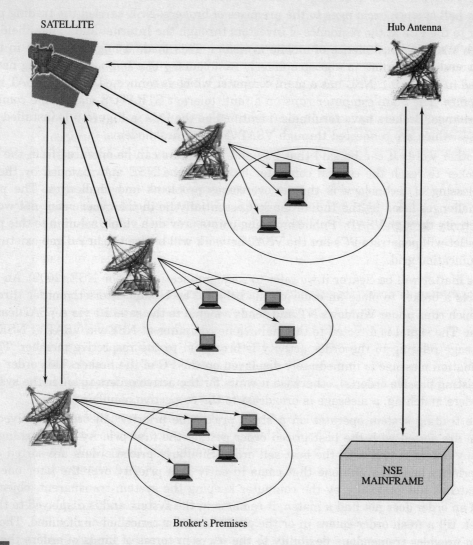

SATELLITE

Hub Antenna

NSE
MAINFRAME

Broker's Premises

Figure 9.1 Internet Trading Network

Source: National Stock Exchange (NSE), Mumbai

enables market participants, irrespective of their geographical locations, to trade with one another simultaneously, improving the depth and liquidity of the market. It provides full anonymity by accepting orders, big or small, from members without revealing their identity, thus providing equal access to everybody. It also provides a perfect audit trail, which helps to resolve disputes by logging in the trade execution process in entirety. Thus it sucked liquidity from other exchanges and in the very first year of its operation, the NSE became the leading stock exchange in the country, impacting the fortunes of other exchanges and forcing them to adopt SBTS also. Today India can boast that almost 100 per cent of its trading takes place through electronic order matching. Technology was used to carry the trading platform from the trading hall of stock exchanges to the premises of brokers. NSE carried the trading platform further to the PCs at the residence of investors through the Internet and to handheld devices through WAP for convenience of mobile investors. This made a huge difference in terms of equal access to investors in a geographically vast country like India. The trading network is depicted in Figure 9.1. NSE has a main computer which is connected through VSAT installed in its office. The main computer runs on a fault tolerant STRATUS mainframe computer at the exchange. Brokers have terminals (identified as the PCs in Figure 9.1) installed at their premises which are connected through VSATs/leased lines/modems.

In other words it can be said that buy and sell orders can be operated from the office of the broker to reach the central computer located at the NSE and matched by the server. The blessing of technology is that it overcomes problems and challenges. The problems and challenges faced by the Indian market essentially lie in the cyber retail net work with connectivity through VSATs. Public browsing points provide a viable solution to this problem. The outlet will penetrate PCs but the VSAT network will bridge the broad gap existing in the communication grid.

The matter will be clearer if we refer to some publications of the NSE (2009). An investor instructs a broker to place an order on his behalf. The broker enters the order through his PC, which runs under Windows NT and sends a signal to the satellite via a VSAT/leased line/modem. The signal is directed to the mainframe computer at NSE via VSAT at NSE's office. A message relating to the order activity is broadcast to the respective member. The order confirmation message is immediately displayed on the PC of the broker. This order matches the existing passive order(s), otherwise it waits for the active orders to enter the system. On the orders matching, a message is broadcast to the respective member.

The trading system operates on a strict price time priority. All orders received on the system are sorted with the best priced order getting the first priority for matching i.e. the best buy orders match with the best sell order. Similarly priced orders are sorted out on a time priority basis, i.e. the one that came in early gets priority over the later one. Orders are matched automatically by the computer keeping the system transparent, objective and fair. If an order does not find a match, it remains in the system and is displayed to the whole market, till a fresh order comes in or the earlier order is cancelled or modified. The trading system provides tremendous flexibility to the users in terms of kinds of orders that can be placed on the system. Several time-related (immediate or cancel), price-related (buy/sell limit and stop loss orders) or volume related (disclosed quantity) conditions can be easily built into an order. The trading system also provides complete market information on-line. The market screens at any point of time provide complete information on total order depth in a security, the five best buys and sells available in the market, the quantity traded during the day in that security, the high and the low, the last traded price, etc.

Investors can also know the fate of the orders almost as soon as they are placed with the trading members. Thus the NEAT system provides an Open Electronic Consolidated Limit Order Book (OECLOB). Limit orders are orders to buy or sell shares at a stated quantity and stated price. If the price quantity conditions do not match, the limit order will not be executed. The term 'limit order book' refers to the fact that only limit orders are stored in the book and all market orders are crossed against the limit orders sitting in the book. Since the order book is visible to all market participants, it is termed as an 'Open Book'.

NEAT SYSTEM

The NEAT system supports an order driven market, wherein orders match on the basis of time and price priority. All quantity fields are in units and prices are quoted in Indian Rupees. The regular lot size and tick size for various securities traded is notified by the exchange from time to time.

MARKET TYPES

The capital market system has four types of markets.

Normal Market

A normal market consists of various book types wherein orders are segregated as Regular Lot Orders, Special Term Orders, Negotiated Trade Orders and Stop Loss Orders depending on their order attributes.

Odd Lot Market

The odd lot market facility is used for the limited physical market. The main features of the limited physical market have been discussed earlier.

RETDEBT Market

The RETDEBT market facility on the NEAT system of capital market segment is used for transactions in retail debt market session. Trading in the retail detail market takes place in the same manner as in the equities (capital market) segment.

Auction Market

In the auction market, auctions are initiated by the exchange on behalf of trading members for settlement related reasons.

CORPORATE HIERARCHY

The trading member has the facility of defining a hierarchy amongst its users of the NEAT system. This hierarchy is shown in Chart 9.1.

The users of the trading system can log on as either of the user types. The significance of each type is explained below.

Corporate manager: The corporate manager is a term assigned to a user placed at the highest level in a trading firm. Such a user receives the 'end of day' reports for all branches of the trading member. The facility to set 'branch order value limits' and 'user order value limits' is available to the corporate manager. The corporate manager can view the outstanding orders and trade of all users of the trading member. He can cancel/modify outstanding orders of all users of the trading member.

Branch manager: The branch manager is a term assigned to a user who is placed under the corporate manager. The branch manager receives 'end of day' reports for all the dealers under that branch. The branch manager can set user order value limit for each of his branches. The branch manager can view outstanding orders and trade of all users of his branch. He can cancel/modify outstanding orders of all users of his branch.

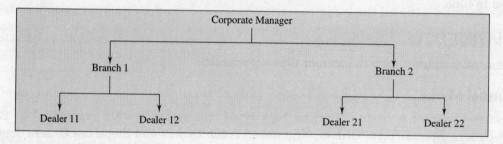

Chart 9.1   Hierarchies of NEAT System Users

Source: National Stock Exchange (NSE), Mumbai

Dealer: Dealers are users at the lowest level of the hierarchy. A dealer can view and perform order and trade related activities only for himself and does not have access to information on other dealers under either the same branch or other branches.

Local Database

The local database provides a faster response time to users. All inquiries made by a user for their own orders/trades are serviced through the local database. If however, a corporate manager/branch manager makes inquiries for orders of any dealer/branch manager of the trading firm, then the inquiry is serviced by the host. The data stored in the local database include system messages, security related information and order/trade related data of the user.

Market Phases

The system is normally made available for trading on all days except Saturdays, Sundays and other holidays. Holidays are declared by the exchange from time to time. A trading day typically consists of a number of discrete stages as explained in the subsequent section.

Opening

The trading member can carry out the following activities after login to the NEAT system and before the market opens for trading:

1. Set up market watch (the securities which the user would like to view on the screen)
2. Viewing inquiry screens

At the point of time when the market is opening for trading, the trading member cannot login to the system. A message 'Market status is changing. Cannot log on for some time' is displayed. If the member is already logged in, he cannot perform trading activities till the market is opened.

Open Phase

The open period indicates the commencement of trading activity. To signify the start of trading, a message is sent to all the trader workstations. The market open time for different markets is notified by the exchange to all the trading members. Order entry is allowed when all the securities have been opened. During this phase, orders are matched on a continuous basis. Trading in all the instruments is allowed unless they are specifically prohibited by the exchange. The activities that are allowed at this stage are 'inquiry,' 'order entry,' 'order modification,' 'order cancellation,' (including quick order cancellation) 'order matching' and trade cancellation.

Market Close

When the market closes, trading in all instruments for that market comes to an end. A message to this effect is sent to all trading members. No further orders are accepted, but the user is permitted to perform activities like inquiries and trade cancellation.

Surveillance and Control (SURCON)

Surveillance and Control (SURCON) is that period after market close during which, the users have inquiry access only. After the end of the SURCON period, the system processes the data for making the system available for the next trading day. When the system starts processing data, the interactive connection with the NEAT system is lost and a message to that effect is displayed at the trader workstation.

Logging On

On starting NEAT application, the log on screen appears with the following detail:

1. User ID
2. Trading Member ID
3. Password
4. New Password

In order to sign on to the system, the user must specify a valid user ID, trading member ID and the corresponding password. A valid combination of user ID, trading member ID and the password is needed to access the system.

1. User ID

Each trading member can have more than one user. The number of users allowed for each trading member is notified by the exchange from time to time. Each user of a trading member must be registered with the exchange and is assigned a unique user ID.

2. Trading member ID

The exchange assigns a trading member ID to each trading member. The trading member ID is unique and functions as a reference for all orders/trades of different users. This ID is common for all the users of a particular trading member.

The trading member ID and user IDs form a unique and valid combination. It is the responsibility of the trading member to maintain adequate control over the persons having access to user IDs. The trading member should request the exchange for changes in user ID user names especially when there are changes in the users who are dealing on behalf of the trading member.

3. Password

When a user logs on for the first time, he has to enter the default password 'NEATCM' provided by the exchange. On entering this password, the system requests the user to enter a new password in the 'New Password' field. On entering the new password the system requests for confirmation of this new password. This new password is known to the user only.

The password should contain a minimum of six characters and maximum of eight characters in length. A combination of characters and numbers is allowed in the password. The password can be changed if the user desires so and a new password can be entered. The new password must be different from the old password. The password appears in the encrypted form and thus complete secrecy is maintained. The system ensures the change in password for all users (password expiry period is parameterized by the Exchange). The user can log on by entering a new password as per the procedure outlined above. In the event of the user forgetting his password, the trading member is required to inform the exchange in writing with a request to reset the password. The user password is reset to the default password set by the exchange. The user can log on by entering a new password as per the procedure outlined above.

If three attempts are made by a user to log on with an incorrect password, then that user is automatically disabled. In case of such an event, the trading member makes a written request to the exchange for resetting of password. The user password is reset to the default password set by the exchange. The user can log on, by entering a new password as per the procedure outlined above.

Earlier, it was possible for members having VSATs at more than one location to use the allotted user IDs interchangeably from either location. This gave rise to various systems security related problems. To reduce such potential risks associated with the member's workstation, the exchange assigns a user ID to a specific location. On account of it, whenever a user attempts to log on to the trader workstation, the system checks for a valid location for that user ID in the database at the host end.

In case there is a mismatch between the user ID and the corresponding VSAT ID, the message is flashed on the log on screen, 'You are trying to sign on from a different location. Sign on is not allowed'. Members connected through leased lines and high speed dial up modems are also checked for the local address of their trading terminals and the corresponding user IDs. In case of mismatch between the two the message, 'You are trying to sign on from a different location. Sign on is not allowed' is flashed on the log on screen. Members may beallowed to log on from different VSAT IDs only on specific written requests, which may be verified by the exchange with reference to the problem specified.

LOG OFF/EXIT FROM THE APPLICATION

One can exit from the application as and when one desires before the SURCON period. On invoking the log off screen, the following options are displayed to the user:

1. Permanent sign off
2. Temporary sign off
3. Exit

1. Permanent Sign Off

As the name suggests, a user can log off permanently from the trading system by selecting this option. The user is logged off and the log on screen appears.

2. Temporary Sign Off

Temporary sign off is a useful feature that allows the user to disallow the use of the trading software without actually logging off. During a temporary signoff period, the application continues to receive all market updates in the background. However, the user cannot enter orders or make inquiries. This allows the user to leave the trading system temporarily inactive and prevents unauthorized access to the system. On selecting the temporary sign off option, a password entry screen is displayed. The use of the NEAT system is enabled on entering the correct password. The temporary sign off is automatically activated when the user is inactive for a period of 5 minutes.

The user has to enter the password to resume activities. If three attempts are made to sign on with an incorrect password, the user is permanently logged off. In this case the user has to log on again.

3. Exit

On selection of this option, the user comes out of the sign off screen.

NEAT SCREEN

The trader workstation screen of the trading member is divided into the following windows:

1. Title bar: It displays the trading system name i.e. NEAT, the date and the current time.

2. Ticker window: The ticker displays information of all trades in the system as and when they take place. The user has the option of selecting the securities that should appear in the ticker. Securities in the ticker can be selected for each market type. On the extreme right hand of the ticker is the on-line index window that displays the current index value of NSE indices namely S&P CNX Nifty, S&P CNX Defty, CNX Nifty Junior, S&P CNX500, CNX Midcap, CNX IT, Bank Nifty, CNX 100 and Nifty Midcap 50. The user can scroll within these indices and view the index values respectively. Index point change with reference to the previous close is displayed along with the current index value.

The difference between the previous close index value and the current index value becomes zero when the Nifty closing index is computed for the day. The ticker window displays securities capital market segments. The ticker selection facility is confined to the securities of capital market segment only. The first ticker window, by default, displays all the derivatives contracts traded in the futures and options segment.

3. Tool bar: The toolbar has functional buttons which can be used with the mouse for quick access to various functions such as Buy Order Entry, Sell Order Entry, Market By Price (MBP), Previous Trades (PT), Outstanding Order (OO), Activity Log (AL), Order Status (OS), Market Watch (MW), Snap Quote (SQ), Market Movement (MM), Market Inquiry (MI), Auction Inquiry (AI), Order Modification (OM), Order Cancellation (OCXL), Security List, Net Position, Online Backup, Supplementary Menu, Index Inquiry, Index Broadcast and Help. All these functions are also accessible through the keyboard.

4. Market watch window: The market watch window is the main area of focus for a trading member. This screen allows continuous monitoring of the securities that are of specific interest to the user. It displays trading information for the selected securities.

5. Inquiry window: This screen enables the user to view information such as Market By Price (MBP), Previous Trades (PT), Outstanding Orders (OO), Activity Log (AL) and so on. Relevant information for the selected security can be viewed.

6. Snap quote: The snap quote feature allows a trading member to get instantaneous market information on any desired security. This is normally used for securities that are not already set in the market watch window. The information presented is the same as that of the market watch window.

7. Order/Trade window: This window enables the user to enter/modify/cancel orders and also to send requests for trade cancellation and modification.

8. Message window: This enables the user to view messages broadcast by the exchange such as corporate actions, any market news, auctions related information etc. and other messages like order confirmation, order modification, order cancellation, orders which have resulted in quantity freezes/price freezes and the exchange action on them, trade confirmation, trade cancellation/modification requests and exchange action on them, name and time when the user logs in/logs off from the system, messages specific to the trading member, etc. These messages appear as and when the event takes place in chronological order.

INVOKING AN INQUIRY SCREEN

All inquiry screens have a selection where the security viewed can be selected. The screen shows the details of the security selected for that inquiry. The details for each inquiry screen are discussed further in this chapter.

Market Watch

The Market Watch window is the third window from the top of the screen that is always visible to the user. The Market Watch is the focal area for users. The purpose of Market Watch is to setup and view trading details of securities that are of interest to users. For each security in the Market Watch, market information is dynamically updated.

Market information displayed: The one line market information displayed in the market watch screen is for current best price orders available in the Regular Lot book. For each security the following information is displayed:

    (a) The corporate action indicator "Ex/Cum"

    (b) The total buy order quantity available at best buy price

    (c) Best buy price

    (d) Best sell price

    (e) Total sell order quantity available at best sell price

    (f) The last traded price

    (g) The last trade price change indicator

    (h) The no delivery period indicator "ND"

If the security is suspended, 'SUSPENDED' appears in front of the security. If a question mark (?) appears on the extreme right hand corner for a security, it indicates that the information being displayed is not the latest and the system will dynamically update it.

Information update: In the market watch screen, changes in the best price and quantities are highlighted on a dynamic basis (in all pages of market watch). For example, if the best price changes as a result of a new order in the market, the new details are immediately displayed. The changed details are highlighted with a change of color for a few seconds to signify that a change has occurred. A blue color indicates that price/quantities have improved, while a red color indicates that the price/quantities have worsened.

If the last traded price is better than the previous last traded price then the indicator '+' appears or if the last traded price is worse than the previous last traded price then the indicator '−' appears. If there is no change in the last traded price, no indicator is displayed.

The list of securities that are available for trading on the capital market segment is available in the security list box. The user has the option to set up securities directly from the security list without typing a single character on the market watch screen. This is a quick facility to set up securities. If the user tries to set up a security which is already present in the market watch one gets a message that the security is already set up. The user also has the option to add and delete the security set up in the market watch screen as many times as one desires. The user can print the contents of the market watch set up by the user. the user can either print the market watch on display or the full market watch.

Market watch download: A user has to set up securities after the first download of the software. After setting up the market watch, it is suggested that the user should log out normally. This will help the user to save the freshly set up market watch securities in a file. If at any given time, when the user has freshly set up a few securities and encounters an abnormal exit, the newly set up securities are not saved and the user may have to repeat the process of setting up securities.

The market watch set up is carried over to subsequent days, thus averting the need to set up the market watch on daily basis. During the log on stage, the relevant market watch details are downloaded from the trading system. The message displayed is 'Market watch download is in progress'. The time taken for the market watch download depends on the number of securities set up.

Special Features of Market Watch Screen

(a) One of the best features of this software is that the user has the facility to set up 500 securities in the market watch. The user can set up a maximum of 30 securities in one page of the market watch screen.

(b) The details of the current position in the market watch defaults in the order entry screen and the inquiry selection screen. It is therefore possible to do quick order entries and inquiries using this feature. The default details can also be overwritten.

(c) Market watch set up can be sorted alphabetically.

(d) An indicator for corporate actions for a security is another feature in market watch. The indicators are as follows:

'XD' - ex-dividend

'XB' - ex-bonus

'XI' - ex-interest

'XR' - ex-rights

'CD' - cum-dividend

'CR' - cum-rights

'CB' - cum-bonus

'CI' - cum-interest

'C*' - in case of more than one of CD, CR, CB, CI

'X*' - in case of more than one of XD, XR, XB, XI

(e) The ex indicator in the market watch screen appears till the end of the no delivery period in which the security goes ex benefit. In case, a security goes ex benefit without having any delivery period, ex indicator is displayed only on the ex day.

Security Descriptor

The following information is displayed in the Security Descriptor – Security Name, Book Closure Start and End Dates, Ex-Date, No-Delivery Start and End Dates, Tick Size, Rating and Remarks. The label DPR i.e. Daily Price Range displays the permissible price band for a security for the current trading day.

Market by Price

The purpose of Market by Price (MBP) is to enable the user to view outstanding orders in the market aggregated at each price and they are displayed in order of best prices.

The fields that are available on the selection screen are Symbol, Series and Book Type. The options available in the book type field are Regular Lot and RETDEBT.

The detailed MBP screen is split into first line, detail line and summary line. The first line displays market type, symbol, series, total traded quantity, highest trade price, lowest trade price, last trade price, per cent change in LTP from previous day close and average traded price. The detail line displays number of buy orders, total buy order quantity at that price, buy order price, sell order price, total sell order quantity at that price and number of sell orders. The summary line displays total buy order quantity and total sell order quantity. For special term orders, the terms are not reflected in the MBP screen. Buy orders are displayed on the left side of the window and sell orders on the right. The orders appear in a price/time priority with the "best priced" order at the top. When any regular lot information, currently displayed on the window, is changed (for example as the result of a trade), this information is automatically reflected in the MBP i.e. the MBP screen is dynamically updated.

All buyback orders are identified by an '*' in the MBP screen. In case a buyback order appears in the best orders in the MBP an '*' will precede such an order record. In addition, an '*' will appear against the 'Total Buy' field in the MBP. Similarly if a buyback order price is among the best five prices in the order book an '*' will appear against the appropriate price and also in the 'Total Buy' field. In case a buyback order is present in the order book but does not appear in the MBP, an '*' will precede the 'Total Buy' field in the MBP screen.

Special Features of MBP

1. Regular lot & special term orders can be viewed in the MBP.
2. The status of a security is indicated in this screen. 'P' indicates that the security is in the pre-open phase and 'S' indicates that the security is suspended.
3. The percentage change for the last traded price with respect to the previous day's closing price and the average trade price of the security in the given market are the additional fields in the screen.
4. No un-triggered stop-loss order will be displayed on the MBP screen.
5. Only information on orders for the best 5 prices is displayed.

Previous Trades

The purpose of this window is to provide security-wise information to users for their own trades. The fields that are available on the selection screen are Symbol, Series, Market Type, Auction Number, Trading Member ID, Branch ID, Dealer, CLI and Time. The options available in the market type field are Normal Market, RETDEBT, Odd Lot and Auction. If the user selects the option to view auction market trade details, the auction number has to be compulsorily entered. The corporate manager can view all the trades for all branches or for a specific branch. Under the specific branch, the user can view trade details for a specific dealer or for all dealers. The branch manager can view all details under that branch i.e. all previous trades for all dealers and for all clients or for all dealers or for a specific dealer. The dealers can view previous trades for own user ID only. The user can select the previous trades up to a particular time period, by entering the relevant time in the time field. The detailed previous trade screen information is split into first line, detail line and summary line. The first line displays market type, symbol, series, last trade price, last trade quantity, last trade time and total traded quantity. The detail line contains buy/sell indicator, PRO/CLI indicator (where P – PRO and C – CLI), order number, trade number, trade quantity, trade price and trade time.

The summary line contains total number of buy trades, total buy quantity traded, total buy traded value, average buy traded price, total number of sell trades, total sell quantity traded, total sell traded value and average sell traded price. Previous trade screen displays the client account number also. Trades are displayed in reverse chronological order. First all buy trades are displayed and then sell trades are displayed.

Special Features of Previous Trades

(a) Trade cancellation can be requested from the previous trade screen. This facility is available only for member's own trades. The corporate manager can request for trade cancellation for any branch or any dealer. The branch manager can request for trade cancellation for any dealer under that branch. The dealer can request for trade cancellation only for trades under that user ID.

(b) Trade modification can be requested from the previous trade screen. The user can request the exchange to modify only the trade quantity field. Moreover, the new quantity requested must be lower than the original trade quantity. Currently trade modification facility is not enabled.

Outstanding Orders

The purpose of Outstanding Orders (OO) is to enable the user to view the outstanding orders for a security. An outstanding order is an order that has been entered by the user, but which has not yet been completely traded or cancelled. The user is permitted to see his own orders.

The fields which are available on the selection screen are symbol, series, book type, auction number, branch ID, dealer, PRO/CLI and time. The options available in the book type field are Regular Lot, RETDEBT, Odd Lot, Negotiated Trade, Stop Loss and Auction. If the user selects the option to view auction market trade details, the auction number has to be compulsorily entered. The corporate manager can view all the OO for all branches or for a specific branch. Under the specific branch, the user can view OO details for a specific dealer or for all dealers. Similarly it is possible to view all OO for a particular client or for all clients under a dealer.

The branch manager can view all OO details under that branch i.e. all OO for all dealers and for all clients or for all dealers or for a specific dealer. The dealer can view OO for his own user ID only. The detailed outstanding orders screen is split into first line and detail line. the first line contains symbol, series, market type, security status, label, current time and current date. The detail line contains book type, User ID, Client A/C number, order number, order quantity pending and order price. The orders are listed on the basis of price/time priority. The orders are displayed in order of Regular Lot orders and then Stop Loss orders. Outstanding order screen is not dynamically updated, but the user has option to refresh the OO screen by re-invoking the inquiry.

Special Features of Outstanding Orders

(a) The user can modify orders from the outstanding orders screen.

(b) The user can cancel orders from the outstanding orders screen.

(c) The user can view status of a particular order from the outstanding orders screen.

Activity Log

The Activity Log (AL) shows all the activities that have been performed on any order belonging to that user. These activities include order modification/cancellation, partial/full trade, trade modification/cancellation. It displays information of only those orders in which some activity has taken place. It does not display those orders on which no activity has taken place.

The fields that are available on the selection screen are Symbol, Series, Market Type, Branch ID. Dealer, PRO/CLI and Client Account Number. The Symbol, Series and Market Type fields are compulsory. The options available in the Market Type field are Normal Market, RETDEBT, Odd Lot and Auction. The detailed AL screen is split into first line and detail line. The first line displays Market Type, Symbol, Series, Current Time and Current Date. The detail line contains User ID, Order Number, PRO/CLI indicator (where P-PRO, C-CLI), Buy/Sell Indicator, Order quantity, Order price, Order Terms/Trade Number, Disclosed Quantity, MF Indicator, MF Quantity, Activity Indicator and Activity Time. One line appears for each activity that has taken place today.

For example, if a buy order is traded against three separate sell orders, then the activity log for the buy order shows three separate lines and the original order details.

The following activities are displayed:

B   For buy orders, this indicates a match.

S   For sell orders, this indicates a match.

OC   This indicates an order was cancelled.

OM   This indicates an order was modified. The details displayed are the order after it was modified.

TC   For both buy and sell orders this indicates that a trade involving this order was cancelled.

TM   For both buy and sell orders this indicates that a trade involving this order was modified.

Special terms associated with the order are displayed to help identify the order.

Special Features of Activity Log

(a) The AL gives details of all activities in chronological order.

(b) Within the order number, the details appear with the oldest activity first and the latest last.

(c) The activity consists only of orders entered by the requesting trading member.

(d) This inquiry option is not available to users in inquiry mode.

Order Status

The purpose of the Order Status (OS) is to look into the status of one of the dealer's own specific orders. The screen provides the current status of orders and other order details. The order status screen is not dynamically updated. In case the order is traded, the trade details are also displayed. In case of multiple trades the display is scrolled.

To view the status of a particular order, enter the order number for which the order status is to be viewed in the selection screen of OS. The first part of the order number (i.e. today's date) is defaulted. The user has to enter the second part of the order number. If the user does not know the order number, then the user can position the highlight bar on the desired order on the outstanding order screen and then invoke the OS screen. The order number is directly defaulted in the order status selection screen.

The detailed OS screen is divided into three parts. The first part covers order related information, the second part covers the trade related information if the order has resulted in a trade and the third part gives summary details.

The first part details are in two lines. The first line gives Book Type, Symbol, Series, Order Number, Type (Buy/Sell), Total Order Quantity, Order Price, PRO/CLI, Client A/C Number and Participant ID. The second line gives Disclosed Quantity, MF/AON Indicator, MF Quantity, Trigger Price, Day, Indicator 1 (Order Modified – MOD), Indicator 2 (Order Cancelled – CXL) and Indicator 3 (Order Traded – TRD). The second part details are Trade Quantity, Trade Price, Trade Time and Trade Number. The third part details are Quantity Traded Today and Balance Quantity (remaining quantity).

Special Features of Order Status

(a) The OS provides the user the current status of the order i.e. whether the order has been modified, cancelled, traded or been partially traded on the previous day.

(b) It shows all the order details. It also shows the trade details for each trade done against this order.

(c) The data are presented in chronological order. One line appears for each activity that has taken place today.

(d) The dealer can view the order status of orders entered under that dealer ID only.

(e) This inquiry option is not available to users in inquiry mode.

Snap Quote

The snap quote is a feature available in the system to get instantaneous market information on a desired security. This is normally used for a security that is not set up in the market watch window. The information displayed for the set up security is the same as that in the market watch window i.e. corporate action indicator 'Ex/Cum', the total buy order quantity, best buy price, best sell price, total sell order quantity, last traded price, last trade price change indicator and the no delivery indicator 'ND'.

The snap quote is displayed for the time specified by the exchange from time to time. The display position of snap quote is reserved and no other information overlaps it. A user can therefore simultaneously view a regular inquiry (e.g. MBP) and the snap quote display.

Market Movement

The purpose of the market movement screen is to provide information to the user regarding the movement of a security for the current day. This inquiry gives the snap shot for a particular security for a time interval as parameterized by the Exchange. The fields that are available on the selection screen are symbol, series and market type. The user can select the market type as normal market, RETDEBT and odd lot market.

The detailed output screen is given in two parts. The first part gives information regarding the security for the entire day namely Symbol, Series, Market Type, Total Buy Order Quantity, Total Sell Order Quantity, Total Traded Quantity, High Price, Low Price, Open Price and Last Traded Price. The second part gives information for a particular time interval namely Time Interval, Buy Order Quantity, Sell Order Quantity, Traded Quantity, High Price and Low Price. The user can save the market movement screen by specifying the directory and file name to save the information. This file can be viewed in MSDOS editor.

Special Features of Market Movement

(a) The market movement screen provides information to the user regarding the movement of a security for the current day on orders/trades done today.

(b) The information displayed is from the time the market was opened today and in chronological sequence.

Market Inquiry

The purpose of the market inquiry is to enable the user to view the market statistics, for a particular market, for a security. It also displays the open price and previous close price for a security. The fields that are available on the selection screen are symbol, series and market type. The user can select market type as normal, RETDEBT and odd lot.

The detailed output screen is given in two parts. The first line displays Symbol, Series, Security Status, Corporate Actions Indicator 1, Corporate Actions Indicator 2, Corporate Actions Indicator 3, Total Traded Quantity, 52 Week High and 52 Week Low. The second line displays Closing Price, Opening Price, High Price, Low Price, Last Traded Price and Net change from closing price. The third line displays Last Traded Quantity, Last Traded Time and Last Traded Date. The fourth line displays Best Buy Order Quantity, Best Buy Order Price, Best Sell Order Price and Best Sell Order Quantity.

Special Features of Market Inquiry

(a) This screen is not dynamically updated. It displays the security status of the security selected. 'S' indicates that the security is suspended, 'P' indicates that the security is in pre open (only for normal market) and in absence of the above indicators the security is open for trading.

(b) An indicator for corporate actions for a security is displayed on the screen. The indicators are as follows:

"CD" = cum-dividend "XD" = ex-dividend
"CR" = cum-rights "XR" = ex-rights
"CB" = cum-bonus "XB" = ex-bonus
"CI" = cum-interest "XI" = ex-interest

(c) The net change indicator for last trade price with respect to the previous day's closing price and the net change percentage for the last trade price with respect to the previous day's closing price are displayed.

(d) The base price of a security for the day is equal to the previous day's closing price of the security in normal circumstances. Thus, in the market inquiry screen the field indicating the closing price also gives the base price for the day.

(e) If the base price is manually changed (due to a corporate action) then the market inquiry will not display the new base price in the closing price field.

Auction Inquiry

The purpose of Auction Inquiry (AI) is to enable the users to view the auction activities for the current trading day. This window displays information about auctions currently going on and auctions that have been completed.

The detailed line in the auction inquiry screen displays: No. – Serial Number, St. – Status of the auction security, Type – Buy/Sell auction, Symbol, Series, Best Buy Qty, Best Buy Price, Best Sell Price, Best Sell Qty, Auction Qty, Auction Price and Settlement Period.

The following are the different status displayed for an auction security:

   S - Auction is in Solicitor Period

   M - System is matching the orders

   F - Auction is over

   X - Auction is deleted

   P - Auction is pending and yet to begin.

The user can view the auction details of a security setup in the market watch, by invoking the auction inquiry screen after highlighting the auction security. To view the auction details for all the securities, the user should blank out the contents of all the fields in the auction inquiry selection screen. To view the auctions after a particular number, the user should blank out the contents in the symbol & series field and enter the number in the auction number field on the selection screen. The auction inquiry screen then displays all auctions from that number onwards. This window is dynamically updated.

Security/Portfolio List

This is a facility for the user for setting up the securities in the market watch screen. This screen also has a new facility of allowing the user to setup his own portfolio.

Security List

The user can select securities based on symbol, series, instrument type and market type. A blank/partial search for symbol and series is also possible. The symbol, series, market type and security name are displayed based on the selection criteria. The user can also print the selected securities.

Portfolio List

Once the security is selected, the same can be used for setting up a portfolio. The user can give a name to the list so selected. The existing portfolio can be modified and/or removed. The user can also set-up a particular portfolio in market watch. Portfolio created can be used for basket order entry also. Order files can be generated based on the portfolio created using basket trading option.

Multiple Index Broadcast and Graph

This screen displays information of NSE indices namely S&P CNX Nifty, S&P CNX Defty, CNX Nifty Junior, S&P CNX 500 and CNX Midcap CNX IT, Bank Nifty and CNX 100. The indices are labeled vertically and the information is displayed against each index horizontally. The data displayed for each index is as follows:

- ❖ Current Index
- ❖ High Index
- ❖ Low Index
- ❖ Open Index
- ❖ Close Index
- ❖ Per cent change in current index (with respect to previous close index)
- ❖ 52 week high
- ❖ 52 week low
- ❖ Up moves
- ❖ Down moves
- ❖ Market capitalization (in Rs. lakhs)

An index graph displays all the indices on a real time basis to the market.

Online Backup

The on line backup is a facility that the user can invoke to take a backup of all order and trade related information for the user. The information available is for the current day only. On the selection screen the user can select the various fields on which the output will be filtered. The fields that can be filtered are CLI, market type, book type, symbol, series, instrument type, date, time, order indicator, trade indicator, buy/sell indicator, order numbers and trade numbers The user is provided the option to copy the files to any drive of the computer. This utility generates two ASCII files namely Order.txt and Trade.txt. The user can specify any filename for orders and trades. This utility will help the user to generate the contract notes. The user is requested to first take a backup on the C:\drive and subsequently copy it to the A:\drive to avoid overloading the PC capacity and causing an abnormal log off.

Basket Trading

The purpose of basket trading is to provide NEAT users with a facility to create an offline order entry file for a selected portfolio. On inputting the value, the orders are created for the selected portfolio of securities according to the ratios of their market capitalizations. An icon has been provided in the toolbar which can be selected by the mouse to invoke the functionality. In the basket trading functionality, the user first selects a portfolio from the combo box. The portfolio in the combo box is user defined portfolios (which can be created or edited from the security list screen which is an existing functionality).

All user defined portfolios are automatically loaded into the combo box. The user then allocates an amount to the portfolio by mentioning the amount in the 'Amount' edit box. The amount entered is in lakhs and must be less than or equal to Rs. 3,000 lakhs. If the amount entered is not sufficient to buy/sell a complete basket, a message "Insufficient amount for creating the basket" is displayed. Then, the user mentions whether he wants to buy or sell the portfolio by selecting a choice from the BUY/SELL combo box. The user has to mention the name of the offline order file which would be generated. The output offline order file is always generated in the basket directory of the current selected login drive. If a file with the given name already exists then it asks whether to overwrite the old file.

A reverse file with the same name is also generated in 'R_Basket' directory of the current login drive. The reverse file contains the reverse order (if the user has selected buy then it contains sell orders and vice-versa). The user can mention the order's duration (IOC or day) by selecting from a check box. The user can also specify PRO/CLI orders by selecting from the combo box. In case of CLI orders it is compulsory to mention the account number in the edit box. The participant's name can be mentioned. If it is already mentioned it is verified whether it is a valid participant or not. The amount mentioned in the 'amount edit' box is divided among the securities of the portfolio, depending on their current market capitalization, and the amount allocated per security is used to calculate the number of shares to be bought/sold for that security which is reflected in the offline order file. The number of shares is rounded off to the nearest integer. If the basket contains any security whose regular lot is not one, then the file will need to be corrected by the user to accommodate shares in tradable lots. If the portfolio contains a security which is suspended/not eligible in the chosen market then an error message is displayed on the screen. All the orders generated through the offline order file are priced at the available market price.

Quantity of shares of a particular security in a portfolio is calculated as under:

$$\text{Number of shares of a security in the portfolio} = \frac{\text{Amount} * \text{Issued capital for the security}}{\text{current portfolio capitalization}}$$

Where

$$\text{Current portfolio capitalization} = [\text{Last traded price (Previous close if not traded)} * \text{Number of issued shares}]$$

In case at the time of generating the basket, any of the constituents are not traded, the weightage of the security in the basket is determined using the previous close price. This price may become irrelevant if there has been any corporate action in the security for the day and the same has not yet been traded before generation of the file. Similarly, basket facility will not be available for a new listed security till the time it is traded.

Buy Back Trades

As per SEBI Notification, dated 14th November, 1998, buyback of securities is permitted in the secondary market. This is termed as 'buyback from the open market'. In the open market, buyback of shares is permitted through stock exchanges having electronic trading facilities and such buyback orders are required to be identified upfront in the electronic trading screen as buyback orders.

The purpose of buyback trade functionality is to give information to the market about the buyback trades executed from the start of the buyback period till the current trading date in the securities whose buyback period is currently on. It provides information about symbol, series, day's high price, day's low price, day's weighted average price, day's volume, total volume, highest/lowest/weighted average prices till previous day; buy back start & end date.

The buyback trade functionality provides users with information about the buyback trades going in various securities. The front screen shows symbol, series, low price (today), high price (today), weightage, average price, volume (today) and previous day volume. The user after selecting a particular row from the buyback list box can view further information viz. symbol, series, start date, end date, total traded quantity (till date), previous high price, previous low price and weighted average, price till date of buyback scheme. The buyback broadcasts updates the information.

Supplementary Functions

This section discusses certain supplementary functions of NEAT such as branch order value limit, most active securities, color selection, report selection, net position and print system message.

The supplementary menu list box has the following options:

- ❖ Report selection
- ❖ Full message display
- ❖ Color selection
- ❖ Print system message On/Off
- ❖ Print order/Trade confirmation slips On/Off
- ❖ Ticker selection
- ❖ Market movement
- ❖ Most active securities
- ❖ Index inquiry
- ❖ Offline order entry
- ❖ Order limits
- ❖ SQUVL
- ❖ Order attribute selection
- ❖ Reprint order/Trade confirmation slip
- ❖ Branch order value limit
- ❖ Net position and net position backup
- ❖ Online backup
- ❖ One line/Tabular slips
- ❖ User order value limit
- ❖ Client master maintenance
- ❖ Index trading

❖ Reverse basket on traded quantity

❖ Reset user ID

❖ About

Report Selection

The report selection window allows the user (corporate manager and branch manager) to specify the number of copies to be printed for each report. The user can update the number of copies for a report. The report selection screen allows the user (corporate manager and branch manager only) to specify the number of copies to be printed for each report. All the reports are generated at the end of day. Once the reports are printed, the report selection screen shows the date and the time the reports were printed. The user can request for reprinting any of the reports.

The reports that are available to the trading member are open order today, order log, trades done today, market statistics and market indices.

Open order: This report gives details about all dealers of the trading member that are currently outstanding or unmatched orders. Regular lot, special terms, odd lot and stop loss outstanding orders are presented in this report.

Order log: The purpose of this report is to give the activity log of the orders for the dealers belonging to a trading member. This report shows orders placed today, orders modified today, orders cancelled and orders deleted by the system. This report shows the activity log for the orders of a trading member. It shows the details of the orders which are entered today, modified today, cancelled by the dealer today. For order modification, the modified order details are shown for each modification done.

Trades done today: The purpose of this report is to show the details of the trading activities of the trading member. This report gives details of trades done today for all dealers belonging to the trading member firm. The report has details for all types of trades i.e. normal market trade, odd lot trade, RETDEBT trade and auction trade.

Market Statistics

The purpose of this report is to show the market statistics of that trading day. This report gives details related to all the securities traded on that day for all markets. A separate market indices report is also disseminated to members, which contains details regarding the open, high, low, close, previous close and per cent change over the previous close of S&P CNX Nifty, S&P CNX Defty, CNX Nifty Junior, S&P CNX500, CNX Midcap, CNX IT, Bank Nifty, CNX 100 and Nifty Midcap 50 indices.

Full Message Display

This option enables the display of all the system messages right from the start of the opening phase. It is also possible to filter the messages depending on the message code, symbol, series, PRO/CLI, client, date and time. The system messages can be printed, if needed.

The message area contains the user ID for order and trade confirmation\modification\ cancellation and rejection. The trade confirmation\modification\cancellation messages displayed in the message area will contain the corresponding remarks entered during the order entry.

The user can filter, print and save messages. In the message filtering screen the message code by default shows 'All'. The user has the option to select the desired message code on which the messages can be filtered. The messages can also be filtered on symbol, series, trading member code, PRO/CLI/ ALL, client A/C number, date and time fields.

In case the user desires to filter messages for the trading member's own order/trade related messages, 'PRO' has to be specified with the trading member code defaulting in the 'Client Account' field. In case the user desires to filter messages for a particular client, 'CLI' has to be specified with the client account code in the 'Client Account' field. In case the user desires to view all messages, 'All' has to be specified and the 'Client Account' field should be blank. The message filter displays 'All' by default when the user invokes the full message display screen.

Message area will contain the machine number along with the message specifying from which machine the message has been generated. An extra filter code has been provided in the message area to filter messages on the machine number parameter.

The messages are filtered as per the selection criteria. The message codes on which the selection can be made are furnished in Table 9.1.

Table 9.1 Message Codes on which the Selection can be Made

Message Code	Description of Messages Selected
ALL	All messages
AUC	Auction order/trade messages
AUI	Auction initiation messages
LIS	All listing related messages
ORD	Order related messages
OTH	Miscellaneous
SPD	Security suspension/De-suspension
SYS	System messages
TRD	Trades

The full message display and filtered messages can be printed by invoking the print command by ensuring that the printer is online. The user can save messages by invoking the 'save' option on the full message display screen and by specifying the directory and file name in the pop up box. Here an option is available to the user to both specify the directory and file name to save messages, or to choose the default directory i.e. NSE cm\user directory. This file can be viewed in MS-DOS editor.

Color Selection

The user can customize the colours for various inquiry and other trader workstation screens as per choice. The background and the foreground colors can be selected by invoking the color selection option. The following is displayed on the color selection list box:

List of screens: Lists all the screens in the NEAT system. The user has the option of changing both the foreground and the background colors of any screen.

Display window: Displays the screen with the changed colors. To change the color of a particular screen, the user has to position the highlight bar on the desired screen and select any one of the sixteen color buttons. The change in the color can be seen in the display window. The user can reset the color to default setting by selecting the default option. It is to be noted that the user cannot select the same color for foreground of an inquiry screen.

Print System Messages On/Off

The 'Print System Messages On/Off' enables/disables printing of the system messages as and when they appear in the messages window. By default the option is set to 'Off'. The user can change the On/Off position by pressing the space bar. The current mode (On/Off) is displayed for this option on the supplementary menu screen itself.

Print Order/Trade Confirmation Slips On/Off

The 'Print Order/Trade Confirmation On/Off' enables/disables printing of the order/trade slips. By default the option is set to 'Off'. The user can change the On/Off position by pressing the space bar. The current mode (On/Off) is displayed for this option on the supplementary menu screen itself.

Ticker Selection

The ticker selection screen allows the user to set up the securities that should appear in the user's ticker window. All the securities available in the system for a particular market are displayed. If a security is deleted from the system, it is also removed from the ticker selection display. The selection of securities can be done for each market separately. The user can select one or all security types for display.

Market Movement

The purpose of the market movement screen is to provide information to the user regarding the movement of a security for the current day. This inquiry gives a snap shot for a particular security for a time interval as parameterized by the exchange.

Most Active Securities

This screen displays the details of the most active securities based on the total traded value during the day. The number 'N' is parameterized by the exchange. The information provided on this screen is not dynamically updated. However, the user can get the latest information by refreshing the screen.

Index Inquiry

Index inquiry gives information on previous close, open, high, low and current index values of S&P CNX Nifty at the time of invoking this inquiry screen. This screen displays information of S&P CNX Nifty at the time the screen was invoked on the current trading day.

At the end of day after market closure the previous close field will display the current day's closing index value. The user can refresh the details of the screen by re-invoking the screen.

CLEARING, SETTLEMENT ROLLING SETTLEMENT

We discussed earlier that till recently, the stock exchanges in India followed a system of account period settlement for cash market transactions. T+2 rolling settlements have now been introduced for all securities. The members receive the funds/securities in accordance with the pay-in/pay-out schedules notified by the respective exchanges. Given the growing volume of trades and market volatility, the time gap between trading and settlement gives rise to settlement risk.

In recognition of this, the exchanges and their clearing corporations employ risk management practices to ensure timely settlement of trades. The regulators have also prescribed elaborate margining and capital adequacy standards to secure market integrity and protect the interests of investors. The trades are settled irrespective of default by a member and the exchange follows up with the defaulting member subsequently for recovery of his dues to the exchange. Due to setting up of the Clearing Corporation, the market has full confidence that settlements will take place on time and will be completed irrespective of possible default by isolated trading members.

Movement of securities has become almost instantaneous in the dematerialized environment. Two depositories viz., National Securities Depositories Ltd. (NSDL) and Central Depositories Services Ltd. (CDSL) provide electronic transfer of securities and more than 99 per cent of the turnover is settled in the dematerialized form. All actively traded scrips are held, traded and settled in demat form. The obligations of members are downloaded to members/custodians by the clearing agency. The members/custodians make available the required securities in their pool accounts with Depository Participants (DPs) by the prescribed pay-in time for securities. The depository transfers the securities from the pool accounts of members/custodians to the settlement account of the clearing agency. As per the schedule determined by the clearing agency, the securities are transferred on the pay-out day by the depository from the settlement account of the clearing agency to the pool accounts of members/custodians. The pay-in and pay-out of securities is effected on the same day for all settlements.

Select banks have been empanelled by the clearing agency for electronic transfer of funds. The members are required to maintain accounts with any of these banks. The members are informed electronically of their pay-in obligations of funds. The members make the required funds available in their accounts with clearing banks by the prescribed pay-in day. The

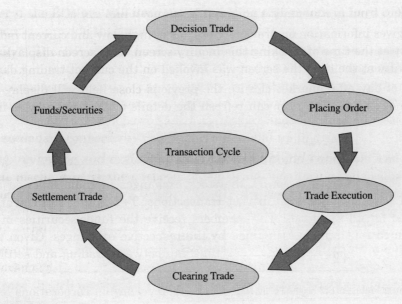

Chart 9.2 Transaction Cycle

Source: National Stock Exchange (NSE), Mumbai

clearing agency forwards the funds obligations file to clearing banks which, in turn, debit the accounts of members and credit the account of the clearing agency. In some cases, the clearing agency runs an electronic file to debit members' accounts with clearing banks and credit its own account.

On pay-out day, the funds are transferred by the clearing banks from the account of the clearing agency to the accounts of members as per the member's obligations. In the T+2 rolling settlement, the pay-in and pay-out of funds as well as securities take place within 2 working days after the trade date.

If a person holding assets (securities/funds), either to meet his liquidity needs or to reshuffle his holdings in response to changes in his perception about risk and return of the assets, decides to buy or sell the securities, he selects a broker and instructs him to place buy/sell order on an exchange. The order is converted to a trade as soon as it finds a matching sell/buy order. At the end of the trade cycle, the trades are netted to determine the obligations of the trading members to deliver securities/funds as per settlement schedule.

The buyer/seller delivers funds/securities and receives securities/funds and acquires ownership of the securities. A securities transaction cycle is presented in Chart 9.3.

SETTLEMENT PROCESS

While the NSE provides a platform for trading to its trading members, the National Securities Clearing Corporation Ltd. (NSCCL) determines the funds/securities obligations of the trading

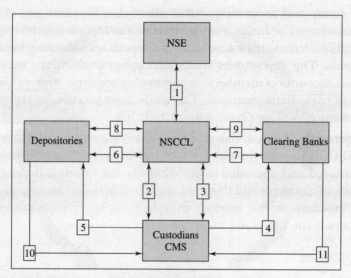

Source: National Stock Exchange (NSE), Mumbai

members and ensures that trading members meet their obligations. The NSCCL becomes the legal counter party to the net settlement obligations of every member.

This principle is called *'novation'* and the NSCCL is obligated to meet all settlement obligations, regardless of member defaults, without any discretion. Once a member fails on any obligations, the NSCCL immediately cuts off trading and initiates recovery.

The clearing banks and depositories provide the necessary interface between the custodians/clearing members (who clear for the trading members or their own transactions) for settlement of funds/securities obligations of trading members. The core processes involved in the settlement process are:

(a) Determination of obligation: NSCCL determines what counter-parties owe, and what counter parties are due to receive on the settlement date. The NSCCL interposes itself as a central counter party between the counter parties to trades and nets the positions so that a member has security wise net obligation to receive or deliver a security and has to either pay or receive funds.

(b) Pay-in of funds and securities: The members bring in their funds/securities to the NSCCL. They make available required securities in designated accounts with the depositories by the prescribed pay-in time. The depositories move the securities available in the accounts of members to the account of the NSCCL. Likewise members with funds obligations make available the required funds in the designated accounts with clearing banks by the prescribed pay-in time. The NSCCL sends electronic instructions to the clearing banks to debit members' accounts to the extent of payment obligations. The banks process these instructions, debit accounts of members and credit accounts of the NSCCL.

(c) Pay-out of funds and securities: After processing for shortages of funds/securities and arranging for movement of funds from surplus banks to deficit banks through RBI clearing, the NSCCL sends electronic instructions to the depositories/clearing banks to release pay-out of securities/funds. The depositories and clearing banks debit the accounts of NSCCL and credit settlement accounts of members. Settlement is complete upon release of payout of funds and securities to custodians/members. The settlement process for transactions in securities in the CM segment of NSE is presented in Chart 9.3.

(d) Risk management: A sound risk management system is integral to an efficient settlement system. The NSCCL has put in place a comprehensive risk management system, which is constantly monitored and upgraded to pre-empt market failures. It monitors the track record and performance of members and their net worth; undertakes on-line monitoring of members' positions and exposure in the market, collects margins from members and automatically disables members if the limits are breached.

Settlement Agencies

The NSCCL, with the help of clearing members, custodians, clearing banks and depositories settles the trades executed on exchanges. The roles of each of these entities are explained below:

(a) NSCCL: The NSCCL is responsible for post-trade activities of a stock exchange. Clearing and settlement of trades and risk management are its central functions. It clears all trades, determines obligations of members, arranges for pay-in of funds/securities, receives funds/ securities, processes for shortages in funds/securities, arranges for pay-out of funds/securities to members, guarantees settlement, and collects and maintains margins/collateral/base capital/ other funds.

(b) Clearing members: They are responsible for settling their obligations as determined by the NSCCL. They have to make available funds and/or securities in the designated accounts with the clearing bank/depository participant, as the case may be, to meet their obligations on the settlement day. In the capital market segment, all trading members of the exchange are required to become clearing members of the Clearing Corporation.

(c) Custodians: A custodian is a person who holds the documentary evidence of the title to property, like share certificates, etc., for safekeeping. The title to the custodian's property remains vested with the original holder, their nominee(s), or custodian trustee, as the case may be. In NSCCL, the custodian is a clearing member but not a trading member. He settles trades assigned to him by trading members. He is required to confirm whether he is going to settle a particular trade or not. If it is confirmed, the NSCCL assigns that obligation to that custodian and the custodian is required to settle it on the settlement day. If the custodian rejects the trade, the obligation is assigned back to the trading/clearing member.

Explanations

1. Trade details from the exchange to the NSCCL (real-time and end of day trade file).
2. NSCCL notifies the consummated trade details to CMs/custodians who reaffirm them. Based on the affirmation, NSCCL applies multilateral netting and determines

obligations. NSCCL notifies the consummated trade details to CMs/custodians who confirm them. Based on the conformation, NSCCL applies multilateral netting and determines obligations.

3. Download of obligation and pay-in advice of funds/securities.

4. Instructions to clearing banks to make funds available by pay-in time.

5. Instructions to depositories to make securities available by pay-in time.

6. Pay-in of securities (NSCCL advises depository to debit pool accounts of custodians/CMs and credits its account. This is carried out by the depository).

7. Pay-in of funds (NSCCL advises clearing banks to debit accounts of custodians/CMs and credit its account. This is done by the clearing bank).

8. Pay-out of securities (NSCCL advises depository to credit the pool accounts of custodians/CMs and debit its account, which is done by the depository).

9. Pay-out of funds (NSCCL advises clearing banks to credit accounts of custodians/CMs and debit its account, which is carried out by the clearing bank).

10. Depository informs custodians/CMs through DPs.

11. Clearing banks inform custodians/CMs.

(d) Clearing banks: Clearing banks are a key link between the clearing members and the NSCCL for settlement of funds. Every clearing member is required to open a dedicated settlement account with one of the clearing banks. Based on his obligation as determined through clearing, the clearing member makes funds available in the clearing account for the pay-in and receives funds in case of a pay-out. Multiple clearing banks provide advantages of competitive forces, facilitate introduction of new products viz. working capital funding, anywhere banking facilities, the option to members to settle funds through a bank, which provides the maximum services suitable to the member. The clearing banks are required to provide the following services as a single window to all clearing members of National Securities Clearing Corporation Ltd. as also to the Clearing Corporation:

❖ A network of branches in cities that cover the bulk of the trading cum clearing members

❖ High level automation including Electronic Funds Transfer (EFT) facilities

❖ Facilities like, dedicated branch facilities, software to interface with the Clearing Corporation and access to accounts information on a real time basis

❖ Value-added services to members such as free-of-cost funds transfer across centers etc.

❖ Providing working capital funds

❖ Stock lending facilities

❖ Services as professional clearing members

❖ Services as depository participants

❖ Other capital market related facilities

❖ All other banking facilities like issuing bank guarantees/credit facilities etc.

(e) Depositories: A depository is an entity where the securities of an investor are held in electronic form. The person who holds a demat account is a beneficiary owner. In case of a joint account, the account holders will be beneficiary holders of that joint account. Depositories help in the settlement of the dematerialized securities. Each custodian/clearing member is required to maintain a clearing pool account with the depositories. He is required to make available the required securities in the designated account on settlement day. The depository runs an electronic file to transfer the securities from accounts of the custodians/clearing member to that of NSCCL. As per the schedule of allocation of securities determined by the NSCCL, the depositories transfer the securities on the pay-out day from the account of the NSCCL to those of members/custodians.

(f) Professional clearing member: The NSCCL admits a special category of members namely, professional clearing members. A Professional Clearing Member (PCM) may clear and settle trades executed for their clients (individuals, institutions etc.). In such an event, the functions and responsibilities of the PCM would be similar to those of custodians. PCMs may also undertake the clearing and settlement responsibility for trading members. In such a case, the PCM would settle the trades carried out by the trading members connected to them. The onus for settling the trade would thus be on the PCM and not the trading member. A PCM has no trading rights but has only clearing rights, i.e. he just clears the trades of his associate trading members and institutional clients.

Settlement Cycle

At the end of each trading day, concluded or locked-in trades are received from the NSE by the NSCCL. The NSCCL determines the cumulative obligations of each member and electronically transfers the data to Clearing Members (CMs). All trades concluded during a particular trading period are settled together. A multilateral netting procedure is adopted to determine the net settlement obligations (delivery/receipt positions) of CMs. The NSCCL then allocates or assigns delivery of securities *inter se*, the members to arrive at the delivery and receipt obligation of funds and securities by each member. On the securities pay-in day, delivering members are required to bring in securities to NSCCL. On pay out day the securities are delivered to the respective receiving members. Settlement is deemed to be complete upon declaration and release of pay-out of funds and securities. Exceptions may arise because of short delivery of securities by CMs, bad deliveries or company objections on the pay-out day.

NSCCL identifies short deliveries and conducts a buying-in auction on the day after the pay-out day through the NSE trading system. The delivering CM is debited by an amount equivalent to the securities not delivered and valued at a valuation price (the closing price as announced by NSE on the day previous to the day of the valuation). If the buy-in auction price is more than the valuation price, the CM is required to make good the difference. All shortages not bought-in are deemed closed out at the highest price between the first day of the trading period till the day of squaring off or closing price on the auction day plus 20 per cent, whichever is higher. This amount is credited to the receiving member's account on the auction pay-out day.

Bad Deliveries (in Case of Physical Settlement)

Bad deliveries (deliveries which are *prima facie* defective) are required to be reported to the clearing house within two days from the receipt of documents. The delivering member is required to rectify these within two days. Un-rectified bad deliveries are assigned to auction on the next day.

With effect from 1st April, 2003 the settlement cycle has been further reduced from T+3 to T+2.

Normal Market

The trades executed each trading day are considered as a trading period and trades executed during the day are settled based on the net obligations for the day.

At NSE, trades in rolling settlement are settled on a T+2 basis i.e. on the 2nd working day. Typically trades taking place on Monday are settled on Wednesday; Tuesday's trades are settled on Thursday and so on.

A tabular representation of the settlement cycle for rolling settlement is given in Table 9.2.

Table 9.2 Settlement Cycle for Rolling Settlement

	Activity	Day
Trading	Rolling settlement trading	T
Clearing	Custodial confirmation	T+1 working days
Delivery	Generation	T+1 working days
Settlement	Securities and funds pay in	T+2 working days
	Securities and funds pay out	T+2 working days
	Valuation of shortages based on closing prices	at T+1 closing prices
Post Settlement	Auction	T+3 working days
	Bad delivery reporting	T+4 working days
	Rectified bad delivery pay-in and pay-out	T+5 working days
	Auction settlement	T+6 working days
	Re-bad delivery reporting and pickup	T+8 working days
	Close out of re-bad delivery and funds pay-in & pay-out	T+9 working days

Source: National Stock Exchange (NSE), Mumbai

Inter Institutional Segment

Trading in this market segment is available for 'institutional investors' only. In order to ensure that the overall FII limits are not violated, selling in this segment is restricted to FII clients. Buying is restricted to institutional clients.

Members are required to enter the custodian participant code at the time of order entry and to ensure that the selling/buying restrictions are strictly adhered to. A sale order entered by trading members on behalf of non FII clients or a buy order entered by trading members on behalf of non institutional (FIIs, FIs, banks, mutual funds & insurance companies) clients, shall be deemed to be invalid. The member entering the invalid order shall further be liable for disciplinary action, which may include penalties, penal action, withdrawal of trading facilities, suspension etc.

Deals executed in this segment are cleared on a T+2 rolling basis. Settlement of all transactions is compulsorily in demat mode only.

The settlement cycle for this segment is given in Table 9.3.

Table 9.3 Settlement Cycle for Inter Institutional Segment

	Activity	Day
Trading	Rolling settlement trading	T
Clearing	Custodial confirmation	T+1 working days
	Delivery generation	T+1 working days
Settlement	Securities and funds pay in	T+2 working days
	Securities and funds pay out	T+2 working days
	Valuation of shortages based on closing prices	at T+1 closing prices
Post Settlement	Close out	T+2 working days

Source: National Stock Exchange (NSE), Mumbai

Securities Settlement

The securities obligations of members are downloaded to members/custodians by NSCCL after the end of the trading day. The members/custodians deliver the securities to the clearing house on the pay in day in case of physical settlement and make available the required securities in the pool accounts with the depository participants in case of dematerialized securities. Members are required to open accounts with depository participants of both the depositories, NSDL and CDSL.

Delivering members are required to deliver all documents to the clearing house (in case of physical settlement) between 9:30 a.m. and 10:30 a.m. on the settlement day. Receiving members are required to collect the documents from the clearing house between 2:00 p.m. and 2:30 p.m.

In case of dematerialized settlement, the members receive their obligation by 2.30 p.m. on T+1 day. The members need to arrange for the securities as per their obligations and give instructions by 10.30 a.m. on the pay-in day. In case of NSDL the members need to give instructions to move the securities to the settlement account of NSCCL, whereas in the case of CDSL the members need to ensure that the necessary quantity of securities are available in their pool account. The members need to ensure that the settlement number and type are correctly entered to avoid any defaults. Pursuant to SEBI directive (*vide* its circular SMDRP/Policy/Cir-05/2001 dated 1st February, 2001) NSCCL has introduced a settlement system for direct delivery of securities to the investors' accounts with effect from 2nd April, 2001.

Direct Payout to Investors

SEBI, *vide* its circular No. SMDRP/Policy/Cir-05/2001, dated 1st February, 2001 had directed stock exchanges to introduce a settlement system for direct delivery of securities to the investors' accounts with effect from 2nd April, 2001. Accordingly, NSCCL introduced the facility of direct payout to clients' accounts on both the depositories. It ascertains from each clearing member, the beneficiary account details of their respective clients who are due to receive pay out of securities. NSCCL has provided its members with a frontend for creating the file through which the information is provided to NSCCL. Based on the information received from members, the Clearing Corporation sends payout instructions to the depositories, so that the client receives the pay out of securities directly to their accounts on the pay-out day. The client receives payout to the extent of instructions received from the respective clearing members. To the extent of instructions not received, the securities are credited to the CM pool account of the member.

Salient Features of Direct Payout to Investors

❖ Clearing members are required to provide a file to NSCCL for effecting pay out to investors' accounts for a particular settlement type, settlement number and delivery type. The file is to be provided as per the structure specified by NSCCL.

❖ Clearing members are provided with an application in the clearing front end for the purpose of capturing the requisite data and generating the file. This front end is a part of the Clearing Front End Version 4.2, which is available on the extranet in the 'common/clearing' directory.

❖ The time limit for submission of files is up to 9.30 a.m. on the pay out day.

❖ The files are uploaded by NSCCL in its system and returned with the indication of the success/rejection of the file and the records. This is purely a validation of the correctness of the file and record formats.

❖ Clearing members shall provide details of beneficiary accounts of the clients of the trading members in any one of the depositories.

❖ Credit to the accounts of various constituents (i.e. client account and CM Pool/CM clearing account) would be in the same order as specified by the clearing member in the file given to NSCCL.

❖ If for any client account record, the quantity requested for direct payout is more than the balance available for pay out to the clearing member in that depository, the quantity available in that depository shall only be directly credited to the member's settlement account in that depository.

❖ If the member receives all the shares in NSDL, the same will be transferred to the member's pool account in NSDL.

   (a) In the following situations, the payout shall be credited to the CM pool/Clearing account of the clearing members:

- Where the clearing members fail to provide the details of the beneficiary account or where the credit to the beneficiary accounts of the clients fail, or any account whatsoever.
- The remaining quantity received from any other depository as pay out shall be credited to the CM pool/Clearing account of the clearing member with the respective depositories.
- If the member's client has not paid the dues to the member for the said securities or for any other reason, the member has valid justification not to release the payout of a client directly. In such a situation the member may not be given the beneficiary account details of such clients in the file. In case the investor has paid the dues for delivery of securities and there is no valid justification for not releasing pay-out directly to the client, the member has to provide the details of its client's beneficiary account so that direct credit can be given to the client.

Funds Settlement

Currently, NSCCL offers settlement of funds through 13 clearing banks namely Canara Bank, HDFC Bank, IndusInd Bank, ICICI Bank, Bank of India, UTI Bank, IDBI Bank, Standard Chartered Bank, HSBC Ltd., Kotak Mahindra Bank, State Bank of India, Union Bank of India, Citibank NA.

Clearing Account

Every clearing member is required to maintain and operate a clearing account with any one of the empanelled clearing banks at the designated clearing bank branches. The clearing account is to be used exclusively for clearing operations i.e., for settling funds and other obligations to the Clearing Corporation including payments of margins and penal charges. Clearing members are required to authorize the clearing bank to access their clearing account for debiting and crediting their accounts, reporting of balances and other information as may be required by NSCCL from time to time as per the specified format. The clearing bank will debit/credit the clearing account of clearing members as per instructions received from the Clearing Corporation.

A clearing member can deposit funds into this account in any form, but can withdraw funds from this account only in self-name.

Change in Clearing Bank

In case a clearing member wishes to shift a clearing account from one designated clearing bank to another, the procedure is as follows:

1. The CM clearing member while requesting the Clearing Corporation for a change in the clearing bank account shall either: Furnish the No Objection Certificate (NOC) received by the member from the existing clearing bank for shifting of account, or in case no response was received by the clearing member from the existing clearing bank in respect of the NOC request even after a minimum waiting period of a fortnight, a

declaration to the above effect along with an acknowledged copy of the NOC request made by the member to the existing clearing bank.

2. The Clearing Corporation would thereon issue a letter of introduction to the other designated clearing bank.

3. On opening the account with the other designated clearing bank, the clearing member shall submit to the Clearing Corporation the account particulars issued by the bank and also the acknowledged copy of the letter issued by the clearing member to the clearing bank.

4. The Clearing Corporation shall thereon communicate the date from which the new clearing account will be operational and also the date after which the existing clearing account may be closed by the clearing member.

Funds Settlement

Members are informed of their funds obligation for various settlements through the daily clearing data download. The daily funds statement gives date-wise details of each debit/ credit transaction in the member's clearing account whereas the summary statement summarizes the same information for a quick reference.

The member account may be debited for various types of transactions on a daily basis. The member is required to ensure that adequate funds are available in the clearing account towards all obligations, on the scheduled date and time. The member can refer to his various obligation statements and provide for funds accordingly. To ensure timely fulfillment of funds obligations, members may avail of the facility of standing instructions to transfer the requisite amount from some other account to the clearing account or a temporary overdraft facility from the bank. In case the member has availed of such a facility, the member may furnish details of his obligation to the bank to ensure timely transfer of funds towards the same to avoid inconvenience. The member with a funds pay-in obligation is required to have clear funds in his account on or before 11.00 a.m. on the scheduled pay-in day. The payout of funds is credited to the clearing account of the members on or after 1.30 p.m. on the scheduled payout day.

On-line Exposure Monitoring

NSCCL has put in place an on-line monitoring and surveillance system whereby exposure of the members is monitored on a real time basis. A system of alerts has been built in so that both the member and NSCCL are alerted as per pre-set levels (reaching 70 per cent, 85 per cent, 90 per cent, 95 per cent and 100 per cent) when the members approach their allowable limits. The system enables NSSCL to further check the micro-details of members' positions, if required and take pro-active action.

The on-line surveillance mechanism also generates various alerts/reports on any price/ volume movement of securities not in line with past trends/patterns. For this purpose the exchange maintains various databases to generate alerts. Alerts are scrutinized and if necessary taken up for follow up action. Open positions of securities are also analyzed. Besides this, rumors in the print media are tracked and where they are price sensitive, companies are contacted for verification. Replies received are informed to the members and the public.

Off-line Monitoring

Off-line surveillance consists of inspections and investigations. As per regulatory requirements, a minimum of 20 per cent of the active trading members are to be inspected every year to verify the level of compliance with various rules, bye-laws and regulations of the exchange. Usually, inspection of more members than the regulatory requirement is undertaken every year. The inspection verifies if investor interests are being compromised in the conduct of business by the members. The investigation is based on various alerts, which require further analysis. If further analysis reveals any suspicion of irregular activity, which deviates from the past trends/patterns and concentration of trading at the NSE at the member level, then a more detailed investigation is undertaken. If the detailed investigation establishes any irregular activity, then disciplinary action is initiated against the member. If the investigation suggests suspicions of possible irregular activity across exchanges and/or possible involvement of clients, then the same is informed to SEBI.

International Securities Identification Number

SEBI being the National Numbering Agency for India has permitted NSDL to allot International Securities Identification Numbers (ISINs) for demat shares. While allotting ISINs, NSDL ensures that:

1. The ISINs allotted by NSDL do not at any point of time breach the uniqueness of the ISIN of the physical form for the same security.
2. The ISIN for a security is allotted only when the security is admitted to NSDL or on receipt of request for ISIN from CDSL.
3. The numbering system is simple.
4. The numbering system of ISIN is in compliance with the structure of ISIN adopted by SEBI.

Numbering system of ISIN: The numbering structure for securities in NSDL is a 12 digit alpha numeric string. The first two characters represent the country code i.e. IN (in accordance with ISO 3166). The third character represents the issuer type as detailed in Table 9.4.

Table 9.4 Distribution of Codes According to Issuers Types

Issuer Type	Code Allotted
Central Government	A
State Government	B
Municipal Corporation	C
Union Territories	D
Company, Statutory Corporation, Banking Company	E
Mutual Funds including UTI	F

Note: ISINs for Government Securities (Gsec) i.e. loans raised by Central and State Government are allotted by Reserve Bank of India (RBI).
Source: National Stock Exchange (NSE), Mumbai

The list may be expanded as per need. The maximum issuer types can be 35 (A to Z and 0 to 8. The partly paid up shares are identified by 9). The next 4 characters (fourth to seventh character) represent company identity of which first 3 characters are numeric and fourth character is alpha character. The numbering begins with '001A' and continues till '999A' and proceeds to '001B'. The next two characters (the eighth and ninth characters) represent the security type for a given issuer. Both the characters are numeric. The next two characters (the tenth and eleventh characters) are serially issued for each security of the issuer entering the system. The last digit is a check digit. The security types may be expanded as per the need as detailed in Table 9.5.

Table 9.5 Distribution of Codes According to Securities Types

Security Type	Code
Equity Shares	01
Postal Savings Scheme	02
Preferential Shares	03
Bonds	04
Deep Discount Bonds	05
Floating Rate Bonds	06
Commercial Papers	07
Step Discount Bonds	08
Regular Return Bonds	09
Certificate of Deposits	10
Securitized Instruments	11
Debentures	12
Units	13
Government Securities	14
Warrants	15
Commodities	16
RBI Relief Bonds	17

DEMATERIALIZATION AND ELECTRONIC TRANSFER OF SECURITIES

Traditionally, settlement systems on Indian stock exchanges gave rise to settlement risk due to the time that elapsed before trades were settled by physical movement of certificates. There were two aspects: The first related to settlement of trade in stock exchanges by delivery of shares by the seller and payment by the buyer. The stock exchange aggregated trades over a period of time and carried out net settlement through the physical delivery of securities. The process of physically moving the securities from the seller to his broker to the Clearing Corporation to the buyer's broker and finally to the buyer took time with the risk of delay somewhere along the chain. The second aspect related to transfer of shares in favor of the purchaser by the issuer. This system of transfer of ownership was grossly inefficient as every transfer involved the physical movement of paper securities to the issuer for registration, with the change of ownership being evidenced by an endorsement on the security certificate. In many cases the process of transfer took much longer than the two months stipulated in the Companies Act, and a significant proportion of transactions wound up as bad delivery due to faulty compliance of paper work. Theft, mutilation of certificates and other irregularities were rampant, and in addition the issuer had the right to refuse the transfer of a security. Thus the buyer did not get a good title of the securities after parting with good money. All this added to the costs and delays in settlement, restricted liquidity and made investor grievance redressal time-consuming and at times intractable.

To obviate these problems, the Depositories Act, 1996 was passed to provide for the establishment of depositories in securities with the objective of ensuring free transferability of securities with speed, accuracy and security by:

(a) Making securities of all companies, whether listed or unlisted, freely transferable subject to certain exceptions.

(b) Dematerializing the securities in the depository mode.

(c) Providing for maintenance of ownership records in a book entry form.

In order to streamline both the stages of settlement process, the Depositories Act envisages transfer of ownership of securities electronically by book entry without making the securities move from person to person. The Act has made the securities of all companies whether listed or unlisted, freely transferable by restricting the company's right to use discretion in effecting the transfer of securities, and dispensing with the transfer deed and other procedural requirements under the Companies Act.

A depository holds securities in dematerialized form. It maintains ownership records of securities and effects transfer of ownership through book entry. By law, it is the registered owner of the securities held with it with the limited purpose of effecting transfer of ownership at the behest of the owner. The name of the depository appears in the records of the issuer as registered owner of securities. The name of the actual owner appears in the records of the depository as beneficial owner. The beneficial owner has all the rights and liabilities associated with the securities. The owner of securities intending to avail of depository services opens an account with a depository through a DP. The securities are transferred from one account to another through book entry only on the instructions of the beneficial owner.

In order to promote dematerialization of securities, NSE joined hands with leading financial institutions to establish the National Securities Depository Ltd. (NSDL), the first depository in the country, with the objective of enhancing the efficiency in settlement systems as also to reduce the menace of fake/forged and stolen securities. This has ushered in an era of dematerialized trading and settlement. SEBI has made dematerialized settlement mandatory in an ever-increasing number of securities in a phased manner, thus bringing about an increase in the proportion of shares delivered in dematerialized form. The settlement of trades on stock exchanges is almost 100 per cent in demat form.

CDSL was set up in February, 1999 to provide depository services. All leading stock exchanges like the National Stock Exchange, Calcutta Stock Exchange, Delhi Stock Exchange, The Stock Exchange, Ahmedabad, etc. have established connectivity with CDSL.

Note: The above discussions have been taken almost entirely from the NSE publication division and are mostly reproduced here for clear understanding of the general investors and readers of this book.

It is quite obvious that dematerialization will accelerate the e-revolution whose potentiality is enormous in India. The Indian consumer is fast accepting the changing ideas as they are computer savvy and have a basic knowledge of English as India produces the highest number of graduates in the world. The advantages of e-commerce lie in the vast choice, economy in transaction and wealth of information. Since 14th March, 1995 BSE On-line Trading (BOLT) has been used by members from their Trader Work Station (TWS) by replacing the long standing open outcry trading system. The system is fully automated; the scrips traded in the stock exchange have been classified into Groups A, B1, B2, C, F and Z. Where A, B1 and B2 represent equity segments, but Group C represents odd lot securities falling in Groups A, B1 and B2. Group F represents debt market securities and Group Z represents securities that are investor unfriendly and either a winding up petition is filed or a winding up notification dispatched.

The trades done by the trading members every week from Monday to Friday of the scrips falling in Groups A, B1, B2, C, F and Z are settled by payment and delivery of securities in the following week routed through the Clearing House. The delivery order states the information regarding the scrip, quantity and price and also provides the name of the member to whom delivery has been made through the Clearing House and will provide details of receipts and payments of the respective settlement.

BSE software is able to tackle capital adequacy norms. Capital adequacy norms and a member's security deposit will be considered as a part of the carry forward system and surveillance function accordingly.

The member has to maintain a minimum capital of Rs. 10 lakhs apart from an amount of cash deposit with the exchange, long–term fixed deposit with the bank the exchange has a lien on and approved margin with the exchange that would have a cover on it. Capital adequacy of 3 per cent would imply that the member's gross option position does not exceed 33.33 times the capital adequacy norms. Salient features of the system are:

1. Members deposit of cash and securities with the bank
2. The volume of the securities deposited by the members is calculated at the daily closing rate
3. Calculation of required capital and shortfall of members be determined
4. Members must be informed about shortfall
5. Members will be cautioned if shortfall capital has not been covered within a stipulated period of time

6. Carry forward system calculates the capital adequacy on a daily basis by collecting the transaction data from the BOLT and latest capital adequacy data to the BOLT to truckle short fall on the subsequent day (see also Chart 1.2 in Chapter-1, for more details).

DEMATERIALIZED TRADING SYSTEM (DEMAT) AND BOLT

The exchange started dematerialized (demat) trading right from 29th December, 1997 by replacing physical delivery of securities. Auction session for shortage in the demat segment, carried out by BOLT is held after pay-in and pay-out of scrips of different group. The pay-in and pay-out of money will be made through Electronic Clearing System (ECS) in the member's bank account. Electronic payment is carried out in the form of Business-to-Business (B2B), Business to Customer (B2C), Customer to Business (C2B) and Customer to Customer (C2C). Payment below US \$10 will be settled by C2C or B2C, payment between US \$10 to \$500 is settled by B2C category and payment above US \$500 falls under the B2B category which constitutes 95 per cent of the volume of transactions, with the remaining 5 per cent falling under other categories.

The introduction of the Modified Carry Forward System along with BOLT throughout the country has improved the volume of transactions and liquidity of the exchange. As a result of that margin, risk management and surveillance system have improved significantly. In tandem with the philosophy of self regulation, the BSE developed the BSE On-Line Surveillance System (BOSS) which is unique and was inaugurated by the then Finance Minister Shri Jashwant Sinha on 15th July, 1999.

As a part of Mission 2000, the Bombay Stock Exchange has taken a series of initiatives to make it 'investor friendly, self-regulated and efficient exchange'. With the introduction of web based trading facilities for members there has been a sea change in the way the exchange members deal with customers. The style of trading has also led to transparency of information, improvement in efficiency, cost efficiency, enhanced service to customers and an opportunity for investors to avail of execution facility.

Under Mission 2000, the BSE has set objectives to become technologically superior, investor friendly and the premier stock exchange. The plan includes leadership in products, technology and volumes; enhancing investors' wealth; persuading the government and regulator by strategic initiatives by attaining a high level of investor protection and education to meet features challenges. SEBI had appointed a committee under the chairmanship of Justic Kania for corporatization and dematerialization of stock exchanges and submitted its report on 28th August, 2002. The NSE on 23rd March,2005 and OTCEI on 15th September, 2005 notified for corporatization (converting from non-corporate structure to corporate structure) and dematerialization (separation of ownership, management and trading). The IPO through on-line (BOLT) and introduction of internet trading made the exchange corporatized. The strategic objective of Mission 2000 is enabling Vision 2005 from the point of view of a long term plan in terms of success and growth. The BSE has appointed Price Waterhouse Coopers as a consultant to execute the road map. Vision 2005 took into account organization of the stock exchange, trading and settlement system, new products and e-commerce and certainly e-brokerage as a part of the plan.

A new concept has emerged in the name of e-brokerage where members of stock exchanges will be members of the BSE or NSE to become net brokers. Here brokers have to invest in membership cards, incur expenses for physical infrastructure, invest in software including exchange connectivity, settle trade through surveillance system and take into account risk management. Investment has to be made in hardware and networking equipment including front office and back office with costs varying from Rs. 3 crores to Rs. 15 crores.

OVER THE COUNTER EXCHANGE OF INDIA (OTCEI)

Started from 1992, Over the Counter Exchange of India (OTCEI) has ring and ring-less, electronic, screen based, nation-wise stock exchange links for small investors across the country, providing them the benefits of transparency and quick settlement. OTCEI is an exchange meant for listing of small companies, that is, companies which have a paid-up capital of between Rs. 3 crore to Rs. 5 crore. As the OTCEI is not doing well due to the debate between market forces versus state control, with the collapse of the erstwhile Soviet Union and the Republic of China taking the path of market socialism.

The recommendations of the Malegam Committee Report of 1995 may change the fate of this unique exchange provided recommendations are implemented in full. The public issue of a company below Rs. 10 crore and issue for diversification are routed through the OTCEI.

An interesting feature is that brokers will no longer call the shots as OTCEI will look after the settlement of small investors' funds. As small investors are the backbone of scrip trading OTCEI will take care of them. In the USA, Canada and Europe use of Electronic Data Interchange (EDI) is mandatory and skilled personnel are necessary. In line with the aforesaid countries the Ministry of Commerce and Industry has launched a course conducted by All India Management Association (AIMA) on EDI for providing specialized software for stock exchanges and banks. Stock investors invest their money in stock exchanges through an EDI firm. The concept of OTCEI will succeed and thrive only if retail investors make a handsome profit out of the bourses.

C-STAR

The Calcutta Stock Exchange (CSE) also has an on-line trading system called C-Star. According to CSE representatives, the regional stock exchanges will float 100 per cent subsidiaries with the power to take up corporate membership in any other stock exchange. It will also register members of its stock exchange as sub-brokers and traders of regional stock exchanges. The CSE will treat these subsidiaries at par with its other members. Thus, if a whole lot of smaller stock exchanges become members of the CSE, their members will inevitably take a C-Star screen too. A greater spread means more business and hence more turnover. For the smaller stock exchange brokers, there is a lot to gain as the smaller stock exchanges, through their subsidiaries, will be members of the CSE. To the individual broker of a small stock exchange, therefore, the cost of trading at the NSE, BSE or the CSE presumably becomes cheaper (Basistha Basu, *Economic Times*, Calcutta, Sept. 27, 1999).

INTERNET SERVICE PROVIDERS

As a result of disinvestment, the erstwhile Videsh Sanchar Nigam Limited (VSNL) came into the fold of the Tata Group from 2002 and was renamed as Tata Communication Services (TCS). It had a monopoly over the international telecom voice traffic till 2004 and is considered as the country's single gateway provider in the country for transmitting voice traffic. After that the government had to allow private Internet Service Providers (ISPs) to establish their own gateway. The telecom gateway is a switching infrastructure which connects the domestic telecom network with foreign telecom networks and ensures a smooth flow of international traffic between countries. The Internet telecom gateway normally transmits data for internet purposes. The Department of Telecommunication (DoT) has been entrusted as the Centre for the Development of Telemetric (C-DOT) for monitoring the installation of equipment at the gateway. By using this gateway BSE, NSE and OTCEI have opened up the horizon and go to the public in line with other international exchanges including Australia and Singapore.

The new economy is breaking the long-standing axioms, principles, postulates, doctrines and conventions relating to investors, brokers and stock market. The e-economy redefines many perspectives based on old wisdom, which has not evaporated with time, technology and the e-commerce system but realities and corollaries have changed accordingly. To become a rule breaker, rule shaker, rule maker or rule taker depends on one's risk taking ability. The strategy of the organization depends on the e-economy and value rendered to customers or users. The value of the e-business matrix provides results between the level of risk and level of reward. The horizontal axis is considered as value and the vertical axis is considered as risk. A rule breaker takes more risks and expects much value addition but those who believe in rules are reluctant to take risks and their value addition is insignificant. On the flip side, rule shakers added much value with low risk by way of innovative ideas but those who follow rules lead the industry added potential value with high risk.

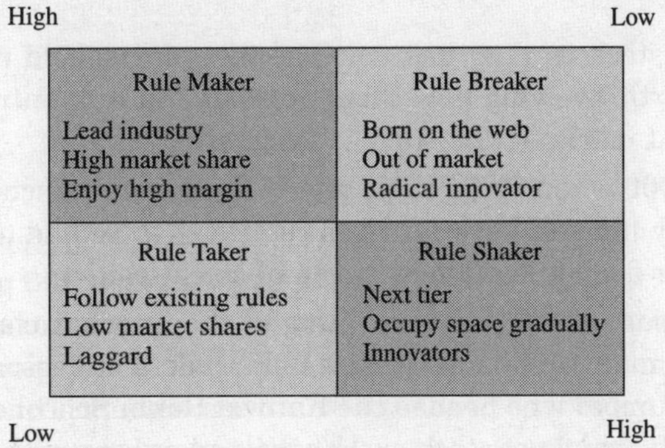

	High		Low	
	Rule Maker		**Rule Breaker**	
	Lead industry		Born on the web	
	High market share		Out of market	
	Enjoy high margin		Radical innovator	
	Rule Taker		**Rule Shaker**	
	Follow existing rules		Next tier	
	Low market shares		Occupy space gradually	
	Laggard		Innovators	
	Low		High	

Chart 9.4 E-Business Value Martrix

[Idea taken from *Net Ready @* by Amir Hartman, John Sifonis and John Kadar, McGraw-Hill]

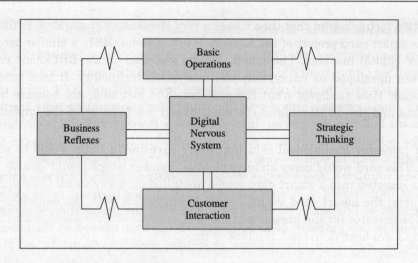

Digital Nervous System of Business Activity

Source: Bill Gates (2000), *Business @ the Speed of Thought,* Warner Books, New York

The man behind the digital economic success is Bill Gates. Bill Gates' keys to digital success lie in his book, *Business @ The Speed of Thought.* Bill Gates opined that, 'If the 1980s were about quality and the 1990s were about reengineering then the 2000s will be about velocity.'[1] In the words of Gates, '*A digital nervous system comprises the digital processes that closely link every aspect of a company's thoughts and actions.*'

Basic operations such as finance and production, plus feedback from customers, are electronically accessible to a company's knowledge workers, who use digital tools to quickly adapt and respond. The immediate availability of accurate information changes strategic thinking from a separate, stand-alone activity to an ongoing process integrated with regular business activities.[2]

In India, Internet stock trading has now become a household name to stock players and investors, but it is worth knowing how this happened. To new entrants of the stock markets and students of capital markets, the story is fascinating.

On February 1st 2000 when SEBI chairman D.R. Meheta punched a keyboard for the first internet trade, he may himself have failed to realize that he had opened the door for Indian stock markets to enter a completely new world of stock trading.

During the latter part of 1999, at a meeting of the internet trading committee set up by SEBI, the committee's main architect, Deepak B. Pathak, a professor from the Indian Institute of Technology (IIT), Mumbai who headed the Kanwal Rekhi School of Information Technology, placed a proposal to the chiefs of stock exchanges and other members of the committee.

---

[1]Bill Gates, 2000, *Business @ the Speed of Thought: Succeeding in the Digital Economy,* Warner Books, New York, p. xvii
[2]*Ibid* p. 16

Information technology at that time was at a very elementary stage, Prof. Pathak suggested that like the smart card project of the Reserve Bank of India (RBI), a similar project could be developed for capital markets. This could then be mounted on the RBI smart card platform as it has been developed as encryption and decryption technology. It took members of the committee some time to digest what the professor had just said, not because he had asked the exchanges and the SEBI to fund the pilot project but because of the implications of the move.

In effect professor Pathak had said that every investor in India would be armed with a smart card. This card would carry an identification number which would identify the investor when it was inserted into a smart card reader installed on a keyboard. Once an investor put in a sale quote, the smart card would automatically check with the depository participant account of the investor for the presence of the said number of shares and block these. As soon as the shares have been delivered, the lock or flag on the shares would be lifted. In the case of a buy transaction, the cash account with the concerned bank would be checked for funds the funds would be transferred at the time of settlement. The same technology can be extended to applying for IPOs and accessing critical information through websites where companies could be asked to file all information on-line.

This system has completely redefined the role of brokers. At present, the brokers perform two major functions; firstly, they handle the logistics, place orders on behalf of the clients and undertake the settlement of these orders. Secondly, the brokers stand guarantors for making the payment or delivering the shares on behalf of clients. There is a third dimension also; brokers perform the role of providing the correct investment advice to investors. According to the manager of the NSE, at present a broker is not just an intermediary but more importantly the credit risk guarantor. The credit risk of a client can be known and a check can be done before any transaction goes through. The identity of the client can be known through this technology and hence two major fears, that of seeing a client flee after placing an order and secondly not being able to bring in settlement dues would be eliminated. In short, the role of brokers would change from trading agent to investors' advisor. In an internet trading environment, the role of the broker will be that of providing value addition and quality information to investors on the basis on which they can trade.

Thus the way a computer now comes with a CD-Rom drive or with flash drive (pen drive), every computer in India would have a smart card reader. Even if this does not happen, it would be available to most small investors at an affordable cost and they could install a smart card reader and carry out their trading in the comfort of their homes.

Security of Investors

10

To overcome the operational inefficiencies arising from the traditional paper based trading and settlement system, the Government of India introduced electronic trading and settlement system through National Stock Market System (NSMS). The NSMS has been initiated by the NSE with the help of the National Clearing and Depository System (NCDS) and Stock Holding Corporation of India (SHCIL), Securities Trading Corporation of India Limited (STCI) in conformity with Central Listing Authority (CLA).

With the implementation of the new economic policy in 1991, the magnitude of the capital market has increased manifold over time. Needless to say the volume of transactions and their settlement has also mounted day by day and investors face a number of problems. To overcome these different problems that crop up with investments, the National Clearance and Depository System (NCDS) has developed to fulfil the needs. NCDL will provide two sets of financial intermediaries' depositories and clearing corporations:

- Depository service providers viz. NSDL and CSDL
- Clearing corporations viz. NSCCL and CCLL

The Gazette notification on SEBI (Depositories and Participants) Regulation, 1996 made on 16th May, 1996 and the first depository National Securities Depositories Limited (NSDL) came into existence on 8th November, 1996, but the actual trading of dematerialised securities was initiated by the NSE on December 26th 1996. The Central Depository Services (India) Limited (CDSL) obtained recognition on February 8th 1999 and started limited operations at the BSE on March 22nd 1999. NSDL and CSDL have introduced inter depository connectivity on and from September 20th 1999.

NSDL was the first depository and was promoted on 20th September 1995 by IDBI, UTI and NSE as a public limited company by promulgating the Depository Ordinance, 1995 and started commercial operations on November 8th 1996 following the laws and bye-laws of the Depositories Act, 1996 and SEBI (Depositories and Participants) Regulations, 1996. The board of directors of the National Securities Depository Limited, organize, maintain, control, manage, regulate and facilitate the operation of depository and security transactions by participants of the depository subject to the provisions of the Depositories Act, 1996. Holding and handling of securities in electronic form eliminates multifarious problems associated with physical form of transaction like loss in transit, problems of bad delivery, duplication and sticky settlement cycles that are undergone through clearing houses.

Securities in physical form are cancelled and converted to highly secured electronic form as maintained by the NSDL.

The functions of the NSDL are as follows:

1. To convert the securities in dematerialization and then re-materialize securities.
2. Maintain investors' holdings in electronic form.
3. Allotment of securities may be made in electronic form in case of IPOs.
4. Stock lending and borrowing of securities in electronic form.
5. Freezing of securities in d-mat accounts of investors.
6. Receipt of bonus, rights, sweat equity shares, employee stock option in electronic form.
7. Hypothecation of dematerialization.

Any person willing to act as a participant shall file an application as per the specified format along with fees specified by the SEBI through the depository. A net worth certificate based on the books of accounts certified by a chartered accountant shall be submitted to the depository. A participant shall act as an agent of the depository and shall be liable to the client for depository activities as per deed. The depository may suspend a depository participant for violating rules and regulations. The executive committee can take the initiative to form participants' fund and investors' protection fund. The disbursement of dividend or interest will be provided by the registrar, but the distribution of securities entitlement will be made by the depository on the basis of the information provided by the registrar.

According to the Depositories Act, 1996, an investor has the option to hold shares either in physical or in dematerialized form. Only shares of companies that have registered for participation with NSDL can be dematerialized. The BSE and NSE have distinct trading systems, viz. physical and depository. Before using the electronic form of shares, dematerialization can be carried out in the following ways:

1. Ascertain from the Depository Participant (DP), whether the securities can be dematerialized.
2. Open an account with a DP (as simple as opening a bank account).
3. Surrender your share certificates to a DP along with a dematerialization request Form.
4. Participation in NSDL system is through a DP.

A DP could be a financial institution, bank, custodian, a clearing corporation, a stock broker, or a non-banking financial company. A depository participant is an intermediary between the investor and NSDL and is authorized to maintain accounts of dematerialized shares of anybody. Anyone can choose any DP. The depository system is a paperless trading system that holds the scrips in electronic form. The move was initiated by the Stock Holding Corporation of India Ltd. In 1992 SEBI constituted a committee to study the pros and cons of the depository system. Thereafter the Government of India promulgated the Depository Ordinance, 1995 leading to the foundation of the depository system in India and ultimately the Depository Act, 1996 was enacted in parliament and received the assent of the President of India.

Table 10.1 Depositories and Custodian Service Providers in India

Depository and Custodian Service Provider	Promoter/s	Date when it Came into Existence
National Securities Depository Limited (NSDL)	IDBI, UTI and NSE	November, 1996
Central Depository Services (India) Limited (CDSL)	BSE, SBI, Bank of India, Bank of Baroda and HDFC Bank	March, 1999

As a depository company, NSDL provides services to the investors through a DP's network. The NSDL operates accounts of investors via DPs. An investor can open an account in a DP with a customer ID and will get a statement from time to time in the same way as commercial banks provide statements to their account holders. Investors do not have to send shares to the company for transfer, he/she would thus save courier costs of Rs. 30 per transfer in addition to 0.5 per cent stamp duty of Rs. 50 for transfer of shares worth of Rs. 10,000. Purchasing shares for long-term investment in the physical form involves risks and costs, whereas demat delivery eliminates the risks and reduces costs.

Table 10.2 Comparative Cost of Shares in the Physical Form and Demat Form

Items	Physical (Rs.)	NSDL (Rs.)	Savings (Rs.)
Brokerage	75-100	50-75	25-50
Stamp Duty	50	Nil	50
Postal Charges	10-30	Nil	10-30
Company Objection	10-30	Nil	10-30
Settlement Charges	Nil	5-10	(5-10)
Custody (5 Years)	Nil	25-50	(25-50)

The biggest benefit is that brokers do not have any fear of bad delivery of dematerialized shares and charge the minimum brokerage. The rolling settlement system is much faster than physical settlement. There is no chance of losing the shares in transit or any theft during the process of transfer and no need of stamp duty. Transaction charges under the book entry system are much lower than for the physical segment. Since the pay in and pay out of securities is made electronically, it involves less paper and fulfills the 'go green' slogan. The handling cost of holding physical shares is negated. There is no possibility of bad delivery but

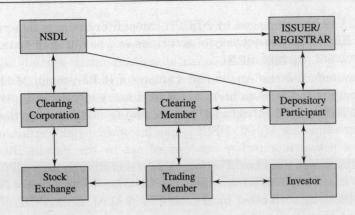

Chart 10.1   The Depository Environment

Source: The flow chart designed by Purnendu Panda in his article *Reviving the Market Sentiment* published in the *Economic Times* on August 24, 1996

investors have to be as careful in operating DPs as in handling bank accounts. Transfer or deposit slip must not be handed over to any one without taking the proper safety measures.

There is no restriction on opening accounts with DPs. An investor can open accounts with more than one depository. The depository has not prescribed any minimum balance of securities; the balance can be zero. Dematerialization of certificates is possible only for certificates that have already been registered in the name of the investor and securities admitted for dematerialization with the NSDL. The integrated system National Electronic Settlement and Transfer (NEST) can be used through the VSAT satellite link or through the land line.

Clearing corporations have the operational capability to provide services relating to clearing and settlement of transactions of securities admitted to the depository made in the dematerialized form.

CSDL was initiated by BSE, SBI, Bank of India and Bank of Baroda, and HDFC Bank received the certificate of commencement on February 8th 1999 but commenced operations on March 22nd 1999 as the second depository in India. NSDL and CCDL have come out with a memorandum of understanding for inter-depository settlements. Both have ultimately established inter-connectivity with effect from September 20th 1999. CSDL is also a member of the Asia–Pacific Central Securities Depository Group. The legal frame work and style of operation is similar to that of NSDL. CSDL was established to accelerate the scripless (dematerialized) trading system and to provide trust worthiness among the individual investors in India. CSDL also provides competitive environment in favor of investors.

Facing cumbersome clearing facilities and settlement systems, NSE set up the National Securities Clearing Corporation Limited (NSCCL) in April, 1995 but started operations in April, 1996. NSCCL operates in tandem with clearing members, depositories, banks and customers. The settlement of Government Securities (G–Sec) entrusted by the RBI has been accorded to the NSE is also managed by NSCCL through Subsidiary General Ledger (SGL) accounts with the RBI to ensure delivery of securities and payment in time; which has also widened the government security market.

The NSCCL has enforced the Automated Lending and Borrowing Mechanism (ALBM) which helps members of the NSE to borrow and lend securities determined by the market. Moreover, from 2001 the BSE introduced the Borrowing and Lending Securities Scheme (BIESS) on the same lines as ALBM. NSCCL has introduced risk containment mechanism through NEST. The actual monitoring was carried out by the Parallel Risk Management System (PRISM) which uses Standard Portfolio Analysis of Risk System (SPAN(r)) on lines of margin calculation based on SEBI parameters. The Clearing Corporation of India (CCIL) was promoted by the SBI along with other banks and FIs in April, 2001. CCIL acts as a clearing house of government securities and a money market instrument.

The Stock Holding Corporation of India Limited (SHCIL) was promoted as a corporation by IDBI, IFCI, ICICI, LIC, GIC and UTI along with the RBI in 1986 but commenced its operations in 1988. The basic objective was to provide quick transfer of shares, clearing, depository, information and development along with a support system. It also acts as the largest custodian of FIS and MFs for UTI, LIC and Morgan Stanley.

The Securities Trading Corporation of India Limited (STCIL) was promoted by the RBI and LIC in 1994, as a custodian of debt instrument of the money market especially for call money market.

As per Section 73 of the Companies Act, 1956, listing is mandatory for shares and debentures subscribed to by the public through prospectus. The SEBI (Central Listing Authority) Regulation, 2003 has initiated the formation of the Central Listing Authority (CLA) and provides adequate manpower and infrastructure for it to open branches throughout the country. It is mandatory for an issuer to seek prior approval from the respective stock exchanges where the securities are listed before going into public issue. It is also mandatory for the issuer to obtain a Letter Precedent to Listing (LPTL) from the CLA before public issue and before putting the application to the stock exchanges. Non-compliance with CLA regulations or terms of the listing agreement is liable to the penalty clause mentioned in Sections 15A or 15B of the SEBI Act, 1992.

CREDIT RATING

The seeds of credit rating were sown during the world wide depression, which started in the 1930s. The first mercantile credit rating agency was set up in New York, USA in 1841 for rating the financial ability of merchants. It was subsequently acquired by Mr. Robert Dun, who published first Rating Guide in 1859. The second rating agency was formed by Mr. John Bradstreet in 1849, and published a rating book in 1857.

In 1900 Mr. John Moody established Moody's Investor service and in the early 1920s it took the responsibility of rating bonds issued by corporations and municipalities in the USA. In

1933 firms owned by Mr. Dun and Mr. Bradstreet were merged to form Dun and Bradstreet. Another development was made in the case of Standard and Poor. Mr. Henry Vernum Poor's publishing company published its own first rating in 1916 and Standard Statistics Company also published their rating in 1922. But, in 1941 Standard Statistics Company and Mr. Poor's publishing company were merged to form the world famous rating agency Standard and Poor's. This major rating agency was acquired by McGraw Hill in 1966. Credit Rating and Information Services of India Limited (CRISIL) was floated on January 1st 1988 as India's first rating agency jointly by ICICI and UTI. Subsequently, the Investment Information and Credit Rating Agency of India Limited (ICRA Ltd.) was promoted by IFCI with other FIs in 1991. The Credit Analysis and Research Limited (CARE) was promoted by FIs and private sector companies (IDBI, UTI, Canara Bank, Kotak Mahindra Finance Ltd., etc) in November 1993, UTI Credit Rating Limited, ONIDA Individual Credit Rating Agency of India Ltd. (ONICRA) were established in November 1993 at the initiative of Onida Finance Ltd., Duff and Phelps Rating Agency of India Ltd. (DCR) was established in 1995 as a private sector credit rating agency. Later on FITCH India, a joint venture of a Chicago based Credit Rating Company and Alliance Credit Capital Company of India acquired Duff and Phelps Rating Agency of India Ltd. In the Indian credit rating scenario, CRISIL, CARE and ICRA are the main players and on the international scenario, Standard and Poor's and Moody's play significant roles.

Credit rating is defined by Prof. L.M. Bhole[1] *'as an act of assigning values to credit instruments by estimating or assessing the solvency i.e. the ability of the borrower to repay debt, and expressing them through pre-determined symbols.'* The SEBI (Credit Rating Agencies) Regulations, 1999 state that a *'credit rating agency means a body corporate which is engaged in or proposes to be engaged in, the business of rating of securities offered by way of public or right issue.'*

In India, credit rating is mandatory subject to certain conditions. SEBI (Credit Rating Agencies) Regulation, 1999 states that public issue of debentures and bonds both comestible and redeemable issued for more than 18 months have to be credit rated. Moreover, if the maturity period is less than 18 months credit rating is not mandatory. As per RBI guidelines commercial papers issued in India have to acquire rating grades not below P2 from CRISIL, or A2 from ICRA or PR2 from CARE. A Non Banking Financial Company (NBFC) having net funds less than Rs. 25 lakhs have to acquire minimum rating of FA – from CRISIL or MA – from ICRA or CARE, BBB from CARE or BBB – from DCR as per the Public Deposit (Reserve Bank) Directions, 1999.

Methodology

Generally, it can be said that the objectives of different credit rating agencies are to provide guidance to investors or creditors in determining the credit risk associated with a financial instrument or equity. Agencies try to provide reliable information on the relative quality of equity or other financial instruments like, debentures, bonds, preference shares and long term

[1]L.M. Bhole, 2004, *Financial Institutions and Markets – Structure, Growth and Innovations*, Tata McGraw-Hill Publishing Company Ltd., New Delhi, India

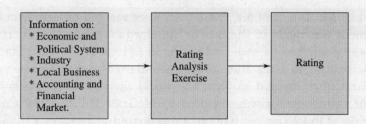

Chart 10.2 General Rating Process

Source: *Investment Banking and Finance Service, Vol-1,* The ICFAI University, Hyderabad, India.

instruments. For this, agencies undertake a scientific analytical exercise to examine most of the fundamental (and sometimes also the technical) parameters of the company to assess and grade its equity or other instruments.

Almost all the international and national credit agencies follow the general rating process. This is furnished in Chart 10.2.

Rating Methodology of CRISIL

Though there is a general process of rating, different agencies have developed their own processing methods. CRISIL's methodology includes the following risk exposures of the corporate or borrower:

- ❖ Industry risk analysis
- ❖ Business risk analysis
- ❖ Financial risk analysis
- ❖ Management risk analysis
- ❖ Fundamental risk analysis

Main Objectives of CRISIL

- ❖ To assist both individual and institutional investors in making investment decisions in fixed income securities.
- ❖ To enable corporates to raise large amount of funds at fair cost from a wide spectrum of investors.
- ❖ To enable intermediaries in placing their debt instruments with investors by providing them with an effective marketing tool.
- ❖ To provide regulators with a market-driven system to bring about discipline and healthy growth of the capital market.

Table 10.3 (A & B) CRISIL Rating Symbols

A. In Case of Debenture/Long-term Investment Rating	
Highest safety	FAAA
High safety	FAA
Adequate safety	FA
Inadequate safety	FB
High risk	FC
Default or expected to be default	FD

B. In Case of Short-term Instruments	
Highest safety	P_1
High safety	P_2
Adequate safety	P_3
Inadequate safety	P_4
Default or is expected to be default	P_5

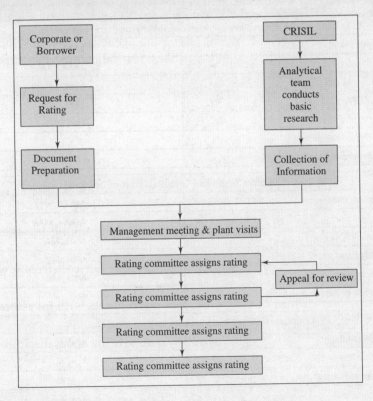

Chart 10.3   CRISIL Rating Process

Source: Investment Banking and Finance Service, Vol-1, The ICFAI University, Hyderabad, India.

Rating Methodology of CRISIL

ICRA's rating methodology of debt instruments is more or less similar to that of CRISIL or other credit rating agencies. The method for grading equity depends on requisites of the prospective equity issuer and equity assessment process commences at the request of the investor (ICFAI, 2004).

ICRA formed a group called Earning Prospect and Risk Analysis (EPRA) to provide authentic information on the relative quality of equity. This group examines almost all

Tables 10.4   Main Differences of Equity Grading and Assessment

Equity Grading	Equity Assessment
Grading is at the request of the equity issuer.	Assessment is at the request of the investor.
Imparts greater visibility for a large number of potential investors.	It is for the use of the specific investors only.
It is kept under surveillance once the issuer accepts and uses the grade.	It is a one time exercise.
It is in the form of a symbolic indicator and a rationale.	It is in the form of a report.

Tables 10.5   (A, B & C) ICRA Rating Symbols

A. In Case of Debentures, Bonds, Preference Shares/Long-term Instruments	
Highest safety	LAAA
High safety	LAA+, LAA
Adequate safety	LBBB+, LBBB
Inadequate safety	LBB+, LBB
High risk prone	LB+, LB
Adequate risk prone	LC+, LC
Default or default possibility	LD

B. In Case of Medium Term Fixed Deposits/Company Deposits	
Highest safety	MAAA
High safety	MAA+, MAA
Adequate safety	MA+, MA
Inadequate safety	MB+, MB
Risk prone	MC+, MC
Default or default possibility	MD

C. In Case of Short–term Security Instruments/CPs	
Highest safety	A_1+, A_1
High safety	A_2+, A_2
Adequate safety	A_3+, A_3
Risk prone	A_4+, A_4
Default or default possibility	A_5+

the parameters relating to the fundamentals of the company including respective sectoral perspectives and offers two services like equity grading and equity assessment. Though the procedure of analysis for grading and assessing equity is similar in nature, the end results differ from one another. These differences are given in Table 10.4.

Rating Methodology of CARE

CARE offers a wide range of products and services in the area of credit information and equity research. Its credit rating covers all types of debt instruments like: (i) debentures, (ii) fixed deposits, (iii) certificates of deposits, (iv) commercial papers and (v) structured obligations.

CARE is also engaged in general credit analysis rating of companies on request of banks, other lenders and business counterparties.

CARE's rating methodology and rating process are more or less similar to those of CRISIL.

Table 10.6 (A & B) CARE Rating Symbols

A. In Case of Long-term or Medium-term Instruments/Securities	
Highest safety	CARE AAA
High safety	CARE AA
Appropriate/Suitable safety	CARE A
Adequate/Sufficient safety	CARE BBB
Speculative	CARE BB
High risk prone	CARE B
High investment risk or may be default	CARE C
Lowest category, either in default or likely to be default soon	CARE D

B. In Case of Short-term Instruments/Securities	
Highest safety	PR1
High safety	PR2
Adequate safety	PR3
Minimum safety	PR4
May be in default	PR5

In India the credit rating process has been initiated by the client or issuer company on a case to case basis and the process of rating is started after gathering all operational features and financial features provided by the company or from an in house data base or data from reliable source. The primary objectives of credit rating are to judge future cash generating ability and how to how to mitigate debt obligation in adverse situations. The focus of the analysis is to determine fundamentals on a long-term basis and also to determine the probability of change of this fundamental and how it will affect the credit worthiness of the borrower in particular.

Table 10.7 Comparative Credit Rating Symbols by CRISIL, ICRA and CARE

Terminology	CRISIL Rating	ICRA Rating	CARE Rating
Long-term:			
Highest safety	AAA	LAAA	CARE AAA
High safety	AA	LAA	CARE AA
Adequate safety	A	LA	CARE A
Moderate safety	BBB	LBBB	CARE BBB
Inadequate safety	BB	LBB	CARE BB
Risk prone	B	LB	CARE B
Substantial risk		LC	CARE C
Default		LD	CARE D
Medium-term:			
Highest safety	FAAA	MAAA	CARE AAA
High safety	FAA	MAA	CARE AA
Adequate safety	FA	MA	CARE A
Moderate safety			CARE BBB
Inadequate safety	FB	MB	CARE BB
Risk prone	FC	MC	CARE B
Substantial risk			CARE C
Default	FD	MD	CARE D
Short-term:			
Highest safety	P-1	A1	PR-1
High safety	P- 2	A2	PR-2
Adequate safety	P-3	A3	PR-3
Moderate safety			
Inadequate safety	P-4	A4	PR-4
Risk prone			
Substantial risk			
Default	P-5	A5	PR -5

Source: www.CARE.com, www.ICRA.com, www.CRISIL.com (Accessed on 5.12.2011)

INTERNATIONAL CREDIT RATING ENVIRONMENT

The objective of credit rating is to serve the investor's need at the time of offering credit. They will judge the credit worthiness of the issuer on the basis of available information provided by rating for every credit instrument. The rating process followed by two international rating agencies, Standard and Poor's and Moody's is more or less the same.

Information is based on fundamental analysis including business risk and financial risk in conformity with managerial efficiency and effectiveness and operational efficiency, bearing in mind the regulatory and competitive environment. The rating system offered by Credit

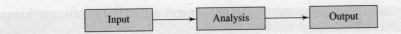

Chart 10.4 Exercises of Rating Analysis

Rating Agencies (CRAs) for various credit instruments are based on rates and grades. Two basic grades are well known nationally and internationally for identifying risk free and risk prone securities, one is the investment grade and the other is the speculative grade. Standard and Poor's four highest rated categories, "AAA", "AA", "A", "BBB" fall into the investment grade category with highest capacity, very strong capacity, strong capacity and adequate capacity respectively. On the other hand, Moody's "Aaa", "Aa", "A", "Baa" ratings fall into the investment category with different investment grades. Standard and poor's "AAA" is equivalent to Moody's "Aaa". Standard and Poor's speculative grade of debt rating varies from BB, B, CCC, CC and C, and reflects uncertainties and risk exposure in relation with principal and interest payment. Equivalent ratings of Moody vary from Ba, B, Caa, Ca to C. Standard and Poor's rating from AAA to C with attachment of plus (+) or minus (–) may indicate varying degrees of risk but Moody's rating variation with attached 1, 2 or 3 indicates high, mid-range ranking and low end rank respectively.

Table 10.8 Rating Structure of Standard and Poor and Moody

(On the basis of investment grades and speculative grades)

Investment Grades	Standard and Poor	Moody
Highest quality	AAA, AAA-, AA+	Aaa, Aaa1, Aaa2, Aaa3
Excellent	AA, AA-, A+	Aa, Aa1, Aa2, Aa3
Good	A, A-, BBB+	A, A1, A2, A3
Medium	BBB, BBB-, BB+	Baa, Baa1, Baa2, Baa3
Speculative Grades		
Questionable	BB, BB-, B+	Ba, Ba1, Ba2, Ba3
Poor	B, B-, CCC+	B, B1, B2, B3
Very poor	CCC, CCC-, CC+	Caa, Caa1, Caa2, Caa3
Extremely poor	CC, CC-, C+	Ca, CA1, Ca2, Ca3
Lowest	C	C
Default in interest payment	C1	
Default in payment	D	

Source: Investment Analysis and Portfolio Management – Prasanna Chandra, p331 and Investment Banking and Financial Services, Volume–I, p474-477

Recently, the US was degraded from AAA to AA+ by S & P's rating. We will take a quick look at US credit worthiness. How did the United States get in debt to the tune of US $14.3 trillion? And who are the creditors?

Table 10.9 US Debts and the Creditors

When the US debts was accumulated and who holds the US debt	Amount in Trillion US$	When the US debts was accumulated and who holds the US debt	Amount in Trillion US$
President Obama: Oct 2009 - July 2011, stimulus spending tax, tax cards and the effects of 2007 - 09 recessions in lost revenues and in spending on unemployment compensation, etc.	2.4	George Bush: Oct 1989 – Sep 1993, cost from the first gulf war and lower revenue due to the recession.	1.5
George W. Bush: Oct 2001 – Sep 2009 tax cuts, the wars in Iraq and Afghanistan, economic down turn in 2001 and recession in 2007.	6.1	Ronald Reagan Oct 1981 – Sep 1989, peacetime defense spending and permanent tax cut.	1.9
Bill Clinton: Oct 1993 – Sep 2001 despite two years of budget surplus, deficit spending in other years added to debt.	1.4	Before Reagan: Deficit spending from previous war and economic down turn.	1
Who holds the debt?			
The public including debt held by individuals, corporations, banks and insurance companies, pensions and mutual funds, state and local government	3.6	Other countries	1.9
Foreign countries: China	1.2	The US Government Federal Reserve System includes collateral for US currency and store of liquidity for emergency need (includes by 855 billion since July 2010).	1.6
Japan	0.9	Social Security Trust Funds generated by the program that have been invested in Government bonds	2.7
Britain	0.3	Other Government Trust Fund	1.9
Oil exporting countries	0.2		

Content source: New York Times; *Image source:* Department of Treasury, Financial Management Service, Bureaus of Public Debt, Federal Reserve Bank of New York cited in Trade Tiding on 18th August, 2011 (www.iitrade.ac.in 10.11.2011)

Moody's Investors Service on 9th November, 2011 lowered India's banking outlook from stable to negative on the basis of the possibility of bad loans. Profit will be hit accordingly as per a study made on 15 commercial banks which together constitute 66 per cent of the total assets as on March, 2011.

Note: For writing this chapter we have taken help from our previous publication titled *Share Bazarer Riti Niti*, New Central Book Agency, Kolkata, India, 1999

Appendix:
Investment Terminology

EARNINGS PER SHARE – EPS

What does *Earnings Per Share - EPS* Mean?

It is the portion of a company's profit allocated to each outstanding share of common stock. Earnings per share serve as an indicator of a company's profitability.
They are calculated as:

$$= \frac{\text{Net Income - Dividends on Preferred Stock}}{\text{Average Outstanding Shares}}$$

When calculating EPS, it is more accurate to use a weighted average number of shares outstanding over the reporting term, because the number of shares outstanding can change over time. However, data sources sometimes simplify the calculation by using the number of shares outstanding at the end of the period.

Diluted EPS expands on basic EPS by including the shares of convertibles or warrants outstanding in the number of outstanding shares.

INVESTOPEDIA EXPLAINS *EARNINGS PER SHARE – EPS*

EPS is generally considered to be the single most important variable in determining a share's price. It is also a major component used to calculate the price-to-earnings valuation ratio.

For example, assume that a company has a net income of $25 million. If the company pays out $1 million in preferred dividends and has 10 million shares for half of the year and 15 million shares for the other half, the EPS would be $1.92 (24/12.5). First, the $1 million is deducted from the net income to get $24 million, then a weighted average is taken to find the number of shares outstanding, i.e.

$$(0.5 \times 10M + 0.5 \times 15M) = 12.5M.$$

An important aspect of EPS that is often ignored is the capital that is required to generate the earnings (net income) in the calculation. Two companies could generate the same value of the EPS, but the company that could do so with less equity (investment) would be more efficient at using its capital to generate income and, all other things being equal, would be a "better" company. Investors also need to be aware of earnings manipulation that will affect the quality of the earnings number. It is important not to rely on any one financial measure, but to use it in conjunction with statement analysis and other measures.

TYPES OF EPS

While the math may be simple, there are many variations of EPS being used these days, and investors must understand what each one represents if they are to make informed investment decisions. For example, the EPS announced by a company may differ significantly from what is reported in financial statements and in headlines. As a result, a stock may appear over or undervalued depending on the EPS being used. Here we will define some of the variations of EPS and discuss their pros and cons.

By definition, EPS is net income divided by the number of shares outstanding; however, both the numerator and denominator can change depending on how you define "earnings" and "shares outstanding". Because there are so many ways to define earnings, we will first deal with shares outstanding.

SHARES OUTSTANDING

Shares outstanding can be classified as either primary (primary EPS) or fully diluted (diluted EPS).

Primary EPS is calculated using the number of shares that have been issued and held by investors. These are the shares that are currently in the market and can be traded.

Diluted EPS entails a complex calculation that determines how many shares would be outstanding if all exercisable warrants, options, etc. were converted into shares at a point in time, generally the end of a quarter.

We prefer diluted EPS because it is a more conservative number that calculates EPS as if all possible shares were issued and outstanding. The number of diluted shares can change as share prices fluctuate (as options fall into/out of the money), but generally the Street assumes the number is fixed as stated in the 10-Q or 10-K.

Companies report both primary and diluted EPS, and the focus is generally on diluted EPS, but investors should not assume that this is always the case. Sometimes, the diluted and primary EPS are the same because the company does not have any "in-the-money" options, warrants or convertible bonds outstanding. Companies can discuss either, so investors need to be sure which is being used.

EARNINGS

As has been evident in recent headlines, EPS can be whatever the company wants it to be, depending on assumptions and accounting policies. Corporate spin-doctors focus media attention on the number the company wants in the news, which may or may not be the EPS reported in documents filed with the Securities & Exchange Commission (SEC). Based on a set of assumptions, a company can report a high EPS, which reduces the P/E multiple and makes the stock look undervalued. The EPS reported in the 10Q, however, can result in a much lower EPS and an overvalued stock on a P/E basis. This is why it is critical for investors to read carefully and know what type of earnings is being used in the EPS calculation.

We will focus on five types of EPS and define them in the context of the type of "earnings" being used.

REPORTED EPS (OR GAAP EPS)

We define reported EPS as the number derived from Generally Accepted Accounting Principles (GAAP), which are reported in SEC filings. The company derives these earnings according to the accounting guidelines used. (Note: A discussion of how a company can manipulate EPS under GAAP is beyond the scope of this book, but investors should remember that it is possible. Our focus is on how earnings can be distorted even if there is no intent to manipulate results.)

A company's reported earnings can be distorted by GAAP. For example, a one-time gain from the sale of machinery or a subsidiary could be considered as operating income under GAAP and cause the EPS to spike. Also, a company could classify a large number of normal operating expenses as an "unusual charge" which can boost EPS because the "unusual charge" is excluded from calculations. Investors need to read the footnotes in order to decide what factors should be included in "normal" earnings and make adjustments in their own calculations.

ONGOING EPS

This EPS is calculated based upon normalized or ongoing net income and excludes anything that is an unusual one-time event. The goal is to find the stream of earnings from core operations which can be used to forecast future EPS. This can mean excluding a large one-time gain from the sale of equipment as well as an unusual expense. Attempts to determine an EPS using this methodology is also called "pro forma" EPS.

PRO FORMA EPS

The words "pro forma" indicate that assumptions were used to derive whatever number is being discussed. Different from reported EPS, pro forma EPS generally excludes some expenses/ income that were used in calculating reported earnings. For example, if a company sold a large division, it could, in reporting historical results, exclude the expenses and revenues associated with that unit. This allows for more of an "apples-to-apples" comparison.

Another example of pro forma is a company choosing to exclude some expenses because the management feels that the expenses are non-recurring and distort the company's "true" earnings. Non-recurring expenses, however, seem to appear with increasing regularity these days. This raises questions as to whether management knows what it is doing or is trying to build a "rainy day fund" to smooth EPS.

HEADLINE EPS

The headline EPS is the EPS number that is highlighted in the company's press release and picked up in the media. Sometimes it is the pro forma number, but it could also be an EPS number that has been calculated by the analyst/*pundit* that is discussing the company. Generally, sound bites do not provide enough information to determine which EPS number is being used.

CASH EPS

Cash EPS is operating cash flow (not EBITDA) divided by diluted shares outstanding. We think cash EPS is more important than other EPS numbers because it is a "purer" number. Cash EPS is better because operating cash flow cannot be manipulated as easily as net income and represents real cash earned, it is calculated by including changes in key asset categories such as receivables and inventories. For example, a company with reported EPS of $0.50 and cash EPS of $1.00 is preferable to a firm with reported EPS of $1.00 and cash EPS of $0.50. Although there are many factors to consider in evaluating these two hypothetical stocks, the company with cash is generally in better financial shape.

Other EPS numbers have overshadowed cash EPS, but we expect it to get more attention because of the new GAAP rule (FAS 142), which allows companies to stop amortizing goodwill. Companies may start talking about "cash EPS" in order to differentiate between pre-FAS 142 and post-FAS 142 results; however, this version of "cash EPS" is more like EBITDA per share and does not factor in changes in receivables and inventory. Consequently, I feel it is not as good as operating-cash-flow EPS, but is better in certain cases than other forms of EPS.

The Bottom Line

There are many types of EPS being used, and investors need to know what the EPS represents and determine if it is a valid representation of the company's earnings. A stock may appear as great value because it has a low P/E, but that ratio may be based on assumptions with which you may not agree.

CASH EARNINGS PER SHARE - CASH EPS

What Does *Cash Earnings Per Share - Cash EPS* Mean?

Cash EPS is a measure of financial performance that looks at the cash flow generated by a company on a per share basis. This differs from basic (EPS), which looks at the net income of the company on a per share basis. The higher a company's cash EPS, the better it is considered to have performed over the period. A company's cash EPS can be used to draw comparisons to other companies or to the company's own past results.

$$\text{Cash EPS} = \frac{\text{Operating Cash Flow}}{\text{Diluted Shares Outstanding}}$$

INVESTOPEDIA EXPLAINS *CASH EARNINGS PER SHARE - CASH EPS*

You may sometimes see cash EPS defined as either EPS plus amortization of goodwill and other intangible items, or net income plus depreciation divided by the number of outstanding shares.

Whatever the definition, the point of cash EPS is that it is a stricter number than other variations on EPS because cash flow cannot be manipulated as easily as net income.

EARNINGS

What Does *Earnings* Mean?

Earnings are the amount of profit that a company produces during a specific period, which is usually defined as a quarter (three calendar months) or a year. Earnings typically refer to after-tax net income. Ultimately, a business's earnings are the main determinant of its share price, because earnings and the circumstances relating to them can indicate whether the business will be profitable and successful in the long run.

INVESTOPEDIA EXPLAINS *EARNINGS*

Earnings are perhaps the single most studied number in a company's financial statements because they show a company's profitability. A business's quarterly and annual earnings are typically compared to analyst estimates and guidance provided by the business itself. In most situations, when earnings do not meet either of those estimates, a business's stock price will tend to drop. On the other hand, when actual earnings are greater than estimates by a significant amount, the share price is likely to surge.

CONSENSUS ESTIMATE

What Does *Consensus Estimate* Mean?

Consensus estimate is a figure based on the combined estimates of the analysts covering a public company. Generally, analysts give a consensus for a company's earnings per share and revenue; these figures are most often made for the quarter, fiscal year and next fiscal year. The size of the company and the number of analysts covering it will dictate the size of the pool from which the estimate is derived.

INVESTOPEDIA EXPLAINS *CONSENSUS ESTIMATE*

When you hear that a company has "missed estimates" or "beaten estimates", these are references to consensus estimates. Based on projections, models, sentiments and research, analysts strive to come up with an estimate of what the company will do in the future.

Obviously, consensus estimates are not an exact science. This leads some market *pundits* to believe that the market is not as efficient as it is often purported to be, and that the efficiency is driven by estimates about a multitude of future events that may not be accurate. This might help to explain why a company's stock quickly adjusts to the new information provided by quarterly earnings and revenue numbers when these figures diverge from the consensus estimate.

EARNINGS ESTIMATE

What Does *Earnings Estimate* Mean?

Earnings estimate is an analyst's estimate for a company's future quarterly or annual earnings.

INVESTOPEDIA EXPLAINS *EARNINGS ESTIMATE*

Analysts use forecasting models, management guidance, and fundamental information on the company in order to derive an estimate.

STOCK SCREENER

What Does *Stock Screener* Mean?

Stock screener is a tool that investors can use to filter stocks given certain criteria of their choice.

INVESTOPEDIA EXPLAINS *STOCK SCREENER*

By using a stock screening tool an investor is able to follow a strict set of criteria that he or she requires prior to investing in a company. For example, an investor could screen stocks by entering the following criteria: "listed on the NYSE", "in the telecommunications industry", "has a P/E ratio between 15-25", and "has an annual EPS growth of at least 15% for the past three years". The screener would then produce a list of stocks that displayed all these attributes. In this example stocks are screened using only four criteria; however, you can screen stocks by as many criteria as the particular screener you are using will allow.

The stock screener has replaced many days' worth of research with a few clicks of a mouse.

DIVIDEND YIELD

What Does *Dividend Yield* Mean?

Dividend yield is a financial ratio that shows how much a company pays out in dividends each year relative to its share price. In the absence of any capital gains, the dividend yield is the return on investment for a stock. Dividend yield is calculated as follows:

$$= \frac{\text{Annual Dividends Per Share}}{\text{Price Per Share}}$$

INVESTOPEDIA EXPLAINS *DIVIDEND YIELD*

Dividend yield is a way to measure how much cash flow you are getting for each dollar invested in an equity position - in other words, how much "bang for your buck" you are getting from dividends. Investors who require a minimum stream of cash flow from their investment portfolio can secure this cash flow by investing in stocks paying relatively high, stable dividend yields.

To better explain the concept, refer to this dividend yield example: If two companies both pay annual dividends of $1 per share, but ABC company's stock is trading at $20 while XYZ company's stock is trading at $40, then ABC has a dividend yield of 5% while XYZ is only yielding 2.5%. Thus, assuming all other factors are equivalent, an investor looking to supplement his or her income would likely prefer ABC's stock over that of XYZ.

DIVIDEND

What Does *Dividend* Mean?

Dividend can be defined as follows:

1. A distribution of a portion of a company's earnings, decided by the board of directors, to a class of its shareholders. The dividend is most often quoted in terms of the dollar amount each share receives (dividends per share). It can also be quoted in terms of a percent of the current market price, referred to as dividend yield. It is also referred to as "Dividend Per Share (DPS)."

2. Mandatory distributions of income and realized capital gains made to mutual fund investors.

INVESTOPEDIA EXPLAINS *DIVIDEND*

1. Dividends may be in the form of cash, stock or property. Most secure and stable companies offer dividends to their stockholders. Their share prices might not move much, but the dividend attempts to make up for this. High-growth companies rarely offer dividends because all their profits are reinvested to help sustain higher-than-average growth.

2. Mutual funds pay out interest and dividend income received from their portfolio holdings as dividends to fund shareholders. In addition, realized capital gains from the portfolio's trading activities are generally paid out (capital gains distribution) as a year-end dividend.

EX-DIVIDEND

What Does *Ex-Dividend* Mean?

Ex-dividend is a classification of trading shares when a declared dividend belongs to the seller rather than the buyer. A stock will be given ex-dividend status if a person has been confirmed by the company to receive the dividend payment.

Investopedia Explains *Ex-Dividend*

A stock trades ex-dividend on or after the ex-dividend date (ex-date). At this point, the person who owns the security on the ex-dividend date will be awarded the payment, regardless of who currently holds the stock. After the ex-date has been declared, the stock will usually drop in price by the amount of the expected dividend.

EX-DIVIDEND DATE

What Does *Ex-Date* Mean?

Ex-Date is the date on or after which a security is traded without a previously declared dividend or distribution. After the ex-date, a stock is said to trade ex-dividend.

INVESTOPEDIA EXPLAINS *EX-DATE*

This is the date on which the seller, and not the buyer, of a stock will be entitled to a recently announced dividend. The ex-date is usually two business days before the record date. It is indicated in newspaper listings by an *x*.

Glossary

Aa

Above par: The par value of a share is its face value, when the share price is above its face value, it is termed as above par.

Accelerated depreciation: In accelerated depreciation larger amounts are written off in the earlier years of an asset's life, to enable the company to qualify for larger tax deduction at the initial stage, and invest in expansion and growth.

Across the board: A movement of stock prices that affects almost all stocks.

Acting in concert: When two or more investors act together with the same goal, that is buying or selling shares of a particular company to push the price up or down, or accumulating stock with the eventual purpose of securing a controlling interest in a company, they are acting in concert. These investors are also called as concert parties.

Active market: This market is characterized by frequent and large volumes of trading of a particular share or shares in general. In such a market the gap between buying and selling prices is narrow. Also, in such a market the buying or selling activities of financial institutions tend to have a lower impact than in a dull market.

Active shares: Shares in which there are frequent and day to day dealings, as distinguished from partly active shares in which dealings are not so frequent. Most shares of leading companies are likely to be active, particularly those which are sensitive to economic and political events and are, therefore, subject to sudden price movements. Some market analysts prefer to define active shares as those which are bought and sold at least three times a week and hence are easy to buy or sell.

Actuals: Trading which results in delivery of a physical commodity like grain, gold, meat etc. to the buyer at the expiry of the contract. If futures and options contracts are terminated before expiry of the contract, these do not end in actual delivery; even then since the trading is in physical commodities it would qualify as actual trading.

A-D index or Advance-Decline index: It is a useful tool for detecting a bullish or bearish trend in the stock market in which one divides the number of traded shares which have risen in price by those which have fallen. For example, if 200 shares have advanced and 100 shares declined in a particular day, then the A-D index will be 200/100 = 2. Numbers more than 1 indicate a bullish trend and less than 1 a bearish market.

Ad hoc margin: When a member of a stock exchange has an unusually large outstanding position the exchange collects this margin from him.

Admission to dealing: When a particular share of a company is allowed to be entered in the official list of a stock exchange, it is admitted to dealing.

ADR: American Depositary Receipt is a certificate issued by an American bank stating that a number of shares in a foreign company have been deposited with them. The receipt can be traded in US markets. Instead of having to buy shares of foreign companies in foreign markets, Americans can buy them in the US in the form of ADRs. ADRs are issued by the company in the USA as per the Securities and Exchange Commission (SEC), USA. Indian companies like Reliance, Wipro etc. tap the American market through placement of ADRs or GDRs.

Additional volatility margin: The BSE had imposed an Additional Volatility Margin (AVM) from 18th September, 2000 ranging from 10 per cent to 25 per cent on 66 scrips. The scrip's attaching AVM include DSQ Software, EIH, Global Tele, Gramophone Company and others.

Advance decline line: This is a measurement of the number of stocks that have advanced or declined over a period of time. The market is considered bullish if more stocks advance than decline on a particular day. It is a bearish sign if declines outnumber advances.

Air pocket stocks: Where, as a result of sudden unfavorable news affecting a company (such as a trading loss) or an industry (such as price control or liberalization of imports) there is a steep fall in the price of a share, creating a large gap between a day's closing price and considerably lower opening price on the following day, an air pocket appears. Shares which are particularly prone to such falls are usually over priced in the first instance. In short, air pocket stock can be termed as a stock that falls sharply in the wake of negative news as a result of unexpected poor earnings.

Allotment advice: A letter sent to a successful applicant for shares and debentures of a company informing him that he has been allotted so many shares or debentures. This is not saleable.

Allotment letter: Communication was made in the pre-digital era by the company to its investors regarding allotment of securities in response to application.

Alpha factor: The difference between what portfolios actually earned and were expected to earn at the level of systematic risk as measured by Jensen to measure portfolio management.

Alpha stocks: The most frequently traded shares are often termed as alpha stocks.

Annuity: An investment scheme offered by banks, Life Insurance Corporation of India, Unit Trust, and other non-banking financial institutions, in which persons in lieu of lump sum payment, or regular payment over a period of time, receive a specified sum for life or a fixed period. On death or expiry of the fixed period the investment fund may be refunded, sometimes with a small premium, to the investor or his nominee. Annuities do not provide life cover.

Appropriations: A term featuring on the balance sheet of a company showing how the net profits are deployed in distribution of dividends on preference shares and equity shares, transfer to general reserves, and balance carried forward.

Arbitration: The settlement of disputes between clients, brokers and sub-brokers through arbitrators.

Asset: What is owned by the business like fixed assets, current assets and semi-current assets.

Asset-backed fund: A fund in which investment comprises only tangible assets such as shares or real property, and not loans to banks or financial institutions. These funds can grow in a manner like fixed interest loans account. At the same time, depression is bad news for these funds. They blossom with inflation.

Asset coverage: When a company goes to liquidation, this concept becomes important. From the total book value of assets are deducted the claims of creditors, and the ratio of what remains to the total number of preference shares represents the asset coverage for such shares. The asset coverage of equity shares is the ratio obtained after deducting all the creditor's dues and the value of the preference shares, divided by the number of equity shares. The result is also called the net book value of equity shares.

Asset play: A term used for a stock that is attractive because the current price does not reflect the value of company's stock.

Asset stripping: Selling off assets of a company for quick profit, rather than running the company for steady gain. The asset stripper is usually left with a shell company which he keeps alive, not for regular business, but for other, usually dishonest purposes, such as tax evasion.

Asset value: See NAV.

At best: When an investor places an order with a broker at best, he is not setting a price limit for buy or sell, but is leaving it to the discretion of the broker to transact the deal at the best possible price. Such orders are usually filled, whereas orders with buy or sell limits may not always be executed.

Averaging: Buying of a particular share at different times, in different quantities, and different prices, so that an advantageous average price is obtained. That is, if one buys 100 shares of a particular company at Rs. 80 in a rising market; when the price falls to Rs. 60 he buys another 200 shares of the same company. By averaging he has obtained a price of Rs. 66.33 for that share.

Average down: A strategy to lower the average price paid for a company's share. This strategy is not recommended as it can result in huge losses.

Averaging up: Buying in a rising market to lower the overall cost. If prices move up further there is a profit. This strategy involves a fair degree of risk.

Averaging in/Averaging out: Buying or selling at different prices in order to build up, or liquidate, a substantial holding over a long period.

Away from the market: When a limit order to buy is lower than the current market price, or a limit order to sell is above the current market price, it is away from the market. The broker may hold such an order for a period of time, but if within this period he cannot fill it, he kills it.

Bb

Back up: When a stock market has backed up it has shown a sudden reversal of trend – a sudden fall in a rising market, or sudden rise in a falling market.

Badla: This is an additional payment made by an investor or speculator to carry over the transaction to the next settlement period. The badla financer provides an amount equal to the make-up price multiplied by the number of shares.

Balance sheet: Balance sheet is a snap shot of the financial situation of a concern at a particular moment of time. It is a statement of assets owned by a business and how they are financed from shareholders' funds and liabilities. It does not reflect the market value of a business.

Barometer stock: A share, usually a blue chip, whose price is taken to show the state of the stock market. It is a widely held, frequently traded share with stable price record. Its Beta Coefficient is 1.

Bear: A bear is a person with a pessimistic market outlook, who expects the market will go down and derive benefit from the declining situation of the market.

Bear cycle: An extended period, usually shorter than a bull cycle, when the share prices generally keep falling and stock market indices keep going down.

Bear hammering: Persistent selling pressure by bears, bringing the price down.

Bear hug: A takeover strategy of acquiring the company without giving previous warnings. In this case a proposal letter is sent to the directors of the target company so they can take a quick decision.

Bear raid: An attempt by investors to manipulate the price of a stock by short selling a large number of shares. These manipulators earn profit from the difference between the higher initial price and the new low price after such a makeover.

Bear spread: It is an option market strategy in which one buys a combination of calls and puts on the same security at different strike or exercise prices to profit from a fall in prices. Alternatively, one buys a put option of short maturity and another of long maturity to profit from the difference between the two put options as the price falls.

Bear trap: An erratic movement of share prices downwards, encouraging investors to sell short. When the market corrects itself and prices go up, unwary investors get caught in the bear trap.

Beta coefficient or beta factor: It is a measure of the performance of a particular share or class of shares in relation to the general movement of the market. If a share has a beta of 1 its rise and fall correspond exactly with the market; with a beta of 2 its rise or fall is double, that is, when the market rises 10 per cent it rises by 20 per cent and when the market falls by 10 per cent it falls by 20 per cent. With beta of 0.5 the particular share will rise by only 5 per cent if the market rises by 10 per cent; fall by 5 per cent if market falls by 10 per cent. Shares with negative betas are *contrarian shares*.

Beta shares: These shares are listed but infrequently traded, shares of companies with a beta, generally have low equity capital.

Big bang: Major changes in the operation of the stock trading on the London Stock Exchange, introduced on 27th October 1986. The requirement that the jobber and the stockbroker should be different entities, under the dual-capacity system, was abolished, as were the fixed commission rates chargeable by the brokers. The big bang also started modernization and globalization of trading on the London Stock Exchange.

Blue chip: Stock of a well known company that has a long record of profit growth and dividend payment and reputation of quality management, products and services.

Bottom fisher: An investor who buys stocks that have fallen to the bottom prices before going up. In the extreme situation, bottom fishers buy stocks of bankrupt or near bankrupt companies.

Book closure: The company keeps the register of members updated for payment of dividend, write issue and bonus issue every year for a certain period of time.

Business cycle: A recurrence of periods of boom and recession in economic activity, which impact inflation, growth and unemployment.

Buy back: A public limited company can buy back its own equity shares at a tender price offered in the market or negotiated price of buy back offered by large holders. SEBI has allowed the purchase of one's own shares under certain condition.

Buy on bad news: After receiving bad news that the price of a particular stock will plummet, investors purchase at this stage on the assumption that the price will not fall any lower. If there is any adverse development it is temporary and stock prices will begin to rise again.

Bull: A bull is a person who thinks prices will rise or is optimistic about the prospect of an individual stock, the industry or even the economy as a whole.

Bull market: A strong rising market, when the market zooms.

Buy and hold strategy: This is a strategy of accumulating shares of a company over a period of time. This strategy allows the investor to pay favorable long-term gains tax on prices and avoid more active trading strategy.

Buying climax: A rapid rise in the price of stocks sets the stage for a reversal or a quick fall in prices.

Cc

Call option: A call option is an option to purchase a specified number of shares on or before a specific future date at a striking price. Call options of purchase are executed in the expectation that market price of the specific share will rise.

Capital flight: Movement of large sums of money from one country to another to escape economic or political turmoil or to generate higher rates of return. FDI or FII investments are examples.

Capital gains: Profit on sale of assets like stock, a flat, home, land, etc. that appreciated in value. In case of stock sold within one year it is called short-term capital gains and if it is sold after one year, it is known as long-term capital gains. In the case of other assets if they are sold within three years it indicates short-term capital gains and if more than three years it indicates long-term capital gains. Short-term capital gains are liable to full taxation, while long-term capital gains carry some rebate as per the Income Tax Act, 1961.

Capital gearing: Capital gearing is the ratio between fixed interest bearing securities to owners equity.

Cartel: When a group of individuals or businesses or nations agree to influence prices by regulating production or marketing of a product. The Oil and Petroleum Exporting Cartel (OPEC) is the best example as it controls oil prices throughout the world.

Cash cow: A share which yields a consistently high rate of dividends. Also, a currently profitable business that does not have very bright growth prospects and is therefore used to fund other enterprises.

Cats and dogs: Speculative stocks that have short historic sales, earnings and dividend payment. In bull market analysts forecast that even cats and dogs stocks are going up.

Circuit breakers: These preventive measures are used by stock exchanges to halt trading temporarily in stocks, when a particular stock has fallen or risen by a specific amount in a specific period. These types of measures are used to stabilize prices.

Clearing house: As a part of stock exchange execution of the delivery and settlement of stock between member brokers.

Closely held company: When the majority of shares of a company are held by a few shareholders for the purpose of controlling the company.

Company law board: The company law board administers within the purview of the Companies Act, 1956.

Consolidated financial statement: Financial statement consisting of assets and liabilities of parent company and subsidiary company. As per the Indian Companies Act, 1956 it is not obligatory but as per Accounting Standard it is mandatory.

Convertible debenture: A debenture that provides a fixed interest before conversion and after a certain period of time it will be fully or partially converted into a certain number of shares at par or at a premium.

Cooking the books: Falsifying the financial accounts of a company to keep share holders happy and to attract investors with the lure of high profit. A high level of accounting skill combined with cunning is necessary to achieve this end. Certain expenses are omitted, liabilities are concealed, write-offs delayed, valuation reserves not provided for, and other such fraudulent practices are followed to present a false picture.

Cornering the market: Effective control on the price of a specific stock by purchasing a large number of stocks.

Corporate tax: This type of direct tax is to be levied on the profit of a company.

Correction: Correction indicates a reverse movement, usually a downward movement of stock or index. This correction happens within the rising trend to book profit.

Covered call: A covered call is a contract to sell certain shares at a certain price on a future date. If the seller actually possesses the shares the contract or the call is covered. If he does not, he will have to buy the shares from the market, and if the price has fallen by then he will make profit. If it has risen above the contracted price, he will have to buy the shares at a loss, since he is not covered.

Crash: This is nothing but a sharp drop in stock prices. It is followed by highly inflated stock prices or massive change of economic issues.

Creeping takeover: It means a slow, imperceptible acquisition of the controlling interest in a company by buying its shares in the stock market over a period of time.

Crossing: It is a method adopted by specialist institutional brokerage firms to handle large buy or sell orders, which would, in the normal course, distort the price movement of shares. In this kind of negotiated transaction, the brokerage firm matches the buyers with the sellers. Once the deal is closed, the prearranged orders are sent to the exchange floor for execution. Sometimes it is also referred as secondary distribution.

Cross-border listing: It means the listing of shares of a company on the stock exchanges of different countries to create a larger market.

Cross holding: Companies under the same group of promoters holding shares in one another's companies. It is a common practice in the corporate world.

Current yield: Current yield is calculated by dividing the annual interest or dividend on a debenture or stock derived on face value by its market price.

Current ratio or Quick ratio: It is the ratio of current assets to current liabilities. If it is more than 1, the company's operations are in a healthy state.

Cushion theory: This refers to a strong bearish market. If many investors are taking a short position in a particular share, the theory holds that prices must rise, as the bears will have to cover their short positions. Technical analysts read it as a particularly bullish sign if the short positions in a share are twice as high as the number of shares traded daily, because price rises will force bears to cover their positions, thus pushing up prices further.

Cyclical shares: Shares which rise and fall in price with the state of the national economy, such as those of construction, automobile, cement and engineering companies; or those affected by international economy, such as shipping, aviation, and tourism; also shares which are affected by natural phenomena, like fertilizers and tea. Examples of non-cyclical shares would be drugs, insurance, basic foodstuffs and a number of consumer products.

Dd

Daily margin: An amount, to be decided by the stock exchange, to be deposited by a member, on a daily basis, for purchase or sale of securities. The amount is to be deposited at the stock exchange. The margin is imposed to curb excessive speculation.

Daisy chain: Stock market manipulators buying and selling amongst themselves to give the impression that the share is being vigorously traded and the price is rising. At a certain point of the rise the manipulators unload their shares to unwary investors, who then discover that there is no one to sell them to.

Dartboard investing: It is the strategy of investing in randomly selected shares in the belief that this is perhaps better, than shares carefully selected after technical or fundamental analysis. It is sometimes also referred to as Random Walk Theory.

Day order: It is an order which is only good for the day it is placed, to a stockbroker to buy or sell particular shares. If the order is to be held till it can be executed. It is called a good-till-cancelled order.

Day trading: Buying and selling the same share during a single day, hoping to make a profit from price fluctuations. It also refers to in-and-out trader.

Death-valley curve: It is a period during which a company is using up its venture capital (shareholders' equity + long-term loan) before supporting its operations from its own earnings.

Deep in the money: It is an option trading term, referring to a call or put option whose market price has risen well above (for calls) or well below (for puts) the exercise price. It is a very profitable situation for the holder of the option.

Defensive share: Shares which are more stable than others and tend to fall less in a bear market, providing safe return of the investor's money. Blue chip shares fall in this class.

De-gearing: It is a process of replacing fixed interest loans by issuing equity shares of a comparable value. This is done to lower the company's capital gearing or leverage.

Delayed opening: A delayed opening refers to a delay in starting of trading in a stock due to gross imbalance in buy and sell order for good or bad news of a particular stock.

Delisting: Striking the name of shares of a company from a stock exchange because the firm did not abide by the regulations specified by the stock exchange under the purview of SEBI.

Delta Stocks: These are the least liquid shares of a stock exchange.

Disinvestment: When reduction of investment is made by sale of equity in the stock market to raise funds for the government exchequer.

Depository: An institution recognized by NSDL and SEBI which holds securities in electronic form on behalf of an investor like the Stock Holding Corporation.

Depression: Depression indicates an economic condition of falling prices, reducing purchasing power, rising unemployment, an excess supply over demand and general decrease in business activity.

Debentures: Debentures may be defined as a financial instrument for raising long-term finance. The company has to repay interest and principal amount within a stipulated period of time. At the time of liquidation debenture holders get their money back prior to equity holders.

Descending tops: A chart pattern observed by a technical analyst where the new high price level of a stock is lower than the preceding one. This type of chart formation comes in a bearish trend.

Dip: A slight fall in the price of a share indicates *buy on dips*.

Dragon markets: Emerging markets of the Pacific Basin such as Indonesia, the Philippines, Malaysia, and Thailand.

Drip feed: To fund a new company in a number of stages, rather than all at once, in relatively small amounts over a period of time.

Dud issues: New public issues, often floated with much publicity, which fail to produce any benefit for the investors. The companies either do not start operations or go into liquidation soon after starting business.

Dumping: Offering for sale a large number of shares all at once, without bothering about the effect of such an action on the market. In the international mode, it applies to selling goods at a very low price, often below cost, to get rid of surplus or outdated production or to gain an advantage over competitors.

Ee

Each way: Commission earned by a broker on both purchase and sale of a trade.

Embargo: Government prohibiting the movement of goods and commodities to other countries. It is commonly used during war. It is also been used in economic recession and economic meltdown situations.

Efficient portfolio: A portfolio that has the maximum expected return for any level of risk or a minimum level of risk corresponding to any expected return.

Efficient market: Efficient market theory says market prices reflect the knowledge and expectation of all investors. Those who follow this theory are unable to forecast market movement.

Enlistment of shares: Enlistment of shares in different stock exchanges gives trading privileges for different types of shares.

EPS: The Earning Per Share (EPS) is one of the most widely used indicators of the worth of the company. It is the ratio between profit after tax (PAT) and number of equity shares of the company.

Equity financing: This is the process of raising funds by issuing equity shares. This is normally done to meet the expense needs of a company.

Eurodollar: US currency held in banks outside the United States, mainly in Europe and commonly used for settling international transactions.

Euro issue: Euro issue made by Indian companies to raise foreign currency from outside India. Lots of funds are available in the European market looking for a high rate of interest.

Evening up: Buying or selling to offset an existing market position – long or short.

Extrinsic value: It is an option market term, signifying the amount by which the market price of an option exceeds the price which would be realized if the option were exercised.

Ff

Fallen angel: A security that has fallen below its original value and now is traded for its yield.

Fighting the tape: Going against the stock market trend. It originates from the New York Stock Exchange, where share prices used to be reported on a ticker tape. If one is buying when the tape is showing a downtrend, or short selling when the share prices are rising, one is fighting the tape. The stock exchange maxim says: Don't fight the tape (unless, that is, you are a contrarian).

Fill or kill: If an order to buy or sell a particular security is not executed immediately then the order stands cancelled. This type of order is called fill or kill order.

Financial institution: An institution that collects funds from the public and invests the funds in financial assets like stocks, bonds, money market instrument, bank deposit or loans etc.

Financial market: A market for the exchange of capital and credit for the economy. Financial market comprises the money market, capital market, credit market and foreign exchange market.

Financial statement: Balance sheet and income statement are the two major financial statements. The former reflects the financial position of the concern at a particular moment of time. On the other hand, the latter measures the performance of the organization over a period of time.

Fixed income investment: This type of investment provides fixed returns over time.

Floating stock: A certain portion of a company's paid up capital that participates in day to day trading is called floating stock.

Foreign collaboration: Foreign collaboration means joint efforts at the micro level between firms of two countries with sanction from the respective governments either between firms in the private sectors, public sectors or joint sectors.

Forward contract: It is an agreement between two parties to exchange financial instruments for cash at a predetermined future date at the price specified today.

Gg

G-5: Group of five nations viz. USA, France, Japan, UK and Germany.

G-7: G-5 plus Canada and Italy. It is also known as the group of seven.

G-20: Group of 20 countries as ranked by Associated Chambers of Commerce and Industry of India (ASSOCHAM) as follows: China, Russia, South Korea, India, Germany, Australia, Mexico, Saudi Arabia, Turkey, Brazil, US, UK, Indonesia, Japan, South Africa, Canada, Argentina, France and Italy.

Gamma stocks: Shares of small companies which are traded very infrequently are known as Gamma stock.

Gambling: Gambling means speculation with study and chance. Gambling is not officially allowed, but prevails in the organized market. Society and economy have to bear the negative impact of gambling.

Glamour stock: FIs and public prefer this stock due to steady earnings, above average sales and wealth accumulation.

Globalization: Globalization may be defined as a stage of development where economic activities can be organized as per economic considerations across national boundaries.

Going public: A phrase used when a private company goes in for a public offer for the first time. Thus the company's ownership is shifted from a few private owners to wide range of public holding.

Go-go fund: When mutual funds invest their money in highly risky but potentially rewarding stocks.

Gold bug: An analyst enamored with gold as an area of potential investment. He is usually worried about economic meltdown, stagflation, hyper inflation and recommended gold as a hedge against inflation.

Gross Domestic Product (GDP): A country's total income derived from domestic sources in terms of money in a year.

Global Depository Receipts (GDR): Global depository receipts or certificates issued by overseas depository banks outside India. Most of the GDRs are listed on the London or New York Stock Exchange.

Growth stock: A stock that gains faster than that of average stock in terms of earnings during the last few years and continues to glitter in future. Over a long period of time, growth stock out perform in comparison with slow growing or stagnant stock.

Hh

Haircut: The difference between the buying price and selling price of a market maker.

Hammering the market: Speculators or bears think that the market is about to fall due to short sell and are said to be bear hammering.

Hedging: By the method of hedging, speculators try to offset loss from one transaction by gain from other transaction.

High-tech stock: Stock of companies in high technology areas such as computers, information technologies, electronics and bio-technologies and so on. High-tech stocks normally have an above average growth rate and are typically volatile.

Hit the bid: If the asking price of a share is higher than the bid price, the seller of a share hit the bid if he accepts the lower bid price.

Hot issue: A newly issued stock that has hot public demand. The price of this stock has risen sharply after listing due to great public demand.

Ii

Inactive stock: A security that has been traded with low frequency. The low volume makes the security illiquid and small investors shy away from such kinds of security.

Initial Public Offering (IPO): An IPO will be considered the first public offer of security of a company since its inception. The company becomes a listed company as a result of IPO.

Inside information: New developments within the corporation are only known to the officers of the firm but not for public consumption. The government is taking steps to make use of inside information a major offence, punishable by a fine and even in jail.

Interest sensitive stock: A special type of stock whose earnings change with change of interest rate.

Investment strategy: This is a plan to allocate assets among different types of stocks, debentures, real assets and precious assets. This plan can be formulated on the basis of investors' outlook on economic growth, interest rate, inflation, risk taking ability, tax bracket, investors' age, future need for capital, children's education, marriage etc.

Ll

Lame duck: When a bear is unable to keep his commitments and make settlement by clearing the difference of prices he is called a lame duck.

Limit order: This is an order to buy or sell a security at a specific price or price range. The broker will execute the trade only with the price restriction as specified by the client.

Mm

Making-up-price: At this price a transaction is closed for the current settlement and carried forward to the following settlement.

Manipulation: Buying and selling a security to create a false appearance of active trading by one person or by a group acting in concert and thus influencing other investors to buy or sell shares. Those found guilty of manipulation are punishable under civil and criminal law of the country.

Market timing: Market timing is a decision of when to buy or sell securities considering the fundamental and technical analysis.

Market tone: General health and vigor of a securities market. The market tone is good when dealers and market makers are trading actively on narrow bid and offer spreads.

Methods of marketing shares: There are three ways in which a company may raise capital: marketing shares from the primary market through public issue or IPO, right issue and bonus issue.

Money market securities: Money market securities are debt instruments that are connected to the security markets. These are short-term instruments and include treasury bills, certificates of deposit and commercial papers and such instruments.

Moving average crossovers: It is the point where the various moving average lines intersect each other. Technical analysts use crossovers to give the base price for buy or sell.

Nn

Near money: Cash equivalent and other assets that are easily convertible into cash are called near money.

Non-voting stock: Corporate securities that do not empower a holder to vote on corporate resolutions or the election of directors. Such stock is sometimes issued in connection with a takeover attempt. This classification is issued in the western stock markets, and is not applicable in the case of the Indian stock market.

Nationalization: Government takeover of private companies' operations and or assets.

Negative cash flow: A situation in which a business spends more cash than it receives through earnings or other transactions in an accounting period. This situation is called a cash crunch situation and leads to paucity of working capital.

NAV: The Net Asset Value (NAV) in the case of a mutual fund scheme is arrived at by calculating the total market price of all the shares by utilizing the corpus of the scheme minus all liabilities and dividing it by the total number of units under the scheme. This figure tends to change quite often as mutual funds are always buying and selling shares at book value.

Non-trading company: An association of persons can register a company whose ultimate objective is not to earn profit. The profit or income earned by the association is not distributed to its members as dividend.

NSE: The Indian economy is governed by the National Stock Exchange (NSE). It has become an integral part of the growing Indian economy. The pulse of business, industry, service or real estate or agriculture reflected through the NSE came into operation in 1985 and 90 per cent of the volume is routed through NSE. NSE is earmarked as the first in stock future turnover, second in Asia for equity derivatives and fourth largest equity market in the world at the beginning of 2010.

Oo

Odd lot: It is quite different from marketable lot. It could be sell out or buy out at a discount rate at the time of physical transaction.

One decision stock: A stock with good growth potential and such shares are ideal for a buy and hold strategy.

Option: An option is a derivative which provides its holders an opportunity to purchase or sell a specific security or an asset at a striking price on or before a specified future date.

Option holder: One who has bought a call (buy) or put (sell) option but not exercised it yet.

Optimum size: The optimum size means the firm in existing conditions of technology and organizing ability has the lowest average cost of production per unit.

Pp

Pay out ratio: That percentage of a firm's profits which is paid out to shareholders in the form of dividend. Young, fast growing companies reinvest most of their earnings in their business and usually pay no dividend.

Per value: The face value or nominal value of a security.

P/E ratio: The Price Earnings ratio (P/E ratio) is an indicator of how highly a company is valued in the market. It is arrived at by dividing the market price of a share on a given date by the EPS. A high P/E ratio does not necessarily indicate a bright future of the company. A low P/E ratio, where the EPS is high often indicates that a share is underpriced.

Pool: A group of investors or speculators who come together and use their combined power to manipulate security prices or obtain control of a company.

Policy board: A policy board consists of part-time directors, either elected or nominated, who generally take policy decisions to be executed by executive directors.

Premium raid: Surplus attempt to acquire a position in a company's stock by offering holders an amount or premium over the market value of their shares. The term raid assumes that the motive is control and not simple investment.

Primary market: A market for new issues of stock including initial public offering. This is distinguished from the secondary market where previously issued stocks are bought and sold.

Prime rate: This is the interest rate that the banks will charge their most credit worthy clients. This rate is determined by the interaction of demand and supply of money during the particular period.

Private limited company: A private limited company must have at least 2 members (maximum members will be 50) and transfer of shares is restricted.

Private placement: Sale of stocks, debentures or other investments directly to an investor, mutual fund or institutional investors, rather than a general public offering through a public issue, is called private placement.

Program trading: Computer driven buying or selling through a program that constantly monitors stock, giving buy and sell signals when opportunities for arbitrage profits occur when market conditions warrant portfolio accumulation or liquidation transaction.

Portfolio: A combination of holding of more than one stock, bond, mutual funds, cash equivalent or other assets by individual or institutional investors. The purpose of a portfolio is to reduce risk by diversification of assets.

Public deposit: A public company can collect their loan fund by issuing a public deposit or fixed deposit. The present ceiling of public deposit is restricted to 15 per cent of the paid up capital and free reserve of the respective company.

Public limited company: A public limited company must have at least 7 members (maximum number of members will be equal to the number of shares of the company) and transfer of shares is allowed.

Public Sector Enterprises (PSEs): Public sector enterprises means all business enterprises which are owned and controlled by the government.

Qq

Quick assets: This indicates the current assets minus inventories.

Quote: High bid for buy or lowest offer for sell given by the jobber.

Quoted share: Quoted shares are those shares enlisted in a particular stock exchange at a different price.

Quoted price: When particular stock exchanges have quoted different prices of different shares for trading, it is called the quoted price.

Rr

Registrar of companies: The registrar of companies acts on a state basis as a trustee officer to preserve documents and returns submitted by the company, keep a vigil over the companies and scrutinize the documents and returns submitted by the company.

Relative strength: The rate at which a stock falls relative to other stocks in a falling market or rises relative to other stocks in a rising market. A stock that holds value in a falling market is expected to be a strong performer on the upside and vice-versa.

Relative strength index: An indicator invented by J. Wellers Wilder and used to ascertain an overbought or oversold and divergent situation.

Repo rate: Short-term rate at which the RBI lends to banks.

Return on sales: Net pre-tax profit as a percentage of net sales. This is used to measure the overall efficiency of a company in comparison to a previous period or with other companies in the same period of time. Returns on sales vary widely from industry to industry.

Reverse repo rate: Short term rate at which banks park funds with other banks.

Rigged market: This is a situation in which the security prices are manipulated to lure unsuspecting buyers and sellers.

Right shares: If a public limited company wants to issue fresh shares to increase its capital, it has to be offered to the existing shareholders on a prorate basis at first.

Rising bottom: A term used in technical analysis. This is a technical price pattern which shows a rise in the price of stock or commodity. This pattern shows a higher bottom or a higher support level signifying a rising trend.

Ss

SEBI: The Government of India set up the Securities and Exchange Board of India in 1988. But SEBI had statutory powers when the SEBI Act, 1992 was passed by parliament and got the assent of the President of India. Now, SEBI acts as a regulatory authority of the Indian capital market.

SEC: Securities and Exchange Commission is the capital market regulatory body of the USA.

Seller's market: A situation when there is more demand than supply for a security or a product. This usually leads to a rise in prices as the sellers can set both the prices and terms of sales.

Selling climax: A term used in technical analysis. When investors panic and dump their stock it leads to a sharp fall in prices. During such a climax there is a sharp increase in volume.

Shakeout: A period when weak security holders are removed from the market, usually at a loss.

Speculation: Speculation comes from the Latin word "Speculare," which means to act looking into the future. To some extent, every bull or bear is a speculator.

Stag: A person who subscribes to a new issue with the primary intention of selling it at a profit no sooner than he gets the shares. The term is used for the speculator who gets in and out of the market at a fast profit or loss, rather than hold securities for investment.

Stock split: Stock split means reduction of par value of the share and the corresponding increase in the number of shares.

Stop loss: A term commonly used by traders of stock and commodities. This is a client's order to a broker to sell a stock in case it drops below a particular price. A stop loss order will protect profits that have already been made or prevent loss if the stock falls.

Synergy: A large, efficient and more profitable company formed by combining the resources of two companies, formed either by a merger or by acquisition. This leads to high earnings per share.

Tt

Takeover: Takeover happens when a person or another company buys the shares of one or more companies.

Top out: A share which has come to the end of its price rise, and is now expected to stay at a flat level or even decline, is said to have topped out.

Trading on equity: When the borrowed capital is higher than their own capital and the business return is higher than the borrowed rate of interest. Equity shareholders earn more by using borrowed capital, hence it is called trading on equity.

Transfer deed: An official document which records the transfer of ownership of securities. In the UK it is called a transfer form.

Transfer register: A book where changes of ownership of a company's shares are recorded.

Turnaround: A favorable reversal of fortune of a company or market or an economy. Some investors prefer to put their money in companies performing poorly but which are likely to turnaround soon or show a marked improvement in case of earnings.

Two-sided market: A market in which both bid and ask prices are firm and both buyers and sellers are assured of completing their transactions. It is also called a two-way market.

Uu

Underwriter: Financial institutions, big brokers, merchant bankers who take the responsibility of selling shares and debentures on behalf of a company are called underwriters. For the task of underwriting the underwriters charge a commission which is called the underwriters' commission. This commission must not exceed 5 per cent of the issue price of shares.

Unlisted securities: These securities are not on the official lists of stock exchanges. This type of securities involves a high degree of risk.

Unloading: Selling of large quantities of stocks at below the market price either to raise cash quickly or to depress the market.

Unit Trust of India: Established in the year 1964. The UTI fund is divided into units. Small investors can buy or sell the units involving list risk. UTI appointed a number of portfolio managers to manage the fund properly and give average returns to the investors by minimizing risk.

Unquoted share: These shares do not have an official buying and selling price in the stock exchanges as listed shares have.

Vv

Venture capital: A source of financing for new start up companies or turnaround companies that entails some investment risk, but also offers immense profit potential if the scheme is successful.

V-formation: Technical chart pattern in v-shape indicating that the stock being charted has bottomed out and is now in a bullish trend. An upside down i.e. inverse v-shape is considered bearish.

Volatile: This is a term use to describe rapid and extreme fluctuations in the price of a stock or commodity. A stock may be volatile because of the low equity capital of the company.

$$Volatility = HP - LP/LP *100$$

Voting right: This is the privilege of the shareholders to vote at company meetings as and when required.

Ww

Wall Street: New York Stock Exchange situated at the corner of Board Street and Wall Street. The New York Stock Exchange, popularly known as Wall Street was established in the year 1792.

Warrant: A warrant is a tradeable instrument which can be traded subject to certain conditions.

Wash sale: In case of a wash sale, the seller repurchases a security immediately after sale. It is not a genuine sale; it is merely recorded as a sale for the purpose of tax evasion or avoidance purposes.

Weak market: A bear market is called a weak market, where the number of sellers is more than the number of buyers resulting in a continuous decline of prices of most of the shares.

White knight: If a person or an organization takes appropriate steps to rescue a company from an unfavorable takeover bid.

Windfall profit: Profit that occurs suddenly as a result of an event not controlled by the person or company profiting from the event.

Winding up: The official closing down of a company under the purview of the law.

Xx

X.D: Ex-dividend means excluding dividend. Shares transfer after the real date of dividend i.e. dividend goes in favor of previous holders.

Yy

Yo-yo stock: Highly volatile stock, which will move up and down like a yo-yo.

Yield: Percentage of money received (dividend) from investment (shares).

Yield curve: Yield curve represents the interest obtained from investment with respect to time taken. Low interest securities have a flat yield curve and high interest securities have a steep yield curve.

Yield gap: Yield gap is the difference between interest received from fixed interest bearing security and equity shares.

Yield to maturity: Return from debt instrument, if it is held till maturity. Discounted cash flow method is applied to compute yield to maturity.

Yankee bonds: Bonds issued in the USA by foreign organizations but denominated in dollars.

Zz

Zero-rated debentures: Debentures bearing no interest and that may be issued at a discount to attract investors. Investors hope to gain from capital appreciation rather than interest.

Zero inflation: Zero inflation indicates stability of prices.

Bibliography

Agarwal, Dhanpat Ram (2009) *Global Meltdown: The Road Ahead*, Swadeshi Research Institute, Kolkata.

Altman, Edward I. (1971) *Corporate Bankruptcy in America*, Heath Lexington Books, New York.

Anand, K.K.R. (1994) *Management Consultancy – A User's Guide*, Vikas Publishing House Pvt. Ltd., New Delhi.

Argenti, John (1976) *Corporate Collapse – The Causes and Symptoms*, McGraw Hill Book Co. Ltd., London.

Avadhani, V.A. (1999) *Marketing of Financial Services and Markets*, Himalayan Publishing House, New Delhi.

Barua, Samir, Verma, J.R., Raghunathan V. (1996) *Portfolio Management*, Tata McGraw-Hill Publishing Co. Ltd., New Delhi.

Bernstein, P.L. and Damodaran, A. (1998) *Investment Management*, John Wiley & Sons Inc., Third Avenue, New York.

Bhalla, V. K. (2004) *Investment Management: Security Analysis and Portfolio Management*, S. Chand and Co. Ltd., 10th revised edition, New Delhi.

Bharat's Manual of SEBI (2000) Bharat Law House Pvt. Ltd., Kolkata.

Bhole, L.M. (2004) *Financial Institutions and Markets – Structure, Growth and Innovations*, Tata McGraw-Hill Publishing Co. Ltd., New Delhi.

Chandra, Prasanna (1994) *Projects Preparation, Appraisal, Budgeting and Implementation*, 3rd edition, Tata McGraw-Hill Publishing Co. Ltd., New Delhi.

Chandra, Prasanna (1995) *Fundamentals of Financial Management*, Tata McGraw-Hill Publishing Co. Ltd., New Delhi.

Chandra, Prasanna (1996) *Investment Game – How to Win*, Tata McGraw Hill Publishing Co. Ltd., New Delhi.

Chandra, Prasanna (2008) *Investment Analysis and Portfolio Management*, Tata McGraw-Hill Publishing Co. Ltd., New Delhi.

Chatterjee, B.K. (1993) *Marketing Management Concepts and Strategies*, Academic Publishers, Kolkata.

Chaturvedi, Hari Om (1999) *Investment Performance of Equity Shares*, Anmol Pulications Pvt. Ltd., New Delhi.

Das Gupta, Gurudas (1994) *The Securities Scandal: A Report to the Nation*, People's Publishing House, New Delhi.

Das, Gurcharan (2000) *India Unbound*, Penguin Books, India.

Davidson, Jeffrey P., Dean Charles W. (1993) *Business Secrets for Reducing Cost and Improving Cash Flow*, Jaico Publishing House, Bombay.

Dey, Amal Krishna (2009) *Readings in Indian Agricultural Development*, E-Book, Published by Cooperjal Limited, London.

Donnahoe, Alan S. (1989) *What Every Manager Should Know About Financial Analysis*, Simon and Schuster Inc., New York.

Drucker, Peter F. (1993) *Managing for the Future – The 1990s and Beyond*, Tata McGraw-Hill Publishing Co. Ltd., New Delhi.

Elton, J. Edwin and Gruber, J. Martin (1999) *Investments: Portfolio Theory and Asset Pricing*, Massachusetts Institute of Technology, Cambridge, Massachusetts.

Fischer, Donald E., Jordan and Ronald J. (1992) *Security Analysis and Portfolio Management*, 5th edition, Prentice-Hall of India Pvt. Ltd., New Delhi.

Focardi, Sergio M. and Fabozzi, Frank J., (2004), *The Mathematics of Financial Modeling & Investment Management*, John Wiley & Sons Inc., Third Avenue, New York.

Focardi, Sergio M., Fabozzi, Frank J. and Kolm, Petter N. (2006) *Financial Modeling of the Equity Market*, John Wiley & Sons Inc., Third Avenue, New York.

Galbraith, J.K. (1955) *The Great Crash*, Houghton Mifflin Harcourt Publishing Co., New York.

Gangadhar, V. and Babu, G. Ramesh (2003) *Investment Management*, Anmol Publications, New Delhi.

Garg, K.C., Sareen, V.K., Sharma, Mukesh (2003) *Business Regulatory Framework*, Kalyani Publishers, New Delhi.

Gates, Bill (2000) *Business @ the Speed of Thought: Succeeding in the Digital Economy*, Warner Books, New York.

Goyal, Alok and Goyal, Mridula (NA) *Financial Market Operations*, V.K. Pulications, New Delhi.

Gray, Tony and Greenbaum, Kurt (1995) *A Thousand Miles From Wall Street*, John Wiley & Sons Inc., Third Avenue, New York.

Hampton, John J. (1989) *Financial Decision Making: Concepts, Problems and Cases,* Prentice-Hall of India Pvt. Ltd., New Delhi.

Hooper, Joseph and Zalewski A. (2007) *Covered Calls and Leaps*, John Wiley & Sons Inc., Third Avenue, New York.

Horngren, Charles T., Foster, George and Datar, Srikant M. (1999) *Cost Accounting – A Managerial Emphasis*, 9th edition, Prentice-Hall of India Pvt. Ltd., New Delhi.

Introduction to Management (2003) ICFAI Centre for Management Research, Hyderabad.

Investment Banking and Financial Services (June 2004) ICFAI University, Hyderabad.

Investment Banking and Financial Services Volume I and II (2004) The ICFAI University, Hyderabad.

Kaplan, Robert S. and Atkinson, Anthony A. (2000) *Advance Management Accounting*, 2nd edition, Prentice-Hall of India Private Limited, New Delhi.

Khan, M.Y. (2007) *Indian Financial System*, Tata McGraw-Hill Publishing Co. Ltd., New Delhi.

Kritzman, Mark P. (1995) *The Portable Financial Analyst*, John Wiley & Sons Inc., Third Avenue, New York.

Kuchhal, S.C. (1982) *Corporate Finance – Principles and Problems,* Chaitanya Publishing House, Allahabad.

Kumar, S.S.S. (2010) *Financial Derivatives*, PHI Learning Pvt. Ltd. New Delhi.

Maringer, Dietmar G. (NA), *Portfolio Management with Heuristic Optimization*, Springer India Pvt. Ltd., New Delhi.

Mergers and Acquisitions (2005) The ICFAI University, Hyderabad.

Mukherjee, S., Ghose, A. and Roy, A. (2006) *Indian Financial System and Financial Market Operations,* Dey Book Concern, Kolkata.

National Securities Depository Limited, *Hand Book for NSDL Depository Operation Module*, National Stock Exchange of India Limited, Mumbai.

Nester, William R. (1993) *European Power and the Japanese Challenge*, Macmillan, printed in Hong Kong.

NSE (NA) *Surveillance in Stock Exchanges Module*, Work Book, National Stock Exchange of India Limited, Mumbai.

Pandian, Punithavathy (2009) *Security Analysis and Portfolio Management*, Vikas Publishing House Pvt., Ltd., Noida.

Rathnam, P.V. and Lalita, P. (2000) *Financial Management – Theory, Problems and Solutions*, Kitab Mahal, New Delhi.

Rudra, Ashok (1970) *Rate of Growth of Indian Economy*, Economic Development in South Asia, Kandy Conference Proceedings, edited by E.A.G. Robinson and M. Kidron, Macmillan, London.

Sayers, R.S. (1976) *Modern Banking*, 7th edition, Oxford University Press, Delhi.

Tripathy, Nalini Prova, *Financial Investment Services*, PHI Learning Pvt. Ltd., New Delhi.

Vohra, N.D. and Bagri, B.R. (2006) *Futures and Options*, 2nd edition, Tata Mc-Graw Hill Publishing Co. Ltd., New Delhi.

Yamane, Taro (1970) *Statistics – An Introductory Analysis*, 2nd edition, Harper & Row Publishers, New York and John Weatherhill Inc., Tokyo.

Yaraswy, N.J. (1992) *PSU Stocks*, Vision Books, New Delhi.

Journals, Newspapers and News Channels

Chakravarty, Manas, 'An Investor Cine to Definition of Profit and a Balancing Act Made Transparent', *Business Standard*, 10 January and 12 January, 1996.

Chaze, Aaron and Murli, B., 'The Bull Sees Red', *Business Standard*, April 8, 1993.

Chobhan, Aman, 'Figuring out the Maze', *Business Standard*, 5 March, 2001.

Chopra, Rishi, 'Indexing Future', *Economic Times*, Calcutta, January 17, 2000.

Choudhury, Utpal, K., 'Derivatives Options: Profit Position', *Business Standard*, April 22, 2002.

Choudhury, Utpal K., 'Leveraging Profits and Sifting through Figures', *Business Standard*, March 19 and May 21, 2001.

Choudhury, Utpal K., 'The Market Gridlock, Smart Investor', *Business Standard*, April 23, 2001.

Datta, Devansu, 'Margin and Leverage', *Business Standard*, January 14, 2002.

Datta, Devenshu, 'Wave Theory', *Business Standard*, December 10, 2001.

Datta, Tapas, 'Modernization at the CSEA', *Business Standard*, February 28, 1995.

Desai, Ashok, 'Mess in the Making', *Business Standard*, 26 September, 1996.

Dey, Ajit, Time for Retrospections and Change, *Business Standard*, February 28, 1995.

ET in the Class Room, 'All about Money Supply', *Economic Times*, January 09, 2001.

ET in the Class Room, 'What are Index Futures', *Economic Times*, Calcutta, July 7, 2000.

ET in the Class Room, 'What are the Various Types of Option Trading', *Economic Times*, Calcutta, May 28, 2001.

Fernand, Larissa, OTCEI, 'Online and Ahead', *Business Standard*, April 26, 2001.

Hand Book for NSDL Depository Operations Module.

Infosys Annual Report 2010-11.

Irani, S.D., an Article on Internet, (e-mail: sdirani@usa.net)

Kajaria, Sunil, 'The Brokerage Business in Liberalized Scenario', *Business Standard*, February 28, 1995.

Laker, Damien, 'Performance Measurement for Short Position', *The Journal of Performance Measurement*, Spring, 2002, p. 8.

Mehta, D.R., 'A Smart Move', *Business Standard*, March 25/26, 2000.

Mehta, Sanjiv, FAQs: Futures and Options, *Economic Times*, Calcutta, June 4, 2001.

Menchero, Jose, 'Performance Attribution with Short Position', *The Journal of Performance Measurement*, Winter, 2002-2003.

Merchant, Minhaz, 'How to Keep India Shining', *The Times of India*, Kolkata, Nov. 2, 2011.

Mohandas Pai, T.V. and Seshadri, Gautam 'Why Borrowing? Reward Yourself', *The Economic Times*, Kolkata, Dec. 16, 2011.

Nair, Rajesh, A series of articles on Technical Analysis, published every week during March 25 to July 16, 2001 in *Business Standard*.

Panchal, Salil, 'Jobbers Back in Business on BSE', *Business Standard*, October 6, 1995.

Panchisia, Naresh, 'The Professional Deal', *Business Standard*, February 28, 1995.

Pandey, Vinay, 'The Change Paradigm', *Business Standard*, December 27, 1997.

Paras Dagli, Circa, 'Capital Market, Smart Investor', *Business Standard*, April 23, 2001.

Parekh, H.T., *The Bombay Money Market,* Book Publication, p.2.

Philipose, Mobis, 'Pricing Futures', *Business Standard*, November 27, 2000.

Raajneelam and Amir, Inslya, 'A-Z of Cutting Costs', *The Times of India*, Dec. 14, 2008.

Reserve Bank of India Bulletin, RBI, June 1960, p. 801.

Roddy, Sale, 'How Safe are Investments in Emerging Indian Market', *Business Standard*, February 28, 1995.

Roy, P.K., 'Genesis and Growth', *Business Standard*, February 28, 1995.

Saxena, Shobhan (April 5, 2012) 'Power of 5', *The Economic Times*, Kolkata.

Securities and Exchange Board of India Bulletins.

Sen, Anjuli, Globalisation of Capital Market, *Business Standard*, February 28, 1995.

Shah, Navinchandra, Future Will Reduce in Spot, *Business Standard*, December 20, 1999.

Stock Exchange Official Directory, Bombay.

T.V. Channels – ET Now, CNBC TV 18, NDTV Profit, Bloomberg UTV.

Think Tank (by PM), *Financial Express*, January 25, 2000.

Vaish, Manoj, 'Deriving Derivatives Knowledge', *Economic Times*, Calcutta, June 12, 2000.

Various Publications of Basistha Basu and Basav Bhattacharya, in *Economic Times*.

Various Publications of National Stock Exchange, 2009, Mumbai.

Vijay, P.N., 'Smart Money – Lines of Fortune', *Economic Times*, Calcutta, November 24, 1990.

Investment Related Websites

www.advfn.com

www.CARE.com

www.CRISIL.com

www.iba.org.in

www.icra.com

www.iitrade.ac.in

www.investopedia.com

www.moneycontrol.com

www.morganstanly.com

WWW.nse.india

www.sebi.in

www.sbimf.com

www.wealth.economictimes.com

www.nse-india.com, (Rao, Purna Chandra, purna623@gmail.com)

www.bseindia.com. (Dr. B.P. Prasad's Article)

www.Articlebase.com, (Future of Derivatives in India, Nair S. Shiny) posted on June 29, 2009

www.Indianmba.com/faculty_column/FC/fc681.html., Derivatives in India (2007) Anwar Shaista

www.en.wikipedia.org/wiki/Derivative_(finance), Derivatives (finance), Podhuvan, Segai, Accessed on 30.12.2011.

www.sushilfinance.com., Derivatives Trading in India, Accessed on 27.12.2011